In Mohawk Co

Laurence M. Hauptman, *Series Editor*

In Mohawk Country

Early Narratives about a Native People

Edited by Dean R. Snow,
Charles T. Gehring,
and William A. Starna

Syracuse University Press

This volume is respectfully dedicated to the memory of
Ron LaFrance, Skaroniate
(1945-1996)

Friend, colleague, Mohawk

First Edition 1996
96 97 98 99 00 01 02   6 5 4 3 2 1

The paper used in this publication meets the minimum requirements
of American National Standard for Information Sciences—Permanence
of Paper for Printed Library Materials, ANSI Z39.48-1984. ∞™

Library of Congress Cataloging-in-Publication Data

In Mohawk country : early narratives about a Native people / edited by
Dean R. Snow, Charles T. Gehring, and William A. Starna. — 1st ed.
p. cm. — (The Iroquois and their neighbors)
Includes bibliographical references.
ISBN 0-8156-2723-8(alk. paper). — ISBN 0-8156-0410-6(pbk. : alk.
paper)
1. Mohawk Indians—History—Sources. 2. Mohawk Indians—Social
life and customs. 3. Ethnohistory—New York (State)—Mohawk River
Valley. 4. Mohawk River Valley (N.Y.)—History—Souces. 5. Mohawk
River Valley (N.Y.)—Social life and customs. I. Snow, Dean R.,
1940- . II. Gehring, Charles T., 1939- . III. Starna, William
A. IV. Series
E99.M8I5 1996
974.7'602—dc20   96-43348

Contents

Tables and Figures

Tables

Figures

Preface

This volume is one of several resulting from the Mohawk Valley Project. William Starna and I started the project together as an archaeological program in 1981 after discussing the possibility for many months. We jointly supervised the first two field seasons in 1982 and 1983. I remain indebted to him for introducing me to the valley and to its modern inhabitants, among whom he had grown up. I could not have begun without him.

The Mohawks were and are one of the five (later six) nations of the Iroquois confederacy, which for centuries dominated what is now upstate New York. The Mohawk nation was the easternmost, living in the Mohawk River valley west of modern Albany. The Seneca nation near Rochester was westernmost. Spaced between them from east to west were the Oneida, Onondaga, and Cayuga nations. The Tuscarora nation joined the confederacy early in the eighteenth century. Some Iroquois peoples remain in their sixteenth-century homelands, but many now live elsewhere in the United States and Canada, dispersed by the forces of war and politics over the centuries.

The Mohawks were probably the most numerous of the Iroquois in the early seventeenth century, and their proximity to Dutch and later English colonists in Albany (Dutch Fort Orange) made them first among equals in many of the Indian-European interactions of the colonial era. Compared to that of other Iroquois nations, the history and archaeology of the Mohawks had not been well developed by 1980, and the time was ripe for renewed investigation.

We initially conceived the project as a cooperative effort between our two State University of New York institutions, the University at Albany and the College at Oneonta. Our purpose early on was to rescue as much information as we could from the rapidly disappearing archaeological record in the Mohawk Valley and to synthesize that information into a chronology that would be as good as those already developed for the Onondaga and Seneca areas in New York.

The project went very well. We were able to pull together information from many sites, virtually all of which had been known for decades, as well as from many public and private archaeological collections. By 1984 Starna's interests had broadened and the Mohawk Valley Project shifted entirely to the University at Albany. By that time it was also clear that demographic problems were becoming the primary scientific focus of the project. Starna (1980) had previously initiated discussion of this subject. By 1989 we were able to discuss methods by which we were able to determine Mohawk population size for any particular year with unexpected accuracy (Snow and Starna 1989). This line of research

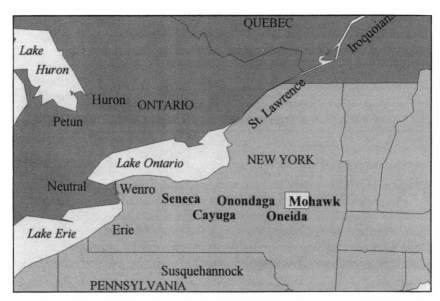

1. Location of the Iroquois nations in 1634. The Iroquois proper are shown in bold face. Other Northern Iroquoian nations are shown in the surrounding states and provinces. The location of Figure 2 appears as a white rectangle.

culminated in part with the publication of a summary of Mohawk population history in *Science* (Snow 1995a). I also published a related paper in *American Antiquity* at about the same time in which I advanced demographic arguments for an alternative hypothesis to explain Iroquois origins (Snow 1995b). Both articles were dependent upon data in two large monographs that detail the findings of the Mohawk Valley Project (Snow 1995c, 1995d). The arguments advanced in the second of these (Snow 1995d) in support of the Mohawk sequence as we currently understand it are dependent not only on archaeology but also on careful readings of the documents. Although many readers may wish to use the narratives for other purposes, they were most crucial to the Mohawk Valley Project for our understanding of the details of Mohawk archaeology from 1634 on.

It became clear during the course of the project that many of our conclusions would depend not only on archaeology but also on historic documentation and the work of ethnologists. I accordingly sought funding for two specific publication efforts. One was the revision and publication of James W. Herrick's doctoral dissertation on Iroquois medical botany. This was recently published by Syracuse University Press (Herrick 1995). The second was the pulling together of historical narratives relating to the Mohawks and their valley. That effort has led to the production of this volume.

Preparation of both books was made possible mainly by the National Endowment for the Humanities. This volume was made possible by an NEH grant (RO-21465-87), which supported the Mohawk Valley Project during the years 1986,

1987, and 1989. The work was also supported by the Littauer, McDonald, Arkell Hall, and Wenner-Gren foundations, without whose support the full benefit of NEH funding could not have been realized. NEH and other public and private sources also provided support to the Mohawk Valley Project both before and after the period during which this volume was produced. Although indirectly so, all of that support provided crucial long-term context.

Most of the narratives reproduced here have been published before, but almost none of them is currently in print. Only van den Bogaert is currently available from a publisher (Syracuse University Press) in acceptable translation. Two sources have never been published before and are appearing here in English for the first time. These are Andreani and Rohde. Van der Donck is currently available in an older translation, but it is so flawed that we have provided a new translation of the portion relating to the Mohawks.

I worked closely with Charles Gehring and William Starna in completing this volume. Gehring is the director of the New Netherland Project, and he is an expert on seventeenth-century Dutch. Starna is an ethnohistorian and archaeologist with a thorough knowledge of Dutch, French, and English sources related to the Mohawk Valley. Both are old friends and superb scholars.

In all cases the narratives have their own biases. They are journals, reports, diaries, or autobiographies written by individuals for their own personal or professional reasons, and the unique perspective of each of them must be appreciated if the work is to be fully understood. Jesuit missionaries were interested in converting Mohawks to Catholicism while English military officers were interested in recruiting them to other purposes. Their perspectives were different, as were the things they considered worth writing about. The reader must take care to evaluate these biases while reading their works.

One of us has provided an introduction to each of the narratives. Our initials indicate which of us is responsible in each case. In all cases the introductions are intended to inform the reader about what is known of the author, the circumstances of his narrative, and its significance to the Mohawks and their valley. Specific source criticism is provided where possible and to the extent that it is relevant to understanding the author's bias. I have also written a general introduction that is designed to help guide the reader through the rest of the volume.

In cases where new translation was not required, we have reproduced previous versions without modification, except that footnotes and other scholarly devices have typically been removed. In many cases these earlier inclusions introduced errors or unnecessarily created confusion. In other cases they were merely unnecessary. In all cases our editions of previously published versions are explained in detail in the chapter introductions.

Charles Gehring translated Friedrich Rohde's narrative from German. This has not been previously published. Gehring also polished the Danckaerts translation. Perhaps most importantly, he acquired and approved the new translation of van der Donck, a crucially important work. I am grateful to him for his willingness to go beyond the writing of introductions in these cases.

I am grateful to Elisabeth Ruthman for her translation of the Paolo Andreani manuscript. Giose Rimanelli later reviewed the Italian manuscript and the English translation, providing a few suggestions for improving the latter. I have made a few additional editorial changes based upon my anthropological background. The manuscript was first brought to my attention by Charles Gehring and George Hamell. Hamell later found biographical information on Andreani with the assistance of Melinda Yates of the New York State Library.

I have included details from nine historical maps. I selected these after several years of informal searching and a more thorough searching of the collections of the Library of Congress and the New York State Archives. Many maps that seemed relevant at first proved to have been drawn at scales too general to provide much detail on the Mohawk Valley. Others provided detail but proved to be derivatives from earlier maps and were therefore out of date by the times they were drawn. Grassmann (1969) made use of maps by Franquelin (1684, 1688) and (perhaps wrongly) assumed that they represented the true locations of Mohawk villages in the years they were drafted. It would certainly be a mistake to assume this of Visscher's 1685 map, which simply repeats data from a 1653 map. Despite these problems, I have reproduced all of the relevant maps, along with necessary cautions regarding their interpretation.

I brought the larger project to its conclusion by 1993 with the continuing advice and assistance of Starna, Gehring, and many others. Before the project began I had the assistance of Robert Funk and Donald Lenig. In the first field season I had the benefit of assistance from Wayne Lenig, who had inherited his knowledge of the valley from his father. Then and later I had the assistance of dozens of graduate and undergraduate students from the University at Albany as well as the State University College at Oneonta. For two seasons I had the help of Earthwatch volunteers, and in all field seasons there were various other adult volunteers from the region.

The members of the Van Epps–Hartley Chapter of the New York State Archaeological Association have also been constant in their support. These included its founder, Vincent Schaefer, and others who provided invaluable assistance at various times. Most important among them has been Donald Rumrill, a natural scholar who has risen from the avocational ranks to produce a series of important articles on Mohawk archaeology. Rumrill (1985) was the first to see many of the currently accepted associations between documentary village names and archaeological sites. Previous speculation by Grassmann (1969:648–664) on this topic had been less successful, and still earlier speculations by others were almost entirely incorrect. Our understanding of Mohawk history has improved with every generation of scholarship, but there is no reason to conclude that we have taken it as far as it can go. There will be further refinements to the brief sketch provided in the introduction that follows, perhaps even major ones. For that the next generation of scholars has my grateful acknowledgment in advance. I hope that this volume will assist them.

William Sturtevant read the book in manuscript and provided many useful comments and criticisms. The work has been much improved by his careful reading and thoughtful suggestions. His is, of course, absolved of responsibility for any lingering errors.

Finally, I thank the Mohawks themselves, past and present. Their existence has made and continues to make a difference in the history of the region. We all continue to study the documents and strive to interpret them accurately in light of other evidence from archaeology, theory, and oral tradition. The dialog has sometimes been heated, but I am convinced that in the long run our inferences will be well tempered by that heat, and that the objective reality of the past will be seen with greater clarity by all of us.

D.R.S.

Introduction

The purpose of this volume is to provide in one place the principal documentary narratives relating to the Mohawk Valley for the years between Harmen van den Bogaert's journey in 1634-1635 and the planning of the Erie Canal in the early nineteenth century. These sources vary substantially in their origins, purposes, and biases. It has become fashionable in recent years to view all sources as so biased that there is no objective reality to be discovered through them. We do not share the cynical view that all accounts of the past are but flawed constructions, or that any interpretation we might make of them will itself necessarily be a politically inspired construction. While admitting that all documents (even this one) are in some sense or at some level self-serving, we maintain that an objective view of the past can be approached if one reads the available sources with skeptical care and thoughtful criticism. There is an objective reality to the past, even though we may never know it with complete accuracy; to assume otherwise is ultimately self-defeating.

The Dutch were primarily merchants, and their business interests never lie very far below the surfaces of their narratives. The French Jesuits were missionaries, and their reports from the Mohawk Valley were concerned mainly with their efforts to convert the Mohawk Indians and the awful but sublime suffering those efforts often entailed. Early English narratives were often political or military in nature, and concerned with the need to secure the Mohawks as allies. Later European travelers were often out to discover the curiosities of America and sometimes to poke fun at its inhabitants. Finally, the latest narratives were written by men interested in the opening of western New York to settlement and commerce by way of the Mohawk Valley.

All of these perspectives and implied biases influenced how authors represented what they saw. All of the authors brought prejudices with them, not the least of which were stereotypes about the Mohawks and other American Indians. Sometimes their preconceptions are obvious from remarks they would not have made at all had they not been previously burdened by some misconception. For example Van de Donck was clearly impressed by the attractiveness of Indian women and the small sizes of their families, points that he would not have made had he not expected something else. One is also struck by Rohde's contempt for the Palatine German's living in the Mohawk Valley, whose rude lifestyle he attributes to their long association with the Indians. In this case we get two stereotypes for the price of one.

People often tend to write about what they find to be unusual or shocking. There is much about torture and mayhem in these pages, mainly because violence is shocking and it engages the attention of both writer and reader. But people also write what is important to their larger agendas. English military officers liked to include detailed counts of warriors, and Jesuit missionaries avoided the long descriptions of domestic activities that interested Dutch traders.

Sorting it all out and finding objectively valid evidence of past reality is what ethnohistorians do best, and it is what they argue about most. It is often the case that what we would like most to know about for our own purposes was simply not of interest to the authors of the only documents we have. Sometimes they give us the information we want only obliquely as chance asides to what they thought was of principal interest. All of this leaves plenty of room for scholarly debate, and we hope that this volume will be a productive venue for future debate about the Mohawks and their valley.

The Mohawk Valley has been a major corridor linking the Atlantic Coast to the interior of North America for thousands of years. In the seventeenth and eighteenth centuries it was the primary conduit of contact between the Dutch and later English colonists and the Mohawks and other Iroquois Indians west of them. It was the eastern door of the League of the Iroquois, which stretched across what is now upstate New York like a great imaginary longhouse. West of the Mohawks were arrayed the Oneidas, Onondagas, Cayugas, and Senecas, the last the keepers of the League's western door (Figure 1). In the eighteenth century the Tuscaroras were added as a sixth nation, and they initally lived near the Oneidas. Indians of many other nations were absorbed in numbers both large and small; before, during, and after that same period. The strategy helped the Mohawks and the other Iroquois nations to survive to the present, even as many others disappeared as identifiable nations. The Mohawks persist today, the same yet different from their ancestors, as all human cultures inevitably are. This volume is as much for them as it is about them.

The Mohawks have been the focus of archaeological and historical attention for well over a century, but prior to the 1980s the archaeological sequence was poorly understood and the associations of documented village names to archaeological sites were erroneous in nearly all cases. Table 1 shows the currently accepted sequence of major Mohawk village sites. Population figures are drawn from two sources resulting from the Mohawk Valley Project (Snow 1995a, 1995d). The place-names in Table 1 are archaeological site names and not necessarily the names by which Mohawk villages are called in the narratives. The locations of the sames sites are shown in Figure 2, along with the locations of modern Fort Plain, Canajoharie, Fonda, Fort Hunter, and the area known as Stone Arabia. The seventeenth-century community of Schoharie, known archaeologically as the Bohringer site, is in the upper Schoharie Valley south of the area included in Figure 2. The area covered by Figure 2 appears as a white rectangle on Figure 1.

Linking village names mentioned in historical narratives to archaeological sites was a major objective of the Mohawk Valley Project. It was a difficult task that took over a decade to complete. Even after that much effort, it should be remembered that the proposed associations of village names and sites are hy-

Table 1. Sequence of Major Post-1626 Mohawk Villages Known as of 1996

Date	Western Series	Central Series		Eastern Series	Population
1776					
	Indian Castle (Ft. Hendrick)			Fort Hunter	640
1755					
	Dekanohage Prospect Hill	Bohringer (Schoharie Valley)		Fort Hunter	580
1712					
	Dekanohage	Prospect Hill Allen		Milton Smith	620
1693		FRONTENAC RAID - MOVE TO SOUTH BANK			
	Lipe #2				
	White Orchard	(undiscovered hamlet)		Caughnawaga	1100
1679					
	White Orchard	Schenck		Fox Farm	2000
	Jackson-Everson (Huron)				
1666		DE TRACY RAID - MOVE TO NORTH BANK			
	Jackson-Everson (Huron)			Freeman	2304
	Allen Fisk	Horatio Nellis Mitchell		Janie Printup	1734
1646					
	Oak Hill #1	Van Evera-McKinney	|		1760
				Bauder	
	Sand Hill #1	Prospect Hill Rumrill-Naylor	|		2835
1635		INITIAL SMALLPOX EPIDEMIC			
	Failing	Brown Yates		Cromwell	7740
1626		MAHICAN RAID - MOVE TO SOUTH BANK			

potheses that best account for the data as we currently know them. Hypotheses are by definition not provable, and they survive for only so long as they can account best for the available data. New archaeological data will probably require future revisions in our inferences and at least a few new hypotheses.

Van den Bogaert provides us with our earliest detailed description and our longest single list of contemporaneous villages. Table 2 lists the villages that van den Bogaert named in 1635 along with the names of the archaeological sites with which those village names are most probably associated. While these associations are the ones that seem most likely at this time, it is possible that new evidence will alter this interpretation in the future. The historical literature is strewn with what are now clearly incorrect associations between names and sites, just as the Mohawk Valley itself is strewn with historical markers that are mostly in the wrong places. Table 2 already represents a slight revision of what we thought only four years prior to this writing (Snow and Starna 1989:145), although the revision in this case was mainly through addition rather than substitution of inference.

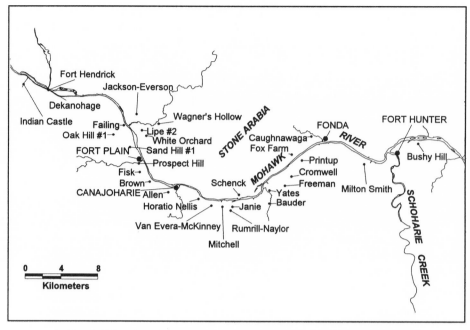

2. Post-1626 archaeological sites and modern place–names of the Mohawk
Valley. Modern names appear in caps. See text to relate site names to village
names mentioned in the narratives.

It appears that van den Bogaert saw four communities, all of which were in the
process of moving to new villages in the wake of a devastating smallpox epidemic. The four old villages would have held 7740 people, while the four new
ones replacing them would have held only 2830, indicating a population loss of
63%. In a matter of a few years the Mohawks contracted further into only three
villages (Snow 1995a).

Isaac Jogues noted in 1642 that there were three Mohawk villages named
Ossernenon, Andagaron, and Tionontoguen. These are probably (but not certainly) the sites known as Bauder, Rumrill-Naylor, and Oak Hill #1 respectively.
Only two years later, the Dutch minister Johannes Megapolensis called the same
three villages Asserué, Banagiro, and Thenondiogo. It is very likely that the
Frenchman and the Dutchman heard the same names, but the example shows
how different their ears were and how difficult it can be to link references in
multiple documents from the period.

Jogues escaped the Mohawks with Dutch help in 1643, the date of his narrative, but the Dutch remained friendly with the powerful Mohawks. Jogues returned briefly in civilian clothes to the Mohawk Valley early in 1646. On his
return to Canada later during the summer, he wrote an account that referred confusingly to "Oneugi8ré, jadis Osserrion." The comment appears in Lalemant's
report for 1646. This has most often been interpreted to mean that the village

3. Detail from *First Figurative Map*, attributed to Adriaen Block (1614). A colored version exists in the Algemeen Rijksarchief, The Hague. This detail is from a 1986 reproduction by Holland Village, Inc. of a copy in the New York Public Library Stokes Collection. Permission to reproduce has been given by the New Netherland Museum. Although the map is usually attributed to Block, the 1986 reproduction caption allows for the possibility that the map was drawn by Captain Cornelis Hendricksz. Both explored New York on the ship De Onrust (or Unrest), the first Dutch ship built in New Netherland.

The map depicts "Niev Nederlandt." The Mohawk Valley is denoted by the words "MAQVAAS" and "cunomakers." Three inscriptions around these two words refer to Fort Nassau, which was built at this time on Castle Island in what is now Albany. As translated by Charles Gehring, they read: "But as far as one can understand by what the Mohawk say and show, the French come with sloops as high up as their country to trade with them," "Fort Nassau is 58 feet wide between the walls and built as a square; the moat is 18 feet wide," and "The house is 36 feet long and 26 feet wide inside the fort."

Table 2. Mohawk Castles and Villages in 1634

Villages	Houses	Hearths	1626-1635 Pop.	1635-1650 Pop.	Probable Sites
Onekagoncka	36	216	2160		Cromwell
Canawarode	6	36	360		Yates
Schatsyerosy	12	72		725	Bauder
Canagere	16	73		730	Rumrill-Naylor
Schanidisse	32	192	1920		Brown
Osquage	9	54		540	Prospect Hill
Cawaoge	14	84		840	Sand Hill #1
Tenotoge	55	330	3300		Failing
TOTALS	180	1057	7740	2835	

Source: Snow 1995d:280

Jogues had called "Ossernenon" three years earlier, and which he was in 1646 calling "Osserïon," had moved and the name of the new village was "Oneugi8ré." However, this does not fit with either what Megapolensis says or the archaeological evidence. I infer that Jogues meant that while he had previously been in Ossernenon, his 1646 visit took him to Oneugi8ré, which was the same as Megapolensis's "Banagiro" and van den Bogaert's "Canagere." In other words, he meant that he had formerly been in one village and was now in another, not that the village had changed its name or both its name and its location. If my inference is correct, then all of these names probably relate to the Rumrill-Naylor site. Mohawk words never begin with a "B," so Megapolensis must have misunderstood what he heard in any case. Further, the phonemically equivalent "K" or "G" sounds are often soft, easily mistaken for the soft glottal stop that most speakers of modern English would use at the beginning of a word like Oneugi8ré, but never think to write down. Thus Van den Bogaert heard the initial sound in the village name as a "K," Megapolensis heard it as a "B," and Jogues either did not hear it, treated it like an initial (silent) glottal, or chose to ignore it.

Jogues's Ossernenon (Osserïon) was probably on the site referred to archaeologically as the Bauder site. This community probably moved to the Printup site after his death in 1646. In no case was the name Ossernenon ever applied to the early eighteenth-century cemetery site known as Auriesville. The modern identification of Auriesville with Ossernenon dates only to the late nineteenth century, when scholars were only just beginning to find and understand relevant documentary sources. Nevertheless, the construction of a Jesuit shrine there to Jogues and other Jesuit martyrs has established the connection in the popular imagination.

Van der Donck's map of 1653 (Figure 4) shows four place names: Caronay, Canagero, Shanatissa, and t'Iounontego. These names probably refer to the

Printup, Mitchell, Horatio Nellis, Allen sites respectively. Three of the names are cognate with names mentioned earlier by van den Bogaert and others, reflecting the common (but not consistent) practice of carrying village names along through successions of site locations. Canagero later turns up as Gandagaro, Gannagaro, Canagora, and similar forms. It applies to the sequence of village relocations on the Rumrill-Naylor, Van Evera-McKinney, Mitchell, and Schenck sites. The name drops out of the documents after 1679, reflecting the reduction of Mohawk communities in the valley from three to two.

The village that starts out in van den Bogaert's account as Tenotoge becomes Tionontoguen, Thenondioga, t'Iounontego, Tionondogue, Tinniontoguen, and similar forms in later references. The name was apparently applied to a succession of sites beginning with Failing and moving through the Oak Hill #1, Allen, White Orchard, and possibly the Lipe #2 sites.

"Kaghnuwage" appears as a new village name in 1659, probably to refer to a new settlement at the Freeman site. This name is later repeated by several authors as Andaraque, Gandaouage, Gandaouaguen, Caghnawaga, Cahaniaga, Kaknnaogue, and Caughnawaga, among other forms. These names were later often applied to the Fox Farm site, the Caughnawaga site proper, and the succession of sites occupied by Mohawk refugees near Montreal from the late seventeenth century on. The reserve there is still known as Kahnawake, a spelling that reflects modern Mohawk pronunciation as well as the unity of "K" and "G" in that language.

After the western Mohawk village moved to the south side of the river in 1693, it came to be called Canijoharie. This was later spelled Kanajohare, Canojaharie, Canajohary, and in other similar ways before reaching its modern standard form of Canajoharie. It was used to refer variously and confusingly to villages at the Allen, Prospect Hill, and Indian Castle sites before coming to rest at the modern village of Canajoharie.

There are many other place names and ethnic names mentioned in the narratives that follow. The above discussion of place names should be sufficient to allow interpretation of those belonging to the Mohawk Valley. Ethnic names that apply to the Mohawks as a people rather than to their villages fall into three main classes. The early French writers referred to the Mohawks as Anniegué, Annieronnons, Agnié, Anniez, Agnez, Agniez, and similar forms borrowed from the Hurons. The Dutch often called them Maquaas, Maques, Maquas, Mahakuaas, and so forth, which they had borrowed from the Mahicans. The English, who consulted first with the Massachusetts and other southern New England nations, referred to the Mohawks as Mahwukes, Mawhawkes, Mohacks, Mohaggs, Mowhakes, and so on before settling on the modern spelling. All of these forms and more are discussed in detailed synonymies that are provided in the *Handbook of North American Indians*, volume 15 (Trigger 1978). None of them are cognate with terms that the Mohawks used to refer to themselves. To themselves the Mohawks were the Kanyenkehaka `people of the place of the flint'. They called their valley Kanyenka `the place of the flint', although there is reason to believe that "flint" meant more specifically the distinctive quartz crystals, now usually called

Herkimer Diamonds, that are found both in quarries and on archaeological sites in the valley.

Some readers will find it useful to cite these narratives as we have presented them. Others will find it necessary to go to the original sources. Still others will want to consult material that we have not been able to include. There are many other documentary references to the Mohawks and their valley, but we have been constrained by space and the need to avoid inclusion of sources in which reference to our main subject was brief or tangential. I trust that our efforts will be useful to a growing number of scholars, and that in the future the subject will enjoy the attention it deserves.

In Mohawk Country

A Journey into Mohawk and Oneida Country

1634-1635

Harmen Meyndertsz van den Bogaert

In 1624 the Dutch West Indian Company established a trading post at Fort Orange (Albany, New York) and was soon fully engaged in a lively and profitable fur trade with the local Indian inhabitants. This followed the earlier explorations of Henry Hudson in the valley that now bears his name and the short-lived Dutch settlement at Fort Nassau. Within a brief period of time the Dutch had convinced the Mohawks, who controlled the major trading route through the Mohawk Valley, that they were not a threat, forming a bond of friendship and mutual interest that was to endure for many years to come.

Along the St. Lawrence River, north of the Dutch, was their only competitor for Indian furs—the French. Both of these European powers, along with their Indian allies, were in regular conflict over control of the fur-trapping regions of the interior, areas located generally west of the Champlain-Hudson valleys. Of most concern to the Dutch was the possibility that the French would capture the fur market around Oneida Lake, using to their advantage the easy water access via Lake Ontario and the Oswego and Oneida rivers. If the French were allowed to negotiate a truce and a trading partnership with the Iroquois in that region, the trading post at Fort Orange would be rendered useless and the West India Company would have little choice but to end its investment in New Netherland. It was in this context that van den Bogaert made his journey to the Iroquois.

In the winter of 1634 the commander of Fort Orange ordered van den Bogaert, a barber-surgeon, and two other Dutchmen, west into the Mohawk Valley and Indian country. The party was to learn why the fur trade had declined, suspected to have been caused by French incursions, and to negotiate a new price structure for furs with the Indians. The expedition, lasting some six weeks, took the Dutchmen through a number of Mohawk villages to the Oneidas, nearly 100 miles from the fort. While on the trail van den Bogaert kept a daily journal, a remarkable chronicle by a keen observer, which described Indian villages, healing rituals, language, subsistence practices, the environment, and many other details of the region and its inhabitants. The journal stands as a unique and compelling document. It is the earliest known record of the interior west of the Hudson.

1

For many years van den Bogaert's journal lay undiscovered in a garret in Amsterdam. In 1895 it was obtained by General James Grant Wilson, a bibliophile and editor, who, from 1900 to 1914, was president of the American Ethnological Society. He published a translation of the journal that same year (Wilson 1895, 1896). It appeared again, with some revision, in J. Franklin Jameson's *Narratives of New Netherland* (Jameson 1909:139-162). The version reproduced here was published in 1988 (van den Bogaert 1988).

W.A.S.

PRAISE GOD above all. At Fort Orange 1634.

11 December. Report of the most important things that happened to me while traveling to the Maquasen [Mohawk] and Sinnekens [Oneidas]. First of all, the reasons why we went were that the Maquasen and Sinnekens had often come to our Commissary Martin Gerritsen and me, saying that there were French Indians in their country, and that they had called a truce with them, so that they, namely, the Maquasen, would trade furs with them there, because the Maquase wanted as much for their furs as did the French Indians. Therefore, I asked Sr. Martin Gerritsen's permission to go there and learn the truth of the matter in order to report to their High Mightinesses as soon as possible, because trade was going very badly. So for these reasons I went with Jeromus la Croex and Willem Tomassen. May the Lord bless our journey.

Between nine and ten o'clock we left with five Maquasen Indians mostly toward the northwest, and at one half hour into the evening, after eight miles, we came to a hunter's cabin where we spent the night by the waterway that runs into their country, and is named Oÿoge. The Indians here fed us venison. The country is mostly covered with pine trees and there is much flat land. This waterway flows past their castle in their country, but we were unable to travel on it because of the heavy flooding.

12 ditto. We continued our journey three hours before dawn. The Indians, who traveled with us, would have left us there, if I had not noticed it; and when we intended to eat something, their dogs had eaten up our meat and cheese so that we had nothing but dry bread to travel on. After we had traveled an hour, we came to the tributary that flows into our river and past the Maquase's villages. Here there was a heavy ice flow. Jeronimus crossed first in a canoe made of tree bark with an Indian because only two men could travel together in it. After this Willem and I [crossed]. It was so dark that we could not see one another without staying close together so that it was not without danger. After crossing over, we went another one and a half miles and came to a hunter's cabin. We entered and ate some venison there. We then continued our journey. After we had gone another half mile, we saw some people coming toward us. When they saw us, they ran away. Throwing down their bags and packs, they ran into a marsh and hid behind a thicket so that we were unable to see them. We looked at their goods and packs, taking a small loaf of bread baked with beans. We ate it up and con-

tinued on mostly along this aforesaid waterway, which flowed most fiercely because of the flood. There are many islands in this waterway, on the banks of
which are 500 or 600 morgens of flatland; indeed, much more. When we, by
estimation, had covered eleven miles, we came at one hour into the evening to a
cabin one half mile from the first castle. No one was there but women. We would
have then continued on, but I could not move my feet because of the rough going; so, we slept there. It was very cold with a north wind.

13 ditto. In the morning we went together to the castle over the ice that had
frozen in the waterway during the night. When we had gone one half mile, we
came into their first castle that stood on a high hill. There were only 36 houses,
row on row in the manner of streets, so that we easily could pass through. These
houses are constructed and covered with the bark of trees, and are mostly flat
above. Some are 100, 90, or 80 steps long; 22 or 23 feet high. There were also
some interior doors made of split planks furnished with iron hinges. In some
houses we also saw ironwork: iron chains, bolts, harrow teeth, iron hoops,
spikes, which they steal when they are away from here. Most of the people were
out hunting for bear and deer. These houses were full of grain that they call
ONESTI and we corn; indeed, some held 300 or 400 skipples. They make boats
and barrels of tree-bark and sew with it. We ate here many baked and boiled
pumpkins which they call ANONSIRA. None of the chiefs was at home, except for
the most principal one called ADRIOCHTEN, who was living one quarter mile from
the fort in a small cabin because many Indians here in the castle had died of
smallpox. I invited him to come visit with me, which he did. He came and bid
me welcome, and said that he wanted us to come with him very much. We would
have gone but we were called by another chief when we were already on the
path, and turned back toward the castle. He had a large fire started at once, and a
fat haunch of venison cooked, from which we ate; and he also gave us two bear-
skins to sleep on, and presented me with three beaver pelts. In the evening I
made some cuts with a knife in Willem Tomassen's leg, which had swollen from
walking, and then smeared it with bear's grease. We slept here in this house, and
ate large quantities of pumpkin, beans, and venison so that we suffered of no
hunger here but fared as well as it is possible in their country. I hope that everything shall succeed.

14 ditto. Jeronimus wrote a letter to the commissary, Marten Gerritsen, asking
for paper, salt, and ATSOCHWAT, i.e., Indian tobacco. We went out with the chief
to see if we could shoot some turkeys, but got none. However, in the evening I
bought a very fat turkey for 2 hands of sewant [wampum], which the chief
cooked for us; and the grease that cooked from it he put in our beans and corn.
This chief let me see his idol which was a marten's head with protruding teeth,
covered with red duffel-cloth. Others keep a snake, a turtle, a swan, a crane, a
pigeon, and such similar objects for idols or telling fortunes; they think that they
will then always have luck. Two Indians left from here for Fort Orange with
skins.

15 ditto. I went out again with the chief to hunt turkeys, but we got none. In
the evening the chief once again let us see his idol. On account of the heavy

snow over the path we decided to stay here another two or three days until the opportunity presented itself to proceed.

16 ditto. In the afternoon a good hunter named SICKARIS came here who wanted us to go with him very much and carry our goods to his castle. He offered to let us sleep in his house and stay there as long as we pleased. Because he offered us so much, I presented him with a knife and two awls; and to the chief in whose home we had stayed I presented a knife and a scissors. Then we departed from this castle ONEKAHONCKA. After we had gone one half mile over the ice we saw a village with only six houses. It was called CANOWARODE, but we did not enter it because he said that it was not worth much. After we had gone another half mile we passed a village with twelve houses called SCHATSYEROSY. This one was like the other, saying also that it was not worth much. After we had gone a mile or a mile and a half past great tracts of flatland, we entered a castle at about two hours in the evening. I could see nothing else but graves. This castle is called CANAGERE and is situated on a hill without palisades or any defense. There were only seven men at home and a group of old women and children. The chiefs of this castle TONNOSATTON and TONIWEROT were out hunting so that we slept in SECKARIS'S house as he had promised us. We counted in his house 120 pelts of marketable beaver that he had caught with his own hands. We ate beaver's meat here everyday. In this castle there are 16 houses, 50, 60, 70, 80 steps long, and one of 16 steps, and one of five steps in which a bear was being fattened. It had been in there almost three years and was so tame that it ate everything given it.

17 ditto. Sunday. We looked over our goods and came upon a paper of sulphur. Jeronimus took some out and threw it on the fire. They saw the blue flame and smelled the odor, and told us that they also had such goods. When SICKARIS came in, they got it out and let us look at it, and it was the same. We asked him how he came by it. He told us that they got it from the foreign Indians, and that they considered it good for healing many illnesses, but principally for their legs when they become very sore from traveling and are very tired.

18 ditto. Three women came here from the Sinnekens with some dried and fresh salmon, but they smelled very bad. They sold each salmon for one guilder or two hands of sewant. They also brought much green tobacco to sell, and had been six days underway. They could not sell all their salmon here, but went with it to the first castle. Then we were supposed to travel with them when they returned. In the evening Jeronimus told me that an Indian was planning to kill him with a knife.

December 19. We received a letter from Marten Gerritsen dated the eighteenth of this year. With it came paper, salt, and tobacco for the Indians and a bottle of brandy. We hired a man to guide us to the Sinnekens, and gave him one half piece of duffel, two axes, two knives and two awls. If it had been summer there would have been people enough to accompany us, but since it was winter they did not want to leave their country because it snowed there often a man's height deep. Today we had a very heavy rain. I gave this Indian a pair of shoes. His name was SQORHEA.

December 20. Then we left the second castle, and when we had gone one mile our Indian SQORHEA came before a stream that we had to cross. This stream was running very hard with many large chunks of ice, because yesterday's heavy rain had broken up the stream so that we were in great danger. Had one of us just fallen, it would have been the end. But the Lord God protected us and we made it across. We were soaked up to the waist. After going another half mile, with wet and frozen clothing, stockings, and shoes, we came to a very high hill on which stood 32 houses, all similar to the previous ones. Some were 100, 90, 80 steps or paces long. In each house there were four, five or six places for fires and cooking. There were many Indians at home here so that we caused much curiosity in the young and old; indeed, we could hardly pass through the Indians here. They pushed one another into the fire to see us. It was almost midnight before they left us. We could not do anything without having them shamelessly running about us. This is the third castle, and it is called SCHANIDISSE. The chief's name is TEWOWARY. This evening I got a lion skin to cover myself with; however, in the morning I had at least 100 lice. We ate here much venison. There is considerable flatland around and near this castle, and the woods are full of oak and walnut trees. We got a beaver here in exchange for an awl.

December 21. We left very early in the morning, intending to go to the fourth castle. However, after we had gone a half mile we came to a village with nine houses called OSQUAGE. The chief's name was OQUOHO, i.e., wolf. Here there was a great stream which our guide would not cross. Because of the heavy rain, the water was over our heads. For this reason we delayed until Saturday. This chief gave us many goods and fed us well, for everything in his house was at our disposal. He told me simply that I was his brother and good friend. Indeed, he also told me how he had traveled thirty days overland, and saw there an Englishman coming from the Minquas in order to learn their language for the fur trade. I asked him whether there were French Indians near the Sinnekens. He said, yes, and I was pleased, and thought that I would then reach my objective. I was asked here to heal a man who was very sick.

December 22. In the morning at sunrise we crossed the stream together. It was over our knees and was so cold that our stockings and shoes quickly froze as hard as armor-plate. The Indians dared not cross there but went two by two with a stick from hand to hand. After we had gone one half mile, we came to a village called CAWAOGE. It had 14 houses and a tame bear. We went in and smoked a pipe of tobacco because the old man, who was our guide, was very tired. An old man came to us and said, "Welcome, welcome, should you have to stay overnight." However, we left in order to continue our journey. I wanted to buy the bear, but they would not part with it. All along the path stood many trees very similar to the savin tree. They have a very thick bark. This village is also located on a high hill. After we had gone a mile overland through a sparsely wooded region we came to the 4th castle called TENOTOGE. It had 55 houses, some 100 steps [in size] and others more or less as large. The waterway that was mentioned earlier ran past here and took the course mostly north-west and south-east. There are more houses on the opposite bank of the waterway; however, we did not enter them because they were mostly full of grain. The houses in this castle are full of grain and beans. Here the Indians looked on in amazement; for most everyone was at home, and they crowded in on us so much that we could barely pass among them. After a long period, an Indian came to us who took us to his house and we went in it. The castle was surrounded with three rows of palisades. However, now there were only 6 or 7 [posts] left, so thick that it was unbelievable that Indians could do it. They pushed one another into the fire in order to see us.

23 Dec. A man came shouting and screaming through some of the houses here. However, we did not know what it was supposed to mean. After a while Jeronimus de la Croix came, and wondered what it meant that the Indians were arming themselves. I asked them what was meant by it and they said [it was] nothing against me, "We are going to play with one another." There were four with clubs, and some with axes and sticks so that there were 20 men under arms; 9 on one side and 11 on the other. Then they went at each other, fighting and striking. Some wore armor and helmets which they made themselves from thin reeds and cord woven together so that no arrow or axe could penetrate to cause serious injury. After they had skirmished in this manner for a long time, the adversaries ran at one another; and the one dragged the other by the hair as they would do with conquered enemies, and would then cut their heads off. They wanted us to fire our pistols, but we went away and left them. Today we feasted on two bears, and we received today one half skipple of beans and some dried strawberries. Also, we provided ourselves here with bread that we could take along on the journey. Some of it had nuts, chestnuts, dried blueberries and sunflower seeds baked in it.

24 Dec. Since it was Sunday I looked in on a person who was sick. He had invited into his house two of their doctors who were supposed to heal him. They were called SUNACHKOES. As soon as they arrived, they began to sing, and kindled a large fire, sealing the house all around so that no draft could enter. Then both of them put a snakeskin around their heads and washed their hands and faces. They then took the sick person and laid him before the large fire. Taking a bucket of water in which they had put some medicine, they washed a stick in it 1/2 ell long. They stuck it down their throats so that the end could not be seen, and vomited on the patient's head and all over his body. Then they performed many farces with shouting and rapid clapping of hands, as is their custom, with much display, first on one thing and then on the other, so that the sweat rolled off them everywhere.

25 Dec. As it was Christmas day we arose early in the morning, intending to go to the Sinnekens. However, on account of the steady snow we were unable to start out, because no one would go with us to carry our goods. I asked them how many chiefs there were and they told me thirty persons.

26 Dec. This morning I was given two pieces of bear's meat to take on the journey. We took our leave amid much uproar that surged behind and before us. They repeatedly shouted: "ALLESE RONDADE," i.e., "Shoot!" However, we did not want to shoot. Finally they went away. Today we passed over much flatland, and also through a stream over our knees in depth. I think that we proceeded

today mostly in a west-north-west direction. The woods through which we traveled were at first mostly oak but after three or four hours underway we encountered mostly birch. It snowed the entire day so that it was very difficult to climb over the hills. After an estimated seven miles, we came to a bark hut in the woods where we kindled a fire and stayed the night. It continued to snow with a strong north wind. It was extremely cold.

Dec. 27 Early in the morning we continued on with great difficulty through two and a half feet of snow in some places. We went over hills, and through thickets, seeing tracks of many bear and elk, but no Indians. Here there are beech trees. After going seven or eight miles, we found at sunset once again a hut in the woods with little bark, but with some tree branches. We again made a big fire and cooked SAPPAEN. It was so cold during the night that I could barely sleep two hours.

Dec. 28 We continued on, proceeding as before. After we had gone one or two miles, we came to a waterway that the Indians told me flowed into the land of the Minquasen. After having gone another mile we came to another waterway that flowed into the South River, so the Indians told me. Here many otters and beavers were caught. Today we passed over many high hills. The woods are full of many large trees, but mostly birch. After going another seven or eight miles we did as above. It was extremely cold.

Dec. 29 We pushed on with our journey. After having traveled awhile, we came to a very high hill. When we had just about reached the top, I fell so that I thought that I had broken my ribs; however, it was only the handle of my sword that had broken. We passed through low lands where many oak trees and ironwood grew. After seven more miles, we found another hut into which we settled ourselves. We made a fire and ate up all the food we had, for the Indians said that we were still about four miles from the castle. It was nearly sunset when another Indian ran on to the castle to tell them that we were coming. We would have gone too, but because we were all very hungry the Indians would not take us along. Course NW.

Dec. 30 We proceeded toward the Sinnekens' castle without eating. After having gone a while, the Indians pointed out to me the tributary of the river before Fort Orange, which passes through the land of the Maquaesen. A woman came along the way, bringing us baked pumpkins to eat. This stretch is mostly full of birch wood and flatlands cleared for sowing. Just before reaching the castle, we saw three graves in the manner of our graves: long and high. Otherwise their graves are round. These graves were surrounded with palisades that they had split from trees, and were so neatly made that it was a wonder. They were painted red, white, and black. Only the chief's grave had an entrance, above which stood a large wooden bird surrounded by paintings of dogs, deer, snakes, and other animals. After having gone four or five miles, the Indians asked us to shoot. We fired our weapons, which we reloaded, and then we went to the castle. North-west of us we saw a very large body of water. Opposite the water was extremely high ground which seemed to lie in the clouds. When I inquired about it, the Indians told me that the French came into that water to trade. After that we confidently went to the castle where the Indians divided themselves into two rows and let us pass in between them through their entrance. The one we passed through was three and a half feet wide. Above the entrance stood three large wooden images, carved as men, by which three locks fluttered that they had cut from the heads of slain Indians as a token of truth, that is to say, victory. This castle has two entrances, one on the east and one on the west side. A lock was also hanging by the east gate, but this gate was one and a half feet smaller than the other. Then we were finally brought into the farthest house, where I found many acquaintances. We were put in the place where the chief was accustomed to sit because he was not home at the time. We were cold, wet, and tired. We received food immediately, and they built a good fire. This castle is also located on a very high hill and was surrounded with two rows of palisades, 767 steps in circumference, in which there are 66 houses; but built much better and higher than all the others. There were many wooden gables on the houses which were painted with all sorts of animals. They sleep here mostly on raised platforms, more than any other Indians. In the afternoon, one of the councilors came to ask me what we were doing in his country and what we brought him for gifts. I said that we brought him nothing, but that we just came for a visit. However, he said that we were worth nothing because we brought him no gifts. Then he told how the French had traded with them here with six men and had given them good gifts; for they had traded in the aforementioned river last August of this year with six men. We saw there good timber axes, French shirts, coats, and razors. And this councilor derided us as scoundrels, and said that we were worthless because we gave them so little for their furs. They said that the French gave them six hands of sewant for one beaver and all sorts of other things in addition. The Indians sat so close to us here that we could barely sit. If they had wanted to do anything to us we could have done nothing, but there was no danger to our persons. In this river already mentioned, there are six or seven or even 800 salmon caught in one day. I saw houses with 60, 70 and more dried salmon.

31 Dec. On Sunday the chief of this castle returned home. He was called ARENIAS. He came with another man, saying that they came from the French Indians. Some of the Indians gave a scream, saying JAWE ARENIAS, which meant that they thanked him for coming. I told him that we would fire three shots this evening, and they said that it was good and they were very pleased. We asked them for the locations of all of their castles and for their names, and how far they were from one another. They put down kernels of corn and stones, and Jeronimus made a map from them. We reckoned everything in miles; how far every place was from one another. The Indians here told us that in that high country that we had seen near the lake there lived people with horns. They also said that many beavers were caught there; however, they dared not travel so far because of the French Indians. For this reason, therefore, they would make peace. This evening we fired three shots in honor of the year of our Lord and Redeemer JESU CHRISTO.

PRAISE THE LORD ABOVE ALL
IN THE CASTLE ONNEYUTTEHAGE
OR SINNEKENS 1635 January

1 January. An Indian once again called us scoundrels, as has been previously told, and he was very malicious so that Willem Tomassen became so angry that the tears ran from his eyes. The Indian seeing that we were upset, asked us why we looked at him with such anger. We were sitting during this time with their 46 persons around and near us. Had they had any malicious intentions, they could have easily grabbed us with their hands and killed us without much trouble. However, when I had heard his screaming long enough, I told him that he was the scoundrel. He began to laugh and said that he was not angry and said "You must not be angry. We are happy that you have come here." Jeronimus gave the chief two knives, two scissors, and some awls and needles that we had with us. In the evening the Indians hung up a belt of sewant and some other strung sewant that the chief had brought back from the French Indians as a token of peace that the French Indians were free to come among them; and they sang HO SCHENE JO HO HO SCHENE I ATSIEHOENE ATSIHOENE. Whereupon all the Indians shouted three times NETHO NETHO NETHO, and then hung up another belt, singing KATON KATON KATON KATON. Then they shouted in a loud voice H_ H_ H_. After long deliberation they concluded the peace for four years, and then each went to his house.

Jan. 2 The Indians came to us and said that we had to wait another four or five days; and if we could not go sooner, then they would provide us with all necessities. However, I said that we could not wait long. They answered that they had sent for the ONNEDAEGES, which is the castle next to them. But I said that they mostly let us starve, whereupon they said that henceforth we would receive sufficient food. Today we were twice invited to feast on bear's meat and salmon.

January 3. Some old men came to us and said that they wanted to be our friends, and that we must not be afraid. Whereupon I told them that we were not afraid. Toward midday they gathered their council here with 24 men. After they had conferred for a long time, an old man came to me and felt whether my heart was beating against his hand. When he shouted that we were not afraid, six more men came from the council, and they presented us with a beaver coat. They gave it to me saying, "It is for your journey, because you are so tired." And pointing to my feet and his, said, "That is also because you have walked through the snow." When we accepted it, they shouted three times NETHO, NETHO, NETHO, which means that they were pleased. At once they laid five more beaver skins at my feet, and thereby requested that they would like to have four hands of sewant and four hands of long cloth for each large beaver because "We have to travel so far with our pelts and when we arrive we often find no cloth, no sewant, no axes, kettles or anything else; and thus we have labored in vain. Then we have to go back a long way carrying our goods." After we had sat for a time, an old man came to us for whom they translated us in another language, and he said, "You have not said whether we shall have four hands or not." Whereupon I told him that we had no authority to promise them that, but that we would tell the chief at the Manhatas [Manhattan], who was our commander, and that I would inform him of everything in the spring, and come myself into their country. Then they said to me WELSMACHKOO, "You must not lie, and come in the spring to us and bring us all an answer. If we receive four hands, then we shall trade our pelts with no one else." Then they gave me the five beavers and shouted again in a loud voice NETHO NETHO NETHO; and so that everything should be firm and binding, they shouted or sang: HA ASSIRONI ATSIMACHKOO KENT OYAKAYING WEE ONNEYATTE ONAONDAGE KOYOCKWE HOO SENOTO WANYAGWEGANNE HOO SCHENEHALATON KASTEN KANOSONI YNDICKO, which was to say that I should go to all these places, by naming all the castles, and I would go there freely and be free there in every place; I would have house and fire, wood and anything else. Whatever I received there would be mine; and if I wished to go to the French, then they would go with me and bring me back wherever I desired. Thereupon they again shouted in a loud voice three times, NETHO NETHO NETHO, and I was again made a present of a beaver. This day we were invited to eat bear's meat. In this chief's house three or four meals were eaten everyday. Whatever was not cooked there was brought in from other houses in large kettles, because the council came here everyday to eat; and whosoever is in the house, receives a wooden bowl full of food, for it is the custom that every man who comes here, receives a bowl full. If bowls are lacking, then they bring their own bowls and spoons. They then sit down next to one another where the bowls are fetched and brought back full, because an invited guest does not stand up until he has eaten. Sometimes they sing and sometimes not. They then thank the host and each returns home.

Jan. 4 Two men came to me and said that I should come and see how they would drive out the devil; but I said that I had seen that before. However, I had to go along anyway. There were twelve men here who were to drive him out; and because I would not go alone, I took Jeronimus with me. When we arrived, the floor of the house was completely covered with tree bark over which the devil-hunters were to walk. They were mostly old men who were all colored or painted with red paint on their faces because they were to perform something strange. Three of them had garlands around their heads upon which were five white crosses. These garlands were made of deer's hair which they dyed with the roots of herbs. In the middle of this house was a very sick person who had been languishing for a long time, and there sat an old woman who had an empty turtle shell in her hands, in which were beads that rattled while she sang. Here they intended to catch the devil and trample him to death, for they stomped all the bark in the house to pieces, so that none remained whole. Wherever they saw but a little dust on the corn, they beat at it with great excitement, and then they blew that dust toward one another and were so afraid that each did his best to flee as if he had seen the devil. After much stomping and running, one of them went to the sick person and took an otter from his hand, and for a long time sucked on the sick man's neck and back. Then he spit in the otter and threw it on the ground, running away with great excitement. Other men then ran to the otter and performed such antics that it was a wonder to see; indeed, they threw fire, ate fire, and threw around hot ashes and embers in such a way that I ran out of the house. Today I received another beaver.

Jan. 5 I bought four dried salmon and two pieces of bear's meat that was nine inches thick; there was some here even thicker. Today we ate beans cooked with bear's meat. Otherwise nothing occurred.

Jan. 6 Nothing in particular happened other than I was shown some stones with which they make fire when they go into the woods, and which are scarce. These stones would also be good on firelocks.

Jan. 7 We received a letter from Marten Gerritsz dated the last of December by a Sinck who came from our fort. He said that our people were very troubled because we did not return, thinking that we had been killed. We ate here fresh salmon that had been caught but two days ago. Six and a half fathoms of sewant was stolen from our bags and never recovered.

Jan. 8 ARENIAS came to me and said that he would accompany me to our fort with all his pelts for trading. Jerominmus offered to sell his coat here but could not get rid of it.

Jan. 9 The ONNEDAGENS [Onondagas] arrived here in the evening; six old men and four women, who were very tired from the journey. They brought some beaver pelts with them. I went and thanked them for coming to visit us. They welcomed me and because it was late I went again to our house.

Jan 10. Jeronimus badly burned his pants that had fallen from his body into the fire during the night. The chief's mother gave him cloth to repair them and Willem Tomassen sewed them up again.

Jan. 11 The Indians came to me at 10 o'clock in the morning and said, "Come into the house where the ONNEDAGENS sit in council and shall give you gifts." Jeronimus and I went there and took along a pistol. We sat down by an old man named CANASTOGEERA, who was about 55 years old. He said to us, "Friends, I have come here to see you and to speak with you." We thanked him for this, and after they held council for a long time, an interpreter came to me and gave me five wild beavers for my journey and because we came to visit them. I took the beavers and thanked them, whereupon they shouted loudly three times NETHO, and then they laid another five wild beavers at my feet and gave them to us because we had come into his council house. We would have received many pelts as gifts, if we had just come into his country, and he asked me earnestly to visit his country in the summer. Then they gave me another four wild beavers and demanded that they must receive more for their pelts, then they would bring us many pelts. If I returned to their country in the summer, we would have three or four Indians to show us that lake and where the French came to trade with their sloops. When we picked up our fourteen beavers they shouted once again three times NETHO, and we fired three shots and gave the chiefs two pair of knives, some awls, and needles. Then we received the news that we could go. We still had five pieces of salmon and two pieces of bear's meat to eat on the way, and we were given here some bread and meal to take along.

Jan. 12 We said goodbye, and when we thought that everything was ready, the Indians would not carry our goods: 28 beavers and five salmon with some bread, because they all had enough to carry. However, after much grumbling and nice words, they went with us in company, carrying our goods. There were many people here who walked along with us shouting ALLE SARONDADE, that is to say, "Shoot!" When we passed the chief's grave, we fired three shots, and then they left us and went away. It was about nine o'clock when we left here. We walked only about five miles through two and a half feet of snow. It was very difficult going so that some Indians had to sleep in the woods in the snow, but we found a hut where we slept.

Jan. 13 Early next morning we were once again on our way. After going another seven or eight miles, we came to a hut where we stopped to cook something to eat, and to sleep. ARENIAS pointed out to me a place on a high hill and said after a ten days' journey we could come to a river here where many people lived and where there were many cows and horses. However, we must sail across the river for a whole day and then travel another six days to get there. This was the place we passed on the 29th of December. He did us much good.

Jan. 14 On Sunday we were ready to go, but the chief wanted to stay in order to go out bear hunting from here. However, because it was nice weather, I went on alone with two or three Indians. Two Maquaesen came to us here because they wanted to go to trade elks skins and SATTEEU.

Jan. 15 In the morning two hours before daybreak, after having eaten with the Indians, I continued my journey. When it was almost dark, the Indians built a fire in the woods for they would go no farther. About three hours into evening I came to a hut where I had slept on December 26th. It was very cold and I was not able to start a fire. Therefore I had to walk around the whole night to keep warm.

Jan. 16 In the morning three hours before daybreak, when the moon came up, I looked for the path, which I finally found. At nine in the morning after hard going, I came to a great flat country. After traversing a high hill I came upon a very level path which was made by the Indians who had passed here with much venison when returning home from the hunt to their castles. I saw the castle at ten o'clock and entered it at twelve noon. At least 100 people accompanied me in and showed me a house where I was to stay. They gave me a white hare to eat which they had caught two days ago. It was cooked with chestnuts. I received a piece of wheat bread from an Indian who had come from Fort Orange on the 15th of this month. Toward evening about 40 fathoms of sewant were distributed among them as testimony of the Indians who had died of the smallpox; this in the presence of the chiefs and nearest friends, because it is their custom that they distribute it thus to the chiefs and nearest friends. Toward evening the Indians gave me two bear skins with which to cover myself, and they fetched reeds to put under me. I was also told that our people longed for our return.

Jan. 17 Jeronimus and Willem Tomassen arrived at the castle TENOTOGEHAGE with some other Indians. They were still alert and healthy. In the evening another 100 fathoms of sewant were distributed to the chiefs and friends of closest blood.

Jan. 18 We went again to this castle, that is to say, from this castle to hasten our progress homeward. Although there were in some houses here at least 40 or 50 quarters of venison, cut and dried, they offered us little of it to eat. After proceeding a half mile, we passed through the village called KAWAOGE; and a half mile further we came to the village of OSQUAGO. The chief OSQUAHOO received us well. We waited here for the chief AROMYAS whom we had left in the castle of TENOTOOGE.

Jan. 19 In the morning we continued our journey with all haste. After traveling a half mile we came to the third castle called SCHANADISSE. I looked into some houses to see whether there were any pelts. I found nine ONNEDAGES [Oneidas] there with pelts whom I asked to accompany me to the second castle. The chief TATUROT was at home, that is to say, TONEWEROT was at home, who pronounced us welcome at once and gave us a very fat quarter of venison which we cooked. As we were sitting eating we received a letter from Marten Gerrtsen by an Indian who was looking for us. It was dated the 8th of this month. We decided unanimously to proceed to the first castle as quickly as possible in order to depart for Fort Orange in the morning. We arrived at the first castle while the sun was still three hours high. We had bread baked here and packed the three other beavers that we had received from the chief when we first came here. We ate and slept here this night.

Jan. 20 In the morning before daybreak, Jeronimus sold his coat to an old man for four beavers. We left this place one hour before dawn. When we had covered about two miles, the Indians pointed to a high hill where their castle had stood nine years ago when they were driven out by the Mahicans. Since that time they had not wanted to live there any longer. After traveling seven or eight miles, we found that the hunter's cabin had been burned so that we had to spend the night under the stars.

Jan. 21 Early in the morning we started out once again. After traveling for some time, we came upon a wrong path that was the most traveled, but because the Indians knew the paths better than we, they went back with us. After going eleven miles we came, praise and thank God, to Fort Orange the 21st of January Anno 1635.

Of Incursions by the Hiroquois, and the Captivity of Father Jogues

1642-1643

Barthelemy Vimont

Isaac Jogues was born in Orleans, France, in 1607. He was fifth of nine children in a prosperous family, and he could have had a successful professional career in business. However, he entered a Jesuit college in 1617 and eventually went to study theology at Clermont in Paris. Despite notable success there, he decided to set aside his studies in order to become a missionary in North America. He was ordained in January 1636 and left for New France three months later. By September he had reached his post in the mission of St. Joseph in Huron country.

The first Jesuits had arrived in Canada in 1625, ten years after the first Recollects, and had entered Huronia in 1626. Both orders had been expelled from Canada by the English occupation that began in 1629. Only the Jesuits were allowed to return after the English returned Quebec to France in 1632. Their missions among the Hurons were arduous. In 1637 the Jesuits were blamed for a severe epidemic and sentenced to death by the Indians. The sentences were not carried out, and the Jesuits gained acceptance after the epidemic abated. In 1638 Jogues was given the task of building a central residence for missionaries, and later he was sent to the Tobacco Nation with Father Garnier. In 1641 Jogues traveled west to Sault Ste. Marie with Charles Raymbaut in order to explore mission potential among the Chippewas (Ojibwas).

In 1642 Jogues was assigned to a convoy of twelve Huron canoes sent back to Quebec. They were ambushed and captured by Mohawks on the return trip. Jogues, René Goupil, and Guillaume Couture were taken to the Mohawk village of Ossernenon. Goupil was killed, but Jogues was given to an old Mohawk woman as a servant. Although the Iroquois frequently adopted prisoners as substitutes for lost family members, it appears that Jogues did not enjoy this status. Perhaps partly because of his physical mutilation, he was not given the position and prerogatives of a Mohawk man. Nevertheless, he was able to write an account while in captivity. After a year of servitude, Jogues escaped to Rensselaerswyck, now Albany, and helped to escape to France (via England) by the Dutch.

Jogues's account was included as part of the relation for 1642-1643 written by Barthelemy Vimont. It arrived in Trois-Rivières as a letter from Jogues, delivered by a Mohawk envoy. The portion reproduced here was published by

Reuben Thwaites in chapter 12 of volume 24 of the *Jesuit Relations* (JR 24:270-297). Vimont's secondhand characterization of Iroquois torture that follows the letter from Jogues has been omitted. Technical changes for the current publication have been limited to removal of endnote superscripts, deletion of bracketed references to original page breaks, and the dropping of hyphens caused by word breaks at the ends of lines in earlier versions. Readers seeking these particulars should refer to the Thwaites edition.

D.R.S.

THERE ARE TWO divisions of Iroquois,—the one, neighbors of the Hurons and equal to them in number, or even greater, are called Santweronons. Formerly, the Hurons had the upper hand; at present, these prevail, both in number and in strength. The others live between the three Rivers and the upper Hiroquois [Iroquois], and are called Agneronons [Mohawks]. There are among these latter only three villages, comprising about seven or eight hundred men of arms. The settlement of the Dutch is near them; they go thither to carry on their trades, especially in arquebuses [guns]; they have at present three hundred of these, and use them with skill and boldness. These are the ones who make incursions upon our Algonquins and Montagnais, and watch the Hurons at all places along the River,—slaughtering them, burning them, and carrying off their Peltry, which they go and sell to the Dutch, in order to have powder and Arquebuses, and then to ravage everything and become masters everywhere, which is fairly easy for them unless France gives us help. For, sundry contagious diseases having consumed the greater part of the Montagnais and Algonquins, who are neighbors to us, they have nothing to fear on that side; and, moreover, the Hurons who come down,—coming for trade, and not for war, and having not one Arquebus,—if they are met, as usually happens, have no other defense than flight; and, if they are captured, they allow themselves to be bound and massacred like sheep. In former years, the Iroquois came in rather large bands at certain times in the Summer, and afterward left the River free: but, this present year, they have changed their plan, and have separated themselves into small bands of twenty, thirty, fifty, or a hundred at the most, along all the passages and places of the River; and when one band goes away, another succeeds it. They are merely small troops well armed, which set out incessantly, one after the other, from the country of the Iroquois, in order to occupy the whole great River, and to lay ambushes along it everywhere; from these they issue unexpectedly, and fall indifferently upon the Montagnais, Algonquins, Hurons, and French. We have had letters from France that the design of the Dutch is to have the French harassed by the Iroquois, to such an extent that they may constrain them to give up and abandon everything,—even the conversion of the Savages. I cannot believe that those Gentlemen of Holland, being so united to France, have this wretched idea; but, the practice of the Iroquois being so consistent with it, they ought to apply to it a remedy in their settlement, as Monsieur the Governor has done here,—often preventing our Savages from going to kill the Dutch. That is very easy for them; otherwise, they will have difficulty in clearing themselves and in exculpating themselves from the wrong. Now here is the miserable result of the incursions of the Iroquois this year.

The 9th of last May, as soon as the ice was gone from the surface of the great River, eight Algonquins, coming down from toward the Hurons in two canoes, all laden with peltry, landed one morning four leagues from the three Rivers, in order to make a little fire; it had frozen quite hard all night, and they had paddled during the darkness, fearing surprise from their enemies. Hardly had they been half an hour refreshing themselves, when nineteen Iroquois issue from the wood, and fall upon them, kill two men, and take the others captive, with all their pel- try. Father Buteux had passed by there only two days before, in a canoe, accom- panied by three Hurons. It is a miracle that he was not perceived and taken, with his companions. The nineteen Iroquois were not alone; others were seen six or seven leagues above, moving toward the fort of Richelieu.

A month later, which was the ninth of June, another band of forty made its attack at Mont-Real and the environs; they were in ambush half a league above the settlement of Mont-Real, on the Island itself, a hundred paces from the River. They had erected a little fort there at the time of their arrival, which was a few days before; thence they were watching the Hurons on the River, and the French of Mont-Real on land, in order to surprise any of them who might be scattered about the settlement. Everything succeeded for them to their wish; for on the aforesaid day, the ninth of June, they perceived sixty Hurons coming down in thirteen canoes,—without Arquebuses and without arms, but all freighted with peltries,—who were coming to Mont-Real, and from there to the three Rivers, for their trade. They carried the letters of our Fathers with the Hurons, and a copy of their Relation. The forty Hiroquois issue from the wood, fall upon them, frighten them with their Arquebuses, put them to flight, and take twenty-three of them prisoners, with their canoes and the peltry; the rest escape, and strive to reach the settlement of Mont-Real. The Hiroquois do not stop there; they give their twenty-three prisoners, all naked, into the charge of ten of their comrades, well armed, and send ten others to fall upon five Frenchmen, who were working at some carpentry, two hundred paces from the settlement. Meanwhile the twenty who remain present themselves before the fort, and make a false attack on it, with a discharge of more than a hundred arquebus shots; this gave leisure to the other ten to surprise our five Frenchmen. Three of these they beat to death,—scalping them, and carrying away their hair,—and take the two others captive; then they go to rejoin their companions, and all together betake them- selves to their fort, where the two Frenchmen were bound, and put with the cap- tive Hurons. The Hiroquois passed the night in rejoicing over their prize, and in consulting as to what they should do with it. Morning having come, they rush upon the Huron prisoners, and beat thirteen of them to death, almost without selection. They reserve ten of them alive, along with our two Frenchmen, and then go away to the canoes to get robes of Beaver without number; and after having loaded all that they could of these, they leave even more than thirty on the spot, and thus cross the River, triumphant with joy, and laden with rich spoils. Our French of the settlement see them cross, without being able to offer any remedy. Eight or ten days later, one of the two French prisoners escaped by flight,—pretending to his host to go to fetch some wood, in order to prepare the kettle. He reported that the Iroquois had not done them any harm since their capture, and had kept them bound only two days; that they signified to them that they already had French prisoners, and that all together were tilling the soil in their country. For the rest, in these encounters and attacks, one must not speak of making a sally upon the enemy; for, as neither their coming nor their number is known, and as they are concealed in the woods,—where they are trained for running, very differently from our French,—the sallies would avail only to undergo new massacres; for usually a small party attacks, and the others remain in ambush in the thick of the woods.

Those of the Hurons who could escape by flight arrived in single file at the settlement of Mont-Real,—partly toward evening, partly the next day, and all naked,—and gave news of their disastrous accident, also learning ours. I have had letters from Mont-Real that the five Frenchmen who were captured or killed, as if they had anticipated their death, were preparing themselves for it by notable acts of virtue, and by attendance at the Sacraments,—which they had approached a few days previously, and some, the very day of their capture.

While this band of forty were at Mont-Real, and were making these ravages there, another of like number was on lake Saint Pierre, below the fort of Richelieu; and on the twelfth of June they came to encamp in an old fort, made four years ago by the Iroquois, three or four leagues from the three Rivers, on the same side as the settlement. They had with them three or four Hurons, taken the year before with Father Jogues, among whom were two brothers of that great Joseph, known through the Relation of the Hurons, and by his own virtue. Both escaped from the band of the Iroquois, and came toward evening to the three Rivers, where by good fortune they found Father de Brebeuf, to whom they related plenty of news: that Father Jogues was still alive; that last year after his capture, though able to escape, he would not do it, in order not to separate himself from the captive Hurons till after the combat; he baptized all the prisoners, who were expecting nothing but death, and longed only for Heaven. They said that immediately the Father and the two Frenchmen, Cousture and René Goupil, received many blows with fists and clubs; but that the worst treatment which was dealt them was at their encounter with two hundred and fifty Iroquois, who were returning from their attack on Richelieu, where they lost five of their people, and several were wounded. Yet they were not bound while on the road, except at their entrance into the village, when they were all stripped to their shirts, and received many affronts and outrages,—their beards were plucked out, their nails were torn out, the tips of their fingers being afterward burned in calumets all red with fire. Father Jogues had his left thumb cut off, and they crushed with their teeth the index finger of his right hand, which nevertheless he uses a little at present. We were told they spared the lives of all the Hurons except two, who were burned; that the little Therese, the Seminarist of the Ursulines, was much sought after in marriage; that she had lived near her uncle named Joseph, who is the one who, having escaped, was relating all these tidings to Father de Brebeuf. He said that René Goupil, walking near the village with Father Jogues,—both praying to God together,—was struck down with a blow of a hatchet by an Iroquois, who had just learned the death of some of his people, killed at the Fort of Richelieu; that Father Jogues, seeing René fall at his feet, fell on his knees and offered his head to the Iroquois, who was content with having killed one of them. Guillaume Cousture, in the combat, would not flee or separate himself from the Father; the latter abode all the winter in the cabin of an Iroquois Captain, without having been given to any one after the capture,—contrary to their custom,—and thus it is always free to them to kill him; he passed the winter with a single red cape for all his clothing. He had, nevertheless, liberty to go to the three Villages, to console and teach the Hurons and the captives; the Iroquois did not willingly hear him speak of God. These Hurons said that Cousture had his foot frozen with cold; that two Hollanders, one of whom was mounted on horseback, had come to the village where father Jogues was, and had tried to ransom him, but that the Iroquois would not listen to it; that an Iroquois of that band had been charged with a long letter, by father Jogues, to give to us; that the Iroquois spoke of conducting them back, but that he and the others put no faith in it.

Here follows what Joseph related of himself: "I prayed to God continually," said he to Father Brebeuf; "my fingers served me for a rosary, which I rehearsed every day. I made my examination, and confessed my sins to God, as when I confess to you; I conversed incessantly with God, and spoke to him in my heart as if we had been two who had talked together, and thus I was not weary. If sometimes they gave me wherewith to make a feast, I did so without any ceremony, and the Iroquois let me do it. I know well that God has saved my life; for, having been given to people who had not sufficient means to save my life, by giving presents according to our custom,—he caused that they did not accept me, and that I was, for the second time, given to another, who had the means and the wish to deliver me from death. As soon as I thought I had sinned, I went to find Father Jogues in order to confess. As regards the Father," he said, "he offers his prayers quite openly; but as for us, he told us that we should pray quite low,—that the Iroquois had as yet no sense. The Father," he added, "speaks to them of God: but they do not listen to him; he has only one little book of prayers, and Cousture the other." He added withal, that he had been twice at the habitation of the Flemings [Dutch], and his brother four times; whence he related many things of their trade, houses, etc. But what he had remarked above all was that, when they had given him to eat, and he had made the sign of the Cross, a Hollander said to him that that was not well; "And, in fact," he said, "they do not do so, like you. They smoke and drink without ceasing. I was expecting," said he, "that in the evening they would go to pray to God together, as you do, but they did not come to that." That is what Joseph relates.

Let us return to the band of our Iroquois from which he had escaped with his brother, and a third who arrived shortly after. The Iroquois, no longer seeing the three Hurons, and suspecting what the matter was,—that they had withdrawn to the three rivers,—believed they were discovered, and returned to their country.

But, at the same time, others succeeded them in the same lake of St. Pierre, above the three rivers; so that the Hurons who had escaped to Mont real, and who were coming down to the 3 rivers, were again met and pursued. But it pleased God to deliver them, though with infinite hardships; for most of them, leaving their canoes, rushed into the woods and came all naked to the three rivers, by frightful roads. Some other Hurons, captives of former years, who were with these latter bands of Iroquois, escaped and came to the three rivers, and confirmed all that their companions had said,—especially that there was talk in the country of bringing hither Father Jogues and restoring him to the French; but, as the treachery of the Iroquois is known, no one believed a word of it. Monsieur the Governor, however, who desired the Father's deliverance, and peace if it were reasonable, equipped four shallops and went, prepared for war or peace, to the three rivers, and thence to the Fort of Richelieu, in order to see if the Iroquois would present themselves on the river or before the habitations. But nothing appeared; as soon as they perceived the shallops, they entered further within the woods; and, the shallops having passed, they returned to the edge of the water, and kept watch on the Algonquins and Hurons. Monsieur the Governor often landed, in order to examine their trail, and to see if he might encounter some band of them in their customary Forts, in order to attack them there. Two leagues above Riche-lieu he found a road newly made in the woods, which extended about two leagues, whereby the Iroquois traversed and cut off a point of land in order to come from their river into that of St. Lawrence, bearing their canoes and baggage on their shoulders, and not to pass before the Fort of Richelieu. If Monsieur the Governor had had the soldiers for whom he was hoping from France, he would no doubt have proceeded even into the country of the Iroquois, with 200 or 300 Algonquins and Montagnais who offered themselves to keep him company; and I believe that this would have produced a very good effect, and that he would have constrained those proud Barbarians to an honest peace, or have entirely subdued them. What I have said herein above, need not give extraordinary terror; when the Iroquois have encountered resistance, they have given way as soon as, or sooner than, the others. The Algonquins, being in reasonable number, have often made them tremble and flee. Let us return to their incursions of this year, notwithstanding which the Algonquins failed not to go to the chase; they cannot forego that exercise without dying from hunger. The land does not yet yield enough for them; "As well," they say, "die by the hand, or by the iron of the Iroquois, as of a cruel hunger." The 30th of July, seven young Algonquins went to the chase toward Mont-real,—they were nearly all Christians; they encountered two Iroquois canoes, one of which, in which there were twelve men, ran straightway upon them. These good young men were not frightened; Father le Jeune had said to them on leaving: "If you flee death, you will find it; if you seek it, it will flee from you. Commend yourselves to God, if you meet the enemy." They observe this counsel,—they pray to God fervently in their hearts, and paddle with all their might straight toward the Iroquois, who discharge upon them ten or twelve arquebus shots, without other effect than to pierce one canoe and to wound one Algonquin in the foot. The Algonquins continually advance, and discharge two or three arquebuses that they had; they prostrate two Iroquois, wounded to death in their canoe, and constrain them all to go ashore and retreat. If these Young Algonquins had had powder to continue and pursue further, they would have killed most of the band; but we have always been afraid to arm the Savages too much. Would to God that the Hollanders had done the same, and had not compelled us to give arms even to our Christians,—for hitherto, these have been traded only to the latter.

The 15th of August, twenty Algonquins left the three rivers in order to go to the chase toward Richelieu. When in the lake of St. Pierre, seven or eight leagues from the settlement, at the mouth of a river called saint François, they separated themselves into two bands, in order to hunt better. The one, which was composed of twelve, straightway encounters twenty Iroquois, well armed; then they were in close conflict,—first with the arquebuses, of which the Iroquois had twice as many, then with the javelin, finally with the knife. Some on both sides were killed; the Algonquins, seeing themselves weaker, took flight; three, with a Huron who happened to be in their company, were made prisoners. They burned one of these; God granted the favor to 2 others, who were Christians, to escape. They reported to us that the Iroquois were nearly all wounded, and some, to death. At the same time when that was occurring in the lake of St. Pierre, there were 2 other bands of Iroquois, who were prowling about the Fort of Riche-lieu; they had with them a captive Huron, but an Iroquois by affection. The latter took his place alone in a canoe, and advanced toward the Fort, and requested to speak; they receive him,—they have him enter, they ask him who he is, and what brings him. He answers that he is an Iroquois, and that he wishes to treat of peace for himself and for his companions; he presents some beavers with this object. They ask him if he has news of Father Jogues; he draws forth a letter from him and presents it, then asks to return. They tell him that the letter is addressed to Monsieur the Governor, who is at Kebec [Quebec] or at the 3 rivers, and that he must wait for an answer; he requests that they fire a cannon shot, which is done, and straightway his comrades appear in 3 or 4 canoes. They paddle steadily, in order to come toward the Fort; they are hailed to stop, three or four times,—which not obeying, they are fired upon; that constrained them to go ashore, and flee into the woods, abandoning their canoes and baggage; it is not known whether they were wounded or killed.

Not many days later, a band of about l00 Iroquois appeared at the same place, in eleven great canoes; they had crossed above Mont-real, had remained there several days in ambush, and had presented themselves before the settlement. There, under pretext of some sign of peace, they had essayed to attract near them some Algonquins of the Iroquet nation, who had been sent to parley at a distance, upon whom they treacherously discharged more than a hundred arquebus shots,—but, thanks to God, without effect. They had afterward come down to Richelieu, where, seeing themselves discovered they retreated. Here follows a copy of the letter from Father Jogues, written from the Iroquois, which that Huron of whom I have spoken, brought and gave to Monsieur de Champ-flour: it is addressed to Monsieur the Governor. It is a great pity that three others, which he wrote to us previously, have been lost.

"Monsieur, here is the 4th that I have written since I am with the Iroquois. Time and paper fail me to repeat here what I have already conveyed to you at great length. Cousture and I are still living. Henry (one of those two young men who were taken at Mont-real) was brought here the eve of saint John's day. He was not loaded with blows from clubs at the entrance to the village, like us, nor has he had his fingers cut, like us; he lives, and all the Hurons brought with him into the country. Be on your guard everywhere; new bands are always leaving, and we must persuade ourselves that, until the Autumn, the river is not without enemies. There are here nearly three hundred arquebuses, and seven hundred Iroquois; they are skilled in handling them. They can arrive at the three rivers by various streams; the Fort of Richelieu gives them a little more trouble, but does not hinder them altogether. The Iroquois say that if those who took and killed the French at Mont-real had known what you have done,—in redeeming the Sok-okiois whom you delivered from the hands of the Algonquins,—they would not have done that; they had started in the midst of the winter, and before the news of it came. Nevertheless, quite recently there has departed a band, and the man of Mathurin (Father Brebeuf knows him well) is in it, and leads the band, as at our capture last year. This troop desires and purposes to take some French, as well as Algonquins. Let not regard for us prevent from doing that which is to the glory of God. The design of the Iroquois, as far as I can see, is to take, if they can, all the Hurons; and, having put to death the most considerable ones and a good part of the others, to make of them both but one people and only one land. I have a great compassion for these poor people, several of whom are Christians,—the others Catechumens, and ready for baptism; when shall a remedy be applied to these misfortunes? when they shall all be taken? I have received several letters from the Hurons, with the Relation taken near Mont-real. The Dutch have tried to ransom us, but in vain; they are still endeavoring to do so at present, but it will again be, as I believe, with the same result. I become more and more resolved to dwell here as long as it shall please Our Lord, and not to go away, even though an opportunity should present itself. My presence consoles the French, the Hurons, and the Algonquins. I have baptized more than sixty persons, several of whom have arrived in Heaven. That is my single consolation, and the will of God, to which very gladly I unite my own. I beg you to recommend that prayers be said, and that masses be offered for us, and above all for the one who desires to be forever,

MONSIEUR,
Your very humble servant, Isaac Jogues, of the Society of JESUS.

"From the village of the Iroquois, the 30th of June, 1643."

Of the Deliverance of Father Isaac Jogues, and His Arrival in France

1643-1644

Barthelemy Vimont

The account that follows was part of Vimont's report for 1643-1644. It was published by Thwaites as most of chapter 14 in volume 25 of the *Jesuit Relations* (JR 25:42-73). Vimont actually wrote only a few introductory and connecting passages. The account is composed mainly of the contents of two letters written by Isaac Jogues.

Jogues escaped from Mohawk captivity in 1643 and found refuge with Dutch settlers at Rensselaerswyck, now Albany. His first letter was written from there in August of that year. By January he was back in France, where he wrote two more letters describing his experiences, the first of which is reproduced here. A fourth unattributed letter that describes Jogues's ordeal in third person form has also been omitted.

Jogues, only 37 years old, returned to France so ravaged by his experience that his friends did not recognize him. His mutilated fingers technically barred him from celebrating mass. Papal permission was sought and granted to allow him to celebrate mass despite the disfigurement. Within a few months he would return again to New France.

Endnote superscripts, bracketed references to original page breaks, and hyphens caused by word breaks at the ends of lines in earlier versions can be found in the Thwaites edition but have been deleted here. Thwaites reproduced Vimont's words and Latin passages in roman typeface. The contents of the letters apart from the Latin passages were set in italic typeface by Thwaites. We have reversed this in order to make the narrative easier to read. Now only Vilmont's introduction and the Latin passages appear in italics.

D.R.S.

THIS NEWS will be by so much more agreeable as it was less expected. This poor Father was no longer spoken of, save as one speaks of the dead. Some believed him burned and devoured by the Iroquois; others regarded him as a victim who awaited nothing more but the knife and the teeth of the Sacrificers of Moloch. In fact, the God of the forsaken saved him by a wholly special Provi-

dence, at the moment when he was destined to the fire, and to those other cruel-
ties which pass the malice of men. He is living, and, if his hands are shortened,
his heart is enlarged,—the sufferings of his body have not diminished the
strength of his mind: we are expecting him from day to day. [If] the Printer
were not so hurried, we could learn from his own lips the pleasant ways which
God has taken in order to deliver him. The letter which he writes again from his
captivity to Father Charles Lalemant, speaks to us of these quite amply; but it
does not satisfy all the questions that we might put to him. Let us follow it, nev-
ertheless; for it well deserves its place in this Chapter.

I started the very day of the Feast of Our Blessed Father saint Ignace, from the
Village where I was captive,—in order to follow and accompany some Iroquois
who were going away, first for trade, then for fishing. Having accomplished their
little traffic, they stopped at a place seven or eight leagues below a settlement of
the Dutch, which is located on a river where we carried on our fishing. While we
were setting snares for the fish, there came a rumor that a squad of Iroquois, returned from pursuit of the Hurons, had killed five or six on the spot, and taken
four prisoners, two of whom had been already burned in our Village, with cruelties extraordinary. At this news, my heart was pierced through with a most bitter
and sharp pain, because I had not seen, or consoled, or baptized those poor victims. Consequently, fearing lest some other like thing should happen in my absence, I said to a good old woman,—who, by reason of her age, and the care that
she had for me, and the compassion that she felt toward me, called me her
nephew, and I called her my aunt,—I then said to her: "My aunt, I would much
like to return to our Cabin; I grow very weary here." It was not that I expected
more ease and less pain in our Village,—where I suffered a continual martyrdom, being constrained to see with my eyes the horrible cruelties which are
practiced there; but my heart could not endure the death of any man without my
procuring him holy Baptism. That good woman said to me: "Go then, my
nephew, since thou art weary here; take something to eat on the way." I embarked in the first Canoe that was going up to the Village,—always conducted
and always accompanied by the Iroquois. Having arrived, as we did, in the settlement of the Dutch, through which it was necessary for us to pass, I learn that
our whole Village is excited against the French, and that only my return is
awaited, for them to burn us. Now for the cause of such news. Among several
bands of Iroquois, who had gone to war against the French, the Algonquins, and
the Hurons, there was one which took the resolution to go round about Richelieu,
in order to spy on the French and the Savages, their allies. A certain Huron of
this band, taken by the Hiroquois, and settled among them, came to ask me for
letters, in order to carry them to the French,—hoping, perhaps, to surprise some
one of them by this bait; but, as I doubted not that our French would be on their
guard, and as I saw, moreover, that it was important that I should give them
some warning of the designs, the arms, and the treachery of our enemies, I found
means to secure a bit of paper in order to write to them,—the Dutch according
me this charity. I knew very well the dangers to which I was exposing myself; I
was not ignorant that, if any misfortune happened to those warriors, they would

make me responsible therefor, and would blame my letters for it. I anticipated my death; but it seemed to me pleasant and agreeable, employed for the public good, and for the consolation of our French and of the poor Savages who listen to the word of Our Lord. My heart was seized with no dread, at the sight of all that might happen therefrom, since it was a matter of the glory of God; I accordingly gave my letter to that young warrior, who did not return. The story which his comrades have brought back, says that he carried it to the fort of Richelieu, and that, as soon as the French had seen it, they fired the Cannon upon them. This frightened them so that the greater part fled, all naked,—abandoning one of their Canoes, in which there were three arquebuses, powder and lead, and some other baggage. These tidings being brought into the Village, they clamor aloud that my letters have caused them to be treated like that; the rumor of it spreads everywhere,—it comes even to my ears. They reproach me that I have done this evil deed; they speak only of burning me; and, if I had chanced to be in the Village at the return of those warriors, fire, rage, and cruelty would have taken my life. For climax of misfortune, another troop—coming back from Mont-real, where they had set ambushes for the French—said that one of their men had been killed, and two others wounded. Each one held me guilty of these adverse encounters; they were fairly mad with rage, awaiting me with impatience. I listened to all these rumors, offering myself without reserve to our Lord, and committing myself in all and through all to his most holy will. The Captain of the Dutch settlement where we were,—not being ignorant of the evil design of those Barbarians, and knowing, moreover, that Monsieur the Chevalier de Montmagny had prevented the Savages of New France from coming to kill some Dutch,—disclosed to me means for escape. "Yonder," said he to me, is a vessel at anchor, which will sail in a few days; enter into it secretly. It is going first to Virginia, and thence it will carry you to Bordeaux or to la Rochelle, where it is to land." Having thanked him, with much regard for his courtesy, I tell him that the Iroquois, probably suspecting that some one had favored my retreat, might cause some damages to his people. "No, no," he answers, "fear nothing; this opportunity is favorable; embark; you will never find a more certain way to escape." My heart remained perplexed at these words, wondering if it were not expedient for the greater glory of our Lord; that I expose myself to the danger of the fire and to the fury of those Barbarians, in order to aid in the salvation of some soul. I said to him then: "Monsieur, the affair seems to me of such importance that I cannot answer you at once; give me, if you please, the night to think of it. I will commend it to our Lord; I will examine the arguments on both sides; and to-morrow morning I will tell you my final resolution." He granted me my request with astonishment; I spent the night in prayers, greatly beseeching our Lord that he should not allow me to reach a conclusion by myself; that he should give me light, in order to know his most holy will; that in all and through all I wished to follow it, even to the extent of being burned at a slow fire. The reasons which might keep me in the country were consideration for the French and for the Savages; I felt love for them, and a great desire to assist them,—insomuch that I had resolved to spend the remainder of my days in that captivity, for their salvation; but I saw the face of affairs quite changed.

In the first place, as regarded our three Frenchmen, led captive into the country as well as I: one of them, named René Goupil, had already been murdered at my feet; this young man had the purity of an Angel. Henry, whom they had taken at Mont-Real, had fled into the woods. While he was looking at the cruelties which were practiced upon two poor Hurons, roasted at a slow fire, some Iroquois told him that he would receive the same treatment, and I, too, when I should return; these threats made him resolve rather to plunge into the danger of dying from hunger in the woods, or of being devoured by some wild beast, than to endure the torments which these half Demons inflicted. It was already seven days since he had disappeared. As for Guillaume Cousture, I saw scarcely any further way of aiding him,—for they had placed him in a village far from the one where I was; and the Savages so occupied it on the hither side of that place, that I could no longer meet him. Add that he himself had addressed me in these words: "My Father, try to escape; as soon as I shall see you no more, I shall find the means to get away. You well know that I stay in this captivity only for the love of you; make, then, your efforts to escape, for I cannot think of my liberty and of my life unless I see you in safety." Furthermore, this good youth had been given to an old man, who assured me that he would allow him to go in peace, if I could obtain my deliverance; consequently I saw no further reason which obliged me to remain on account of the French.

As for the Savages, I was without power and beyond hope of being able to instruct them; for the whole country was so irritated against me that I found no more any opening to speak to them, or to win them; and the Algonquins and the Hurons were constrained to withdraw from me, as from a victim destined to the fire, for fear of sharing in the hatred and rage which the Iroquois felt against me. I realized, moreover, that I had some acquaintance with their language; that I knew their country and their strength; that I could perhaps better procure their salvation by other ways than by remaining among them. It came to my mind that all this knowledge would die with me, if I did not escape. These wretches had so little inclination to deliver us, that they committed a treachery against the law and the custom of all these nations. A Savage from the country of the Sokokiois, allies of the Iroquois, having been seized by the upper Algonquins and taken a prisoner to the three Rivers, or to Kebec [Quebec], was delivered and set at liberty by the mediation of Monsieur the Governor of New France, at the solicitation of our Fathers. This good Savage, seeing that the French had saved his life, sent, in the month of April, some fine presents, to the end that they should deliver at least one of the French. The Iroquois retained the presents, without setting one of them at liberty, which treachery is perhaps unexampled among these peoples,—for they inviolably observe this law, that whoever touches or accepts the present which is made to him, is bound to fulfill what is asked of him through that present. This is why, when they are unwilling to grant what is desired, they send back the presents or make others in place of them. But to return to my subject,—having weighed before God, with all the impartiality in my power, the reasons which inclined me to remain among those Barbarians or to leave them, I believed that our Lord would be better pleased if I should take the opportunity to escape. Daylight having come, I went to greet Monsieur the Dutch Governor, and declared to him the opinions that I had adopted before God. He summons the chief men of the ship, signifies to them his intentions, and exhorts them to receive me, and to keep me concealed,—in a word, to convey me back to Europe. They answer that, if I can once set foot in their vessel, I am in safety; that I shall not leave it until I reach Bourdeaux or la Rochelle. "Well, then," the Governor said to me, "return with the Savages, and toward the evening, or in the night, steal away softly and move toward the river; you will find there a little boat which I will have kept all ready to carry you secretly to the Ship." After very humbly returning thanks to all those Gentlemen, I withdrew from the Dutch, in order better to conceal my design. Toward evening, I retired with ten or twelve Iroquois into a barn, where we passed the night. Before lying down, I went out of that place, to see in what quarter I might most easily escape. The dogs of the Dutch, being then untied, run up to me; one of them, large and powerful, flings himself upon my leg, which is bare, and seriously injures it. I return immediately to the barn; the Iroquois close it securely, and, the better to guard me, come to lie down beside me,—especially a certain man who had been charged to watch me. Seeing myself beset with those evil creatures, and the barn well closed, and surrounded with dogs, which would betray me if I essayed to go out, I almost believed that I could not escape. I complained quietly to my God, because, having given me the idea of escaping, *Concluserat vias meas lapidibus quadris, et in loco spatioso pedes meos*: He was stopping up the ways and paths of it. I spent also that second night without sleeping; the day approaching, I heard the cocks crow. Soon afterward, a servant of the Dutch farmer who had lodged us in his barn, having entered it by some door or other,—I accosted him softly, and made signs to him (for I did not understand his Flemish), that he should prevent the dogs from yelping. He goes out at once, and I after him, having previously taken all my belongings,—which consisted of a little office of the Virgin, of a little Gerson, and a wooden Cross that I had made for myself in order to preserve the memory of the sufferings of my Savior. Being outside of the barn, without having made any noise, or awakened my guards, I cross over a fence which confined the enclosure about the house; I run straight to the river where the Ship was,—this is all the service that my leg, much wounded, could render me: for there was surely a good quarter of a league of road to make. I found the boat as they had told me, but, the water having subsided, it was aground. I push it, in order to set it afloat; not being able to effect this, on account of its weight, I call to the Ship, that they bring the skiff to ferry me,—but no news. I know not whether they heard me; at all events, no one appeared. The daylight meanwhile was beginning to discover to the Iroquois the theft that I was making of myself; I feared that they might surprise me in this innocent misdemeanor. Weary of shouting, I return to the boat; I pray God to increase my strength; I do so well, turning it end for end, and push it so hard that I get it to the water. Having made it float, I jump into it, and go all alone to the Ship, where I go on board without being discovered by any Iroquois. They lodge me forthwith down in the hold; and, in order to conceal me, they put a great chest over the hatchway. I was two days and two nights in the belly of that vessel, with such discomfort that I thought I would suffocate and die with the stench. I remembered then poor Jonas, and I prayed our Lord, *Ne fugerem à facie Domini,*—that I might not hide myself before his face, and that I might not withdraw far from his wishes; but on the contrary, *infatuaret omnia consilia quæ non essent ad suam gloriam,*—I prayed him to overthrow all the counsels which should not tend to his glory, and to detain me in the country of those infidels, if he did not approve my retreat and my flight. The second night of my voluntary prison, the Minister of the Dutch came to tell me that the Iroquois had indeed made some disturbance, and that the Dutch inhabitants of the country were afraid that they would set fire to their houses, or kill their cattle; they have reason to fear them, since they have armed them with good arquebuses. To that I answer: *Si propter me orta est tempestas, projicite me in mare:* "If the storm has risen on my account, I am ready to appease it by losing my life;" I had never the wish to escape to the prejudice of the least man of their settlement. Finally, it was necessary to leave my cavern; all the Mariners were offended at this, saying that the promise of security had been given me in case I could set foot in the Ship, and that I was being withdrawn at the moment when it would be requisite to bring me thither if I were not there; that I had put myself in peril of life by escaping upon their word; that it must needs be kept, whatever the cost. I begged that I be allowed to go forth, since the Captain who had disclosed to me the way of my flight was asking for me. I went to find him in his house, where he kept me concealed; these goings and these comings having occurred by night, I was not yet discovered. I might indeed have alleged some reasons in all these encounters; but it was not for me to speak in my own cause, but rather to follow the orders of others, to which I submitted with good heart. Finally, the Captain told me that it was necessary to yield quietly to the storm, and wait until the minds of the Savages should be pacified; and that every one was of this opinion. So there I was, a voluntary prisoner in his house, from which I am writing back to you the present letter. And if you ask my thoughts in all these adventures, I will tell you.

First, that that Ship which had wished to save my life, sailed without me.

Secondly, if Our Lord do not protect me in a manner well-nigh miraculous, the Savages, who go and come here at every moment, will discover me; and if ever they convince themselves that I have not gone away, it will be necessary to return into their hands. Now, if they had such a rage against me before my flight, what treatment will they inflict on me, seeing me fallen back into their power? I shall not die a common death; the fire, their rage, and the cruelties which they invent, will tear away my life. God be blessed forever. We are incessantly in the bosom of his divine and always adorable providence. *Vestri capilli capitis numerati sunt: nolite timere: multis passeribus meliores estis vos quorum unus non cadet super terram sine patre vestro*; he who has care for the little birds of the air does not cast us into oblivion. It is already twelve days that I have been concealed,—it is quite improbable that misfortune will reach me.

In the third place, you see the great need that we have of your prayers and of the holy Sacrifices of all our Fathers; procure us this alms everywhere, *Ut reddat me Dominus idoneum ad se amandum, fortem ad patiendum, constantem ad perseverandum in suo amore, et servitio,*—to the end that God may render me fit and well disposed to love him; that he may render me strong and courageous to suffer and to endure; and that he may give me a noble constancy to persevere in his love and in his service,—this is what I would desire above all, together with a little New Testament from Europe. Pray for these poor nations which burn and devour one another,—that at last they may come to the knowledge of their Creator, in order to render to him the tribute of their love. *Memor sum vestri in vinculis meis*; I do not forget you; my captivity cannot fetter my memory. I am, heartily and with affection, etc.

From Renselaerivich, this 30th of August, 1643.

Novum Belgium
and an Account of René Goupil
1644

Isaac Jogues

Jogues left France and sailed to Quebec for the second time in 1644. He arrived in Quebec in July. Although he wanted to establish a mission among the Mohawks, his former captors, the assignment was judged still too dangerous. He was sent to Ville Marie instead.

Peace was restored between the French and the Mohawks with the release of Father Bressani in August 1644. When Father Jérôme Lalemant was appointed superior-general of the Jesuits in New France, Jogues renewed his request to missionize among the Mohawks. By May 1646 the authorities were sufficiently convinced of the good intentions of the Mohawks to send Jogues as an ambassador to them. Jogues and his party ascended Lake Champlain and Lake George. Jogues may have been the first Frenchman to see Lake George, which he named Saint Sacrement. The trip was a success, and Jogues left a box of supplies behind with the Mohawks, intending to return as a full-time missionary.

Jogues returned to Quebec and Troix Rivières by July to report his success, but his request to return to the Mohawks to spend the winter was refused. Instead he was to be sent with Jean de La Lande to winter with the Hurons.

In August, while waiting in Trois-Rivières to depart for Huronia, Jogues wrote the following description of New Netherland. He describes New Amsterdam (now New York City), the Hudson River, Rensselaerswyck (now Albany), and the country of the Mohawks (Agniehronons). For this description he was drawing on his own observations and experiences of 1642-1643. Following this is Jogues's account of René Goupil, an undated tribute that is usually published with *Novum Belgium*. Goupil had been killed by the Mohawks in 1642 when both he and Jogues had been taken prisoner.

These were among the last writings of Isaac Jogues. In October he was captured again by the Mohawks, along with his companion Jean de La Lande, as they made their way upstream to Huronia. The box Jogues had left behind in the Mohawk village had been blamed for the epidemic and famine that had afflicted the Mohawks following his visit in the spring of the year. Jogues was killed by a blow to the head on October 18, and La Lande was executed shortly thereafter.

Both *Novum Belgium* and the *Account of René Goupil* were published as portions of volume 28 of the *Jesuit Relations* (JR 28:104-135). A letter from Jogues to Andre Castillon, which Thwaites included after the *Account of René Goupil*, has not been reproduced here. The only technical changes from the Thwaites edition have been the removal of endnote superscripts, the correction of a few typographical errors, and the dropping of hyphens caused by word breaks at the ends of lines in earlier versions. A 1630 map by Johannes de Laet, which Thwaites reproduced with his publication of *Novum Belgium,* bears little relevant information and has not been included here.

D.R.S.

Novum Belgium

NEW HOLLAND—which the Dutch call, in Latin, Novum Belgium; in their own language, Nieuw Nederland; that is to say, New Netherlands—is situated between Virginia and New England. The entrance to the River, which some call the River Nassau, or the great River of the North, to distinguish it from another which they call South River,—and some charts, I believe, that I have recently seen, the River Maurice,—is in the latitude of 40 degrees, 30 minutes. Its channel is deep, and navigable by the largest ships, which go up to Manhattes [Manhattan] Island, which is 7 leagues in circumference; thereon is a fort intended to serve as nucleus for a town to be built, and to be called New Amsterdam.

This fort, which is at the point of the island, about 5 or 6 leagues from the river's mouth, is called fort Amsterdam; it has 4 regular bastions, provided with several pieces of artillery. All these bastions and the curtains were, in the year 1643, merely earthworks, most of which had quite given way, and through them the fort could be entered from all sides; there were no trenches. For the defense of this fort,—and of another which they had built, farther on, against the incursions of the savages, their enemies,—there were 60 soldiers. They were beginning to case the gates and the bastions with stone. In this fort there was a house of worship, built of stone, which was quite spacious; the house of the Governor,—whom they call the director General,—built quite neatly of brick; and the storehouses and soldiers' quarters.

There may be, on the Island of Manhate and in its environs, about 4 or five hundred men of various sects and nations,—the Director General told me that there were men of eighteen different languages; they are scattered here and there, up and down the stream, according as the beauty or convenience of the sites invited each one to settle. Some artisans, however, who work at their trades, are located under cover of the fort; while all the others are exposed to the incursions of the Savages, who, in the year 1643, when I was there, had actually killed about forty Hollanders, and burned many houses, and barns full of wheat.

The River, which is very straight, and flows directly from North to South, is at least a league wide before the Fort. The ships are at anchor in a bay which forms the other side of the island, and they can be defended by the Fort.

Shortly before I arrived there, 3 large ships of 300 tons had come to load wheat; two had received their lading, but the 3rd could not be laden, because the savages had burned a part of the grain. These ships had sailed from the West Indies, where the West India Company usually maintains seventeen war vessels.

There is no exercise of Religion except the Calvinist, and the orders declare that none but Calvinists be admitted; nevertheless, that point is not observed,—for besides the Calvinists, there are in this settlement Catholics, English Puritans, Lutherans, Anabaptists, whom they call Mnistes, etc.

When any one comes for the first time to dwell in the country, they furnish him horses, cows, etc., and give him provisions,—all which he repays when he is well settled; and, as for lands, at the end of ten years he gives the Company of the West Indies a tenth of the produce that he harvests.

This country has for limits on the New England side a River which they call the Fresh River, which serves as boundary between them and the English; nevertheless, the English approach them very closely,—preferring to have lands among the Dutch, who require nothing from them, to depending upon English Milords, who exact rents and like to put on airs of being absolute. On the other side,—the Southern, toward Virginia,—it has for limits the River which they call South River, on which there is also a Dutch settlement; but at its entrance the Swedes have another, extremely well equipped with cannon and people. It is believed that these Swedes are maintained by Amsterdam merchants, incensed because the Company of the west Indies monopolizes all the trade of these regions. It is toward this River that they have found, as is said, a gold mine.

See in the book of sieur De Laet, of Antwerp, the table, and the account of new Belgium, as he sometimes calls it; or the great map of "Nova Anglia, Novum Belgium, et Virginia."

During fully 50 years the Dutch have frequented these regions. In the year 1615, the fort was begun; about 20 years ago, they began to make a settlement; and now there is already some little trade with Virginia and New England.

The first comers found lands quite suitable for use, cleared in former times by the savages, who tilled their fields there. Those who have come since have made clearings in the woods, which are commonly of oak; the lands are good. Deer hunting is abundant toward autumn. There are some dwellings built of stone: they make the lime with oyster shells, of which there are great heaps made in former times by the savages, who partly live by that fishery.

The climate there is very mild; as that region is situated at 40 and two-thirds degrees, there are plenty of European fruits, as apples, pears, Cherries. I arrived there in October, and even then I found many Peaches.

Ascending the River as far as the 43rd degree, you find the 2nd settlement, which the flow and Ebb of the tide reaches, but extends no further; ships of 100 and a hundred and twenty tons can land there.

There are two items in this settlement, which is called Renselaerswick,—as if one should say, "the settlement of Renselaers," who is a wealthy merchant of Amsterdam: first, a wretched little fort, named Fort orange,—built of logs, with 4 or 5 pieces of Breteuil cannon, and as many swivel guns,—which the Company of the West Indies has reserved for itself, and which it maintains. This fort was formerly on an Island formed by the River; it is now on the mainland on the side of the Hiroquois, a little above the said Island. There is, secondly, a Colony sent thither by that Renselaers, who is its Patron. This colony is composed of about a hundred persons, who live in 25 or 30 houses built along the River, as each has found convenient. In the principal house is lodged the Patron's representative; the Minister has his own house apart, in which Preaching is held. There is also a sort of Bailiff, whom they call Seneschal, who has charge of Justice. All their houses are merely of boards, and are covered with thatch. There is as yet no masonry, except in the chimneys.

As the forests supply many stout pines, the people make boards by means of their mills, which they have for this purpose.

They have found some very suitable lands, which the savages had formerly prepared, on which they plant corn and oats, for their beer, and for the horses, of which they have a great many. There are few lands fit to be tilled, as they are narrowed by hills, which are poor soil; that obliges them to separate from one another, and they already hold two or 3 leagues of territory.

Trade is free to every one, which enables the savages to obtain all things very cheaply: each of the Dutch outbidding his companion, and being satisfied, provided he can gain some little profit.

This settlement is not more than 20 leagues from the Agniehronons [Mohawks]; there is access to them either by land or by water,—the River on which the Iroquois dwell falling into that which passes by the Dutch; but there are many shallow rapids, and a fall of a short half-league, past which the canoe must be carried.

There are several nations between the two Dutch settlements, which are 30 German leagues apart,—that is to say, 50 or 60 French leagues. The Wolves [Mahicans], whom the Iroquois call Agotsaganens, are the nearest to the settlement of Renselaerswick or to the fort of orange. Several years ago, there being a war between the Iroquois and the Wolves, the Dutch Joined these latter against the others; but, 4 having been taken and burned, peace was made. Later, some nations near the sea having slain some Dutch of the most remote settlement, the Dutch killed 150 savages,—not only men and women, but little children. The savages having, in various reprisals, killed 40 Dutch, burned many houses, and wrought damage reckoned, at the time when I was there, at 200,000*ll*,—two hundred thousand livres,—troops were levied in New England. Accordingly, at the beginning of winter, the grass being short, and some snow on the ground, they gave the savages chase with six hundred men, two hundred being always on the march and one set continually relieving another. The result was, that, being shut up on a great Island, and unable to flee easily, because of the women and children, there were as many as sixteen hundred killed, including women and children. This compelled the remainder of the savages to make peace, which still continues. That occurred in 1643 and 1644.

From 3 Rivers, in New France, August 3, 1646.

Account of René Goupil

René Goupil was a native of Anjou, who, in the bloom of his youth, urgently requested to be received into our Novitiate at Paris, where he remained some months with much edification. His bodily indispositions having taken from him the happiness of consecrating himself to God in holy Religion,—for which he had a strong desire,—he journeyed, when his health improved, to New France, in order to serve the society there, since he had not had the blessing of giving himself to it in old France. And, in order to do nothing in his own right,—although he was fully master of his own actions,—he totally submitted himself to the guidance of the superior of the Mission, who employed him two whole years in the meanest offices about the house, in which he acquitted himself with great humility and Charity. He was also given the care of nursing the sick and the wounded at the hospital. which he did with as much skill—for he understood surgery well—as with affection and love, continually seeing Our Lord in their persons. He left so sweet an odor of his goodness and his other virtues in that place, that his memory is still blessed there.

When we came down from the Hurons in July, 1642, we asked Reverend Father Vimont to let us take him with us, because the Hurons had great need of a Surgeon; he granted our request.

I cannot express the joy which this good young man felt when the superior told him that he might make ready for the journey. Nevertheless, he well knew the great dangers that await one upon the river; he knew how the Iroquois were enraged against the French. Yet that could not prevent him—at the least sign of the will of him to whom he had voluntarily committed all his concerns—from setting forth for 3 Rivers.

We departed thence on the 1st of August,—the day after the feast of Our Blessed Father. On the 2nd, we encountered the enemies, who, separated into two bands, were awaiting us with the advantage which a great number of chosen men, fighting on land, can have over a small and promiscuous band, who are upon the water in scattered canoes of bark.

Nearly all the Hurons had fled into the woods, and, as they had left us, we were seized. On this occasion his virtue was very manifest; for, as soon as he saw himself captured, he said to me: "O my father, God be blessed; he has permitted it, he has willed it,—his holy will be done. I love it, I desire it, I cherish it, I embrace it with all the strength of my heart." Meantime, while the enemies pursued the fugitives, I heard his confession, and gave him absolution,—not knowing what might befall us after our capture. The enemies having returned from their hunt, fell upon us like mad dogs, with sharp teeth,—tearing out our nails, and crushing our fingers, which he endured with much patience and courage.

His presence of mind in so grievous a mishap appeared especially in this, that he aided me, notwithstanding the pain of his wounds, as well as he could, in the instruction of the captive Hurons who were not christians. While I was instructing them separately, and as they came, he called my attention to the fact that a

poor old man, named Ondouterraon, was among those whom they would probably kill on the spot,—their custom being always to sacrifice some one in the heat
of their fury. I instructed this man at leisure, while the enemies were attending to
the distribution of the plunder from 12 canoes, some of which were laden with
necessaries for our Fathers among the Hurons. The booty being divided, they
killed this poor old man,—almost at the same moment in which I had just given
him a new birth through the salutary waters of holy Baptism. We still had this
consolation, during the journey that we made in going to the enemy's country,
that we were together; on this journey, I was witness to many virtues.

Upon the road, he was always occupied with God. His words and the discourses that he held were all expressive of submission to the commands of the
Divine providence, and showed a willing acceptance of the death which God was
sending him. He gave himself to him as a sacrifice, to be reduced to ashes by the
fires of the Iroquois, which that good Father's hand would kindle. He sought the
means to please him in all things, and everywhere. One day he said to me,—it
was soon after our capture, while we were still on the way,—"My Father, God
has always given me a great desire to consecrate myself to his holy service by the
vows of Religion in his holy society; my sins have rendered me unworthy of this
grace until this hour. I nevertheless hope that Our Lord will be pleased with the
offering which I wish now to make him, by taking, in the best manner that I can,
the vows of the society in the presence of my God and before you." This being
granted to him, he uttered the vows with much devotion.

Covered with wounds as he was, he dressed those of other persons,—the
enemies who had received some blow in the fight, as well as the prisoners themselves. He opened a vein for a sick Iroquois; and all that with as much charity as
if he had done it to persons very friendly.

His humility, and the obedience which he rendered to those who had captured
him, confounded me. The Iroquois who conveyed us both in their canoe told me
that I must take a paddle, and use it; I would do nothing of the kind, being proud
even in death. They addressed him in the same way, some time afterward, and
immediately he began to paddle; and when those barbarians tried to drive me, by
his example, to do the like, he, having perceived it, asked my pardon. I sometimes suggested to him, along the way, the idea of escaping, since the liberty
which they gave us furnished him sufficient opportunities for this; but as for myself, I could not leave the french and 24 or 25 huron captives. He would never do
so,—committing himself in everything to the will of Our Lord, who inspired him
with no thought of doing what I proposed.

On the lake we met 200 Iroquois, who came to Richelieu while the French
were beginning to build the fort; these loaded us with blows, covered us with
blood, and made us experience the rage of those who are possessed by the demon. All these outrages and these cruelties he endured with great patience and
charity toward those who ill-treated him.

On approaching the first village, where we were treated so cruelly, he showed
a most uncommon patience and gentleness. Having fallen under the shower of
blows from clubs and iron rods with which they attacked us, and being unable to

rise again, he was brought—as it were, half dead—upon the scaffold where we already were, in the middle of the village; but he was in so pitiful a condition that he would have inspired compassion in cruelty itself. He was all bruised with blows, and in his face one distinguished nothing but the whites of his eyes; but he was so much the more beautiful in the sight of the Angels as he was disfigured, and similar to him of whom it is said: *Vidimus eum quasi leprosum,* etc.; *non erat ei species neque decor.*

Hardly had he taken a little breath, as well as we, when they came to give him 3 blows on his shoulders with a heavy club, as they had done to us before. When they had cut off my thumb,—as I was the most conspicuous,—they turned to him and cut his right thumb at the 1st joint,—while he continually uttered, during this torment: "JESUS, MARY, JOSEPH." During six days, in which we were exposed to all those who wished to do us some harm, he showed an admirable gentleness; he had his whole breast burned by the coals and hot cinders which the young lads threw upon our bodies at night, when we were bound flat on the earth. Nature furnished more skill to me than to him for avoiding a part of these pains.

After they had given us life,—at the very time when, a little before, they had warned us to prepare for being burned,—he fell sick, suffering great inconveniences in every respect, and especially in regard to the food, to which he was not accustomed. In that, one might say most truly, *Non cibus utilis ægro.* I could not relieve him,—for I was also very sick, and had none of my fingers sound or entire.

But this urges me to come to his death, at which nothing was wanting to make him a Martyr.

After we had been in the country six weeks,—as confusion arose in the councils of the Iroquois, some of whom were quite willing that we should be taken back,—we lost the hope, which I did not consider very great, of again seeing 3 Rivers that year. We accordingly consoled each other in the divine arrangement of things; and we were preparing for everything that it might ordain for us. He did not quite realize the danger in which we were,—I saw it better than he; and this often led me to tell him that we should hold ourselves in readiness. One day, then, as in the grief of our souls we had gone forth from the Village, in order to pray more suitably and with less disturbance, two young men came after us to tell us that we must return home. I had some presentiment of what was to happen, and said to him: "My dearest brother, let us commend ourselves to Our Lord and to our good mother the blessed Virgin; these people have some evil design, as I think." We had offered ourselves to Our Lord, shortly before, with much devotion,—beseeching him to receive our lives and our blood, and to unite them with his life and his blood for the salvation of these poor peoples. We accordingly return toward the Village, reciting our rosary, of which we had already said 4 decades. Having stopped near the gate of the Village, to see what they might say to us, one of those two Iroquois draws a hatchet, which he held concealed under his blanket, and deals a blow with it on the head of René, who was before him. He falls motionless, his face to the ground, pronouncing the holy name of JESUS (often we admonished each other that this holy name should end

both our voices and our lives). At the blow, I turn round and see a hatchet all
bloody; I kneel down, to receive the blow which was to unite me with my dear
companion; but, as they hesitate, I rise again, and run to the dying man, who was
quite near. They dealt him two other blows with the hatchet, on the head, and
dispatched him,—but not until I had first given him absolution, which I had been
wont to give him every two days, since our captivity; and this was a day on
which he had already confessed.

It was the [29th] of September, the feast of St. Michael, when this Angel in
innocence, and this Martyr of Jesus Christ, gave his life for him who had given
him his. They ordered me to return to my cabin, where I awaited, the rest of the
day and the next day, the same treatment; and it was indeed the purpose of all
that I should not long delay, since that one had begun. Indeed, I passed several
days on which they came to kill me; but Our Lord did not permit this, in ways
which it would be tedious to explain. The next morning, I nevertheless went out
to inquire where they had thrown that Blessed body, for I wished to bury it, at
whatever cost. Certain Iroquois, who had some desire to preserve me, said to me:
"Thou hast no sense! Thou seest that they seek thee everywhere to kill thee, and
thou still goest out. Thou wishest to go and seek a body already half destroyed,
which they have dragged far from here. Dost thou not see those young men going
out, who will kill thee when thou shalt be outside the stockade?" That did not
stop me, and Our Lord gave me courage enough to wish to die in this act of
charity. I go, I seek; and, with the aid of an Algonquin,—formerly captured, and
now a true Iroquois,—I find him. The children, after he had been killed, had
stripped him, and had dragged him, with a rope about his neck, into a torrent
which passes at the foot of their Village. The dogs had already eaten a part of his
loins. I could not keep back my tears at this sight; I took the body, and, by the
aid of that Algonquin, I put it beneath the water, weighted with large stones, to
the end that it might not be seen. It was my intention to come the next day with a
mattock, when no one should be there, in order to make a grave and place the
body therein. I thought that the corpse was well concealed; but perhaps some
who saw us,—especially of the youths,—withdrew it.

The next day, as they were seeking me to kill me, my aunt sent me to her
field,—to escape, as I think; this caused me to delay until the morrow, a day on
which it rained all night, so that the torrent swelled uncommonly. I borrowed a
mattock from another cabin, the better to conceal my design; but, when I draw
near the place, I no longer find that Blessed deposit. I go into the water, which
was already very cold; I go and come,—I sound with my foot, to see whether the
water has not raised and carried away the body; I find nothing. How many tears
did I shed, which fell into the torrent, while I sang, as well as I could, the psalms
which the church is accustomed to recite for the dead. After all, I find nothing;
and a woman of my acquaintance, who passed there and saw me in pain, told me,
when I asked her whether she knew what they had done with him, that they had
dragged him to the river, which was a quarter of a league from there, and which I
was not acquainted with. That was false: the young men had taken away the
body, and dragged it into a little wood near by,—where, during the autumn and

winter, the Dogs, Ravens, and Foxes fed upon it. In the Spring, when they told me that it was there that they had dragged him, I went thither several times without finding anything. At last, the 4th time, I found the head and some half-gnawed bones, which I buried with the design of carrying them away, if I should be taken back to 3 Rivers, as they spoke of doing. I kissed them very devoutly, several times, as the bones of a martyr of Jesus Christ.

I give him this title not only because he was killed by the enemies of God and of his Church, and in the exercise of an ardent charity toward his neighbor,—placing himself in evident peril for the love of God,—but especially because he was killed on account of prayer, and notably for the sake of the holy Cross.

He was in a Cabin where he nearly always said the prayers,—which little pleased a superstitious old man who was there. One day, seeing a little child of 3 or 4 years in the cabin,—with an excess of devotion and of love for the Cross, and with a simplicity which we who are more prudent than he, according to the flesh, would not have shown,—he took off his cap, put it on this child's head, and made a great sign of the cross upon its body. The old man, seeing that, commanded a young man of his cabin, who was about to leave for the war, to kill him,—which order he executed, as we have said.

Even the child's mother, on a journey in which I happened to be with her, told me that it was because of this sign of the Cross that he had been killed; and the old man who had given the command that he should be slain,—one day when they called me to his cabin to eat, when I previously made the sign of the Cross,—said to me: "That is what we hate; that is why they have killed thy companion, and why they will kill thee. Our neighbors the Europeans do not do so." Sometimes, also, when I was praying on my knees during the hunt, they told me that they hated this way of doing, and on account of it they had killed the other Frenchman; and that, for this reason, they would kill me when I came back to the Village.

I ask Your Reverence's pardon for the haste with which I write this, and for the want of respect of which I am thus guilty. You will excuse me, if you please; I feared lest I should fail at this opportunity, to discharge a duty which I ought to have performed long ago.

A Short Account of the Mohawk Indians
1644

Johannes Megapolensis, Jr.

Johannes Megapolensis, Jr., was born in 1603 or 1604 in North Holland, The Netherlands. Jameson (1909:165) speculates that his surname is a Greco-Latinization of van Grootstede. He apparently became a protestant preacher after abandoning Catholicism as a young man. In 1642 the patroon Kiliaen van Rensselaer selected Megapolensis to minister to the settlers of Rensselaerswyck. The New Netherland patroonship was a vast tract that at the time took up much of what are now Albany and Rensselaer counties.

Megapolensis arrived at Fort Orange in August 1642, committed to six years of service. During that time he lived on the east side of the Hudson River, opposite what is now Albany. He preached to Dutch settlers, and in 1643 he began preaching to Indians as well. He appears to have been liked and trusted by many, not least of them the patroon. He also assisted Isaac Jogues in his escape from the Mohawks.

Megapolensis left for home at the end of his contract in 1649. When he reached Manhattan he was asked to stay on as dominie, Dominie Backerus having recently resigned. He remained in New Amsterdam through the city's surrender to the English in 1664. He died in what had by then been renamed New York in 1669.

The account of the Mohawks that follows was apparently compiled from letters sent by Megapolensis to his friends. It was first published, without the knowledge or consent of the author, at Alkmaar, North Holland, in 1644. A copy of this pamphlet survives in the University of Ghent library. It was reprinted by Joost Hartgers in 1651 and printed in English translation by Ebenezer Hazard in 1792. A revised translation was published by Brodhead in 1857. Further revision was made by A. Clinton Crowell of Brown University, and that version was published by Jameson in 1909. The last is the version reproduced here.

Jameson's footnotes are not essential to understanding the text and are in some cases misleading. Both the footnotes and their superscript numbers in the body of the text have been dropped here. Readers wishing to explore them should refer to the Jameson publication (Megapolensis 1909).

D.R.S.

38

A Short Account of the Mohawk Indians, their Country, Language, Stature, Dress, Religion and Government, thus described and recently, August 26, 1644, sent out of New Netherland, by Johannes Megapolensis the younger, Preacher there.

THE COUNTRY here is in general like that in Germany. The land is good, and fruitful in everything which supplies human needs, except clothes, linen, woollen, stockings, shoes, etc., which are all dear here. The country is very mountainous, partly soil, partly rocks, and with elevations so exceeding high that they appear to almost touch the clouds. Thereon grow the finest fir trees the eye ever saw. There are also in this country oaks, alders, beeches, elms, willows, etc. In the forests, and here and there along the water side, and on the islands, there grows an abundance of chestnuts, plums, hazel nuts, large walnuts of several sorts, and of as good a taste as in the Netherlands, but they have a somewhat harder shell. The ground on the hills is covered with bushes of bilberries or blueberries; the ground in the flat land near the rivers is covered with strawberries, which grow here so plentifully in the fields, that one can lie down and eat them. Grapevines also grow here naturally in great abundance along the roads, paths, and creeks, and wherever you may turn you find them. I have seen whole pieces of land where vine stood by vine and grew very luxuriantly, climbing to the top of the largest and loftiest trees, and although they are not cultivated, some of the grapes are found to be as good and sweet as in Holland. Here is also a sort of grapes which grow very large, each grape as big as the end of one's finger, or an ordinary plum, and because they are somewhat fleshy and have a thick skin we call them *Speck Druyven*. If people would cultivate the vines they might have as good wine here as they have in Germany or France. I had myself last harvest a boat-load of grapes and pressed them. As long as the wine was new it tasted better than any French or Rhenish Must, and the color of the grape juice here is so high and red that with one wine-glass full you can color a whole pot of white wine. In the forests is great plenty of deer, which in autumn and early winter are as fat as any Holland cow can be. I have had them with fat more than two fingers thick on the ribs, so that they were nothing else than almost clear fat, and could hardly be eaten. There are also many turkies, as large as in Holland, but in some years less than in others. The year before I came here, there were so many turkies and deer that they came to feed by the houses and hog pens, and were taken by the Indians in such numbers that a deer was sold to the Dutch for a loaf of bread, or a knife, or even for a tobacco pipe; but now one commonly has to give for a good deer six or seven guilders. In the forests here there are also many partridges, heath-hens and pigeons that fly together in thousands, and sometimes ten, twenty, thirty and even forty and fifty are killed at one shot. We have here, too, a great number of all kinds of fowl, swans, geese, ducks, widgeons, teal, brant, which sport upon the river in thousands in the spring of the year, and again in the autumn fly away in flocks, so that in the morning and evening any one may stand ready with his gun before his house and shoot them as they fly past. I have also eaten here several times of elks, which were very fat and tasted much like venison; and besides these profitable beasts we have also in this country lions, bears, wolves, foxes, and particularly very many snakes, which are large and as long as eight, ten, and twelve feet. Among others, there is a sort of snake, which we call rattlesnake, from a certain object which it has back upon its tail, two or three fingers' breadth long, and has ten or twelve joints, and with this it makes a noise like the crickets. Its color is variegated much like our large brindled bulls. These snakes have very sharp teeth in their mouth, and dare to bite at dogs; they make way for neither man nor beast, but fall on and bite them, and their bite is very poisonous, and commonly even deadly too.

As to the soil of this country, that on the mountains is a reddish sand or rock, but in the low flat lands, and along the rivers, and even in the jutting sides of the mountains for an hundred or two hundred paces up, there is often clay. I have been on hills here, as high as a church, to examine the soil, and have found it to be clay. In this ground there appears to be a singular strength and capacity for bearing crops, for a farmer here told me that he had raised fine wheat on one and the same piece of land eleven years successively without ever breaking it up or letting it lie fallow. The butter here is clean and yellow as in Holland. Through this land runs an excellent river, about 500 or 600 paces wide. This river comes out of the Mahakas [Mohawks] Country, about four leagues north of us. There it flows between two high rocky banks, and falls from a height equal to that of a church, with such a noise that we can sometimes hear it here with us. In the beginning of June twelve of us took a ride to see it. When we came there we saw not only the river falling with such a noise that we could hardly hear one another, but the water boiling and dashing with such force in still weather, that it seemed all the time as if it were raining; and the trees on the hills near by (which are as high as Schoorler Duyn) had their leaves all the time wet exactly as if it rained. The water is as clear as crystal, and as fresh as milk. I and another with me saw there, in clear sunshine, when there was not a cloud in the sky, especially when we stood above upon the rocks, directly opposite where the river falls, in the great abyss, the half of a rainbow, or a quarter of a circle, of the same color with the rainbow in the sky. And when we had gone about ten or twelve rods farther downwards from the fall, along the river, we saw a complete rainbow, like a half circle, appearing clearly in the water just as if it had been in the clouds, and this is always so according to the report of all who have ever been there. In this river is a great plenty of all kinds of fish—pike, eels, perch, lampreys, suckers, cat fish, sun fish, shad, bass, etc. In the spring, in May, the perch are so plenty, that one man with a hook and line will catch in one hour as many as ten or twelve can eat. My boys have caught in an hour fifty, each a foot long. They have three hooks on the instrument with which they fish, and draw up frequently two or three perch at once. There is also in the river a great plenty of sturgeon, which we Christians do not like, but the Indians eat them greedily. In this river, too, are very beautiful islands, containing ten, twenty, thirty, fifty and seventy morgens of land. The soil is very good, but the worst of it is, that by the melting of the snow, or heavy rains, the river readily overflows and covers that low land. This river ebbs and flows at ordinary low water as far as this place, although it is thirty-six leagues inland from the sea.

As for the temperature in this country, and the seasons of the year, the summers are pretty hot, so that for the most of the time we are obliged to go in just our shirts, and the winters are very cold. The summer continues long, even until All Saints' Day; but when the winter does begin, just as it commonly does in December, it freezes so hard in one night that the ice will bear a man. Even the rivers, in still weather when there is no strong current running, are frozen over in one night, so that on the second day people walk over it. And this freezing continues commonly three months; for although we are situated here in 42 degrees of latitude, it always freezes so. And although there come warm and pleasant days, the thaw does not continue, but it freezes again until March. Then, commonly, the rivers first begin to open, and seldom in February. We have the greatest cold from the northwest, as in Holland from the northeast. The wind here is very seldom east, but almost always south, southwest, northwest, and north; so also the rain.

Our shortest winter days have nine hours sun; in the summer, our longest days are about fifteen hours. We lie so far west of Holland that I judge you are about four hours in advance of us, so that when it is six o'clock in the morning with us it is ten in the forenoon with you, and when it is noon with us, it is four o'clock in the afternoon with you.

The inhabitants of this country are of two kinds: first, Christians—at least so called; second, Indians. Of the Christians I shall say nothing; my design is to speak of the Indians only. These among us are again of two kinds: first, the Mahakinbas [Mohawks], or, as they call themselves, *Kajingahaga*; second, the Mahakans [Mahicans], otherwise called *Agotzagena.* These two nations have different languages, which have no affinity with each other, like Dutch and Latin. These people formerly carried on a great war against each other, but since the Mahakanders were subdued by the Mahakobaas, peace has subsisted between them, and the conquered are obliged to bring a yearly contribution to the others. We live among both these kinds of Indians; and when they come to us from their country, or we go to them, they do us every act of friendship. The principal nation of all the savages and Indians hereabouts with which we have the most intercourse, is the Mahakuaas [Mohawks], who have laid all the other Indians near us under contribution. This nation has a very difficult language, and it costs me great pains to learn it, so as to be able to speak and preach in it fluently. There is no Christian here who understands the language thoroughly; those who have lived here long can use a kind of jargon just sufficient to carry on trade with it, but they do not understand the fundamentals of the language. I am making a vocabulary of the Mahakuaas' language, and when I am among them I ask them how things are called; but as they are very stupid, I sometimes cannot make them understand what I want. Moreover when they tell me, one tells me the word in the infinitive mood, another in the indicative; one in the first, another in the second person; one in the present, another in the preterit. So I stand oftentimes and look, but do not know how to put it down. And as they have declensions and conjugations also, and have their augments like the Greeks, I am like one distracted, and frequently cannot tell what to do, and there is no one to set me right. I shall have to speculate in this alone, in order to become in time an Indian grammarian. When I first observed that they pronounced their words so differently, I asked the commissary of the company what it meant. He answered me that he did not know, but imagined they changed their language every two or three years; I argued against this that it could never be that a whole nation should change its language with one consent;—and, although he has been connected with them here these twenty years, he can afford me no assistance.

The people and Indians here in this country are like us Dutchmen in body and stature; some of them have well formed features, bodies and limbs; they all have black hair and eyes, but their skin is yellow. In summer they go naked, having only their private parts covered with a patch. The children and young folks to ten, twelve and fourteen years of age go stark naked. In winter, they hang about them simply an undressed deer or bear or panther skin; or they take some beaver and otter skins, wild cat, raccoon, martin, otter, mink, squirrel or such like skins, which are plenty in this country, and sew some of them to others, until it is a square piece, and that is then a garment for them; or they buy of us Dutchmen two and a half ells of duffel, and that they hang simply about them, just as it was torn off, without sewing it, and walk away with it. They look at themselves constantly, and think they are very fine. They make themselves stockings and also shoes of deer skin, or they take leaves of their corn, and plait them together and use them for shoes. The women, as well as the men, go with their heads bare. The women let their hair grow very long, and tie it together a little, and let it hang down their backs. The men have a long lock of hair hanging down, some on one side of the head, and some on both sides. On the top of their heads they have a streak of hair from the forehead to the neck, about the breadth of three fingers, and this they shorten until it is about two or three fingers long, and it stands right on end like a cock's comb or hog's bristles; on both sides of this cock's comb they cut all the hair short, except the aforesaid locks, and they also leave on the bare places here and there small locks, such as are in sweeping-brushes, and then they are in fine array.

They likewise paint their faces red, blue, etc., and then they look like the Devil himself. They smear their heads with bear's-grease, which they all carry with them for this purpose in a small basket; they say they do it to make their hair grow better and to prevent their having lice. When they travel, they take with them some of their maize, a kettle, a wooden bowl, and a spoon; these they pack up and hang on their backs. Whenever they are hungry, they forthwith make a fire and cook; they can get fire by rubbing pieces of wood against one another, and that very quickly.

They generally live without marriage; and if any of them have wives, the marriage continues no longer than seems good to one of the parties, and then they separate, and each takes another partner. I have seen those who had parted, and afterwards lived a long time with others, leave these again, seek their former partners, and again be one pair. And, though they have wives, yet they will not leave off whoring; and if they can sleep with another man's wife, they think it a brave thing. The women are exceedingly addicted to whoring; they will lie with a man for the value of one, two, or three *schillings,* and our Dutchmen run after them very much.

The women, when they have been delivered, go about immediately afterwards, and be it ever so cold, they wash themselves and the young child in the river or the snow. They will not lie down (for they say that if they did they would soon die), but keep going about. They are obliged to cut wood, to travel three or four leagues with the child; in short, they walk, they stand, they work, as if they had not lain in, and we cannot see that they suffer any injury by it; and we sometimes try to persuade our wives to lie-in so, and that the way of lying-in in Holland is a mere fiddle-faddle. The men have great authority over their concubines, so that if they do anything which does not please and raises their passion, they take an axe and knock them in the head, and there is an end of it. The women are obliged to prepare the land, to mow, to plant, and do everything; the men do nothing, but hunt, fish, and make war upon their enemies. They are very cruel towards their enemies in time of war; for they first bite off the nails of the fingers of their captives, and cut off some joints, and sometimes even whole fingers; after that, the captives are forced to sing and dance before them stark naked; and finally, they roast their prisoners dead before a slow fire for some days, and then eat them up. The common people eat the arms, buttocks and trunk, but the chiefs eat the head and the heart.

Our Mahakas carry on great wars against the Indians of Canada, on the River Saint Lawrence, and take many captives, and sometimes there are French Christians among them. Last year, our Indians got a great booty from the French on the River Saint Lawrence, and took three Frenchmen, one of whom was a Jesuit. They killed one, but the Jesuit (whose left thumb was cut off, and all the nails and parts of his fingers were bitten,) we released, and sent him to France by a yacht which was going to our country. They spare all the children from ten to twelve years old, and all the women whom they take in war, unless the women are very old, and then they kill them too. Though they are so very cruel to their enemies, they are very friendly to us, and we have no dread of them. We go with them into the woods, we meet with each other, sometimes at an hour or two's walk from any houses, and think no more about it than as if we met with a Christian. They sleep by us, too, in our chambers before our beds. I have had eight at once lying and sleeping upon the floor near my bed, for it is their custom to sleep simply on the bare ground, and to have only a stone or a bit of wood under their heads. In the evening, they go to bed very soon after they have supped; but early in the morning, before day begins to break, they are up again. They are very slovenly and dirty; they wash neither their face nor hands, but let all remain upon their yellow skin, and look like hogs. Their bread is Indian corn beaten to pieces between two stones, of which they make a cake, and bake it in the ashes: their other victuals are venison, turkies, hares, bears, wild cats, their own dogs, etc. The fish they cook just as they get them out of the water without cleansing; also the entrails of deer with all their contents, which they cook a little; and if the intestines are then too tough, they take one end in their mouth, and the other in their hand, and between hand and mouth they separate and eat them. So they do commonly with the flesh, for they carve a little piece and lay it on the fire, as long as one would need to walk from his house to church, and then it is done; and then they bite into it so that the blood runs along their mouths. They can also take a piece of bear's-fat as large as two fists, and eat it clear without bread or anything else. It is natural to them to have no beards; not one in an hundred has any hair about his mouth.

They have also naturally a very high opinion of themselves; they say, *Ihy Othkon,* ("I am the Devil") by which they mean that they are superior folks. In order to praise themselves and their people, whenever we tell them they are very expert at catching deer, or doing this and that, they say, *Tkoschs ko, aguweechon Kajingahaga kouaane Jountuckcha Othkon*; that is, "Really all the Mohawks are very cunning devils." They make their houses of the bark of trees, very close and warm, and kindle their fire in the middle of them. They also make of the peeling and bark of trees, canoes or small boats, which will carry four, five and six persons. In like manner they hollow out trees, and use them for boats, some of which are very large. I have several times sat and sailed with ten, twelve and fourteen persons in one of these hollowed logs. We have in our colony a wooden canoe obtained from the Indians, which will easily carry two hundred *schepels* of wheat. Their weapons in war were formerly a bow and arrow, with a stone axe and mallet; but now they get from our people guns, swords, iron axes and mallets. Their money consists of certain little bones, made of shells or cockles, which are found on the sea-beach; a hole is drilled through the middle of the little bones, and these they string upon thread, or they make of them belts as broad as a hand, or broader, and hang them on their necks, or around their bodies. They have also several holes in their ears, and there they likewise hang some. They value these little bones as highly as many Christians do gold, silver and pearls; but they do not like our money, and esteem it no better than iron. I once showed one of their chiefs a rix-dollar; he asked how much it was worth among the Christians; and when I told him, he laughed exceedingly at us, saying we were fools to value a piece of iron so highly; and if he had such money, he would throw it into the river. They place their dead upright in holes, and do not lay them down, and then they throw some trees and wood on the grave, or enclose it with palisades. They have their set times for going to catch fish, bears, panthers, beavers and eels. In the spring, they catch vast quantities of shad and lampreys, which are exceedingly large here; they lay them on the bark of trees in the sun, and dry them thoroughly hard, and then put them in *notasten*, or bags, which they plait from hemp which grows wild here, and keep the fish till winter. When their corn is ripe, they take it from the ears, open deep pits, and preserve it in these the whole winter. They can also make nets and seines in their fashion; and when they want to fish with seines, ten or twelve men will go together and help each other, all of whom own the seine in common.

They are entire strangers to all religion, but they have a *Tharonhijouaagon,* (whom they also otherwise call *Athzoockkuatoriaho,*) that is, a Genius, whom they esteem in the place of God; but they do not serve him or make offerings to him. They worship and present offerings to the Devil, whom they call *Otskon*, or *Aireskuoni*. If they have any bad luck in war, they catch a bear, which they cut in pieces, and roast, and that they offer up to their *Aireskuoni,* saying in substance, the following words: "Oh! great and mighty Aireskuoni, we confess that we have offended against thee, inasmuch as we have not killed and eaten our captive enemies;—forgive us this. We promise that we will kill and eat all the captives we shall hereafter take as certainly as we have killed, and now eat this bear." Also when the weather is very hot, and their comes a cooling breeze, they cry out directly, *Asoronusi asoronusi, Otskon aworouhsi reinnuha*; that is, "I thank thee, I thank thee, devil, I thank thee, little uncle!" If they are sick, or have a pain or soreness anywhere in their limbs, and I ask them what ails them they say that the Devil sits in their body, or in the sore places, and bites them there; so that they attribute to the Devil at once the accidents which befall them; they have otherwise no religion. When we pray they laugh at us. Some of them despise it entirely; and some, when we tell them what we do when we pray, stand astonished. When we deliver a sermon, sometimes ten or twelve of them, more or less, will attend, each having a long tobacco pipe, made by himself, in his mouth, and will stand awhile and look, and afterwards ask me what I am doing and what I want, that I stand there alone and make so many words, while none of the rest may speak. I tell them that I am admonishing the Christians, that they must not steal, nor commit lewdness, nor get drunk, nor commit murder, and that they too ought not to do these things; and that I intend in process of time to preach the same to them and come to them in their own country and castles (about three days' journey from here, further inland), when I am acquainted with their language. Then they say I do well to teach the Christians; but immediately add, *Diatennon jawij Assirioni, hagiouisk,* that is, "Why do so many Christians do these things?" They call us *Assirioni,* that is, cloth-makers, or *Charistooni*, that is, iron-workers, because our people first brought cloth and iron among them.

They will not come into a house where there is a menstruous woman, nor eat with her. No woman may touch their snares with which they catch deer, for they say the deer can scent it.

The other day an old woman came to our house, and told my people that her forefathers had told her "that *Tharonhij-Jagon,* that is, God, once went out walking with his brother, and a dispute arose between them, and God killed his brother." I suppose this fable took its rise from Cain and Abel. They have a droll theory of the Creation, for they think that a pregnant woman fell down from heaven, and that a tortoise, (tortoises are plenty and large here, in this country, two, three and four feet long, some with two heads, very mischievous and addicted to biting) took this pregnant woman on its back, because every place was covered with water; and that the woman sat upon the tortoise, groped with her hands in the water, and scraped together some of the earth, whence it finally happened that the earth was raised above the water. They think that there are more worlds than one, and that we came from another world.

The Mohawk Indians are divided into three tribes, which are called *Ochkari*, *Anaware, Oknaho,* that is, the Bear, the Tortoise and the Wolf. Of these, the Tortoise is the greatest and most prominent; and they boast that they are the oldest descendants of the woman before mentioned. These have made a fort of palisades, and they call their castle *Asserué.* Those of the Bear are the next to these, and their castle is called by them *Banagiro.* The last are a progeny of these, and their castle is called *Thenondiogo.* These Indian tribes each carry the beast after which they are named (as the arms in their banner) when they go to war against their enemies, and this is done as well for the terror of their enemies, as for a sign of their own bravery. Lately one of their chiefs came to me and presented me with a beaver, an otter, and some cloth he had stolen from the French, which I must accept as a token of good fellowship. When he opened his budget he had in it a dried head of a bear, with grinning teeth. I asked him what that meant? He answered me that he fastened it upon his left shoulder by the side of his head, and that then he was the devil, who cared for nothing, and did not fear any thing.

The government among them consists of the oldest, the most intelligent, the most eloquent and most warlike men. These commonly resolve, and then the young and warlike men execute. But if the common people do not approve of the resolution, it is left entirely to the judgment of the mob. The chiefs are generally the poorest among them, for instead of their receiving from the common people as among Christians, they are obliged to give to the mob; especially when any one is killed in war, they give great presents to the next of kin of the deceased; and if they take any prisoners they present them to that family of which one has been killed, and the prisoner is then adopted by the family into the place of the deceased person. There is no punishment here for murder and other villainies, but every one is his own avenger. The friends of the deceased revenge themselves upon the murderer until peace is made by presents to the next of kin. But although they are so cruel, and live without laws or any punishments for evil doers, yet there are not half so many villainies or murders committed amongst them as amongst Christians; so that I oftentimes think with astonishment upon all the murders committed in the Fatherland, notwithstanding their severe laws and heavy penalties. These Indians, though they live without laws, or fear of punishment, do not (at least, they very seldom) kill people, unless it may be in a great passion, or a hand-to-hand fight. Wherefore we go wholly unconcerned along with the Indians and meet each other an hour's walk off in the woods, without doing any harm to one another.

Johannes Megapolensis.

Two Letters of Bressani

1644

Francesco Giuseppe Bressani

Bressani was born in Rome in 1612. He joined the Society of Jesus at the age of fourteen and went to New France as a missionary in 1642. After some time at Quebec and later Trois-Rivières, he set off for Huron country early in 1644. He and his companions were attacked and made prisoners by one of several Iroquois war parties that were active at that time. His experiences at the hands of the Mohawks were similar to those of Isaac Jogues. However, after extended torture, he was handed over to a Mohawk woman for adoption, a replacement for a relative who had been killed by the Hurons. The reprieve gave him the time and strength to write the first letter that follows here in July. He did not live up to the expectations of his Mohawk captor, so she ransomed him to the Dutch for a pittance. He wrote his second letter in New Amsterdam in August.

Bressani returned to France late in 1644, but was back in Trois-Rivières by the middle of the following year. He returned to service among the Hurons, sharing with them the difficulties brought on by nearly constant attacks from the Iroquois. The Iroquois nearly wiped out the Hurons by 1649, despite repeated trips to Quebec by Bressani to plead for help from the government of New France. He finally led a rescue column to Huron country in 1651, but met the surviving Hurons and Jesuit missionaries retreating towards Quebec. With the Huron mission in collapse, Bressani returned to Italy, where he died in 1672.

The two letters reproduced here are from volume 39 of the *Jesuit Relations* (JR 39:55-83). The originals were written in Italian. They were included in the relation for 1653 along with some editorial comments. The comments, which add nothing to this introduction, are deleted here. Moreover, the letters themselves, which Thwaites published in italics, are reproduced here in roman typeface. Bressani's occasional Latin lines are reproduced in italics here. We have omitted bracketed references to original manuscript page breaks. Superscripted references and hyphens caused by word breaks in the Thwaites edition have also been deleted.

D.R.S.

I

I KNOW NOT whether Your Paternity will recognize the letter of a poor cripple, who formerly, when in perfect health, was well known to you. The letter is
badly written, and quite soiled, because, in addition to other inconveniences, he
who writes it has only one whole finger on his right hand; and it is difficult to
avoid staining the paper with the blood which flows from his wounds, not yet
healed: he uses arquebus [gun] powder for ink, and the earth for a table. He
writes it from the country of the Hiroquois [Iroquois], where at present he happens to be a captive; and desires herewith to give you a brief report of that which
the divine providence has at last ordained for him. I started from three rivers by
order of the Superior, on the 27th of last April,—in company with six Christian
Barbarians, and a young Frenchman, with three canoes,—to go to the country of
the Hurons. The first evening, the Huron who was guiding our canoe, wishing to
shoot at an Eagle, was the occasion of our wreck in the lake named for St. Peter;
two Hurons, by swimming, dragged me to land, as I did not know how to swim,
and there we spent the night, all drenched. The Hurons took this accident for a
bad omen, and counseled me to return whence we had started as we were not yet
more than 8 or 10 miles distant thence. They declared that certainly the journey
would not result well for us; but I, who suspected some superstition in this discourse, judged it best to proceed to another French fort, 30 miles farther, where I
hoped that we might refresh ourselves. They obeyed me, and we started for that
place on the following morning, quite early; but the snow and the bad weather
prevented us from making much progress, and obliged us to end the day at noon.
The third day, when not distant more than 22 or 24 miles from three rivers, and 7
or 8 from the fortress of Richelieu, we were taken captive by 27 Hiroquois, who,
having killed one of our Barbarians, captured the others, and me with them. We
might have fled, or indeed killed some Hiroquois; but I, for my part, on seeing
my companions taken, judged it better to remain with them,—accepting as a sign
of the will of God the inclination and almost resolution of those who conducted
me, who chose rather to surrender than to escape by flight. Those who had captured us made horrible cries, *Sicut exultant victores capta præda*; and, after
many thanks to the Sun for having in their hands, among the others, a "black
robe,"—as thus they call the Jesuits,—they changed our canoes. Then, having
taken from us everything,—that is, provisions for all of ours who lived among
the Hurons, who were in extreme necessity, as they had not been able for several
years to obtain help from Europe,—they commanded us to sing. Meanwhile,
they led us to a little neighboring river, where they divided the spoils, and tore
away the scalp and hair, from the slaughtered Huron, in order to carry it as in
triumph, attached to a pole; they also cut off his feet and hands, along with the
most fleshy parts of the body, to eat them, with the heart. Then they made us
cross the lake, to spend the night in a place somewhat retired, but very
damp,—in which we began to sleep, bound and in the open air, as during the
remainder of the journey. It consoled me in this matter to know that this was the
will of God, as I had undertaken this journey through obedience; and I hoped

much from the intercession of the Virgin, and that of many souls who were praying for me.

On the following day, we embarked on a river upon which we had hardly made a few miles when they commanded me to throw into the water my writings, which they had left with me till then,—as if these had been the cause, as they superstitiously believed, of the wreck of our canoe; and they were astonished that I showed some feeling on that score, not having shown any at the loss of everything else. We still voyaged two days against the current of the river, until we were constrained by the rapids to go ashore; and we traveled six days in the woods. The second day,—which was a Friday, the sixth of May,—we met other Hiroquois, who were going to war. They accompanied many threats with some blows which they gave us; and, having related to our party the death of one of theirs, killed by a Frenchman, the result was that my captors began to treat me more harshly than before.

When they seized us, they were dying with hunger; therefore in two or three days they consumed all our provisions, and for the remainder of the journey there was no food except from either hunting or fishing, or from some wild root, if any were found. During the extreme hunger which we suffered, they found on the shore of the river a dead and putrid beaver, which at evening they gave to me, that I might wash it in the river; but, having thrown it away,—persuading myself that this was their intention, so stinking it was,—I paid for that with a severe penance. I will not write here what I suffered on that journey; enough to know that we marched, carrying burdens, in the woods, where there is no road at all, but only stones, or young shoots, or ditches, or water, or snow,—which was not yet everywhere melted. We traveled without shoes; fasting sometimes till three and four o'clock in the afternoon, and often whole days; exposed to the rain, and soaked in the water of the torrents and rivers which we had to cross. At evening, my office was to gather the wood, carry the water, and do the cooking, when there was any; and if I came short in anything, or did not understand well, the blows were not lacking,—and much less did these fail, when we happened to meet people who were going either fishing or hunting; besides, I was hardly able to rest at night, for being bound to a tree and exposed to the severity of the air, which was still quite cold. We finally reached their lake, on which—when they had made other canoes, at which it was necessary for me to assist them—we sailed five or six days, after which we landed, and there we made three days' journey on foot. On the fourth day, which was the 15th of May,—about the 20th hour, being still fasting, we arrived at a river where about 400 Barbarians were assembled for fishing; being already apprised of our arrival, they then came to meet us. At about two hundred paces from their cabins, they stripped me naked, and made me go first; on either side, the young men of the country stood in line, every one with his stick in hand, but the first of them had, instead of the stick, a knife. Then, as I began to proceed, this one suddenly stopped me; and, having taken my left hand, with the knife which he held, he made in it an incision between the little finger and the ring-finger, with so much force and violence that I believed he would split my whole hand; and the others began to load me with blows as far as the stage prepared for our torment. Then they made me mount upon some great pieces of bark, about nine palms above the ground,—in order that we might be seen and mocked by the people. I was now bruised all over, and covered with blood, which was flowing from all parts of my body,—and exposed to a very cold wind, which made it suddenly congeal over the skin; but I greatly consoled myself to see that God granted me the favor of suffering in this world some little pain in place of that which I was under obligation, because of my sins, to pay in the other with torments incomparably greater. Meanwhile, the warriors arrived, and were magnificently received by the people of this village; and, when they were refreshed with the best that they had from their fishing, they commanded us to sing; it may be imagined how we could do so, fasting, weak from the journey, overwhelmed with blows, and trembling with cold from head to foot. Some time after, a Huron slave brought us a dish of turkish [Indian] corn; and a Captain, seeing me tremble with cold, at my urgency finally tossed back to me the half of an old summer garment, all torn, which covered rather than warmed me. They made us sing until the warriors went away; and they left us in the hands of the young men of the place, who finally made us come down from that stage, where we had been about two hours,—in order to make us dance in their manner; and because I did not do so, or know how to, they beat me, pricked me, tore out my hair and beard, etc. They kept us in this place five or six days for their pastime, exposed to the discretion or indiscretion of everybody. It was necessary to obey the very children, and that in things little reasonable, and often contrary. "Get up and sing," said one. "Be quiet," said the other; and if I obeyed one, the other ill-used me. "Here, give thy hand, which I will burn for thee;" and the other burned me because I did not extend it to him. They commanded me to take the fire in my fingers, and put it into their pipes, in which they took tobacco; and then they purposely made it fall four or five times in succession, in order to make me burn my hands by picking it up again from the ground. This was usually done at night. Toward evening, the Captains shouted through the cabins with frightful voices: "Up! assemble yourselves, O young men, and come to caress our prisoners." At this invitation they arose and gathered themselves into some large cabin; and, lifting from my back that poor rag of clothing which they had returned to me, they left me naked. Then some pricked me with sharp sticks, others with firebrands; these burned me with red-hot stones, those with hot ashes and lighted coals. They made me walk around the fire, where they had fixed in the earth sharp sticks between the burning ashes; some tore out my hair, others my beard; and every night, after having made me sing, and tormented me as above, they would burn one of my nails or fingers for the space of eight or ten minutes; of ten that I had, I have now only one whole one left,—and even from this one they had torn out the nail with their teeth. One evening, they burned one of my nails; on another, the first joint or section of a finger; on the next, the second. In six times, they burned nearly six of my fingers,—and more than 18 times they applied the fire and iron to my hands alone; and meanwhile it was necessary to sing. Thus they treated us till one or two hours after midnight, and then they left me on the bare ground, usually tied to the spot, and exposed to the rain, without other bed or cover than a small skin, which covered not the half of my body,—even at times without anything, because they had already torn up that piece of garment; although, out of pity, they made of it for me enough to cover that which decency does not permit to be uncovered, even among themselves, but retained the rest.

I was treated in this way, and worse, for a whole month; but, at this first place, no longer than eight days. I would never have believed that a man could endure so hard a life. One night, while they were tormenting me as usual, a Huron who had been taken captive with me,—perhaps because he had seen that one of his companions, having declared himself against us, had freed himself from the torments,—shouted, in the midst of the assembly, that I was a person of rank, and a Captain among the French. He was heard with great attention, and then they uttered a loud shout in token of joy,—resolving to treat me still worse,—and, on the following morning, condemned me to be burned alive, and eaten. They then began to guard me more strictly, not leaving me alone even in the necessities of nature,—wherein both the men and the boys molested me, in order to make me return as soon as possible to the cabin, fearing lest I should escape.

We started thence on the 26th of May; and, four days later we arrived at the first Village of this nation. On this journey,—made on foot, amid rains and other hardships,—my sufferings were greater than before. The barbarian who conducted me was more cruel than the first, and I was wounded, weak, ill fed, and half naked; moreover, I slept in the open air, bound to a stake or to a tree, trembling all night with cold, and from the pain of these bonds. At difficult places in the road, I had need of some one to aid me because of my weakness, but all help was denied me; for this reason, I often fell, renewing my wounds; and to these they added new blows, in order to urge me to proceed,—thinking that I was feigning for the sake of staying behind, and then taking flight. On one occasion, among others, I fell into a river, and came near being drowned; however, I got out, I know not how; and all drenched with water, together with a quite heavy bundle on my shoulders, I was obliged to complete about six miles more marching until evening. They, meanwhile, jeered at me, and at my stupidity in having allowed myself to fall into the river; and they did not omit, at night, to burn off one of my nails. We finally arrived at the first village of that nation, where our entrance was similar to the former, and still more cruel, because—in addition to the blows with their fists, and other blows which they gave me on the most sensitive parts of the body—they split, for the second time, my left hand between the middle finger and the forefinger; and I received beatings in so great number that they made me fall to the ground, half dead. I thought that I would lose my right eye, with my sight; and, although I did not rise from the ground, for I could not, they did not cease to beat me, chiefly on the breast and on the head. Indeed, without some other hindrance they would have ended by killing me, had not a Captain caused me to be dragged—as it were, by force—upon a stage of bark, similar to the first, where, soon afterward, they cut off the thumb of my left hand and wounded the forefinger. Meanwhile a great rain came up, with thunder and lightning; and they went away, leaving us there, naked in the water, until some one, I know not who, taking pity on us, toward evening led us to his cabin. Here they tormented us with greater cruelty and impudence than ever, without a moment of rest: they forced me to eat filth; burned the rest of my nails, and some fingers; wrung off my toes, and bored one of them with a firebrand; and I know not what they did not do to me once, when I feigned to be in a swoon, in order to seem not to perceive something indecent that they were doing. Surfeited with tormenting us here, they sent us to another Village, nine or ten miles distant, where, besides the other torments, already mentioned, they suspended me by the feet,—sometimes with cords, again with chains, which they had taken from the Dutch; with these, at night, they left me bound—hands, feet, and neck—to several stakes,—as usual, upon the bare ground. Six or seven nights they tormented me in such fashion, and in such places, that I could not describe these things, nor could they be read, without blushing. On those nights, I was awake almost all night, and they appeared to me very long, although they were the shortest of the year. "My God, what will purgatory be?" This thought appeased my pains not a little. In this manner of living I had become so fetid and horrible that every one drove me away like a piece of carrion; and they approached me for no other purpose than to torment me. Scarcely did I find any one to feed me,—although I had not the use of my hands, which were abnormally swollen, and putrid; I was thus, of course, still further tormented by hunger, which led me to eat Indian corn raw,—not without concern for my health,—and made me find a relish in chewing clay, although I could not easily swallow it. I was covered with loathsome vermin, and could neither get rid of them nor defend myself from them. In my wounds, worms were produced; out of one finger alone, more than four fell in one day. *Putredini dixi: Pater meus es; mater mea, et soror mea, vermibus; factus eram mihimet ipsi gravis*: so that I would have regarded, by the very judgment of self-love, *mori lucrum*,—death as gain. I had an abscess in the right thigh, caused by blows and frequent falls, which hindered me from all repose,—especially as I had only skin and bone, and the earth, for bed Several times the Barbarians had tried, but to no purpose, to open it, with sharp stones,—not without great pain to me. I was compelled to employ as Surgeon the renegade Huron who had been taken with us. The latter—on the day which, as was believed, was the eve of my death—opened it for me with four knife-thrusts, and caused blood and matter to issue from it, in so great abundance and with such stench that all the Barbarians of the cabin were constrained to abandon it. I desired and was awaiting death, but not without some horror of the fire; I was preparing for it, however, as best I could, and was heartily commending myself to the Mother of mercy, who is truly *Mater amabilis, admirabilis, potens, et clemens, consolatrix afflictorum*,—who was, after God, the sole refuge of a poor sinner, forsaken by all creatures in a strange land, *in loco horroris, et vastæ solitudinis*, without a language to make himself understood, without friends to console him, without Sacraments to strengthen him, and without any human remedy for alleviating his ills. The Huron and Algonquin prisoners (these are our Barbarians), instead of consoling me, were the first to torment me, in order to please the Hiroquois. I did not see the good Guillaume, except afterward, when my life was granted me; and the lad who had been taken in my company was no longer with me, especially after they perceived that I had him say his prayers,—a thing which they did not favor. But they did not leave him without torments, for, although he was no more than twelve or thirteen years old, they tore out five of his nails with their teeth; and, at his arrival in the country, they bound his wrists tightly with thongs, causing him the acutest pain,—and all in my presence, in order to afflict me the more. Oh, at such times, what a different opinion is held of many things which are commonly much esteemed! Please God that I remember it, and profit thereby. The days being irksome to me, and having no rest at night, I counted in the month five days more than I should; but, seeing the Moon one evening, I corrected my error. I knew not why they deferred my death so long; they told me that it was to fatten me before eating me, but they took no means to do so. One day, at last, they assembled in order to despatch me. It was the 19th of June, which I reckoned as the last of my life; and I entreated a Captain that they would commute, if it was possible, the death by fire into some other, but another man exhorted him to remain firm in the resolution already taken. The first, nevertheless, assured me that I should die neither by fire nor by any other death; I did not believe him, and know not whether he himself spoke in good faith. But, finally, it was as he said, because such was the will of God and of the Virgin Mother,—to whom I acknowledge my life, and that which I esteem still more,—a great strength in my troubles; may it please the Majesty of God that this redound to his greater glory and to my good. The Barbarians themselves marveled at this result,—contrary to their every intention, as the Dutch have reported and written to me; they therefore gave me, with the ceremonies of the country, to an Old woman, in place of her Grandsire, killed some time before by the Hurons. She, instead of having me burned,—as all desired, and had already resolved,—ransomed me from their hands at the price of some beads, which the French call "porcelain." I live here among the shadows of death, not hearing anything spoken of but murders and assassinations. They have recently slain in a cabin one of their own nation, as being useless, and as one who did not deserve to live. Of course, I suffer somewhat here; my wounds are not yet healed over, and many do not regard me with a favorable eye. One cannot live without crosses, and this one is of sugar in comparison with the past one. The Dutch cause me to hope for my ransom, and that of the Lad who was taken with me; the will of God be done, in time and in Eternity. I shall hope for it with greater reason if you will make me a partaker of your Holy Sacrifices and prayers, and of those of our Fathers and brethren,—especially of those who were formerly acquainted with me. From the Hiroquois, the 15th of July, 1644.

II

I have not met any one to carry the inclosed letter; you will therefore receive it along with the present, which is intended to give you news of my ransom, effected by the Dutch, from the hands of the Barbarians who kept me a prisoner. The matter was not very difficult, and they ransomed me cheaply, on account of

the small esteem in which they held me, because of my want of skill for everything, and because they believed that I would never get well of my ailments. I
was twice sold, the first time to that Old woman who was to have me burned; and
the second to the Dutch, quite dear,—that is, for the price of 15 or 20 doppias. I
sang my *in exitu Israel de Ægypto* on the 19th of August,—a day which is in the
octave of the Assumption of the Virgin, who was my deliverer,—when I had
been a captive in the country of the Hiroquois four months,—a small thing in respect of what my sins deserved. I could not, in the time of my servitude, render
to those unfortunates, for the evil which they did me, the good which I desired
for them, which was, to give them the knowledge of the true God. Not knowing
the language, I tried to instruct, by means of a captive interpreter, an old man
who was dying; but pride hindered him from listening to me,—he answered me
that a man of his age and standing should teach, and not be taught. I asked him
whether he knew whither he would go after death; he answered me, "To the Sunset;" and here he began to relate their fables and delusions, which those wretched
people, blinded by the Demon, regard as the most solid truths. I baptized no one
except a Huron, whom they conducted to the place where I was, in order to burn
him; those who were guarding me urged me to go to see him. I went thither with
repugnance,—they having falsely told me that he was not one of our Barbarians,
and that I would not have understood him. I pass through the crowd; they form in
line for me, and allow me to approach that man who was already quite disfigured
by the tortures. He was lying on the bare ground, without being able to rest his
head in any place; I, seeing near him a stone, push it with my foot as far as his
head, that he may use it for a pillow. Then,—looking at me, and, either by some
wisp of beard which I had left, or by some other sign, judging that I was a
stranger,—he said to the person who had him in custody: "Is not this the European whom you hold captive?" And, the other having answered him "Yes,"
looking at me the second time with a somewhat pitiful glance, "Sit down" (he
said to me), "my brother, near me, for I desire to speak to thee." I do so, not
without horror at the stench which emanated from that body already half roasted,
and ask him what thing he desires,—rejoicing to understand him a little, because
he spoke Huron, and hoping through this opportunity to be able to instruct him
for baptism; but his answer, to my utmost consolation, anticipated me. "What do
I ask," he says; "I ask nothing else than baptism: make haste, because the time is
short." I undertook to question him, in order not to offer a Sacrament with pre-
cipitation, and I found him perfectly instructed,—having been received among
the Catechumens, even in the country of the Hurons. I baptized him then, with
great satisfaction to both him and myself; but although I had done so with some
artifice,—having used a little water which I had had brought for giving him to
drink,—the Hiroquois nevertheless perceived it. The Captains, being, as soon as
possible, informed of this, suddenly drove me from the cabin with anger and
threats,—beginning to torment him again as before; and the following morning
they finished roasting him alive. Then, because I had baptized him, they carried
all his limbs, one by one, into the cabin where I abode,—skinning, in my presence, and eating, his feet and hands. The husband of the mistress of the cabin put

at my feet the dead man's head, and left it there a considerable time,—reproaching me with what I had done, by saying: "And what indeed have thy enchantments" (speaking of the baptism, and of the prayers that we had said together) "helped him? have they perhaps delivered him from death?" I then felt great sorrow at not being able, for want of language, to explain to them at so excellent an opportunity the virtue and effects of holy Baptism. But that time has not yet arrived; their sins—and especially pride—are a great obstacle to the grace of God, *Qui humilia respicit, et alta à longe cognoscit.* They all account themselves Champions, and as Mars: they despise the Europeans as vile and cowardly people, and think that they themselves were born to subjugate the world; *evanuerunt in cogitationibus suis*, and therefore *tradidit illos Deus in desideria cordis eorum.* Your most holy prayers and sacrifices, and those of the whole Society, which always prays for the conversion of the infidels, will avail to obtain that God may regard them with an eye of pity, and me with them,—especially in the dangers of the sea whereinto I am entering,—assuring yourself that not only in health, but maimed, I shall be always Your Paternity's unworthy son and most humble servant.

F.G.B.
From new Amsterdam, the 31st of August, 1644.

Of the Mission of the Martyrs, Begun in the Country of the Iroquois

1646

Jérôme Lalemant

Jérôme Lalemant was born in Paris in 1593. He entered the Jesuit novitiate in 1610 and was extensively schooled and experienced by the time he went to Canada in 1638. He served as superior of the Huron mission (1638-1645) and later served twice as superior of the Jesuits in Canada (1645-1650 and 1659-1665). He was responsible for a historically important Huron census, which was made shortly after his arrival in 1638.

During his 1645-1650 period of service, Lalemant had to deal with the deaths of several Jesuit missionaries, including Isaac Jogues, Jean de Brébeuf, and his own nephew, Gabriel Lalemant. In the account that follows here, Lalemant describes the trip of Jogues and Jean Bourdon to Mohawk country. Although it is not a first person account, it is included here because it supplements Jogues's own description with important information on the Mohawks. Lalemant dated his report and sent it to France on October 28, 1646, only ten days after Jogues was killed.

This report was published as a portion of volume 29 of the *Jesuit Relations* (JR 29:45-63). Technical changes from the Thwaites edition include removal of endnote superscripts, the dropping of hyphens caused by word breaks at the ends of lines in earlier versions, and the dropping of bracketed references to page breaks in the original manuscript. The reader is reminded that the word "porcelain" in Jesuit usage refers to tubular shell wampum.

D.R.S.

WHEN I SPEAK of a Mission among the Iroquois, it seems to me that I speak of a dream, and yet it is a truth. It is with good right that it is made to bear the name of the Martyrs; for—besides the cruelties which those Barbarians have already inflicted upon some persons impassioned for the salvation of souls; besides the pains and fatigues which those who are destined to this Mission are bound to incur—we may say with truth that it has already been crimsoned with the blood of one Martyr; for the Frenchman who was slain at the feet of Father Isaac Jogues lost his life for having expressed the sign of our creed to some little Iroquois children, which so greatly offended their parents that they—imagining that there might be some spell in this action—made of it at once a crime and a martyrdom.

Add this, that—if it be permitted to conjecture, in things which indicate great probabilities—it is credible (if this enterprise succeed) that the designs which we have against the empire of Satan, for the salvation of these peoples, will not yield their fruits before they be sprinkled with the blood of some other Martyrs. Nevertheless, the principal design of this denomination is that this Mission may be assisted with the influence and favor of those blessed and consecrated victims who have the honor to approach nearest to the Lamb, and to follow him everywhere. But let us begin the discourse.

Monsieur our Governor having resolved to send two Frenchmen to the country of the Annierronnons [Mohawks],—in order to convey to them his word, and to betoken to them his joy and satisfaction over the peace happily concluded, —Father Isaac Jogues was presented to him, to be of the party. As he had already purchased an acquaintance with these peoples and their language, with a coin more precious than gold or silver, he was soon accepted; the Iroquois welcomed him, and he who had sustained the weight of war, was not for retreating in time of peace. He was very glad to sound their friendship, after having experienced the rage of their enmity. He was not ignorant, however, of the inconstancy of these Barbarians; the difficulty of the roads was patent to him, as a man who had experienced it; he saw the dangers into which he was throwing himself; but he who never risks for God will never be an extensive dealer in the riches of Heaven. He was ready sooner than the proposition was made to him. Monsieur the Governor thought proper to send, besides, the sieur Bourdon, a settler in the country,—who showed his zeal for the public welfare all the more that he forsook his own family, in order to throw himself into hazards which are never small among these Barbarians.

The Algonquins, seeing that a Father was embarking, gave him warning not to speak of the Faith at the very first; "for there is nothing," said they, "so repulsive at the beginning as our doctrine, which seems to exterminate everything that men hold most dear; and, because your long robe preaches as well as your lips, it would be expedient to walk in shorter apparel." This warning was heeded, and it was considered necessary to treat the sick as sick, and to behave among the impious as one does among the heretics,—that one must become all things to all men, in order to gain all to JESUS CHRIST.

They started on the 16th of May from three Rivers; and on the 18th, the eve of Pentecost, they embarked at Richelieu on the river of the Iroquois. They were conducted by four Annierronnon Iroquois; two young Algonquins accompanied them, in their own separate canoe, laden with the gifts which they were going to make for the confirmation of the peace. The Holy Ghost,—to whom is dedicated the largest village of the Iroquois,—whose feast was about to begin in the Church at the moment of their departure, gave them even then a foretaste of the good fortune of their voyage.

They arrived, on the eve of the Blessed Sacrament, at the end of the lake which is joined to the great lake of Champlain. The Iroquois name it An-diatarocté, as if one should say, "there where the lake is shut in." The Father named it the lake of the Blessed Sacrament.

They left it, the day of that great Feast, continuing their way by land with great fatigues, for they had to carry on their backs their bundles and their baggage; the Algonquins were obliged to leave a great part of theirs on the shore of the lake.

Six leagues from this lake, they crossed a small river which the Iroquois call Qiogué; the Dutch, who are located along it, but lower down, name it the River van Maurice.

On the first day of June, their guides, overcome by their burdens and the toil, turned aside from the road which leads to their villages, in order to pass by a certain place called in their language Ossaragué; this spot (according to the Father's report) is very remarkable as abounding in a small fish, the size of the her-ring. They were hoping to find some assistance there; and indeed they were loaned some canoes to carry their baggage as far as the first settlement of the Dutch, distant from this fishery about eighteen or twenty leagues.

God has a guidance all full of love: his goodness caused this detour to be made in order to give some assistance to the poor Therese, a former Seminarist of the Ursulines; our party met her at this place. The Father refreshed her memory con-cerning her duty, and heard her confession, to the great satisfaction of her soul.

On the 4th of June, they landed at the first settlement of the Dutch, where they were Very well received by the Captain of the fort of Orange; they departed thence on the sixteenth of the same month, accompanied and assisted by the Iro-quois who happened to be in that quarter. The next day, at evening, they arrived at their first small village, called Oneugiouré, formerly Osserrïon. There it was necessary to stay two days, in order to be gazed at and welcomed by those peo-ples, who came from all parts to see them; those who had formerly ill-used the Father no longer showed any inclination to do so; and those whom natural com-passion had touched at the sight of his torments, were evidently delighted to see him in another position and employed in an important office.

On the 10th of June, honored by the feast of the holy Trinity, he gave this Most holy name to that village. There was held, at the same time, a general as-sembly of all the principal Captains and elders of the country; there were exhib-ited the gifts which the sieur Bourdon brought with the Father; there were also present the two Algonquins who accompanied them.

Silence procured, the Father sets forth the word of Onontio and of all the French, betokened by the gifts of which I have given the explanation in the pre-ceding Chapter. He indicates the joy that was caused by the sight of the Ambas-sadors, and the satisfaction of all the people at the conclusion of the peace between the French, the Iroquois, the Hurons, and the Algonquins. He assures them that the council fire is lighted at three Rivers; he presents a necklace of 5000 Porcelain beads [wampum], in order to break the bonds of the little Frenchman captive in their country, and the like for the deliverance of Therese; he thanks them for having refused the heads [scalps] of the montagnais or of the

Algonquins massacred by the Sokoquiois. He made a special present of 3000 Porcelain beads to one of the great families of the Annierronnon scattered through their three villages, in order to keep a fire always lighted when the French should come to visit them.

His harangue was favorably heard, and his gifts very well received. He spoke next for the Algonquins, who were not acquainted with the Iroquois language, and who were somewhat ashamed at the lack of a great part of their presents; for, of 24 robes of Elk skins, they had left 14 on the way, as we have remarked. The Father excused them by reason of the injury received by one of those two young men, through the weight of his burden, and the difficulty of the roads. He failed not to give the sense of all these speeches, and to specify all these gifts, insomuch that the assembly was satisfied therewith,—to the extent that afterward the Iroquois responded with two gifts which they made to the Algonquins; and they sent two others for the Hurons.

As for what concerned Onontio and the French,—as a favor to whom they had made peace with their allies,—they answered with more pomp and with a great manifestation of affection.

At the request of the little Frenchman, they drew forth a necklace of 2000 beads. "There," said they, "is the bond which held him captive; take the prisoner and his chain, and do with them according to the will of Onontio."

As for Therese, whom they had given in marriage after her captivity, they answered that she would be restored as soon as she should return to their country; and, in token of the truth of their word, they offered a necklace of 1500 Porcelain beads. The family of which we have spoken—which is named "the Wolf family"—assured the French, by a beautiful gift of 36 palms of Porcelain, that they should always have a secure dwelling among them, and that the Father, in particular, would always find his little mat all ready to receive him, and a fire lighted to warm him. All this was done with great demonstrations of good will.

But some distrustful minds did not look with favor on a little chest, which the Father had left as an assurance of his return; they imagined that some misfortune disastrous to the whole country was shut up in that little box. The Father, to undeceive them, opened it, and showed them that it contained no other mystery than some small necessaries for which he might have use.

I was almost forgetting to say that the Father, having remarked in the assembly some Iroquois from the country of the Onondaëronnons [Onondagas], made them in public a gift of 2000 Porcelain beads, in order to make them understand the design which the French had in going to see them in their country; and told them that he made them this gift in advance, so that they would not be surprised at seeing the faces of the French. He said that, furthermore, the French had three roads by which to go to visit them,—one through the Annierronnons; another, by the great Lake which they name Ontario, or Lake of St. Louys; the third, through the land of the Hurons. Some of the elders manifested surprise at this proposition. "It is necessary," they said, "to take the road which Onontio has opened; the others are too dangerous; one meets in them only people of war, men with painted and figured faces, with clubs and war hatchets, who seek only to kill,"—adding that the way which leads into their country was now excellent, entirely cleared, and very secure. But the Father followed up his point, not considering it expedient to depend on the Annierronnons, in order to go up into the Nations above. He put his gift in the hands of the Iroquois, who promised, in presence of the Onondaëronnons, to go and present it to the Captains and elders of their country. Thus ended the public affairs, in which the Father was not forgetful of those more private and important. He gathered some few Christians,—who are still there,—instructed them, and administered to them the Sacrament of Penance; he often made the round of the cabins, visited the sick, and sent to Heaven by the waters of Baptism some poor dying creatures,—predestined, however, to riches.

After all these assemblies, the Annierronnons urged the departure of the French,—saying that a band of Iroquois from above had started in order to await, at the passage, the Hurons who were to come down to the French; and that those warriors would move thence to Montreal, in order to come and cross before Richelieu, and go back to their own country by the river of the Iroquois. "We do not believe," said they, "that they will do you any harm when they meet you; but we fear for the two Algonquins who are with you."

The Father thereupon told them, very pertinently, that he was astonished to see how they permitted those upper Iroquois to come down into their district, and proceed to make war within their limits, descending the rapids and waterfalls which were of the jurisdiction and within the marches of the Annierronnons. "We have given them warning of this," they answered. "What then?" said the Father, "do they despise your commands? Do you not see that all the lawless acts that they may commit will be imputed to you?" They opened their eyes at this argument, and promised to apply to the matter an efficacious remedy.

In conclusion, the Father, our French, and their guides left the village of the holy Trinity on the 16th of June. They journeyed for several days by land, not without difficulty: for it is necessary to do like the horses of Arabia,—carry one's own provisions and baggage; the brooks are the hostelries that one meets. Having arrived on the shore of the Lake of the Blessed Sacrament, they made canoes or little boats of bark; having embarked in these, they made their way by paddling until the 27th of the same month of June, when they landed at the first settlement of the French, situated where the river of the Iroquois empties into the great flood of St. Lawrence.

Such is the beginning of a Mission which must furnish an opening to many others among well-peopled Nations. If these roads are strewn with Crosses, they all are also filled with miracles; for there is no human skill or power which could have changed the face of affairs so suddenly, and have drawn us out of the utmost despair, to which we were reduced. There are neither gifts nor eloquence which could have converted, in so short a time, hearts enraged for so many years. I know not what may not be hoped for, after these acts at the hand of the Almighty; may he be blessed beyond ages and beyond eternity.

Father Isaac Jogues, entirely attentive and devoted to this Mission, after having rendered account of his commission, thought of nothing but undertaking a second voyage in order to return thither and especially before the winter; for he could not endure to be so long absent from his spouse of blood. At last, he succeeded so well that he found the opportunity therefor, toward the end of September; and he started from three Rivers on the 24th of that month, in company with a young Frenchman, and some Iroquois and other Savages. We have learned that he was abandoned on the way by most of his companions, but that he continued his voyage. He goes intending to spend the winter there, and, on all the occasions which shall present themselves, to influence the minds and affections of the Savages,—but especially to care for the affairs of God and the riches of Paradise. He has much need of earnest prayers for the success of an enterprise so difficult.

Voyages of Pierre Esprit Radisson

1651-1654

Pierre Esprit Radisson

Pierre (Peter) Radisson was born in about 1636 in France. He arrived in Canada in about 1651 and was captured by the Mohawks while hunting near Three Rivers. His narrative is useful for what it tells us about Iroquois adoption practices and Mohawk culture generally. He could have escaped earlier than he did, but he was not simply a war captive. It is clear that he was incorporated into a family as a replacement for a lost member, and his life among the Mohawks was not a harsh one.

Radisson returned to Europe early in 1654 after his escape via Fort Orange. He returned almost immediately to Canada. Meanwhile, his widowed sister had married Médard Chouart at Three Rivers. Chouart was known as Sieur des Groseilliers. They were both members of several expeditions westward and became involved in the developing beaver trade. This brought them into conflict with the governor of Canada by 1660. Radisson and Chouart refused to share their profits with the governor and angrily entered English service at Boston and Port Royal. Radisson knew the fur trade and how it could be exploited through an alliance with the Iroquois. Some believe that he was instrumental in the English conquest of Dutch New Netherland. He later participated in the founding of the Hudson's Bay Company, and he made several voyages on behalf of that organization. He died in 1710.

Radisson wrote most of his accounts in imperfect English. The account reproduced here is part of a manuscript covering the years 1651 to 1684 that is now in the Bodleian Library, Oxford. An edition by Gideon Scull was published by the Prince Society in 1885. This was reprinted by Burt Franklin in 1967. Scull's footnotes have been omitted here. English abbreviations have been replaced with complete words in order to ease reading. The reader should note especially that Radisson used the word "head" to have both the standard meaning and the meaning of "scalp." Most words in brackets were part of the 1885 published version. I have inserted a few additional clarifications in brackets where they seemed necessary. Otherwise, Radisson's English has been left as he wrote it.

D.R.S.

The Relation of my Voyage, being in Bondage in the Lands of the Irokoits [Iroquois], *which was the next yeare after my coming into Canada, in the yeare 1651, the 24th day of May.*

BEING PERSUADED in the morning by two of my comrades to go and recreat ourselves in fowling, I disposed myselfe to keepe them Company; wherfor I cloathed myselfe the lightest way I could possible, that I might be the nimbler and not stay behinde, as much for the prey that I hoped for, as for to escape the danger into which wee have ventered ourselves of an enemy the cruelest that ever was uppon the face of the Earth. It is to bee observed that the french had warre with a wild nation called Iroquoites, who for that time weare soe strong and so to be feared that scarce any body durst stirre out either Cottage or house without being taken or killed, saving that he had nimble limbs to escape their fury; being departed, all three well armed, and unanimiously rather die then abandon one another, notwithstanding these resolutions weare but young mens deboasting; being then in a very litle assurance and lesse security.

At an offspring of a village of three Rivers we consult together that two should go the watter side, the other in a wood hardby to warne us, for to advertise us if he accidentaly should light [upon] or suspect any Barbars [barbarians] in ambush, we also retreat ourselves to him if we should discover any thing uppon the River. Having comed to the first river, which was a mile distant from our dwellings, wee mett a man who mett a man who kept cattell, and asked him if he had knowne any appearance of Ennemy, and likewise demanded which way he would advise us to gett better fortune, and what part he spied more danger; he guiding us the best way he could, prohibiting us by no means not to render ourselves att the skirts of the mountains; ffor, said he, I discovered oftentimes a multitude of people which rose up as it weare of a sudaine from of the Earth, and that doubtless there weare some Enemys that way; which sayings made us looke to ourselves and charge two of our fowling peeces with great shot the one, and the other with small. Priming our pistols, we went where our fancy first lead us, being impossible for us to avoid the destinies of the heavens; no sooner tourned our backs, but my nose fell ableeding without any provocation in the least. Certainly it was a warning for me of a beginning of a yeare and a half of hazards and of miseryes that weare to befall mee. We did shoot sometime and killed some Duks, which made one of my fellow travellers go no further. I seeing him taking such a resolution, I proferred some words that did not like him, giving him the character of a timourous, childish humor; so this did nothing prevaile with him, to the Contrary that had with him quite another issue then what I hoped for; ffor offending him with my words he prevailed so much with the others that he persuaded them to doe the same. I lett them goe, laughing them to scorne, beseeching them to helpe me to my fowles, and that I would tell them the discovery of my designes, hoping to kill meat to make us meate att my retourne.

I went my way along the wood some times by the side of the river, where I finde something to shute att, though no considerable quantitie, which made me goe a league off and more, so I could not go in all further then St. Peeter's, which is nine mile from the plantation by reason of the river Ovamasis, which hindered me the passage. I begun'd to think att my retourne how I might transport my fowle. I hide one part in a hollow tree to keep them from the Eagles and other devouring fowles, so as I came backe the same way where before had no bad incounter. Arrived within one halfe a mile where my comrades had left me, I rested awhile by reason that I was looden'd with three geese, tenn ducks, and one crane, with some teales.

After having layed downe my burden uppon the grasse, I thought to have heard a noise in the wood by me, which made me to overlook my armes; I found one of my girdle pistols wette. I shott it off and charged it againe, went up to the wood the soffliest I might, to discover and defend myselfe the better against any surprise. After I had gone from tree to tree some 30 paces off I espied nothing; as I came back from out of the wood to an adjacent brooke, I perceived a great number of Ducks; my discovery imbouldened me, and for that there was a litle way to the fort, I determined to shute once more; coming nigh preparing meselfe for to shute, I found another worke, the two young men that I left some tenne houres before heere weare killed. Whether they came after mee, or weare brought thither by the Barbars, I know not. However [they] weare murthered. Looking over them, knew them albeit quite naked, and their hair standing up, the one being shott through with three boulletts and two blowes of an hatchett on the head, and the other runne thorough in severall places with a sword and smitten with an hatchett. Att the same instance my nose begun'd to bleed, which made me afraid of my life; but withdrawing myselfe to the watter side to see if any body followed mee, I espied twenty or thirty heads in a long grasse. Mightily surprized att that view, I must needs passe through the midst of them or tourne backe into the woode. I slipped a boullet uppon the shott and beate the paper into my gunne. I heard a noise, which made me looke on that side; hopeing to save meselfe, perswading myselfe I was not yet perceived by them that weaare in the medow, and in the meane while some gunns weare lett off with an horrid cry.

Seeing myselfe compassed round about by a multitude of dogges, or rather devils, that rose from the grasse, rushesse, and bushesse, I shott my gunne, whether un warrs or purposly I know not, but I shott with a pistolle confidently, but was seised on all sids by a great number that threw me downe, taking away my arme without giving mee one blowe; ffor afterwards I felt no paine att all, onely a great guidinesse in my heade, from whence it comes I doe not remember. In the same time they brought me into the wood, where they shewed me the two heads [scalps] all bloody. After they consulted together for a while, retired into their boats, which weare four or five miles from thence, and wher I have bin a while before. They layed mee hither, houlding me by the hayre, to the imbarking place; there they began to errect their cottages, which consisted only of some sticks to boyle their meate, whereof they had plenty, but stuncke, which was strange to mee to finde such an alteration so sudaine. They made [me] sitt downe by. After this they searched me and tooke what I had, then stripped me naked, and tyed a rope about my middle, wherin I remained, fearing to persist, in the same posture the rest of the night. After this they removed me, laughing and howling like as many wolves, I knowing not the reason, if not for my skin, that was soe whit in respect of theirs. But their gaping did soone cease because of a false alarme, that their scout who stayed behind gave them, saying that the ffrench and the wild Algongins, friends to the ffrench, came with all speed. They presently put out the fire, and tooke hould of the most advantageous passages, and sent 25 men to discover what it meant, who brought certaine tydings of assurance and liberty.

In the meanewhile I was garded by 50 men, who gave me a good part of my cloathes. After kindling a fire againe, they gott theire supper ready, which was sudenly don, ffor they dresse their meat halfe boyled, mingling some yallowish meale in the broath of that infected stinking meate; so whilst this was adoing they combed my head, and with a filthy grease greased my head, and dashed all over my face with redd paintings. So then, when the meat was ready, they feeded me with their hodpot, forcing me to swallow it in a maner. My heart did so faint at this, that in good deede I should have given freely up the ghost to be freed from their clawes, thinking every moment they would end my life. They perceived that my stomach could not beare such victuals. They tooke some of this stinking meate and boyled it in a cleare watter, then mingled a litle Indian meale put to it, which meale before was tossed amongst bourning sand, and then made in powder betwixt two rocks. I, to shew myselfe cheerfull att this, swallowed downe some of this that seemed to me very unsavoury and clammie by reason of the scume that was upon the meat. Having supped, they untyed mee, and made me lye betwixt them, having one end of one side and one of another, and covered me with a red Coverlet, thorough which I might have counted the starrs. I slept a sound sleep, for they awaked me uppon the breaking of the day. I dreamed that night that I was with the Jesuits at Quebuc drinking beere, which gave me hopes to be free sometimes, and also because I heard those people lived among Dutch people in a place called Menada, and fort of Orang, where without doubt I could drinke beere. I, after this, finding meselfe somewhat altered, and my body more like a devil then anything else, after being so smeared and burst with their filthy meate that I could not digest, but must suffer all patiently.

Finally they seemed to me kinder and kinder, giving me of the best bitts where lesse wormes weare. Then they layd [me] to the watter side, where there weare 7 and 30 boats, ffor each of them imbark'd himselfe. They tyed me to the barre in a boat, where they tooke at the same instance the heads [scalps] of those that weare killed the day before, and for to preserve them they cutt off the flesh to the skull and left nothing but skin and haire, putting of it into a litle panne wherein they melt some grease, and gott it dry with hot stones. They spread themselves from off the side of the river a good way, and gathered together againe and made a fearfull noise and shott some gunns off, after which followed a kind of an incondit singing after nots, which was an oudiousom noise. As they weare departing from thence they injoyned silence, and one of the Company, wherein I was, made three shouts, which was answered by the like maner from the whole flocke; which done they tooke their way, singing and leaping, and so past the day in such like. They offered mee meate; but such victuals I reguarded it litle, but could drinke for thirst. My sperit was troubled with infinite deale of thoughts, but all to no purpose for the ease of my sicknesse; sometimes despairing, now againe in some hopes. I allwayes indeavoured to comfort myselfe, though half dead. My resolution was so mastered with feare, that at every stroake of the oares of these inhumans I thought it to be my end.

By sunsett we arrived att the Isles of Richelieu, a place rather for victors then for captives most pleasant. There is to be seen 300 wild Cowes together, a number of Elks and Beavers, an infinit of fowls. There we must make cottages, and for this purpose they imploy all together their wits and art, ffor 15 of these Islands are drowned in Spring, when the floods begin to rise from the melting of the snow, and that by reason of the lowness of the land. Here they found a place fitt enough for 250 men that their army consisted [of]. They landed mee & shewed mee great kindnesse, saying Chagon, which is as much [as] to say, as I understood afterwards, be cheerfull or merry; but for my part I was both deafe and dumb. Their behaviour made me neverthelesse cheerfull, or att least of a smiling countenance, and constraine my aversion and feare to an assurance, which proved not ill to my thinking; ffor the young men tooke delight in combing my head, greasing and powdering out a kinde of redd powder, then tying my haire with a redd string of leather like to a coard, which caused my haire to grow longer in a short time.

The day following they prepared themselves to passe the adjacent places and shoote to gett victualls, where we stayed 3 dayes, making great cheere and fires. I more and more getting familiarity with them, that I had the liberty to goe from cottage, having one or two by mee. They untyed mee, and tooke delight to make me speake words of their language, and weare earnest that I should pronounce as they. They tooke care to give me meate as often as I would; they gave me salt that served me all my voyage. They also tooke the paines to put it up safe for mee, not takeing any of it for themselves. There was nothing else but feasting and singing during our abode. I tooke notice that our men decreased, ffor every night one other boate tooke his way, which persuaded mee that they went to the warrs to gett more booty.

The fourth day, early in the morning, my Brother, viz., he that tooke me, so he called me, embarked me without tying me. He gave me an oare, which I tooke with a good will, and rowed till I sweate againe. They, perceaving, made me give over; not content with that I made a signe of my willingnesse to continue that worke. They consent to my desire, but shewed me how I should row without putting myselfe into a sweat. Our company being considerable hitherto, was now reduced to three score. Mid-day wee came to the River of Richlieu, where we weare not farre gon, but mett a new gang of their people in cottages; they began to hoop and hollow as the first day of my taking. They made me stand upright in the boat, as they themselves, saluting one another with all kindnesse and joy. In this new company there was one that had a minde to doe me mischiefe, but prevented by him that tooke me. I taking notice of the fellow, I shewed him more friendshipe. I gott some meate roasted for him, and throwing a litle salt and flower over it, which he finding very good tast, gave it to the rest as a rarity, nor did afterwards molest mee.

They tooke a fancy to teach mee to sing; and as I had allready a beginning of their hooping, it was an easy thing for me to learne, our Algonquins making the same noise. They tooke an exceeding delight to heare mee. Often have I sunged in French, to which they gave eares with a deepe silence. We passed that day and night following with litle rest by reason of their joy and mirth. They lead a dance, and tyed my comrades both their heads att the end of a stick and hopt it; this done, every one packt and embarked himselfe, some going one way, some another. Being separated, one of the boats that we mett before comes backe againe and approaches the boat wherein I was; I wondered, a woman of the said company taking hould on my haire, signifying great kindnesse. Shee combs my head with her fingers and tyed my wrist with a bracelett, and sunged. My wish was that shee would proceed in our way. After both companys made a shout wee separated. I was sorry for this woman's departure, ffor having shewed me such favour att her first aspect, doubtlesse but shee might, if neede required, saved my life.

Our journey was indifferent good, without any delay, which caused us to arrive in a good and pleasant harbour. It was on the side of the sand where our people had any paine scarce to errect their cottages, being that it was a place they had sejourned [at] before. The place round about [was] full of trees. Heare they kindled a fire and provided what was necessary for their food. In this place they cutt off my hair in the front and upon the crowne of the head, and turning up the locks of the haire they dab'd mee with some thicke grease. So done, they brought me a looking-glasse. I viewing myselfe all in a pickle, smir'd with redde and black, covered with such a cappe, and locks tyed up with a peece of leather and stunked horridly, I could not but fall in love with myselfe, if not that I had better instructions to shun the sin of pride. So after repasting themselves, they made them ready for the journey with takeing repose that night. This was the time I thought to have escaped, ffor in vaine, ffor I being alone feared least I should be apprehended and dealt with more violently. And moreover I was desirous to have seene their country.

Att the sun rising I awaked my brother, telling him by signes it was time to goe. He called the rest, but non would stirre, which made him lye downe againe. I rose and went to the water side, where I walked awhile. If there weare another we might, I dare say, escape out of their sight. Heere I recreated myselfe running a naked swoord into the sand. One of them seeing mee after such an exercise calls mee and shews me his way, which made me more confidence in them. They brought mee a dish full of meate to the water side. I began to eat like a beare.

In the mean time they imbark'd themselves, one of them tooke notice that I had not a knife, brings me his, which I kept the rest of the voyage, without that they had the least feare of me. Being ready to goe, saving my boat that was ammending, which was soone done. The other boats weare not as yett out of sight, and in the way my boat killed a stagg. They made me shoot att it, and not quite dead they runed it thorough with their swoords, and having cutt it in peeces, they devided it, and proceeded on their way. At 3 of the clock in the afternoone we came into a rappid streame, where we weare forced to land and carry our Equipages and boats thorough a dangerous place. Wee had not any encounter that day. Att night where we found cottages ready made, there I cutt wood as the rest with all dilligence. The morning early following we marched without making great noise, or singing as accustomed. Sejourning awhile, we came to a lake 6 leagues wide, about it a very pleasant country imbellished with great forests. That day our wild people killed 2 Bears, one monstrous like for its biggnesse, the other a small one. Wee arrived to a fine sandy bancke, where not long before many Cabbanes weare errected and places made where Prisoners weare tyed.

In this place our wild people sweated after the maner following: first heated stones till they weare redd as fire, then they made a lantherne with small sticks, then stoaring the place with deale trees, saving a place in the middle whereinto they put the stoanes, and covered the place with severall covers, then striped themselves naked, went into it. They made a noise as if the devil weare there; after they being there for an hour they came out of the watter, and then throwing one another into the watter, I thought veryly they weare insensed. It is their usual Custome. Being comed out of this place, they feasted themselves with the two bears, turning the outside of the tripes inward not washed. They gave every one his share; as for my part I found them [neither] good, nor savory to the pallet. In the night they heard some shooting, which made them embark themselves speedily. In the mean while they made me lay downe whilst they rowed very hard. I slept securely till the morning, where I found meselfe in great high rushes. There they stayed without noise.

From thence wee proceeded, though not without some feare of an Algonquin army. We went on for some dayes that lake. Att last they endeavoured to retire to the woods, every one carrying his bundle. After a daye's march we came to a litle river where we lay'd that night. The day following we proceeded on our journey, where we mett 2 men, with whome our wild men seemed to be acquainted by some signes. These 2 men began to speake a longe while. After came a company of women, 20 in number, that brought us dry fish and Indian corne. These women loaded themselves, after that we had eaten, like mules with our baggage. We went through a small wood, the way well beaten, untill the evening we touched a place for fishing, of 15 Cabbans. There they weare well received but myselfe, who was stroaken by a yong man. He, my keeper, made a signe I should to him againe. I tourning to him instantly, he to me, taking hould of my haire, all the wild men came about us, encouraging with their Cryes and hands, which encouraged me most that non helpt him more then mee. Wee clawed one another with hands, tooth, and nailes. My adversary being offended I have gotten the best, he kick't me; but my french shoes that they left mee weare harder then his, which made him [give up] that game againe. He tooke me about the wrest, where he found himselfe downe before he was awarre, houlding him upon the ground till some came and putt us asunder. My company seeing mee free, began to cry out, giving me watter to wash me, and then fresh fish to relish me. They encouraged me so much, the one combing my head, the other greasing my haire. There we stayed 2 dayes, where no body durst trouble me.

In the same Cabban that I was, there has bin a wild man wounded with a small shott. I thought I have seen him the day of my taking, which made me feare least I was the one that wounded him. He knowing it to be so had shewed me as much charity as a Christain might have given. Another of his fellowes (I also wounded) came to me att my first coming there, whom I thought to have come for reveng, contrarywise shewed me a cheerfull countenance; he gave mee a box full of red paintings, calling me his brother. I had not as yett caryed any burden, but meeting with an ould man, gave me a sacke of tobacco of 12 pounds' weight, bearing it uppon my head, as it's their usuall custome. We made severall stayes that day by reason of the severall encounters of their people that came from villages, as warrs others from fishing and shooting. In that journey our company increased, among others a great many Hurrons that had bin lately taken, and who for the most part are as slaves. We lay'd in the wood because they would not goe into their village in the night time.

The next day we marched into a village where as wee came in sight we heard nothing but outcryes, as from one side as from the other, being a quarter of a mile from the village. They satt downe and I in the midle, where I saw women and men and children with staves and in array, which put me in feare, and instantly stripped me naked. My keeper gave me a signe to be gone as fast as I could drive. In the meane while many of the village came about us, among which a good old woman, and a boy with a hatchet in his hand came near mee. The old woman covered me, and the young man tooke me by the hand and lead me out of the company. The old woman made me step aside from those that weare ready to stricke att mee. There I left the 2 heads of my comrades, and that which comforted me that I escaped the blowes. Then they brought me into their Cottage; there the old woman shewed me kindnesse. Shee gave me to eate. The great terror I had a litle before tooke my stomack away from me. I stayed an hower, where a great company of people came to see mee. Heere came a company of old men, having pipes in their mouthes, satt about me.

After smoaking, they lead me into another cabban, where there weare a company all smoaking; they made [me] sitt downe by the fire, which made [me] apprehend they should cast me into the said fire. But it proved otherwise; for the old woman followed mee, speaking aloud, whom they answered with a loud ho, then shee tooke her girdle and about mee shee tyed it, so brought me to her cottage, and made me sitt downe in the same place I was before. Then shee began to dance and sing a while, after [she] brings downe from her box a combe, gives it to a maide that was neare mee, who presently comes to greas and combe my haire, and tooke away the paint that the fellows stuck to my face. Now the old woman getts me some Indian Corne toasted in the fire. I tooke paines to gether it out of the fire; after this shee gave me a blew coverlett, stokins and shoos, and where with to make me drawers. She looked in my cloathes, and if shee found any lice shee would squeeze them betwixt her teeth, as if they had ben substantiall meate. I lay'd with her son, who tooke me from those of my first takers, and gott at last a great acquaintance with many. I did what I could to gett familiarity with them, yeat I suffered no wrong att their hands, taking all freedom, which the old woman inticed me to doe. But still they altered my face where ever I went, and a new dish to satisfy nature.

I tooke all the pleasures imaginable, having a small peece at my command, shooting patriges and squerells, playing most part of the day with my companions. The old woman wished that I would make meselfe more familiar with her 2 daughters, which weare tolerable among such people. They weare accustomed to grease and combe my haire in the morning. I went with them into the wilderness, there they would be gabling which I could not understand.

They wanted no company but I was shure to be of the number. I brought all ways some guifts that I received, which I gave to my pursekeeper and refuge, the good old woman. I lived 5 weeks without thinking from whence I came. I learned more of their maners in 6 weeks then if I had bin in ffrance 6 months. Att the end I was troubled in minde, which made her inquire if I was Anjonack, a Huron word. Att this I made as if I weare subported for speaking in a strang language, which shee liked well, calling me by the name of her son who before was killed, Orinha, which signifies ledd or stone, without difference of the words. So that it was my Lordshippe. Shee inquired [of] mee whether I was Asserony, a french. I answering no, saying I was Panugaga, that is, of their nation, for which shee was pleased.

My father feasted 300 men that day. My sisters made me clean for that purpos, and greased my haire. My mother decked me with a new cover and a redd and blew cappe, with 2 necklace of porcelaine [wampum]. My sisters tyed me with braceletts and garters of the same porcelaine. My brother painted my face, and [put] feathers on my head, and tyed both my locks with porcelaine. My father was liberall to me, giving me a garland instead of my blew cap and a necklace of porcelaine that hung downe to my heels, and a hattchet in my hand. It was hard for me to defend myselfe against any encounter, being so laden with riches. Then my father made a speech shewing many demonstrations of vallor, broak a kettle full of Cagamite [sagamite = porridge] with a hattchett. So they sung, as is their usual coustom. They weare waited on by a sort of yong men, bringing downe dishes of meate of Oriniacke, of Castors [beavers], and of red deer mingled with some flowers. The order of makeing was thus: the corne being dried between 2 stones into powder, being very thick, putt it into a kettle full of watter, then a quantity of Bear's grease. This banquett being over, they cryed to me Shagon, Orimha, that is, be hearty, stone or ledd. Every one withdrew into his quarters, and so did I.

But to the purpose of my history. As I went to the fields once, where I mett with 3 of my acquaintance, who had a designe for to hunt a great way off, they desired me to goe along. I lett them know in Huron language (for that I knew better then that of the Iroquoits) I was content, desiring them to stay till I acquainted my mother. One of them came along with mee, and gott leave for me of my kindred. My mother gott me presently a sack of meale, 3 paire of shoos [moccasins], my gun, and tourned backe where the 2 stayed for us. My 2 sisters accompanied me even out of the wildernesse and carried my bundle, where they tooke leave.

We marched on that day through the woods till we came by a lake where we travelled without any rest. I wished I had stayed att home, for we had sad victu-alls. The next day about noone we came to a River; there we made a skiffe, so litle that we could scarce go into it. I admired their skill in doing of it, ffor in lesse then 2 hours they cutt the tree and pulled up the Rind, of which they made the boat. We embarked ourselves and went to the lower end of the river, which emptied it selfe into a litle lake of about 2 miles in length and a mile in breadth. We passed this lake into another river broader then the other; there we found a fresh track of a stagge, which made us stay heere a while. It was five of the clock att least when 2 of our men made themselves ready to looke after that beast; the other and I stayed behind. Not long after we saw the stagge crosse the river, which foarding brought him to his ending. So done, they went on their cours, and came backe againe att 10 of the clocke with 3 bears, a castor, and the stagge which was slaine att our sight. How did wee rejoice to see that killed which would make the kettle boyle. After we have eaten, wee slept.

The next day we made trappes for to trapp castors, whilst we weare bussie, one about one thing, one about another. As 3 of us retourned homewards to our cottage we heard a wild man singing. He made us looke to our selves least he should prove an ennemy, but as we have seene him, called to him, who came immediately, telling us that he was in pursuite of a Beare since morning, and that he gave him over, having lost his 2 doggs by the same beare. He came with us to our Cottage, where we mett our companion after having killed one beare, 2 staggs, and 2 mountain catts, being 5 in number. Whilst the meat was a boyling that wild man spoake to me the Algonquin language. I wondred to heare this stranger; he tould me that he was taken 2 years agoe; he asked me concerning the 3 rivers and of Quebuck, who wished himselfe there, and I said the same, though I did not intend it. He asked me if I loved the french. I inquired [of] him also if he loved the Algonquins? Mary, quoth he, and so doe I my owne nation. Then replyed he, Brother, cheare up, lett us escape, the 3 rivers are not a farre off. I tould him my 3 comrades would not permitt me, and that they promised my mother to bring me back againe. Then he inquired whether I would live like the Hurrons, who weare in bondage, or have my owne liberty with the ffrench, where there was good bread to be eaten. Feare not, quoth he, shall kill them all 3 this night when they will bee a sleepe, which will be an easy matter with their owne hatchetts.

Att last I consented, considering they weare mortall ennemys to my country, that had cutt the throats of so many of my relations, burned and murdered them. I promised him to succour him in his designe. They not understanding our lan-guage asked the Algonquin what is that that he said, but tould them some other story, nor did they suspect us in the least. Their belly full, their mind without care, wearyed to the utmost of the formost day's journey, fell a sleepe securely, leaning their armes up and downe without the least danger. Then my wild man pushed me, thinking I was a sleepe. He rises and sitts him downe by the fire, behoulding them one after an other, and taking their armes a side, and having the hattchetts in his hand gives me one; to tell the truth I was loathsome to do them mischif that never did me any. Yett for the above said reasons I tooke the hattchet and began the Execution, which was soone done. My fellow comes to him that was nearest to the fire (I dare say he never saw the stroake), and I have done the like to an other, but I hitting him with the edge of the hattchett could not disingage [it] presently, being so deep in his head, rises upon his breast, butt fell back sudainly, making a great noise, which almost waked the third; but my comrade gave him a deadly blow of a hattchet, and presently after I shott him dead.

Then we prepared our selves with all speed, throwing their dead corps, after that the wild man took off their heads, into the watter. We tooke 3 guns, leaving the 4th, their 2 swoords, their hattchetts, their powder and shott, and all their porselaine; we tooke also some meale and meate. I was sorry for to have ben in such an incounter, but too late to repent. Wee tooke our journey that night alongst the river. The break of day we landed on the side of a rock which was smooth. We carryed our boat and equippage into the wood above a hundred paces from the watter side, where we stayed most sadly all that day tormented by the Maringoines; we tourned our boat upside downe, we putt us under if from the raine. The night coming, which was the fitest time to leave that place, we goe without any noise for our safty. Wee travelled 14 nights in that maner in great feare, hearing boats passing by. When we have perceaved any fire, left off rowing, and went by with as litle noise as could [be] possible. Att last with many tournings by lande and by watter, wee came to the lake of St. Peeter's.

We landed about 4 of the clock, leaving our skiff in among rushes farr out of the way from those that passed that way and doe us injury. We retired into the wood, where we made a fire some 200 paces from the river. There we roasted some meat and boyled meale; after, we rested ourselves a while from the many labours of the former night. So, having slept, my companion awaks first, and stirrs me, saying it was high time that we might by day come to our dweling, of which councel I did not approve. [I] tould him the Ennemys commonly weare lurking about the river side, and we should doe very well [to] stay in that place till sunnsett. Then, said he, lett us begon, we [are] passed all feare. Let us shake off the yoake of a company of whelps that killed so many french and black-coats, and so many of my nation. Nay, saith he, Brother, if you come not, I will leave you, and will go through the woods till I shall be over against the french quarters. There I will make a fire for a signe that they may fetch me. I will tell to the Governor that you stayed behind. Take courage, man, says he. With this he tooke his peece and things. Att this I considered how if [I] weare taken att the doore by meere rashnesse; the next, the impossibility I saw to go by myselfe if my comrad would leave me, and perhaps the wind might rise, that I could [only] come to the end of my journey in a long time, and that I should be accounted a coward for not daring to hazard myselfe with him that so much ventured for mee. I resolved to go along through the woods; but the litle constancy that is to be expected in wild men made me feare he should [take] to his heels, which approved his unfortunate advice; ffor he hath lost his life by it, and I in great danger have escaped by the helpe of the Almighty. I consent to goe by watter with him.

In a short time wee came to the lake. The watter very calme and cleare. No liklyhood of any storme. We hazarded to the other side of the lake, thinking ffor more security. After we passed the third part of the lake, I being the foremost, have perceaved as if it weare a black shaddow, which proved a real thing. He at this rises and tells mee that it was a company of buzards, a kinde of geese in that country. We went on, where wee soone perceaved our owne fatall blindnesse, ffor they weare ennemys. We went back againe towards the lande with all speed to escape the evident danger, but it was too late; ffor before we could come to the russhes that weare within halfe a league of the waterside we weare tired. Seeing them approaching nigher and nigher, we threw the 3 heads in the watter. They meet with these 3 heads, which makes them to row harder after us, thinking that we had runn away from their country. We weare so neere the lande that we saw the bottom of the watter, but yett too deepe to step in. When those cruel in-humans came within a musquett shott of us, and fearing least the booty should gett a way from them, shott severall times att us, and deadly wounding my comrade, [who] fell dead. I expected such another shott. The litle skiff was pierced in severall places with their shooting, [so] that watter ran in a pace. I defended me selfe with the 2 arms. Att last they environed me with their boats, that tooke me just as I was a sinking. They held up the wild man and threw him into one of their boats and me they brought with all diligence to land. I thought to die with-out mercy.

They made a great fire and tooke my comrade's heart out, and choped off his head, which they put on an end of a stick and carryed it to one of their boats. They cutt off some of the flesh of that miserable, broyled it and eat it. If he had not ben so desperately wounded they had don their best to keepe him alive to make him suffer the more by bourning him with small fires; but being wounded in the chin, and [a] bullet gon through the troat, and another in the shoulder that broake his arme, making him incurable, they burned some parte of his body, and the rest they left there. That was the miserable end of that wretch.

Lett us come now to the beginning of my miseries and calamities that I was to undergo. Whilst they weare bussie about my companion's head, the others tyed me safe and fast in a strang maner; having striped me naked, they tyed me above the elbows behind my back, and then they putt a collar about me, not of porce-laine as before, but a rope wrought about my midle. So [they] brought me in that pickle to the boat. As I was imbarqued they asked mee severall questions. I being not able to answer, gave me great blowes with their fists. [They] then pulled out one of my nailes, and partly untied me.

What displeasure had I, to have seen meselfe taken againe, being almost come to my journey's end, that I must now goe back againe to suffer such torments, as death was to be expected. Having lost all hopes, I resolved alltogether to die, being a folly to think otherwise. I was not the [only] one in the clawes of those wolves. Their company was composed of 150 men. These tooke about Quebucq and other places 2 frenchmen, one french woman, 17 Hurrons, men as [well as]

women. They had Eleven heads [scalps] which they sayd weare of the Algonquins, and I was the 33rd victime with those cruels.

The wild men that weare Prisners sang their fatal song, which was a mornfull
song or noise. The 12 coulours (which weare heads) stood out for a shew. We
prisoners weare separated, one in one boat, one in an other. As for me, I was put
into a boat with a Huron whose fingers weare cutt and bourned, and very [few]
amongst them but had the markes of those inhuman devils. They did not premitt
me to tarry long with my fellow prisoner, least I should tell him any news, as I
imagine, but sent me to another boat, where I remained the rest of the voyage by
watter, which proved somewhat to my disadvantage.

In this boat there was an old man, who having examined me, I answered him
as I could best; tould him how I was adopted by such an one by name, and as I
was a hunting with my companions that wildman that was killed came to us, and
after he had eaten went his way. In the evening [he] came back againe and found
us all a sleepe, tooke a hattchett and killed my 3 companions, and awaked me,
and so embarked me and brought me to this place. That old man believed me in
some measure, which I perceived in him by his kindnesse towards me. But he
was not able to protect me from those that [had] a will to doe me mischief. Many
slandred me, but I tooke no notice.

Some 4 leagues thence they erected cottages by a small river, very difficult to
gett to it, for that there is litle watter on a great sand [bank] a league wide. To
this very houre I tooke notice how they tyed their captives, though att my owne
cost. They planted severall poastes of the bignesse of an arme, then layd us of a
length, tyed us to the said poasts far a sunder from one another. Then tyed our
knees, our wrists, and elbows, and our hairs directly upon the crowne of our
heads, and then cutt 4 barrs of the bignesse of a legge & used thus. They tooke 2
for the necke, puting one of each side, tying the 2 ends together, so that our
heads weare fast in a hole like a trappe; likewayes they did to our leggs. And
what tormented us most was the Maringoines and great flyes being in abundance;
did all night but puff and blow, that by that means we saved our faces from the
sting of those ugly creatures; having no use of our hands, we are cruelly tormented. Our voyage was laborious and most miserable, suffering every night the
like misery.

When we came neere our dwellings we mett severall gangs of men to our
greatest disadvantage, ffor we weare forced to sing, and those that came to see us
gave porcelaine to those that most did us injury. One cutt of a finger, and another
pluck'd out a naile, and putt the end of our fingers into their bourning pipes, &
burned severall parts in our bodyes. Some tooke our fingers and of a stick made
a thing like a fork, with which [they] gave several blowes on the back of the
hands, which caused our hands to swell, and became att last insensible as dead.
Having souffred all these crueltyes, which weare nothing to that they make usually souffer their Prisoners, we arrived att last to the place of execution, which is
att the coming in to their village, which wheere not [long] before I escaped very
neere to be soundly beaten with staves and fists. Now I must think to be no lesse

traited by reason of the murder of the 3 men, but the feare of death takes away the feare of blowes.

Nineteen of us prisoners weare brought thither, and 2 left behind with the heads. In this place we had 8 coulours. Who would not shake att the sight of so many men, women, and children armed with all sorte of Instruments: staves, hand Irons, heelskins wherein they putt halfe a score [of] bullets? Others had brands, rods of thorne, and all suchlike that the Crueltie could invent to putt their Prisoners to greater torments. Heere, no help, no remedy. We must passe this dangerous passage in our extremity without helpe. He that is the fearfullest, or that is observed to stay the last, getts nothing by it butt more blowes, and putt him to more paine. For the meanest sort of people commonly is more cruell to the fearfullest then to the others that they see more fearfull, being att last to suffer chearfuly and with constancy.

They begun to cry to both sides, we marching one after another, environed with a number of people from all parts to be witnesse to that hidious sight, which seriously may be called the Image of hell in this world. The men sing their fatall song, the women make horrible cryes, the victores cryes of joy, and their wives make acclamations of mirth. In a word, all prepare for the ruine of these poore victimes who are so tyed, having nothing saving only our leggs free, for to advance by litle and litle according [to] the will of him that leades; ffor as he held us by a long rope, he stayed us to his will, & often he makes us falle, for to shew them cruelty, abusing you so for to give them pleasure and to you more torment.

As our band was great, there was a greater crew of people to see the prisoners, and the report of my taking being now made, and of the death of the 3 men, which afflicted the most part of that nation, great many of which came through a designe of revenge and to molest me more then any other. But it was alltogether otherwise, for among the tumult I perceaved my father & mother with their 2 daughters. The mother pushes in among the Crew directly to mee, and when shee was neere enough, shee clutches hould of my haire as one desperat, calling me often by my name; drawing me out of my ranck, shee putts me into the hands of her husband, who then bid me have courage, conducting me an other way home to his Cabban, when he made me sitt downe. [He] said to me: You senselesse, thou was my son, and thou rendered thyselfe enemy, and thou rendered thyself enemy, thou lovest not thy mother, nor thy father that gave thee thy life, and thou notwithstanding will kill me. Bee merry; Conharrassan, give him to eate. That was the name of one of the sisters. My heart shook with trembling and feare, which tooke away my stomack. Neverthelesse to signifie a bould countenance, knowing well a bould generous minde is allwayes accounted among all sort of nations, especially among wariors, as that nation is very presumptious and haughty. Because of their magnanimity and victories opposing themselves into all dangers and incounters what ever, running over the whole land for to make themselves appeere slaining and killing all they meete in exercising their cruelties, or else shewing mercy to whom they please to give liberty. God gave mee the grace to forgett nothing of my duty, as I tould my father the successe of my voyage in the best tearme I could, and how all things passed, mixturing a litle of their languag with that of the Hurrons, which I learned more fluently then theirs, being longer and more frequently with the Hurrons.

Every one attentively gave ears to me, hoping by this means to save my life. Uppon this heere comes a great number of armed men, enters the Cabban, where finding mee yett tyed with my cords, sitting by my parents, made their addresses to my father, and spak to him very loud. After a while my father made me rise and delivers me into their hands. My mother seeing this, cryes and laments with both my sisters, and I believing in a terrible motion to goe directly on to the place of execution. I must march, I must yeeld wheere force is predominant att the publique place.

I was conducted where I found a good company of those miserable wretches, alltogether beaten with blowes, covered with blood, and bourned. One miserable frenchman, yett breathing, having now ben consumed with blowes of sticks, past so through the hands of this inraged crew, and seeing he could [bear] no more, cutt off his head and threw it into the fire. This was the end of this Execrable wofull body of this miserable.

They made me goe up the scaffold where weare 5 men, 3 women, and 2 children captives, and I made the Eleventh. There weare severall scaffolds nigh one an other, where weare these wretches, who with dolefull singings replenished the heavens with their Cryes. For I can say that an houre before the weather approved very faire, and in an instant the weather changed and rayned Extremely. The most part retired for to avoid this hayle, and now we must expect the full rigour of the weather by the retiration of those persidious [persons], except one part of the Band of hell who stayed about us for to learn the trade of barbary; ffor those litle devils seeing themselves all alone, continued [a] thousand inventions of wickednesse. This is nothing strang, seeing that they are brought up, and suck the crueltie from their mother's brest.

I prolong a litle from my purpose of my adventure for to say the torments that I have seen souffred att Coutu, after that they have passed the sallett, att their entering in to the village, and the rencounters that they meet ordinarily in the wayes, as above said. They tie the prisoners to a poast by their hands, their backs tourned towards the hangman, who hath a bourning fire of dry wood and rind of trees, which doth not quench easily. They putt into this fire hattchets, swords, and such like instruments of Iron. They take these and quench them on human flesh. They pluck out their nailes for the most part in this sort. They putt a redd coale of fire uppon it, and when it is swolen bite it out with their teeth. After they stop the blood with a brand which by litle and litle drawes the veines the one after another from off the fingers, and when they draw all as much as they can, they cutt it with peeces of redd hott Iron; they squeeze the fingers between 2 stones, and so draw the marrow out of the boanes, and when the flesh is all taken away, they putt it in a dishfull of bourning sand. After they tye your wrist with a corde, putting two for this effect, one drawing him one way, another of another way. If the sinews be not cutt with a stick, putting it through & tourning it, they make them come as fast as they can, and cutt them in the same way as the others. Some others cutt peeces of flesh from all parts of the body & broyle them, gett you to eat it, thrusting them into your mouth, puting into it a stick of fire. They breake your teeth with a stoane or clubbs, and use the handle of a kettle, and upon this do hang 5 or 6 hattchetts, red hott, which they hang about their neck and roast your leggs with brands of fire, and thrusting into it some sticks pointed, wherein they put ledd melted and gunnepowder, and then give it fire like unto artificiall fire, and make the patient gather it by the stumps of his remaining fingers. If he cannot sing they make him quack like a henne.

I saw two men tyed to a rope, one att each end, and hang them so all night, throwing red coales att them, or bourning sand, and in such like bourne their feet, leggs, thighs, and breech. The litle ones doe exercise themselves about such cruelties; they deck the bodyes all over with hard straw, putting in the end of this straw, thornes, so leaves them; now & then gives them a litle rest, and sometimes gives them fresh watter and make them repose on fresh leaves. They also give them to eat of the best they have that they come to themselves againe, to give them more torments. Then when they see that the patient can no more take up his haire, they cover his head with a platter made of rind full of bourning sand, and often getts the platter a fire. In the next place they cloath you with a suit made of rind of a tree, and this they make bourne out on your body. They cutt off your stones and the women play with them as with balles. When they see the miserable die, they open him and pluck out his heart; they drink some of his blood, and wash the children's heads with the rest to make them valient. If you have indured all the above said torments patiently and without moanes, and have defied death in singing, then they thrust burning blades all along your boanes, and so ending the tragedie cutt off the head and putt it on the end of a stick and draw his body in quarters which they hawle about their village. Lastly [they] throw him into the watter or leave [him] in the fields to be eaten by the Crowes or doggs.

Now lett me come to our miserable poore captives that stayed all along [through] the raine upon the scaffold to the mercy of 2 or 300 rogues that shott us with litle arrowes, and so drew out our beards and the haire from those that had any. The showre of rayne being over, all come together againe, and having kindled fires began to burne some of those poore wretches. That day they plucked 4 nailes out of my fingers, and made me sing, though I had no mind att that time. I became speechlesse oftentimes; then they gave me watter wherin they boyled a certain herbe that the gunsmiths use to pollish their armes. That liquour brought me to my speech againe. The night being come they made me come downe all naked as I was, & brought to a strang Cottage. I wished heartily it had ben that of my parents. Being come, they tyed me to a poast, where I stayed a full houre without the least molestation.

A woman came there with her boy, inticed him to cutt off one of my fingers with a flint stoan. The boy was not 4 yeares old. This [boy] takes my finger and begins to worke, but in vaine, because he had not the strength to breake my fingers. So my poore finger escaped, having no other hurt don to it but the flesh cutt round about it. His mother made him suck the very blood that runn from my finger. I had no other torment all that day. Att night I could not sleepe for because of the great paine. I did eat a litle, and drunk much watter by reason of a feaver I caught by the cruel torment I suffred.

The next morning I was brought back againe to the scaffold, where there were company enough. They made me sing a new, but my mother came there and made [me] hould my peace, bidding me be cheerfull and that I should not die. Shee brought mee some meate. Her coming comforted me much, but that did not last long; ffor heare comes severall old people, one of which being on the scaffold, satt him downe by me, houlding in his mouth a pewter pipe burning, tooke my thumb and putt it on the burning tobacco, and so smoaked 3 pipes one after another, which made my thumb swell, and the nayle and flesh became as coales. My mother was allwayes by me to comfort me, but said not what I thought. That man having finished his hard worke, but I am sure I felt it harder to suffer it. He trembled, whether for feare or for so much action I cannot tell. My mother tyed my fingers with cloath, and when he was gon shee greased my haire and combed my haire with a wooden comb, fitter to combe a horse's tayle then anything else. Shee goes back againe.

That day they ended many of those poore wretches, flinging some all alive into the midle of a great fire. They burned a frenchwoman; they pulled out her breasts and tooke a child out of her belly, which they broyled and made the mother eat of it; so, in short, [she] died. I was not abused all that day till the night. They bourned the soales of my feet and leggs. A souldier run through my foot a swoord red out of the fire, and plucked severall of my nailes. I stayed in that maner all night. I neither wanted in the meane while meate nor drinke. I was supplied by my mother and sisters. My father alsoe came to see me & tould me I should have courage. That very time there came a litle boy to gnaw with his teeth the end of my fingers. There appears a man to cutt off my thumb, and being about it leaves me instantly & did no harme, for which I was glad. I believe that my father dissuaded him from it.

A while after my father was gon 3 came to the scaffold who swore they would me a mischiefe, as I thinke, for that he tied his leggs to mine, called for a brand of fire, and layd it between his leggs and mine, and sings: but by good lucke it was out on my side, and did no other effect then bourne my skin, but bourned him to some purpos. In this posture I was to follow him, & being not able to hould mee, draweth mee downe. One of the Company Cutt the rope that held us with his knife, and makes mee goe up againe the scaffold and then went their way.

There I stayed till midday alone. There comes a multitude of people who make me come downe and led mee into a cottage where there weare a number of sixty old men smoking tobacco. Here they make mee sitt downe among them and stayed about halfe an houre without that they asked who and why I was brought thither, nor did I much care. For the great torments that I souffred, I knew not whether I was dead or alive. And albeit I was in a hott feavor & great pain, I rejoyced att the sight of my brother, that I have not seene since my arrivement. He comes in very sumptuously covered with severall necklaces of porcelaine, & a hattchett in his hand, satt downe by the company and cast an eye on me now and then. Presently and comes in my father with a new and long cover, and a new porcelaine about him, with a hatchett in his hands, likewise satt downe with the company. He had a calumet of red stoane in his hands, a cake uppon his shoulders, that hanged downe his back, and so had the rest of the old men. In that same cake are incloased all the things in the world, as they tould me often, advertising mee that I should [not] disoblige them in the least nor make them angry, by reason they had in their power the sun, and moone, and the heavans, and consequently all the earth. You must know in this cake there is nothing but tobacco and roots to heale some wounds or sores; some others keepe in it the bones of their deceased friends; most of them wolves' heads, squirrels', or any other beast's head. When there they have any debatement among them they sacrifice to this tobacco, that they throw into the fire, and make smoake, of that they puff out of their pipes; whether for peace or adversity or prosperity or warre, such ceremonies they make very often.

My father, taking his place, lights his pipe & smoaks as the rest. They held great silence. During this they bring 7 prisoners; to wit, 7 women and 2 men, more [then] 10 children from the age of 3 to 12 years, having placed them all by mee, who as yett had my armes tyed. The others all att liberty, being not tyed, which putt me into some despaire least I should pay for all. Awhile after one of the company rises and makes a long speech, now shewing the heavens with his hands, and then the earth, and fire. This good man putt himselfe into a sweate through the earnest discours. Having finished his panigerique, another begins, and also many, one after another.

They gave then liberty to some, butt killed 2 children with hattchetts, and a woman of 50 years old, and threw them out of the cottage (saving onely myselfe) att full liberty. I was left alone for a stake, they contested together [upon] which my father rose and made a speech which lasted above an houre, being naked, having nothing on but his drawers and the cover of his head, and putt himselfe all in a heate. His eyes weare hollow in his head; he appeared to me like [as if] mad, and naming often the Algonquins in their language [that is, Eruata], which made me believe he spoake in my behalfe. In that very time comes my mother, with two necklaces of porcelaine, one in her armes, and another about her like a belt. As soone as shee came in shee began to sing and dance, and flings off one of her necklaces in the midle of the place, having made many tourns from one end to the other. Shee takes the other necklace and gives it mee, then goes her way. Then my brother rises and holding his hattchett in his hand sings a military song. Having finished [he] departs. I feared much that he was first to knock me in the head; and happy are those that can escape so well, rather then be bourned. My father rises for a second time and sings; so done, retired himselfe. I thought all their guists, songs, and speeches should prevaile nothing with mee.

Those that stayed held a councell and spoake one to an other very long, throwing tobacco into the fire, making exclamations. Then the Cottage was open of all sides by those that came to view, some of the company retires, and place was made for them as if they weare Kings. Forty staye about me, and nigh 2000 about my cottage, of men, women, and children. Those that went their way retourned presently. Being sett downe, smoaked againe whilest my father, mother, brother, and sisters weare present. My father sings a while; so done, makes a speech, and taking the porcelaine necklace from off me throws it att the feet of an old man, and cutts the cord that held me, then makes me rise. The joy that I receaved att that time was incomparable, for suddenly all my paines and griefs ceased, not feeling the least paine. He bids me be merry, makes me sing, to which I consented with all my heart. Whilst I did sing they hooped and hollowed on all sids. The old man bid me "ever be cheerfull, my son!" Having don, my mother, sisters, and the rest of their friends [sung] and danced.

Then my father takes me by the arme and leads me to his cabban. As we went along nothing was heard but hooping and hollowing on all parts, biding me to take great courage. My mother was not long after me, with the rest of her friends. Now I see myselfe free from death. Their care att this was to give me meate. I have not eaten a bitt all that day, and for the great joy I had conceaved, caused me to have a good stomach, so that I did eat lustily. Then my mother begins to cure my sores and wounds. Then begins my paines to [break out] a new; ffor shee cleans my wounds and scrapes them with a knife, and often thrusts a stick in them, and then takes watter in her mouth, and spouts it to make them cleane. The meanwhile my father goes to seeke rootes, and my sister chaws them, and my mother applyes them to my sores as a plaster. The next day the swelling was gone, but worse then before; but in lesse then a fortnight my sores weare healed, saving my feete, that kept [me] more then a whole month in my Cabban. During this time my nailes grewed a pace. I remained onely lame of my midle finger, that they have squeezed between two stoanes. Every one was kind to mee as beforesaid, and [I] wanted no company to be merry with.

I should [be] kept too long to tell you the particulars that befell me during my winter. I was beloved of my Parents as before. My exercise was allwayes a hunting without that any gave me the least injury. My mother kept me most brave, and my sisters tooke great care of mee. Every moneth I had a white shirt, which my father sent for from the Flemeings [Dutch], who weare not a farr off our village. I could never gett leave to goe along with my brother, who went there very often. Finally, seeing myselfe in the former condition as before, I constituted as long as my father and fortune would permitt mee to live there. Dayly there weare military feasts for the South nations, and others for the Algonquins and for the French. The exclamations, hoopings and cryes, songs and dances, signifies nothing but the murdering and killing, and the intended victory that they will have the next yeare, which is in the beginning of Spring. In those feasts my father heaves up his hattchett against the Algonquins. For this effect [he] makes great preparations for his next incamping. Every night [he] never failes to instruct and encourage the young age to take armes and to reveng the death of so many of their ennemy that lived among the french nation. The desire that I had to make me beloved, for the assurance of my life made me resolve to offer myselfe for to serve, and to take party with them. But I feared much least he should mistrust me touching his advis to my resolution. Nevertheiesse I finding him once of a good humour and on the point of honnour encourages his son to break the kettle and take the hattchett and to be gon to the forraigne nations, and that was of courage and of great renowne to see the father of one parte and the son of another part, & that he should not mispraise if he should seperat from him, but that it was the quickest way to make the world tremble, & by that means have liberty everywhere by vanquishing the mortall enemy of his nation; uppon this I venture to aske him what I was. [He] presently answers that I was a Iroquoite as himselfe. Lett me revenge, said I, my kindred. I love my brother. Lett me die with him. I would die with you, but you will not because you goe against the ffrench. Lett me a gaine goe with my brother, the prisoners & the heads that I shall bring, to the joy of my mother and sisters, will make me undertake att my retourne to take up the hattchett against those of Quebecq, of the 3 rivers, and Monteroyall [Montreal] in declaring them my name, and that it's I that kills them, and by that you shall know I am your son, worthy to beare that title that you gave me when you adopted me. He sett [up] a great crye, saying, have great courage, son Oninga, thy brother died in the warrs not in the Cabban; he was of a courage not of a woman. I goe to aveng his death. If I die, aveng you mine. That one word was my leave, which made me hope that one day I might escape, having soe great an opportunity; or att least I should have the happinesse to see their country, which I heard so much recommended by the Iroquoites, who brought wondrous stories and the facilitie of killing so many men.

Thus the winter was past in thoughts and preparing for to depart before the melting of the snow, which is very soone in that Country. I began to sett my witts together how I should resolve this my voyage; for my mother opposed against it mightily, saying I should bee lost in the woods, and that I should gett it [put] off till the next yeare. But at last I flattered with her and dissembled; besides, my father had the power in his hands. Shee daring not to deny him any thing because shee was not borne in my father's country, but was taken [when] little in the Huronit's Country. Notwithstanding [she was] well beloved of her husband, having lived together more then fourty years, and in that space brought him 9 children, 4 males and 5 females. Two girls died after a while, and 3 sons killed in the warrs, and one that went 3 years before with a band of 13 men to warre against a fiery nation which is farre beyonde the great lake. The 5th had allready performed 2 voyages with a greate deale of successe. My father was a great Captayne in warrs, having ben Commander in all his times, and distructed many villages of their Ennemy, having killed 19 men with his owne hands, whereof he was marked [on] his right thigh for as many [as] he killed. He should have as many more, but that you must know that the Commander has not amused himselfe to kille, but in the front of his army to encourage his men. If by chance he tooke any prisoners, he calles one of his men and gives him the captives, saying that it's honour enough to command the conquerors, and by his example shews to the yong men that he has the power as much as the honour. He receaved 2 gunn shots and 7 arrows shotts, and was runne through the shoulders with a lance. He was aged 3 score years old, he was talle, and of an excellent witt for a wild man.

When our baggage was ready, my father makes a feast to which he invites a number of people, & declares that he was sorry he had resolved to go to warre against an Ennemy which was in a cold country, which hindred him to march sooner then he would, but willing to see his sonnes before him, and that this banquett was made for his 2 sons' farewell. Then he tould that his adopted son was ready to go with his owne son to be revenged of the death of their brothers, and desired the Commander to have a care of us both. This Commander loved us both, said that the one which [was] meselfe should be with him to the end. If anything should oppose he would make me fight him. I was not att home when he spoke those words, but my mother toald me it att my retourne. I was a fishing by with my sisters & brother. When wee came back wee found all ready, butt with a heart broken that our mother and sisters lett us goe. Few days after I was invited to a military banquett where was the Captayne, a yong gallant of 20 years old, with a company of 8, and I made the 10th. We all did sing and made good cheare of a fatt beare. We gave our things to slaves, we carried only our musquetts. Our kindred brought us a great way. My sister could not forbeare crying, yett tould me to be of a stout heart. We tooke att last [leave and] bid them adieu. We tooke on our journey over great snowes for to come to the great Lake before the Spring. We travelled 7 days through woods and indifferent country, easie in some places and others difficult. The Rivers weare frozen, which made us crosse with a great deale of ease.

Wee arrived the 7th day in a village called Nojottga, where we stayed 2 days. From thence came a young man with us. We arrived into another village, Nontageya, where we stayed foure days. Wee had allways great preparations, and weare invited 9 or tenne times a day. Our bellyes had not tyme to emptie themselves, because we feeded so much, and that what was prepared for us weare severall sortes, Stagg, Indian corne, thick flower, bears, and especially eels. We have not yett searched our baggs wheare our provision was. In this place wee mended them. For my part I found in myne 6 pounds of powder and more then 15 pounds of shott, 2 shirts, a capp, 8 pairs of shoes, and wherewith to make a paire of breeches, and about 1000 graines of black and white porcelaine, and my brother as many. Wee had new covers, one to our body, another hung downe from our shoulders like a mantle. Every one [had] a small necklace of porcelaine and a collar made with a thread of nettles to tye the Prisoners. I had a gunne, a hattchett, and a dagger. That was all we had. Our slaves brought the packs after us.

After we marched 3 dayes, we came to a village, Sononteeonon, there we layd a night. The next day, after a small journey, we came to the last village of their confederates. Heere they doe differ in their speech though of [our] nation. It's called Oiongoiconon. Here we stay 2 dayes, and sent away our slaves and carryed our bundles ourselves, going allwayes through the woods. We found great plaines of 2 leagues and a halfe journey without a tree. We saw there stagges, but would not goe out of our way to kill them. We went through 3 villages of this nation neare one another. They admired to see a frenchman accompanying wild men, which I understood by their exclamations. I thought I grewed leane to take litle voyage, but the way seemed tedious to all. The raquett [snowshoes] allwayes with the feet and sometimes with the hands, which seemed to me hard to indure, yett have I not complained. Att the parting of the slaves, I made my bundle light as the rest. We found snowes in few places, saving where the trees made a shaddow, which hindred the snow to thaw, which made us carry the raquetts with our feete, and sometimes with the hands.

After 10 days' march [we completed our journey] through a country covered with water, and where also are mountaines and great plaines. In those plaines wee killed stagges, and a great many Tourquies [turkeys]. Thence we came to a great river of a mile wide which was not frozen, which made us stay there 10 or 12 dayes making skiffs of the rind of walnut trees. We made good cheere and wished to stay there longer. We made 3 skiffs to hould 3 men, and one to hould two. We imbarked though there weare ice in many places, and yett no hinderance to us going small journeys, fearing least what should befall us. In 4 dayes we came to a lake much frozen; covered in some places with ice by reason of the tossing of the wind, and the ground all covered with snow. Heere we did our best to save us from the rigour of the aire, and must stay 15 dayes. The wild men admired that the season of the yeare was so backward. Att the end the wind changes southerly, which made the lake free from Ice and cleare over all the skirts of it, without either snow or ice. There was such a thawing that made the litle brookes flow like rivers, which made us imbarque to wander [over] that sweet sea. The weather lovely, the wind fayre, and nature satisfied. Tending forwards, singing and playing, not considering the contrary weather past, continued so 6 days upon the lake and rested the nights ashore.

The more we proceeded in our journey, the more the pleasant country and warmer. Ending the lake, we entered into a beautifull sweet river, a stoan-cast wide. After halfe a day we rid on it, weare forced to bring both barks and equipage uppon our backs to the next streame of that river. This done about 20 times, hawling our boats after us all laden. We went up that river att least 30 or 40 leagues. Att last [it] brought us to a lake of some 9 miles in length. Being comed to the highest place of the lake, we landed and hid our boats farr enough in the woods, [and] tooke our bundles. We weare 3 dayes going through a great wildernesse where was no wood, not so much as could make us fire. Then the thickned flower did serve us instead of meate, mingling it with watter. We foorded many litle rivers, in swiming & sayling. Our armes, which we putt uppon some sticks tyed together of such wood as that desolat place could afford, to keepe them from the weatt. The evening we came on the side of a violent river, uppon which we made bridges of trees that we [made] to meet, to go over.

We left this place after being there 3 dayes. We went up that river in 2 dayes; there we killed stagges. After we came to a mouth of another river. We made a litle fort, where it was commanded by our captayne to make no noise. They desired me to be very quiet, which I observed strictly. After refreshment we imbarked, though unseasonably, in the night, for to make som discovery. Some went one way, some another. We went a great way, but not farr off our fort. The next day we meet altogether & made Some Councell, where it was decreed that 2 should go to the furthermost part of a small river in a boat, to make a discovery, and see if there weare tracks of people there, whilst the other 9 should take no-

tice of a villag, that they knew'd to be nigh, and because it was lesse danger to
make there a discovery. The youngest of the company and me are pitched [upon]
to goe into the river. We tooke the lightest boat. It was well, [for] that in some
places of the river there was not watter enough to carry us. We weare fained to
draw the boat after us. I believe not that ever a wild man went that way because
of the great number of trees that stops the passage of the river.

After we have gon the best part of the day, we found ourselves att the end of a
small lake some 4 mile in length, and seeing the woods weare not so thick there
as wheare wee passed, we hid our boat in some bushes, taking onely our armes
along, intending on still to pretend some discovery. We scarce weare in the
midle of the lake when we perceave 2 persons goeing on the watter side, att the
other side of the lake; so my comrade getts him up a tree to discerne better if
there weare any more. After he stayed there a while [he] comes [down] & tells
me that he thought they weare 2 women, and that we might goe kill them.
Doubtlesse, said I, if they are women the men are not afarre from them, and we
shall be forced to shoote. Wee are alone, and should runne the hazzard of 2
women for to be discovered. Our breethren also would be in danger that knowes
nothing. Moreover it's night; what dost thou intend to doe? You say well, replyes
he; lett us hide ourselves in the wood, for we cannot goe downe in the river in
the night time. Att breake of day we will [go] back to our companions where we
will finde them in the fort.

Here we came without any provisions, where we must lie under a rotten tree.
That night it rayned sadly. We weare wett; but a naturall Exercise is good fire.
We weare in our boat early in the morning, and with great diligence we came
back better then we went up, for the river grewed mighty high by reason of so
much that fell of raine. I will not omitt a strange accident that befell us as we
came. You must know that as we past under the trees, as before mentioned, there
layd on one of the trees a snake with foure feete, her head very bigg, like a Turtle, the nose very small att the end, the necke of 5 thumbs wide, the body about 2
feet, and the tayle of a foot & a halfe, of a blackish collour, onto a shell small
and round, with great eyes, her teeth very white but not long. That beast was a
sleepe upon one of the trees under which wee weare to goe; neither of us ever
seeing such a creature weare astonished. We could not tell what to doe. It was
impossible to carry our boat, for the thicknesse of the wood; to shoot att her wee
would att least be discovered, besides it would trouble our Company. Att last we
weare resolved to goe through att what cost soever, and as we weare under that
hellish beast, shee started as shee awaked, and with that felled downe into our
boat, there weare herbes that served [to secure] us from that dreadfull animal.
We durst not ventur to kill her, for feare of breaking of our boat. There is the
question who was most fearfull? As for me, I quaked. Now seeing shee went not
about to doe us hurt, and that shee was fearfull, we lett her [be] quiet, hoping
shortly to land and to tourne upsid downe of our boat to be rid of such a devill.
Then my comrad began to call it, and before we weare out of the litle river our
feare was over; so we resolved to bring her to the fort, and when once arrived att
the great river, nothing but crosse over it to be neare our fort. But in the mean

while a squirrell made us good spoart for a quarter of an houre. The squirrell would not leap into the water; did but runne, being afraid of us, from one end of the boat to the other; every time he came nearer, the snake opened her wide mouth & made a kind of a noise, & rose up, having her 2 fore feet uppon the side of the boat, which persuaded us that shee would leave us. We leaned on that side of the boat, so with our owers thrusted her out; we seeing her swime so well, hasted to kill her with our owers, which shee had for her paines. The squirrell tooke the flight, soe we went, longing to be with our comrades to tell them of what we have seene. We found one of our company watching for us att the side of a woode, for they weare in feare least wee should be taken, & expected us all night long. As for their part they neither have seen nor heard anything. Wherefore resolved to goe further, but the news we brought them made them alter their resolution. Wee layd all night in our fort, where we made good cheare and great fires, fearing nothing, being farr enough in the wood.

The next day before the breaking of the day we foorded the river, & leaving our 3 boats in the wood, went a foot straight towards the place where we have seene the 2 persons; & before we came to the lake we tooke notice of some fresh trakes which made us look to ourselves, and followed the trakes, which brought us to a small river, where no sooner came but we saw a woman loaden with wood, which made us believ that some cottage or village was not afar off. The Captaine alone takes notice of the place where abouts the discovery was, who soone brought us [to see] that there weare 5 men & 4 women a fishing. We wagged [sic] att this the saffest [way] to come unawarre uppon them, and like starved doggs or wolves devoured those poore creatures who in a moment weare massacred. What we gott by this was not much, onely stagges' skins with some guirdles made of goate's hair, of their owne making. These weare in great estime among our wild men. Two of ours goes to the cabban which was made of rushes, where they founde an old woman. They thought it charity to send her into the other world, with two small children whome also they killed; so we left that place, giving them to the fishes their bodyes. Every one of us had his head, and my brother two; our share being considerable [we] went on along the river till we came to a small lake. Not desiring to be discovered, we found a faire road close by a wood, withtooke ourselves out of it with all haste, and went towards a village. There we came by night, where we visited the wildernesse to find out a secure place for security to hide ourselves; but [finding] no conveniencies we [went] into the wood in a very cleare place. Heere we layd downe uppon our bellies. We did eat, among other things, the fish we gott in the cabban of the fishermen. After dispatching one of the Company bouldly into the village, being thirsty after eating, for heere we had no water, [which] brings us [so] that we are all very quiett. The great desire we had to catch and take made us to controule the Buissinesse.

Early in the morning we came to the side of the wildernesse, where we layd in an ambush, but could see nobody that morning. Att two of the clock in the after non we see 20, as well men as women, a great way from us. We went to the wood, whence we perceived many att worke in the fields. Att evening [they] passed by very nigh us, but they neither see nor perceived us. They went to cutt wood; whilst they weare att worke there comes foure men and three women, that tooke notice of our ambush. This we could not avoid, so weare forced to appeare to their ruine. We tooke the 3 women and killed 2 men. The other 2 thought to escape, but weare stayed with our peeces; the other 2 that weare aworking would runne away, but one was taken, the other escaped. The news was brought over all those parts. Thence we runne away with our 4 prisoners and the 4 new heads with all speed. The women could not goe fast enough, and therefore killed them after they went a whole night; their corps we threwed into the river; heere we found a boat which served us to goe over. We marched all that day without any delay; being come to an open field we hid ourselves in bushes till the next day. We examined our Prisoners, who tould us no news; non could understand them, although many Huron words weare in their language. In this place we perceived 2 men a hunting afarre off; we thought [it] not convenient to discover ourselves, least we should be discovered and passe our aime. We tooke another day, 2 before and the rest after, the prisoners in the midle. We speedily went the rest of the day through a burned country, and the trees blowne downe with some great windes. The fire over came all, over 15 leagues in length and 10 in breadth. We layd in the very midle of that country upon a faire sandy place where we could see 3 or 4 leagues off round about us, and being secure we made the prisoners sing which is their Acconroga before death. There we made a litle fire to make our Kettle boyle a tourkey, with some meale that was left. Seeing no body persued, we resolved to goe thence before daylight to seeke for more booty. We stayed 14 nights before we turned back to the village, during which time we mett with nothing, and having gon on all sides with great paines without victualls. Att last we came to kill 2 Stagges, but did not suffice 12 of us. We weare forced to gather the dung of the stagges to boyle it with the meat, which made all very bitter. But good stomachs make good favour. Hunger forced us to kill our Prisoners, who weare chargeable in eating our food, for want of which have eaten the flesh. So by that means we weare freed from the trouble.

The next day we came neere a Village. Att our coming we killed a woman with her child, & seeing no more for us that way we tourned backe againe for feare of pursueing, and resolved to goe backe to the first village that was 3 days' journey; but on the way we mett with 5 and 20 or 30 men and women, who discovered us, which made [us] go to it. They fought & defended themselves lustily; but [there is] no resisting the Strongest party, for our guns were a terrour to them, and made them give over. During the fight the women ranne away. Five of the men weare wounded with arrowes and foure escaped, but he that was sent with me att first to make a discovery was horribly wounded with 2 arrowes and a blow of a club on the head. If he had stuck to it as we, he might proceed better. We burned him with all speed, that he might not languish long, to putt ourselves in safty. We killed 2 of them, & 5 prisoners wee tooke, and came away to where we left our boats, where we arrived within 2 days without resting, or eating or drinking all the time, saveing a litle stagge's meate. We tooke all their booty, which was of 2 sacks of Indian corne, stagges' skins, some pipes, some red and green stoanes, and some tobacco in powder, with some small loaves of bread, and some girdles, garters, necklaces made of goats' haire, and some small coyne of that country, some bowes and arrowes, and clubbs well wrought. The tournes of their heads weare of snakes' skin with bears' pawes. The hayre of some of them very long, & all proper men. We went on the other side of the river the soonest we could, and came to our fort. After we looked about us least we should be surprised, and perceiving nothing, we went about to gett meat for our wants & then to sleepe.

Att midnight we left that place. Six of us tooke a boate, 5 an other, and 2 the litle one. We row the rest of the night with all strength, & the breaking of the day hid ourselves in very long rushes & our boats. The litle boat went att the other side of the river, those hid it in the wood. One of them went up a tree to spie about, in case he could perceive any thing, to give notice to his comrades, & he was to come within sight of us to warne us. We weare in great danger going downe the streame of that river in the night time. We had trouble enough to carry all our baggage without the least noise. Being come to the end of the river which empties it selfe into a lake of some 8 or 9 leagues in compasse, we went into a small river to kill salmons, as in deed we tooke great many with staves, and so Sturgeons, of which we made provision for a long while. Att last finding our selves out of all feare & danger, we went freely a hunting about the lake, where we tarried 3 dayes, and 2 of our Company mett with 2 women that runned away from the Sanoutin's country, which is of the Iroquoit nation. Those poore creatures having taken so much paines to sett themselves att liberty to goe to their native country, found themselves besett in a greater slavery then before, they being tyed [and] brought to us.

The next day we went from thence with the 5 prisoners & the 22 heads. So much for the litlenesse of our boats as for the weight we had to putt upon them, being in danger, which made us make the more hast to the place where we intended to make new boats. For 9 days we went through dangerous places which weare like so many precipices with horrible falling of watters. We weare forced to carry our boats after the same maner as before, with great paines. We came att last to a lake where we contrived other boats, and there we parted our acquisited booty, and then each had care of his owne. We ordered the biggest boat should hould 4 men and 2 prisoners; the next 3 men and the 2 women that last weare taken; the 3d should hould 3 and the other prisoner. My brother and I had a man & woman with 4 heads to our share, and so the rest accordingly without dispute or noise.

We wandered severall dayes on that lake. It was a most delightfull place, and a great many islands. Here we killed great many bears. After we came to a most delightfull place for the number of stagges that weare there. Thence into a straight river. From thence weare forced to make many carriages through many stony mountains, where we made severall trappes for castors. We tooke above 200 castors there, and fleaced off the best skins. There weare some skins so well dressed that [they] held the oyle of beares as pure bottles. During that time we mett severall huntsmen of our country; so we heard news of our friends. Only our father was not yett retourned from the warrs against the french and algonquins. We left our small boats, that weare purposely confected for our hunting, & tooke our great boats that could carry us and all our luggage.

We went up the same river againe, not without great labour. Att last with much ado we arrived at the landing place where wee made a stay of 4 days; where many Iroquoites women came, and among others my 2 sisters, that received me with great joy, with a thousand kindnesses and guilts, as you may think. I gave them the 2 heads that I had, keeping the woman for my mother, to be her slave. There was nothing but singing & dancing out of meere joy for our safe retourne. I had 20 castors for my share, with 2 skins full of oyle of beare and another full of oriniack and stagge's grease. I gave to each of my sisters 6 stagges' skins to make them coats. I kept the grease for my mother, to whome it is convenient to give what is necessary for the family. We made our slaves carry all our booty, & went on to litle journeys through woods with ease, because the woods weare not thick and the earth very faire and plaine. All the way the people made much of me, till we came to the village, and especially my 2 sisters, that in all they shewed their respects, giveing me meate every time we rested ourselves, or painting my face or greasing my haire or combing my head. Att night they tooke the paines to pull off my stokins, & when I supped they made me lay downe by them and cover me with their coats, as if the weather had ben cold.

This voyage being ended, albeit I came to this village, & twice with feare & terror, the 3d time notwithstanding with joy & contentment. As we came neare the village, a multitude of people came to meete us with great exclamations, and for the most part for my sake, biding me to be cheerfull & qualifying me dodcon, that is, devil, being of great veneration in that country to those that shew any vallour. Being arrived within halfe a league of the village, I shewed a great modesty, as usually warriors use to doe. The whole village prepares to give the scourge to the captives, as you [have] heard before, under which I myselfe I was once to undergoe. My mother comes to meet mee, leaping & singing. I was accompanied with both [of] my sisters. Shee takes the woman slave that I had, and would not that any should medle with her. But my brother's prisoner, as the rest of the captives, weare soundly beaten. My mother accepted of my brother's 2 heads. My brother's prisoner was burned the same day, and the day following I received the sallery of my booty, which was of porcelaine necklaces, Tourns of beads, pendants, and girdles.

There was but banqueting for a while. The greatest part of both young men & women came to see me, & the women the choicest of meats, and a most dainty and cordiall bit which I goe to tell you; doe not long for it, is the best that is among them. First when the corne is greene they gather so much as need requireth, of which leaves they preserve the biggest leaves for the subject that followes. A dozen more or lesse old women meet together alike, of whome the greatest part want teeth, and seeth not a jott, and their cheeks hange downe like an old hunting-dogg, their eyes full of watter and bloodshott. Each takes an eare of corne and putts in their mouths, which is properly as milke, chawes it, and when their mouths are full, spits it out in their hands, which possibly they wash not once one yeare; so that their hands are white inside by reason of the grease that they putt to their haire & rubbing of it with the inside of their hands, which keeps them pretty clean, but the outside in the rinknesse of their rinkled hands there is a quarter of an ounze of filth and stinking grease.

And so their hands being full of that mince meate minced with their gumms and [enough] to fill a dish. So they chaw chestnutts; then they mingle this with bear's grease or oyle of flower (in french we call it Tourne Sol) with their hands. So made a mixture, they tye the leaves att one end & make a hodgepot & cover it with the same leaves and tye the upper end so that what is within these leaves becomes a round ball, which they boile in a kettle full of watter or brouth made of meate or fish. So there is the description of the most delicious bitt of the world. I leave you taste of their Salmi gondy, which I hope to tell you in my following discourses of my other voyages in that country, and others that I frequented the space of tenne years.

To make a period of this my litle voyage. After I stayed awhile in this village with all joy & mirth, for feasts, dances, and playes out of meere gladnesse for our small victorious company's hapy retourne, so after that their heads had sufficiently danced, they begin to talke [of going] to warre against the hollanders. Most of us are traited againe for the castors we bestowed on them. They resolve unanimously to goe on their designe. Every thing ready, we march along. The next day we arrived in a small brough of the hollanders, where we masters them, without that those beere-bellies had the courage to frowne att us. Whether it was out of hope of lucre or otherwise, we with violence tooke the meate out of their potts, and opening their coubards [cupboards] we take and eat what we [can] gett. For drinking of their wine we weare good fellowes. So much that they fought with swords among themselves without the least offer of any misdeed to me. I drunk more then they, but more soberly, letting them make their quarrells without any notice.

The 4th day we come to the fort of Orange, wher we weare very well received, or rather our Castors, every one courting us; and was nothing but pruins and reasins and tobbacco plentifully, and all for ho, ho, which is thanks, adding *nianonnha,* thanke you. We went from house to house. I went into the fort with my brother, and have not yett ben knowne a french. But a french souldier of the fort speaks to me in Iroquois language, & demanded if I was not a stranger, and did veryly believe I was french, for all that I was all dabbled over with painting and greased. I answered him in the same language, that no; and then he speaks in swearing, desiring me [to tell him] how I fell in the hands of those people. And hearing him speake french, amazed, I answered him, for which he rejoyced very much. As he embraces me, he cryes out with such a stirre that I thought him senselesse. He made a shame for all that I was wild but to blush red. I could be no redder then what they painted me before I came there. All came about me, ffrench as well as duch, every one makeing [me] drink out of the bottles, offering me their service; but my time yett was not out, so that I wanted not their service, for the onely rumour of my being a frenchman was enough. The flemish women drawed me by force into their houses, striving who should give, one bread, other meate, to drinke and to eate, and tobacco. I wanted not for those of my nation, Iroquoise, who followed me in a great squadroon through the streets, as if I had bin a monster in nature or a rare thing to be seen.

I went to see the Governor, & talked with me a long time, and tould him the life that I lead, of which he admired. He offred me to buy me from them att what price so ever, or else should save me, which I accepted not, for severall reasons. The one was for not to be behoulding to them, and the other being loathsome to leave such kind of good people. For then I began to love my new parents that weare so good & so favourable to me. The 3^d reason was to watch a better opportunity for to retyre to the french rather then make that long circuit which after I was forced to doe for to retyre to my country more then 2,000 leagues; and being that it was my destiny to discover many wild nations, I would not to strive against destinie. I remitted myselfe to fortune and adventure of time, as a thing ordained by God for his greatest glorie, as I hope it will prove. Our treatis being done, overladend with bootyes abundantly, we putt ourselves in the way that we came to see againe our village, and to passe that winter with our wives, and to eat with them our Cagaimtie in peece, hoping that nobody should trouble us during our wintering, and also to Expect or finde our fathers retourning home.

Leaving that place, many cryed to see me among a company of wolves, as that souldier tould me who knowed me the first houre; and the poore man made the tears come to my eyes. The truth is, I found many occasions to retire for to save me, but have not yett souffred enough to have merited my deliverence. In 2 dayes' journey we weare retourned to our cabbans, where every one of us rendered himself to his dearest kindred or master. My sisters weare charged of porcelaine, of which I was shure not to faile, for they weare too liberall to mee and I towards them. I was not 15 dayes retourned, but that nature itselfe reproached me to leade such a life, remembering the sweet behaviour and mildnesse of the french, & considered with meselfe what end should I expect of such a barbarous nation, enemy to God and to man. The great effect that the flemings shewed me, and the litle space was from us there; can I make that journey one day? The great belief that the people had in me should make them not to mistrust me, & by that I should have greater occasion to save me without feare of being pursued.

All these reasons made one deliberat to take a full resolution, without further delay, of saving meselfe to the flemings; ffor I could be att no safty among such a nation full of reveng. If in case the ffrench & algonquins defeats the troupe of theirs, then what spite they will have will reveng it on my boanes; ffor where is no law, no faith to undertake to goe to the ffrench. I was once interrupted, nor have I had a desire to venture againe for the second time. I should delight to be broyled as before in pitifull torments. I repented of a good occasion I lett slippe, finding meselfe in the place with offers of many to assist me. But he that is of a good resolution must be of strong hopes of what he undertakes; & if the dangers weare considered which may be found in things of importancy, you ingenious men would become cooks. Finally, without expecting my father's retourne, putting away all feare & apprehension, I constituted to deliver meselfe from their hands at what ever rate it would come too. For this effect I purposed to faine to goe a hunting about the brough; & for to dissemble the better, I cutt long sticks to make handles for a kind of a sword they use, that thereby they might not have the least suspition.

One day I tooke but a simple hattchett & a knife, if occasion presented to cutt some tree, & for to have more defence, if unhappily I should be rencountred, to make them believe that I was lost in the woods. Moreover, as the whole nation tooke me for proud, having allways great care to be guarnished with porcelaine, & that I would fly away like a beggar, a thing very unworthy, in this deliberation I ventured. I inquired [of] my brother if he would keepe me company. I knewed that he never thought, seeing that he was courting of a young woman, who by the report of many was a bastard to a flemish. I had no difficulty to believe, seeing that the colour of her hayre was much more whiter then that of the Iroquoits. Neverthelesse, shee was of a great familie. I left them to their love. In shorte, that without any provision I tooke journey through the forests guided by fortune. No difficulty if I could keepe the highway, which is greatly beatten with the great concours of that people that comes & goes to trade with the flemings; but to avoid all encounters I must prolong a farre off. Soe being assisted by the best hope of the world, I made all diligence in the meene while that my mother nor kindred should mistrust me in the least.

I made my departure att 8 of the clock in the morning the 29th 8bre, 1663 [1653]. I marched all that journey without eating, but being as accustomed to that, without staying I continued my cours att night. Before the breaking of the day I found myselfe uncapable because of my feeblenesse and faintnesse for want of food and repose after such constraint. But the feare of death makes vertu of necessity. The morning commanded me to goe, for it's faire and could ayre, which [was] somewhat advantageous to keepe [me] more cheerfull. Finally the resolution reterning my courage, att 4 of the clocke att evening, the next daye I arrived in a place full of trees cutt, which made mee looke to myselfe, fearing to approach the habitation, though my designe was such. It is a strange thing that to save this life they abhorre what they wish, & desire which they apprehend. Approaching nigher and nigher untill I perceived an opening that was made by cutting of wood where was one man cutting still wood, I went nearer and called him. [He] incontinently leaves his work & comes to me, thinking I was Iroquoise. I said nothing to him to the contrary. I kept him in that thought, promissing him to treat with him all my castors att his house, if he should promise me there should be non of my brother Iroquoise there, by reson we must be liberall to one another. He assured me there was non then there. I tould him that my castors were hidden and that I should goe for them to-morrow. So satisfied [he] leads me to his cabban & setts before me what good cheare he had, not desiring to loose time because the affaire concerned me much. I tould him I was savage, but that I lived awhile among the ffrench, & that I had something valuable to communicate to the governor. That he would give me a peece of paper and Ink and pen. He wondered very much to see that, what he never saw before don by a wildman. He charges himself with my letter, with promise that he should tell it to nobody of my being there, and to retourne the soonest he could possible, having but 2 litle miles to the fort of Orange.

In the meane while of his absence shee shews me good countenance as much as shee could, hoping of a better imaginary profit by me. Shee asked me if we had so much libertie with the ffrench women to lye with them as they; but I had no desire to doe anything, seeing myselfe so insnared att death's door amongst the terrible torments, but must shew a better countenance to a worse game. In the night we heard some wild men singing, which redoubled my torments and apprehension, which inticed me to declare to that woman that my nation would kill [me] because I loved the ffrench and the flemings more than they, and that I resolved hereafter to live with the flemings. Shee perceiving my reason hid me in a corner behind a sack or two of wheat. Nothing was to me but feare. I was scarcely there an houre in the corner, but the flemings came, 4 in number, whereof that french man [who] had knowne me the first, who presently getts me out & gives me a suite that they brought purposely to disguise me if I chanced to light upon any of the Iroquoits. I tooke leave of my landlady & landlord, yett [it] grieved me much that I had nothing to bestow upon them but thanks, being that they weare very poore, but not so much [so] as I.

I was conducted to the fort of Orange, where we had no incounter in the way, where I have had the honnour to salute the Governor, who spoake french, and by his speech thought him a french man. The next day he caused an other habit to be given me, with shoos & stokins & also linnen. A minister that was a Jesuit gave me great offer, also a Marchand, to whom I shall ever have infinit obligations, although they weare satisfied when I came to france att Rochel. I stayed 3 dayes inclosed in the fort & hidden. Many came there to search me, & doubt not but my parents weare of the party. If my father had ben there he would venture hard, & no doubt but was troubled att it, & so was my mother, & my parents who loved me as if I weare their owne naturall Son. My poore sisters cryed out & lamented through the town of the flemings, as I was tould they called me by my name, ffor they came there the 3d day after my flight. Many flemings wondered, & could not perceive how those could love me so well; but the pleasure caused it, as it agrees well with the Roman proverbe, "doe as they doe." I was imbarked by the governor's order; after taking leave, and thanks for all his favours, I was conducted to Menada, a towne faire enough for a new country, where after some 3 weekes I embarked in one of their shipps for holland, where we arrived after many boisterous winds and ill weather, and, after some six weeks' sayle and some days, we landed att Amsterdam the 4th of January, 1664 [1654]. Some days after I imbarked myselfe for france and came to Rochelle well & safe, not without blowing my fingers many times as well as I [had] done before [when] I arrived in holland. I stayed till spring, expecting the transporte of a shippe for new france.

Of the Capture and Deliverance of Father Joseph Poncet

1653

Françcois-Joseph le Mercier and Joseph-Antoine Poncet de la Riviére

---

This narrative is taken from volume 40 of the *Jesuit Relations* (JR 40:119-155). Bracketed references to original manuscript page breaks and hyphens due to word breaks in the Thwaites edition are all omitted here. Two endnotes and their superscripted references have also been omitted. Poncet wrote a first-person account of his experiences at the request of his new superior, François-Joseph le Mercier, then in his first of two appointments as superior of the Jesuits of Canada. Le Mercier included Poncet's account in his report for 1653. Le Mercier's third-person description (**I**) precedes Poncet's account (**II**). An editor in Paris added the first paragraph and some other sentences connecting the fragments that survived an attack at sea by the English. These are printed here in brackets to distinguish them from the accounts of le Mercier and Poncet. We have eliminated the large number of quotation marks that Thwaites used to distinguish Poncet's and le Mercier's portions of the report and the comments of the editor in Paris. All bracketed insertions are part of the original. We have used braces { } to set off our own insertions.

A sketch of François-Joseph le Mercier, who wrote a small portion of what follows, has been provided below with the more lengthy account for 1664-1665 that he authored alone. Poncet was born in Paris in 1610. He was admitted to the novitiate of the Jesuits in 1629 and sailed to Quebec in 1639. He was posted to the Huron mission for a year and later carried out duties at Trois-Rivières and Montreal. He lost his left index finger under torture by the Mohawks after his capture in 1653. Poncet was treated in a manner similar to but less brutal than that shown Jogues and Bressani. He returned to France in 1657, and he later went to serve on Martinique, where he died at the age of 65.

D.R.S.

[THE IROQUOIS, having butchered some Frenchmen in the month of June, at Cap rouge,—a place distant three leagues, or thereabout, from the fort of Quebec,—surprised in the same place, on the twentieth of the month of last August, Father Joseph Poncet and a Frenchman named Maturin Franchetot. This good

Father, seeing that a poor French widow had some grain in the field, and lacked help to gather it in, went off in that direction to hunt up some good people who would be willing to aid in garnering her little harvest. He had just spoken to the Frenchman mentioned above, when some Iroquois, issuing from the neighboring forest, where they had been hidden in ambush, rushed upon them separately and unexpectedly, and dragged them away. The Father was bidden, upon his return, to commit to paper his capture and all his adventures; he obeyed with reluctance, desiring that his Crosses be known only to the King of the crucified; but a part of his account was torn up by the English. After citing two or three short passages from a letter written on this subject, we shall follow, in this Chapter, what has come into our hands.]

I

As soon as the news was brought to Quebec that the Iroquois had carried off Father Poncet, not only was general sadness felt on his account, as he was beloved by all; but thirty or forty Frenchmen, and some Christian Savages, firmly resolved to rescue him from the hands of those Barbarians, whatever it might cost them to do so. They launched their canoes on the day following his capture, purposing to forestall the Enemy by going to wait for them in some spot which they must pass, in order to surprise them as they went by. So many prayers have been offered here, in public and in private, since their departure, that I can but think either that God will restore him to us, or that by his means he will give peace to this poor country, both within and without its borders. [And, farther down in the same letter:] Father Poncet was captured on the twentieth of August, toward evening; on the twenty-first, toward night, our scouts followed him; and on the twenty-sixth, one of the canoes that had gone in pursuit of the robbers who were carrying him off brought back news to us that those scouts had stopped at Three Rivers to give help to the Village, as it was harassed by five hundred Iroquois,—who were holding it closely beset, and were prowling about the neighborhood in all directions. Those who returned in this canoe told us that they found, near the Island of saint Eloy, two faces drawn with charcoal on a tree from which the bark had been removed, and the names of Father Poncet and Mathurin Franchetot written beneath these. Furthermore, they said they had found in the same place a book in which was written, in substance, these words: "Six Hurons, turned Iroquois, and four Anniehronnons {Mohawks} are carrying off Father Poncet and Mathurin Franchetot. They have not yet done us any injury. It is their custom to treat their prisoners gently as long as they are still in fear of being overtaken." [That is what was written to me concerning this good Father's capture. Let us now come to the tattered remnants of his own account, of which I shall make a brief abridgment.]

II

We arrived [says he] at a very rapid River, where the army that had gone to Three Rivers had camped. The Barbarian who had captured me at Cap rouge took away from me the Reliquary which I was wearing on my neck, and hung it to his own. One day, when he was running in the woods, this Reliquary flew open and all the Relics were lost,—there remaining in the little copper box composing the Reliquary only a small piece of paper on which I had written in my own blood, when I was still in the country of the Hurons, the names of our Fathers martyred in America, and a short Prayer in which I asked Our Lord for a violent death in his service, and the grace to shed all my blood for the same cause. It so happened that, when I had adroitly removed this paper from that Barbarian's grasp, I saw constantly before my eyes the sentence of my death written in my own blood, so that I could not revoke it. Nevertheless, I had a feeling that those great souls and stout hearts who had preceded me in this conflict had been actually immolated, as having genuine virtues; and that I, who had only the shadows and faint likenesses thereof, would be crucified only in appearance.

I still had in my Breviary a Picture of St. Ignatius, with Our Lord bearing his Cross,—a mystery which well suited our Society; and in which, as I had always felt a strong affection for it, he was pleased to give me some share, in the extraordinary hardships that I underwent on this journey. The Picture of Our Lady of Pity, surrounded by the five wounds of her Son, was also left me, and formed my greatest recreation, and my consolation in distress. But the fear that these hallowed portraits might meet with some indignity, made me decide to forego their possession and hide them in a bush.

I kept a little Crown of Our Lord, which was the only thing left me of all that I had on my person when I was captured. I concealed it so well that it was never perceived by those Barbarians.

To return to our journey: when it came to crossing the Stream of which I have spoken, I was ordered to wade through it. I was already soaking wet, having passed the night in the tall grass, which was all saturated with drizzling rain and the dew of night, the nights being very cold. I was wet up to the waist in this Stream; and all that, with the want of nourishment, caused me a severe colic and excessive pains. I did not, however, cease to perform all my devotions as usual, taking comfort quietly with Our Lord, from whose hand, and not from the hand of men, I received this Cross.

Amid these labors, I was seized with so great numbness in the left leg, and was so severely inconvenienced by a large blister under this same left foot, that my hosts were compelled to halt for a time, a thing which they had not expected. They had only a morsel of boiled meat left, which they had kept from their last meal, thinking to reach a place where they would find provisions. They ate it at the same inn where we had lodged throughout our journey,—under the vault of Heaven; and, as I felt extremely exhausted, I had recourse to my two Patrons, Saint Raphael and Saint Martha, saying to them softly in my heart that I greatly needed some refreshment in the thirst from which I was suffering, and a little broth in my exhaustion. Scarcely had these feelings arisen in my breast, when one of our conductors brought me some wild plums that he had found in the woods,—by great good luck, for more than six hundred men had passed that spot. Toward night, after experiencing much difficulty in finding a little clean water, because we were in a nasty swamp, I lay down and went to sleep, with no other comfort than what I gained from my weakness; but when my host aroused me and offered me some broth, I was much surprised, not knowing how he could have made it.

On the following morning I was compelled to set out without breakfasting, and walk with one leg and one foot crippled, and my whole body disabled. The strength that God gave me I attribute to my dear Patrons, especially to St. Joseph, to whom I had frequent recourse. At two o'clock in the afternoon, reaching a spot near the river which flows down to the territory of the Dutch, and across which is situated the principal Village of the Iroquois, we were ordered to strip ourselves, and give up what was left us of our French garments. When I had nothing left on me but a breech-clout, a blue great-coat, all in rags, was thrown over my back; and to my companion was left an old linen doublet, badly tattered. Some Savages of our band, who had gone on ahead, had returned as far as this river with their wives, bringing some ears of Indian corn and some native squashes to our conductors; but they never offered us a single morsel. It was late; we were fasting, extremely fatigued by our journey, and covered with very dirty rags; but for refreshment were ordered to sing as we walked, thus attired. It was the beginning of our victors' triumph. I intoned the Litany of the blessed Virgin, the *Veni Creator,* and other Hymns of the Church.

As we crossed the river of the Dutch, I confessed my companion, who wished to prepare himself for death, having caught sight of about forty or fifty Iroquois who appeared to be waiting for us with staves in their hands. We were stripped entirely naked, except our breech-clouts, and were made to pass through these Barbarians, who were drawn up in line. They gave me some blows on the back with their switches; but as I was quickening my steps, one of those executioners stopped me short, taking me by the arm and stretching it out, in order to give me a blow with a short, thick stick that he raised aloft. I gave my arm to Our Lord, thinking the man was about to break and shatter the bone between the elbow and the wrist; but, the blow falling on the joint, I came off with a wound which disappeared in course of time. When we had entered the Village, I was made to take the lead in ascending a scaffold erected in the middle of the public place, and raised about five feet from the ground. My companion joined me there soon afterward, bearing the marks of the blows he had received; and, among others, were seen the traces of a troublesome and painful lashing across his breast.

I felt so firm and calm on this stage, and faced, with so serene an eye and mind, those who were looking at me, that I wondered at myself. Nevertheless, I felt some alarm at the sight of a certain One-eyed man who carried a knife in one hand, and a piece of their bread in the other. I remembered that the good Father Isaac Jogues had lost one of his thumbs on a similar scaffold; and, not feeling then disposed to give the man my fingers, I appealed to his good Angel; and the man, approaching us, gave my companion the bread that he was holding, and then withdrew without doing any injury. A shower, coming up suddenly, dispersed the spectators, and we were conducted to the shelter of a little roof at the entrance to a cabin. There we were made to sing; and God put me in such a state of submission to those Barbarians, and I abandoned myself with such fortitude to all sorts of indignities, that there was nothing I would not have done, provided it were bidden me and were not contrary to God's Law. [I will say here, in passing, what I have noticed in a private letter,—namely, that, as the Father did not succeed in all these apish tricks in a manner satisfactory to the Savages,—who, in consequence, would have been inclined to condemn him to death,—a young Huron, a captive among these people, came forward to sing and dance, and execute all the grimaces, in the Fathers place, the latter having never learned that trade.]

Toward evening [continues the Father] we were conducted to the cabin of him who had captured me, and there I was given a dish of their sagamité, or porridge made of Indian corn and water. The old men having assembled in this cabin, a woman presented a brasse of Porcelain {a fathom of wampum} to enforce her request that one of my fingers should be cut off. I felt no farther reluctance at giving up my hands, especially as—in the hope which I had entertained, during my journey, of saving my life, and in my desire to work afterward in the cause of peace—I always believed it expedient that I should bear the marks of my experience, and that it should cost me one of my fingers. As a result, I no longer appealed to the Angels of these Barbarians, in order to avoid that cross, but rather to Saint Gabriel, that I might gain strength to suffer it cheerfully. The One-eyed man, who had approached our scaffold with a purpose which he did not execute at the time, took my right hand and examined my fingers; and, just as I was thinking that the fingers of that hand were a little more necessary to me than those of the left, he took the latter and dropped the right. Then calling a child, from four to five years of age, he gave him his knife, took the index or forefinger of my left hand, and made the child cut it off. I offered my blood and my sufferings in the cause of peace, regarding this little sacrifice with a mild eye, a serene countenance, and a stout heart; I sang the *Vexilla,* and I remember that I repeated two or three times the couplet, or Strophe,—*Impleta sunt quæ concinit David fideli carmine, dicendo nationibus, regnavit à ligno Deus.*

The Hymn completed and the finger cut off, that man hung around my neck a part of the Porcelain beads which the woman mentioned above had given; and with the rest he encircled my severed finger, and carried it to my captor. Now, as the blood flowed from the wound in abundance, the One-eyed man wished to apply to it the fire of his tobacco-pipe, in order to stanch it—which would have caused me intense pain. But he was anticipated by others, who had a glowing coal applied to it by the same child who had done the cutting. As the blood did not cease flowing, they wrapped the wound for me, some time afterward, in a leaf of Indian corn; and that was all the dressing applied to it until my life had been granted me. I shall abridge what follows [adds the Father], since it appears to me as if it were being snatched out of my hands.

On the following day, we were conducted to another Village, where there was to be held a great Assembly of the notables of the country. A woman took away my shoes from me, thinking perhaps that we were going to be put to death; accordingly I made that journey barefooted and bareheaded. For three days and two nights—namely, the Friday, Saturday, and Sunday immediately preceding the Nativity of the blessed Virgin—we were exposed to the ridicule, the taunts, and the insolence of the children and of every one. We shared in the promise that was made to the Son of God before his birth: *Saturabitur opprobriis,*—"He shall be filled with reproaches." It was our principal dish, from morning until evening, in the great public place where we were exposed. Some gave me blows with their pipes on my cut finger, others applied to it burning ashes; some gave me fillips on it; others applied thereto the fire from their tobacco, and others the hot stone of their pipes. In a word, every one did us some injury, according to his fancy. Behold what we suffered outwardly, while inwardly we were expecting, as the last act of this tragedy, only horrible and frightful torments.

In the night from Friday to Saturday they burned in the fire of their pipes the two Index-fingers, both right and left, of poor Mathurin, my companion,—an operation which he bore with admirable patience, singing the *Ave maris stella* in his sufferings. We were very rigorously bound during these two nights, the cords around our hands and feet being made fast at such a height, and in a manner so extremely uncomfortable, that we were half suspended in the air; we suffered in consequence, a pain of such excruciating severity that a good old man, seeing plainly that it was unbearable, loosened our bonds and relieved us a little.

On one of these nights, the Elders ordered the young people to content themselves with making us sing and dance, without causing us further torments. But that did not prevent those who were around the fires in the cabin from touching glowing firebrands to our flesh as we passed. I received a good part of these burns.

Sunday was spent in councils and assemblies, in order to determine what should be done with us. Toward evening, our sentence was pronounced, but in terms which I did not understand. I took it for a sentence of death, and my mind was so well prepared for this that I seemed to see the divine grace all ready to sustain me in the cruelty of the last torments. But my sentence was milder: I was given to a good old woman in place of a brother of hers, who had been captured or killed by those on our side. Nevertheless, my life was not yet safe; for that woman could have made me die in all the torments that could have been suggested by revenge. But she had pity on me and delivered me from death, at the season when the Church is wont to honor the birth of the blessed Virgin. I pray God to reward that goodness. As soon as I had entered her cabin, she began to sing a song of the dead, in which two of her daughters accompanied her. I was near the fire during these doleful chants and was made to sit down on a kind of table slightly raised from the ground; and then I became aware that I was given in return for a dead man, the last mourning for whom these women were renewing,—causing the departed to become alive again in my person, according to their custom. In this cabin I met a captive Algonquin woman, who had been adopted into that family, into which I saw myself also adopted. As I had seen her before, and as I understood her language, I was delighted. I found also a Huron of my former acquaintance, which increased my joy.

As soon as I had been made a relative of my house, they began to dress my finger after the manner of the Savages,—applying to it I know not what roots or barks, previously boiled, which they wrapped in a linen rag that was greasier than a kitchen-cloth. This poultice lasted me a fortnight, so that it became hard, in such a manner as to cause me great inconvenience. I was given half a blanket, to serve me as robe and as bed; and, some time afterward, they made me some stockings and shoes after their fashion; I was also presented with an old and very greasy shirt,—and all that with so much savage kindness and so great affection, that I have not experienced more cordiality among the Savages who are friendly to us. Moreover, they went to my captor, and paid him for my life with several thousand Porcelain beads.

As for my poor companion, he was conducted on Sunday to another Village and was burned on Monday, the day of the Nativity of the blessed Virgin, who had delivered me at the beginning of her festival.

Three days thereafter, there was brought to the Village where I was news of the army that had gone to Three Rivers. For a considerable time I was in fear of death, not knowing whether the news was good or bad, and being well assured that I would be the object of their vengeance, in case it were bad.

But at length there came a Captain, who was commissioned to grant my life, and to conduct me back to Three Rivers. It happened, by a very special providence, that this man was a member of the family to which I had been given, and a brother of her who had adopted me as her brother. He lived in another Village, whence he sent two Hurons to invite me to go and see him. These good people told the Iroquois marvels about me, assuring them that I was mourned by all the French, and that on my life and my return depended the lives of their fellow-countrymen who had been left as hostages at Three Rivers. These words caused me to receive as much consideration as I had before met with indignity. The Captain whom I have just mentioned was delighted to see me still alive; and he gave me an old hat, which was very acceptable to me, inasmuch as I had been going bareheaded for twelve days. He promised to conduct me to the Dutch, in order to have me clothed, and then to take me back to the country of the French.

Upon this Captain's report, they began to call assemblies and hold councils, for the purpose of concluding peace with the French. Meanwhile, I was conducted to fort Orange, occupied by the Dutch, where I arrived on the twentieth of September. The first family to whom I came received me with much charity: I was given a dinner and, among other things, I there ate some apples,—a fruit which I had not tasted for fifteen years; and I was also presented with a white shirt. A young man who had been captured at Three Rivers by the Iroquois, and ransomed by the Dutch, whom he served as interpreter, came to find me, and, after some conversation, told me that he was coming to make his confession on the next day, which was Sunday.

A good Scotch Lady, who has shown herself on all occasions very charitable toward the French,—and who had done all in her power to ransom Monsieur Petit's little son, who has since died among the Iroquois,—conducted me to her house, to remove the dressing of bark or roots which those good Iroquois women, of whom I have spoken, had applied to my finger; and, when she saw that it was still very far from being healed, she sent me to fort Orange, to have it dressed by a Surgeon. There I met the Governor of that fort, to whom the Iroquois Captain had presented a letter from Monsieur de Lauzon, Governor for the King over the great river saint Lawrence in new France. This man received me very coldly, although the letter which bad been brought to him commended me in the highest terms. As night was approaching, and I was going away to lie down on the bare floor, without bed or supper, a Savage asked the Governor for leave to take me to a family who were friendly to him. I was conducted thither, and found there an old man who received me with much kindness. The Frenchman whom I mentioned above was living in that house; and he set his conscience in order during the three nights that I spent with him under the roof of that worthy man,—whose courtesy I wish I could acknowledge by any kind of service, so handsomely did he treat me when I was in the most despicable condition in the world. I could not lack coats, as this worthy Gentleman presented me a very decent one; and, at the same time, a good Walloon, knowing nothing of this kindness, went to search through the houses, to find me the means of clothing myself. I was also told that that good Scotch Lady was preparing to do me the same charity; but I thanked them all, and would not accept anything but a hooded cloak, and some stockings of the Savage fashion, with some French shoes, and a blanket that was to serve me for bed on my return journey. That Lady took charge of all this, with so much skill and affection as to include every conceivable provision for my comfort. My hosts urged me to take some food for my journey; but I contented myself with some peaches from a Brussels Merchant, a good Catholic, whom I confessed at my departure. I had to promise them all to come back and see them the next Summer, so much affection and kindness did they manifest toward me.

Leaving the Dutch settlement, I was conducted to the Village of the man who had captured me. Upon going to visit him, he returned to me my Breviary. Thence we proceeded to the Village and to the cabin where I had been adopted, where I remained only two days; for some one came to conduct me, together with my sister who had given me my life, to the largest of the Iroquois Villages, for the purpose of attending the councils and assemblies in which the question of peace was to be discussed. I observed that presents were being everywhere collected, to accompany my escort back to Quebec. There was nothing but feasting, and I was given the best possible reception at these gatherings. At length, on St. Michael's day, it was decreed that they should solicit and conclude a treaty of peace with the French and their Allies. This conclusion was reached in the Village where the first Frenchman, the good René Goupil, companion to Father

Isaac Jogues, had been killed by the Iroquois on that very day of St. Michael. I had always expected that this festival would not pass without some important occurrence.

Three days after this resolution, I was told that the Captain who had escorted me to the Dutch settlement would be my conductor to the country of the French,—not by water, because of the storms which ordinarily prevail at this season upon lake Champlain, over which we must have passed; but by another route, which was very fatiguing to me, as we had to proceed on foot through those great forests for seven or eight days, and I had neither strength nor legs for so great an undertaking. At the end of these eight days is found a river upon which we proceed by boat for about two days, and then we come to the great river saint Lawrence, into which the first empties its waters, sixty leagues or thereabout above the Island of Montreal, and not far from the lake called Ontario.

I at that time recalled to mind St. Joseph, who bore Our Lord to Egypt through the deserts of Arabia, as is believed; and I prayed him to serve me as guide and support in the fatigues of this journey. I had always had frequent recourse to his protection in all my labors, as also to that of St. Michael, protector of the Church and of France; and it happened, as I have since learned, that on the fourth of September, the day on which I entered an Iroquois Village for the first time, the *Te Deum* was sung at Kebec {Quebec} in a little Church dedicated to St. Joseph. This was in thanksgiving at my deliverance and my return to Three Rivers,—a report having arisen, though the first author of it could never be discovered, that I had escaped from the hands of the Enemy. On that same day, too, the Sacrifice of the Mass was offered for the same reason at the Cove of St. Joseph [Sillery], in a Church dedicated to God under the name of St. Michael,—whom we may call the Angel of our peace, since that was concluded in the country of the Iroquois on the day of his festival.

At length, on the third of October, I left behind me the last Village of the Iroquois, to return to Quebec. On a little hill at a short distance from the Village, I met the Captains and Elders of the country, who were waiting for me with the presents which they sent in ratification of the peace. They made me their last harangue, urging me to bind our new alliance firmly. My conductor having taken charge of the presents, we pursued our journey, accomplishing only four leagues on that first day. All those whom we met bestowed some endearment on me, according to their custom, and begged me to use my influence in concluding a satisfactory peace with the French.

I began and completed this journey by land, with inconceivable fatigues. We started upon a Friday, the third of October; and we arrived at the first river that I mentioned above on Saturday, the eleventh of the month. We proceeded in company with several Iroquois who were going to hunt the Beaver about lake Ontario. The rains, and the mountains and valleys; the mountain-streams and brooks, and four rivers of considerable size which we had to cross by fording, wetting ourselves thereby up to the waist; another larger one, that had to be crossed on rafts, insecure and badly put together; very short rations, consisting solely of Indian corn just picked, without bread, without wine, without meat and without game, those regions having been hunted bare,—all these things, I say, formed a Cross for me that was so formidable and unceasing that it seems to me a perpetual miracle that I was able to bear it, suffering, as I was, such intense pain and such extreme weakness. It was also very remarkable that my Guide never lost his gentleness and patience, although he saw what a bad traveler I was. In this return journey, I seem to have participated a little in the weakness and exhaustion of the King of the afflicted,—as on my outward journey, after my capture, I had shared in his bonds and his agony.

But now, at the end of this nine days' labor, there appeared three young men, sent by the Elders of the country to notify my Conductor that a Captain, to whom presents had been given at Three Rivers for my deliverance, had just arrived in the country with a report that the Iroquois hostages who had been left in the French fort had been put in irons, and that some of them had already had their heads broken. This Captain declared that he had learned that news from the mouth of a Savage, a friend of his. Upon leaving, they warned my Conductor and his attendants to be on their guard, if they were to involve themselves farther in conducting me home. They asked me if I wished to go on, as affairs then stood, and I had no answer. My Conductor, with great courage, said to me that if I would give him my word to try to save his life, he would expose it to all sorts of dangers for the sake of leading me back, safe and sound, among the French. I gave it to him very freely, and that many times; for he constantly asked me for it. The promise given and accepted, we embarked and pursued our journey. I have since learned that this false rumor was based on the fact that irons had been put on the feet of an Algonquin Savage who had become intoxicated. These alarms came to us from time to time, and some took pleasure in reporting them to me, thinking to intimidate me; but those persons were not of the number of my Guides, who always treated me with much gentleness.

As we began to draw near the Island of Montreal, my people were afraid of meeting with some Algonquins; and meanwhile they took such great pleasure in hunting—game being very plenty in those regions of the great river saint Lawrence—that this delay seemed tiresome to me. Our final Cross was the danger of being swallowed up in the whirlpools of the saint Louys rapids, within sight of the Montreal settlement. I almost thought I would find my grave in those currents, but they did me no further harm than to wash away the rest of my sins.

At last, we landed safely at that settlement on the twenty-fourth of October,—nine weeks having passed, in honor of St. Michael and all the holy Angels, since the beginning of my captivity. We left Montreal on the twenty-fifth, toward evening, and arrived on the twenty-eighth at Three Rivers, where we remained until the third of November. On the fifth we set foot on shore at Quebec; on the sixth our Iroquois, my Conductors, made their presents in the cause of peace, which were responded to with other presents; and thus, upon a Sunday evening, eighty-one days after my capture,—that is to say, just nine times nine days,—the great affair of the peace, so ardently desired, was brought to a close. The Holy Angels made manifest by this number, nine, which is dedicated to them, the share which they had in this sacred work,—which was conducted in an entirely different manner from the affairs managed by the Savages, who protract to extreme length their assemblies and proceedings. I spent only one month in the country of the Iroquois, entering it on the fourth of September, and leaving it on the third of October; and in this short time I held communication with the Dutch, saw fort Orange, and thrice entered the four Villages of the Anniehronnon Iroquois,—the rest of the period of my captivity being consumed by my journey thither and back. I was taken by way of the River of the Iroquois and Lake Champlain, and then proceeded, for two days only, by land; and I returned by another way, so that I passed over the two routes taken by their armies and warriors when they come to seek us. That, approximately, is what obedience required me to relate concerning my journey.

Description of New Netherland

1653

Adriaen Cornelissen van der Donck
Translated by Diederik Goedhuys

Adriaen Cornelissen van der Donck came from a prominent family in Breda, a city in the province of North Brabant, Netherlands. Adriaen studied jurisprudence at the University of Leiden, which conferred on him the degree of *juris utriusque doctor*, doctor of both civil and canon law. In 1641 Kiliaen van Rensselaer, former director of the West India Company and patroon of Rensselaerswijck, recruited Adriaen for the position of *schout* in his colony along the Hudson, a Dutch office combining the duties of sheriff and prosecuting attorney. When Adriaen arrived in the colony, Arent van Curler, the grand nephew of the patroon and business manager of Rensselaerswijck, assigned him a farm on the southern end of Castle Island. With the arrival of van der Donck, New Netherland had acquired its first lawyer and most highly educated inhabitant. Adriaen's position as *schout* and the location of his farm near the mouth of the Normanskill (one of the routes to the Mohawk) afforded him excellent opportunity to observe the natives as they came into the colony to trade. Soon dissatisfied with the crowded conditions on the island, Adriaen found a more suitable location at the northern end of the colony, close to the mouth of the Mohawk River. Proximity to this major Mohawk trading route probably pleased Adriaen as much as it displeased Kiliaen van Rensselaer to have his law enforcement officer so far from the center of his patroonship.

When his three-year contract with the patroon expired in 1644 he decided to remain in Rensselaerswijck until Kieft's war with the Indians down river had ended. Shortly after his retirement from the patroon's service he married the daughter of Francis Doughty, a religious dissident from New Plymouth.

Van der Donck's observations of the natives were enhanced by contact with individuals such as Isaac Jogues and Harmen Meyndertsz van den Bogaert. By 1645 his knowledge of the Indians had developed to such a stage that Willem Kieft, director of New Netherland, called upon his assistance at treaty negotiations with the Mohawks. As soon as peaceful relations were established in the Manhattan area, Kieft granted van der Donck a 24,000 acre estate in the southwest corner of present-day Westchester County. Adriaen named this land, which was a reward for his assistance with the Mohawk negotiations, Colendonck.

Adriaen lived on his estate in gentlemanly splendor as a *jonkher* (landowner) with his wife Mary until he ran afoul of the new director-general, Petrus Stuyvesant. In 1648 Adriaen was elected to the Board of Nine Men, an advisory council selected from a double list of nominations presented by the inhabitants. When Stuyvesant learned that van der Donck was keeping a journal of complaints against the administration, he ordered it seized. Rather than desisting from his criticism, Adriaen assembled evidence and sailed to the Netherlands with two other members of the board to present their case to the states-general.

Although Adriaen ostensibly won several concessions, the states-general later refused him permission to return to New Netherland. While an exile in his native land, Adriaen wrote his *Beschrijvinghe van Nieuw Nederlandt* [Description of New Netherland]. In 1653, after receiving a copyright for his manuscript, he was allowed to return to his family at Colendonck. The book was published in Amsterdam in 1655, the same year that Jonkher Adriaen van der Donck died on his estate in the New World, and again in 1656. The place name Yonkers still bears testimony to the man regarded by many as the most reliable source of information on the natives of the upper Hudson and Mohawk Valley.

The first translation was completed in 1833 by Jeremiah Johnson, a former mayor of Brooklyn and descendant of original settlers of New Netherland. Johnson's effort was eventually published in the Collections of the New York Historical Society (1841). It was reprinted by Syracuse University Press in 1968. It has been recognized for some time that Johnson's translation was inadequate. Not only is it deficient because of Johnson's misreading of the text, but some passages have been omitted without comment. The translation below by Diederick Goedhuys is completely new, drawing on research and related materials that were unavailable to Johnson. The following selection from van der Donck's work represents only that section concerning his description of the Native Americans.

C.T.G.

Of the Manners and Extraordinary Qualities of the Original Natives of New Netherland

Their Bodily Shape, and Why They Are Called Savages

Having briefly spoken of the attributes of the land as far as needful, it will also be worthwhile to treat in the following of the nature of its original natives, so that when the Christians shall have multiplied there, and the savages melted away, we may not suffer the regret that their manners and customs have likewise passed from memory

In figure, build and shape of the body, both men and women are equal to the average and well-proportioned sort here in the Netherlands. In height, and as between height or weight and girth they vary as elsewhere, the one less, the other more, and rarely deviate from the average. Their limbs are nimble and supple, and they can run prodigiously with striking stamina, carrying big and heavy packs with them. They are very good at voluntary physical exercise when so inclined, but quite averse—chiefly the menfolk—to heavy sustained labor of a slavish type. They arrange all their tasks and affairs accordingly, so that they will not need to do or work much. Congenital defects and deformities are very seldom seen amongst them, and in all my time in that country I never encountered more than one who was born with an unsound body. Cripples, hunchbacks or otherwise misshapen persons are so rarely seen that one may in truth say that such do not exist there, and if one does occasionally observe a maimed or infirm individual, it will appear upon inquiry that the defect resulted from an accident or was inflicted in war. All are slender and clean-limbed, and none is particularly heavy, fat, or gross. Although generally speaking nature has not endowed them with surpassing wisdom, and they must develop their best judgment without formal training, yet one finds no fools, madmen, maniacs, or lunatics among them. Both men and women tend to be broad-shouldered and slim-waisted. The hair of the head, before it is changed by old age, is always jet-black, quite sleek and uncurled, and almost as coarse as a horse's tail. Any other color or kind of hair they regard as conspicuously ugly. On the chest, under the arms and on the chin and the private parts of the body they have no or very little hair; any hair that does come up sparsely in the said places they pluck out at the root. It rarely regrows, other than on old men, some of whom are a little stubble here and there around the chin. All, men and women alike, have fine faces, with black-brown eyes and snow-white teeth. Purblind or cross-eyed persons are very seldom found amongst them. Of those born blind I have never heard or been told, and they seldom lose their sight by accident. I have known of only one with cataracts on both eyes, whom smallpox had left blind. In great old age their sight fails, but not as early as in this country. The hue or color of their bodies is generally not as white as ours, though some quite fair-skinned ones are to be found, and most are born white. The rest tend towards a yellowish complexion like the Gypsies or heathens who roam through our country, or like the country folk who are much in the open, as they are, without guarding against the sun and air. Their yellowness is no fault of nature, but only an acquired feature due to the heat of the sun which burns more powerfully than in this country. Passed from generation to generation, the effect is all the stronger. Despite the yellowness they all share, some more than others, one finds many handsome and graceful persons and faces among both men and women. It is true that at first sight they appear somewhat strange to our people, because color, speech, and dress are so different, but for those who associate with them frequently the strangeness soon passes. And it seems that their womenfolk have an attractive grace about them, for several Hollanders (before many Holland women were to be had there) became infatuated with them. Their countenance and facial features are as theirs and as varied as in this country, seldom strikingly beautiful and even more rarely very ugly, and if they were instructed as our women are, they would no doubt differ little from them, if at all.

The original natives of that country (for there are now also many natives not originally from there, but Christians born of Christians), were all called savages by our people as a general appellation, though they are divided into many different tribes. That name, as far as can be ascertained, was given them from the first, and is quite appropriate for a number of reasons. First, on account of religion, because they have none or so little as to be virtually in a state of nature. Second, as regards marriage and in the recognition of landed property they deviate so far from the general laws that they may well be called savage, because they act in those matters almost at will. Third, as the Christians, to set themselves apart, give some foreign nation the name of Turks or Mamelukes or Barbarians, because the term heathen is too general and little used abroad, they did not wish to include the American natives within it either. Similarly, the terms black and white are customary among those who have business overseas, to distinguish the Negroes from our and similar nations, but neither of these names quite fitted the American natives, who tend towards the olive-colored. Therefore our people on the spur of the moment rather than with forethought, it may be supposed, called them savages, as the first name that occurred to them. And since the first opinion or notion of women and the uneducated is best, it seems appropriate that they be called savages, since they are quite wild and are strangers to the Christian religion.

Fare and Food of the Indians

In food and drink, even on their feast days, the Indians are not at all excessive, spendthrift, frivolous, or lavish, and easily contented so long as they have something to keep body and soul together and satisfy hunger and thirst. Nor is it customary among them as it is with us that the highest-placed, noblest, or richest expects to be treated accordingly and better than a poor devil or a common man, but always and everywhere their food and drink are sufficient and, according to season, the same for all. Their usual drink has always been water, from a fountain or spring if they can get it, as they rarely fail to do. When they are well provided they will occasionally drink grape juice with fresh meat or fish, if it is in season. They drink the juice fresh and never turn it into wine. Beer, brandy, or strong liquor are unknown to them, except to those who frequently move among our people and have learnt that beer and wine taste better than water. The Indian languages are varied and very rich, yet none has a word denoting drunk. Drunkenness they call madness, and to drunken men they refer as fools, such as those few who associate often with our people or are otherwise able to obtain liquor, for most of them have no taste for liquor at all. In order to prevent insolence, the government has forbidden the sale of strong liquor to them. They drink greedily in getting drunk and are then quite difficult and virtually, as the saying goes, *sint felten in specie*.[1] Before they become accustomed to it [alcohol], they are easily made drunk, a small beer or two being enough to do it. But in time they learn to tolerate liquor equally well as the Hollanders do. Gout, podagra, pimply and red noses or similar snares are unknown amongst them, as are drink-related accidents.

Their food is normally fish and meat of every kind, depending on the time of year and the locality where they happen to be. They have no pride or particular fashion in preparing and serving these, and cook fish or meat simply in water without any herbs, salt or lard, other than may be naturally present in it. They are also ignorant of stewing, braising, baking, frying, etc., and rarely heat or grill anything, unless it be morsels of meat and small fish when traveling or hunting and having to make do. For bread they use maize, or Turkish corn; mills being unknown to them, their women beat or pound it, as the Hebrews did their manna in the wilderness, and bake cakes of it. They will also add the grits to meat, to make a broth, the way some use barley or rice here. But their common fare, for which this corn is most often used, is porridge, known locally as samp. Its use among the Indians is so general that rarely a day passes without their eating it, unless they are traveling or hunting, and one can hardly ever enter an Indian dwelling or this porridge is being eaten or prepared. All of them, including women, children, and old people, are so attached and accustomed to it that when they visit us or each other they first of all ask and look for it. Without samp one cannot really entertain them properly, nor can they, so it seems, eat their fill. They will often cook it together with meat or fish when available, mostly not fresh, but dried and pounded into meal. They generally do this towards the end of winter and the approach of spring when the hunting season is past and their stock of provisions is nearly exhausted. They also eat a lot of beans which they consider a delicacy when boiled with fresh meat in plenty of water. Further they take as food and sustenance all sorts of meat, fish, and fruit which the country yields and they can obtain. They do not observe customary or fixed meal times as our people usually do, and judge it best to eat when they are hungry. They have tremendous control over their appetite, stomachs, and bodies, so that they can get by with very little for two, three, or four days. When supplies are ample once again they will quickly make up for the loss or delay, yet this does not upset their stomachs or make them ill. Though all of them are stout trenchermen, no gluttons are to be found amongst them. Ceremonies of seating at the upper or lower end of the table, being the first or last to fall to or to be served or waited upon, I have not been able to notice. Except on the major festivals, they very seldom invite one another, but those under their roof when meal time comes around will be served as well. No one is passed over and it is not their custom to accept payment. Exceptional treats for their guests are beaver tails, fatty meat, rockfish heads, and roasted corn pounded into meal with high-fat gravy poured over it. Also chestnuts boiled for a while, shelled, crushed, and prepared by stewing in gravy and fat.

When they intend to go on a long journey to hunt or to wage war, and know or surmise they will not find supplies, they provide themselves with parched meal made of roasted corn. Such meal goes so far and is so nourishing that a small bag lasts them for many days. Less than a quarter of the contents is used up in a day, because it is so concentrated and swells out again when moistened. They carry the little parcel with them and when hungry they take a small handful from it and drink some water and feel themselves well enough looked after to carry on for another day. But if they can get some meat or fish to go with it, the corn meal serves them as a substitute for fine bread as it needs no baking.

Of the Dress and Ornaments of Men and Women

Most of them wear the same kind and shape of clothing and are not showy or luxurious in that respect, except for some young lads who soon forget about it when they grow older. The women, however, are much more inclined to adorn and decorate themselves than the men are, though they do not go to nearly the lengths seen in this country. The young males up to twelve or thirteen years of age go about quite naked; the girls generally cover themselves as soon as they begin to walk. Around the waist they all wear a belt made of leather, whalefin, whalebone, or wampum. The men pull a length of duffel cloth—if they have it—under this belt, front and rear, and pass it between the legs. It is over half an ell [35cm] wide and nine quarter-ells [155cm] long, which leaves a square flap hanging down in front and at the back. It suits them well, is quite comfortable and also airy in summer when they often wear nothing else. It covers their nakedness and hence bears the name of loin cloth. Before duffel cloth was common in that country, and sometimes even now when it cannot be had, they took for that purpose some dressed leather or fur, cut it like such a cloth and made it fit. Our people everywhere refer to it by the vulgar name of *clootlap* [breech cloth], which word may appear unseemly to some in this country, but this shows that words simply have their usage, and in that country it is such that the word does not offend the ear of delicate women and maids. The women also wear a length of woolen cloth of full width [165cm] and an ell and a quarter [90cm] long, which comes halfway down the leg. It is like a petticoat, but under it, next to the body, they wear a deerskin which also goes around the waist and ends in cleverly cut pointed edging and fringes. The wealthier women and those who have a liking for it wear such skirts wholly embroidered with wampum, often worth between one and three hundred guilders. As covering for the upper part of the body both men and women use a sheet of duffel cloth of full width, i.e., nine and a half quarter-ells, and about three ells [210cm] long. It is usually worn over the right shoulder and tied in a knot around the waist and from there hangs down to the feet. By day it serves them as a cloak and by night as a bed and a blanket. Men's and women's stockings and shoes are of deer or moose skin, which some decorate richly with wampum, but most wear it as it comes. Some of them also make shoes out of corn husks, but those do not last. A few now buy their stockings and shoes from our people and that appears to suit them best. The men mostly go bareheaded and the women with uncovered hair which is tied at the back of the head and folded into a tress of about a hand's length, like a beaver tail. Over it they draw a kerchief, often exquisitely worked with wampum. When they want to appear rather splendid and lovely they wear around the forehead a strap of wampum shaped like the headband that some believe was worn in olden times. It holds the hair neatly together, is tied in a bow to the tress behind and so makes quite a graceful and lively show. Then around the neck they wear various trinkets mostly made of wampum and regarded by them as very fine and elegant, as pearls are among us. They also wear bracelets of wampum around the wrists and prettily wrought figures on the chest which is halfway and not closely covered. Many of them drape beautiful girdles of wampum around the waist and wear fine little ornaments through the earlobes. The women and maids, [even] when they are decked out at their finest and smartest, paint their faces little or not at all, except for a small black beauty spot here and there, and maintain a very stately, quiet, steady, and yellowish mien from which all playful coquetry seems to have been banished, more so than it really is. The men are painted all over, though mostly the face, in all kinds of vivid colors so that when one is not accustomed to seeing them thus, one does not recognize them. And when it is parade time they look so stately, proud, and self-possessed that they will scarcely deign to turn their heads. Some wear in addition a circular headdress of very long and fine deer hair, dyed red, rather like the haloes that used to be painted over the heads of saints, and which looks very handsome. They further have short plaits of very fine and shiny hair hanging over the chest. When a young fellow is dressed up like that he is almost too haughty to open his mouth. They rarely adorn themselves to that extent, however, with the exception of a few maidens in the flower of their years. At other times all of them are by nature dirty and careless of their persons. In winter when it is cold the women and children especially do not often leave their shelter. As was mentioned, they cover themselves with duffel cloth and some wear it folded double. They further arm their bodies against the cold with bear and raccoon fat which they rub on the skin, and by wearing a jerkin and sleeves of bear skin. They also have clothes made of the skins of weasels, bears, deer, and moose in which they can withstand the winter quite comfortably. In a word, they have the necessary clothing to cover their bodies and withstand the cold, yet they also know how to dress up for show or for formal occasions. White linen used to be unknown to them, but many are now beginning to look for shirts and buy them from our people; they tend to wear the shirts without washing until worn out.

Their Houses, Castles, and Settlements

Their houses are mostly of one and the same shape, without any special embellishment or remarkable design. When building a house, large or small,—for sometimes they build them as long as some hundred feet, though never more than twenty feet wide—they stick long, thin, peeled hickory poles in the ground, as wide apart and as long in a row as the house is to be. The poles are then bent over and fastened one to another, so that it looks like a wagon or arbor as are put in gardens. Next, strips like split laths are laid across these poles from one end to the other. On large houses the strips below are laid rather closer together than on the roofs, and upwards in proportion until they are a foot or so apart. This is then well covered all over with very tough bark. For durability everything is peeled, so that no worms can get in it. Then they go out and get the bark of ash, elm, and chestnut trees; if it is late in summer, rather than peel those, though they need the

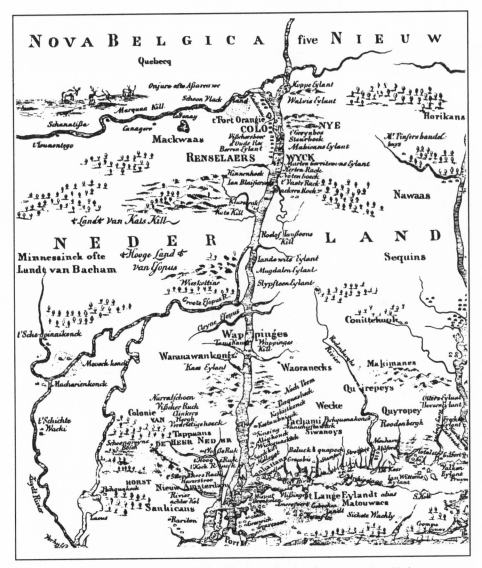

4. Detail from the van der Donck (1968:facing iv) *Map of the New Nether-lands, With a View of New Amsterdam, A.D. 1656.* Van der Donck was the first to show the Mohawk villages of t'Iounontego, Schanatissa, Canagero, and Carenay, all on the south side of the river. The map was already out of date, for other sources make it clear that the Mohawks had consolidated themselves into only three villages at least a decade earlier. The Mohawk details on the map were copied repeatedly by cartographers such as Visscher and Homann until 1710.

bark, they take yew trees that grow near the waterside, whose bark yields easily even when the others are dry. With such pieces of bark of about a fathom square, the smooth side turned inward, they cover the entire wooden frame, [the members of which are] up to a foot apart near the top, as has been stated, and tie the bark down securely where needed. If there is a hole or tear in the bark they know how to plug it up, and against shrinking, they let the [sheets of] bark overlap one another. In sum, they arrange it so that their houses repel rain and wind, and are also fairly warm, but they know nothing about fitting them out with rooms, salons, halls, closets, or cabinets. From one end of the house to the other along the center they kindle fires, and the area left open, which is also in the middle, serves as chimney to release the smoke. Often there are sixteen or eighteen families in a house, fewer or more according as the houses are large or small. The door is in the middle, and the people on either side. Everyone knows his space and how far his place extends. If they have room for pot and kettle and whatever else they have, and a place to sleep, they desire no more. This means that often a hundred or a hundred and fifty and more lodge in one house. Such is the arrangement of a house as they commonly are found everywhere, unless they are out hunting or fishing, then they merely put up a makeshift. In the villages and castles they always do solid and good work. As sites for their castles they tend to prefer, if possible, a high or steep hill near water or a riverside, which is difficult to climb up and often accessible on one side only. They always take care also that it is flat and even on top. This they enclose with a very heavy wooden stockade constructed in a peculiar interlocking diamond pattern. First they lay a heavy tree along the ground, sometimes with a lighter one on top, as wide and as broad as they intend to make the foundation. Then they set heavy oak palisades diagonally in the ground on both sides, which form a cross at the upper end where they are notched to fit tighter together. Next another tree is laid in there to make a very solid work. The palisades stand two deep, sufficiently strong to protect them from a surprise attack or sudden raid by their enemies, but they do not as yet have any knowledge of properly equipping such a work with curtains, bastions, and flanking walls. They also build some small forts here and there on the level and low land near their plantations to shelter their wives and children from an assault, in case they have enemies so nearby that they could be fallen upon by small parties. They think highly of their forts and castles built in that fashion, but these actually are of little consequence, and cause them more harm than good in war with the Christians. In such a castle they often put twenty or thirty houses, up to a hundred feet and some even longer, like those measured by our people at up to 180 paces. Seeing that they manage with so little space in these castles, as related above, they cram such a multitude of people inside that it is unbelievable and leaves one amazed when he sees them come out. Besides these castles they have other settlements that lie in the open in the manner of villages. Most of them have the woods on one side and their corn fields on the other. They also have settlements at some places near waterways where they are accustomed to do much fishing every year, and at the same time do some planting, but those places they leave toward winter and go to live in the castles or in the deep woods where it is warm and firewood is close at hand. There as well no wind can trouble them, and they have good opportunity for hunting, by which they nourish themselves in place of fishing. They seldom abandon their secure castles and large settlements completely; otherwise they find it very easy to pack up and move. They seldom remain long in one place, but follow the season and time of the year. That is, in the summer, when the fishing is good, they move to the watersides and rivers; in the autumn and winter, when meat is best, they seek the woods. Sometimes, but mostly in the spring, they go in droves to the sea shore to eat oysters and to stock up on all kinds of shellfish, which they know how to dry and preserve for a long time.

Ways of Marriage and Childbirth

Having treated of bodily shape and care, dress and ornaments, and described the communal dwellings, we shall now indicate the sequel, without which all that was related before would come to naught, that is, marriage and its consequences. Since it is the only sustenance and continuation of all the world, no nation is to be found anywhere so primitive that does not benefit from its effects and has not retained some of its features. In New Netherland, among the original natives (for among our people it is the same as at home), one can still just perceive the early traces of marriage, but if this is to be improved it must be done soonest. The words man and wife, father and mother, sister, brother, uncle, aunt, niece, nephew, married and single are well known and customary among them, and this is a sure sign, even if no other evidence or more direct proof could be furnished, that something resembling marriage exists. To speak more clearly, the Indians do marry, and usually but one wife, except for chiefs or rich and powerful persons, who may have two, three, or four wives at the same time, generally of the hand-somest and most diligent. It is remarkable that they, guided only by the light of nature, so manage their womenfolk that one never hears, or can learn on inquiry, that any hatred, quarrel or discord prevails among these women, or arises over the upbringing of the children, domestic affairs, and preferences regarding the husband, in which respect they follow his pleasure alone. Weddings are not nearly as ceremonious as among decent people in this country, and the 'every-man' of the Indians can have it as casual as he likes. They observe no definite marriageable age and judge this by competence alone, which they are not loath to try out beforehand. The marriages of young folks who are friends or are ac-quainted through mutual friends are normally arranged with the latter's knowl-edge and advice, having regard to family and standing, but in the case of wid-owed or separated persons, of whom there are many, it is not usual to involve friends. The men, according to wealth and condition, must always present some gift or tribute to their future bride, like the wedding coin of old or token of their mutual pledge. Yet if a widow and widower were married without the counsel of friends and they afterwards disagree, or one of them is unfaithful, or some other misunderstanding arises, the husband may take back his gifts and deny his bed to his wife, and if she does not leave by herself, turn her rudely out of doors. For

among the Indians no marriages are so firm and binding that they cannot be dis-
solved at once and completely by one or both parties whenever the wife or husband misbehaves or some misunderstanding causes discontentment. It is indeed
in those parts a common and usual occurrence, so much so that I have known
men who habitually changed wives every year, sometimes for little or no reason.
One sees as well that when a marriage breaks down or marriage partners are
changed, it is the husband's doing more often than the wife's. In a divorce the
children stay with the mother; many nations reckon descent accordingly, also for
greater certainty. All the same, the longer the spouses stay together and keep
their marriage vows, the more laudable and honorable that is held to be. During
marriage, prostitution and adultery are considered most disgraceful, particularly
among the women, who would sooner face death than consent to it. Viler still
they think it when done by the light of day or in the open fields where someone
might watch or the sun shine on it and, so they say, see it. No man will keep his
wife, however much he loves her, when he becomes aware of such conduct. If
the woman is single or otherwise unattached, however, it does not matter and she
may do as she pleases, provided she accepts payment. Free favors they regard as
scandalous and whore-like, but they are not blamed for what else may happen to
them, and no one will scruple later to propose marriage to such a woman. It also
happens that a free woman cohabits with someone for a time so long as he satis-
fies her and gives her enough, whom she would nevertheless not want to marry.
They are actually proud of such liaisons and will in later years boast of having
slept with many chiefs and brave men. I was amazed to hear how sedate and
steady women, of the worthiest among them, thought highly of themselves when
speaking of such conduct on their part as if it were praiseworthy and glorious.
When a girl reaches marriageable age—they speak of 'ripe'—and, still being
single, is desirous of marrying, she covers head, face, and body all over, leaving
no skin exposed, as a sign of her purpose. Then someone will soon present himself and propose to her. That is the usual procedure over there, even for girls
who in any case have enough suitors, but yet wish to proceed in that manner in
order to make their intentions known to everyone and so likely improve their
prospects, seeing that the menfolk rarely propose in vain. When pregnant,
whether in or out of wedlock, they guard very carefully against anything that
could injure the unborn child. They rarely experience bad or painful days during
pregnancy. When their time is near, which they estimate fairly closely, and they
fear heavy labor or it is their first confinement, some of them take a potion of
local roots and herbs. They then commonly go into the woods, though it be in the
depth of winter, where they give birth unaided. For this they prefer a quiet, sheltered spot near running water, where they put up a simple hut or screen of mat-
ting and the like, having brought some provisions with them. If the child is a boy
they immerse it straightaway in the nearby streamlet and leave it there for some
time, even in freezing weather. The child must be hardened from the first, they
say, so as to grow up a brave man and a good hunter. Then they dress the infant
and wrap it in warm fur clothing, and keep a close watch on it lest it die accidentally. After spending a few more days in that place they return to their home and

friends. It is curious that confinement causes them no illness or any lasting indisposition, nor do they die in childbirth. The reason given by some is that they have less knowledge of good and evil than we have and are also less sinful, since labor pains are not natural, but are a punishment for sin imposed on the first mother. Others hold that it is due to the wholesome climate, their well-formed bodies, and their mostly primitive state.

Of Suckling, and the Relations between Men and Women

It is unknown in that country for women to have their children breast-fed or nursed by others. They all, of whatever rank, do so themselves. This is true in and around New Amsterdam to a distance of a few days' travel, but I have heard that farther inland some women are not so particular. While suckling or with child, the women will not consort with men, simply for the reason they themselves give, that it would harm the infant or unborn child. They do not object, however, to the husband seeing another woman, but as for themselves, they keep strictly to their rule and consider it shameful and defamatory for any woman to do otherwise. Nor do they see this as a reason for weaning their children early, as they normally continue breast-feeding for a year. During their monthly period as well, they are averse, distant, and shy, keep apart and rarely appear or let themselves be seen by men. Only if it comes upon them during some festivity, meeting, or social occasion will they stay on if at all possible, rather than leave and return when it is over. At other times, though, when all is well and they are unattached, they make light of their virtue, both men and women being extremely liberal and uninhibited in their relations. But foul and improper language, which many of our people think amusing, they despise. Kissing, romping, pushing, and similar playful frolicking, popularly known as petting, and other suggestive behavior one is unlikely to see among these people. They speak scornfully of it when done in their presence. And if they see Hollanders behaving in that fashion they tell them sarcastically: "Shame on you; if you are so inclined, wait till nighttime or you are alone." Could anything be funnier? Yet at the right time they will decline no proposition, and almost all of them are available and ready to carry on with abandon. Some, like chiefs and prominent persons, having two or more wives, will readily accommodate a visiting friend with one of their wives for a night, but if it happens without their knowledge they resent it and repudiate the woman or, as they say, send her packing.

Ways of Burial, Lamentation, and Mourning

When someone among the Indians departs this life, all around take great care in committing the dead body to earth. Even though the deceased was a complete stranger, having no friends or relations there and hardly known to anyone, they do not neglect the usual ceremonies. If he was a person of some standing they observe the same customs, with variations according to his position. During the terminal illness they all give faithful support, but once the soul has parted from the body, it is the nearest relations who come to straighten the limbs and shut the eyes. After a few days and nights of vigil and lamenting, they carry the corpse to the grave where they do not lay it down, but seat it supported by a stone or block of wood as if sitting in a chair. Then they place money, a pot, kettle, dish, and spoon with some provisions next to it in the grave in case, they say, the departed has need of it in the other world. Next they stack as much wood around the corpse as will keep the earth away from it, and over the grave they build a great mound of wood, stone, and earth with a wooden palisade on top like a little house. All the places of burial are secluded and held to be sacred, and it is to them a serious offense or villainy to disturb, damage, or desecrate such places. The nearest relations, chiefly the women, observe a set period of lamentation. They call out the name of the departed with hideous howling and strange gestures, beat their chests, scratch their faces, and display every bodily sign of mourning. When a mother has lost a child her lamenting exceeds all bounds, for she wails and rants whole nights through as though she were stark mad. If the deceased died young or fell in war the lament is adapted to it. The mourners shave their heads and burn the hair on the grave at a specific time in the presence of relations. In sum, they are much affected and dismayed by someone's passing, particularly if they were related or close to that person. In order to put the mourning and grief behind them the sooner and avoid distressing the deceased's relations, those of the same family and neighborhood dislike having the bereavement mentioned, recounted, or asked after and feel that doing so is meant to hurt and grieve. Mourning attire is not usual, other than by relations, and then only in the form of a few black markings on the body. When a woman's husband dies, however, she shaves her head and blackens her whole face, as a man does when his wife dies, and wears a deerskin dress next to the skin. They mourn and do not re-marry for more than a year and even if they were recently married or had not been happy together they observe these ceremonies strictly.

Their Festivities and Special Gatherings

Feasts and big meetings are not regular events among them, but are sometimes held to deliberate concerning peace, war, contracts, alliances, and agreements. Also, to consult the devil on some future matter or outcome, or on the crops and the productiveness of the season; or else to rejoice over a success with dancing, and merriment. Peace or war with neighbors and surrounding nations are not decided in haste or by the few, but debated in all their councils. There, persons of some authority are free to state their opinions at such length and as amply as they please without anyone interrupting them, no matter how long the speech or whether it goes against the mood of many. But if they fully approve of what is said they voice their acclamation towards the end of the address. The councils always meet before noon and do not normally continue beyond noon. If no conclusion is reached by then they resume in good time in the morning. When they plan to practice witchcraft, however, and conjure the devil to reveal the future, as is their way, the meeting takes place in the afternoon towards evening. Some of their number are wonderfully able to consort with the devil and perform great magic, or so at least they make the common people believe. They begin by jumping, shouting, ranting, and raving as though they were mad and possessed, light big fires and dance around, beside and right through them. They tumble and roll head over heels, beat themselves and perform such queer pranks that they break out all over in a sweat that trickles down their bodies. With such sickening behavior and grimaces they seem to have become devils themselves, so that it is horrible to see for someone not used to it. When properly in a trance, the devil charmers start a dismal jabbering and howling, and scream at one another as if demon-possessed. After this has gone on for a while the devil appears to them, so they say, in the shape of an animal; if a ferocious animal, it is a bad omen; a harmless animal is better. The apparition tells them strange things in reply to their questions, but seldom so clear and detailed that they can rely on it or fully comprehend it. They learn or appear to learn something from it and grope for the meaning, like a blind man reaching for an egg. If the matter turns out differently it is their fault not to have understood. Sometimes they read more into the message than it contains. Any Christians who may be present can observe the hubbub, but while they are there the devil will not make an appearance. The sorcerers can cast a spell on some of the common folk so that the subject foams at the mouth as if possessed, in a way not otherwise seen, for he throws himself into the glowing hot fire without feeling it. After a while someone whispers in his ear and he is once again as quiet and meek as a lamb. To celebrate some or other success or to dance they assemble in the afternoon. First a spokesman explains the matter, then food is served, as may also be done following a council meeting. They are hearty eaters and everyone consumes so much that it ought to last them for three days. Nothing must be left over; food not eaten there is to be taken home or fed to the dogs. When they have gorged themselves so fully they can only move their flushed heads, the old and staid have a smoke to round off the feast, while the young and not-so-young take to singing, skipping, and dancing, often the whole night through.

How Human Beings and Animals First Came to That Country

Various arguments are put forward when one undertakes to investigate how those we now call savage people first came to that part of the world which seems always to have been separated by the ocean from the other three continents. Some say they were settled there, but others ask by whom and how did lions, bears, wolves, foxes, snakes, and other vermin get there? No one would carry such creatures in ships for the purpose of transplanting them. When discussing the creation with the Indians, we have never been able to satisfy them or give them answers they believed. Many think, with reference to an unknown chronicler, that long ago in legendary times a group of people sailed well equipped from parts of Sweden and Norway to look for a better country, led by a chief named Sachema, and that it has never been determined where they ended up. And since all the chiefs in New Netherland who live by waterways and seashores are known as Sachemaes it is concluded that they descend from those settlers. That conclusion is not easy to accept, but the matter remains puzzling. Others advance the view that the people of that part of the world did not originate with Adam and that a separate creation of humans and animals took place there. Many reasons are given purporting to prove that no Deluge passed over those lands which are represented as a completely new world that differs in all respects from the old. That is true enough, but from another perspective. The same persons also trouble their heads over the question whether on Doomsday when all the world ends, the new world also will be judged. They argue some of the population being of recent date and the greater part innocent, that portion of the globe is not so accursed and defiled by sin and therefore will not incur the same just punishment as the more sin-laden rest of the world. Then there are some who say that most probably in ages past the sea between Cape Verde and America may have been so narrow, even narrower than between Calais and Dover, that people and animals were able to cross from Africa to America by way of the islands. That is hard to believe; but if not there, they add, it was elsewhere. The latter seems to us the best-advised view, the more so as certain studies show that the Chinese visited Brazil and that along the indented shore of the Strait of Magellan or somewhere on the other side of America, a narrows or contiguity of land existed. For the peopling of America must necessarily have happened by migration and not by creation, or the very foundation of Scripture would be ruined. Those of a contrary opinion ask, if America could actually be seen from Cape Verde or thereabouts, did Petrus Columba [Christopher Columbus?] and Americus [Amerigo Vespucci?] discover what had never been lost? To pursue those disputes is not to our purpose, however, and we leave everyone his freedom to judge and to write more on the subject.

Of the Different Nations and Languages

The variety of nations, tribes, and languages in that part of the world is as great as in Europe. Those of one tribe or nation tend to keep together and have a particular chief and their own form of government. There are also higher chiefs, to whom the others submit. All appear to have sprung from one original stock, however. They will not lightly marry into another tribe, for each is jealous of its strength and tries to increase its numbers. Just as tribes, settlements and places have their chiefs, so has every house. He who is the most prominent and respectable of each such community has the authority and eminence. Rank is established correspondingly, though not always observed in practice. Their languages are very diverse and differ as much from one another as Dutch, French, Greek, and Latin. Declension and conjugation resemble those in Greek, for they, like the Greeks, have duals in their nouns and even augments in their verbs. To render their speech in one or other European language is impossible, and they have no taste or inclination for it. Until one makes the effort to learn their language, he understands as little of it as if he heard a dog bark. Some omit to sound the letter R in their language, but others voice it so often that they hardly utter a syllable without it. Apart from that, the pronunciation varies little, and they can mostly understand each other. Their languages can conveniently be divided into four main groups. Though there are appreciable differences between these, the speakers readily manage to communicate. The divisions are: Mahatans, Minquaes, Siavanoo, and Wappanoo. By Matanse are meant those living, in that part [Manhattan], along the North River, on Long Island, in Newesinck [Navesink, N.J.], Achtertoe,[2] etc. The Minquaas are those living far inland, like the Macquaas [Mohawks] and the Sinnekes [Senecas]. The Siavanoos [Delawares] live to the southward, and the Wapanoos [New England Algonquians] reside northeast of us. Their languages are very rarely learnt fully and perfectly by our people, though there are some who by conversing in those tongues over an extended period have reached a point where they can understand and say everything. Not being learned men, however, they are unable to teach others or identify the principles of the language.

Of Money and Their Manufacture of It

That there should be no greedy desire for precious metals in that country no one believes who has ever looked the place over. Yet the use of gold and silver or any other minted currency is unknown there. In the areas which the Christians frequent the Indians use a kind of currency they call zeewant. Anyone is free to make and acquire it, so that no counterfeiters are to be found amongst them. The currency comes in white and black, the black being worth half as much again as the white. It is made of conch shells, which are cast up by the sea about twice a year or taken from it They knock off the thin shell wall all around, keeping only the middle standard or pillar that is surrounded by the outer shell. These they grind smooth and even, and trim them according as the sticks are thick or thin. They drill a hole in each, string them on tough stalks, and file them down to equal size. Finally they restring the sticks on long cords and issue them in that form. This is the only money circulating among the Indians and in which one trades with them. Among our people, too, it is in general use for buying everything one needs. It is also traded in quantity, often by the thousand, because it is made in the coastal districts only and is mostly drawn for spending in the parts where the pelts come from. Among the Hollanders, gold and silver currency also circulate, and in increasing amounts, though as yet much less than in this country.

The Innate Character and the Pastimes of the Indians

The Indians are notably melancholy, unaffected, calm, and of few words. If some few have a different disposition, that does not upset the general rule. The little they do say is long considered, slowly spoken, and long remembered. When buying, trading, or having other business they say no more than is necessary. For the rest they speak of nothing very worthwhile other than concerns their hunting, fishing, and warfare, though the young men will chat to each other about the girls. While not given to gross lies, they are not very careful of the truth or in keeping their word either. Cursing, swearing, and scolding are foreign to them, unless they learnt it by mixing with our people. Surpassing wisdom and outstanding intelligence are not encountered among them, merely a reasonable knowledge based on experience. Nor are they keen to learn or diligent in that respect. Good and evil they are quick to recognize. By themselves they are simple and ignorant, but when they have spent some time among our people they become quite clever and trained for everything. They are dirty, slovenly, and careless, with all the faults arising from it; also most vengeful and headstrong, and unconcerned at facing death if it comes to that. They scorn any pain inflicted on them and take pride in singing until they succumb. Avarice and begging are in their nature, and they must not be entrusted with too much, or they tend to become thievish. Yet they are by no means upset when refused even a trifling request. Strongly independent, they do not tolerate domination. They resent being struck, unless they have done wrong, when they endure it passively. Delicacies in food and drink do not tempt them. Cold, heat, hunger, and thirst they bear remarkably well, and they disregard hardship. From the youngest age they swim like ducklings. Outdoors, they spend their time fishing, hunting, and making war; at home, they relax, smoke a pipe, frolic in the brook, or play with reeds, which is to them as keeping company and card playing are with us. Grown old, they knot fishing nets, and carve wooden bowls and spoons. The men do no regular work; such work as needs to be done falls to the women.

Their Bodily Care and Medicine

They incur no expense whatever and dislike medication and purgatives. When something ails them, fasting is their cure and if that does not help they go into a sauna and sweat it all out. They do this mainly in the mild season of the year, and may drink some potion with it, though very little. The sauna is made of clay, let into the ground, fully enclosed and fitted with a small door through which they can just pass. They heat a quantity of pebbles and shove them in, all around the sides. Then the patient sits down in the middle, quite naked, cheerful and singing, and endures the heat as long as he can. Emerging, he lies down in cold spring water. This method benefits them greatly, they declare, and is a sufficient remedy for various ailments. Fresh wounds and dangerous injuries they know how to heal wonderfully with virtually nothing. They also have a cure for lingering sores and ulcers. They can treat gonorrhea and other venereal diseases so easily as to put many an Italian master to shame. They do all this with herbs, roots, and leaves from the land, having medicinal properties known to them, and not made into compounds. Of course, nature assists them greatly, because they do not eat and drink to excess, else they could not accomplish so much with such limited means. When someone falls seriously ill and may die, all of them or their nearest relations only resort to conjuring the devil, and make noise enough to dispatch at once a person who is at death's door. Actually, as they would have us believe, the devil is supposed to reveal whether the patient will live or die; also, what remedy must be used to get him back on his feet, in cases where there is hope of recovery. They seldom receive a clear answer, however, and must apply some remedy anyway. If there is hope, the patient is straightaway served food which he is persuaded to eat heartily whether he feels like it or not.

The Farming, Planting, and Gardening of the Indians

The women do all the farming and planting. The men are hardly concerned with it, unless they are very young or very old when they help the women under the latter's direction. They grow no wheat, oats, barley, rye, etc., are unacquainted with plowing and spadework, and do not keep their lands tidy. Grain for bread and porridge they obtain by planting Turkish wheat, or corn, together with assorted beans, as mentioned above.[3] They plant tobacco for their own use, but of a different variety that is not as good as ours and requires less work and looking after. Garden vegetables they have none but pumpkins and squashes, also discussed earlier. Their plots and gardens are not fenced off from the open field and they give little attention to them. Nevertheless they raise so much corn and beans [Turcksche boonen] that we purchase these from them in fully loaded yachts and sloops. They know nothing of manuring, fallow seasons, and proper tillage. The labor they devote to farming is all manual, using small adzes that are sold to them for the purpose. Not much more is to be said of their husbandry; yet they regard their methods as better than ours which, in their view, involve far too much bother, care, and effort than is to their liking.

Special Account of Their Hunting and Fishing

They all have a passion for hunting and fishing, and observe set times of the year for it. Spring and part of summer are given over to fishing, but when the game begins to increase in the woods and the early hunting season approaches, many young men quit fishing. The elderly go on longer, until winter and the main hunting season, but do in the meantime take part to the extent of setting snares. They fish in inland waters, excepting those who live on the coast or sea islands and there enjoy special opportunities. It is done with the seine, pound nets, small fykes, gill nets, and gaffs. They are not accustomed to salting or curing fish, but dry a few for pounding into meal while the fish still smells. In winter, the meal is added to their porridge, as stated earlier. Youths and fit men often go out hunting bears, wolves, fishers, otters, and beavers. Deer are hunted and killed in great numbers in the coastal areas and near river banks, where most of the Christians live. They used to catch deer only in traps or shoot them with arrows; now they also use guns. What they enjoy most is to form a team of one or two hundred, storm across a broad field and bag much game. They also know how to construct game traps of thick poles joined together, having two wide wings in front and narrowing to a throat at the end. Into this they drive a horde of game and slaughter them. In a word, they are clever hunters, well trained to capture all kinds of game in various ways. Beavers are caught far inland—for near us there are not many—mainly by the black Minquaes [Eries?], who are not actually black, but are so called because they wear a black square on the chest. Likewise by the Sinnekes [Senecas], Macquaas [Mohawks] and Rondaxkes [Adirondacks], or French Indians, also known as Euyrons [Hurons]. The Indians set out on the beaver hunt in big parties that are gone for a month or two and meanwhile live on what else they can catch and meal or corn they have with them. They catch as many as 40 to 80 beavers each, and other game like otters and fishers as well. All told, an average of 80,000 beavers per year are caught in this part of the country, not counting moose, bears, otters, and deer. Some people worry that in time all the game may be exterminated, but there is no need for concern; hunting has gone on for many years and the yield is not diminishing. The country is full of lakes, streams, and creeks and its vast expanse stretches as far as the Pacific Ocean, indeed beyond travel and cultivation, so that the animal life in many parts remains undisturbed.

Distinctions of Birth, Rank, and Quality

Social differences among the Indians are not nearly as great and obvious as among us. They say frankly they are unable to understand why one person is so much higher-placed than another, as they are in our estimation. Still, the Indians recognize some as noble born and the others as commoners, and these will seldom marry outside their station. No chief has the power to confer rank; authority and chieftainship are hereditary and continue as long as the chief's family produces persons suited to that rank. A guardian may govern in the name of a minor. The oldest and foremost of the ruling houses together with the supreme chief represent the whole nation. Commissioned rank is conferred in time of war only and on merit without regard to family or standing. Thus the lowliest person can become the greatest military chief, but the rank dies with the person. If his descendants follow in his footsteps, however, they may continue to be accounted noble, and this may well be the origin of the Indian nobility. The nobles themselves esteem their rank highly, though not so much as in this country. The commoners show little respect for rank unless it is accompanied by courage and energy, and then it really counts. Such a person they call Monitto or Ottico by analogy with the devil who is a wizard.

Of Their Warfare and Weapons

The principal order, authority, and structure of command of the Indians is revealed in time of war and matters pertaining to war, but is not so firm that they can maintain platoons, companies, and regiments whenever they wish. They march in separate files and out of step, even when in their best formation. They attack furiously, are merciless in victory, and cunning in planning an assault. If it is a dangerous one they operate by stealth, very quietly, and under cover of darkness. They will always attempt to ambush and deceive the enemy, but face to face on a plain or water they are not particularly combative and tend to flee in good time, unless they are besieged, when they fight stubbornly to the last man as long as they can stand up. Captives are not ransomed, nor can they be certain of their lives before they are handed over to someone who had previously lost a bosom friend in war. They will seldom kill women and children in the heat of the attack and never afterwards. Instead, they take away with them as many as they can capture. The women they treat as their own and the children are brought up as though born amongst them, in order to strengthen the nation. They all fight as volunteers and are not retained in regular service by pay. They cannot pursue a campaign strategy or conduct a siege for very long. The men will not lightly divulge a planned attack to us, but they do tell their womenfolk, and no sooner do these learn of it than they make it known to the Christians (for whom they generally have a liking) if they reckon the action may hurt them. When some undertaking is being planned or an approaching danger feared the women and children are removed to places of safety until the attack has taken place or the danger has passed. Their weapons used to be, always and everywhere, bow and arrow, a war club on the arm and, hanging, from the shoulder, a shield big enough to cover all of the body up to the shoulders. They paint and do up their faces in such a manner that they are barely recognizable even to those who know them well. Then they tie a strap or snake skin around the head, fix a wolf's or fox tail upright on top and stride as imperiously as a peacock. Nowadays they make much use in their warfare of flintlock handguns which they learn to handle very well, prize highly, and spare no money to buy in quantity at high prices from the Christians. With it they carry a light ax in place of the war club and so they march off.

Of Their Administration of Justice and Penalties

The proper pursuit, order, and administration of justice, as they ought to be exercised to protect the virtuous and punish the wicked, do not exist among these people or at any rate to such small extent that the Hollanders out there, observing the proceedings with concern, are amazed that a human society can remain in existence where no stronger judicial authority prevails. All personal misdeeds such as theft and related crimes, adultery, lechery, lying, cheating, false witness, or similar offenses against the law remain unpunished. This goes so far that in my time there I knew of a woman (an unmarried harlot) who did away with her own child and though it was widely known nothing happened in consequence. Also, that someone on several occasions violated women whom he encountered in the woods and other lonely places and nothing was done about it. For the rest, I never heard of any serious transgressions during the nine years I was there, other than theft, which is fairly common among them, though not in large hauls; it may be a knife, an ax, a pair of shoes or stockings, and suchlike. If one catches the thief in the act, one may boldly repossess the item and box his ears, but if the loss is discovered later it must be reported to the chief. He will usually return the article to you and sharply reprimand the thief. Even though the chief punishes his subjects no worse than in words, it is incredible how they fear this and how little mischief is done, by and large much less than in our community with its energetic administration of justice.

Manslaughter and injuries to the person concern the chiefs and the culprit's connections only in so far as atonement can be made. They not only promote this strongly, but will also contribute liberally should the culprit lack the means, as is frequently the case, for manslaughter is not expiated without much money. The closest relative is always the avenger and if he can get his hands on the killer within twenty-four hours he slays him in turn and with impunity. If the killer can avoid capture and death for a while, the avenger is protected by a friend during that time, but after the twenty-four hours have elapsed action is seldom taken. Even so, the killer must flee and stay under cover as friends try to settle the terms of the atonement. These would include that the culprit must keep away from his relations, wife, husband, or children and turn aside should he encounter them. It is rare for any one to be condemned to death, other than prisoners of war charged with infringing the law of nations. Such are sentenced to death by fire and are burned very slowly at the hands and feet, so that it takes as long as three days before the sufferer expires. Meanwhile he does nothing but sing and dance right to the end since to scorn pain and suffering is one of the principal virtues they praise and esteem.

Of the Universal Law of Nations

Of all the rights, laws, and maxims observed anywhere in the world, none in particular is in force among these people other than the law of nature or of nations. Accordingly, wind, stream, forest, field, sea, beach, and riverside are open and free to everyone of every nation with which the Indians are not embroiled in open conflict. All those are free to enjoy and move about such places as though they were born there. Safe conduct is not obstructed and quarter given in time of war is respected, while indefensible sites are spared. They do not break a pact they have concluded, even with enemies, except with great reluctance when compelled to do so either because they have suffered an injustice or by popular demand. State envoys may come and go unhindered, are received with ceremony, and usually seen off with gifts for the people and their ruler. If an envoy is in any way grieved or wronged, it is a grave affront and severe reprisals are taken. When the envoys are unwelcome they confront a somber mien and in the absence of a desire to negotiate the gifts that are normally presented beforehand are not accepted. This shows them that they had better leave sooner than later and, moreover, their lives may be in danger. Were any harm to befall the envoys the only redress is strict retaliation. It may be that their nation is already engaged in other wars or does not feel itself strong enough. In that case they may defer taking action in order to seek help or gain an advantage later, but they will never forget it.

Of the Gifts and Offerings

All their treaties, accords, peace negotiations, atonements, proposals, requests, contracts, and pledges are sealed and sanctioned with gifts and offering. Without these, their acts and promises are not worth much, but when followed or preceded by a presentation, they are regarded as duly executed and attested. That is why an offering is commonly made with each point requested or agreed, the points being represented and remembered by means of wooden sticks that they have with them to that end. While each subject, article, or point is being stipulated, determined, and recapitulated, the person making the request or speech has the offering either before him or in his hand. At the close of the parley he places it before the one for whom it is intended. Matters thus concluded with and among them they will exactly remember and perform to the utmost by all possible means. The offerings they make usually consist of zeewant, pelts, duffel cloth, and munitions of war; very seldom of corn. They are ever ready to conduct business by proffering gifts among themselves and also with our nation, who are not keen on it, however, because the Indians tend to demand too much in return and appropriate what the other party does not give of his own accord. When making a request to one of them or generally, one sends an offering to the respective person or locality. The offering is hung up, the request is put, and those to whom it is addressed examine and deliberate the proposition seriously. If they take the offering the request as made is accepted and consented to, but if it remains where it hangs for over three days the matter is held in abeyance and the petitioner has to alter the conditions or augment the offering or both.

Of the Indians' Government and Public Policy

Public policy in the proper sense they have none, but there is a glimmer of government and something that in broad terms suggests policy. Government is of the popular kind, so much so that it is in many respects defective and lame. It consists of the chiefs, nobles, and the tribal and family elders. Only when military matters are being considered are the war chiefs consulted as well. Those together constitute all there is of council, governance, and rule. They consider everything at great length and spare no time when the matter is of any importance. No particular order of seating, is observed, though when traveling, rank is to some extent recognized in that the worthiest of them walks in front. In case of equal claims, the oldest or the one who is on home ground has precedence, but without noticeable ceremony or compliment. When a matter has been decided in the aforesaid manner the populace is summoned to the chief's house or wherever the council has met. A person gifted with eloquence and a strong, penetrating voice is called upon to speak. He recounts in the fullest detail in a formal address and as agreeably as he can what was deliberated, decided, and resolved. Then there is silence all around, and meanwhile the chiefs try to gain the community's approval of their decisions. If they encounter difficulties they have various means of securing acceptance, for the community usually has to carry out what has been decided, and without its consent they cannot make much progress. Therefore, each of them recommends the matter very particularly and earnestly to the family in which he is foremost. It may happen occasionally during the assembly that the chiefs face impertinent and unseemly behavior by a suspicious, unruly and biased person. Then one of the younger chiefs will jump up and in one fell swoop smash his skull with an ax in full view of everyone. No one will intervene or become involved beyond carrying off and burying the body. This happens but seldom and never without persuasion having been tried first. Yet I have heard from prominent Indians that sometimes a resolution adopted by such means and having only the appearance of upholding the rights of council members is approved, praised, and loudly acclaimed, whereafter it has great force and rarely fails to be given effect.

Their Religion and Whether They Can Be Christianized

They are all heathens, have no particular religion or devotion, and no known idols or images they venerate, let alone worship. When swearing an oath they take as witness the sun, regarded as all seeing. They have great affection for the moon, as governing all growth, yet do not worship or pay homage to it. The other planets they know by name, and through that knowledge and from other signs they are fairly weather-wise. To pray and celebrate holy days, or anything like it, is not known amongst them. They do know something of God, as we shall remark later, and are in great fear of the devil, for he harms and torments them much. When they have been out fishing or hunting they customarily throw a portion of the catch in the fire and say without ceremony, there, devil, eat you that. They appreciate hearing about God and our religion, and during our services and prayers they keep very quiet and seem to pay attention, but in reality they have no notion of these matters. They live without religion and inner or outward devotions; even superstition and idolatry are unknown to them and they follow the dictates of nature alone. For that reason some suppose that they may all the easier be led to the knowledge and fear of God. Only one of the Indian nations has a word for Sunday, which they call *Kintowen*. The oldest among them say that in early times a greater knowledge and fear of God existed, but, they say, because we are unable to read and write and the people are becoming more wicked, the Sunday has fallen into disuse and oblivion. When talking earnestly with them about this, they show some signs of regret, but none of emotion. When one berates them, individually or generally, for some wicked act or speech on the ground that it incurs the wrath of God in heaven, they reply, we do not know that God or where he is and have never seen him; if you know and fear him, as you say you do, how come there are so many whores, thieves, drunkards, and other evildoers among you; surely that God of yours will punish you severely, since He warned you of it. He never warned us, and left us in ignorance, therefore we do not deserve such punishment. Very seldom do they adopt our religion, nor have any particular official measures been resorted to or applied to induce them to do so. When their children are still young it happens that our people take them into the home as servants, and as opportunities arise give them some slight religious instruction, but when they grow to be young men and women, and begin to mix with the other Indians, they soon forget what they never learnt thoroughly, and revert to Indian ways and manners. The Jesuits in Canada have made an effort and led many to the Roman Catholic religion, but because they have no inner inclination towards it or were not properly taught the principles and have regard to appearances only, they easily lapse from the faith and actually mock it. Thus it happened when a certain merchant who still resides amongst us went up to trade with the Indians in the year 1639 and got into a discussion on religion with a chief who spoke French well, which the merchant also understood. After they had downed five or six glasses of wine the chief said, I myself had so far been instructed in religion by your people that I frequently said mass among the Indians; once upon a time the place in which the altar stood accidentally caught fire and the people rushed forward to quench it, but I checked them, saying, the God standing there is almighty and will shortly make the fire go out by itself; then we waited expectantly, but the fire burned steadily on until it had consumed everything, including even your almighty God and all the fine objects around him. Ever since I have disliked religion and esteemed the sun and the moon much more and better than all your gods, for they (the sun and the moon) warm the earth and make the crops grow, and your God cannot save himself from fire. In all that country I know no more than just one person who is an ornament to religion. Nor is it to be expected, so long as the matter is thus suffered to drag, that many Indians will through instruction be led to religion. Public authority ought to become involved and provide for sound teaching of our language and the elements of the Christian religion to their youth in good schools established in suitable localities in that country, so that in due course they could and would teach each other further and take pleasure in doing so. It would take a deal of effort and preparation, but without such measures not much good can be achieved among them. The neglect of it is a very bad thing, since the Indians themselves say they would be happy to have their children instructed in our language and religion.

Of Their Sentiments Regarding Hope of Afterlife

It is cause for great wonder and powerful evidence against all unbelieving freethinkers that these people who are so barbaric and wild, as has been shown, nevertheless are able to distinguish between body and soul, and believe, as in fact they do, the one to be perishable and the other immortal. The soul, they say, is that which animates and rules the body, and from which spring all the virtues and vices. When separated from the body at death the soul travels to a region to the southward so equable one never needs protective covering against the cold, yet not so hot as to be uncomfortable. That is the destination of the souls who were good and virtuous in this life, and where they enjoy everything in abundance, for all things needed are in infinite supply without requiring, any labour. Those who in this life were wicked and evil will be in another place differing completely in condition and qualities from the first, nor will they enjoy anything like the contentment of the virtuous. Whether the body will at some time be reunited with the soul, I have never been able to ascertain from them. I have spoken with Christians who thought to have heard them say so, but I cannot affirm it. When they hear voices or sounds coming from the woods in the dead of night that we reckon were made by a wild animal, they say in consternation, what you hear calling there are the souls of wicked persons who are doomed to wander about and haunt woods and wilderness in the night and at unseasonable times. For fear of them the Indians will not go anywhere at night, unless in a group when they must; otherwise they always take a torch. They are frightened of evil spirits who, they believe, remain intent on hurting and terrifying them. They confess and believe also that the soul comes from, and is given by, God. That is what one may on occasion learn from them when talking in a serious vein with the old and wise; more could perhaps be gotten from them if one knew their language thoroughly. Among the common people or the youngsters one never hears those matters spoken of, but one can nevertheless see the righteousness of God who through the universal light of mankind's nature has made these people understand, recognize, and surmise that the reward for doing good and evil awaits men after this life.

Of the Knowledge of God and the Fear of Devils

Although the original natives of New Netherland are heathens and unbelievers they all know and confess that there is a God in heaven, eternal and almighty. Since God is in the highest degree good and merciful, they aver, and unwilling to hurt or punish any human being He does not concern Himself at all with the ordinary affairs of the world. The devil takes advantage of the scope thus given him, and all that happens to man here below, they believe, the devil disposes, guides, and governs at will. God, or the supreme chief, who dwells in heaven is no doubt much greater and higher than the devil and also has dominion over him, but declines to become involved in all those troubles. When we respond to this by saying that the devil is evil, cunning, and wicked, they frankly admit that to be true and also that he takes great pleasure in directing all matters in as baneful a way as he can. They further maintain that every misfortune, scourge, calamity, and infirmity is inflicted on them by the devil. They express by the general appellation of devil all accidents and illnesses they suffer, for example, in case of an internal disorder they say there is a devil within my body, and if something ails them in an arm, leg, foot, hand, shoulder, or the head they say, pointing to the affected part, there is a devil inside. Since the devil is so malicious and merciless towards them they have no choice but to fear and yet keep on friendly terms with him and sometimes throw a morsel into the fire to please him, as stated above. When we refute those absurdities easily we do so by saying to them that God is omniscient and omnipotent; knows the nature of devils exactly; quietly observes their doings; and will not permit a puffed-up and faithless servant to tyrannize man, who is the most glorious creature of all and made in God's im-

age, provided he duly puts his trust in God and does not forsake His commandments in favor of evil. To that they respond with a weird and fantastic argument:
You Dutch say so, and seen superficially it may seem to be as you maintain, but
you do not understand the matter aright. This God, who is supremely good, almighty, and beneficent, Lord of all heaven and earth and all its host, is not alone
up there in heaven without any company or diversion, but has with him a goddess or woman who is the fairest the eye has ever seen or can see. With this goddess or beauty He passes and forgets the time, being deeply attached to her, and
meanwhile the devil lords it on earth and does whatever he wishes. That conviction is firmly inculcated in them and no matter how far one pursues the argument
and reasons with them, whatever abominable absurdities they resort to, and
whether one checkmates them in debate, in the end they return to the view, like
the dog that licks up its own vomit, that the devil must be served because he has
power to harm them.

Their Thoughts on the Creation and the Propagation of Mankind and Animals in the World

From the younger Indians or those leading an unsettled life and often met with
among our people no certainty or reply concerning this subject is to be had. One
must await a suitable opportunity to discuss it with riper and wiser persons if one
is to get some indication of it. It may happen during serious discourse that they
themselves inquire after our views on the origin of mankind. When we then relate the creation of Adam, in broken language and to the best of our ability, they
cannot or will not understand it in regard to their own nation or the Negroes, on
account of the difference in skin color. As they see it the world was not created
the way we believe it was and as told in Genesis 1 and 2. They say that before
the world and the mountains, humans, and animals had come into existence God
was with the woman who dwells with him, and no one knows when that was or
where they had come from. Water was all there was or at any rate water covered
and overran everything. Even if an eye had existed at that time it could not have
seen anything but water wherever it might have been, for all was water or covered by water. What then happened, they say, was that the aforementioned beautiful woman or idol descended from heaven into the water. She was gross and big
like a woman who is pregnant of more than one child. Touching down gently,
she did not sink deep, for at once a patch of land began to emerge under her at
the spot where she had come down, and there she came to rest and remained.
The land waxed greater so that some areas became visible around the place
where she sat, like someone standing on a sandbar in three or four feet of water
while it ebbs away and eventually recedes so far that it leaves him entirely on dry
land. That is how it went with the descended goddess, they say and believe, the
land ever widening around her until its edge disappeared from view. Gradually
grass and other vegetation sprang up and in time also fruit-bearing, and other
trees, and from this, in brief, the whole globe came into being such as it appears
to this day. Now whether the world you speak of and originally came from was

then created as well, we are unable to say. At the time when all that had been accomplished the high personage went into labor and, being confined, gave birth to three different creatures: the first was in every respect like a deer as they are today, the second resembled a bear, and the third a wolf. The woman suckled those creatures to maturity and remained on earth for a considerable time during which she cohabited with each of the said animals and was delivered a number of times of various creatures in multiple births. Thus were bred all humans and animals of the several kinds and species that can still be seen in our day. In due course they began to segregate according, to the families and species still existing, both from an innate urge and for the sake of propriety. When all those things had thus been disposed and made self-perpetuating the universal mother ascended again to heaven rejoicing at having accomplished her task. There she continues to dwell forever, finding her entire happiness and delight in keeping and fostering the supreme Lord's love for her. To that she is devoted and from it derives her complete enjoyment and satisfaction; therefore, God vouchsafes her his fondest love and highest esteem. Here below meanwhile humans and animals of all the various species that were the result of miscegenation increase and multiply, as does all creation the way we find it still. That is why human beings of whatever condition still exhibit the innate characters of one or other of the three animals mentioned, for they are either timid and harmless in the nature of deer, or vindictive, cruel, bold, and direct in the nature of bears, or bloodthirsty, greedy, subtle, and treacherous like wolves. That all this has changed somewhat now and is no longer obvious or implicit, they attribute to the times and people's guile in disguising it. This, they say, is all we have heard on the subject from our ancestors, and believe to be true; had they been able to write like yourselves they might have left us a more complete account, but they could not. There you have, dear reader, all that I have been able to ascertain and that was worth writing down generally and in detail concerning the folkways of the Indians in New Netherland, including most of what from the beginning individual Christians over there have come to know. Even where it is fantastic and contrary to truth I thought fit to put it simply before you in writing. The wise, as I have heard them philosophize, think and speculate deeply about it and, as the saying goes, know like Virgil how to distill gold from Euvius's dung.[4]

ENDNOTES

1. This is a reference to Saint Valentine, the patron saint of the falling sickness, here a condition related to drunkenness; St. Velten and St. Felten are both attested reflexes of his name. Coupled with the *Bargoens* or thieves' language meaning of *specie* as "strong drink," the expression could be translated as "epileptic from the bottle."

2. Probably a misprint for Achtercol, a settlement along the Hackensack River in New Jersey.

3. In an earlier part of the work, not included in this selection.

4. The name Euvius in this final passage is probably a misprint for the Roman poet Quintus E. Ennius (239-169), sometimes called the father of Roman literature. He was noted for his *Annales,* an epic poem that told the story of Rome from Aeneas to Ennius's own period of the second Punic War. As Ennius's version of Aeneas and the founding of Rome was no match for Vergil's *Aeneid,* the allusion in this passage is clear.

Of the Condition
of the Country of the Iroquois,
and of Their Cruelties

1659-1660

Jérôme Lalemant

Jérôme Lalemant is the presumed author of the relation of 1659-1660, although his name does not appear on the original. The portion reproduced here appears as chapter 2 in the report (JR 45:202-215).

Jérôme was brother to Charles Lalemant and uncle to Gabriel Lalemant. He was born in 1593 and extensively educated in France prior to traveling to Huron country in 1638. He was named superior of the Huron Mission the year he arrived, succeeding Jean de Brébeuf. One of his first acts was to conduct a census of the Hurons, which has since been of great importance to historians and anthropologists. Lalemant supervised construction of the Jesuit residence at Sainte Marie Among the Hurons, beginning in 1639. Lalemant assumed the post of superior of the Jesuits in Canada in 1645, an appointment that required him to move his residence to Quebec. During his first term, 1645-1650, many Jesuits lost their lives and the Hurons were nearly annihilated by the Iroquois. He returned to France in 1650 to plead his case for the missions in Canada. He returned to Quebec in 1651 to serve under his successor, Paul Ragueneau. He was recalled to France in 1656, but was sent back to New France to serve again as superior of the Jesuits in 1659. He served with distinction until 1665 and died in 1673 at Quebec.

Bracketed references to original page breaks and hyphens caused by word breaks in the Thwaites edition have been deleted here.

D.R.S.

WHAT A POET has said of fortune,—that her most customary game is to break scepters, abase crowned heads, and, in rolling her wheel, raise some to the throne by the same movement whereby she casts others down, *Ludum insolentem ludere pertinax,*—and what History teaches us of the overthrow of States, of the downfall of Republics, and of the revolutions that have so often changed the face of the Empires of the Greeks, Persians, Romans, and other nations, may be applied here, *si parva licet componere magnis.*

This blind and fickle dame does not refrain from taking her diversion in Savages' cabins and amid forests, as well as in Kings' palaces and in the midst of great Monarchies. She can play her game everywhere, and everywhere she deals her blows, which in truth are more remarkable when they fall on gold and scarlet than when they strike only States of wood and destroy only towns of bark. But, after all, she causes equal vexation to both classes.

Of the five tribes constituting the entire Iroquois nation, that which we call the Agnieronnons [Mohawks] has been so many times at both the top and the bottom of the wheel, within less than sixty years, that we find in history few examples of similar revolutions. Insolent in disposition, and truly warlike, they have had to fight with all their neighbors,—with the Abnaquiois [Abenakis], who are Eastward of them; on the south, with the Andastogehronnons [Susquahannocks], a people inhabiting the shores of Virginia; with the Hurons on the West; and with all the Algonkin Nations scattered throughout the North. We cannot go back very far in our researches in their past history, as they have no Libraries other than the memory of their old men; and perhaps we should find nothing worthy of publication. What we learn then from these living books is that, toward the end of the last century, the Agnieronnons were reduced so low by the Algonkins that there seemed to be scarcely any more of them left on the earth. Nevertheless, this scanty remnant, like a noble germ, so increased in a few years as to reduce the Algonquins in turn to the same condition as its own. But this condition did not last long; for the Andastogehronnons waged such energetic warfare against them during ten years that they were overthrown for the second time and their nation rendered almost extinct, or at least so humiliated that the mere name Algonkin made them tremble, and his shadow seemed to pursue them to their very firesides.

That was at the time when the Dutch took possession of these regions and conceived a fondness for the beavers of the natives, some thirty years ago; and in order to secure them in greater number they furnished those people with firearms, with which it was easy for them to conquer their conquerors, whom they put to rout, and filled with terror at the mere sound of their guns. And that is what has rendered them formidable everywhere, and victorious over all the Nations with whom they have been at war; it has also put into their heads that idea of sovereign sway to which they aspire, mere barbarians although they are, with an ambition so lofty that they think and say that their own destruction cannot occur without bringing in its train the downfall of the whole earth.

But what is more astonishing is, that they actually hold dominion for five hundred leagues around, although their numbers are very small; for, of the five Nations constituting the Iroquois, the Agnieronnons do not exceed five hundred men able to bear arms, who occupy three or four wretched Villages.

The Onneioutheronnons [Oneidas] have not a hundred warriors; the Onnontagehronnons [Onondagas] and Oiogoenh-ronons [Cayugas] have three hundred each, and the Sonontwaehronons [Senecas], who are the farthest removed from us and the most populous, have not more than a thousand combatants. If any one should compute the number of pure-blooded Iroquois, he would have difficulty in finding more than twelve hundred of them in all the five Nations, since these are, for the most part, only aggregations of different tribes whom they have conquered,—as the Hurons; the Tionnontatehronnons [Petuns], otherwise called the Tobacco Nation; the Atiwendaronk, called the Neutrals when they were still independent; the Riquehronnons [Eries], who are the Cat Nation; the Ontwagannhas [Shawnees in this case], or fire Nation [usually applied to the Mascoutens]; the Trakwaehronnons, and others,—who, utter Foreigners although they are, form without doubt the largest and best part of the Iroquois.

It is therefore a marvel that so few people work such great havoc and render themselves so redoubtable to so large a number of tribes, who, on all sides, bow before this conqueror.

It is true, they have performed some valiant deeds, and have, on certain occasions, distinguished themselves as highly as could be expected from the bravest warriors of Europe. Savages although they are, they still understand warfare very well; but it is usually that of the Parthians, who gave the Romans of old so much trouble, fighting them just as the Savages fight us. The Agnieronnons especially have always excelled in this kind of warfare, and sometimes even in that which demands courage only. They defeated two thousand men of the Cat Nation in the latter's own intrenchments; and, although they were only seven hundred in number, they nevertheless climbed the enemy's palisade, employing against it a counter-palisade which they used, in place of shields and ladders, to scale the fortress, receiving the hail of shot that fell on them from every direction. It is said of them that, while there are no Soldiers more furious than they when they form an army, so there are none more cowardly when they are only in small bands, whose glory it is to break a number of heads and carry off the scalps. Yet they have not failed to demonstrate, on several occasions, that the courage of individuals went even to the point of rashness,—as when one of them passed the night at the entrance to a Huron village, hiding in a dunghill; thence he suddenly emerged at dawn of the following day, like a man risen from the dead, and hurled himself upon the first comer, taking flight again after breaking his head in this most unexpected manner. Two others showed themselves still braver. Under cover of the darkness, they stealthily approached a sentry post, where careful watch was being kept after the manner of the Savages, which is to sing at the top of one's voice all night long. When they had allowed the sentry to shout for a considerable time, one of the two nimbly mounted the sentry post, and delivered a blow with his hatchet upon the first man whom he encountered; then, throwing the other to the ground, he took his leisure to kill him and remove the scalp from his head, as the noblest trophy of his victory. Last year, an Agnieronnon went all alone to war against Tadoussac; he accomplished a journey of two or three hundred leagues, making his way alone by sea and land, to find an Algonkin who was his enemy and whom he killed at last with his own hand, almost in the very midst of the French and of a large body of Savages. It is true, he lost his life in the act; but he lost it in defying them and in making his retreat as if he were walking for pleasure,—a haughtiness that caused his death.

But these traits of bravery are not found in all the Iroquois; knavery is much more common with them than courage, and their cruelty far exceeds their knavery; and it may be said that, if the Iroquois have any power, it is only because they are either knavish or cruel. All the treaties that we have made with them are proofs of their perfidy; for they have never kept a single one of the promises that they have so often and so solemnly sworn to us. And as for cruelty, I would make this paper blush, and my listeners would shudder, if I related the horrible treatment inflicted by the Agnieronnons upon some of their captives. This has indeed been mentioned in the other relations; but what we have recently learned is so strange that all that has been said on the subject is nothing. I pass over these matters, not only because my pen has no ink black enough to describe them, but much more from a fear of inspiring horror by recounting certain cruelties never heard of in past ages.

It is only a neat trick with them to make a cut around the thumb of a captive, near the first joint; and then, twisting it, to pull it off by main strength, together with the sinew, which usually breaks toward the elbow or near the shoulder, so great is the violence employed. The thumb, thus removed with its sinew, is hung to the sufferer's ear like an ear-pendant, or attached to his neck in place of a carcanet. Then they will do the same with a second and a third finger, while, to replace the fingers that have been pulled off, they force into the wounds splinters of hard wood, which cause pains quite different from the foregoing, although excessive, and very soon produce a great inflammation and a huge swelling of the entire hand and even of the whole arm. Even if this first game were all, is it not with reason that the French of this country have so long asked the destruction of so cruel an enemy? since, after all, five or six hundred men are unable to withstand a courageous undertaking, if it be executed in such manner as the glory of God and the compassion due to them demand. The Iroquois have the disposition of women; there are none more courageous when no resistance is offered them, and none more cowardly when they encounter opposition. They deride the French, because they have never seen them wage war in their country; and the French have never done so because they have never made the attempt, hitherto believing the roads more difficult to pass than they really are. With our present knowledge of these barbarians,—having seen, when we were in their midst, how alarm was everywhere felt when they beheld themselves attacked in their own country,—it may be said with full assurance that, if an army of five hundred Frenchmen should arrive unexpectedly, it could say, *Veni, vidi, vici.*

I have stated that there are only five or six hundred men to destroy; for it is beyond doubt that, if the Agnieronnons were defeated by the French, the other Iroquois Nations would be glad to compromise with us, and give us their children as hostages of their good faith. Then those fair Missions would be revived at Onnontagué [Onondaga], at Oiogoen [Cayuga], and in all the other remaining Iroquois Nations, among whom we have already sown the first seeds of the faith. These have been so well received by the common people that we may not, without distrusting the divine Providence, despair of one day reaping therefrom very abundant fruits. Moreover, the great door would be open for so many old and new missions toward the tribes of the North, and toward those newly discovered ones of the West, all of whom we embrace under the general name of Algonquins. But it is a subject of too wide a scope and demands a separate Chapter.

Letter from a Frenchman in Captivity
Among the Agnieronons,
to a Friend of His at Three Rivers

1660-1661

Jérôme Lalemant

Thwaites credits Lalemant with writing the relation of 1660-1661, which was subsequently edited by Paul le Jeune in Paris. The section reproduced here is an unattributed letter from one of several French captives held by the Iroquois during the period (JR 47:86-93). The author of the letter was released along with others, and he was able to deliver his letter himself. Lalemant identifies neither the writer nor his friend. Thwaites (JR 47:315) adds a little biographical information on Louis Guimont and Antoine de la Meslé, both of whom are mentioned in the letter. Neither these endnotes nor the superscripts leading to them have been included here. Bracketed references to original page breaks and hyphens caused by word breaks in the Thwaites edition have also been omitted.

At the time this letter was written, Lalemant was in his second term of appointment as superior of the Jesuits in Canada. The Hurons called Lalemant "Achiendassé." The Hurons subsequently used this personal name for Lalemant as a name for succeeding superiors of the Jesuits of Canada. This is consistent with the Northern Iroquoian custom of imbuing names with some of the meaning of titles and transferring names to successors when their current holders died.

D.R.S.

MY DEAR FRIEND,

I have scarcely any fingers left, so do not be surprised that I write so badly. I have suffered much since my capture, but I have also prayed much. There are three of us Frenchmen here who were tortured in company. We had agreed that, while one of the three was being tortured, the other two should pray for him—which we never failed to do; and we had also agreed that, while the two were praying, the one under torture should chant the Litany of the blessed Virgin, or else the *Ave Maris stella,* or the *Pange lingua*—which was done. It is true, our Iroquois scoffed and hooted in great derision upon hearing us sing in this manner; but that did not prevent us from doing it.

136

They made us dance around a great fire, in order to make us fall into it, they standing about the fire, to the number of forty and more, and kicking us violently from one to another, like the ball in a game of tennis; and, after giving us a severe burning, they put us out in the rain and cold. I never suffered such severe pain, and yet they did nothing but laugh. We pray to God with good courage; and, if you ask me whether I did not lose my patience, and wish ill to the Iroquois who were so maltreating us, I shall answer you, "No," and that, on the contrary, I prayed for them.

I must give you tidings of Pierre Rencontre, whom you knew well. He died like a Saint. I saw him while he was being tortured, and he never said aught but these words: "My God, take pity on me,"—which he repeated continually until he ceased to breathe.

Did you know Louys Guimont, who was captured this Summer? He was beaten to death with clubs and iron rods, receiving so many blows in succession that he perished under them. But yet he did nothing but pray to God, so that the Iroquois, enraged at seeing him constantly moving his lips in prayer, cut away his upper and lower lips entirely. What a horrible sight! And still he ceased not to pray, which so irritated the Iroquois that they tore his heart, still throbbing with life, out of his breast and threw it in his face.

As for Monsieur Hebert, who was wounded with a musket-ball in the shoulder and arm, he was given to the Iroquois of Onneiout [Oneidas], and was there stabbed with knives by some drunken men of the country. As for little Antoine de la Meslée, that poor child moved my compassion deeply; for he had become the servant of these barbarians, and then they killed him too with the knife, when out Hunting.

There are yet many more Frenchmen in bondage, but I write you nothing about them, for I would never finish,—they arrive here almost every day,—and then my fingers give me much pain. We are indeed a pitiful sight to behold, we who are alive; for they think more of their dogs than of us, and we are glad sometimes to eat the scraps left by the dogs. On our way hither, although we all had our feet raw with wounds, our captors nevertheless made us walk barefoot, and loaded us with their entire luggage,—hastening our steps with blows from sticks, as one would drive a horse. Whenever they met any of their own people, they would pull out some of our finger-nails before their eyes, in order to welcome them; but we always prayed to God, and always those barbarians jeered at us. Pray heartily for me, for I sadly need your prayers. Father le Moine is said to be at Onnontagué [Onondaga] for the purpose of making peace, but he will never make peace with the Iroquois of this country; for they say they will not have it, and they regard the French as dogs. Still, one would never believe how few they are—they have at no time amounted to two hundred men, all told, in the country; while their three villages have no palisades, except here and there some stakes as large as one's leg, through which one can easily pass. If Father le Moine could deliver me from this place, he would do me a great charity; and the same can be said of the other Frenchmen here, for we are indeed wretched and worthy of compassion. The Dutch are no longer willing to secure our freedom, as it costs them too dearly; on the contrary, they tell the Iroquois to cut off our arms and legs, and kill us where they find us, without burdening themselves with us. I commend myself to your kind prayers and to those of all our good friends. In saying this last Farewell to them, I cannot refrain from weeping bitterly; for I know not what will become of me.

Notable Embassy of the Iroquois

1663-1664

Jérôme Lalemant

Lalemant was near the end of his service as superior of the Jesuits in Canada when he wrote this chapter to his relation of 1663-1664. The chapter describes an Iroquois embassy sent to Quebec in the spring of 1664. The Iroquois delegates were sent to seek peace and to ask that Jesuits be sent to live amongst them. The French were suspicious of Iroquois motives. Whatever they might have been, the project was ruined by an Algonquin ambush.

The relation contains valuable information on the Mohawks (Agniehronnons) and other Iroquois nations. Their relations with the Mahicans and other Algonquian-speaking nations are also discussed.

The chapter is reprinted essentially as translated and edited by Thwaites (JR 49:136-153). The exceptions are that we have omitted bracketed numbers indicating page breaks in the original and hyphens caused by word breaks at the ends of lines in the Thwaites edition have been omitted.

D.R.S.

SINCE WAR BROKE OUT between the Iroquois and ourselves, we have not yet seen on their part a more solemn Embassy—whether in point of the number and rank of the ambassadors, or the beauty and number of the presents—than that which they despatched last Spring.

Upon investigating the causes of such an extraordinary event, it is not easy to hit on the true one. They proclaim that they wish to unite all the nations of the earth and to hurl the hatchet so far into the depths of the earth that it shall never again be seen in the future; that they wish to place an entirely new Sun in the Heavens, which shall never again be obscured by a single cloud; that they wish to level all the mountains, and remove all the falls from the rivers—in a word, that they wish peace. Moreover, as an evidence of the sincerity of their intentions, they declare that they are coming—women, and children, and old men—to deliver themselves into the hands of the French,—not so much in the way of hostages for their good faith as to begin to make only one Earth and one Nation of themselves and us.

All these words are specious, but for more than five years we have known from our own experience that the Iroquois is of a crafty disposition, adroit, dissembling, and haughty; and that he will never descend so low as to be the first to ask peace from us, unless he has a great scheme in his head, or is driven to it for some very pressing reason.

Some think that the Agniehronnons [Mohawks]—the nation nearest to us and the most arrogant and cruel—ask us for peace because they are no longer in a condition to make war, being reduced to a very small number by famine, disease, and the losses that they have suffered in the last two or three years, on all sides whither they have directed their arms. Quite recently they suffered a bleeding which greatly weakened them. We learn that an army of six hundred Iroquois, the greater part of whom were Agniehronnons, went out to sack a Village composed of certain Savages called Mahingans [Mahicans] or the Wolves. The latter saw that the army which was about to pounce upon them would put the whole place to fire and sword, if it were allowed to approach the Village; and so they resolved to advance against it and take it unawares. They accordingly went out, to the number of a hundred only, and after going two leagues, encountered the Enemy and gave battle. The fight lasted a very long time with great loss on both sides. Nevertheless, superior numbers prevailing, the Mahingans were forced to retire into their Village, leaving the Field of battle to the Iroquois, who found themselves so hardly used in this first engagement that they thought only of retreat. But when they saw such a large number of their men fallen on the spot, they resolved to revenge themselves for this loss, although they should all perish in the attempt. In order not to give the Mahingans time to recover and rally, they set out on that very evening, and at daybreak made the attack on the Village with great fury and frightful yells, as if they had already made themselves masters of the place. The heat of the combat was great on both sides, and the Iroquois lost many men, because they made the assault without taking the precaution to cover themselves, which obliged them at last to retreat, leaving many dead around the Enemy's Village. This check, with some others that occurred at the same time, humbled them greatly, and brought them very low; and that is thought to have been the reason which forced them to come to us and ask for peace. Others think that the Sonnontouaehronnons [Senecas]—the nation farthest distant from us, simplest in nature, and most numerous—asked us for peace in order to be able to make head against the Andastogueronons [Susquehannocks]; these are Savages of new Sweden, very warlike, and better able than any others to exterminate the Iroquois. In order to secure themselves against so redoubtable an Enemy, the Sonnontouaehronnons ask the French to come in large numbers and settle among them. They ask this, hoping that the French will surround their Villages with flanked palisades, and furnish them with the munitions of war,—which they hardly dare any longer to go and obtain of the Dutch, as the Mahingans render the roads very dangerous. Finally, they beg that some black gowns be sent them, to take control of an entire Village of old Huron Christians, and to convert the others. Father Simon le Moyne had already gone to Montreal with this design; he was delighted at being destined to expose his life for the sixth time to the Iroquois; and would be there now, if the Embassy had succeeded.

As for the Onnontaehronnons [Onondagas], some think that they desire peace, others believe that they are far from it; and both may be said to be right. For Garakontié, that famous liberator of the French Captives, has done too much not to wish for peace; on the other hand, there are other families who are too envious and too much opposed to him to suffer him to have the glory of concluding a general peace with the French. Nothing of that sort, however, is apparent; but as the Iroquois are more crafty than is imagined, both the one side and the other may conceal some knavish trick under that fair appearance; and the richer the presents are that they wish to make, the more are they to be mistrusted.

But, without pausing longer to examine the designs of this Embassy, let us see how it succeeded. The Onnontaehronnons, its prime movers, did not wish to expose rashly the most prominent men of their entire country; and so, in order to assure themselves fully in the matter, they sent to Montreal, as early as the month of August, advance couriers, as it were, to sound the way, and find out whether the envoys would be well received there. They appeared, accordingly, above our settlement with a white flag in their Canoe, in order not to be taken for Enemies. Under such protection they landed at Montreal, and made some presents as a declaration that all the Iroquois nations, except that of Onneiouté [Oneidas], asked for peace, and that even the Agnehronnons were thus inclined,—confirming the whole with a letter written to Monsieur de Mesy, our Governor, by one of the prominent men of new Holland, who gave his guarantee of their good faith. This proposition was listened to with joy, but nevertheless with distrust, since at the very moment when they were talking to us of peace, they were making war on us in our Fields, where murders were being committed upon our Husbandmen. Yet, in order not to rebuff them entirely, they were sent back from Montreal with friendly words; and they departed with a resolution to go and hasten the departure of the Ambassadors.

In fact, a short time afterward, Captain Garakontié—who was the soul, as it were, of this enterprise—joined the Sonnontouaehronnons, together with those of his nation; and to this end he made a prodigious collection of porcelain, which is the gold of the country, in order to make us the most beautiful presents that had ever been given us. There were, among other gifts, a hundred collars, some of which were more than a foot in width. They embarked to the number of thirty, laden with these riches; and, in order to be still more welcome, they took with them the two Frenchmen of whom I spoke in the preceding Chapter, to begin their presents by giving these men their liberty.

But their ill luck seems to have accompanied them wherever they went. After they had made some days' journey, our Algonkins, who were waging war in that part of the country, perceiving traces of these Ambassadors, laid an ambuscade for them below the great sault, and, attacking them unexpectedly, put them all to rout. Some were killed on the spot, others were made prisoners, and the rest took flight. As for the two Frenchmen, they sustained the first onset, and had great difficulty in making themselves recognized as Frenchmen by the Algonkins,—who, in the heat of the conflict, throwing aside their guns to take their hatchets, were striking right and left without considering on whom the blows fell. They were finally recognized, but had the grief of seeing that their liberty would cost their liberators their lives or their freedom.

Thus the grand project of this Embassy has vanished in smoke, and instead of the peace which it was bringing us, we have on our hands a more cruel war than before; for the Iroquois would cease to be Iroquois if they did not make every effort to avenge the deaths of those Ambassadors. Perhaps they will dissimulate for some time, if they find themselves too much weakened by their late losses; and then—if they are not either entirely exterminated or put into such a condition that they cannot stir again—sooner or later they will take vengeance on the French, as they did on the Hurons, ten years after having become reconciled with them.

Beyond this, it is very difficult to judge whether this defeat is advantageous or disadvantageous to us. There is much to be said on both sides. In general, we can assert that the great body of the Iroquois do not love us, and that they have a deadly hatred for the Algonkins. Consequently, when we see them so remarkably urgent for making peace with us, we do not doubt that they are afraid of the victorious arms of our triumphant Monarch, and that for once they really fear the plan which he has adopted to exterminate them, learning of it, as they have—partly from new Holland, and partly from some French Captives. And so, seeing themselves within two finger-breadths of total destruction,—famine and disease having begun it; the Andastoguehronnons, Mahingans, Algonkins, and other Savages having advanced it; and the French being interested in completing it, if they undertake it,—feeling, then, in this way the approach of their ruin, they pretend to wish for peace, or rather necessity forces them to wish for it. But they do so to let the storm pass, and to renew the war more vigorously than ever after they shall have evaded this blow, and recovered from the extremity to which divine Providence has reduced them. It is, without doubt, a last punishment for so much opposition which they have offered to the Faith; and it enables our great King to acquire the glory of extending the Kingdom of Jesus Christ by enlarging his own, and of bearing his victorious arms over more than a thousand leagues of very fine territory. Thither our Missionaries will afterward bear the torch of the Faith, and make conquests for Heaven, which will increase the Blessings that God confers upon those conquests which our August Prince is about to make as far as the ends of the world.

Extract from a Letter Written at Quebec on the 22nd of September

Since despatching the Relation by the Ship which sailed from here on the 31st of August, the Onionenhronnons [Oneidas] have come on an Embassy, reaching Quebec on the 18th of September. Its Chief is one of our old friends; he was Father René Menard's host when the latter was Missionary among the Iroquois. They spoke through twenty presents, of which six of the finest were for the Ecclesiastics,—Monseigneur the Bishop of Petræa, and the Fathers of our Society, for whom they ask with urgency to instruct them in the Faith,—and for the Hospital Nuns and the Ursulines, whose kind offices they hope to receive when they shall be sick here, and when they bring their daughters here to receive instruction.

Ten of these twenty presents were for the Algonquins, their old Enemies, with whom they testify their desire to form a friendship which shall never be broken.

They spoke for all the Iroquois Nations except that of Onneiout [Oneidas].

Had we not been often deceived by such Embassies, which have concealed deadly treasons under these appearances of Peace, we might have been deceived in this; but our experiences make us mistrust these faithless Barbarians, even when they trust us implicitly.

To render more lucid the information desired regarding the Iroquois Nations, let it be stated that there are five of them,—forming, as it were, five different Cantons, leagued against their common Enemies.

The Anniehronnons [Mohawks] are the nearest to us, and neighbors to New Holland, where they obtain firearms, powder, and lead; with the Dutch, too, they carry on all their trading.

The Onneiochronnons [Oneidas] are two days' journey farther distant.

The Onnontaehronnons [Onondagas] are still farther away.

The Onionenhronnons [Cayugas] are about three days' journey beyond the last-named tribe.

The Sonnontouehronnons, [Senecas] who are the most populous and have several Villages, are the farthest distant, by about three days' journey.

They are all situated along the great Lake of the Iroquois called Ontario, from 20 to 30 leagues inland.

They are settled in Villages, and till the soil, raising Indian corn, otherwise called Turkish corn. Wheat grows there very well, but they do not use it.

Behind them, farther southward, they have Savage Enemies who for some time past have been making vigorous war on them,—the Nation of the Wolves, the Abnaquinois [Abenakis], allied with New England, and the Andastoehronnons [Susquehannocks], allied with New Sweden.

Thus seeing themselves attacked on both sides, they fear the arms of France, and that with reason.

END

Of the Iroquois Country, and the Routes Leading Thither

1664-1665

François-Joseph le Mercier

Jérôme Lalemant served as superior of the Jesuits of Canada until August 1665, at which time he was succeeded by François-Joseph le Mercier. Le Mercier had been born in 1604 in Paris and had followed a typically Jesuit religious education there. He was ordained in 1633 and spent two more years training as a Jesuit. He arrived in Quebec in the summer of 1635, and within days he was headed for Huronia and service as a missionary under the authority of Jean de Brébeuf.

Le Mercier was called "Chaüosé" by the Huron, and he was uncommonly successful in learning their language. He moved to the new residence at Sainte Marie Among the Hurons after Lalemant had it constructed in 1639, but continued to travel around the Huron villages. Eventually Sainte Marie Among the Hurons became a center for retreats and rest under le Mercier's supervision. Jean de Brébeuf and Gabriel Lalemant (nephew of Jérôme Lalemant) were killed in the spring of 1649 during the Iroquois campaign against the Hurons. Le Mercier and Paul Ragueneau burned Sainte Marie Among the Hurons and fled with the surviving Huron refugees to Christian Island. A year later they fled to safer refuge near Quebec.

Le Mercier was appointed rector of the College at Quebec and superior of the Jesuits of Canada in 1653. However, he left those positions in 1656 in order to join a missionary expedition to Iroquois country. He returned to Quebec the following year and carried out various duties until August 1665, when he was reappointed to his former post as superior. Part of his new mandate was to develop missions among the Ottawas around Sault Ste. Marie. Le Mercier returned to France in 1672. A year later he was sent to the West Indies, where he died in 1690.

Le Mercier wrote his account of the Iroquois country based on his own first-hand experience in 1656-1657, along with information that he had gathered since then. The French were increasing their military presence in the direction of the Iroquois, and in another year de Tracy would conduct his raid against Mohawk villages.

The map of Iroquois country published by Thwaites with this chapter (JR 49:256-267) has been reproduced here as well. Bracketed numbers indicating page breaks in the original relation have been dropped. Hyphens inserted by Thwaites where words were broken at the ends of lines have also been omitted.

D.R.S.

IT MUST BE STATED that the Iroquois are composed of five Nations, of which the nearest to the Dutch is that of Anniegué [Mohawk], embracing two or three villages, which contain perhaps three to four hundred men able to bear arms.

These people have always made war upon us, although they have at times pretended to ask for peace.

Forty-five leagues Westward is situated the second Nation, called Onneiout [Oneida], which has at most only a hundred and forty warriors, and has never consented to any peace parleys, but has always embroiled our relations whenever an understanding seemed to be at hand.

Fifteen leagues farther Westward lies Onnontagué [Onondaga], which has fully three hundred men. We were, in times past, received there as friends, and then treated like enemies; and this treatment forced us to abandon that post—which, as being the center of all the Iroquois Nations, we had occupied for two years, and from which we had proclaimed the Gospel to all those poor people; we were aided by a garrison of Frenchmen sent by Monsieur de Lauson, then Governor of New France, to take possession of those regions in his Majesty's name.

Twenty or thirty leagues thence, still in a Westerly direction, is the village of Oiogouen [Cayuga], containing three hundred warriors. Here, in the year 1657, we had a Mission which, amid this barbarism, formed a Church filled with piety.

Toward the end of the great lake called Ontario is situated the most populous of the five Iroquois Nations, called Sonnontouan [Seneca], and embracing fully twelve hundred men in the two or three villages which compose it.

These last two Nations have never made open war upon us, and have ever maintained a neutral attitude.

This entire stretch of country, to the distance of a hundred or a hundred and fifty leagues, lies partly Southward and partly Westward of the French settlements.

For the most part, this region is fertile and covered with fine woods,—whole forests of chestnut and walnut trees, among others,—interspersed with many lakes and rivers, very rich in fish.

The climate there is temperate, the seasons succeeding regularly as in France, while the soil, in various parts, is adapted to the growth of all the products of Touraine and Provence.

Snow is not deep or lasting, the three Winters which we passed among the Onnontagueronnons [Onondagas] having been mild in comparison with those of Quebec,—where for five months snow covers the earth to the depth of three, four, or five feet.

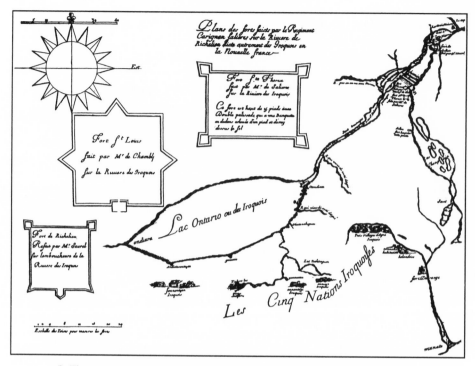

5. *The Iroquois Country* is a map from the Jesuit relation of 1664-1665 (JR
49:facing 266). The map shows the five nations of the League of the Iroquois
and specifies three Mohawk (Agne) villages on the south side of the river.

As we occupy the Northern part of New France, and the Iroquois the Southern,
it is not to be wondered at if their lands are pleasanter, better adapted to cultivation, and productive of fruits of superior quality.

There are two principal rivers leading to the Iroquois,—one to those living
near New Holland, namely, the Richelieu river, of which we shall speak presently; the other leading to the remaining Nations, which are farther from us, by
ascending our great river Saint Lawrence, which, above Montreal, is in a certain
sense divided into two branches, one of them conducting to the former country
of the Hurons, the other to that of the Iroquois.

It is one of the most notable rivers to be seen, considering rather its beauty
than its utility; for there are found, throughout almost its entire course, many
beautiful Islands, some large and others small, but all covered with fine forests.
These Islands are full of deer, bears, and wild cows, which furnish in abundance
the provisions necessary for travelers, who find everywhere such game, and,
occasionally, whole herds of animals of the deer species.

The banks of the river are usually shaded with great oaks and other full-grown
forest-trees, which cover excellent soil.

Before reaching the great lake Ontario, we cross two others, one of which adjoins the Island of Montreal, while the other lies midway on the journey. The latter is ten leagues long by five broad, ending in many small Islands very pleasing to the view, and we have named it Lake Saint François.

But what detracts from this river's utility is the waterfalls and rapids extending nearly forty leagues,—that is, from Montreal to the mouth of lake Ontario,—there being only the two lakes I have mentioned where navigation is easy.

In ascending these rapids, it is often necessary to alight from the canoe and walk in the river, whose waters are rather low in such places, especially near the banks.

The canoe is grasped with the hand and dragged behind, two men usually sufficing for this—one at the prow, and the other at the stern; and as the canoe is very light, being only of bark and unladen, it glides with the greatest ease over the water, and meets with but little resistance.

Occasionally one is obliged to run it ashore, and carry it for some time, one man in front and another behind—the first bearing one end of the canoe on his right shoulder, and the second the other end on his left. One is forced to do this either on account of waterfalls and whole rivers, which sometimes fall straight downward from a prodigious height; or owing to the excessive swiftness of the current; or because, the water being too deep, it is impossible to walk and drag the canoe; or for the reason that one wishes to go across the country from one river to another.

But on gaining the mouth of the great lake, the navigation is easy, the water being calm there, and broadening out,—at first imperceptibly, then becoming about a third wider, afterward more than a half, and finally stretching away farther than the eye can reach. This is especially so after one has passed countless small Islands lying at the entrance to the lake, in such great numbers and variety that the most experienced Iroquois Pilots sometimes lose their way among them, and have much difficulty in recognizing the right course in the confusion and labyrinth, so to speak, formed by these Islands—which, moreover, have nothing pleasing about them but their multitude. For they are nothing but great rocks projecting above the water, and covered only with moss or some firs and other fruitless trees, whose roots spring from clefts in these rocks—which can furnish those barren trees with no other nourishment or moisture than such as the rains are able to supply.

Extricating oneself from this gloomy retreat, one discovers the lake, which appears like a sea, without Islands and without shores, on which barks and ships can sail from one end to the other in perfect safety. Hence communication would be easy between all the French Colonies that could be planted on the shores of this great lake, which is more than a hundred leagues long by thirty or forty wide.

Thence one can go by different rivers to all the Iroquois Nations except that of the Annieronnons, who are reached by way of the Richelieu river; to this stream we can well devote a few words, since on its banks our troops have already erected the three forts mentioned by us.

It is called the Richelieu river, from the fort of the same name that was built at its mouth at the beginning of the wars; it has been quite recently rebuilt, to guard the entrance to that river.

It is also styled "the river of the Iroquois," as it forms the highway leading to them; and by that route those Barbarians have most often come to attack us.

The bed of this river is a hundred to a hundred and fifty feet wide throughout almost its entire course, although it is a little narrower at its mouth. Its banks are clothed with beautiful pines, through which it is easy to walk; and, in fact, fifty of our men made their way on foot there for nearly twenty leagues, from the mouth of the river up to the Falls, so called—although there is really no waterfall there, but merely a swift current, filled with rocks which impede its course and render navigation almost impossible for three-quarters of a league. Yet in time the passage can be freed from obstructions.

As for the rest of the river, it has from its source a very fine bed, in which occur as many as eight Islands before the basin below the Falls is reached.

This basin is a sort of little lake, a league and a half in circumference, and from six to eight feet deep, in which fish are very plentiful at almost any season.

At the right of this basin, going up, one sees fort Saint Louis, very recently erected on that spot; it is an extremely advantageous place for the purpose in view concerning the Iroquois, since its situation renders it well-nigh impregnable, and gives it the command of the entire river.

After passing the rapids of the Falls, which extend for nearly three leagues, one sees the third fort, which marks the end of all these rapids; for thereafter the river is found to be very beautiful and easy to navigate up to the lake called Champlain, toward the end of which one enters the territory of the Annieronnon Iroquois.

Of the Mission of Sainte Marie Among the Iroquois of Agnié

1667-1668

François-Joseph le Mercier

Le Mercier was nearly 64 years old when he wrote thia report. He was still in his second appointment as superior of the Jesuits in Canada. Other details regarding his life are provided in the introduction to his report for 1664-1665.

The report was written by le Mercier in a time of peaceful relations with the Iroquois. He drew upon the written comments of Frémin, Pierron, and Bruyas, and these statements appear as quotations. Missionaries were active among all five Iroquois nations at this time, and the account of the Mohawks (Agnié) is especially detailed. Although Dutch settlements were growing not far from the Mohawks, they were now under English control. The English had conquered New Netherland and renamed the province New York in 1664.

The translated relation reproduced here is taken from volume 51 of the *Jesuit Relations* (JR 51:179-219). Bracketed numbers indicating page breaks in the original manuscript have been dropped here. Hyphens inserted by Thwaites where words were broken at the ends of lines have also been omitted. Endnotes and the superscripted references leading to them have also been omitted, although one useful note is preserved in brackets.

D.R.S.

THE FATHERS Fremin, Pierron, and Bruyas, having set out in July of the year 1667, to go to the lower Iroquois, in order to restore the Missions there which the wars had discontinued; and having been detained a long time in Fort sainte Anne, at the entrance to Lake Champlain, by the fear of a band of Mahingan [Mahican] Savages,—called by us the Loups, who are enemies of the Iroquois,—left this Fort at last, resolved to run the same risks and pass through the same dangers as were to be encountered by the Iroquois Ambassadors, in whose company they were going to their country. We cannot give a clearer knowledge of their journey, their arrival, their reception, and the success they have begun to realize in planting the Faith in these desert and barbarous regions, than by listening to their own account in the Journal which they kept from their departure up to their fixed and permanent abode in the Iroquois Villages. It begins thus:

Article I. Journey of Three Jesuit Fathers to the Lower Iroquois

The delay which our fear of the nation of the Loups caused us to make in the Forts gave us an opportunity of rendering some service there to the Soldiers, by a kind of Mission that we gave them. But at last, on the eve of St. Bartholomew's day, about four o'clock in the afternoon, we embarked to go and take shelter at a league's distance from the last Fort of the French, which is that of sainte Anne; and thereafter we went on our way, both day and night, without any mishap, and without discovering any trace of the enemy. They had taken a Southerly direction, to return to their own country, while we kept to the Northern part of Lake Champlain.

We admired at the outset the care that our Christian Iroquois had to pray to God, all together, immediately after embarking, although they had been present at holy Mass, which we celebrated very early every morning. These prayers finished, we all set about paddling, like poor galley-slaves, from morning until evening. Not one of us three had learned this exercise, but, because we had so few men for performing the necessary work, we were obliged to take part therein. We gaily crossed this entire great Lake, which is already too renowned by reason of the shipwreck of several of our Frenchmen, and, quite recently, by that of sieur Corlart [Arendt van Curler], commandant of a Hamlet of the Dutch near Agnié [Mohawk country],—who, on his way to Quebec for the purpose of negotiating some important affairs, was drowned while crossing a large bay, where he was surprised by a storm.

Arriving within three-quarters of a league of the Falls by which Lake St. Sacrement [Lake George] empties, we all halted at this spot, without knowing why, until we saw our Savages at the water-side gathering up flints, which were almost all cut into shape. We did not at that time reflect upon this, but have since then learned the meaning of the mystery; for our Iroquois told us that they never fail to halt at this place, to pay homage to a race of invisible men who dwell there at the bottom of the lake. These beings occupy themselves in preparing flints, nearly all cut, for the passers-by, provided the latter pay their respects to them by giving them tobacco. If they give these beings much of it, the latter give them a liberal supply of these stones. These watermen travel in canoes, as do the Iroquois; and, when their great Captain proceeds to throw himself into the water to enter his Palace, he makes so loud a noise that he fills with fear the minds of those who have no knowledge of this great Spirit and of these little men. At the recital of this fable, which our Iroquois told us in all seriousness, we asked them if they did not also give some tobacco to the great spirit of Heaven, and to those who dwell with him. The answer was that they do not need any, as do people on the earth. The occasion of this ridiculous story is the fact that the Lake is, in reality, often agitated by very frightful tempests, which cause fearful waves, especially in the basin where sieur Corlart, of whom we have just spoken, met his death; and when the wind comes from the direction of the Lake, it drives on this beach a quantity of stones which are hard, and capable of striking fire.

"I passed a fine Slate-quarry," says one of the three Fathers, "that we found five leagues from Lake St. Sacrement, a cannon-shot from a little Islet of about 20 feet in diameter. This quarry is not of the nature of all those that I have seen on the seashore, or in the neighborhood of Quebec, which have only the appearance of quarries; but this one is quite like those I have seen in the Ardennes of our France, its color being a beautiful blue and its laminæ easily detached,—large or small, as one wishes,—very fragile and very soft.

"While I paused at this Slate-quarry, our sailors landed at the end of Lake St. Sacrement, and made preparations for the portage, which is barely half a league long through the woods, each one taking his burden, of baggage or of canoes. When we had embarked again, we at last, after some strokes of our paddles, quitted these canoes, very glad to have arrived safely at the end of the Lake, from which point there remained only thirty leagues of journey by land, to reach the goal to which we had so long aspired."

The whole country of the Iroquois was at that time so overcome with fear of a new French army, that for several days fourteen warriors had been constantly on the watch at the entrance to this Lake, in order to discover the army's line of march, and bear news of it with all haste to the whole Nation. Their purpose was to lay ambuscades for it in the woods, by means of which they intended to attack it at an advantage, and harass it in the defiles; accordingly, there was also a third band posted there, for the purpose of making this reconnaissance. But, by great good fortune for them and for us, instead of being enemies to them, we were Angels of peace; while on their part, from being Lions as they had been, they became our menials, and served us very opportunely as porters,—being furnished us by Providence to take charge of our baggage, which we would have had much difficulty in transporting to their country by land.

We proceeded accordingly in company, by short marches, and came to within three-quarters of a league of their chief Village, called Gandaouagué, the one which the late Father Jogues watered with his blood, and where he was so maltreated during eighteen months of captivity. We were received there with the customary ceremonies, and with all imaginable honor. We were conducted to the cabin of the foremost Captain, where all the people crowded in, to contemplate us at their ease,—quite delighted to see among them Frenchmen, so peaceably inclined, who not long before had made their appearance there as if infuriated, setting fire to everything.

The first care of Father Fremin was to go through the cabins, and find the Huron and Algonquin captives, who alone compose two-thirds of the Village. He baptized at once ten of their children, offering to God these blessed first-fruits of the new Mission.

Article II. First Baptism Conferred on an Iroquois Woman

This is the place to relate a miracle of grace wrought by Divine goodness in the person of a poor Iroquois woman, whom the warriors of the loup [Mahican] nation had, a short time before, scalped in plain sight of the Town. Father Fremin, entering the Cabin where this poor unfortunate was,—all bathed in her blood, and more dead than alive from the wounds she had just received,—approached her. Seeing that she was drawing near her end, he spoke to her about the other life—the tortures of hell, into which she was going to fall if she did not embrace the Faith; and the joys of Paradise, which were assured to her if she became a Christian. To these teachings she turned a deaf ear, and the Father was obliged to go out without having made any impression upon her mind. While we were at prayers for the salvation of this poor Soul, the Father returned to the charge; but he had no sooner entered the cabin than he found a new obstacle there, in the person of an old woman who not only repulsed him, but confirmed the sick woman in her obstinacy. The hour marked by Providence was not yet come. He returned for the third time, but without success; and we almost despaired of the salvation of this dying woman, because we were about to depart from that Village, much grieved at leaving this prey to the demon.

Nevertheless, the Father was urgently inspired to make one last attempt, while we raised our hands to heaven to move God's Pity. He went in, and drew near; he spoke, was heard, and found this poor woman quite changed. She listened to him with pleasure, repeated the prayers with fervor, and, in a word, was found so well prepared—the Holy Ghost having been her Master and Teacher—that before she died we gave her Holy Baptism, that she should be the first Soul of this Barbarian community who should pray to God in Heaven for us, and for the conversion of her countrymen. It had not been our intention to remain that day at Gandaouágué; but God, who has his designs, made the salvation of this poor woman spring from her own misfortune, and from the delay caused by the warriors who had gone in pursuit of the loups, who had inflicted this blow.

Article III. Severe Trial of Another Iroquois Woman after her Baptism

But here follows another marvel of grace, much more considerable than the first. It will doubtless give consolation to the Readers, and at the same time will make them see that the force of true Christianity and the Spirit of JESUS CHRIST is found not less among Barbarians than among civilized nations, *ubi non est Gentilis et Judeus, Barbarus et Scytha, sed omnia et in omnibus Christus.* Father Fremin relates it, with all possible fidelity, in these terms:

"Arriving in the country of the Iroquois, we were obliged to remain three days in the first Village which we found on our way, called Gandaouágué; fear of the warriors of the loup nation kept us shut up there, and prevented us from going on without a considerable escort.

"During this time, which God very opportunely gave me, I tried to reassemble our old Christians of the Huron Nation, who had been for several years deprived of the sight of their Pastor. I made them all assemble in a Cabin apart, in order to prescribe all the exercises of Christianity which they were to practice.

"In this little band there happened to be an Iroquois woman, twenty-five years of age, who wished to remain and hear what I was going to say. At the close of my discourse she addressed me, and told me that she wished, in all sincerity and without pretense, to be a Christian. I answered her that I could judge of her sincerity from her perseverance; and that, meantime, I would instruct her, and would little by little make her understand the great blessing to which she aspired. She on her part did not fail to perform all that I could expect from a fervent Catechumen. She was present at all our meetings, with a fervor worthy of the first Christians; and when I had to go away, and had designated the Cabin where all were to assemble, morning and evening, to say their prayers in public, and had named a good Christian woman to take the charge of informing all the others of the hour of these meetings, our Iroquois woman offered herself for this office of Charity and humility. Then, with a courage altogether heroic, she surmounted the natural and usual shame that young Iroquois women feel in going from Cabin to Cabin to give that kind of invitation, which is not done without receiving taunts and insults from those who are not Christians.

"When I was ready to depart, as she saw that she could not yet obtain the grace of Baptism, she said to me with a charming simplicity: 'At least, Baptize my only son; he has not sinned yet, to render himself unworthy of that blessing.' I granted her this request, and comforted her greatly, promising her to come back in a fortnight, in order to instruct her.

"The fortnight having expired, as I was unable to get away from more important duties which were overwhelming me, I could not keep my promise to visit her; but she came herself to find me in the Village of Tionnontonguen. I was delighted to see her, and when I told her that I was going to begin in good earnest to teach her the prayers and principal Rites of our Faith, she answered me: 'I know them; I learned them perfectly during thy absence, from a good Huron woman, who has not ceased to instruct me every day.' Then, proceeding to recite without error all the prayers and principal articles of the Faith, 'What is the reason,' she added, 'that thou dost not Baptize me? Thou oughtest now to keep thy word.'

"As I did not yet know her sufficiently, I put her off until another time, as gently as I could, and won her consent to go back to her home with the hope that I would, as soon as possible, comply with her desires. In fact, some time afterward I visited her Village, Gandaouagué; and as I entered she came to meet me, in order to ask me for Baptism. I tried then to ascertain from our good Huron Christian women how she had conducted herself during my absence. They assured me that she had been an example for all the other women, both in fervor and in constancy at prayers, every morning and every evening, without ever failing to be there; and that she even added her words to her example, exhorting them with an admirable ardor.

"Accordingly, I spoke to her in private, in order to sound the depths of her heart a little; and I found a woman of rare innocence, of good intelligence, and of an excellent memory. She was accustomed to tell her beads five or six times every day; and I can affirm that, from morning till night, she was continually praying. All these excellent dispositions obliged me at last to confer on her Holy Baptism.

"This virtue was too great not to be tested. After the lapse of only two days, her son fell ill; and I trembled with fear for this poor woman, not thinking her yet sufficiently established; but I perceived plainly that hers was no common virtue. She did not weaken in her holy resolves, but continued her devotions as usual, and merited by her constancy the cure of her son.

"But it was only to encounter a more severe test. Scarcely had her son recovered when her husband was killed, very near the village, by the Mahingans. She loved this man more than herself, and, while she was physically well formed, she had also a good mind, and was related to the best families of the country. All these good qualities had brought about their marriage, which had been confirmed during the last eight or ten years by a reciprocal love, very tender and constant; and it was regarded as the most complete union that existed among the Savages.

"From this it can be judged what must have been this woman's affliction; and whether her faith, which was yet only in its infancy, was not in great danger of destruction. But so far from relaxing in her devotions, she on the contrary increased them, in order to fortify herself constantly more and more against the assaults of the devil. He incited the relatives of the deceased to come all pouring into her Cabin, and cast at her a thousand reproaches,—imputing to her both the illness of her son and the death of her husband, whom she had killed by becoming a Christian. Her own relatives also took part in this effort; and they, all together, spent a week with her, loading her with all the most atrocious insults that passion could suggest to them, and inflicting upon her all the ill treatment one can imagine in such circumstances.

"The strongest courage would falter under such conditions; and a week of suffering was enough to throw her into a state of dejection, both of mind and of body; but she had no sooner perceived this than she sent for me to come and comfort her. At our interview, she redoubled her tears, and I could not restrain my own; but her tears were all innocent, and I found her heart perfectly resigned to the decrees of God, and her Soul as pure and guiltless amid all this wrangling as on the very day of her Baptism. But what I most admired was her firmness in her faith and in all her exercises of devotion, in which she continued always unshaken, even to telling her beads eight and ten times a day; in this she experienced a marvelous peace amid her greatest afflictions.

"After that, I thought that God was satisfied with these tests; but scarcely had twenty days' time begun to dry her tears, when she was seized with an inflammation of the eyes which greatly disfigured her face and made her lose the use of her eyes. At this mishap all her relatives, as well as those of her dead husband, redoubled their persecutions. 'Art thou not yet content with having killed thy husband?' they asked her. 'Wilt thou kill thyself too? Seest thou not that it is the Faith that causes all these ills? Take pity on thy child and thy other relatives, if thou art determined to abandon thyself a prey to all calamities.' For a whole week, they kept up reproaches like these; and she, during all that persecution, had no other consolation than that which God gave her in her prayers, which she increased in proportion as she was persecuted.

"Several times the jugglers of the country were brought to her, to try to effect her cure by feasts and superstitious ceremonies; but she would never consent to this. Those who know how great is the complaisance of the Savages toward their relatives, will easily judge that the virtue of this woman was heroic, and that God visited her with very extraordinary graces.

"Having, then, refused the jugglers of the country, she had recourse to one of our Huron Christians who knew a good remedy for her disease; and, God blessing it, she has recovered, after using it three months, both the sight of her eyes and the health of her body. In gratitude, she continues in her fervor and inspires the same in her son,—who is only four years old, and whom she has already taught some of the prayers. If perseverance places the seal upon so blessed a life, I shall have no difficulty—knowing, as I do, her innocence—in likening her to the Christians of the first Centuries of the Church." But let us return to the journey of our Missionaries, which the narration of these two rather important events has interrupted. Let us see how he continues to speak.

Article IV. Of the Reception of the Fathers in the Other Iroquois Villages, and of a Notable Council which was Held there after their Arrival

From Gandaouagué we went on to another Village, two leagues distant, where we were received even more kindly than at the first one; this place we consecrated by the Baptism of three children, one of whom, Orphaned of both parents, was at the point of death. Was not this a rich recompense in advance for our past labors, and a powerful incentive to embrace with courage those which should present themselves in the future?

However, we had to leave this second Village, in order to journey on to the Capital of this whole country, called Tionnontoguen,—which the Iroquois have rebuilt, at a quarter of a league from that which the French burned down last year. We were escorted thither by two hundred men, who marched in good order; we went last, immediately in front of the hoary Heads and the most considerable men of the country. This march was executed with an admirable gravity until, when we had arrived quite near the Village, every one halted, and we were complimented by the most eloquent man of the Nation, who was awaiting us with the other Deputies. After this, he conducted us into the Village, where we were received with the discharge of all the artillery,—each one firing from his Cabin, and two swivel-guns being discharged at the two ends of the Village.

The entire harangue which this man made us consisted of these few words: that they were glad that the Frenchman was coming to clear the air from the mists with which the nation of the Wolves was clouding it, and to restore calm to their minds by the assurance of peace that our arrival gave them. After this followed the feast, which consisted of a dish of porridge made with Indian corn, cooked in water, with a little smoked fish, and, for dessert, a basket of squashes.

Perhaps some will be astonished that Missionaries accept honors which are paid them with so much ceremony, and are present at feasts with which these peoples are accustomed to regale their Ambassadors. But both these honors and these feasts are after the manner of the Savages,—that is to say, of such a nature that they conflict neither with humility nor with Christian temperance; on the contrary, they furnish opportunities to practice advantageously both these virtues. We must then hold St. Paul's opinion: *Scio et humiliari, scio et abundare, et satiari et esurire.*

The day of the exaltation of the Holy Cross having been fixed upon for making our presents,—that is to say, for speaking in public on the subject of our coming,—all the six Villages of Agnié assembled here, men, women, children, and old men. After having begun the ceremony by the *Veni Creator,* the chanting of which was accompanied by the notes of a small musical instrument, which these peoples listen to with pleasure and wonder, Father Fremin made a harangue before all this great assembly, adapting himself in discourse and gestures to the usage of their most celebrated Orators, who speak not less by gesticulation than by language. He made them see the great blessings produced by peace, and the evils that accompany war—of which they had felt the effects, a year before, in the destruction of their Village by fire. He reproached them for the acts of perfidy and cruelty that they had committed, with such barbarity, upon our Frenchmen, without having received any ill treatment from these. Then he declared to them that he came for the very purpose of changing this barbarous disposition, by teaching them to live like men, and then to be Christians; and that our great Onnontio [King] would then receive them as his subjects, and would take them thenceforth under his Royal protection, as he had all the other tribes of those regions; and that, moreover, they must take good heed in the future not to commit any act of hostility, either upon us or upon our allies.

But, in order to inspire them with greater terror, and make more impression on their minds, as these peoples are greatly influenced by external phenomena, the Father caused to be erected, in the middle of the place where the Council was being held, a pole forty or fifty feet in length, from the top of which hung a Porcelain necklace. He declared that, in like manner, should be hanged the first of the Iroquois who should come to kill a Frenchman or any one of our Allies; and that they had already had an example shown them in the public execution, which took place at Quebec in the preceding year, of a man of their country who had violated some of the terms of peace.

It is incredible how much this present, so unusual, astounded them all. They remained for a long time with their heads down, without daring either to look at this spectacle or to talk about it, until the most prominent and most eloquent of their Orators—having recovered his spirits—arose and performed all the apish tricks imaginable about this pole, to show his astonishment. It is impossible to describe all the gesticulations made by this man, who was more than sixty years old. What looks of surprise at the sight of this spectacle, as if he had not known its meaning! What exclamations, upon finding out its secret and interpretation! How often he seized himself by the throat with both his hands, in a horrible manner,—squeezing it tightly to represent, and at the same time to inspire a horror of, this kind of death, in the multitude of people who surrounded us! In a word, he employed all the artifices of the most excellent Orators, with surprising eloquence; and, after discoursing on this theme a very long time, continually manifesting mental traits which were out of the ordinary, he ended by delivering to us the captives for whom we asked, and giving us the choice of a site for the erection of our Chapel, in the construction of which they offered to cork with all diligence. They delivered to us also a Frenchman whom they had held a prisoner for some time, and promised us the liberty of twelve Algonquins,—part from the Nation of the Nez Percez [Ojibwa], part from that of the Outaouacs [Ottawa],—whom they will put into our hands, to send back each to his own country.

Article V. Of the Establishment of Christianity
in the Country of the Iroquois of Agnié

Our Chapel having been built by the efforts of the Iroquois themselves, who applied themselves to the task with incredible ardor, we opened it, and began to have our old Christians, who had formerly been instructed in their own Huron country by our Fathers, hear the holy Mass. It must here be confessed that we could not help shedding tears of joy at seeing these poor captives so fervent in their devotions, and so constant in their Faith, after so many years during which they had been deprived of all instruction. Such is the reward that God gives us, in advance, for the little labors in which this kind of life, so barbarous in its character, engages us from love to him. The days slip by without our realizing their passage; and, as we are obliged to employ eight consecutive hours in directing the prayers of those who come to the Chapel, the rest of the time passes very quickly in other Apostolic functions.

The mothers bring us their little children, that we may make the sign of the Cross on their foreheads; and they themselves are accustomed to do the same before putting them to bed. Their ordinary conversation in the Cabins is about Hell and Paradise, of which we often speak to them.

The same custom is followed in the other Villages, in imitation of this one; and we are from time to time invited to go and administer the Sacraments to them and put these Infant Churches in such condition as this state of Barbarism admits.

At the very first visit made by Father Fremin to one of these Villages, he found there forty-five old-time Christians, who gave him, and who themselves received in return, much consolation. He was obliged to render this testimony to the truth, that he would never have believed—what he has seen and experienced—how well rooted piety is in the souls of these poor Captives, who far surpass in devotion the generality of Christians, although for so long a time they have had no help from their Pastors. They came to the Sacraments, they had their children Baptized, and they showed the place where they assemble every evening, without fail, to maintain their fervor by the public prayers which they offer together. There, too, some Iroquois are to be found, attracted by the odor of this good example, and persuaded, by so noble a constancy, of the truth of our holy Faith.

As the Iroquois have made conquests in all parts of Canada, they give us means of opening the Treasures of grace to every kind of Nation, by instructing their Captives.

A poor Slave woman, taken in war and brought from the North Sea, is experiencing a blessing, as the effect of this instruction. When at the point of death, she received Holy Baptism, with a marvelous aptness for it.

Another Captive woman, of the Nation of the Loups, was prepared for Baptism, before being burned according to the Sentence that was pronounced upon her. Oh, what pleasure there is in encountering such souls!

We take not less care for the preservation of peace than for the establishment of Christianity, because one depends upon the other. For that reason, we put forth all our efforts to save the life of an Outaouac [Ottawa] whom the Iroquois of Onneiout [Oneida] had sent hither as a victim destined for the fire. "They brought him to this Village in order to keep all knowledge of the matter from us; and the fires were prepared which were to have lighted up that horrible night chosen for this cruel execution. Unfortunately, it happened that there was not here, at that time, any one of the Elders, to whom it belonged to arrest these acts of violence. The young people, who breathe only war, had already seized this prey, and had shut the man up in a Cabin which had all its fires lighted, in order to execute their usual cruelties there in concealment, when an Iroquois woman came to notify me secretly of the affair." (It is Father Fremin who is speaking.) "I ran to the spot in haste; I spoke, I exhorted, but in vain. I threatened; I made the women and children retire. All obeyed me, with the exception of two men who, notwithstanding all my efforts, continued to burn this wretch. Through all the streets of the Village I raised the cry: 'Old men, you are dead! Children, no life remains to you! The peace is broken. Behold the Loups coming on one side, and, on the other, I see Onontio with his army. Your land is going to be devastated, your Fields, your Cabins, your Villages are going to be ruined.' After running through all the streets with these cries, I halted before the Cabin where the prisoner was being burned—contrary to one of the principal articles of the Peace; but the door was barricaded. I called more loudly, saying that the whole country was lost; but I received no answer. By good luck, I found an old man, a relative of those who were the authors of this tragedy. I spoke to him so vigorously, and my menaces had such an effect upon him, that, with the authority which his age and his kinship gave him, he proceeded to rescue this poor man from the midst of the flames, and handed him over into my keeping. He was cured of his wounds, indeed; but the acuteness of the pain, together with the fear, caused him a fever, which afforded me abundant leisure to instruct him at my convenience, and to prepare him for his end. In fact, 24 days after this accident he died a good Christian; and I no longer doubt that it was by a very special Providence that I made all those efforts for his liberty, in order to deliver him at the same time from the fires of the Iroquois and from those of hell."

We interred him with much joy, and with all the solemnity that can be observed amid this state of barbarism. All our Christians were present, in fine order, and with a modesty of bearing that delighted the Iroquois, who wished to see this ceremony, which was so extraordinary to them, and had never been observed among them. Thus, little by little, we shall establish the Kingdom of JESUS CHRIST upon the ruins of that of Satan, who is exerting all his efforts to the contrary, as we are about to see in the following article.

Article VI. Of the Drunkenness of the Iroquois of Agnié, and its Unfortunate Effects

There are many hindrances to the establishment of the Faith among these peoples, to which sufficient reference has been made in the preceding Relations; but one of the greatest, which has not yet been mentioned, of which the devil avails himself very advantageously, is drunkenness, caused by the brandy that the Europeans of these coasts began to sell to the natives some years ago.

It is so common here, and causes such disorders, that it seems sometimes as if all the people of the Village had become insane, so great is the license they allow themselves when they are under the influence of liquor. Firebrands have been thrown at our heads, and our papers set on fire; our Chapel has been broken into; we have been often threatened with death; and during the three or four days while these disorders last,—and they take place very often,—we have to suffer a thousand acts of insolence without complaint, without eating, and without repose. Meanwhile, these furious creatures overthrow everything they come to, and even massacre one another, without sparing either relatives or friends, compatriots or strangers. These acts sometimes go to such an excess that the place seems to us no longer tenable; but we shall leave it only with our lives. Meanwhile, we are constantly working to gather up the precious remnants of the blood of JESUS CHRIST, which was shed not less for these poor Barbarians than for the rest of the world.

When the storm has passed, however, we can perform our functions peaceably enough; and, among others, we have celebrated the Christmas holiday with all the devotion imaginable on the part of our Neophytes, several of whom were present at six consecutive Masses. In this way, God does not leave us always in bitterness.

We have fully forty Hurons who make public profession of Christianity; for the most part, they are making very good progress, and are very zealous. During the first three months we Baptized fifty persons, of whom two Iroquois and two Algonquin women are in the way of salvation, as we have reason to believe, in view of the pious feelings in which they died. Since then, we have Baptized fully fifty more; and of this entire number thirty children are, with all certainty, in Paradise.

That is, for the present, all that we can say about this Mission of Sainte Marie, for which we conceive great hopes if the peace lasts, and if our Iroquois are humbled. To promote this end, we thought it advisable that Father Pierron, after having visited the Dutch,—or rather, the English, who have made themselves Masters of new Holland,—should undertake the journey to Quebec on the ice, in order to inform Monsieur the Governor and Monsieur the Intendant of the state of this country—to the end that they may, having all the information necessary, be able to continue this great work of the peace, which they have so happily begun.

Of the Mission of the Martyrs in the Country of the Anniez, or Lower Iroquois

1668-1669

François-Joseph le Mercier

This narrative is part of the report written by le Mercier for the years 1668 and 1669 (JR 52:117-143). Le Mercier was in his second appointment as superior-general at this time. He paraphrases and quotes letters from Jean Pierron, who was Jesuit missionary to the Mohawks during that time. Pierron was born in 1631 in France and died there in 1700. He became a Jesuit in 1650 and arrived in Canada in 1667. He reopened missions among the Mohawks and other Iroquois along with Frémin and Bruyas, staying amongst them from 1667 to 1674. After traveling in disguise through the English colonies, he spent three more years with the Iroquois and returned to France in 1678.

Pierron reported that in 1668-1669 he ministered to seven Mohawk villages that were scattered over seven and a half leagues of the valley. For the years just before and just after those reported on here, the relations of the Mohawk mission indicate that there were six Mohawk villages (JR 51:158-203, 53:137-139, 153). However, in both cases only three community names are provided. The number of "castles" had been rather consistently given as three from 1640 to 1665, and it was three again in 1672-1673 (JR 57:91, 111). This suggests that the three un-named villages might have been new villages under construction in 1667-1668 and three old villages in the process of abandonment in 1669-1670. However, the seventh village mentioned here can probably be accounted for only as a satellite hamlet. There was an increase in the number of villages to four and then five in 1666 (JR 50:203; NYCD 3:135), before reaching a maximum of seven in this narrative. The total of three reported in 1672-1673 is followed by a count of five in 1677, of which four are named (NYCD 3:250). Once again, one is probably a supplementary settlement, not just a double counting of a single community on the move. Mohawk demography for the period 1666-1677 was probably complicated by both village fissioning and the incorporation of refugee communities from elsewhere in the region.

Bracketed references to page breaks in the original manuscript have been omitted in this reprinting. Similarly, hyphens that appear at the ends of lines and endnotes in the published version of the *Jesuit Relations* have also been dropped.

D.R.S.

THE PEOPLE of Agnié were formerly one of the most flourishing Iroquois Nations, and have always, up to the present time, passed for one of the most valiant, and one of the proudest. That martial spirit, which occupied them in war, separated them so effectually from the Faith that it was thought that the Agnez [Mohawks] would be the last to submit to the Gospel. But God employed the arms of France to give their conversion a beginning; their courage weakened after their defeat; and they are now, of all the Iroquois tribes, the one that gives the greatest hopes of its conversion to the Christian Faith.

Father Jean Pierron, after making a journey to Quebec, arrived safely at Tinniontoguen, the principal Village of that nation, on the 7th day of October, in the year 1668, and took the entire charge of that new Church,—which Father Fremin left him, after himself fostering it with incredible exertions. The living is so meager there that hardly any meat or fish is eaten; but God, by his grace, causes the Missionaries to live very contentedly in this deprivation of all things. "No one could be poorer than are our Agniez," said the Father in one of his Letters; "but, in spite of that, I love them more than myself, seeing how well disposed they are toward Christianity.

"I know enough of the Iroquois language," continues this Father, "to explain all that I wish in matters of religion, and to hear the Confessions of the new Christians; and, without the occupation given me by the Pictures that I paint with my own hand, I would be better versed in the language than I am. But I find the effect of these paintings so great, that I deem a part of my time well spent in this exercise; for by these Pictures I bring it about, in the first place, that our Savages see a graphic representation of what I teach them, by which they are more powerfully moved.

"Moreover, I reap this advantage, that they act as Preachers to themselves; and that those who would not come to pray from devotion, do come at least from curiosity, and thus suffer themselves to be insensibly influenced by that attraction. Finally, I have myself discovered the secret of teaching myself; for, in hearing them describe our Mysteries, I learn much of the language through the medium of these Pictures.

"Among the pictures that I have made, there is one which represents the deaths of the pious and the wicked. What obliged me to make it was, that I saw that the old men and women used to stop their ears with their fingers, the moment I tried to speak to them of God, and would say to me, 'I do not hear.' Accordingly, I put in one part of my Picture a Christian who is dying a holy death, with hands so joined that he holds the Cross and his Rosary; then his soul is borne upward to Heaven by an Angel, and the Spirits of the Blessed appear, awaiting him. In the other part, and in a lower position, I placed a woman, bent with age and dying, who, being unwilling to listen to a Missionary Father who is showing her Para-

dise, is stopping both her ears with her fingers. But there issues from Hell a Demon, who seizes her arms and hands, and puts his own fingers in the ears of this
dying woman, whose soul is carried away by three Demons; while an Angel,
coming out of a cloud, sword in hand, hurls them down into the depths.

"This sketch gave me an excellent theme for discoursing on the immortality of
our souls, and on the pleasures and pains of the other life; and no sooner was the
meaning of my Picture perceived than not another person was found who dared
to say, 'I do not hear.' Now, if that Picture had such an effect, I hope that the representation of Hell, on which I am working, will have a still greater one in the
future."

The invention of these Pictures is not altogether new: it had already been put
to a holy use by a celebrated Missionary of our France; and there is no one who
has read the life of Monsieur le Noblez, who does not admit that this was one of
the most admirable devices which he employed to instruct the various peoples in
our sacred Mysteries.

Father Pierron has been able to imitate that great man, and to introduce in the
depths of our forests a practice that has been of so great use in a nation already
civilized. It was known that this holy method had been infinitely useful; but it
would serve for very little if the Father did not add to these sanctified industries
the great labors that he has necessarily to undergo, in order to visit constantly
each week seven large Villages, covering seven and a half leagues of distance,
that he may prevent any child or any sick adult from dying without receiving
Baptism. And, if occasionally some one escapes his diligence, it is the keenest
affliction that he suffers, and makes him ask that assistance be sent to him immediately. What he desired has been granted him: Father Boniface was chosen,
immediately after his arrival from France at Quebec, to go this year and second
his zeal.

It is difficult to say whether the war which the Iroquois are waging with the
nine nations of the Loups [Mahicans and others], who are scattered all the way
from Manhate [Manhattan] to the environs of Quebec, is more advantageous
than peace to the Christian faith. War humbles them by diminishing their numbers; but it also, by preventing them from remaining in one place, opposes obstacles to the conversion of the warriors, who separate into a number of bands,
for the purpose of proceeding in detachments against the enemy. The Agniez and
the Loups make war on each other, as far as the vicinity of new Orange; and,
having taken captives on both sides, they burn and eat them. But the Loups have
this advantage, that, having a great number of men, and being wandering tribes,
they cannot be easily destroyed by the Iroquois, while the Iroquois can be more
easily destroyed by the Loups.

Nevertheless, we do not cease to win over some souls to JESUS CHRIST, amid
this tumult of arms. Two old men seemed to be only waiting for Baptism, in order that they might die; and they received it with all possible consolation. But a
third,—who, in perfect possession of his faculties, saw death approaching,—in
order to justify his obduracy, took as pretext, that he forgot all the instructions
that the Father gave him, the moment he was out of his Cabin. At last, being

urged to become converted, he said that he had committed too many crimes in his lifetime to be converted in the hour of death. Indeed, as the Divine Providence never permits a man, Savage though he may be, to die without Baptism, if he has tried his best to keep the natural law; so, by a just punishment, God often suffers those who have lived wickedly to be deprived of Baptism.

Another Old man, more than a hundred years old,—a man of excellent judgment, and formerly the head of the country,—was also baptized. He had prepared himself for this grace by his constancy in coming to pray to God, in the presence of all the people, in spite of the continual raillery of some of his nation who were still infidels.

One thing which acts as the greatest obstacle to the conversion of these barbarians is what is called among them "jugglery," or the art of healing the sick by criminal superstitions. Nevertheless, the Father, by his address, has rendered this art so ridiculous that no one dares to operate on a sick person in his presence,—the Jugglers pretending that they have already executed their manipulations, when he enters the Cabin. What gains him credit in this matter is, that he, much better than those pretended Physicians, procures for the sick health of body, as well as that of the soul.

Another care of the Missionaries has to do with the Captives, whom they teach how to die like true Christians in the midst of the flames, after Baptizing them; and sometimes it has happened that the Iroquois themselves have acted as interpreters to teach these victims our mysteries. It can be shown, by a number of examples, that God works in the souls of these infidels, by striking them with fear of him; here is one, that is quite remarkable. A war-Captain, belonging to the nation of the Agnez, intending to set out on the following day to proceed against their enemies, the Loups, went to the Chapel, built by the Savages themselves, and asked the Father what he should do and what he should say, in order to go to Heaven, if it should happen that he were taken in war and were to be burned. This demand touched the Father's heart, and constrained him to teach the man the method of performing an act of contrition. This the Savage rehearsed to himself for an hour, in order to learn it thoroughly; and then repeated it often to the Father—which is a sign that these Barbarians are beginning to apprehend another life; and it may be reasonably believed that that fear which is the beginning of true wisdom will be salutary for them.

While the fear of death makes itself felt in those who are not yet baptized, the contempt for life is admirable in those who have received Baptism. "Those who believe in God," said an Iroquois woman who had lain two nights all alone in the fields, in danger of being carried off by some one of the nation of the Loups, "need not fear death, since it serves them as a passage to Heaven."

Although there are among the Agniez those who have not the Faith, nevertheless many among them have a veritable hunger and thirst after Righteousness; and it comes to pass that God causes some of them to learn their prayers in a way that seems to border on the miraculous. There are Savage women so fervent in prayer that they pass whole nights in it; and so devout toward the blessed Virgin that they say their Rosary several times every day.

The first thing that they do, when they go to work in their fields, is to invite those who are of their company to unite in offering to the Mother of God a prayer,—to which they add, all together, a great many ejaculatory Orisons, which they address to God. Does not that show that they are capable of receiving Christianity?

True piety is beginning to take form in the hearts of the Agniez, in such a manner that the Father who has charge of them writes that he celebrated the last Easter Festival with much solemnity; that he has given holy Communion to his new Christians; and that the ceremony of Good Friday was performed as in France, all adoring our Lord on the Cross.

The Catechism is taught twice a day,—once for the men, and again for the women,—and the fervor there displayed is so great that married persons are not ashamed to be publicly catechized. One woman has been found sufficiently qualified to learn the form of Baptism, and all that is necessary for administering this first Sacrament of the Church, which is the door to all the others,—although she has not yet been allowed the use and practice of it.

This woman came near being included in a massacre inflicted by the Loups on a number of Agniez, almost within a hundred paces of the palisade of one of their Villages, where the enemy had stationed themselves in ambuscade. It happened that this woman, having to go with the others to work in her field, sent them on ahead of her with the assurance that she would follow them immediately afterward. Thereupon she suddenly fell asleep; and, at the same moment, the cry of the persons being massacred was heard. "Ah!" said that good Christian, "I recognize clearly that it was God's will to preserve me, and I do not cease to thank him for that favor."

Here is an occurrence that is not less remarkable. One of those women wounded by their enemies, the Loups, relates that she was attacked by one of the latter, who gave her three blows on the head with a hatchet, while she defended herself courageously against him. But another blow, which was given her near her right eye, threw her to the ground, and left her faint and bleeding. Then—as she reported the event to the Father—she uttered this prayer: "JESUS, you are the master of my life; take pity on me, for if I die in the condition in which I am, without being baptized, I shall be eternally burned in the fires that are never extinguished." Scarcely had she finished these words, when she felt a strength diffused through her whole body. She straightway arose, and as she was about to seize the hatchet of her enemy, who was easily able to kill her, he at the same instant fled. That constrained the woman to ask for Baptism, and to say, "I will believe in and honor, for the rest of my days, JESUS my liberator."

Certainly those are very propitious beginnings; and, although there are not a great many adults in the new Church of the Agniez, because they are baptized only with great precaution, it does not fail to have heroic souls among the women Catechumens,—who make a great impression on their husbands' minds, and gain illustrious victories every day over those who wish to involve them in crime. When one of these new Christians was being urged, even to the point of threats, to give up prayer, she was spirited enough to answer her husband on this occasion: " I am my own mistress, I do what I choose; and do thou what thou choosest." Others mock at insults, and boldly exclaim: "No matter, let them kill us; for this life is a small matter, and we hope God will have mercy on us."

Not less estimable is the constancy of some new Christians in one of their Villages called Gandaouaguen, under the direction of a fervent Catechist; and, although these tribes are infinitely sensitive to raillery, they do not fail to bear it nobly for the love of JESUS CHRIST. "We bend our heads to these insults," they say to the Father; " and, when we are assembled, we pray God to open the eyes of those scoffers, in order that they may see what we see." In a word, experience shows every day more than ever that the Savages (as well as the French) are capable of everything in matters that concern piety and the service of God. They know all that is most difficult in the Mystery of the holy Trinity; they distinguish the two natures in JESUS CHRIST; they are familiar with what the Church teaches about the immortality of our souls, the judgment, mortal sin, venial sin, and original sin; and as particular attention is being given to teaching them the ordinary prayers, and the Commandments of God and of the Church,—which they sing, every Sunday, in Iroquois verses—in this, too, the knowledge of which is absolutely necessary when they are admitted to Baptism, they are not ignorant any more than in the rest.

Even the little children appear susceptible to the most beautiful impressions of the faith. One example, among others, will show this. An Iroquois woman had bestowed especial care on the instruction of one of her children, who was about three years old. Upon her falling ill, he asked her, at the height of her illness, what was the matter with her, that she complained so. "I am ill, my son," his mother answered him. Then this little child, addressing himself to our Lord, said to him: "Lord, who art the master of our lives, take pity on my mother and restore her health." This child is the same to whom was given a picture in which our mysteries are illustrated; he knows them perfectly, and shows an intelligence capable of all things. The Embassy of the principal warriors of Agnié—who came in the spring to Monsieur de Courcelle, our Governor, with presents, asking for some of our Fathers, in order to assist him who has charge of their Church—is a sign that they are well disposed toward the Faith, and that there is reason to conceive great hopes for their conversion. Moreover, the peace, which they themselves took the initiative in coming to ratify with new presents, will contribute greatly to the advancement of Religion, through the just fear inspired in them by the arms of the King, under the command of Monsieur de Courcelle. They fear his courage; and, at the same time that he treats them in a manner best fitted to hold them to their allegiance, he inspires in them, by his words, the respect that they owe to the Christian Faith and to the Preachers of the Gospel.

These Barbarians have now so high an idea of the valor of the French, that they think there is nothing but the King's protection that can defend them from their enemies. That is why they came to ask help of Monsieur our Governor against the nation of the Loups, as for the defense of a country which already belongs to the King by force of arms, and which they hold only because he is pleased to let them have it. It is thus that the Ambassadors from Agnié explained themselves in their harangue.

All these things, joined to the courage that is natural to the nation of the Agniez, confirm more than ever the belief that a flourishing Church can be formed among them: very illustrious are the victories of modesty there. "I admired the virtue of a young woman, newly converted, and solicited to sin with the assurance that the Mission Father would not know about it. 'If he does not know,' replied she, 'God will know it, from whom nothing is hidden, and who alone is more to be feared than all the men in the world.' This answer curbed the insolence of the one who was urging her to do wrong. She is the same woman who has since imitated saint Thomas, holding a glowing firebrand in her hand, as he did, to guard her chastity." It is self-deception to think that Savages are incapable of Christian strength. When an old man, ninety years of age, was being exhorted to bear suffering in this world, considering that he would no longer suffer in Paradise, he replied: "I do not need to be encouraged; Paradise, with its joys, encourages me enough." This man, who had governed the whole country, was baptized on all Saints' day, the name of which he bears. The Agniez have of their own accord considered the fact that a single thing was capable of destroying these fair beginnings of Christian piety; and that there was in their midst a foreign Demon, more to be feared than those that they worshipped in their dreams. This Demon is the intoxicating liquor that was coming to them from new Orange. They sought means, in a public Council, to put a stop to those disorders, that were utterly ruining both the Faith and the bodies of their youth. Having learned from Father Pierron that the most efficacious means was to present, personally, a petition to this end to the Governor-general of Manhate, the most influential men among them went thither, and presented to him a memorial that had been drawn up for them. Following is the reply made by the Governor of Manhate, both to the petition of the Agniez, and to the letter of the Father which he had added to it. These are the very terms, taken word by word from the original:

FATHER:

By your last letter, I learn your complaint, which is seconded by that of the Iroquois Captains, the Sachems, and the Indians, as appears more clearly in their petition, enclosed in yours, touching the great quantity of liquors that some men in Albanie [Albany] take the liberty to sell to the Indians, thereby causing them to commit great disorders, more of which are still to be feared unless measures be taken to prevent them. In reply, you will learn that I have taken all possible care, and will continue to do so, to restrain and prevent, under very severe penalties, the furnishing of any excess to the Indians. And I am very glad to hear that such virtuous thoughts proceed from the Infidels, to the shame of some Christians. But that is to be ascribed to your pious teachings—you who, being well versed in a strict discipline, have

shown them the path of mortification, not only by your precepts, but
by your practice.

Your very humble,
From Fort James, affectionate servant,

November 18, 1668.   FRANCIS LOVELACE

We will finish this Chapter with the number of those who have been baptized
at Agnié, either by Father Fremin or by Father Pierron, during these two years,
1668 and 1669. The list of baptized amounts to a hundred and fifty-one, more
than half of whom were children or old people who died very soon after their
Baptism. That harvest may be regarded as tolerably abundant in a land not under
cultivation, and we ought to hope for much after such prosperous beginnings.

The birth of this flourishing Church is due, next to God, to the death and the
blood of the Reverend Father Jogues. He poured out his blood on the same spot
where this new Christianity is beginning to be born; and we seem to be able in
our day to verify, in his person, those beautiful words of Tertullian,—that "the
blood of the Martyrs is the seed of the Christians." And, if the death of the Martyrs is, as a Father of the Church well says, the science of eternity, *scientia
æternitatis,* we can affirm that the death of Father Jogues has earned for those
Infidels, who murdered him in time past, that God should give them, by means of
his successors, the science of the Gospel. This is the true science of the blessed
eternity that he had proclaimed to them, at three different times when he went
into their country, without fearing the cruelty of those Barbarians.

Of the Mission of the Martyrs in the Country of Agnié, or of the Lower Iroquois

1669-1670

Jean Pierron

Jean Pierron was born in France in 1631 and died there in 1700. He became a Jesuit in 1650 and arrived in Canada in 1667. He reopened the Mohawk mission along with Frémin and Bruyas, and lived amongst the Mohawks from 1667 to 1674. After leaving the Mohawk Valley, Pierron traveled around the English colonies in disguise. Still later, he spent another three years with the Iroquois before returning to France in 1678.

This account reports the well-known attack by Mohegans on the easternmost Mohawk village. Readers should be careful to distinguish between the Mohegans of coastal Connecticut, the Mahicans of the Hudson Valley, and the fictional Mohicans invented by James Fenimore Cooper. Spellings used by Pierron and other early writers do not always facilitate these distinctions.

Once again, François-Joseph le Mercier (superior of the Jesuits in Canada) used Pierron's report verbatim, adding only one introductory sentence of his own. This has been deleted, as have the numerous quotation marks that enclose everything else in the Thwaites edition from which this narrative is taken (JR 53:137-159). Brackets identifying page breaks in the original manuscript have also been omitted.

D.R.S.

I. Of the War of the Agniés [Mohawks] with the Nation of the Loups [Mahicans]

ONE OF THE MOST important things I have to write is the attack on Gandaouagué, which is one of our best Villages, and situated nearest to the enemy's country. On the eighteenth of August, 1669, three hundred of the Nation of the Loups—who live along the Sea, toward Baston [Boston], in new England—presented themselves at daybreak before the Palisade, and began to make so furious a discharge of musketry that the balls, piercing both the stockade and the cabins, soon awakened men, women, and children, almost all of whom were, at the time, sound asleep. The men at once took gun and hatchet in hand; and, while they defended the palisade, the women began, some to make bullets, and others to arm themselves with knives and defensive weapons, in view of an irruption.

Four Iroquois were killed at the outset, in the heat of the combat; and two were wounded, one of whom died a very short time afterward. The neighboring Village, alarmed, took flight in all directions, and carried to Tionnontoguen, distant four leagues from those first two Forts, the news that the whole country was lost, that Gandaouagué was besieged by an army of Loups, that all the young men had already fallen, and that perhaps Gandagaro, which is the neighboring Fort, was at present in desperate straits.

When this news had spread through all the district, at eight o'clock in the morning our Warriors, without becoming disconcerted, dressed themselves promptly in all the most precious things they had, according to the custom observed by them on these occasions; and all, without any other chief to command them than their own courage, advanced on the enemy with force.

I was among the first to march, in order to see whether, amid all the carnage that was going on at the palisade of the Village, where so many infidel souls were being lost, I could not save some one of them.

At our arrival, we heard only mournful outcries over the death of the bravest of this Village. The enemy had already retreated, after about two hours of very obstinate fighting on both sides. There was only a single warrior of the Nation of the Loups left on the place, and I saw that a Barbarian, having cut off his hands and feet, skinned him and separated the flesh from the bones, in order to make from it a detestable repast.

All our warriors, arriving and finding the enemy no longer there, promptly had cornmeal prepared, that they might pursue him in his retreat. The provisions being ready, they immediately embarked in Canoes on our river, which is very swift; and, as they followed the current of the stream, they made very good progress, But, night overtaking them on their march, they had some of their people go forward to search for the enemy, and discover, without any noise, the place where he lay encamped. When these scouts had reached this spot, they wished, in order better to observe its situation, to approach very close to it; but they could not do this so quietly that one of the Loups, who were posted tolerably near them, did not hear a noise, and cry out, according to their custom, *Koué, Koué*—(the Savage equivalent of "Who goes there?"). However, as there was no answer, and as he could discover nothing, he did not think best to give the alarm.

When the spies had returned, and had made their report on the situation of the enemy, it was resolved not to attack him in his redoubt, where he seemed too strongly intrenched; but to lay an ambuscade for him, on the route that it was thought he must take.

To execute this plan, the Iroquois made a wide detour, and went to lay their ambuscade in a place that was precipitous—a very advantageous spot, from which all the road leading toward the Dutch was commanded. In the morning, the Loups broke camp; and, as they were marching in single file, according to the custom of the Savages, twelve of their number became involved unawares in the ambuscade. A shower of balls, with which they saw themselves all at once received, immediately put to flight those whom chance had spared. Frightful yells at once arose on all sides in the forest, and the Loups, having rallied on the same spot where they had encamped, were hotly pursued thither by the Iroquois,—who, upon overtaking them there, made a furious assault upon them. At first the Loups made a vigorous resistance; but, the cowardice of some of their number forcing them to yield to the fury of the Iroquois, ten from out the entire band intrenched themselves in the earth, in order to defend themselves to the last. This new intrenchment caused our Agniés terrible vexation; but, as they are a tireless and valiant people, they lost neither courage nor the hope of dislodging them. And, in order to do it with less danger, they made use of an old tree that they found there, which they carried before them, to shield themselves,—which they could do, going up only one by one to the place where the enemy had fortified himself. Nevertheless, that manoeuver was of no use to them,—for, in spite of this device, the Loups ceased not to keep up an active fire on them from all sides, and to kill and wound a great many of our people; and the combat would assuredly have been much more disastrous to them, had not night overtaken them, and put an end to it. Our Savages had, in the beginning, taken four women of the enemy, out of twenty-four who had come on this expedition; and afterward six men, in the heat of the combat.

On the following morning, when they returned to the charge, they found that the enemy had taken flight in the night and had left them masters of the battlefield. The victors, following the custom of the Savages, cut off the heads of those of the Loups who bad been left on the place, in order to remove the scalps from them; and then they took care to bury those of their own people that had died in the battle.

It was said that there were nearly a hundred Warriors, on the side of the enemy, that perished—by being either slain in the engagement, or drowned in the flight. Yet I found it difficult to believe that their number was so great, because the Iroquois brought back only nineteen scalps from that defeat.

A short time ago, I learned, from some Loups who had been in this combat, that they had lost only fifty men; and the Iroquois nearly forty, counting those that the Loups killed,—on their march before the siege of the Iroquois Village, in the siege, and in the fight that occurred some days later. Nevertheless the Iroquois hold that they lost only thirteen on the battle-field.

While these things were taking place, I was at Gandaouagué, whence I was preparing to make my customary visit to the neighboring Village—not having thought it best to follow our Savages, in the uncertainty of a dangerous issue. But as soon as I learned of the victory,—it was about three o'clock in the afternoon,—I set out alone to go to find our Warriors, to see if I could not induce some of them to acknowledge him from whom they obtained the fortunate success of their arms. I made such haste that I arrived, even before night, at the place where the fight had occurred, which was nearly eight leagues distant from our Village. I testified to them the interest I took in their victory, for which they showed themselves greatly obliged to me; and each one of them was eager to tell me all the particulars of a day that had been so glorious for them. But as my principal purpose was to visit the wounded, to try to render them capable of receiving the truths of our Faith, through the hope I should give them of an eternal and blessed life, I saw every one of them. After this, I had permission to speak to the captives, and I tried to instruct them on that very spot, for fear I would not be able to do it so conveniently in our Villages, because of the ill treatment being prepared for them by the animosity of each and all.

I found two of them that heard me willingly enough; but God so favored me on the following day that, having spoken to them very fully about our mysteries, I observed that they took pleasure therein, and that they were not far removed from the Kingdom of God.

We set out two days after the battle, in company with a great number, both of those that had been in the fight and of persons who had come to see them. The victors carried the scalps, finely painted, on the ends of poles made to bear these trophies. The Slaves, divided into several bands, sang as they marched; and, as I perceived that one of the captive women had a sick child, which she carried at her breast, I thought I would do well to baptize it, seeing it in danger of dying. Therefore approaching it, at a time when we were crossing a brook, I baptized it. This poor child seemed only to have been waiting for that grace, to depart this life; for it died soon afterward, to live eternally in Heaven.

You can judge whether I did not esteem myself well rewarded for the fatigues of my journey, in having been so fortunate as to snatch from the Demon a prey that he was hoping to carry off. But the Baptism which all the captives asked me for, a few days later, was to me a crowning consolation and joy, exceeding all that can be imagined concerning it.

Accordingly, after I had allowed a little abatement to the fire and wrath of the hatred of the Iroquois toward these wretched persons, seeing that they bad been left alone on the scaffold where they had just been tormented,—and where they were still surrounded with all their countrymen's scalps, which were serving as trophies to the glory of the victors,—I approached them; and, making them descend from the scaffold, led them into a neighboring Cabin, in order to prepare them there for a Christian death. While I was earnestly talking to them about their salvation, I heard some of the Iroquois saying to one another, "Seest thou how he loves our enemies?" and others adding that I ought to let people who had done them so many injuries burn in hell also. But there were some among them who acknowledged that I was doing well to instruct them; and that man in his vengeance ought not to carry his resentment beyond the limits of his enemy's life.

Thereupon I embraced the opportunity to say to our Agniés that I loved their enemies—but with the same love wherewith JESUS CHRIST loves us all—because, as they had souls that were immortal, and so capable of being happy in Heaven, it was part of a Christian's duty to procure the same happiness for them all; that, besides, we were to form in Paradise only one beautiful family of true friends, because there is only one God—who, loving us all with the same love, unites in himself all our hearts; and for that reason I was under obligation to love their enemies. But, I added, as for them, besides that common obligation that bound me to love all men in that wise, I had also a very special love for them, because JESUS CHRIST, who is the Master of our lives, had sent me into their country to show them the way to Heaven, and not into the country of the Loups, their enemies. I said in conclusion that it was just that I should love them more than the Loups, since I was being maintained by them; since they were acquainted with me, and suffered me to live in peace in their midst; and since I did not know whether the Loups felt the same kindness toward me.

I prolonged this little discourse with all the emphasis I was able, and dwelt particularly on the description of Hell, the frightful torments of which I depicted to them in lively colors, in order to inspire in them some compassion for those wretched victims whom they were about to put to death with torture. My words, aided by grace, made such an impression on these Barbarians that they all told me that I was doing well to instruct the prisoners.

I accordingly began by giving them very full instruction in all that I deemed necessary to render them capable of receiving the Christian Faith; and they heard me in admirable silence. It is true, I received an altogether extraordinary help from God, who furnished me then with fitting words and powerful arguments,—which made good the deficiencies caused by the shame that the interpreter whom I used felt at teaching in public what she had not yet well learned herself.

As soon as the instruction was ended, I saw one of the captive women begin, of her own accord, to address a long prayer to JESUS CHRIST, for the purpose of asking from him her salvation, Then one of the bravest and greatest warriors of that Nation, who had, with his own hand, killed several Iroquois in the fight, also offered his prayer to God in public. I made a happy use of the new-born fervor of these Neophytes; and after I had induced them all to follow the example of those first ones, and had, by means of the ceremonies that I made them perform, prepared them all for holy Baptism, I baptized them.

After such a consolation, which was capable of alleviating all the pains and fatigues of my occupation, the good God gave me another, which crowned me with joy. I learned that another band of warriors had just arrived at a Village tolerably near the place where I was, and that they had a captive, a woman. I betook myself thither immediately, to see whether I could not win over this soul to God. It happened by the greatest good fortune in the world that, in the midst of the cruelties that were being inflicted on her, I had abundant leisure to instruct her fully in our Mysteries, because she listened to me with so much pleasure and joy that I seemed to see on her countenance sure signs of Predestination; and as she longed only for Paradise, her Baptism undoubtedly opened to her the way thither, her death occurring immediately after she had received it. How admirable is God's Providence toward his Predestined ones! Who would have believed that that woman was destined to find her salvation in her captivity; and, in the midst of the fires of the Iroquois, an eternal glory that she never could have obtained, had she always remained in her own country?

During all these engrossing occupations, there came to me from Onnontagué [Onondaga] a Letter, in which our Fathers besought me to repair thither as soon as possible. This news obliged me to retrace my steps promptly to Agnié, and to visit all the wounded in the six Villages belonging to my Mission. One must needs confess that God well knows how to alleviate the bitterness and toil of the Missionaries, when he so chooses. In ten days I had accomplished more than a hundred leagues, that I might try, amid these forests and frightful solitudes, to meet some souls whom I might be able to win over to God and—as if his goodness had chosen to reward me for what little suffering I had undergone, by giving me what I was most ardently desiring—besides the Loups and that captive woman whom I had the good fortune to baptize, I conferred the same Sacrament on twenty-four more persons, three days before setting out for Onnontagué. Among these last, I found children who were only waiting for that happy moment to go to Heaven, and who almost all died after being prepared therefor by Baptism.

These wars weaken the Agnieronnon [Mohawks] terribly; and even his victories, which always cost him bloodshed, contribute not a little to exhaust him. On the contrary, I learn that our French Colonies are becoming stronger every day, by reason of the great number of families that are settling there, and the aid sent over every year from France. So, from the knowledge I have of the two countries, I can say with truth that that old and redoubtable enemy is no longer so greatly to be feared by our French people as he was; that, on the contrary, he now fears our Arms, and has only respect for those whom he despised before—which is a marvelous advantage for his conversion.

II. Enterprise of four Iroquois Nations
Against a Fort of the Loups, Their Ememies

The victory of our Agniés over the Loups was more glorious than profitable, because they are very few in numbers, compared with their enemies, who can bring against them fifty men to their one. Yet it did not fail to inspire them with courage; and—without considering that even their victories weaken them, and that they lose much more in a single one of their warriors than their enemies do in fifty of theirs—they came to the resolution to avenge themselves for the affront which they thought they had received from the Loups. The four Lower Nations having joined forces, as being interested in this common cause, a troop of four hundred warriors was made up; and the plan was formed to attack one of the Forts of the enemy situated near Mannate [Manhattan], and to seize it rather by some stratagem than by open force. Their plan was concerted in this wise: a band of eight or nine young warriors was to go and make some murderous assault near the Palisade or Fort, in order that, at the noise of this massacre, the enemy might make a sortie from the place and be drawn into the ambuscade, and the other side be enabled to make themselves masters of the Fort without difficulty, when it should be stripped of its garrison.

Accordingly, arriving in sight of the Fort, they laid the ambuscade, and sent men to make the first approaches to the Palisade; but as they saw no one come out, and as every one kept himself intrenched in the Fort, they resolved to proceed to open war and to attack the place in the same manner that the Loups had attacked Gandaouagué. But, in truth, it was with much less success; for meeting with a Palisade impervious to all their blows, they despaired of being able to force it, and were at length obliged to retire in much confusion, without having killed or wounded a single one of the enemy, while two of their own number had been wounded.

At the time when these four hundred men were coming back without having succeeded in their undertaking, a little band composed of only five warriors arrived from another direction, all boastful at having brought back a scalp and led home a prisoner.

I was not, at that time, at Gandaouagué, to prepare him for Baptism; but one of our Christian women, named Marie Tsinouentes,—who had already sometimes performed the office of Catechist, with much success,—repairing to the place where this prisoner was, was greatly surprised to see that he was offering his prayer to God, according to what he had learned among Christian Savages, who were instructed by those of our Fathers who have charge of the Algonquin Missions. She drew near him and instructed him in our mysteries; and that poor man, quite filled with consolation, thanked this generous Christian for showing him such charity in a hostile country, where he had thought that he could find nothing else than a cruel death. In fact, he was put to death some days afterward; but he died as one predestined, having been baptized a little while before. These are the first-fruits, so to speak, of that numerous Nation of the Loups, where I hope God will some day give entrance to the faith; and I also hope that some children of that country, who have gone to Heaven by means of a happy Baptism, will there secure for their relatives the blessings of Heaven and the light of the Faith.

Of the Mission of Sainte Marie Among the Lower Iroquois and of the Mission of Gandaouagué, or of Saint Pierre, in the Country of Agnié

1672-1673

Jean de Lamberville

This report on the Mohawk mission was written by Jean de Lamberville, missionary to the Onondagas, with editorial alterations by Claude Dablon. Dablon was superior of the Jesuits of Canada from 1671 to 1680, and again from 1686 to 1693. Passages that were written by Lamberville and later stricken by Dablon are reproduced in italics. A little original Latin also appears in italics. Material that Dablon inserted is reproduced here within brackets. What Lamberville wrote and Dablon let stand is presented in roman type. These are the same conventions used by Thwaites in volume 57 of the *Jesuit Relations* (JR 57:81-111), from which this narrative is taken. I have added a few additional clarifications in braces { }.

Much of what Lamberville wrote came to him from Jacques Bruyas, Jesuit missionary at the largest and westernmost Mohawk village. Bruyas is quoted in some places, paraphrased in others. Bruyas had arrived in Mohawk country with Frémin and Pierron, following the de Tracy expedition against the Mohawks in 1666, and just two years after the English conquest of New Netherland. Peace with the Algonquian-speaking Indians of the Hudson and New England had reopened trade with the Dutch settlers and English authorities in Albany by 1673. This resulted in new waves of drunkenness and disease. Moreover, the schism between converted and traditional Mohawks was deepening and hostility between the factions increasing. Some converted Mohawks were already moving to Canada. These trends were interrupted briefly by the Dutch reconquest of New York in 1673. However, the English returned to power in 1674, and this was followed by a new influx of refugee New England Indians into Mohawk villages. By 1677 the traditional Mohawks would form a strong alliance with the English, and by 1679 the remaining Catholic Mohawks would move with their missionaries to Canada.

D.R.S.

Chapter 1
Of the Mission of Sainte Marie Among the Lower Iroquois

WHEN THE AGNIERONNON {Mohawk} *Iroquois concluded peace with their enemies, they had not sufficient Prescience to foresee What disadvantages would befall them, and that The hatchet of the mahingan* {Mahicans} *would be less redoubtable to them than the liberty of going as often as they pleased to trade for brandy in new holland. As soon as that baleful peace between them and the Loups* {Mahicans} *was concluded at new orange, the Road was at once opened to them to go there at all times in perfect safety, and afterward to become intoxicated daily during the greatest Heat of The summer. Formerly, they used to drink here only at intervals and at certain seasons; many had to band together and keep themselves in readiness to resist The enemy in case of attack. But since they have no Fear of being insulted by the Loups, drunkenness has become so continual that they cease to drink only on leaving the village; and some have even been known to carry their kegs of brandy to the place where they fish, situated at a distance of over twenty-five Leagues from here.*

This general dissipation was quickly followed by a kind [This country has been greatly afflicted this year by a kind] of pestilence, which began in the month of June, and ceased only in september. It was a fever of so malignant a character that in less than Five days one would either recover, or succumb to its violence. "It was a very sad spectacle for us," says Father Bruyas, "to see brought into the village from all sides the dead and dying, whom two or three days' illness had either carried off or reduced to The last extremity. Most of those who were attacked by the disease felt such violent pains in the head that they lost Their reason. Father Boniface and I had a great deal to do while this General affliction lasted. The fatigue and continual watching, which gave us an opportunity of practicing Charity while endeavoring to relieve the poor dying people, seemed to us to be very Trifling in comparison with The anxiety that we felt at seeing many of those miserable people deprived of reason, and unable to make use of the last moment of Their lives to avert the greatest of all evils after their death. I had The happiness of Administering baptism to those whom I found in possession of Their faculties; when they observed that I would have liked to relieve them, they became very docile in listening to all that I told Them.

"Now, there is no reason to be astonished if the faith has made so little progress since that time, and if we have to deplore the frustration of the bright hopes that we had for the conversion of the agniés
{Mohawks} *of Tionnontoguen or sainte Marie.*

"When I saw what little prospect there was here of making new Christians, [The disease finally coming to an end,] I applied myself chiefly to Instructing the old people, and to bringing back to The fold many of the sheep who had strayed from it,—I mean, many agniés who called themselves Christians, but were so only in name. Bad example and Profligacy had so corrupted Their morals, and they had so completely forgotten their duty, that they barely remembered that they had been baptized. God has granted me The grace of withdrawing a consid-

erable number from Their evil ways, and of seeing at present a little Church, *which is beginning to give as much edification as it formerly caused scandal.* [full of fervor.] I know not when it will increase; but The Fear that I have of making Apostates of the savages renders me more cautious, until they have given me proofs of a sincere heart and of true repentance.

"I have conferred that favor upon a man and a woman. The former is an old man, sixty years of age, who at one time was a person of note, but whom a natural infirmity has caused to be so despised by the agniez that they look upon Him As a slave. God chooses the humble, and has nothing but contempt for the proud. This good man is very assiduous at prayer, and endures with admirable patience The affliction that God has sent Him, in The hope that he will some day receive consolation. The other is only twenty-five years of age. She had Long resisted grace, which urged Her to abandon her Idolatry; but the dread that she felt that baptism would send her to Heaven sooner than she wished, caused her to have An aversion for that sacrament. The error still prevails, in The minds of many Iroquois, that baptism shortens life; and it is no slight obstacle to Their conversion.

"I also baptized four little children, at the request of Their parents—all the more willingly because it is a pledge on their part that they wish to go where Their children will be blessed.

"The Greatest gain that I have had has been among the sick. *God has granted me the grace of preparing* [I have prepared] twenty-two for death, most of whom *in Jesus Christ,* have very probably gone to enjoy the blessedness that the blood of Jesus Christ has earned for them. I hope that The coming year will be more fruitful; and that the good example of the Agniez of The mission of saint Pierre, who are being converted every day, will produce such an impression on the minds of those of sainte Marie that, in the end, these will imitate Them."

Chapter 2
Of the Mission of Gandaouagué, or of Saint Pierre, in the Country of Agnié

In the two villages that lie nearest to new holland, which are situated at a distance of about five Leagues from Tionnontoguen, a second mission has been established, the care of which has for the past four years been *conferred upon* [given to] Father boniface. *To this mission The name of saint Peter has been given, because, after his majesty's arms had conquered The lower Iroquois, it was at Gandaouagué that the faith was embraced with more constancy than in any other district of agnié. There it was, properly speaking, that a nascent Church was first seen; there The Christian courage of those who compose it has manifested itself more strikingly than in any other Place.* [There the faith is embraced with more constancy, and there Christian courage manifests itself more strikingly, than in any other place.] *Therefore we call It The first and principal mission that we have among the Iroquois.*

It is true, this Church exists in the two smallest villages in the whole Iroquois country; a single village of the upper Iroquois is larger and more populous than the two of which I speak. But on the other hand it has, to a certain extent, The advantage over The other Iroquois missions that the small Tribe of Judah had over all the other tribes of Israel, who were much larger and more populous than that of Judah. "Notus in Judæa Deus." I admit that considerable evil conduct and Infidelity still prevail at Gandaouagué, as well as elsewhere; nevertheless, in these two small villages there are more faithful ones who worship God in spirit and in truth, and more souls who are truly Christian than in the other Iroquois villages. As the agniés were The first to shed The blood of the missionaries who bore The faith to Them, they were also the first to receive the fruit of their merits in greater abundance than the other Iroquois nations. In new france, as well as in other countries of the world, what Tertullian said of the martyrs of The early Church is verified, that the blood of martyrs gives birth to new Christians.

[In fact,] For ten months heaven has so favored the operations of *the missionary in that quarter,* [God,] that he counts thirty adults who have been solemnly baptized in his Chapel. *This number may perhaps appear small to those who live in Europe, which is as populous as the Canadian forests are solitary. But, When it is known that these are thirty adults baptized with the ceremonies of The Church, in a country where there are not more than four hundred souls, and where superstition, Impunity, and Profligacy contend against The Gospel, it will be admitted that, even if a missionary wins only those thirty souls, he still accomplishes more than the most zealous preacher in Europe can flatter himself upon having done in converting sinners after many eloquent sermons pronounced before a large assembly.*

Add *to this* that, while contagious diseases were carrying off a great many people, *that Father* [he] administered baptism to fourteen persons on the very Spot where they died. These are so many elect who now enjoy the blessedness that he procured for Them, and who constitute his crown and all his joy.

This success that God has been pleased to grant him has so greatly astonished those who formerly jested at our mysteries, that at present they speak of them only with reserve; and they needs must say that they begin to see that before long they will all become french.

In Fact, prayers are said as regularly, morning and evening, as in the best-ordered families in france. Nothing can be more consoling than to see these good Christians praying aloud, all together, and concluding that holy action by singing various spiritual songs. Many little children, seven or eight years of age, also Have Their own little choir, and do on earth what The angels never cease to do in heaven. It is a pleasure to see these little Innocents forming in ranks in The Chapel, and rendering Their homage to God, as well as Those who are more advanced in years.

A Little Cradle which he arranged at Christmas, illuminated with a number of Candles and adorned with green boughs, wonderfully excited The devotion of the Christians; and they gave The infant Jesus proofs of Their gratitude and love by Singing. It was impossible to resist the persistent requests of those who are still infidels to be allowed to enter, and gratify Their Curiosity by gazing for a

Long time at everything that rendered the Spot agreeable to Their eyes. The festival was spent in Singing and in praying for a Longer time than usual, in spite of The severe cold. *Because of The great concourse of all sorts of people, it was necessary to remain at the door of the Chapel and allow only Chosen persons to enter, while the Christians enjoyed, quite at their Leisure, the representation of the birth of our lord.* So great is their devotion for that lovable mystery that, in order to promote their piety, The Father allowed Them to continue Their Christmas airs and Hymns Until Easter. Can anything more fervent or touching be desired in a country that at first seemed inaccessible to the faith? *The great maxim of the missionaries is: "Patientia pauperum non peribit in finem."*

But *would you believe* [will it be believed] that the ceremony of offering the blessed bread is performed every Sunday by all at Agnié? That means, that this is done among people who have hitherto been known as Cannibals; who have formerly glutted themselves, not only with the flesh of their enemies, but even with that of those who announced The gospel to Them. They practice this ancient custom of The church with all the more pleasure since they are taught that it is The token that they are all brothers and children of God,—whose bread they eat, until he makes Them taste eternal delights. She who offers the blessed bread gives a modest entertainment to all the Christians in her Dwelling, where they say the prayer before and after meals. The Civilities that they pay to her who has invited them indicate nothing of the savage, and these gatherings serve wonderfully to foster fervor and Charity. *"Justi exultent et delectentur in lætitia."* It must truly be said that The finger of God is in this, and that He alone can effect such Changes and so alter The brutal nature of the natives as to make Wolves worthy of being among the number of the sheep belonging to the great pastor of souls.

I say nothing of The esteem manifested by this new Church for all The outward signs of our holy Religion. Crosses, medals, and other similar Articles are Their most precious jewels. So fondly do they preserve These that they wear them around their Necks, even at preaching in new Holland, where The heretics have never been able to tear away from Them a single bead of Their Rosaries.

The zeal of a good Christian woman went so far as to make her drive her husband out of their Dwelling, because he had thrown her Rosary into the fire. But when she was told of The meekness that Jesus Christ enjoined upon all the faithful, she profited so well by that instruction that her husband was won over by her self-restraint, and wished to become a Christian. He commenced to make his intention publicly known by means of a solemn feast, to which The most notable men of the village were invited. He said that he had forgotten his old formula of invocation to Agriskoué,—this is a spirit to whom they are in the habit of addressing themselves, as to a divinity, for all sorts of Things; and therefore he begged The Father to speak for Him to the master of men's lives, who is in heaven, and to whom alone he would in future present all his petitions. The Father pronounced The blessing and thanksgiving, and highly Praised this practice of thanking him who gave us our daily food, and not a demon, who Desired nothing better than to make us The companions of his misery in Hell.

Another Christian woman has been sought in marriage, for two years, by an Iroquois who enjoys great renown in his country. Any other but she would consider herself fortunate in meeting a suitor so worthy of honor, and so good a hunter as he is; but that good Christian, whose name is anastasie, prefers to be alone and to endure The Trials of widowhood, rather than to marry that man. She has declared to him that she would never have any affection for Him so long as he would continue to detest prayer and to prevent by his authority the conversion of several who intended to be baptized—for this is what he is doing. God tries The virtue of this woman by sending afflictions upon Her, and she endures them with great courage and faithfulness. Last year, she saw three of her relatives die in her Dwelling; but she would not allow the jugglers to approach them. She has since been urged to call Them in to give some relief to her children, who were said to be in A critical condition because she would not permit the remedies of the medicine-men of the country to be employed. She has constantly resisted all These solicitations, and has stated that she would rather see The children dead, and be assured of Their salvation, than have Them cured after having been The object of the criminal superstitions of those false physicians.

Disease—which Generally diminishes The devotion of the most fervent, and so weighs upon The mind that it experiences difficulty in uplifting itself to God—has not caused the Christians of this Church to relax their fervor in prayer. On the contrary, it was in the midst of their greatest sufferings that they embraced It most tenderly. They have asserted that it served as an Alleviation of Their evils; and it is now The custom, When any one is dangerously ill, for The Christians to assemble near the dying man, to pray all together for Him, and by Their example to incite Him to have recourse to God.

One day, while the Father was exhorting The Christians in The Dwelling of his hosts to perform an act of Charity, a child died there. The relatives of the dead child at once began to express Their grief by the cries customary on such sorrowful occasions. The Christians who were present, without being astonished, asked to be allowed to commence The works of Charity recommended to them, by themselves laying out The dead child in the Chapel, and accompanying It to its grave while reciting The Rosary. To the Father this ceremony seemed too great an innovation. He deemed it advisable to defer It, lest that funeral array should bury The devotion of some other new Christians, who would have imagined that prayer had caused the death of this baptized child, and that they also would soon be borne to their graves.

In the first Chapter, I spoke of the evils caused by brandy in the Country of Agnié. You have seen that the diseases which afflicted The inhabitants were among the results of that baleful liquor; so I will say no more about it. Here your Reverence will learn only the following. The Father writes that he saw [One could see] nothing more touching than The misfortune of a little child—if, indeed, one can call that a misfortune which caused its blessedness. The mother having died two days after her confinement, and The Father being at The point of death, the child was carried to Him in order to learn who should be Its nurse. The Relatives had resolved to strangle It, that It might be buried with Its mother, who in Cruel compassion had wished that they might be buried in the same grave. However, many of the women deplored The sad fate of the little unfortunate, and by Their Doleful wailings increased The sorrow of the dying Father. The missionary, who was a witness of the spectacle, saw that baptism must not be deferred any Longer, *and that he had reason to apprehend that the Father's silence would be construed into a confirmation of The sentence of death which The relatives had already pronounced. At once, without Heeding whether or not he were observed, he took some water that was fortunately being carried into The Cabin, and baptized the child.* [Some one warned the Missionary to baptize the child before it was placed in the grave with its mother.] Nevertheless, God permitted that It was not killed. It lived three months longer; and, on the day when The Church celebrated The festival of all saints, it went to Heaven to increase Their number [—a happiness that it would probably never have enjoyed had it not been for the Zeal of the christian women].

Another child, about four years old, who was dying of a hectic fever, was asked several times to what Place it would go when it died. As it was unable to speak, it looked upward and pointed with Its finger to The Place where it hoped to go.

A young Boy, fifteen years old, who had become so emaciated by a Protracted illness that he resembled a living skeleton, was several times urged, but in vain, to let himself be baptized; he contented himself with saying some prayers with The father. Finally, when he felt his end approaching, he asked for baptism of his own accord; he received It, and two days afterward he died.

A fourth, who was younger, observing the Father passing, left his Comrades to come and tell Him that he wished to become a Christian. This, which he said merely in jest, really came to pass; for two months later he fell very ill, and when called upon to remember his word, said that now he really wished to become a Christian. The Father made him pray to God, and baptized Him; he died the death of the predestined.

Let us add to these happy deaths that of a good Christian woman, named Christine, who had lived very innocently since her baptism. As the violence of The fever that carried Her off increased, She also increased the fervor of her prayers, and prepared herself for death by acts of the three principal virtues. Shortly before she died, she repeated very frequently that she was at last going to Heaven, whither she had Long desired to go. She gave directions for her funeral, and died in wonderful peace and presence of mind, holding her Rosary in her hand.

I shall conclude by relating to you what I have just learned from a Letter of the same Father boniface. He writes to a missionary that a woman who had been baptized only six months before was [I shall conclude with what happened to a woman who had been baptized only six months Before. She found herself] abandoned by her husband, The most noted Captain of the locality where he resided. He had Left Her an only daughter, whose cheerful nature made Her beloved by all The village, while she was her mother's only consolation and hope. But God was pleased to call Her unto himself, and thus to try The courage of that

Christian woman by so great a loss and so deep an affliction. Every one at once blamed Her for having adopted The customs of the strangers by becoming a Christian, it being said throughout The village that The faith had caused her daughter's death. The Demon took advantage of these murmurings, and made use of wicked tongues to try to make Her apostatize. That virtuous Savage woman courageously scorned all The reports that hatred and Calumny spread against her. She remained as constant as ever in her devotion, being regularly seen to go to The Chapel both morning and evening, communing often with God by means of The sacraments, and leading a most exemplary life. God, who is The Father and consoler of the afflicted, did not Long delay to reward her faithfulness. For, shortly after this storm, in exchange for a little daughter whom he had taken away from Her, he restored to Her, as a Christian, her husband who had abandoned Her, While he was still an infidel, on account of that very daughter. He now took Her back, and loudly proclaimed that he condemned his superstitions in order to embrace our religion. *This man,—who had been won partly by conversation with Father fremin near montreal, and partly by The good example given Him by his Christian countrymen, whose piety The same Father maintains,—*[This man,—who had been won by The striking virtues and good examples to which is due the flourishing condition of the church of the savages who dwell at la prairie de la Magdeleine, near Montreal,—] immediately upon his return to Gandaouagué, spoke highly in favor of The faith in the presence of a great number of persons, and also of the advantages of dwelling near the french. The account given by that Captain, as well as the declaration of his intention to set out, as soon as possible, to go and live with The Christian agniez who are settled *near montreal,* [as I have stated, at la prairie de la Magdeleine,] so greatly astonished and affected The majority of the agnié that they are following Him with a number of women and children, leaving Their country, and Their relatives who persist in remaining behind, to go and dwell as Christians among The french. To witness Their eagerness and diligence in starting at early dawn, you would say that it is The representation on a small scale of what happened of old in Egypt, when The Israelites stole away at night from Pharaoh's Tyranny, to go to a Free country and one abounding in comforts of all kinds.

[It is no slight proof of the faith of These good savages that they have abandoned Their Native country, Their petty household effects, and Their fields abounding in corn; and have sought a foreign land, to live there,—in poverty and want, it is true; but also that they may be able publicly to profess Christianity there, which they could not do at home on account of the great disorders caused by intemperance.]

A resolution so quickly taken and so promptly carried out aroused astonishment in the savages. The agniez of Tionnontoguen, who are not yet fully inclined toward The faith, expressed to Father Bruyas Their resentment, and The reason they had for complaining of the black gowns, who seemed intent upon making a desert of their country and completely ruining Their villages. The Father replied, by a porcelain Collar, that he felt compassion for Them on seeing Them thus abandoned by their people; that neither Father Boniface nor He had in-

spired the Agniés of Gandaouagué with the idea of going away; but that The example and voice of Their bravest warrior had exerted such an influence upon Them that they thought that they should not remain any Longer in Their country while he was absent from it. The Father told them that, moreover, the change would not ruin Their villages, as they thought; but on the contrary These would increase and become more flourishing than before, under The protection of Monsieur our governor. The latter would inform his majesty that we were now convinced of The sincerity of the Agniez, who formerly stated, in one of Their embassies, that The french and The agniez were like two bodies animated by one soul, or like two brothers who acknowledge the same Father.

This address, Delivered by The mouth of a person who fully possesses The Hearts of the Agniez, Appeased The rising storm, and The entire assembly had nothing to say against so clever an answer.

We are further assured that The other agniez, who in very small number have remained in The two villages of Gandaouagué and Gannagaro, are so dismayed by this departure that there is no doubt that they will soon follow the example of Their countrymen.

Of the Agnié Mission

1673-1674

Claude Dablon

The Jesuit report for 1673 and 1674 in New France was written by Claude Dablon (JR 58:171-177). He had been born in France in 1619 and died at Quebec in 1697. He was assigned to a mission among the Onondaga in 1655, and to other assignments in later years. He was named superior of the western missions at Sault Ste. Marie in 1669. His appointment as superior of all the Jesuit missions in New France brought him back to Quebec in 1671. He wrote the annual reports from 1673 to 1679.

The 1673-1674 report for the Mohawk mission was a synopsis of letters received from the Jesuit missionary Jacques Bruyas. Bruyas had been part of the team of missionaries sent to the Mohawks in 1667, after the 1666 de Tracy expedition. The French had destroyed Mohawk villages on the south side of the river, and the Indians had rebuilt them on the north side.

The narrative is notable for its discussion of the steady departure of converted Mohawks to Canada. The English had taken New Netherland in 1664. In 1673 the Dutch recaptured what was now called New York, but held it for only a year. The return of the English in 1774 was accompanied by an influx of New England Indians into Mohawk villages. Half of the Mohawks were already living in Canada. Pressure on the Catholic Mohawks and their Jesuit missionaries was growing, and by 1677 the English and traditional Mohawks had forged an alliance in Albany. The Jesuit mission at Caughnawaga was abandoned in 1679.

D.R.S.

THE AGNIERONNONS [Mohawks], who, among all the Iroquois, have most cruelly waged war against the French, have also been those who, among these savage nations, have embraced the Christian religion in greatest numbers, and with the most fervor. Besides the fact that their villages have dwindled away to an extraordinary degree through the departure of their people,—who have gone to la Prairie de la Magdeleine or to Notre Dame de Foye, to live there as true Christians,—many of those who have remained in their own country are either preparing for baptism, or, having already received it, thoroughly fulfill all the obligations that it entails. Father Bruyas, who has charge of this Mission, has been compelled to ask for assistance; for he writes us that, if things continue as they have for some time, he alone will not suffice for confirming these new Christians in the faith, for perfecting the older ones, for instructing the catechumens, and for performing the other duties that devolve upon a missionary.

The conversion and baptism of one of the elders, one of the most notable men of that nation, named Assendasé, has greatly contributed to furnish him all these occupations. This man, aged about sixty-five years, has always been greatly esteemed in his country, on account of his intelligence and his experience in affairs. In addition to the fact that he is the head of one of the leading families, his arrogance and his treacherous and dissembling character rendered his conversion very difficult. Interest as well as human respect retained him in infidelity, because he derived considerable profit from the practice of superstitions; while, on the other hand, if he renounced them at so advanced an age, he could not avoid raillery, which Savages cannot bear. Assailed by all these motives, he resisted for two years the influence of grace, which constantly impelled him to ask for baptism. But, in the end, the discourse addressed by Monsieur the count de Frontenac at Montreal to the deputies of the five Iroquois nations, to induce them to embrace the Faith, had so powerful an effect upon him that he resolved to overcome all human considerations in order to obey divine inspiration. In fact, as soon as he returned to his country, he earnestly requested Father Bruyas to instruct and baptize him; he manifested such fervor, and renounced all the superstitions of the country in so noble and so public a manner that, although the same Father had resolved to subject him to a rather prolonged trial, he was compelled to shorten the time of his probation, and to grant his request in a comparatively short time. On the day following his baptism, Assendasé gave a public feast, at which he declared to all the guests that he had renounced dreams and the other superstitious customs; and he asserted that he would never again be present at the meetings over which he was accustomed to preside when dreams were discussed. He has so faithfully kept this promise, and practiced all the Christian exercises, that he is the model for all the Christians. Animated by holy emulation, he proposes to equal, if not surpass, Garakontié in fidelity; and by his example to bring Prayer into credit at Agnié [the Mohawk mission], as that excellent Christian has done at Onnontagué [Onondaga]. In the fervor of his conversion, he makes use of energetic words to express his inviolable attachment to the Faith. "I have," he says, "entered into an everlasting brotherhood with him who has baptized me. If the French declare war once more, and come to kill us, I will not, on that account, relinquish the affection I feel for him; and I shall always know how to distinguish him who shall deprive us of the life of our bodies from him who has given me that of the soul, and who will always continue to preserve it for me so long as I obey him." Father Bruyas asserts that, among all the Christians, he has none more obedient or more docile than Assendasé; and that he is every day compelled more and more to admire the power and efficacy of grace in this Savage.

The conversion of this elder has caused a great stir, and has produced a deep impression on the minds of the others, so that Father Bruyas finds himself solicited daily to baptize children and even adults; but he has deemed advisable to grant this favor to a very small number only. There is reason to hope that this willingness will extend to all, at least to the majority of the Savages of Agnié; and that, as the devil formerly made use of the elders in maintaining superstitions, God will also make use of them in overturning the same, and in establishing religion. A still better reason for this hope lies in the fear that the devil himself seems to have of such a result,—a fear which he sufficiently manifests by the fresh efforts that he constantly makes to stay the progress of the Faith. For some time, the Father has daily received new insults from those who will not be converted, and an elder reproached him publicly with destroying their country, because he destroyed dreams and superstitions; and, at the same time, he threatened that, if the Father did not leave the village where he then was, he would have him expelled from the entire country. But a missionary pays little heed to threats of this kind; on the contrary, they are his consolation, because they make his labors resemble still more those of Jesus Christ, which were ever accompanied by similar oppositions.

Observations of Wentworth Greenhalgh
in a Journey from Albany
to the Indians Westward

1677

Wentworth Greenhalgh

Wentworth Greenhalgh was an official in the English colonial government. Edmund Andros, governor of New York from 1674 to 1681, became concerned about French influence on the Mohawks in the early months of 1677. He accordingly sent Greenhalgh and Arnout Cornelise west to secure the Mohawks and the other Iroquois nations as English allies. The trip was successful, and the formation of the alliance in 1677 established the Covenant Chain between the English and the Iroquois. Andros represented himself as speaking for all the English. For their part, the Iroquois were seen and saw themselves as speaking for both the Five Nations and various tributary Indian nations.

Andros was recalled in 1681, but was later sent back to govern the ambitious Dominion of New England, which eventually included all of modern New England, New York, and New Jersey. The Iroquois were encouraged to assume the similar authority with regard to all the Indian nations they represented. The unpopular Andros was imprisoned and sent back to England by the colonists in 1688 when they heard of the overthrow of James II. He later served as governor of Virginia and Maryland.

The manuscript written by Greenhalgh (1677) has been published several times. The most available of these are listed in the bibliography (Greenhalgh 1849-1851, 1853-1883, 1860-1963). The transcription provided here was taken directly from photocopies of the manuscript and checked against the published versions. The manuscript is preserved in the Public Record Office, Kew, Richmond, Surrey, England. Variations between this and the other versions are the result of our efforts to remain faithful to the original. English abbreviations have been replaced with complete words in order to ease reading except in the case of ampersands, which we have left as he wrote them. Greenhalgh's spellings of unabbreviated words have not been changed. We have retained Greenhalgh's punctuation, including even the apostrophe that he occasionally used with plural nouns. The passage in italics was added by Greenhalgh as a marginal note after the main portion of the text had been completed. I have inserted a few clarifications in brackets.

D.R.S.

Observations of Wentworth Greenhalgh
in a Journey from Albany to the Indyans Westward;
Begun May the 20th 1677 and Ended July the 14th following

THE MAQUES [Mohawks] have four towns (viz.) Cahaniaga, or Canagora, Canajorha, Tionondogue; Besides one small village about 110 miles from Albany.

Cahaniaga is double stockadoed round has four ports about four foott wide a piece, contayns about 24 houses, & is situate upon the Edge of an Hill, about a bow shott from the river side.

Canagora is only singly stockadoed, has four Ports like the former, contayns about 16 houses itt is situate upon a Flatt, a stones throw from the water side.

Canajorha is also singly stockadoed and the like manner of Ports and quantity of Houses as Canagora, the like situation, only about two miles distant from the water.

Tionondogue is double Stockadoed round, has four Ports, four foott wide a piece, contains about thirty houses, is scituated on a hill a Bow shott from the river.

The small Village is withoutt Fence & contayns about ten houses, lyes close by the river side, On the North side, as do all the former.

The Maques passe in all fore aboutt 300 fighting men.

Their Corne grows close by the River side.

Of the Situation of the Onyades and the Onondago's and their strength

The Onyades [Oneidas] have butt one towne which lys aboutt 130 miles westward of the Maques, itt is situate aboutt 20 miles from a small river which comes out of the hills to the Southward and runs into the Lake Teshiroque, and aboutt 30 miles distant from the Maques river, which lyes to the Northward; the towne is newly settled, double stockadowed, butt little cleared ground, so thatt they are forced to send to the Onondago's to buy Corne; The towne consists of aboutt 100 houses, they are said to have about 200 fighting men, their Corne growes round about the towne.

The Onondago's [Onondagas] have butt one towne, butt itt is very large consisting of about 140 houses, nott fenced, is situate upon a hill thatt is very large, the Banke on each side extending itt selfe att least two miles, all cleared land, whereon the Corne is planted; They have likewise a small Village about two miles beyound thatt, consisting of about 24 houses. They ly to the Southward of the West, about 36 miles from the Onyades. They plante aboundance of Corne which they sell to the Onyades.

6. Detail from *Carte de la Louisiane* (Franquelin 1684). The map names five Mohawk villages and places them all on the north side of the river. The westernmost, Onontiage, is a misplaced Oneida or Onondaga castle. Tionontogen, Canagaro, and Canaoage are consistent with Greenhalgh's (1677) Tionondogue, Canagora, and Cahaniage. They appear to identify villages at the White Orchard, Schenck, and Fox Farm sites respectively. Ganatebiobiare matches Greenhalgh's reference to Canajorha in placement, and both names might refer to a Huron refugee village that was probably located on the Jackson-Everson site. Three of the four sites, excepting only White Orchard, were abandoned around 1779 when Catholic Mohawks left for Canada. Thus Franquelin's map of 1684 was already about five years out of date when it was drafted.

The Onondago's are said to Bee about 350 fighting men.
They lye about 15 miles from Teshiroque.

Of the Caiougo's and Senecques, their Situation and Strength

The Caiougo's [Cayugas] have three towns about a mile distant from each other, they are nott stockadoed; they doe in all consist of about 100 houses, they ly about 60 miles to the Southward of the Onondago's, they intend the next spring to build all their houses together and Stockado them, they have aboundance of Corne they ly within two or three miles of the Lake Tiohero. They passe for about 300 fighting men.

The Senecques [Senecas] have four towns (viz.) Canagaroh, Tiotohatton, Canoenada, & Keint:he; Canagareh and Tiotohatton lye within 30 miles of the Lake Frontonacque, and the other two ly about four or five miles apiece to the Southward of these; they have aboundance of Corne, none of their towns are stockadoed.

Canagorah lyes on the top of a greatt hill, and in thatt as well as the bignesse much like Onondago, contayning 150 houses; Northwestward of Caiougo 72 miles. *Here the Indyans were very desirous to see us ride our horses, which wee did; they made feasts & dancing, & invited us, that when all the maides were together, both wee & our Indyans might choose such as liked us to ly with.*

Tiotohatton lyes on the brinke or edge of a hill, has nott much cleared ground, is neare the river Tiot:hatton which signifies bending, itt lyes to Westward of Canagorah about 30 miles, contains about 120 houses being the largest of all the houses wee saw, the ordinary being 50 or 60 foott, and some 130 or 140 foott long, with 13 or 14 fires in one house, they have good store of Corne growing about a mile to the Northward of the towne.

Being att this place the 17th of June, there came 50 prisoners from the Southwestward, they were of two nations some whereof have few gunns, the other none att all; One Nation is about ten days Journey from an Christians and trade only with one greatt house nott farre from the Sea, and the other trade only as they say with a black people; this day of them was burnt two women and a man, and a child killed with a stone, att night wee heard a greatt noyse as if the houses had all fallen butt itt was only the Inhabitants driving away the ghosts of the murthered.

The 18th, going to Canagaroh, wee overtooke the prisoners; when the Souldiers saw us, they stopped each his prisoner and made him sing, & cutt of their fingers, & Slasht their bodys with a knife; and when they had sung each man confessed how many men in his time hee had killed; thatt day att Canagaroh there were most cruelly burned four men, four women and one boy. the cruelty lasted aboutt seven hours, when they were almost dead letting them loose to the mercy of the boys, and baking the hearts of such as were dead to feast on.

Canoenada lyes about four miles to the Southward of Canagorah, contayns about 30 houses, well furnished with Corne.

Keint:he lyes aboutt four or five miles to the Southward of Tiotohatton, contayns aboutt 24 houses well furnished with corne.

The Senecques are counted to bee in all aboutt 1000 fighting men.

The French call	By the name of
The Maques	Les Añuiz
The Onyades	Les Onoyauts
The Onondago's &	Les Mantagneurs
Onondago the towne	La Montagne
The Caiaugo's	Les Petuneurs.
The Seneques	Les Caisans.
Cangaro	St. Jaques
Tiotehatton	La Conception.

The townes are called by the names of the Chappells.

Journal of a Voyage to New York and a Tour in Several of the American Colonies in 1679-1680

1680

Jasper Danckaerts

Jasper Danckaerts was born in Vlissingen, Zeeland, in the Netherlands in 1639. A convert to the Protestant religious sect called Labadism after its founder Jean de Labadie, he traveled to New York in 1679 in search for land to settle a religious colony. Danckaerts was accompanied by Petrus Sluyter of Wesel, Germany, one of the sect's main theological spokesmen.

The two Labadists traveled from one end of the former Dutch colony to the other—from Albany (Fort Orange) in the north to New Castle (Nieuwer Amstel) in the south. Danckaerts recorded in diary fashion the events of each day: persons encountered, conversions attempted (mostly failed), customs of the people, descriptions of the countryside, food and spirits consumed, and detailed notes on the Indians. Most of the original comments and observations of the latter came from their visit to the Albany/Schenectady region, where they became acquainted with Robert Sanders, a long-time resident of the area and local expert on the Mohawks.

In 1864 Henry Cruse Murphy, United States envoy to the Netherlands and long-time political figure in Brooklyn, purchased the journal from an Amsterdam book dealer. Murphy's ancestral ties to the original Dutch settlers and his deep interest in the history of New Netherland led him to undertake a translation of the journal. His work was published by the Long Island Historical Society (now the Brooklyn Historical Society) in 1867 under the title *Journal of a Voyage to New York and a Tour in Several of the American Colonies in 1679-80 by Jasper Dankers and Peter Sluyter*. The Long Island Historical Society purchased the manuscript at the auction of Murphy's library in 1884. The second edition appeared in the series entitled Original Narratives of Early American History, edited by Bartlett Burleigh James and J. Franklin Jameson as *The Journal of Jasper Danckaerts* (1913). Some revisions of Murphy's translation were undertaken at this time. This revised edition has been reprinted twice by Barnes and Noble (1941 and 1969).

All editions omitted a fifteen-page section (manuscript pages 216-231) on the Indians, which Murphy thought to be derivative from the work of Adriaen van der Donck. Danckaerts does seem to refer to van der Donck in eight places as "the writer." However, a close examination reveals the observations of Danckaerts to be original material acquired mostly from Robert Sanders. This fragment of the journal has been translated and edited by Charles T. Gehring and Robert S. Grumet (1987:104-120). The section is different from the journal style of the main portion of the manuscript and follows a hiatus (manuscript pages 192-215) that remains lost.

The first of two sections reproduced here begins with the arrival of Danckaerts and Sluyter at the mouth of the Mohawk River north of Albany on April 23, 1680. It ends with their departure from Albany on May 7, 1680. Gehring has revised this extract, which was taken from James and Jameson's 1913 edition of the journal. The second section, which begins with WEAPONS, is taken from Gehring and Grumet (1987:106-120). This remarkably sympathetic section describes Indians generally, but appears to be especially relevant to the Mohawks. The pages still missing from the manuscript probably contained some additional information on Indians.

C.T.G.

[APRIL] 23*d, TUESDAY.* Mr. Sanders having provided us with horses, we rode out about nine o'clock to visit the Cahoos [Cohoes Falls], which is the falls of the great Maquaas Kill [Mohawk River], which are the greatest falls, not only in New Netherland, but in North America, and perhaps, as far as is known, in the whole New World. We rode for two hours over beautiful, level, tillable land along the river, when we obtained a guide who was better acquainted with the road through the woods. He rode before us on horseback. In approaching the Cahoos from this direction, the roads are hilly, and in the course of half an hour you have steep hills, deep valleys, and narrow paths, which run round the precipices, where you must ride with care, in order to avoid the danger of falling over them, as sometimes happens. As you come near the falls, you can hear the roaring which makes everything tremble, but on reaching them and looking at them you see something wonderful, a great manifestation of God's power and sovereignty, of His wisdom and glory. We arrived there about noon. They are on one of the two branches into which the North River is divided up above, of almost equal size. This one turns to the west out of the high land, and coming here finds a blue rock which has a steep side, as long as the river is broad, which according to my calculation is two hundred paces or more, and rather more than less, and about one hundred feet high. The river has more water at one time than another; and was now about six or eight feet deep. All this volume of water coming on this side fell head-long upon a stony bottom, this distance of an hundred feet. Any one may judge whether that was not a spectacle, and whether it would not make a noise. There is a continual spray thrown up by the dashing of the water, and when the sun shines the figure of a rainbow may be seen through it. Sometimes there are two or three of them to be seen, one above the other, according to the brightness of the sun and its parallax. There was now more water than usual in consequence of its having rained hard for several days, and the snow water having begun to run down from the high land.

On our return we stopped at the house of our guide, whom we had taken on the way up, where there were some families of Indians living. Seeing us, they said to each other, "Look, these are certainly real Dutchmen, actual Hollanders." Robert Sanders asked them how they knew it. We see it, they said, in their faces and in their dress. "Yes," said one, "they have the clothes of real Hollanders; they look like brothers." They brought us some ground-nuts, but although the Dutch call them so, they were in fact potatoes, for of ground-nuts, or *mice with tails,* there are also plenty. They cooked them, and gave us some to eat, which we did. There was a canoe made of the bark of trees, and the Indians have many of them for the purpose of making their journeys. It was fifteen or sixteen feet or more in length. It was so light that two men could easily carry it, as the Indians do in going from one stream or lake to another. They come in such canoes from Canada, and from places so distant we know not where. Four or five of them stepped into this one and rowed lustily through the water with great speed, and when they came back with the current they seemed to fly. They did this to amuse us at the request of Mr. Sanders. Leaving there for home, we came again to the house of one Fredrick Pieters, where we had stopped in riding out. He is one of the principal men of Albany, and this was his farm; he possesses good information and judgment. My comrade had some conversation with him. He expected us, and now entertained us well. My comrade was in pain from eating the ground-nuts. On arriving home in the evening, the house was full of people, attracted there out of curiosity, as is usually the case in small towns, where every one in particular knows what happens in the whole place.

24th, Wednesday. My comrade's pain continued through the night, although he had taken his usual medicine, and he thought he would become better by riding on horseback. The horses were got ready, and we left about eight o'clock for Schoonechtendeel [Schenectady], a place lying about twenty-four miles west or north-west of Albany towards the country of the Mohawks. We rode over a fine, sandy cart road through woods of nothing but beautiful evergreens or fir trees, but a light and barren soil. My companion grew worse instead of better. It was noon when we reached there, and arrived at the house of a good friend of Robert Sanders. As soon as we entered my comrade had to go and lie down. He had a high fever, and was covered up warm. I went with Sanders to one Adam, and to examine the flats which are exceedingly rich land. I spoke to several persons of the Christian life, each one according to his state and as it was fit.

25th, Thursday. We had thought of riding a little further on, and so back to Albany; but my comrade was too sick, and had the chills and fever again. The weather, too, was windy and rainy. We concluded therefore to postpone it till the following day; and in the meantime I accompanied Sanders to the before mentioned Adam's. While we were there, a certain Indian woman, or half-breed, that is, from a European and an Indian woman, came with a little boy, her child, who

was dumb, or whose tongue had grown fast. It was about four years old; she had
heard we were there, and came to ask whether we knew of any advice for her
child, or whether we could not do a little something to cure it. We informed her
we were not doctors or surgeons, but we gave her our opinion, just as we
thought. Sanders told me aside that she was a Christian, that is, had left the Indians, and had been taught by the Christians and baptized; that she had made profession of the reformed religion, and was not of the unjust. Not contenting
myself with this account, and observing something in her that pleased me, I
asked her to relate to me herself how it had gone with her from the first of her
coming to Christendom, both outwardly and inwardly. Looking at me she said,
"How glad am I that I am so fortunate; that God should permit me to behold such
Christians, whom I have so long desired to see, and to whom I may speak from
the bottom of my heart without fear; and that there are such Christians in the
world. How often have I asked myself, are there no other Christians than those
amongst whom we live, who are so godless and lead worse lives than the Indians, and yet have such a pure and holy religion? Now I see God thinks of us, and
has sent you from the other end of the world to speak to us." She had heard me
give reasons to the others, and address them generally, before I made this request
of her. I answered, that all who professed the Christian religion did not live as
that religion required, that such were false professors, and not Christians, bearing
the name only, but denying the truth. She had said all this with a tender and affectionate heart, and with many tears, but tears which you felt proceeded from
the heart, and from love towards God. I was surprised to find so far in the woods,
and among Indians—but why say among Indians? among Christians ten times
worse than Indians—a person who should address me with such affection and
love of God; but I answered and comforted her. She then related to me from the
beginning her case, that is, how she had embraced Christianity. She was born of
a Christian father and an Indian mother, of the Mohawk tribes. Her mother remained in the country, and lived among the Mohawks, and she lived with her,
the same as Indians live together. Her mother would never listen to anything
about the Christians, or it was against her heart, from an inward, unfounded hate.
She lived then with her mother and brothers and sisters; but sometimes she went
with her mother among the Christians to trade and make purchases, or the Christians came among them, and thus it was that some Christians took a fancy to the
girl, discovering in her more resemblance to the Christians than the Indians, but
understand, more like the Dutch, and that she was not so wild as the other children. They therefore wished to take the girl and bring her up, which the mother
would not hear to, and as this request was made repeatedly, she said she would
rather kill her. The little daughter herself had no disposition at first to go; and the
mother did nothing more with the daughter than express continually her detesta-
tion and abhorrence of the Christians. This happened several times, when the
daughter began to mistrust that the Christians were not such as the mother told
her; the more so, because she never went among them without being well treated,
and obtaining something or other. She therefore began to hearken to them; but
particularly she felt a great inclination and love in her heart towards those Chris-

tians who spoke to her about God, and of Christ Jesus and the Christian religion. Her mother observed it, and began to hate her and not treat her as well as she had done before. Her brothers and sisters despised and cursed her, threw stones at her, and did her all the wrong they could; but the more they abused and maltreated her, the more she felt something growing in her that attracted and impelled her towards the Christians and their doctrine, until her mother and the others could endure her no longer; while she, feeling her love of the Christians, and especially of their religion, which she called their doctrine, to increase more and more, could no longer live with the Indians. They ceased not seeking to wrong her, and compelled her to leave them, as she did, and went to those who had so long solicited her. They gave her the name of Eltie or Illetie. She lived a long time with a woman, with whom we conversed afterwards, who taught her to read and write and do various handiwork, in which she advanced so greatly that everybody was astonished. She had especially a great desire to learn to read, and applied herself to that end day and night, and asked others, who were near her, to the vexation and annoyance of the other maids, who lived with her, who could sometimes with difficulty keep her back. But that did not restrain her; she felt such an eagerness and desire to learn that she could not be withheld, particularly when she began to understand the Dutch language, and what was expressed in the New Testament, where her whole heart was. In a short time, therefore, she understood more about it than the other girls with whom she conversed, and who had first instructed her, and, particularly, was sensible in her heart of its truth. She had lived with different people, and had very much improved; she spoke of it with heart-felt delight. Finally, she made her profession, and was baptized. Since that time, she said, the love she felt in her heart had not diminished, but had increased, and she sighed to live near Christians, who were good and faithful, and lived up to their religion. Therefore it was that she was so glad to see us, and that God, who had so loved her before, still so loved her as to permit her to see and speak to us, "*me,*" she said, "who have been such a heathen." I told her that God had showed her still more love, as she well knew. She believed it, she said, melting into tears, but she could not express her heart. "Might I only live with such people, how would my heart do good." "Blessed are they who hunger and thirst after righteousness, for they shall be satisfied," I repeated to her, and further expressed what was necessary. "How many times," said she, "have I grieved over these Christians, not daring to speak out my heart to any one, for when I would sometimes rebuke them a little for their evil lives, drunkenness, and foul and godless language, they would immediately say: 'Well, how is this, there is a sow converted. Run, boys, to the brewer's, and bring some swill for a converted sow,' words which went through my heart, made me sorrowful and closed my mouth. But I see that God still thinks of me and loves me, now that he causes me to see and converse with such people as you." We told her she must so much the more receive with love and affection what we said to her, out of regard to God and her soul. "Oh!" said she, "what you have told me is as dear to me as my heart," and she spoke with such feeling and tenderness, such depth of love, that I cannot describe it, and it affected me. Yes, she expressed to me more reality of the truth of Christianity, through the emotions of her heart, although in language according to the genius of the person, which nevertheless was nothing but loving—more, I said, than any one, whether minister or other person, in all New Netherland. She had a brother who was also a half-breed, who had made profession of Christianity, and bad been baptized, and who was not by far as good as she, but on the contrary very wicked; though, I believe, he has been better, and has been corrupted by the conversation of impious Hollanders; for this place is a godless one, being without a minister, and having only a homily read on Sundays. He was married, and so was she. She has some children; her husband is not as good as she is, though he is not one of the worst; she sets a good example before him, and knows how to direct him.

She has a nephew, a full-blooded Mohawk, named Wouter. The Lord has also touched him, through her instrumentality. Wouter speaks no Dutch, or very little. He has abandoned all the Indians, and his Indian friends and relations, and lives with his uncle, the brother of Illetie. He has betaken himself entirely to the Christians and dresses like them. He has suffered much from the other Indians and his friends. He has such a love and comprehension of God, such reverence and humility towards Him and what is godly, that it is a joy to hear him speak. His thoughts are occupied night and day with God and Jesus Christ, wondering about God and His mercy, that he should cause him to know Him, to comprehend Him, and to serve Him. He is endeavoring to learn the Dutch language, so as to be instructed in Christianity, and to be among good Christians who live like Christians. That was all his desire, thinking all the time about it, speaking always with Illetie about it, who assisted and instructed him as much as she could, and always with love, with which God much blessed her. His uncle, with whom he lived, was covetous, and kept him only because he was profitable to him in hunting beaver. He therefore would hardly speak a word of Dutch to him, in order that he might not be able to leave him too soon, and go among the Christians and under Christianity. He sent him to the woods and among the Indians, for the sake of the devilish profit of the world—these are the words of Robert Sanders, and Illetie said not much less; yet this poor creature has, nevertheless, such a great inclination and longing after Christianity.

Besides this inward desire, propensity and feeling, God, the Lord, has given him outward proofs of His love and protection, and among other instances I will relate these two which I well remember. It happened once that his uncle went out a shooting with him in the woods, when the uncle began to sneer at him, saying that he, a mere stupid Indian, could not shoot, but a Christian was a different character and was expert and handy: that he, Wouter, would not shoot anything that day, but he himself would have a good hunt. To which Wouter replied, "It is well, I cannot help it; I will have whatever God sends me." Upon this they separated from each other in the woods, and each went where he thought best. "Now when I was tired out," said Wouter, for we heard it from himself, as well as from his aunt, "and had traveled and hunted the whole day without finding any game, with the evening approaching, grieved that I had shot nothing and troubled at the reproach of my uncle, my heart looked up to God; I fell upon my knees and prayed to Him, that although I was no Christian (he meant baptized), I loved God, and only longed to learn the language in order to be instructed in Christianity, and would receive it with my whole heart; that God would be pleased to send to me a wild animal to shoot, so that the slur, which my uncle had thrown upon me, might be wiped off." While thus down on his knees, with his hat hanging upon a bough which was bent down, his prayer not finished, there comes and stands before him a very young deer, not twenty paces off; it comes softly up to him; his gun rests alongside of him loaded; he takes aim, shoots, and hits the deer in the breast, and the creature drops before him on its two fore feet and there remains. Without going to the deer, he thanks God upon his knees that he had heard his prayer and had turned back the reproach. "Oh," said he, "now do I know there is a God, who is in the woods also, and hears, loves, and thinks of me there." He comes to the deer, which is a young buck two or three years old, as fat and beautiful as he had ever seen in his life, and takes it upon his shoulders and goes with joy to his uncle, whom he found, and asked where was his good hunt and the game he had shot. His uncle was angry and spoke angrily, saying he had been going the whole day, tired and weary, without seeing or shooting anything, and had come there to look after chestnuts. "That is well, that is good," said Wouter, "reproach the Indians no more for not being good shooters. Look at what God has given me upon my prayer;" for he was very glad at what had occurred. The uncle stood and looked, and knew not what to say, being ashamed at what he heard and saw, and of himself. Wouter said further, "I know there has been no wild animal round about here, for I have explored the whole place, far and near, without being able to discover any; and now in so short a time this one presented itself before me, and it is, therefore, certain that God placed it there or caused it to come there. I have no doubt of it." Although the uncle was ashamed, he was not much affected by the circumstance, and still less humiliated or improved. But Elletie had taken it strongly to heart, and when they both told it to us, we were affected by it ourselves, and saw God in it more than he had done.

Another occasion was during the last harvest, in the year 1679, while he was out in the woods hunting beavers. He had then had a successful time and had killed some beavers, the flesh of which he used for food, and had nothing else to eat. The flesh of the beaver, although we never relished it, is esteemed by others a great delicacy. Nevertheless, as we have been told by those who are well acquainted with it, it is a kind of food with which they soon become satiated. He also became tired of it; and not having anything else became sad. He felt his heart boil—this is his own expression—and fell down upon his knees and prayed that God who had heard him before, might be pleased now again to hear him and give him other food, not so much to satisfy him, as to show that he was God and loved him—a God whom the Indians did not know, but for whom he felt he had a greater hunger than his hunger for outward food, or for what the Indians usually were satisfied with, which is beaver and beaver meat, that is, to hunt successfully and trade the skins, which is all they go out hunting for; but that he felt something else, a hunger which could not be satisfied with this food and such like; that he felt more hunger after other food than what the Indians satisfied themselves with; and sought to be a Christian, and no longer to be an Indian.

While in the midst of his prayer, there stood a fine deer before him, which he aimed at and felled at one shot. He quickly loaded his gun again, and had scarcely done so, when he saw close to him a young buffalo. He leveled his gun and brought it down; but on running up to it, he came to himself, his heart was disturbed, and he became anxious and ashamed in considering his covetousness, that he had not thanked God for the first small animal; so that he could go no further from joy and fear. He fell upon his knees before God, in great humility, shame, and reverence, confessing his fault and his want of gratitude, praying God to forgive him, and thanking Him now for both; saying that through his un-thankfulness for the first one, he was not worthy to have the second and larger one.

This may be believed as the true meaning and almost the very words of the Indian, for they were repeated to us from him in his presence, Illetie, who first told us, interpreting after him in the presence of five or six persons who were well versed in the Mohawk language, and bore testimony that he said what she interpreted, and that it was not enlarged.

Thus continuing to long after something which he did not have, and being yet in the woods returning home, he came to a bush which was growing in the shape of a man's hand, and which he stopped to look at and speculate upon. He wondered at it, and his heart was disturbed and began to *boil*. He fell down upon his knees by the bush, striking his hands into it, and prayed: "Oh God! you cause to come before me a sign or image of what I want and for which I hunger and long. It is true I have two hands with which I hunt and shoot and do other things, but I feel I still require a hand to help me, more serviceable than those I have and use, and stronger and wiser than mine. I am in want of a third hand. It is true I have forsaken the Indians and have come among Christians, but this cannot help me unless a third power make me a true Christian, and enable me to learn the language, that I may inquire, read, and enter into the grounds of Christianity." This he did with great tenderness and love; and being so much affected, he cut off the bush and took it with him in remembrance of his feelings and the outpouring of his heart to God, more than for the rarity of the figure in which it had grown. This stick or bush we have seen ourselves and had in our hands. He presented it to Robert Sanders, who carried it to Albany.

His aunt, Illetie, had taught him as well as she could, how he must pray, which she recommended to him to do every time he returned home, morning or evening, or on any other occasion which might happen to him, which he always did with concern and anxiety of heart. He always rejoiced at the proofs of God's [care] over him, and was sorry that he could not improve them, hoping and believing that God would yet give him what he still wanted and hungered after. I asked Illetie, who first told me all this, why they did not take him to some place where he could learn the language, and some handiwork, with reading and writing and the like, and especially where he might be brought to the knowledge and practice of Christianity. She said there were two impediments, first his uncle, whom we have mentioned, who only kept him as a kind of servant, such as the English have, for the sake of vile gain; and, although he was free, and bound to nobody, would never speak a word of Dutch to him, so that he might not lose him. The other difficulty was, that as he was of age, 24 or 26 years old, or thereabouts, no one would receive him for his board and clothing, fearful he would not learn the one or other handiwork, and would therefore be a loss to them. Whereupon I said if he would go with us we would give him board and clothing for all his life, and he should never be our servant or slave, and would be free and clear of all obligation; and if God should give him further the grace he would be our brother and as free as we were. "Oh," said she, "how happy he would be if he should be so fortunate, and God so honored him, as I must shame myself for the honor and happiness He causes me in enabling me to speak with you about these things." I spoke to her further what I thought would serve for her edification and consolation; and told her as my comrade was sick and not able to go out, and the weather was too rainy, she must come to us in the evening, and bring Wouter with her, that we might see him, and converse with him.

I thereupon went home and told my comrade my adventure, who was rejoiced at it, and would expect her in the evening. Meanwhile he had become stronger. The parish prelector, who is the son of minister Schaets, came to visit my comrade, and said he had heard of us, and had been desirous to converse with us. He was a little conceited, but my comrade having heard that he was the prelector, gave him a good lesson, at which he was not badly content, and with which he went away.

When evening came, so came Illetie with her husband, and Wouter, and Adam and his wife, with two or three others besides. We conversed together through Illetie, who interpreted to him from us, and to us from him, and he himself repeated all that Illetie had told me, as before related. We spoke to him from the bottom of our hearts, and he to us from the bottom of his heart and out of love to us. We exhorted, encouraged, and comforted him as much as he required, and his condition would permit. He thanked us with tenderness, that God had vouchsafed to cause him to see and speak with true Christians, with people whom he had so longed for, and with whom he wished to spend his life. "What would you be willing to give to do so?" my comrade asked. "Oh," said he, "all that I have in the world, and more if I had it, or it were in my power." We told him he must leave it to God's liberty, who would do what he pleased, would hear him, and release him when his time should come. After several episodes, we inquired of him what was his greatest wish and desire, his greatest hunger and strongest longing. "I know not justly what it is," he replied, "but I am like a person who has three knives or some other articles which are valuable, useful, and necessary, but has lost the one he has most need of, or is the most serviceable and necessary, and without which the others are of little service. Thus I have forsaken my relatives, and all my friends, my nation and country, which is good, and that is one of the articles. Moreover, I have come among Christians, and Dutch, and begun to know something of God, and that also is good, and is the second one. But I am wanting something more than these, and without which they are of no service to me, namely, a knowledge of the Dutch language, ability to enter into the grounds of Christianity, and become a good Christian." We encouraged him, and assured him of the way of the Lord, that God would hear his prayer, and fulfill his desire, according to the words of the Lord Jesus: "Blessed are they who hunger and thirst after righteousness, for they shall be satisfied." "Oh," said he to Illetie, "how I love people who speak so kindly and mildly, and know how to utter such sweet and beautiful comparisons. Oh, what love I have for them!"

After we had addressed him and her, earnestly and in love, and also the by-standers, to their shame and conviction, for their godless lives, whereby they repelled the heathen and wronged such as began to be drawn [to God] like these, and as having a terrible judgment to expect which they could not escape, Illetie said, yes, there were many Mohawk Indians, who, if they were taught, as they seek to be, and had good examples set before them by the Christians, by their lives, and were not so deceived and cheated by the Christians who ought to assist them, would listen; but now they were repulsed, and the Jesuits who were among them, and whom Wouter had heard preach several times in his own language, corrupted them all. Having said all that was proper to them at this time, we invoked upon them the blessing of God.

26th, Friday. Wouter was early at our house, in order to assist in getting the horses ready. My comrade finding himself better, but still weak, we determined to leave, two of us on horseback and he in a wagon belonging at Albany, which we had the good fortune of meeting at Schoonechten, and in which he could ride over a very comfortable road. It had frozen quite hard during the night, but when the sun rose a little, it became warm enough, especially in the woods, where the wind, which was northwest, could not blow through. I went to take my leave of several persons with whom I had conversed, and also of Illetie, consoling and strengthening her once more and committing her to God and His grace, and she leaving us with tenderness and many tears. At a place where we were taking our leave, the uncle of Wouter had come, who commenced saying in very good Dutch: "Well, gentlemen, I understand Wouter is going to Holland with you." We answered, we did not know it, nor had we thought of it, but nevertheless our hearts were good and tender enough to help him, both body and soul, in what-ever the Lord had wrought in him, or should work in him, as far as we could, which we considered to be our duty, and not only our duty, but the duty of all Christians. If he wished to go to Holland, we would not prevent him, because any person who is free may go there if he chooses; and if he wished to go with us in the same ship in which we should go over, he was free and might act his mind; yes, if he wished to be in our company we should not be able to hinder him, and while he was free no one could prevent him, or ought to, but on the other hand should aid him; especially as all who bore the name of Christians ought to assist in bringing to Christ any one who hungered and thirsted after him as Wouter did. "Well," he asked, without any feeling, "what trade would you teach him?" "Whatever God wished," we answered. "And if he should be taken by the Turks," he continued, "who would be his security, and who would redeem him?" "Well," we asked, "if we were taken by the Turks who would be our security and redeem us? God gives no security and makes no agreement. Whoever wishes to be a Christian must believe and trust in Him, and follow Him in faith, and so must you, and I, and every one, who wishes to be a Christian." Some hard words passed also between Robert Sanders and him, about something relating to himself, namely, that Sanders had said the uncle only sought to keep Wouter on account of the profit to him. As the time called us to depart, we took our leave and left him standing there abashed. Having mounted our horses and entered the wagon, we rode from there about ten o'clock, over a smooth sandy road, and arrived at half-past three at Albany, or Fort Orange, where Sanders's wife was glad to see us, and where we were well received by his whole family.

This Schoonechtendeel is situated, as we have said, twenty-four miles west of Fort Albany, toward the country of the Mohawks, upon a good flat, high enough to be free from the overflowing of the water of the river, which sometimes overflows their cultivated lands which lie much lower. Their cultivated lands are not what they call in that country *valleyen,* but large flats between the hills, on the margin or along the side of the rivers, brooks or creeks, very flat and level, without a single tree or bush upon them, of a black sandy soil which is four and sometimes five or six feet deep, but some times less, which can hardly be exhausted. They cultivate it year after year, without manure, for many years. It yields large crops of wheat, but not so good as that raised in the woodland around the city of [New] York and elsewhere, nor so productively; the latter on the other hand produce a smaller quantity, but a whiter flour. The wheat which comes from this place, the Hysopus [Esopus], and some other places is a little bluer. Much of the plant called dragon's blood grows about here, and also yearly a kind of small lemon or citron, of which a single one grows upon a bush. This bush grows about five feet high, and the fruit cannot be distinguished from any other citron in form, color, taste or quality. It grows wild about the city of New York, but not well. I have not heard of its growing in any other places.

The village proper of Schoon echten [Schenectady], is a square, set off by palisades. There may be about thirty houses, and it is situated on the side of the Maquas Kill [Mohawk River], a stream however they cannot use for carrying goods up or down in yachts or boats. There are no fish in it except trout, sunfish, and other kinds peculiar to rivers, because the Cohoes stops the ascent of others, which is a great inconvenience for the *menage* and for bringing down the produce.

As soon as we arrived in Albany we went to our skipper Meus Hoogboom, to inquire when he was going to the city. He said to-morrow, but he said he would come and notify us of the time. We saw it would run on a much longer time, as it usually does in these parts.

27th, Saturday. We went to call upon a certain Madam Rentselaer [Rensselaer], widow of the Heer Rentselaer, son of the Heer Rentselaer of the colony named the colony of Rentselaerswyck, comprising twelve miles square from Fort Orange, that is, twenty-four miles square in all. She is still in possession of the place, and still administers it as *patroonesse,* until one Richard van Rentselaer, residing at Amsterdam, shall arrive in the country, whom she expected in the summer, when he would assume the management of it himself. This lady was polite, quite well informed, and of good life and disposition. She had experienced several proofs of the Lord. The breaking up of the ice had once carried away her entire mansion, and every thing connected with it, of which place she had made too much account. Also, in some visitations of her husband, death, and others before. In her last child-bed, she became lame or weak in both of her sides, so that she had to walk with two canes or crutches. In all these trials, she had borne herself well, and God left not Himself without witness in her. She treated us kindly, and we ate here exceedingly good pike, perch, and other fish, which now began to come and be caught in great numbers. We had several conversations with her about the truth, and practical religion, mutually satisfactory. We went to look at several of her mills at work, which she had there on an ever-running stream, grist-mills, saw-mills, and others. One of the grist-mills can grind 120 schepels of meal in twenty-four hours, that is, five an hour. Returning to the house, we politely took our leave. Her residence is about a quarter of an hour from Albany up the river. This day we went to visit still other farms and milling establishments on the other side of the river, where there was a water-fall but not large, sufficient to keep about three mills going. This is indeed, I think, the highest that I have seen.

28th, Sunday. We went to church in the morning, and heard Domine Schaets preach, who, although he is a poor, old, ignorant person, and besides is not of good life, yet had to give utterance to his passion, having taken his text largely upon us, at which many of his auditors, who knew us better, were not well pleased, and blamed, condemned, and derided him for it, which we corrected.

In the afternoon, we took a walk to an island upon the end of which there is a fort built, they say, by the Spaniards. That a fort has been there is evident enough from the earth thrown up and strewn around, but it is not to be supposed that the Spaniards came so far inland to build forts, when there are no monuments of them to be seen elsewhere and down on the sea coasts, where, however, they have been according to the traditions of the Indians. This spot is a short hour's distance below Albany, on the west side of the river.

29th, Monday. We should have left to-day, but it was not yet to happen, for our skipper, so he said, could not obtain his passport. We called upon several persons, and among others, upon the woman who had brought up Illetie, the Indian woman, and had first taken her from the Indians, and to whom we have alluded before. This woman, although not of openly godless life, is more wise than devout, although her knowledge is not very extensive, and does not surpass that of the women of New Netherland. She is a truly worldly woman, proud and conceited, and sharp in trading with *wild* people, as well as *tame* ones, or what shall I call them, not to give them the name of Christians, or if I do, it is only to distinguish them from the others. This trading is not carried on without fraud, and she is not free from it, as I have observed. She has a husband, which is her second one, and he I believe is a Papist. He remains at home quietly, while she travels over the country to carry on the trading. In fine she is one of the Dutch female traders, who understand their business so well. If these be the persons who are to make Christians of the heathen, what will the latter be? But God employs such means as pleases Him to accomplish His purposes. He had given Illetie more grace than to her, we are very certain.

We were also invited to the fort by the Heer commandant, who wished to see us, but left it to our convenience. We went there with Robert Sanders, who interpreted for us. This gentleman received us politely. He said he was pleased to receive us, and to learn how we liked the lands up above, and made a few such common observations. He seemed to be not unreasonable, and a reliable person. If he was not a Scotchman, he seemed nevertheless to be a good Englishman, and, as we thought, a Presbyterian. We soon took a friendly leave, and returned home.

We spoke seriously to Robert Sanders about his pride, arrogance, temper, and passion, although according to the world's reputation he is not of bad character. His wife is more simple and a better person; we spoke to her also, as well as to their children, especially to the oldest, named Elizabeth, who was tender-hearted and affectionate. He and all of them promised to improve and reform themselves somewhat, and we saw with consolation that they in some things commenced to do so.

30th, Tuesday. We were ready to leave early, but it ran well on towards noon, when with a head wind, but a strong current down, we tacked over to Kinderhoeck, lying on the east shore sixteen miles below Albany.

Before we quit Albany, we must say a word about the place. It was formerly named the Fuyck by the Hollanders, who first settled there, on account of two rows of houses standing there, opposite to each other, which being wide enough apart in the beginning, finally ran quite together like a *fuyck,* and, therefore, they gave it this name, which, although the place is built up, it still bears with many, especially the Dutch and Indians living about there. It is nearly square, and lies against the hill, with several good streets, on which there may be about eighty or ninety houses. Fort Orange, constructed by the Dutch, lies below on the bank of the river, and is set off with palisades, filled in with earth on the inside. It is now abandoned by the English, who have built a similar one behind the town, high up on the declivity of the hill, from whence it can command the place. From the other side of this fort the inhabitants have brought a spring or fountain of water, under the fort, and under ground into the town, where they now have in several places always fountains of clear, fresh, cool water. The town is surrounded by palisades, and has several gates corresponding with the streets. It has a Dutch Reformed and a Lutheran church. The Lutheran minister lives up here in the winter, and down in New York in the summer. There is no English church or place of meeting, to my knowledge. As this is the principal trading-post with the Indians, and as also they alone have the privilege of trading, which is only granted to certain merchants there, as a special benefit, who know what each one must pay therefor, there are houses or lodges erected on both sides of the town, where the Indians, who come from the far interior to trade, live during the time they are there. This time of trading with the Indians is at its height in the months of June and July, and also in August, when it falls off; because it is then the best time for them to make their journeys there and back, as well as because the Hollanders then have more time outside their farm duties.

We came to anchor at Kinderhook, in order to take in some grain, which the female trader before mentioned had there to be carried down the river.

MAY 1st, *Wednesday.* We began early to load, but as it had to come from some distance in the country, and we had to wait, we stepped ashore to amuse ourselves. We came to a creek where, near the river, lives the man whom they usually call the Child of Luxury, because he formerly had been such an one, but who now was not far from being the Child of Poverty, for he was situated poorly enough. He had a saw-mill on the creek, on a water-fall, which is a singular one, for it is true that all falls have something special, and so had this one, which was not less rare and pleasant than others. The water fell quite steep, in one body, but it came down in steps, with a broad rest sometimes between them. These steps were sixty feet or more high, and were formed out of a single rock, which is unusual. I reached this spot alone through the woods, and while I was sitting on the mill; my comrade came up with the Child of Luxury, who, after he had shown us the mill and falls, took us down a little to the right of the mill, under a rock, on the margin of the creek, where we could behold how wonderful God is even in the most hidden parts of the earth; for we saw crystal lying in layers between the rocks, and when we rolled away a piece of the rock, there was, at least on two sides of it, a crust or bark, about as thick as the breadth of a straw, of a sparkling or glassy substance, which looked like alabaster, and this crust was full of points or gems, which were truly gems of crystal, or like substance. They sparkled brightly, and were as clear as water, and so close together that you could obtain hundreds of them from one piece of the crust. We broke some pieces off, and brought them away with us as curiosities. It is justly to be supposed that other precious stones rest in the crevices of the rocks and mines as these do. I have seen this sort of crystal as large and pointed as the joint of a finger. I saw one, indeed, at the house of Robert Sanders as large as your fist, though it was not clear, but white, like glassy alabaster. It had what they call a table point. Robert Sanders has much of this mountain crystal at his farm, about four miles from Albany, towards the Cahoos, on the east side of the river, but we have not been there.

On returning to the boat, we saw that the woman-trader had sent a quantity of bluish wheat on board, which the skipper would not receive, or rather mix with the other wheat; but when she came she had it done, in which her dishonesty appeared, for when the skipper arrived at New York he could not deliver the wheat which was under hers. We set sail in the evening, and came to Claver Rack, sixteen miles further down, where we also took in some grain in the evening.

2d, Thursday. We were here laden full of grain, which had to be brought in four miles from the country. The boors who brought it in wagons asked us to ride out with them to their places, which we did. We rode along a high ridge of blue rock on the right hand, the top of which was grown over. This stone is suitable for burning lime, as the people of the Hysopus, from the same kind, burn the best. Large, clear fountains flow out of these cliffs or hills, the first real fountains and only ones which we have met with in this country. We arrived at the places which consist of fine farms; the tillable land is like that of Schoonechtendeel, low, flat, and on the side of a creek, very delightful and pleasant to look upon, especially at the present time, when they were all green with the wheat coming up. The woodland also is very good for tillable land, and it was one of the locations which pleased me most, with its agreeable fountains. Coming back to the shore, I made a sketch, as well as I could, of the Catskill mountains, which now showed themselves nakedly, which they did not do to us when we went up the river. They lie on the west side of the river, deep in the country, and I stood on the east side of it. In the evening we obtained a still more distinct view of them.

3d, Friday. We took on board early the rest of our lading. Our tradress [sic] left us here in order to go back to Albany, and we received two other passengers in her stead, a young man of this place, named Dirck, to whom we made mention of our crystal. He said they had at his place a rock, in which there was a yellow, glittering substance like gold, as they firmly believed it was; he did not know we were there, otherwise he would have presented us with a specimen. We spoke to him, as he was a good hearted youth, several times of God and Christ, and of the Christian life, and each time he was much concerned. Truly we discover gradually more and more there is here a hunger and thirst after God, and no one to help them. They go everywhere wandering without a shepherd, and know not where they shall turn. We also spoke to the skipper's daughter, a worldly child, who was not affected by what we said. The Lord will, in His own time, gather together those who are of His elect.

We sailed from there about nine o'clock, but after going eight or twelve miles got aground in consequence of our heavy lading, where we were compelled to remain until four o'clock in the afternoon, waiting for high water. But what was unfortunate, we missed a fine, fair wind, which sprang up about eleven o'clock. Meanwhile the passengers went ashore. I walked a small distance into the country, and came to a fall of water, the basin of which was full of fish, two of which I caught with my hands. They were young shad. I went immediately after the other passengers for assistance to catch more, but when they came, they made such an agitation of the water, that the fish all shot to the bottom, and remained there under the rocks. We therefore could obtain no more; but if we had had a small casting net, we could have caught them in great numbers, or if I had remained there quiet alone. But as it was, we had to abandon it. These fish come at high water from the North River into these little streams, where they find clear, fresh water, and weeds and herbs. They remain there eating and sporting, and in the meantime at low water they are left in these holes or basins, and they are thus caught in great numbers in many of the streams by the Indians.

The water having risen, and the wind being favorable, we went on board, and as soon as we were afloat, got under sail. We proceeded rapidly ahead, and at sundown came to anchor before the Hysopus, where we landed some passengers who lived there.

4th, Saturday. We went ashore early, and further inland to the village. We found Gerrit the glass-maker there, with his sister. He it was who desired to come up here in company with us, and he was now happy to see us. He was engaged putting the glass in their new church, but left his work to go with us through the country, where he was better acquainted than we were. We found here exceedingly large flats, which are more than three hours' ride in length, very level, with a black soil which yields grain abundantly. They lie like those at Schoonecte and Claver Rack, between the hills and along the creek, which sometimes overflows all the land, and drowns and washes out much of the wheat. The place is square, set off with palisades, through which there are several gates; it consists of about fifty houses within the stockade. They were engaged in a severe war with the Indians during the administration of the Heer Stuyvesant, which is therefore still called the Hysopus war, partly because it was occasioned on account of the people of Hysopus, and because they have had to bear there the largest burden of it. In returning to the village we observed a very large, clear fountain bubbling up from under a rock. When we arrived there, we went to the house of the person who was the head of the village, where some people had assembled, who, having no minister, and hearing that my comrade was a theologian, requested him to preach for them the next day. But our skipper having finished what he had to do, we left there. Here and in Albany they brew the heaviest beer we have tasted in all New Netherland, and from wheat alone, because it is so abundant. The glass-maker informed us that Willem, the son of our old people, was going to follow the sea, and had left for Barbados; that Evert Duyckert, our late mate on our voyage out, who had gone as captain of a ketch to Barbados and Jamaica, had arrived; that it was his ship we had seen coming in, when we were leaving the city, and that perhaps he would go with her to Holland. This place is about three-quarters of an hour inland. At the mouth of the creek, on the shore of the river, there are some houses and a redoubt, together with a general storehouse, where the farmers bring in their grain, in order that it may be conveniently shipped when the boats come up here, and wherein their goods are discharged from the boats, as otherwise there would be too much delay in going back and forth. The woodland around the Hysopus is not of much value, and is nothing but sand and rock. We had hardly reached the river, when a man came running up to us as hard as he could, requesting to speak to us. We inquired of him what he desired, when he complained of being sorely afflicted with an internal disease, and said he had heard we well understood medicine, and knew what to prescribe for him. We told him we were no doctors, and had only brought a few medicines with us for our own use, and most of them we had given away. My comrade told him what he thought of his disease, and that we could not help him: whereupon this poor wretched man went sorrowfully back again, for he had spent much to be cured. We told him, however, we would send him a brackish powder which had done good in several cases, and which, if it pleased God to bless it, would perhaps help him. We went on board the boat, and immediately got under sail, with a favorable but light wind, and by evening arrived at the entrance of the Highlands.

5th, Sunday. The wind was ahead, but it was calm. When the tide began to fall, we tacked, or rather drifted along, but with little progress. We passed through the Highlands however, and came to anchor by the time the ebb was spent. The weather was very rainy.

6th, Monday. The wind was still contrary, and blew hard, therefore we tacked, but in consequence of our being very heavily laden we advanced but little. We anchored again when we went ashore at a place on the east side of the river, where there was a meadow on fire. We saw there a beautiful hard stone, as white and as clean as I have ever seen either here or in Europe, very fine for building; and also many cedar trees of beautiful color and strong perfume. Some Indians came alongside of us in their canoes, whom we called on board, and bought from them a very large striped bass, as large as a codfish in the Fatherland, for a loaf of stale bread worth about three stivers, Holland money, and some other fish for a little old salt meat.

7th, Tuesday. At daylight the tide served, but the wind was still ahead, though steady. We continued tacking with considerable progress, and at ten o'clock arrived before the city of New York, where we struck upon a rock. The water was falling, and we therefore immediately carried out an anchor, and wore the yacht off. A slight breeze soon afterward sprang up, and took us to the city. The Lord be praised and glorified for His grace. We delivered our letters, and executed the orders which were committed to us. We inquired for Ephraim and de la Grange, but they had not yet arrived.

Weapons

Their weapons were usually the same as those of all other Indians, bow and arrow, etc.; but when they saw the firearms of the Europeans, they found them an improvement to their security and coveted them. However, when the Europeans saw that their people's sale of such weapons was as giving them a knife to cut their throats, as one says, then the higher authorities decided not to sell any guns, muskets, or any firearms to them, as can be seen by the law of the land. Nevertheless, because the Indians desired them so much, they gave everything they had to acquire them; add to this the insatiable and cursed greed of the Europeans who sold them guns and other weapons, and at much higher prices because it was forbidden to do so and had to be done in strict secrecy. Even those appointed to uphold the law and punish the smugglers (which they did) brought them over by the thousands for sale, including governors and directors. Toward this end everyone did as much as they could, but always in secrecy; and if one was unwilling to do it, there were others who would, so that for every one against there were three for. Finally, when they saw that it was going to be done anyway, they did not want to deny themselves the profit. So it continued. It was also the case if one nation did not do it, then the others located around it did, such as the English and French, so that now they [the Indians] all are equipped with them and are as accustomed to carrying them as the Europeans. It was also the case in selling them gunpowder that was always being used up. Now everything is done pretty much in the open. However, they have tasted its fruits, and whereas they were not much to be feared before with their bows and arrows, they have now become bold and dare to show the muzzle of the gun as does the Hollander.

However, in spite of all this it is apparent that they will not lightly undertake anything again against the Europeans as long as there is good government; indeed, they would never have done it (so I believe) if there had been good government. For they are melting away rapidly, whether it be because of war with one another, or whether it be because of sickness, especially the smallpox from which many occasionally die at the same time. And also, the Europeans grow strong, whether it be because of their own generation's vigorous reproduction, or whether it be because of those who migrate in, which happens now more than ever before. For I have heard tell by the oldest New Netherlanders that there is now not 1/10th part of the Indians there once were, indeed, not 1/20th or 1/30th; and that now the Europeans are 20 and 30 times as many. More continue to come every day, so that it is quite apparent that this nation [of Indians] shall eventually melt away and disappear without being able to submit themselves much to the Europeans, whose godlessness has and continues to retard them [the Indians].

When they have been at war or in a battle and return home, they have a certain kind of scream or shout which they use as they pass the houses of other members of their tribe in order to indicate how many have been lost in the conflict or how many they have slain of the other side. If someone listening in a house hears that one of their own people has been lost, then they respond with a mournful countercry and begin to inquire about who it may be of their friends. If they have prisoners, they have another joyful cry and then they begin to be happy and shout for joy.

Of Their Contracts and Agreements

Their contracts are concluded as [Adriaen van der Donck] the writer of the [1653] history demonstrates, that is, with shells or counters. They hold one in their hand as long as that point is being discussed, and when that point or article has been decided upon and the entire gathering on both sides is satisfied with it, then the counter is marked, or they make it understandable and then put it away. When they come to another article, they take another counter and do as with the other until the whole contract has been concluded. Then they add up their counters, representing so many articles and the specific meaning which each signifies. As they can neither read nor write, they are gifted with a powerful memory; and as it is done so solemnly, they consider it absolutely unbreakable. And because they cannot leave it to their posterity in written form, after the conclusion of the matter all the children who have the ability to understand and to remember it are called together, and then they are told by their fathers, sachems or chiefs how they entered into such a contract with these parties. Then the markers are counted out to them, showing that the contract consists in so many articles and explaining the significance given to the markers and the story of how it was done. Thus they acquire understanding of each article in particular. Then these children are commanded to remember this treaty and to plant each article in particular in their memory, and they and their children [are commanded] to preserve it faithfully so that they may not become treaty-breakers, which is an abomination to them. Then all these shells or counters are bound together with a string in such a manner, signifying such a treaty or contract with such and such a nation. After they have been bound together, the bundle is put in a bag and hung up in the house of the sachem or chief where it is carefully preserved. Robbert Sanders witnessed this as deputy to various treaty conferences with them.

Of Their Intellect and Understanding

They appear to be somewhat sluggish in comprehension and learning ability. However, it is not so much a defect as it is a characteristic of their nature. For it is not only evident in their comprehension but also in their thinking as well as in their speech, and it pervades essentially the course of their life. They do everything intensely, penetrating matters thoroughly and speaking only when absolutely necessary, as one says, so that I frequently had the occasion to be amazed by it. Indeed, the most insolent of our people, as well as many of those with the best knowledge and who do not despise the Indians, as the coarse people commonly do, say that they are all equally dumbfounded by their speech because it is so pregnant with meaning, as we ourselves have noticed; and even those who understand their language fluently have told us many times that they were unable to say certain things in Dutch that were said to them because it was so "sweet" and full of meaning. However, the common and coarse of our nation, who are more evil than full of meaning, despise this. To us it seems to be more of a virtue than a fault. One wishes that what they despise in them would be found more in our people. Also, the Indians hate the precipitancy of comprehension and judgment, the excited chattering, often without knowing what is being said, the haste and rashness to do something, whereby a mess is often made of one's good intentions. Thus they have a very good natural understanding and whatever they do comprehend thoroughly, they understand completely and do not forget it easily; and it should be kept in mind that their sluggishness should be rectified by civilization, because experience teaches that those Indians who traffic with Europeans become quicker and swifter in comprehension than the others and begin to improve little by little.

It is true that they possess no knowledge of specific arts and sciences. Concerning medicine, they perform good cures which dumbfound the Europeans, as reported to us by those who have experienced it. However, with regard to the principles and elements of this art I believe that they are Indian in nature. And I would it were so that those of the Europeans had better principles or foundations, or knowledge of the truth. Perhaps, as coarse as theirs are, they are better than ours, because whatever they do produces better effects in many things; although much worse in others. Also, there are among them no simpletons, lunatics or madmen as among us.

It is not true that they have any knowledge of the stars and planets, nor any knowledge of their movement. If they do, it is minimal; because a certain Jesuit, who was preaching among them, took advantage of an eclipse of the moon to preach to them a few days before the event. He said, "Behold! so that you, Oh dogs and beasts! believe that I am a god, and that what I tell you is the truth, and that I have power over the heavens and its master, so shall you see at a certain time that the moon shall do such and such, reproaching you for your stubbornness and grieving for your disbelief." All the Indians were amazed by the papist's pronouncement and awaited the appointed time with anticipation. When the time came, the scoundrel set up some tubs of water and brought little mirrors in order to show them the eclipse. With wide eyes they watched it approach and when it happened they began to lament and cry out, begging him for forgiveness, etc. A few days later some of these Indians came into Albany to Mr. Robbert Sanders's house and began to tell him and others with great fervor about the Jesuit's pronouncement and its outcome. Whereupon Robbert Sanders and others said that the Jesuit was a scoundrel and had deceived them, and was seeking to mislead them through lies. The Indians were amazed by this remark, because what the papist had told them did actually happen. "I certainly believe it," said Robbert Sanders. "Ask my smallest girl when such things will happen 10, even 20, years from now. She will be able to tell you in less than an hour. We have little books which we can buy for only a few stivers. In them anyone who can read can find all of this. Therefore, what he told you was no great miracle, but rather it happens every year, and has to happen although we do not always see it when it happens or we do not give it much notice; and it would have happened even had he not pronounced it or even had he not been there. At this the Indians ran off joyfully and shamed the Jesuit (how it turned out with him I do not know)." We heard this from Robbert Sanders. If they had had the least knowledge of what the writer relates, they certainly would have known about the eclipse of the moon and have seen it with more anticipation and at least have considered that a much greater miracle, because the eclipse is something that is foremost in the knowledge of the planets.

Burial Place and Condolence

Burials occur just as the writer says. Except that I have noticed that they sometimes set off the mound which they make over the grave with a circular fence the upper ends of which are twisted together or braided to one another so that no animal may enter. They also continually keep the mound clean and weed every day with tears and lamentation; namely, the closest friend or relative and especially the women. Whether it be her husband, father, mother, sister or brother, the longer that the grave is kept clean, the more honor it is for her.

You find these burial places everywhere in the woods, but especially along the banks of rivers or streams near where they live or have lived. Sometimes you also see near these graves some markers hanging in a tree, such as a child's carrying plank or board, which we mentioned before. And it signifies that there lies or sits buried there a woman with a small child or a pregnant woman. This I saw at *Claverrack.* Or it is one or another marker signifying what kind of a person it was who is buried there. However, this is uncommon. But, if a woman has lost her husband or brother, etc., in war, then she mourns him sometimes at night but especially in the morning when she wakes up. Then she will begin to scream, "Oh, my husband! Oh, my husband! Oh, my husband! my husband! Oh, my husband! or brother, etc." This screaming lasts about an hour, every night and every morning, and because everyone in a family lives in one house, the others are frequently unable to sleep because of it. This troubles them greatly and as it continues it pains and saddens them very much, inciting them with anger and revenge toward their enemies until the men say to one another: "Come on, do we have to keep listening to this? Come on, we are getting tired of it. Let's go take revenge." And so they go back there if the war is continuing and return with a prisoner who is then offered to this widow, etc., just as we have said.

It is true that the Indians paint their faces in wondrous fashions; however, I don't believe that only the women paint themselves completely black for their husbands, because between the falls of the South River and the Raritans I have seen father, mother, wife, sister, or brother sitting together who were all painted as black as pitch, looking very aggrieved, sitting there quietly mourning.

Of Their Virtues and Vices

I do not want to speak here of their natural depravities which I know all humans share, but have in mind the exorbitances that manifest themselves in the general course of life. And then this people will have to be viewed on a higher level; I mean, before the Europeans came into their country. And then certainly one will have to admit that this people was simple, sincere, and innocent, and lived together in this manner. All histories attest to this, even those of the Spaniards; and especially those by d'Acosta, a Spaniard and himself a Dominican monk, who was there in person and saw them at the very first. However, in addition to that he considers reasons to demonstrate their innocence: because their language is unable to express drunkenness, it is a clear sign that it did not exist among them, for if it had existed there, it would have surely had a name. And with what would they have drunk themselves drunk? They had nothing but water and, according to the writer, they drink the juice pressed from grapes, which is just the same as our children sometimes do with a bunch of grapes, for they knew neither wine nor strong drink.

They also did not have theft because it could also not be expressed; and what would they have stolen from one another? There was nothing there, and no one sought to have anything, because *zeewant* [wampum], which they all treasure and now serves as their money, did not exist previously but was only their decoration as beads are for children. They had no need for it in order to live, for they obtained it elsewhere and in sufficient amounts. Also not for clothes, because they got them from animals. However, it was just their decoration, and what was then their decoration is now their money—not by their statutes but by the greed of the

Europeans, because they now trade with the Europeans for their decoration who do not want to give it the value which they set on the *zeewant*. But the Europeans have changed it several times so that it now takes three times as much *zeewant* as before, and so that they always come up short. And what did I say about stealing! Avarice was also unknown to them, because everything was held in common: land, fisheries, hunting grounds; and why would they have stolen or have been greedy, when there was simply nothing to steal? But [there was] enough to eat and drink according to their situation then. And for whom would they have done it, when no one inherited anything among them? And they still show no greed but are generous, according to various examples we have thereof. However, it is true that the Europeans do their best to teach it to them by word and deed, as we shall soon demonstrate.

Lying and deceit are unknown among them because they cannot say it. However, while joking and jeering they will say things other than they are, but that is mostly among the youth and that they have also learned from the Europeans, because with what would they have deceived one another, and why? If they lack greed and no one inherits anything? And with regard to trust, what they earnestly promise is demonstrated sufficiently by experience unless it is obstructed by another source.

They are, or were, unfamiliar with cursing and swearing, because their language has no words for it; nor have they used others for this purpose, nor has anyone ever heard such from their mouths. It is true that the Dutch who say "You lie!" and want to use it against them, as they casually do, are unable to do it in the Indian language. Nevertheless, in order to express their anger they then say "That's not the truth!" and now the Indians use the same phrase, although it is not done in the malicious spirit that the words "You lie!" connote.

Of Manslaughter

Manslaughter was almost unknown among them, because if you take away greed, drunkenness, deceit and thievery, and everything else mentioned before, and consider their apparent unconcern about fornication and adultery, then manslaughter has lost most of its power. So it is with all enmities. This has already been demonstrated with regard to nations: that it is mostly revenge and retaliation, because why would they wage war otherwise without having a cause? And this revenge and retaliation are even less among individuals who are able to give so little cause. Although it is not unknown among them, as appears from their custom of atonement or blood-feud. Nevertheless, it can also be that this has emanated from a general enmity; and that it is very rare among them and was even rarer, is shown sufficiently in what the writer says about it under the title "Of their Justice and Punishment," as well as other exorbitances which they have learned from the Europeans.

Fornication

I have little to say about their fornication or adultery, except that I can see that it was not as common before the arrival of the Europeans as was thought, because everyone was allowed to marry as was suitable and could marry as many women as he wanted (which I still doubt was the practice or was much practiced). And he could leave them as he wanted, even if there was no cause or reason. And from this you can even draw another conclusion. However, what happened when the Europeans arrived is revealed by the fruits. And it amazes me that the writer is not ashamed, because anyone can readily see that all of what he says about them on this subject must be attributed mostly to the Europeans, especially if you have any knowledge about what goes on in the countryside and what used to go on was much worse. It is certain that the Indians have imitated them because just as the Europeans have done when they have no or few women, so they have done. And the *Hoere Kil* and its name is their stigma.

I have forgotten to relate in the material under "manslaughter" that it is untrue that they are especially vengeful, because they can have their arms and legs placed in stocks, after they have been convinced that they have done wrong. And they will endure it all without uttering a word. I myself have seen two Indians who were drunk in [New] York. However, the one was more drunk than the other. The less drunk Indian was accompanied by a female Indian who was the sister of the one most drunk. This one who was most drunk had been alone in the city for a period of time; and in the meantime [the less drunk Indian] had beaten the other one's [sister], for what reason I am unaware. Whereupon the other one came out of the city and noticed that the less drunk Indian had beaten his sister. First he began to scold him and show that he was wrong; then he hit and kicked him. After that he took an oyster shell and with the sharpest edge cut and slashed his whole face open so that the blood ran down on his clothes. His face looked as if it had been cut with knives. The hands of the one who did it were bloodied as if he had slaughtered an animal. All three of them then went away together, the one beating the other until the end of Smits Valey, where they sat down together without the one, who was so injured and beaten and much stronger than the one beating him, ever uttering a word, lifting a hand or foot to help or to defend himself. This happened before our door and when we heard the noise we ran out and watched it.

It is true that when they are drunk they are at first wonderful chums with one another, singing and cavorting. However, as it increases, the women and children have to get out of the way and hide all weapons because then it turns into terrible fighting and foaming at the mouth as if they were possessed; indeed, they resemble the devil himself. They beat one another almost to death with pieces of firewood. They throw and kick one another into the fire. Finally, they badly injure one another, although on the following day they are good friends as before, and instead of seeking revenge, they come to one another begging forgiveness, saying "We were drunk; the wine or rum did it." And that is not just once but every time when they have been drunk. Indeed, I have still more to say. It is upon this that the Europeans depend, when they make them drunk. For when they are drunk they have to fight and thrash about, turning the whole house upside down. (Although there are some who are quiet and cheerful when drunk, it is uncommon.) If then a European begins to beat anyone in general or some one person, cracking arms and legs, the next day they are all good chums again. And should someone, whether European or otherwise, say, "Phew! What did you do to get beaten up like this?," rather than complain about it or express feelings of revenge, they will say, "Just what did you do?" "I got drunk. I did wrong." And they will even thank the person who beat them and beg forgiveness, saying that the wine did it.

The most objectionable thing about them, which they abide by as before, is their extreme griminess and filthiness. For I can overlook their heads and hair smeared with bear's grease or other fat; however, I have never seen them wash themselves. For this reason they always look so grimy as if they have been shut up in the smoke, which is not too far wrong.

With regard to work, they do nothing at all comparable to labor. Everything they do is a diversion, as nobles go hunting and fishing, and go off to war. That is all they do. But I don't know. I don't want to be their spokesman but if you consider the matter a bit closer, then you will see that they may not be completely without blame but are at least most excusable. Because, concerning work, I don't know what they would have produced. It is true that agriculture requires much work; however, how would they have done that living in a land where there was nothing but trees, and without the simplest tool to fell trees or to cultivate the fields? Because all that they cut was done with a piece of stone; and even though the land had all been cultivated, what would they have sown or planted in it? Because they had no seed at all, and what they did have grew sufficiently to maturity by itself. And for whom would they have labored? For their children inherited nothing, nor could they inherit anything, because there was nothing but the ground and this was so immense and spacious that it would have been absurd to make oneself the owner of a small plot, and it was all free for them, and freer than a single plot. It is true that they have mines of iron, copper, and other things from which they could have made tools; however, they had as much knowledge of what iron, steel, copper, etc., was as if it was no part of their life. Their language had no words for it—a proof that it was unknown to them, although their language has an abundance of descriptive words and is as rich as one can be. Besides, they lacked the knowledge to refine it and so forth. In a word, they were satisfied and could not be otherwise, because it is certain that most labor arises from want or need, or from avarice and greed. Until recently they were cut off from the means and the fuel (although by nature they are corrupted) by mere sufficiency of necessities and by the total lack of desire, although they live in a land full of treasures. However, if they [the means and the fuel] were unknown to them or were not treasures to them and they were ignorant regarding their preparation, and if that was bad, it was, however, not dead or rooted out but buried as under the ash of a deficient abundance lacking fuel for further consumption. And the necessity that often goes only as far as one reaches, did not concern them because they had found enough and had no knowledge to increase it. Therefore these three things were wedded therein, namely, a sufficient abundance of necessities; no external example of more or greater that could cause them to judge themselves deficient; and then a total impossibility, whether through ignorance or inability, to achieve it at all.

All of this has often caused me to think whether these people have not been sent off and driven into or toward this region, or even whether they are refugees driven from other lands. Just as when one flees, taking nothing along and only seeking to save one's life, they have come here. Otherwise it is hard to imagine how they would have been so totally stripped of all scientific knowledge for accomplishing anything. Or they must be such an old people, separated from the others before all these things came into being.

I can find no excuse for their filthiness or grubbiness except that they are always crawling, sitting and lying on the ground and in the ashes, and are in the smoke so much that they must be smoked. As a result, the elderly among them almost always suffer from bad eyes, although I believe that there are other reasons for it. And also that they grease their bodies, and the particles, ash, and other filth contained in it or sticking to it create a sort of bark by which they are somewhat more protected from the sharp bite of the cold that is so severe in these lands. This is not so strange because it is learned by experience.

This is all that I can observe about the Indians' condition and actions before the arrival of the Europeans. However, if one regards the Indians today, especially those who traffic mostly with the Europeans, then one sees that they have changed as day and night, because they have done and taught them much evil, such as drunkenness. It is certain that they have learned it from the Europeans and now they are so fond of drink that they give all they have for it: clothes and everything on their person, guns, canoes, and everything that they can carry in. This is the practice of the merchants near them: first they attempt to attract them with a sweet tune, giving them first a little pure wine or brandy; then when they soon fall into drunkenness, they talk about what they would like to buy. Then the merchants have the opportunity to cheat them. If they want more rum or brandy, as is usually the case, they get it half or more diluted with water. If they want some other goods, then they are cheated in the fabric, the measure, and the weight. Because, although there are official weights and measures, they have little use near the Indians, who are given as much as one wants to give them. For if they insist on a whole piece of cloth, they will be measured out a fourth of it and pushed away—a fourth or a half to the pound of goods, without even being aware of the deception in it. It is so coarse that the most callous merchants have troubled consciences over it. Now it is not necessary to ask who taught them to steal and deceive, to lie, and to be unfaithful. And this should be so excessive as to call for revenge, as even those who do it say themselves. They have already taught them much about fornication and immorality; however, that was earlier on, when there was no order in the land among the Europeans and everyone did as he wished. Also, there were no women from Europe, but now there are enough and there is better order; nevertheless, these things are still so coarse, especially among the English, that it is a horror. Add to this that when this land was first intended to be populated, scoundrels, whores, and peasants were sent here; indeed, the houses of correction there were emptied repeatedly for this place, as is well known. And you can imagine how such an unconstrained and chosen horde went to work in a barren and wild land, mostly without authority. They [the Indians] are not backbiters, and it is a slander to accuse them of it. For when they are sometimes asked, when they come out of the woods, "How fares this or that one of your neighbors?" they say, "I just saw him in the woods and he is still in good health." If they are questioned further, "But weren't you in his house and don't you know what its condition is?" then they would probably respond, "Phew, what kind of talk is that?" "Isn't the man free in his own house?" "Isn't he capable of taking care of his own things?" "Are we supposed to concern ourselves with it?" "Everyone has enough to do with his own things." "No, that would be very bad, so we don't do it, etc." Therefore, you can plainly see that they did not previously do it. What they now do to please the Europeans and their merchants in particular they learned from them. Just as the merchants did it in front of them, backbiting about their fellow merchants in order to attract the Indians and lure them into their store.

The young among them used to pass their time sitting at home playing with markers and shells. However, now they are completely familiar with playing cards and are as nimble at it as Europeans. These are the virtues which they have been taught and for which they have given their goods.

They knew nothing of delicacy in food or drink, excess or pride in dress, because they had neither the occasion nor the means. However, now the others have made them wiser, whether by their example or instruction, and make them pay dearly for their wares of sugar, syrup, salt, and spices. Thus the Indians also are beginning to sample what tastes best.

They knew nothing about pride in clothing. Now the Europeans stir them up as Jean Potagies, with coats, stockings, and other clothing of various colors sewn together, such as half blue, half red, or yellow or with stripes, just to kindle their pride and to sell their merchandise, and always to satisfy their greed.

Of Their Knowledge of God and Religious Practices

We have already told in our story, far removed from our journey, mostly what we have heard. Therefore, we shall relate here that the Indians in New Netherland acknowledge a primal, supreme, and omnipotent being who is sacred, good, true, and just; exceedingly perfect and blessed, omniscient and omnipresent, etc.; first cause and source of all things, who made and continues to sustain everything, from whom nothing but good flows; and who rules over evil and all evil persons, and according to his righteousness and goodness administers punishment to evil persons and assists good persons. This one they call by the general name among all of them *kicheron*. However, I have been able to learn from them something about the various persons in the divine being.

We have previously spoken about their understanding of the creation of the world and of mankind. They say that God first made a turtle which rose out of the water and began to expose its curved back. This lasted until the back was entirely exposed, and that was the earth. (It can be seen from this that they consider the turtle to be only an emblem.) Then a tree grew in the middle of the earth and on this a man. However, because there also had to be a woman, this tree tipped its top to the ground. It cast roots once more and grew up, producing a woman (so that they acknowledge man and woman as having come forth from the same beginning and in two special times and creations), and all races of the earth came forth from these two.

They acknowledge a general depravity of human nature whereby one is constantly inclined toward evil and does evil if not prevented by God. They say that all evil comes forth from the devil (whom they name *meneto*) and that they are in his power, although he does them nothing but evil, and that for this reason they have to keep him as a friend. Anything artistic or miraculous or terrifying and wondrous they call *menitto;* even artists or bold heroes they call *menitto,* because they resemble the devil.

They acknowledge the immortality of the soul, an eternal life, punishment for evil after this life, and reward for good in a pure and good land where everything is abundant and they live in happiness ever after. When asked how they know this, they say that one of them died and came back to life again and had been there (whether this has any relationship to the Lord Jesus, I do not know).

They have neither images nor idols, nor appointed times for their worship or *kintekayen,* because everything which pertains to the worship of God is called *kintekayen,* even by the Europeans. During this time they are very rigid and quiet.

Their *kintekayen* or devil-chasing has been described sufficiently by the writer. However, I did hear this from Jan Theunnissen Backer who saw that the *kintekayer* at the end fell to the earth in a faint or as in a trance and lay there sweating as if he lay in water, and his breast no longer went up and down as usual but heaved as a bellows. After lying on the ground for a while he tells the gathering what *menitto* has told him and what they must do.

From all of which can be plainly seen that they belong to those whom God has given over to the god and prince of this world and has let them wander, as forsaken ones, in their own paths, without concerning Himself with them, as the writer says and they themselves say by experience. He will have pity on them and in His own time draw near, as He is doing, and let us who are unworthy of it see the first fruits. His name be praised and may the living, flowing water flow out of Jerusalem to here in the west.

About the Wondrous Nature of the Beavers

Just as they are very ingenious in the building of their houses, they are no less in the construction of dams whereby they dam up water in a kil [creek] near where they live or want to live so that in the summer time or during dry spells they do not lack it. For this purpose they choose a large tree standing on the side of the kil and hanging over it. They drop it so that it falls into the water with all its branches. Then they go upstream and bring as much dry wood as they find sufficient and can manage, and then they float them crosswise or at angles or however against this tree and its branches and leaves so that it begins to hold. Then they bring clay or earth for the dam, so that nothing can wash through, until the flow stops. Then again they float smaller pieces of wood into the remaining holes and then put more earth on it so that it becomes very tight. Then by beating on it and plastering it with their tails they make it into such a firm and strong work that it is amazing. By such means they sometimes dam up great amounts of water; indeed, they can put entire areas under water. Mr. Robbert Sanders told us that a Frenchman named La Fleur, whom we also saw on the point of Lisbeth's *Kil Achter Koll,* this La Fleur was coming with another in a canoe out of Canada when they reached an area, which was a kil, where they had insufficient water to continue with their canoe, so that they were forced to break open a beaver dam. They got so much water by doing this that they had enough to go on for three days and had to do nothing more.

The lions, bears or other ferocious animals in New Netherland are not as ravenous as elsewhere; indeed, they will do nothing unless they are harmed or pursued. This is also so with the rattlesnake.

The bears sit the entire winter in a hollow tree with their young. They make the hole so narrow that you could barely put a *kaetsbal* through it and it serves to provide them with air. It sits in it the entire winter without coming out, sucking on its paw. It sucks itself so thin that, when it comes out, it and its young can barely walk. It is then that the young are taken away after the big one has been killed. This was told to us by people who saw it done.

A Narrative of an Attempt Made
by the French of Canada
upon the Mohaques Country

1692

Nicholas Bayard

Nicholas Bayard (Beyard) was born in 1644 in Alphen, Holland. He was of French ancestry, the son of a wealthy merchant and the nephew of Peter Stuyvesant. He grew up in New Amsterdam speaking French, English, and Dutch. He was influenced by Stuyvesant, director-general of the province of New Netherland, and with his uncle's help he secured his first position as a clerk in the office of the provincial secretary. When the English conquered New Netherland in 1664, Bayard's knowledge of English facilitated his rapid rise. In 1666, Bayard married Judith Varlet (Varlith), who had been imprisoned as a suspected witch in Hartford, Connecticut, in 1662. He was well positioned by the time the Dutch temporarily retook the province in 1673. He had political and financial problems after the English returned a year later, but by 1685 had risen once again, this time to the position of mayor of New York. Jacob Leisler seized control of the government and threw Bayard in jail for over a year. Leisler and Bayard changed places when a new governor arrived from England. His journal dates to 1692, after these events (Bayard 1692). A transcription of the journal can be found in the Montgomery County Department of History and Archives, but I have been unable to locate the original. Still later, in 1701, Bayard was again accused, this time of sedition and mutiny, and sentenced to hang. Another new governor (Edward Hyde, Viscount Cornbury) arrived to save Bayard and his fortune by appeal to Queen Anne.

Bayard's spellings are irregular and inconsistent, but I have left his narrative as he wrote it. A few clarifications have been added in brackets where I judged they would be helpful to the reader.

D.R.S.

A Journal kept by Coll. Nicholas Beyard
and Lieut. Coll. Charles Lodwick,
who Attended His Excellency in this Expedition

SUNDAY, THE 12TH of February, 1692, about ten a Clock at night, an express from Lieut. Coll. Beekman of Vulster [Ulster] Country, gave his Excellency an account of Advice from Albany of the French and Indians, consisting of 550 being within 20 miles of Schenectady on the 8th instant, an hour before day, ready to fall upon the two first Castles of the Mohaques [Mohawks].

Whereupon his Excellency ordered the Collonol of the Militia of the City of New York to draw out his Regiment the next Morning.

Monday the 13th, Orders were sent to Coll. Courtland of Kings County, and Coll. Willet of Queens County, to detach out of their Regiments a hundred and fifty men, to be forth with ready to imbarque at the Ferry.

About eight a Clock in the Morning the City Regiment being under Arms, his Excellency on Horse-back at the head of the Regimint, demanded, Why were willing to follow him to the Frontiers against the Enemy? They unanimously threw up their Hats, and cryed, One and all. Upon which the Collonol was ordered to detach 150 of the fittest men, to be under the Command of 3 Captains, with their Subalterns, ready at the first Beat of Drum, and dismissed the Regiment, and ordered all Sloops for Transportation to be secured. About ten a Clock his Excellency did send the express forward to Coll. Beekmen, with orders to get all the Horses in the County of Ulster together in readiness, to carry his Excellency and the Detachments from Kingstone to Albany by Land, in case the River was not open, and to forward any Confirmation of the News to his Excellency.

Tuesday the 14th, by break of day came an express from Major Ingoldsby, confirming the former News, and that the two first Castles were taken by the French and Indians. Whereupon eight Sloops were ordered, with necessary Provisions and Amunition to go round the Fort, and be ready to sail, and the Detachment of the City Regiment did immediately imbarque. About four a clock afternoon the Tide offering, his Excellency attended with the Officers of the Detachments, and several Volunteers, did imbarque and set sail.

Friday the 17, about 9 a clock his Excellency arrived at Albany, being 50 leagues distant from New York, with five of the Sloops, having met with much Ice in the River, which gave some difficulty; the rest arrived towards evening.

As soon as they came on shore, his Excellency ordered Capt. Schuyler to march 50 of the men for Schenectady; about 11 a clock his Excellency followed, with 26 Horse, leaving Instructions with Coll Beyard to forward all the rest of the Detachments, as they did [   ] about half of time together with the Amunition and Provisions.

About 3 a clock afternoon, his Excellency met Major Ingoldsby about 8 miles from Schenectady, on his return for Albany, having gone from thence to visit Schenectady that morning. His Excellency arrived at Schenectady, being 20 miles from Albany, about 5 a clock. About 9 a clock at night Capt. Schuyler, with his men arrived, and found Provisions & Quarters in Readiness for his men.

Saturday morning the 18th, by break of day the men were ready to be trans-ported over the River but a violent Storm did hinder their Transportation till af-ternoon, and Sundry Indian Woman Loaden with Provisions, were sent along with them. This day about Noon Major Merrit, with the rest of the City Detach-ment, did arrive at Schenectady, and were immediately furnished with Quarters, Amunition and Provisions, ready to march next morning.

Sunday the 19th, by break of day, the rest of the Forces that were fit to march, did attempt to get over, but great Quantities of loose ice did hinder, till at out ten a clock the Ice settling, they got over it on foot, which in two hours was dis-persed, and the River open again. This partly carried a further supply of Provi-sions and Amuniton.

Monday the 20th, by break of day, those of the City Detachments, who were not able to march the day before, being refreshed, his Excellency detached from the Garrison of Schenectady, so many of them as made 42 who did immediately march with 13 Horses Loaden with Provision and Amunition.

About 2 a clock afternoon arrived at Schenectady Capt. Stillwell, with the Detachment of Kings County, consisting of 50 men, who were ordered to refresh themselves till next morning, and three Horses with Provisions ordered to be in readyness to attend them.

Tuesday the 21st, the Horses being carried over the River, and the men ready to be transported, came an express from Major Schuyler, giving intellegence of his being near at hand on his Return, who arrived about 4 a clock afternoon; upon which the men and Horse were remanded, and sent back to their own homes. There marched by his Excellency's order (to joyn Major Schuyler) since his arrival 208 effective men, besides Guides and Carriers of Supplyes, with considerable quantities of Provisions and Amunition, which are since returned.

Wednesday the 22d his Excellency returned for Albany, accompanied with Major Schuyler, and Several of the Forces come from pursuit of the Enemy, and arrived about 3 a clock afternoon, much dissatisfied at the Enemies escape.

His Excellency did order Major Schuyler, with some other Officers, to give the Journal of their Action in the Woods.

At 4 a clock arrived Coll. Willet at Albany, with 120 men from Queens County, who were next morning remanded home to their Habitations, together with the rest of the Detachments. At night his Excellency sent to call those Indi-ans that were returned from the Fight, to meet him next morning at Albany.

Thursday the 23d, a Proclamation issued, requiring all the out Farmers to draw themselves into Neighbourhoods, for their better security against the scalking Enemy, and to fortify Stockadoes.

Fryday the 24th, his Excellency received an Address from the Corporation of Albany, congratulating his safe return, and returning Thanks for his early Assis-tance with his Personal Presence for their Relief, etc.

Saturday the 25th, the Indians being arrived last night, and giving their atten-dance, this morning his Excellency, being accompanied with the Magistrates of this City, and the Souldiers and Militia in Arms, came to the City Hall, and made his Speech to the Indians, which was interpreted to them by the Interpretess

Helle. In the afternoon they gave their Answer to his Excellency by the same Interpretess.

Sunday the 26th, about 8 a clock in the morning, four of the chief Sachims [sachems] came to his Excellency, with saome further Propositions, which he immediately answer'd to their Satisfaction.

Monday the 27th, his Excellency caused a Proclamation to be published, prohibiting the selling of Rum to the Indians, and did imbarque for New York, where he arrived Thursday morning following, and was received with such Expressions of Joy and Thankfulness, as the place could afford.

NICHOLAS BEYARD, COLL.
CHARLES LODWICK, LIEUT, COLL.

Report on the French Attack
on the Mohawks

1693

Peter Schuyler

Peter Schuyler was born in Albany (then Beverwyck) in 1657, seven years before the English conquest of New Netherland. He was the father of Philip Schuyler, who was a major military figure in the American Revolution. Peter Schuyler was an army officer and the first mayor of Albany (1686). He maintained friendly relations with the Iroquois generally and the Mohawks in particular.

The account reproduced here is Schuyler's report on his efforts to defeat French and Canadian Indian raiders who attacked the Mohawks in 1693. His report was first published by E.B. O'Callaghan (Schuyler 1854). The episode is commonly referred to as the Frontenac Raid of 1693. The attack, which took place in February, was one of two devastating French raids against the Mohawks in the seventeenth century. Both resulted in burned villages and forced relocations to new village sites. In this case the Mohawks left their burned villages on the north side of the Mohawk River and built new settlements on the south side. The previous raid was that led by de Tracy in 1666.

Schuyler visited the court of Queen Anne in 1710, accompanied by three Mohawks and a Mahican. One of these men was the grandfather of Joseph Brant. Another was Tee Yee Neen Ho Ga Row (Hendrick), later a leading Iroquois League chief and friend of William Johnson. The four Indians were subjects of a well-known series of paintings by John Verelst, done while they were in London. Schuyler died in 1724.

Schulyer's account contains some spellings that are no longer standard. These have been left as he wrote them, and they should not impede understanding. Typographical errors in the earlier published version have been corrected.

D.R.S.

IN OBEDIENCE to his Excellency's Command, Peter Schuyler Mayor, with the other Officers under his Command, give this following Account of their proceedings since the first intelligence of the Enemy's descent into the Country of the Mohaques.

February the 8th, being Wednesday, about 2 a clock afternoon, we had the alarm from Schenectady, that the French and their Indians had taken the Mohaques Castles; soon after we had the News, that a young man, called Jan Baptist van Eps, (taken at Schenectady 3 years a go) was run over from the French, as they were to attack the first Castle of the Mohaques, and come to Schenectady, who related, that the French were 350 Christians and 200 Indians. Major Ingoldesby sent forth with his Warrants, to command in the Farmers of Capt. Genits and Capt. Tunis's Companies of Militia. This night Lieut. John Schuyler and Cornet Abeel with 35 Horse marched to Schenectady.

February 9. Cornet Abeel came express from Schenectady, and desired that Major Schuyler or Major Wessels might be sent thither to pacifie the Indians, who were enraged that no Christians went out in pursuit of the Enemy. Upon which Major Schuyler at his own request was permitted to go that Evening. As soon as Major Schuyler arrived there, he sent out scouts to spy the Forts, and the Enemies motion, and withal to go & warn the Tionondoge Indians of the Enemies coming, but they having gone 12 miles, returned, about 12 a clock at night, saying, they could not get over the River.

Feb. 10. Major Schuyler sent Lieut, Johannes Schuyler and Lieut. John Sanders, and six more to view the Mohaques Fort that was possessed by the Enemy, who brought news, that the French were in both the Forts; of all which he gave advice to Major Ingoldsby at Albany.

Feb. 11. Major Schuyler sent 10 Christians and 40 Indians to lie near the Enemy, and to watch their motion, who made a small Fort to retreat into, and so spyed what the Enemy did.

Feb. 12. News was brought to Schenectady by some of the said Scouts, that they had heard firing at the Mohaques Forts, which was supposed the Tionondoge Indians against the French; which News Major Schuyler sent forward to Albany. Whereupon Major Ingoldsby detached about 200 men out of the several Companies of the Militia Fuzileer and Troop, commanded by Capt. Peter Matthews, Capt. Arent Schuyler, Capt. Benj. Phips, Capt. Kinad van Renslaer, and Capt Tho. Gartin, who arrived at Schenectady about 2 a clock afternoon and joyned Major Schuyler; The Waggons with Bread arrived that night. This day our scouts brought us the News, that the French were there still, & that they had also cut off the third Castle of the Mohaques, called, Tionondoge, and that none of the upper Indians were come down; all which was advertised to Major Ingoldsby forthwith, and Major Schuyler sent to him for Orders to march.

Feb. 13. This morning having received no answer of the said Express, Major Schuyler sent another for Orders to march, and being pressed with the Indians, who threatened else to desert us, was forced to march the men over the River without Orders, which came about 4 a clock in the afternoon, when most of the men were got over the River. This very time we had News by our Scouts, that the French had burnt the Mohaques three Castles, and were marching away, which Major Schuyler ordered Lieut. Young to signifie to Major Ingoldsby. We marched 12 miles that evening, being 273 Christians. In the night about 10 a clock one of our scouts came in, and told us, that 600 of our uppermost Indians were coming down; Major Schuyler forthwith sent the same Messenger, that brought us the News, to Major Ingoldsby, and desired that provision and Amuniton should be sent after us, not knowing what the Indians might have occasion for.

Feb. 14. About 1 or 2 a clock in the morning we decamped, and marched to the small Fort which was made by our 50 scouts, about six a clock in the morning, where we had advice. that the Enemy was not above eight miles from us; upon which Lieut. Harms van Slyk and two Indians were sent to discover the Enemy, who brought us word, they were marched; two Indians came to us with News, that there were 300 of our upper Indians within 20 mile of us, whereupon we sent two Indians back to hasten them up, and to let them know we were there to joyn them. We sent out three Mohaques to discover the Enemy; about 4 a clock in the afternoon we decamped, and marched to the place where the Enemy had lain the night before.

Feb. 15. In the morning two of our Indian Scouts returned (the third being run over to the Enemy) who brought us news they had seen the Enemy within ten miles. Our Indians came up with us about 12 a clock, being 290 men and boys, some armed, and some without arms, a Consult being had we marched about 4 a clock, and encamped all together, having marched about ten miles that afternoon. This night a Consult was held, and Spyes sent to discover the Enemy.

Feb. 16. We marched early in the morning, and having gone ten miles, found the place where the Enemy, had lain two nights before; we halted there, an Oneyde [Oneida] Indian came from the Enemy, being sent to our Indians to debauch them over to the French, which Messenger we did not think fit to sent back, being one of the Prisoners taken at Tionondoge. We sent an express to Major Ingoldsby to acquaint him that the Enemy had built a "Fort, and were resolved to fight us, and sent for supplies of Provision, Amunition and Men, We marched on toward the Enemy, and met with one of our wounded Indians, who informed, that the Enemy stayed for us in a Fort; upon which we marched about two miles, where a Christian Boy (Arnant the Interpreters Son) came to us, who had been three years a Prisoner among the French, he gave account, that the Enemy were about 6 or 700 men, and within three miles, we marched forward to find some convenient place to encamp, and to fortifie our selves from the Enemy that night; we had Scouts out (Christians and Indians) all night to watch the Enemies motion, who brought account in the morning that we were within a mile of their Fort.

Feb. 17. We decamped, and marched toward the Enemy, with Scouts before us, and did not take a direct line, but went round, for fear of an Ambuscade, and came in sight of their Fort about eight a clock in the morning, where our Scouts came and showed us where the Enemy lay, upon which all the Officers were commanded to take their Posts, and make ready to engage, being 250 Christians, and 290 Indians, the Enemy seing us, gave three War'cy which we answered with as many, and as loud as they, and made the woods ring; our Indians went to work to fall Trees and fortifie, but the Enemy sallyed out immediately, we engaged them, and beat them back into their Fort, our Indians fell to work again,

7. Detail from *North America* (Franquelin 1688). This later map by Franquelin shows three Mohawk [Anniez] villages on the north side of the river and
one on the south, but names none of them. These probably identify the White
Orchard and Caughnawaga sites as well as an archaeologically undiscovered
hamlet that is known to have existed just west of Caughnawaga at the time of
the Frontenac raid of 1693. The village on the south side of the river might
refer to the Allen site, which was certainly occupied after 1693 and might
have been founded prior to 1688.

and desired our Christians to help, which they did; the Enemy sallyed out with
all their strength a second time, encouraging their men, crying, They run, we will
cut them all off, and get their Provisions; We received them briskly, & beat them
back into their Fort, with the loss of several of their men: Our men fell to work
again about the Fort; the Enemy sallyed out the third time, but were as well repulsed as before, and beat into their Heads and Scalps into our Fort; after this the
Enemy was quiet, and we finished our Fort; as soon as this Skirmish was over,
we sent an Express to Major Ingoldsby, to acquaint him what had passed, praying him to hasten our Recruits with Provisions and Amunition, for that greatest
part of our men had not had any provision in two days time; we sent out Scouts

of Christians and Indians all that night, to discover the Enemy's motion, and lay all night in our Fort; it was extream bad cold snowy weather.

Feb. 18. Being cold stormy weather, and Snow, insomuch that we could scarce see any Tract, our Scouts came in this Morning, which gave account that the Enemy were in their Fort, some being still popping at our People. About nine a clock an Indian that left the French in their Fort told us, He thought the Enemy would Retreat, that they were packing up their Baggage. Upon which Major Schuyler ordered the Captains to draw out their men to march round the Enemy's Fort to stop them; but the same time had an account they were fled; he commanded the officers to pursue them, and to hinder their Retreat, till men and Privisions came up, but the Men wanting Provisions, refused to march; the Officers with 60 Christians and some Indians pursued the Enemy till they had made a small Fortification, but the Officers not having men to engage them, nor to make a Fort, returned back, leaving two Officers with 40 men and 100 Indians to watch their motion, expecting our Provision to come up that night.

Feb. 19. About 7 a clock in the morning we had an account, that our Provisions were near at hand, which came up to us about nine or ten a Clock, with 80 men, commanded by Capt. Simms; the provisions being immediately distributed among the men, those that were first served, were commanded away after the Enemy, with five Biskets a man: About four a clock, the van being commanded by Capt. Peter Matthews and Capt. Arent Schuyler, came up near the rear of the Enemy, the Scouts telling us, the Enemy were within less than an English mile; we desired the Indians to joyn with us to fall upon their Rear, till the rest of our men came up, sending in the meantime to our People, to march up in all haste, but the Indians halted, and could not be perswaded to march, the Mohaques being most unwilling, because the Enemy had dropt several Prisoners, who told them that if they pursued them, they would kill all their wives and Children, whom they had Prisoners; after an hours Consultation of the Indians, most of our men came up, we marched with all speed, thinking to overtake the Enemy before they got to the River side, but there being a flake of Ice in one part of the River, and all open above and below, the Enemy got over before we got up so We encamped by the River side that night.

Feb. 20. In the morning Major Schuyler resolved to march over the River, to pursue the Enemy, ordering the Officers to get the men ready for that purpose, but many of the men being wearied with fatigue, their Shoes being quite wore out, and Provisions scarce, were not able to make any further pursuit. But that which did most of all discourage us, was, that the Indians had great averseness to pursue or fall upon the Enemy, because of their Wives and Children; whereupon we marched back.

In this Engagement we lost four private Souldiers, & four Indians, two Officers and twelve Christians, and Indians wounded; and we had an account by some of our Indian Prisoners that made their escape, that we killed of the Enemy 33, whereof we found but 27, among which was their Commandant, one Captain, and two others Officers, with two of their commanding Indians, and 26 wounded. We rescued between forty and fifty Prisoners.

Since their Retreat we are informed by divers of the Prisoners, who come home daily, that all our men Prisoners except five, have made their escape, or are set at liberty, and but few Women and Children left with them, not being able to carry the Prisoners off, by reason of their wounded men, whereof they carry thirteen.

As we did not hear, so we could not expect that your Excellency should in so short time (at that season of the Year) be advanced so near us as to Schenectady, and that so considerable Supplies be so speedily got together: And we observed it was no small encouragement to our Indians to see your Excellency at the head of 300 men, besides Volunteers, for our Relief, and theirs; of which we are all sensible.

PETER SCHUYLER, MAJOR
PETER MATTHEWS, CAPT.
K.V. RENSELAER, CAPT.
ARENT SCHUYLER, CAPT.
BENJ. PHIPPS, CAPT.

An Account of the Military Operations in Canada Against the English and the Iroquois, Since the Month of November 1692

1693

Jean Bochart de Champigny, Sieur de Noroy et de Verneuil

Bochart de Champigny was born in France after 1645. He was educated first at a Jesuit college and later studied law. He was apparently an able but humorless administrator (Eccles 1969:71-80). He sailed to Canada from La Rochelle in 1686 and served as intendant of New France from his arrival until 1702. He was involved in Denonville's 1678 campaign against the Iroquois and implicated in the enslavement of Iroquois captives. He later worked with Governor Frontenac, but his bureaucratic style did not mesh well with Frontenac's flamboyance.

French Jesuit missionaries retreated from the Mohawk Valley by 1679, and the French feared that the English would come to dominate all of the Indian nations from Albany westward. King William's War began in 1688 as the competition between English and French interests heated up again. Champigny introduced reforms in the ways the French army was equipped and supplied, mandating new uniforms that made French soldiers look more like *coureurs de bois*.

Champigny was eventually able to persuade Frontenac that a direct assault on the Mohawks would be more effective than raids on border settlements. The attack in 1693 devastated Mohawk villages, which had been located on the north side of the Mohawk River since an earlier French attack in 1666. The Mohawks subsequently relocated their villages on the south side of the Mohawk River in two widely separated areas, near the mouths of Schoharie Creek and East Canada Creek respectively. These became the upper and lower Mohawk communities of the eighteenth century. Champigny returned to France after completing his service as intendant of New France. He died in 1720 at Hâvre-de-Grâce.

The narrative was previously published in English translation in volume 9 of the *Documents Relative to the Colonial History of the State of New-York* (NYCD 9:550-555). It is reproduced here without the footnotes supplied by Edmund O'Callaghan in that earlier publication. The sometimes curious spellings of that translation have been preserved.

D.R.S.

THE IROQUOIS not liking to wage war except secretly, ordinarily select the season when the trees are full of leaves, to approach the French settlements on the frontier of the Colony. When they see the leaves fall and the ground covered with snow, they retire home and do not appear any more, or at least very rarely, during winter.

Count de Frontenac being desirous to take advantage of the season of their retreat in order to strike a heavy blow on them, dispatched from Montreal in the month of January a force of six hundred and twenty-five men, consisting of one hundred soldiers, two hundred Indians, and the remainder the most active young men of the country, under the command of Sieurs de Mantet, Courtemanche and de Lanoue, Canadian officers, accompanied by Sieur de L'Invilliers and twenty other officers, with orders to proceed against and destroy the Mohawks, and afterwards to commit as great ravages as possible around Orange. This party provided with every thing necessary for so long and fatiguing a march on snow shoes through woods and over frozen rivers, dragging their provisions after them, were guided so correctly by our Indians that they arrived near the three Mohawk villages, within fifteen leagues of Orange without being discovered. At nightfall, on arriving, our Indians in company with some Frenchmen went to reconnoitre two of the Villages, situate a quarter of a league the one from the other. On approaching these, they heard the enemy sing which obliged them to wait until the Indians should retire in order to surprise them whilst sleeping. The main body, in the meantime, advanced in two divisions, so as to be able to make a simultaneous attack on both Villages. Our scouts did not delay reporting that the enemy made no more noise. The Villages, which were surrounded by strong pallisades and closed with gates, were approached; our Indians scaled the inclosure in order to open the gates. A crowd entered and became masters of all the cabins without resistance. The small Village, after having been burnt with all its contents, was abandoned at day break, and the Indians and their families brought prisoners to the large Village where the commanders left a portion of their force to guard them. Early next morning our party set off for the third Village, distant seven or eight leagues, where they arrived in the evening, and surprised it on the following night in the same manner as they had the others; set it on fire and brought the prisoners to the principal Village.

The Count's orders were not to give any quarter to the men who would be found under arms, and to bring away the Women and Children for the purpose of augmenting our Indian villages. But this order was not strictly executed, because they surrendered at discretion and expressed themselves pleased at having this opportunity to come and live with our Indians, to whom they were closely related; so that, of about eighty fighting men found in those three villages, only eighteen or twenty were killed, and the others, with the women and children, were made prisoners to the number of two hundred and eighty persons.

This expedition having succeeded as much as could possibly be desired, and our Frenchmen having perceived that a young Englishmen, a prisoner of our Indians whom they brought with them on this march, had made his escape during the night on which the two Villages were taken, and that he would undoubtedly notify the English of their design, judged it unsafe to remain any longer in the enemy's country, as the smallest delay might prevent their retreat, having to travel over the lakes and rivers on which the ice was beginning to rot. Therefore, after they had sojourned only one day at the principal Village, they burnt it, and set out with all the prisoners. On the first and second days of their homeward march, several Mohawks, who, whilst hunting in the neighborhood, had learned the destruction of their Villages, came to join them, expressing their desire to follow their wives and children. They reported that the English and Iroquois had received intelligence, the former by the young Englishman who had escaped, and the latter by four Iroquois who on their way to Orange discovered the trail of our party and then returned to their village to notify the warriors, who were then assembled there to the number of seven hundred, deliberating on the expeditions they were to organize in the spring, and who they believed were on their march to attack our party. On the third day the avant-couriers of the Iroquois did, in fact, overtake our Indians, and submit several propositions to them from their people and the English, to induce our people to wait for them on pretext of having a talk about peace which they represented, on the part of the English, was already concluded in Europe. The Commanders correctly judging it a feint to enable the English and Iroquois to overtake them, for the purpose of attacking them, resolved not to wait; but our Indians having received new assurances of good faith from the enemy who asserted that the Iroquois were in great consternation at the destruction of the three Mohawk Villages; that they were almost certain of their being inclined for peace in order to avoid similar treatment with which our Indians were threatening them; and that, moreover, our party being come to wage war, it must oppose the enemy in case they should dare attack it, so that the resolution was adopted to wait for them and to construct a fort of stockades, for the purpose of security and the confinement of the prisoners.

Two days afterwards, the Iroquois to the number of three or four hundred men arrived, in company with some Englishmen, within musket shot of the fort, where they at once entrenched themselves behind a large abatis of trees. Our Frenchmen and Indians judging correctly thereby, that their design was not to talk of peace resolved on immediately attacking them. They sallied from the fort and advanced towards the enemy and some shots were exchanged on both sides and the foe repulsed within their retrenchments which it was not deemed expedient to force, for fear of falling into some ambush. We lost on this occasion [eight men] and the enemy as many according to their report.

Our Frenchmen having learned from some Mohawks who came over to them, that the English were coming with a large body to reinforce the Iroquois and attack our people, abandoned the fort an hour after the last action, and continued their march the remainder of the day, conveying the wounded on litters. The enemy pursued and encamped within half a league. Some Iroquois came again to assure our Indians that the English Commander was approaching to make peace, and pressed them to wait for him; but our officers aware that this was merely to amuse them, made answer that they had been waiting too long for them, and if they wished to come, let them repair to the centre of Lake Champlain, where they would again wait for them, either to receive their propositions or to fight them. Our party marched the whole of next day, followed by the enemy, and reached the lake on the day following; the ice on it was found all rotten, and the men sunk in some places up to the waist. The greater number of our Indians separated from our Frenchmen with intention of striking across the woods, and the prisoners being too much embarrassed by their baggage (*equipages*) and the women by their children, were almost all forced to remain on the lake-shore. Only fifty of them followed, and the other prisoners promised to come in the spring. Our Frenchmen having arrived at a place where they had secreted, when on their way up to the Mohawk country, a portion of their provisions to serve them on their return, discovered these entirely spoiled by the rain; so that they found themselves entirely destitute at a distance of nearly fifty leagues from our nearest settlements, having to carry the wounded also, under these unfavorable circumstances. They dispatched four Indians and one Frenchman to advise us of the circumstances, that assistance may be promptly sent them; and those messengers reached Montreal in five days. M. de Callières immediately dispatched one hundred and fifty men to them with provisions on their backs. Never was there such distress. They were four or five days without food. About one hundred and twenty, overpowered by fatigue, remained behind until they should be somewhat restored by the supplies that we forwarded to them. Two or three died of hunger; many threw down their arms, and almost all arrived without blankets (*couvertes*) and half naked, scarcely able to drag their heels after them. What was surprising under such untoward circumstances was, that the enemy did not pursue them; they did not dare to follow over the lakes, as the ice melted under their feet. Certain it is, had it not been for this special interposition of Providence, not a solitary Frenchman would have returned.

Whilst this party was out, letters from Acadia and from Sieur d'Iberville commander of *le Poly*, were received at Quebec, stating that two Frenchmen who had deserted from that place last summer with some English prisoners, had repaired to Boston whence they had been sent to Acadia by Governor Phips to carry off or assassinate Sieur St Castin, a gentleman esteemed among our Indians—and that these two Frenchmen having been arrested, had confessed every thing, and reported that warlike preparations were in progress on a large scale at Boston preliminary to coming next spring to attack Quebec by sea with ten thousand, and Montreal by land with two thousand, men. This led Messrs de Frontenac and de Champigny to make the necessary preparations for the extensive fortification of these two posts, and to put them in a complete state of defence.

At the opening of spring, M. de Callieres sent out a detachment of nine Indians in the direction of the English to procure some prisoners, in order to ascertain the designs of the enemy. They went within two leagues of Orange where they discovered five or six men at work in the bush. They killed all except one whom they brought off a prisoner. He was a Frenchman who had been taken at Placentia four years ago; he assured us that the English had issued a proclamation calling on the people to prepare to attack Quebec; that orders had been sent throughout the entire country to muster the settlers; that the rendezvous was fixed at Boston; that they were to leave on the 10th of May and that there were to be ten thousand men exclusive of the crews. This news confirming what had been brought by the French who attempted the murder or seizure of Sieur Saint Castin at Acadia, obliged Mess[rs] de Frontenac and de Champigny to urge on the fortifications of Montreal and Quebec, so as not to be surprised, and to notify the Acadian Indians to hold themselves in readiness to march to the assistance of Quebec at the first notice they should receive of the sailing of the fleet.

And in order to have some reliable news of the enemy's departure and movements, M. de Callières dispatched from Montreal different parties of Christian Indians in the direction of Boston and of the Iroquois Villages. Those who proceeded towards Boston took some English prisoners whose heads they were obliged to break, being unwilling to accompany them; the others did not find an opportunity to strike a blow, so that nothing could be ascertained through them.

In the month of May, M. de Frontenac dispatched four canoes with twenty-three men, escorted by twenty-seven others, to convey his orders to Missilimaki-nac [Michilimackinac] and to adopt measures for bringing down the peltries. They went through in safety, but the escort, in returning, was attacked above the Island of Montreal by a party of the enemy in ambush on the margin of the River, who fired a volley on the canoes, killed [number unspecified] men and took [number unspecified] prisoners; Among the number of those was Sieur de la Valterie, a Canadian officer, who commanded the party.

Three or four parties of Abenakis and Canibas {Kennebecs] arrived at Quebec from Acadia in the course of the same month and in June, bringing some English children whom they had captured, and the scalps of several men whom they had killed in the neighborhood of Boston. Those who arrived last have informed us that the English had sailed from Boston and that an English lady, whom they had taken and left in Acadia, had assured them that several of her relatives were gone on board the fleet.

This intelligence caused the works at Quebec to be hastened. The settlers within twenty-five leagues were commanded to repair thither, and in less than a month the town was inclosed by pallisades fraised after the new fashion, and having a sodded parapet from fifteen to eighteen feet in thickness; the platforms were placed within the bastions, on terre-plains of eighty feet from the parapet; two extensive pieces of Masonry were constructed, one on Cape Diamond, which commands the entire town, for sixteen pieces of cannon, and the other on a height which defends the Cape. M. de Frontenac visited the settlements below Quebec in order to dispose the people to retire into the woods with their movables, cattle and provisions, on the first news of the enemy, so that the latter may not find any thing—not even a blade of grass or any refreshment.

In the latter end of June, an Iroquois Indian belonging to a Village called Oneida, arrived at Quebec with a Frenchman who was a prisoner there. This Indian said that he came on behalf of his family and a portion of his Village, to ascertain whether there were not some means to negotiate a peace, and that he was disposed to mediate with the other Iroquois to induce them to agree thereto in case the Governor should consent on his part to lend a hand to it. M. de Fron-

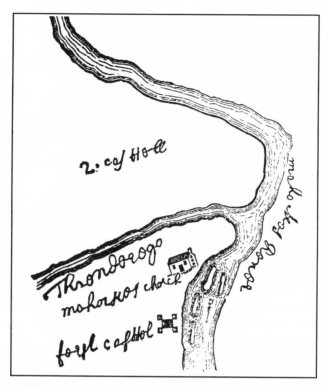

8. Lower Mohawk Castle. This sketch map, on which north is to the right, is from a survey dating to October 23, 1712 (DHSNY 3:543). The "first casttol" was probably on the Bushy Hill site at that time. A second castle was on the Milton Smith site. The two were later consolidated around Fort Hunter at the mouth of Schoharie Creek, noted here as the site of the Mohawk's church. There the settlement became known as the Lower Mohawk Castle, and distinguished from the Upper Mohawk Castle west of modern Canajoharie.

tenac told him that, before listening to any proposals, the Chiefs of the Tribes must come and wait on him to assure him of their good dispositions, and that their persons would be entirely safe.

Seven or eight days after this Indian had taken his departure, there arrived at Quebec a Frenchman named Saint Michel who had been two years a prisoner among the Iroquois. Having been condemned by them to the stake, he preferred to expose himself to perish in the woods. He slipped out at one of the Village gates, which he fortunately found open some hours before the time fixed for his being burnt and, nearly naked, without food, arms or any thing else, he traveled more then two hundred leagues through the forest in twenty-five days, living on grass and roots. He informed us that eight hundred Iroquois were preparing to come and attack us, and that the Indian who had come to speak to M. de Frontenac was acting in good faith, but his adherents were not considerable. He reported also, that the Outawas [Ottawas] and other Nations at a distance from the French, had been harrassing the Iroquois around their Villages, and had killed some of them; that a Frenchman, a prisoner among the Iroquois, being out hunting with seven men and two women, had with an axe killed the seven men whilst sleeping, and conveyed the two women to the Outawas.

News was brought at the same time to Quebec by a canoe from Hudson's bay, that the posts there in the occupation of the French, were guarded by only four men, and that the rest had left for want of provisions; that one Guillory, the Company's armorer, had assassinated the Surgeon and Father Dalmas, the Jesuit; the first by a shot of a gun outside the fort in consequence of a slight difference that had arisen between them whilst the garrison was engaged hunting; and the Father with a blow of an axe, being apprehensive, on confiding the crime to him after serving his mass, they two only being in the fort, that the Father would denounce him to the Commandant. This post will be victualled by some canoes that the Proprietors sent thither in the Spring, and by the Company's ship which sailed from Quebec in the beginning of June, with a full supply of necessaries.

At the close of July, two of our Indians having escaped from the enemy by whom they had taken them prisoners, notified M. de Callières that eight hundred Iroquois were coming down to cut off the harvest; this intelligence caused him to determine on mustering all the forces in his government, so as to form an expedition eight hundred strong, at the head of which he placed himself, to go and meet them.

M. de Frontenac, on learning this movement sent him three hundred Regulars, under the command of Sieur de Vaudreuil, who started from Quebec eight days after his arrival from France, and took up, at Three Rivers in passing, forty-five settlers and 63 Indians. On arriving at Montreal they found M. de Callières returned with his party, without having encountered the enemy. He had taken the precaution to station French Scouts at the passes so as to prevent surprisals, and sent two detachments of Indians to Lakes Champlain and Saint Francis, on the route to Orange and the Iroquois, in order that no party might pass unnoticed, and that the harvest may be gathered in security. He sent at the same time, under the command of Sieur Hertel, who was ennobled by the King in 1691, a detachment of seventy Indians and some Frenchmen to the Grand River of the Outawas to facilitate the passage of the Indians of that name, and of the French who were bringing down the Peltries.

In the beginning of August a party of the enemy made its appearance at the place called Saint Francis, ten leagues above Three Rivers; surprised a gentleman named Crevier, the Seigneur of that quarter, and fifteen or sixteen men who were cutting their grain. They carried off Sieur Crevier and a soldier, and killed a farmer; the others fled into the fort from which they were distant only about a musket shot.

Done at Quebec the 17th of August 1693.

CHAMPIGNY

A Journey to Onondaga

1750

Christian Daniel Claus and Conrad Weiser

Translated and edited by Helga Doblin and William A. Starna

Conrad Weiser was sent to Onondaga country by way of the Mohawk Valley in 1750 by Thomas Lee, president of the Virginia Council. Weiser was instructed to invite the Iroquois to a council at Fredericksburg, where Lee hoped to reconcile them with the Catawbas. Weiser met Daniel Claus in Philadelphia and invited him along. Both had come from Württemberg in Germany and they formed a close friendship. Weiser had been in America for twenty years, but Claus was new to the country. The Iroquois preferred to meet at Albany, but this was not acceptable to Weiser. The meeting was probably doomed by the death of Canasatego only two days before Weiser arrived. Canasatego had been an English ally, and he was replaced by a pro-French Catholic.

After their trip to Onondaga, Claus attached himself to William Johnson. Weiser died in 1760. Two years later Claus married Johnson's daughter, Ann (Nancy). Claus died in 1787 in England, having been forced to leave the Mohawk Valley by the American Revolution.

The journal of Claus and Weiser, from which this brief section is extracted, is in the collections of the *Archives nationales du Québec* at Saint-Foy. The complete journal includes the Christian creed in Mohawk and an incomplete Mohawk-German dictionary, among other things not relevant to this volume. Weiser wrote some sections in English, while Claus wrote others in German. The section dealing with the Mohawks, which is reproduced here, was written by Claus. It has been translated and edited by Helga Doblin and William A. Starna. Clarifications have been included in brackets. The complete journal is scheduled for publication. This complete version will include extensive endnotes.

D.R.S.

ON TUESDAY, the 28th of th[is] m[onth], we set out early on the way to Schoharie in good weather but because of a badly constructed road we could not progress very fast. On the way, we were riding through a valley when Mr. Weiser told how he together with his father-in-law and several others had once been in Albania [Albany] during wintertime. On their way back, they were overtaken by nightfall and not being able to reach Schoharie, they had to spend the night in the

238

bush with an Indian where they were completely snowed in. After 17 miles, we arrived about one o'clock in the afternoon in Schoharie, where Mr. Weiser 20 years and then some ago had lived and thus still had some friend or good acquaintance here and there. We turned in at a Justice [by the name of] Johannes Lawyer, who after lunch led us to a church newly under construction. There we met Mr. Sommers, the minister of the place, who had been sent here from Hamburg [Germany]. This afternoon we walked around the place to visit some acquaintances. The next day Mr. Weiser rode to his half-sister, who lived 10 or 12 miles from Schoharie; I, however, decided to remain in order to get more information about this place and the region as a whole; AB DESCRIPTIO[NE]: Since Mr. Weiser stayed away for 2 days and did not return before the evening of the 30th, we intended to advance a good stretch on the next day. But we could not depart on Friday the 31st before *Brackfest time* because the Reverend Sommers accompanied us part of the way under overcast sky. We begged him, however, to stay back at the last plantation while we continued our journey toward the aforementioned Cornet Johnson's place in Mohawk land on a narrow and rather bad Indian path. On the way, however, we were surprised by such a heavy rain that we were completely drenched. [*several illegible words*] place where there was a natural salt-lick and [we] saw that there were various paths made by the animals. Because of this we missed the right way and again got on another unknown to us. As we were now erring along through bush and hedges completely drenched—Mr. Weiser had also lost one flap of his coat as well as the heel of one of his boots—, we finally encountered 2 Indians, one of whom was sick. Mr. Weiser inquired from them whether this path led to Cornet Johnson's but they did not want to understand any of this but said that this was a way to Schoharie and that we were 5 miles off the beaten path and if we had stayed on the right way, we could by now be at the desired place. Fate had been both favorable and unfavorable to us for if we had not encountered the Indians, we could have reached no place anymore in day light and would have had to spend the night in the bush in drenched clothes without having eaten or drunk. Quite willingly, we turned around with our guides and after crossing the Mohawk River reached the English Fort Hunter at nightfall. This castle had a garrison of [*left blank*] soldiers, otherwise most of the inhabitants were Indians [who lived] in houses built of tree bark. We had to take up quarters at one of the Indian chiefs, by the name of Brant, in German, Brand, and we really could not find fault with it; for he lived in a well built, 2 story house, provided with furniture like that of a middle class family; there was nothing wanting in our food or drink or in our beds. In the morning, we had a good breakfast. We then wanted to pay our respects to the commanding officer, Capt. Butler, but he must already have heard of Mr. Weiser's arrival wherefore he anticipated us in making the [special] effort to come to our lodging.

After informing himself now about this piece of news now [*sic*] about that one from Mr. Weiser, he [turned to me] asking from which country I was and how I happened to be on this journey. Complying with his wish I answered him whereupon he told how he had gotten around quite a bit in northern Germany, yet no farther than the Rhine River while he was in [the] English Military Service. He wanted to take us to his lodging but since we had to hurry on, we asked him to excuse us and hastened to get to Johnson's, which we accomplished after covering 3 additional English miles. At 9 o'clock in the morning we stopped by the aforementioned plantation of Cornet Johnson and asked whether he was at home. He came out immediately and invited us into his room. Mr. Weiser delivered his letter whereupon he asked where we came from and how far we intended to go. Mr. Weiser gave him the answer. He [Johnson] said that last Thursday a gentleman (mailing address: Kalm staying in Philad. at present), sent by the Royal Swedish Academy of Science, had departed for Albany from here after having stayed a few days with him. He had come from Onondaga and on his trip had made various observations about plants and herbs. He [Kalm] had also told him about all sorts of things which he had researched as something very special with the Indians; among others he had asked him [Johnson] about the geometrical shapes of flowers and how the Indians executed their salicalion [salicin] cures with little effort and without any danger to their life. He [Kalm] had been most interested in it and asked Mr. Johnson to do him the great favor of sending out a few Indians after the seeds before he returned. He [Johnson] promised him to do so. It turned out a bit different because even for the Indians they [the seeds] were something very rare to get a hold of. But yesterday the Indians arrived with the seeds; so today he sent out 2 young Indians to bring him live rattlesnakes, which Mr. Kalm had also requested. All this would please Mr. Kalm when he returned. Mr. Weiser gave him [Johnson] to understand that he regretted not to be able to meet said gentleman here as they had agreed in Philadelphia to meet each other in Onondaga. Mr. Johnson replied that he expected him tonight according to [the message that] he [Kalm] had left behind whereupon Mr. Weiser decided to remain. In the meantime, various Indians, acquaintances of Mr. Weiser, came by, greeted him and sat down with him. Mr. Johnson mentioned that since the last war, the Indians all of a sudden no longer came to his house and only sporadically did one or the other drop in without, however, wanting anything. One should not be annoyed that it made no great difference to them whether these were times of war or peace since anyway every means was employed by France to win the English Indians over to their side. And indeed, a French clergyman was placed at the border, who was provided with all the materials belonging to the Indian attire. When one or the other English Indian or their children came to him, he welcomed them very amicably, took them into his store and whatever clothes they chose, he would order them made completely gratis for them; such things made a great impression on these people. It was the same with the religion, and since the French knew that the Indians were great admirers of [French] pictures and decorations catching their [the Indians'] eyes with their extremely beautiful French adornments, they presented their religion to these people through all those pictures. Besides, he [Johnson] wanted to do all kinds of things as e.g. giving the Indians provisions of ammunition from his own bag together with 4 pockets full of advanced money, which [originally] was to be paid to the province. He then led us into a room where he kept his library in a safe place together with his globe and other rarities as e.g. Indian weapons of war. Among them were 1 spear, 2 big arrows and 1 club whose head was of black agate. It was completely round with a little hollow out of which they also smoked; it was about one hand long and the haft about 2 Schl[ag] long. When they defended themselves with it, the blow landed either on the chest or in between the shoulders. Otherwise, Mr. Johnson was rather well provided with a blunderbuss, rifles, muskets and other guns. He also had a charming scarlet and silver habit, which he wore in the last war since he himself had to face great danger and much worry although his house was surrounded by block houses. He likewise led us around the house, whose upper part was still under construction. But as could be judged from the lower part and other features, nothing would be wanting in it in regard to comfort and elegance once it was finished. Anyway, Mr. Johnson showed us many courtesies and treated us well as we drank a good glass of wine first of all to the head of the country and to his own superior but then, we did not forget those we left at home in Germany.

The bigger of Mr. Johnson's dogs makes everyone laugh. When I sat down near him, he came at once, looked at my shirt buttons, ring, boots and spurs and as I, coming from the bush, still had some [leaves or twigs] hanging down from the bottom of my coat, he neatly took them down from me. But when his master came along and had something to eat for him, he embraced, kissed and pressed him to his heart. When he offered him watermelon and bread, he took each in one of his paws and ate them in turn like a human. Mr. Johns[on] said that this animal was a great lover of dram. When the hogshead in the cellar had been opened, he [the dog] smacked around the tap and rattled it until it poured out and all ran onto the floor. This caused great damage not only to him, but also to the many pelts of wild animals that were stored there; the young moor had to be baptized by force.

On Sunday morning, Sept. 2, we departed in hot weather which, however, turned cooler after a rain shower. We walked along the Mohawk [River] on a rather good road and passed through one of the most fertile regions of which I had learned before and now saw for myself. It was only regrettable that the people who cultivated it were so poor that they left the best land untilled and only hoed around the edges; bears and wolves also did much damage. After covering 25 miles we came to one Barthol Pickert, the brother of Mr. Weiser's brother-in-law. On Monday, the 3rd of th[is] m[onth], several good acquaintances accompanied us to Mr. Weiser's sister. Since on the way we visited a man, called Nie Fuchs, who was more than 100 years old, we did not arrive at the sister's house before 2 o'clock in the afternoon. Because M. W.'s horse while being shod had been injured by the Smith John, he had to rent another from that one's brother-in-law; at the same time they took one of his sons, N[ie] John, along, who took care of the provisions that were prepared for the bush.

Description of the Country Between Oswego and Albany—1757

1757

Anonymous

This brief description of the river route between Oswego and Albany was previously published in volume 1 of the *Documentary History of the State of New York* (DHSNY 1:338-343). It was published in translation from French as *Paris Document XIII.* The author is unknown. Notes found with the original are reproduced here as endnotes. Additional notes made by O'Callaghan are unnecessary and have been omitted here. Parenthetical and bracketed clarifications made by O'Callaghan have been rendered consistently in brackets here for clarity. A few obvious typographical errors have been corrected, but spellings have otherwise been left unchanged. The narrative is valuable for the details it provides regarding batteau traffic on the river, and sites along the Mohawk River in the middle of the eighteenth century.

D.R.S.

ITINERARY FROM THE MOUTH of the river Chouegen [Oswego] in Lake Ontario to Lake Oneida, then up Vilcrick [Wood creek] to the Summit level which is the source of the river of the Mohawks, or *des Agniés,* by which we can descend to Corlar or Chenectedi whence Albany or Orange can be reached.

The entrance of the River Chouegen is easy; the harbour is formed of a cove. The English had a fort on each side of this River by which this entrance was defended.

From Chouegen to the Great fall is an ascent of four leagues. In this space the navigation is intricate, the river rapid and encumbered by large rocks. Good pilots, familiar with the shoals, are requisite to be able to pass through it. Batteaus must be unloaded at the Great fall where a portage occurs of about 40 to 50 paces. The batteaus are dragged along the ground.[1] It is estimated to be about four leagues from the Fall to the mouth of the River of the Five Nations, [river Seneca] which mouth is called the Three Rivers; its navigation is good. About a quarter of a league before coming to the Three Rivers there is, however, a current where precaution is requisite.

From the Three Rivers to Lake Oneida is computed at 8 leagues; the navigation is good; the river is about 60 paces wide; it is at all times passable with loaded vessels. This river is the outlet of Lake Oneida. There is neither fall nor rapid at its entrance.

Lake Oneida is twelve leagues long by about one league wide. Its navigation is beautiful and practicable at all times, unless there be a strong contrary wind. It is best on the right of the lake which is the north side.

From Lake Oneida we enter the River Vilcrick,[2] which empties into that Lake, & ascent nine leagues to Fort Bull. This river is full of sinuosities, narrow and sometimes embarrassed with trees fallen from both banks. Its navigation is difficult when the water is low. It is, however, passable at all times with an ordinary batteau load of 14 to 1500 weight. When the waters of this stream are low, an ordinary batteau load cannot go by the river further than within a league of Fort Bull. It becomes necessary then to unload and make a Carrying place of the remainder by a road constructed to the Fort, or to send back the batteaux for the other half load.

Fort Bull which was burnt in 1756 by a detachment under the orders of M. de Lery, was situated on the right bank of this River near its source on the height of land.

From Fort Bull to Fort Williams is estimated to be one league and a quarter. This is the Carrying place across the height of land. The English had constructed a road there over which all the carriages passed. They were obliged to bridge a portion of it, extending from Fort Bull to a small stream near which a fort had been begun though not finished; it was to be intermediate between the two Forts, having been located precisely on the Summit level.

Fort Williams was situated on the right bank of the River Mohawk or *des Agniés,* near the rise of that river on the height of land. It was abandoned and destroyed by the English after the capture of Chouegen.

Leaving Chouegen there is a road over which the English used to drive cattle & horses. This road follows the border of the left bank of the River Chouegen. The Five Nations river is passed at a fall near its entrance into the River Chouegen, after which the road proceeds along the edge of the right bank of the Five Nation's river to the Village of the *Onnontagués* [Onondagas] whence it proceeds across the country to the village of the Caskarorins [Tuscaroras] and the Oneidas[3] whence we can go to Forts Bull and Williams; also to fort Kouary without being obliged to pass the said two forts. The path or road taken by M de Belhêtre in his expedition against the village of the Palatines may be also used. He went from the mouth of the Famine River [now Sacketts Harbor] ten leagues below Chouegen; ascended this river for the distance of four leagues, and leaving it on the left followed the path leading to Oneida Lake on his right, and came to the Summit level at Fort Williams.

The Country through which he passed is fine; there being but few mountains. The soil is soft only in the latter part of the season. He forded three rivers the waters of which were very high during the four days that he was going from the River Famine to Fort Williams, a distance estimated at 24 to 30 leagues.

From Fort Williams the Mohawk river is navigable. Batteaux carry the same load as in the river Vilcrick to the portage at the Little Falls, which is about two leagues below the village of the Palatines and Fort Kouari.

From Fort Williams to Fort Kouari, situated on the right bank of the Mohawk river, is estimated to be 12 leagues. The road follows the right bank of the river which is the south side.

Leaving Fort Williams there is a road that unites with that by which horses and cattle pass from Fort Kouari and Chouagen. This road is bad for about four leagues after leaving Fort Williams. The Country is marshy. Carriages [*les trains*] travel it in winter and during the summer, and it can be easily passed on horseback at all times, though in some places, there is a great deal of mud. After these four leagues, carts can easily go as far as Fort Kouari. Having traveled three leagues on this road which is five leagues from Fort Kouari, we come to the forks of two roads one of which, to the left, leads to the Palatines' village by fording the Mohawk river.

Continuing along the high road, which is on the right bank of the River Mohawk, to go to Fort Kouari, a creek is met that must be forded. Here was a gristmill that has been burnt. One league before reaching Fort Kouari another small stream is encountered over which there is a bridge. This stream is fordable almost at all seasons. There was, also, a saw mill on this creek which has been burnt.

Fort Kouari is situate on the right side of the Mohawk river, on a small hill on the edge of that river's bank. It is a large three story stone house with port holes [*crénelée*] at each story, and likewise in the basement for the purpose of cross firing. There are some small pieces above. The house is covered with plank and shingles. It was built as a store and depot for Choueguen. It is surrounded by a ditch at a distance of about 30 feet. This ditch is six feet deep and seven wide. The crown of the ditch inside is planted with palisades in an oblique form; they are well jointed the one to the other. Behind these there is a parapet of earth so as to be able to fire over the palisades. The four angles of this parapet which is at the back of the ditch, form as it were, four little bastions that reciprocally flank each other. On the West side there is a house apart from the large one. It backs against the parapet of the palisades and serves as a barrack and guard house. There are two doors to the large building; the one at the North is a small swing door. It is used only in going to the river for water. At this side of the house there is no ditch; only palisades fixed in boards set against the brow of the right bank of the river to support the earth. The large door of the house is on the south side; it is folding but not ironed. To go outside the palisades and ditch through this large door, you must leave the house to the left and turn to the Eastward where there is a passage. The ditch has not been excavated. The earth serves as a bridge and road. There are palisades to the right and left; on both sides of the way the whole width of the ditch. Outside the ditch there is a folding gate. There is no other barrier nor chevaux-de frise in front. The nearest house outside the fort is about 150 paces. Opposite this fort in the river is a small cultivated island which can be reached at low water by fording.

From Fort Kouari to that of Cannatchocary [Canajoharie] is four leagues. Some twenty houses are located at a distance one from another, within the space of one league of this road, which is through a flat country. After making this league we go up a mountain that occupies two hours to ascend and descend. The country throughout the whole of this space is covered with wood. After descending, two houses somewhat distant the one from the other are in the league which is still to be travelled to get to Cannatchocari.

The Inhabitants of this Country are Palatines or Germans. They form a Company with some who dwell above the Fall on the other side of the River which is the left bank. This company consists of about 80 men. The road from one to the other of these two forts is good for all sorts of carriages.

Fort Cannatchocari is situated at the side of the Mohawk River on the right bank. It is a square of four bastions of upright pickets joined together with lintels. They are fifteen feet high, about one foot square with port holes inserted from distance to distance with a stage all around to fire from.

This Fort is one hundred paces on each side. It is not surrounded by a ditch. There are some small pieces of cannon at each of its bastions, and a house at each curtain to serve as a store and barrack. Five or six families of Mohawk Indians reside outside the fort.

From Fort Cannatchocari to Fort Hunter is about 12 *leagues;* the road is pretty good; carriages pass over it; it continues along the banks of the Mohawk river. About a hundred houses, at a greater or less distance from one another are found within this length of road. There are some situated also about half a league in the interior. The inhabitants of this section are Germans who compose a company of about 100 men each.

Fort Hunter is situated on the borders of the Mohawk river, and is of the same form as that of Cannatchocari, with the exception that it is twice as large. There is likewise a house at each curtain. The cannon at each bastion are from 7 to 9 pounders. The pickets of this Fort are higher than those of Cannatchocari. There is a church or temple in the middle of the Fort; in the interior of the fort are also some thirty cabins of Mohawk Indians, which is the most considerable village. This fort, like that of Cannatchocari, has no ditch; there's only a large swing door at the entrance.

Leaving Fort Hunter a creek is passed at the mouth of which the fort is located. It can be forded, and crossed in batteaux in summer and on the ice in winter. There are some houses outside under the protection of the Fort in which the country people seek shelter when they fear or learn that an Indian or French war party is in the field.

From Fort Hunter to Chenectedi [Schenectady] *or Corlar is seven leagues.* The public carriage way continues along the right bank of the Mohawk river. About 20 to 30 houses are found within this distance separated the one from the other from about a quarter to half a league. The Inhabitants of this section are Dutch. They form a company with some other inhabitants of the left bank of the Mohawk river, about 100 men strong.

Chenectedi or Corlar, situated on the bank of the Mohawk river, is a village of about 300 houses. It is surrounded by upright pickets, flanked from distance to distance. Entering this village by the gate on the Fort Hunter side, there is a fort to the right which forms a species of citadel in the interior of the village itself. It is a square, flanked with four bastions or demi-bastions, and is constructed half of masonry and half of timbers piled one over the other above the masonry. It is capable of holding 2 or 300 men. There are some pieces of cannon as a battery on the rampart. It is not encircled by a ditch. The entrance is through a large swing gate raised like a drawbridge. By penetrating the village in attacking it at another point, the fire from the fort can be avoided.

The greatest portion of the Inhabitants of Chenectedi are Dutch.

From Chenectedi to Albany or Orange is estimated to be 6 or 7 leagues.[4] The road is excellent for all sorts of carriages; the soil sandy and the country covered with open timber. There are only a few hills. A league and half from Chenectedi, there is a house on the road which is a tavern. A league and half farther on, that is to say half way, another house is met which is also a tavern.

Orange is situate on the right bank of the river Orange, otherwise called Hudson. It is not fortified on the forest side except by an enclosure of walls, or pickets, without a ditch, which is flanked at certain distances; the river defends the entrance on the other side. It is calculated to be smaller than the enclosure of the town of Montreal. In the interior of Orange there is a fort, a sort of citadel, capable of containing 300 men; here are some cannon.

This is all that relates to the Right bank of the Mohawk river. let us pass to the left bank, which is the North side of that river, departing likewise from near its source at Fort Williams, [Rome.]

Leaving Fort Williams by the left bank of the river Mohawk, the village of the Palatines is estimated to be 12 leagues. The Mohawk river is fordable near Fort Williams whence a path leads to the interior, half a league from the shore, parallel with the river whose borders are so marshy that nothing but hay can be had there.

This path leads over hills and small mountains and can be traveled only afoot or on horseback. Eight leagues must be traversed by this path before reaching the forks of the high road that comes from the other side, or right bank of the river. After having traveled this high road a quarter of an hour, a small creek is found, called *Rassedot.* It can be forded. There were two houses on the left flank of this creek, which were burnt, and nothing remains of them but the ruins. Having passed this creek, the high road is followed for a distance of four leagues to the village of the Palatines. All sorts of vehicles travel this road.

The Palatine Village[5] was situated on the left bank of the Mohawk river, not directly opposite Fort Kouari but about half a quarter of a league above it. You go from this village to the fort by batteau; the river can even be forded in several places.

The Palatine Village which consisted of thirty houses has been entirely destoryed and burnt by a detachment under M. de Belhetre's orders. The inhabitants of this village formed a company of 100 men bearing arms. They reckoned there

300 persons, men, women and children, 102 of whom were made prisoners and the remainder fled to Fort Kouari, except a few who were killed whilst fording the river.

From the Palatine Village to the Little Falls, still continuing along the left bank of the river, is estimated about three leagues. In this distance there had been eight houses which have been abandoned. The inhabitants of these houses compose a company with those of Fort Kouari at the opposite side of the river.

The portage at the Little Falls is a quarter of a league, and is passed with carts. There is a road on both sides of the river, but that on the left bank is preferable, being better.

From the portage at the Little Falls, continuing along the left bank of the river, there is only a foot path which is traveled with difficulty on horseback. Three leagues must be made over this path to arrive at the Canada creek where we meet the high road that passes from the termination of the Little Falls portage, along the right bank of the Mohawk river, where there is a ford above Fort Cannatchocari, opposite the mouth of the Canada Creek. There is also a ferry boat at this place to put carts across when the river is high.

After fording Canada Creek, we continue along the left bank of the Mohawk river and high road which is passable for carts for 12 leagues to Col Johnson's mansion. In the whole of this distance the soil is very good. About 500 houses are erected, at a distance one from the other. The greatest number of those on the bank of the river are built of stone. Those at a greater distance from the river in the interior are about half a league off; they are new Settlements, built of wood.

There is not a fort in the whole of this distance of 12 leagues; There is but one farmer's house built of stone that is somewhat fortified and surrounded with pickets. It is situate on the bank of the river three leagues from where the Canada Creek empties into the Mohawk river.

The inhabitants of this Country are Germans. They form four companies of 100 men each.

Col. Johnson's mansion is situate on the border of the left bank of the River Mohawk; it is three stories high; built of stone, with port holes [*creneleés*] and a parapet and flanked with four bastions on which are some small guns. In the same yard, on both sides of the Mansion, there are two small houses; that on the right of the entrance in a Store, and that on the left is designed for workmen, negroes and other domestics. The yard gate is a heavy swing gate well ironed; it is on the Mohawk river side; from this gate to the river there is about 200 paces of level ground. The high road passes there. A small rivulet coming from the north empties itself into the Mohawk river, about 200 paces below the enclosure of the yard. On this stream there is a Mill about 50 paces distance from the house; below the Mill is the miller's house where grain and flour are stored, and on the other side of the creek 100 paces from the mill, is a barn in which cattle and fodder are kept. One hundred and fifty paces from Colonel Johnson's Mansion at the North side, on the left bank of the little creek, is a little hill on which is a small house with port holes where is ordinarily kept a guard of honour of some twenty men, which serves also as an advanced post.

From Colonel Johnson's house to Chenectedi is counted seven leagues; the road is good; all sorts of vehicles pass over it. About twenty houses are found from point to point on this road.

The Mohawk river can be forded during summer, a league and a quarter west of Chenectedi. Opposite Chenectedi the traverse is usually in a ferry boat and batteaux.

The inhabitants of this country are Dutchmen. They form a Company of about 100 men with those on the opposite side of the river below Fort Hunter.

Going from Chenectedi to the mouth of the Mohawk river where it discharges into that of Orange, there is a Great Fall [Cohoes] which prevents the passage of batteaus, so that every thing on the river going from Chenectedi to Orange, passes over the high road that leads there direct.

From Orange to New York is counted 50 to 60 leagues. Barks from New York ascend to Orange. There is also a high road from one to the other of these towns, on the left bank of the river. The country is thickly inabited on both sides of the river. The inhabitants of Orange are, also, mostly Dutch like those of Chenectedi.

From Orange to Boston is considered about 60 leagues. The road thither is across the country. From Boston to New York is reckoned the same distance following the road along the seaside.

New York, situate on the left bank of the Orange River, near its mouth at the sea, is located on a tongue of land forming a peninsula. It is fortified only on the land side. Opposite New York is a large Island [Long Island] very well inhabited and very wealthy. All sorts of vessels of war and Merchantmen anchor between the town and that Island.

NOTA. In the whole Country of the River Corlar there are nine Companies of Militia under the Command of Colonel Johnson; eight only remain, that of the Village of the Palatines being no longer in existence, the greater portion having been defeated by M. de Belhetre's detachment. Colonel Johnson assembles these companies when he has news of any expedition which may concern the Mohawk river.

In the latter part of April 1757, on receiving intelligence by the savages that there was a strong detachment ascending the river St. Lawrence and entering Lake Ontario, he assembled these Companies and went to the Village of the Palatines where he was joined by another body of 11 @ 1200 men sent him by the commandant of Orange; this formed in all a force of 2000 men. He entrenched himself at the head of the Palatine Village where he remained in Camp fifteen days, and did not retire until he received intelligence that the French detachment seen on the River St. Lawrence had passed by and taken the route to the Belle Riviére [Ohio.]

This was the detachment of 500 men that had been sent last year to reinforce Belle Riviére, and had left Montreal in the latter days of the month of April.

ENDNOTES IN THE ORIGINAL

1. From Chouegen to Fort Bull is estimated to be about 36 leagues. The ordinary batteau load is only 14 to 1500 weight. It takes five days to ascend the River from Chouegen to Fort Bull and three and a half from Fort Bull to Chouegen. The river of the Five Nations [Seneca Riv.] rises in little lakes near which, about six leagues from its entrance into the River Chouegen, the Indians of the Five Nations reside. That river divides into two branches. That from the Right rises in the Lake of the Senecas and Cayugas; that from the left beyond the Lake of the Onononontagués.
2. The River of the Killed Fish [now Fish Creek] flows also into this Lake; the English used it formerly; they abandoned it because there was a Portage, and have preferred Vilcrick which they have cleared.
3. The road goes to the great Oneida Village, about two leagues from the Lake. A picket Fort with four bastions, had been constructed in this Village by the English. It was destroyed by the Oneidas in observance of their promise given at a council held between them & the Marquis de Vaudreuil. Each of its sides might have been one hundred paces. There is a second Oneida Village, called the little village, situated on the bank of the lake. There is not fort in the latter.
4. The total distance from Chouegen to Orange is 78 *a* 79 leagues.
5. It requires a day to descend the river with batteaux from Fort Bull to the Palatine Village and three to return; and to go down from the Palatine village to Corlar requires [a day?] and a day and a half to return.

Journal of Warren Johnson[1]
1760-1761

Warren Johnson

Warren Johnson was a brother of William Johnson (±1715-1774), the superintendent of Indian affairs who dominated eighteenth-century English colonial history in the Mohawk Valley. Warren Johnson lived in Ireland, but visited his brother in New York during 1760-1761. His journal of that trip can now be found in the New York State Library. It is reproduced in volume 13 of the *Sir William Johnson Papers*, edited by M.W. Hamilton, but that source is out of print and often hard to find.

Johnson was very interested in economics, and statistics abound in his narrative. It would have been possible to pick up his journal with his arrival in New York City or perhaps Albany, and leave it there again upon his departure. However, only a few pages at the beginning and end of the full account would have been saved, and some relevant information would have been lost. Johnson's journal is a single coherent piece, with mention of things relevant to the Mohawk on nearly every page. Thus the entire work is reproduced here. The original covers his entire trip. Most usages and spellings are left as he wrote them. However, Johnson used a special symbol to represent the word "per," and we have substituted that word for the symbol throughout. Clarifying footnotes in the earlier published version are included here as endnotes.

D.R.S.

SUNDAY THE 29th of June 1760 I sailed for Pargate, on board the Race horse Capt[n]. Norman, & arrived the 30th. at 11th. at Night, & went to Harrigate Spaw in Yorkshire, Where I stay'd about a fortnight with Captain Tyrrell.[2]

The waters in that spaw, tho: Extreamly disagreable in taste, are very medicinal in Scorbutic Cases, & had a fine & salutary Effect upon me.

The 20th. of July I sett out from London for Lady Warrens in Hants; And sailed the 23d. from Cowes, on board the Resolution Capt[n]. Norman, for Philadelphia.

August the 10th. we lost Mizen-top mast, & sprung a Lake the 12th., which daily Encreased, particularly the three Days before we made the Land.

250

September the 5th. we were very near being ruined by whirlwinds, & water spouts. we went as far southward D:26: M:37: And there we were within 500 Miles of Barbadoes; the weather in that Latitude was soe Excessively warm, that I could bear noe Cloaths night or Day for 5 weeks; Notwithstanding the Cabin-windows were kept open every Night: We then got up Delaware River as far as Chester, & landed there the 9th. of September, it is but sixteen Miles from Philadelphia.—

The 10th. of September we arrived in Philadelphia, where there are prodigious Alterations Since the year 1746 as they generally build 100 new houses yearly they are made of Brick & wooden Shingles: the Town is finely laid out, the Streets spacious, but very miry, even in summer, having very litle Pavement, but where they walk, which is paved with Brick.

There are in that Town three Churches, besides other places of worship. An Admirably fine Market Place, And great Quantities of Provisions of all sorts; Beef sold at 3[d]. ¼ English per Lb. and all other provisions mostly in proportion; their Markets are held on Wednesdays & Saturdays, they have there likewise plenty of Fruit, & Roots of all kinds, Indian Corn per Bushel from 2[s]. to 3[s]. Philad[a]. Currency, & wheat from 4[s]. to 5[s]. per Bushel Since the commencement of this war: they have a very fine assembly house and most of their Members Quakers; they have a speaker & 36 of the Members sit in Night Caps; & arm-Chairs.—There is a Battery of about 32 Gunns from 12 to 32 pounders but much impaired, nay almost rotten by Time; They have a Barracks for about 2000 men, And but a very bad Hospital & poor house, for the country provides for their own poor. &c. their Bedlam is in the Hospital; there the ships come up to the Merchants Doors, who have made considerable Fortunes by Tradeing to the west Indies: but now that Trade is much embarrassed; the English Men of war having Seized their Ships there. They have Pumps in the Streets & Excellent fine water, They sew their wheat in the Latter End of August, & make it up in July, they sow their Indian Corn in Spring & make it up in the Midle of October; their Oats they sow in Spring & their Oats & hay are Ripe at the same time. They put Catle on their wheat. Their crops are very bad, in comparison of our, & odly sowed, as the Land is very indifferent being light & sandy, neither is the country yet much cleared. The weather is [*much hotter*] as hot in summer, & even in the Latter End of septem[r].; here, [*than*] as in Jamaica their Summer Seasons are very wett, which Occasions fevers & agues to a great Degree, few families Escaping them, Except the Negroes, who are not subject to them, yet them disorders have not been generally soe brief as this year.

They have a regular Post twice a week; all their Horses are—almost Pad.[3] size being about 14 hands high, their Roads bad & sandy; they drink lavishly of weak Punch, at 12 O Clock which is very requisite. Flies & Musketoes are trouble-some beyond Naming; the common flie, worse than the horse fly with us, and continues to the End of November. Their Provisions of meat by noe means as [good] as our.

More Ships come to this City of Philadelphia than any Part of America for ab^t. 1800 sail in, & out here yearly. It is surprizing how Tradesmen get soe much Money here, as they are vastly more careless than the Irish—

The weather is here soe variable that one Day the Heat is almost intolerable, & next Day the People can hardly bear leaving the fire, tis soe Excessive Cold; Madeira wine is not soe good here, as at N:york, and is sold at 3^s.-6^d. per or 40£ English per Pipe, & Claret is sold at 4^s. per Botle, the Cyder of this Province is pretty good, but their small beer bad, & sold at 4^d, ¼ per quart. Rum 3^s.-6^d.-English per Gallon. They have three Crops of Hay here of a season, but very bad on some Marshes. They generally Lime their Chief sowing, their Cows, sheep, & swine are small; their buckwheat is sowed in Winter for their Poultry, & for hot Cakes, which they use at Break fast. There are here two or three Coaches, many chairs, & 2 Sedans only: The N: W: Gusts cool the air, the Lands here are low, & wett, there are Numbers of Creeks which usually overflow with two or three hour's Rain. Cyder in the Jerseys this year is generally sold at about 14s.-6^d. per English Barrell, Bristol Beer at 1^s.-3^d. En: per Botle. Septem^r. the 15th. Such violent Heat that there was noe going out, & the 16th. every mortal Sitting over fires Shivering with Cold, & burning Oak, Hickery, with every other Combustible.

Wood is here very dear, the Chord of Oak, being 4 feet, long, & 3 high, is sold at 1£-10^s. English and Hickery at 1£-l4^s.-6^d. A good Pad is sold here at 20£ English, they [have] but few trotting horses, and more valued than Pads. The Inhabitants of this Province bury their Dead in the open fields, making a fence of wood round the Place. They Strip the Indian Corn, about the Midle of Septem^r. that it may dry the better, the Leaves of which when dryed are good feeding for the Catle in Winter. their buck wheat is ripe in October, which is commonly between ten & fifteen Bushels per acre, and is sold at 1^s.-6^d. English per: & Oats the same. Their Cows dont give much Milk which is oweing to the poor Soil that grows in a weak shamrougue [clover]. They make wood, & in some places hedge fences, for which there is a small premium, as it preserves Timber: of which the dread the Scarcity. Coals for forges are made here of burn't Wood. Hay is sold here at 2£ Ster^l: per Ton. The River Delaware runs for Small Sloops or larger Burthen vesels, noe higher than Trent-Town^4 30 Miles from Philadelphia, as there are Rocks, & shoals there, but Boats may goe a good way higher.—

September the 18th. I Set out for N:york the Roads were deep, red & sandy with many ferrys & Creeks hardly fordable: Our Horses Sometime Swim; very wet weather & Rains much Heavier than in Europe; I was obliged to stop on the Road, on acc^t. of high waters; the North East wind makes always bad & rainy weather; the North west good, but cold; the south wind makes it Hot: very litle of the Country, as One travels is cleared; the Inns much worse, & dearer, than in Europe, & one must call for more meat, & drink, particularly the Latter, tho: he don't use it.—

Potatoes there not soe good, as in Europe, they have good Bread, wherein, they most use yeast for Barm.^{5} as in Philadelphia. They generally have 10 Bushels of wheat per Acre, 15 of Indian Corn, & much the same of Oats: In the beginning of Septem^r. their wheat is over ground, but in a very weak plant; and is sowed as Level, as our Oats, Notwithstanding the soil is very Wett.—

The Tobacco plant grows in a broad Leaf 4 feet high, & ripens in October. They plow the Ground very light, and in broad Ridges with Three Horses a breast, & noe plow boy, but a Negroe, Generally holds the Plow.

I hired horses at 5£-10^s. for New York. They have mostly wooden Houses from Philadelphia to N:york, their sheep are small, their Cows & Horses, &:C: are pretty good, & have Bells about their Necks that they may be easily found in the woods.

The Roads in the Jerseys are Extreamly bad, & in Staten Island soe much wind & Rain that it is very difficult travelling.

Septem^r. the 20th. I arrived at the Ferry 10 Miles from york, which, it blew soe fresh, I could not cross. I put up at Major Duglas's bad House & very Dear, where, What may be called bad Hay for a Horse per Night is One Shilling & three pence English, One is, here Charged for his Own & Servant's, Lodging, tho he has horses; & a travelling Days Expences here is at least 7^s.-6^d. & in England but 2-6 for a Servant.

September the 21st. I arrived at New york, at Night, & next day, dined at M^r. Kelly's where I drank 3 Botles of bad dutch Claret, & afterwards supped at a Tavern, with fresh Company, & drank Madeira, which Occasioned a Violent fever, again the next Day. in the Morning of the Saturday following, I had 16 or 18 ounces of Blood taken from me, and took a puke in two Hours after, & drank [26] 23 quarts of water, which by operating downwards gave me 16 Motions. And that Night—alsoe I required to be blooded: In short I had a violent fit of it, & had 2 Doctors & a Nurse, attending me.—

October the 22^d. at Night, I went on board an albany Sloop and was soe very weak that I could hardly get to the Vessel. the 25th. in the Morning, I arrived at Albany; Where there is a fine River, And but a Nasty dirty Town, whose Inhabitants [made] a vast Deal of Mony [money] this War. there I found myself weak, & not rid of my Sickness—October the 28th. arrived at my Brothers.—

New York is much about the Same Largeness with Philadelphia, but not soe regularly laid Out, for the Streets are paved, & Narrow, the Houses made of Brick, & Shingled. Some Odd old Dutch Houses, the People mostly Dutch, & have something Odd about them, their Jail, & College are their best Buildings. They [do] great Trading here; There has been a kind of Smugling from this Place to the French, which is Stopped: The Lands about the Town, (and th [*at I seen*] em I saw as I rode about the Country for ten Days) are very bad & not Cleared, their Meat here is bad, they have no market Place as in Philadelphia, they have Every thing very Dear, they dine mostly at 1 of the Clock & drink very hard, the Weather is not quite as hot here as at Philadelphia, tho: it is very hot for some Days in October, and very Sickly, Almost half the People of the Town & Country Sick of Fevers and great Numbers die. Of a Saturday 500 Chairs & Curricles goe out to drink Tea or Dine. Their Horses, and Pads mostly as at Philadelphia, but not near soe good Soil nor Meat; Maderia 5^s. per Botle; Rum: 6^s. Claret 5^s. Currency &—

My whole body, legs & hands broke out 3 Times in a Violent Rash, & peeled, [*my Urine was*—] & had Pains like the Rheumatism, Nothing would Stay on my Stomach for 14 Days, Neither could I eat or Sleep but when I took things to make me. Schenecktedy is a litle dirty Village 16 Miles from my Brothers, & has 3 Company^s. quartered in it. I took two Days traveling in A Curricle from Albany to fort Johnson, the Roads being but very Indifferent; The 8th. of Novem^r. the Weather very fine, & really warm; I eat Suppan^6 & rode out every Day which did me vast Service—

More Custom at fort Johnson than any Inn in England from the Number of Regular & Provincial officers passing by every Day, as the River Mohawk is within 40 yards of the Door. the Provincial Troops are soe Sickly, particularly the New England Ones, that the bury 40 of a Day, chiefly oweing to their dirtiness which gives them fevers & fluxes, they throw them on the Beech, as they die, & some they bury Just by the House, and Scarcely below the Surface—They Sail in Battoes [bateaux]. the People here are Subject to violent Colds, attended with fevers; There are here vast Numbers of Indians, who are troublesome beyond thought to my brother; they often kill one another in drunken fits, there is noe Law to punish them, but some of the Deceas'd's friends, very often, nay, almost always kills the Killer at an other drunken Bout: The Indian Skwas [squaws] pick the Lice of one another & eat them; Every thing very Scar[c]e, and very dear here, wild fowl very Scarce, there is a kind of Pheasant & wood-Cock—Which is not much Larger than A snipe with us, there are few Ducks, and Some wild Turkeys & Deer to be had in Winter, they are obliged to pin up their Sheep, for fear of the Wolves. New york Currency in October 165£—for 100£ English: in September 160£ for 100£; Their Horses run in the Woods all Winter, their Cows are but small   Every Family kills two or three Cows, & generally as many Hogs for Winter's Provision; A Carpenter has here 8^s. per Day with Meat & Drink, & Common Men 4^s. Current; They sow wheat in spring, which Ripens at the Same Time with the other wheat—They take very litle pains, & Scarcely know any thing about Gardening in America. My Brother gives 30£ a year meat & Drink to One. Madeira at N.york is 80£ per pipe Currency: That of the Best some years agoe was Sold at 30£: News Papers are printed Once a week at N:york & Philadelphia; Noe plenty of Fish at Either Place. There are between 30 & 40 Coaches at York: Indians feast greatly upon Dogs; both white People & Indians Eat bears' Flesh. A Sett of Indifferent Shoes for an Horse Shall cost 6^s. English, Iron per Cw^t. is 40^s. Currency. Brandy was 4 Guineas a Botle at, Montreal before it was taken. The Galletegage Indians^7 goe out a hunting in the Latter End of October, & very often bring their whole Families with them, & stay out till Christmas.

9th. of Novem^r. the Weather Changed to frost, & snow, & Rain, which affects me very much, by giving me Pains in my Bones & headaches: my Apothecary's Bill while at N:york, amounted to 10£-13^s.-6^d.—

There are Shoals of wild Pidgeons here, which are not Shot flying: Fort Hunter the Chief Indian Castle is within two Miles of Fort Johnson; The Indians are very Sickly: The Wood Cocks leave this Country the Latter End of October; & where they goe to noe One knows: the Water is bad at New york, officers Carried Napsacks in Abercrombies Time—About half a Salt of our's at Montreal before taken 120 of our men were drowned at a Water fall going to Montreal, where the french Indians, if we had not got them to be Neuter, might have given us a great Check: The Enemy knowing my Brother's Boat, fired at it in particular from a Fort going up to Montreal, The Indians will not, if they can, fight one another., & take Special Care of the white People who goe out with them, if sick. The Duch are an odd & very bad Sort of People, & there is noe Confidence to be put in them. The Mohawk River was soe frozen The 16 of Novem^r. that One might walk over it at Schenectedy: New England People & others Eat pork & other Meat raw particularly if frost-bitten; if travelling they give their Horses 2 quarts of Oats for a feed, & water at any Time, & Tye them to a stake for many hours when the weather is hot: There are fine Hickery Nuts, Butter Nuts, a kind of Wallnuts, Small Chesnuts in abundance, & Peaches & apples very plentifully As One travels along the Roads. Land Sells here for ever at 20^s. per Acre, if any way good, the midling kind of Land at 10^s. per Acre.

There Oysters are not Salt, their Hare like the Rabbet; 25 Novem^r. tha[n]k God, pretty well recovered, & Strong [*tho my Urine is still foul*] New England Rum (which is very bad,) is 8^s. currency per Gallon, at Fort Hunter, it & all other Kinds of Liquor were very dear last summer in our Camp. they Use Leaf Tobacco instead of Roll, their Horses seldom Littered & badly fed: Otter's Skins very good Furr for Muffs, Some of the Indians are now marryed by our Clergy, & Numbers willing to become Christians. Albany River generally frozen in Novem^r. the Indian Women cutt all their fireing both at home, & when a hunting. the french have been better setled about Montreal than we are in any of our Provinces. all European goods Extreamly dear when the place was taken, having noe supplies from home for Some years. Vast Rewards offered by M. Veaudriuel[8] for the thorn in their Sides; Sir W^m. thought twice he had got his Scalp, & paid Rewards for it. Sir William prevented Several Nations of french Indians from fighting against us & run very great Dangers between his own House & Albany, being fired at several Times. At New york Milk is 6 Currency per Quart. Butter very Dear & bad: Negroes not marryed but their Masters; An Indian makes 40£ & upwards yearly by hunting Winter, Spring, & Fall. The Indian Women make up their Corn & there is 8^s.-6^d. Currency for making A Shirt, there are white Hares above fort Hunter & at this Place there are 100 Indians; the wheat Sewed in Spring, is not Sae good as if in Winter   Oats sowed as late as the Midle of May; Noe High Winds in the Mowhawk's Country until December; Tymothy-Grass Seed sowed on very boggy wet ground, three quarts of clear Seed to an Acre will dry the Ground in 3 years Time. If an Indian tells another, he will kill him, the other Submitts & holds down his head, & even will Stay there, tho his Enemy Should [go] A Mile for an Axe, or other Weapon to doe it. If one of them in a boasting Way says he is a great Man, Another comes & Contradicts him, & tells him he is Nothing, but that he is the great Man, & tell him his Exploits, whereupon he looks foolish & Submitts: General Gage & all the officers. Almost reckon 300 Indians above a Match for 1000 Regulars, in the

Woods, they are very great Walkers, bear Fatigue, & quick sighted. Sir W^m. Johnson brought about a Neutrality with thirteen Nations of French Indians, which proved of the utmost Consequence to us, As they might, if Joined with the french, have Stoped our Army at the great fall or Strong Rifts near Montreal. Indians are not near soe much affraid of fighting against white people as against Indians: the Cheroquee [Cherokee] In Carolina consist of 4000 Men, In the Creeks[9] are Sadle Horses Seldom rid from Novem^r. till April but during that Time are generally turned Out—Pidgeons are soe plenty there is noe driving them of a small piece of Ground of 6 Acres, with many Gunns tho Numbers of them be killed. The Sheep in the west Indies Small & hairy. the Indians goe in Mourning for their Relations, the white people condole with them, by clearing their throats to make them Speak, they wipe away the Tears from their Eyes, & the Blood of the Deceased from their Bed. & out of their Sight, that their Hearts may be chearful: this is done by giving them Strings of Wampum, & black Strouds, & by covering the Grave of the Deceased that they may mournn noe more over, it. Indian Warriors unacquainted with managing affairs, Sachems doe all & seldom goe out to fight, the Indians drink Rum greatly, & have an Ox roasted at a Time & dance all Night: All the Gent: here kill Bullocks for their Own Table: the Indians thank you very much for condoling with them, And don't fight or make their appearance at any Meeting until you doe. Sir Willm. was the first Proposer of the Niagara Expedition to gen^l: Amherst at Ticonderoga, the Highlanders by Mistake gave Our Indians two full fires which killed Numbers: the Indians have noe Notion of a Prisoner's fighting Against them A Second Time, tho: Exchanged, When they take Prisonners in their Own quarrells they keep them for ever, & never Exchange them, even after the Conclusion of a Peace, and are mightily displeased with us for Exchanging Prisonners: Indians dont care to goe in Sloops, or larger Vessels, as they think it would make them Stomack Sick; the Mohawk Indians, are related to, & have great influence over the french Indians: the Indians are not very Easy, & still Suspect that we Intend to cutt them all of & destroy them: Numbers of Indians Encamped with us last Campaign at Oswegoe 1358 wom^n. & Child^n. included. 585 Warriors went against Montreal of Different Nations; Sir William and the Indians were in a Dangerous Situation at Montreal the Night before. the Capitulation, if the french w^d. have fought.—

The Indians were greatly disgusted at not being admitted into fort Levi on Isle Royal after the Surrender; Some however got in, & seen the Grenadiers, who took possession of it, plundering, & pillageing, & themselves, not allowed; but Such as got in, ordered out by the General, they were universally dissatisfied, & many returned home upon that Acc^t. there were some plundered Goods given to them but in all not worth 30£, nor had they Liberty to See the prisonners, Sir Willm. had a great Deal of Trouble to Satisfie them; Deputations came there to Sir W^m. from 8 french Indian Nations, who were afterwards Neuter, which in a great Measure ruined the French.

The French Indians are prodigiously attached to their Priests & religion. The french in Canada never ride, but goe all in Chairs. Sir William, & the Indians at

Isle perault opposite the Island of Montreal, took 300 Prisonners, & got a Considerable Deal of Plunder. The Duch keep the New year always for 6 Days as holy Days, And ride in their Slays to one another's Houses, they dance and lie all together let there be ever soe many men & Women, before the fire; the Men must have on their Breeches, & women their Petty Coats. At Caghnawaga, a large french Setlement & Fort, near Montreal, 500 french Indians, but Neuter by Sir Williams good Management, were assembled on the Shore Side, as our Army rowed up the River S^t. Lawrence, to Montreal, &, behaved very well.

We rested on our Arms the Night before the Surrender of Montreal; there were Neither Tents nor Provisions, particularly with the Indians. & it rained very hard. A Carrying place is where One is Obliged to put ashore, & goe by Land to the next Navigable River; The Indians very often carry their Canoes on their Backs over it, particularly if made of Birch. almost all Indians have Sleas; they are generally crooked ham'd with black Eyes, & hair,—few, red, & of a Large Size, very decent at a funeral, whereof I was Eyewitness, they are Accustomed to keep in their Toes to avoid Stump's in the woods. they bury in the fields after which they drink merrily; if a Child is got by a white person its Hair is never black but brownish &c.—If an Indian of Honour promises you even his Wife in Drink, he will certainly Agree to it after.—

When the Indians lose a man in Action, & chance to take an Enemy prisoner, he belongs to the family of the Deceased, who take great Care of him, & look on him in the Same light as on the Person lost, & even leave him the same fortune. Indians greatly reverence their forefathers, whom they look upon to have been the wisest of Men, & are themselves obliged to Such persons as keep up to their Laws, Ceremonies, & Customs; the Indian War Song is like the Irish Cry &.c—

Indians keep their Corn, over their fires, or on Lofts, & they have some Cocks & Dogs without Tails; there is among them Some, Wood called the Bush; They put Lice on Broth to make it rich.

One may see seven large trees grown from one Root   the Lands are very hilly, & mostly Rich, tho: but litle clear from albany to Fort hendrick, or Lonajoharce[10] They have Trouts plenty, some Pike & few Salmon. Trouts are catched in great Quantities, in Winter, in a kind of Baskets, much like the Colliers, by cutting the Ice & setting the Basket agst. The Stream, 20 at a Time, some a foot & a half long. Turkies are Pretty plenty, Some weigh 60 lb. but generally 30 lb. which are seldom seen till after New year, when the Farmers ride down their grain to Albany in Sleas which the Turkies pick in a hard Season. The Justices of Quorum, & Dutch of the Province of New york are out of the way, very mean People, I think the Indians preferable to the latter,   They all wear Check shirts, & some Ruffles of the Same & alsoe Indian Shoes Stockings, & Night Caps.—

White Pease they have with A worm in them, which greatly destroys them, there are vast Quantities of Snakes whose Bites are mortal, if not immediately prevented by applying Salt or Oyle to the Part affected, Otherwise the Leg swells, which runs upwards, & the Person dies very Shortly: in Winter they goe into Rocks & Holes, & the Latter End of April come out weak & feeble. Most officers this War, wore Check Shirts in the Woods: The Indian Language is very Soft, being quite Guttural, Warraghigagey[11] signifies A man who undertakes great Things. Hats there [*not*] good [*nor*] but not well coloured—& are Sold at 1£-15ˢ. English a piece. the Indian women have very great Influence over the Indians, soe that if the young Warriours are going to War they can almost hinder them. but when going all Sing the War song, & get a Charge from the Old Women, particularly to behave well, & not to be a Discredit to themselves, or their forefathers. The Duch make great Use of Stoves, which keep the Room next to them, very warm, which is intirely disagreable to all Strangers & gives them an Head-ach. An Indian Cradle (which they mostly all use) is a flat Board with a Top over the Childs face, on which hangs a Curtain. & the Child bound round to keep it Straight; They have a belt fixed to the Cradle, which they put round them, & carry it in that Manner—

Decemʳ. the 20ᵗʰ. I Sett out from Fort Johnson, with Sir Willᵐ., for Conajo-harie, where we arrived that Night, but not without great Difficulty in crossing the Mohawk River—being full of Ice, the three Days following we were admitted to their Councils which were very Solemn & decent in form of an House of Lords & Commons. On the Second Day they unanimously gave Sir William a Gift of 100,000, Acres of Land or thereabouts, that is 16 by 10 Miles, & reckoned the very best in the Country opposite Fort Hendrick, & 36 Miles from Fort Johnson. I put up at an Indians house (Brants) at Conajoharie, & lay in my Cloaths on a straw Bed before the fire for 3 Nights. The 23ᵈ. I arrived at Stonaraby [Stone Arabia], a very good German Settlement, & more clear Land, than any Part I have Seen in America, I mean from Philadelphia to that Place, 'tis 20 Miles from Conajaharie, & same Distance from Fort Johnson; lay in my Cloaths alsoe that Night on a Straw bed, (noe Sheets the four Nights) the Next Morning, breakfasted upon Sausages, fryed Bacon & Strong Punch; The 24ᵗʰ. returned to Fort Johnson. Indian Women assist at Councils, the Speakers of both Houses only Speech which they doe very decently. Such of the Dutch Clergy as I have seen, seem very odd People.—

Four Quarts of Oats per Day is reckoned good feeding for an Horse, for one Pint of Oats Extraordinary per Day founders the Horse, that is, it Stiffens their Joints, & requires a year, or two to recover them, & perhaps Never. Strawberries are every where One goes & they Say very good, There are Some Raspberries. Wheat sold the 26ᵗʰ. of Decemʳ. above Albany at about 15ˢ. English per Barrell Oats 7ˢ. & Indian Corn at 10ˢ. English per Do—Six Gallons of Sugar boiled, from Sugar Trees produces two pounds of brown Sugar. At Philadelphia they have a fine flat fish called sheep's-head. The Dutch are very foul feeders, their Women very ordinary, & broke before 25 years of Age, the better Sort of both their Men & Women generally wear black & keep blacks as Servants, in America A good Negroe Slave is worth 70£ English. Dutch and Indians carry knives, And are very Treacherous particularly, if Drunk, Dutch Ladies in the Country bring out their young Children Visiting & have them in their Laps at Table cursedly disagreable, & not over modest in speech. Alegini[12] Mountains, near the River Ohio, the highest in all America, are reckoned 29 Miles higher than[13] Philadelphia, & are Boggy on the Top, like our Mountains: low Swamps & marshy Grounds are vastly the Best, the Earth being generally rich & Black: the Hills are sandy, Large Timber grows on the Low Grounds: And good Land is Easily known by the Trees, tho: it be covered with Snow; there are Lead ore, & mines in them, the Low ground, tho: quite A swamp when the Trees are on, Yet when Cleared, dries wonderfully, by (as they Say) the Heat of the Sun without Draining, or any other Method. The Farmers are very bad & seldom Rent, but buy Land. The Creeks are a vast addition to the Land, as One has there both Saw & Grist-Mills. The Ground is generally covered with Snow from Novem^r. to May: The Rivers break about April; the Winters are much Severer in Canada, but more moderate as the Country is Cleared. Noe riding on Horseback from Novem^r. till May.

Sleas are Excellent Machines for travelling on Snow, & cost 15£ English per. The Indians are prodigiously reduced, Mohawk Castles, when Sir Willm. came to America had 1400 Men now not 300. they were moderate untill we corrupted them, & now love Rum Excessively, & are very troublesome, when drunk, & mighty hard to be got Away: They petitioned, or rather begged of Sir William to allow them a Parson & Schoolmaster to Instruct them, which he has granted.

The Tree, by which Sir Willm. Stood in the Action at Niagara had fourteen Balls Lodged in it.—

New England is bad & Sandy light Soil, Philadelphia Jerseys & above Albany reckoned very Good, Philad^a. produces much wheat. The Germans are preferable to the Dutch in every Respect.—

At N.york 36 shillings English is 3£-3^s.0^d., a Guinea 1£-16^s., a Dollar 8^s. The Currency at Philadelphia is a litle better, for there the Dollar is 7^s.-6^d. The Indians paint their Bodies, legs, & head &C, And in Action have on, only a Lap, & Indian Shoes, & their Amunition Slung round them, with Balls in their Mouths which prevents their being thirsty. Several Indians, & Some white People blue their Faces, (in a kind of Ridges) & nick their Breasts, &:C: which is done by pricking the Skin with Pins, till the Blood comes, & then applying Gunpowder to it; which will remain for ever: 'tis a great Torture, however it makes them look desperate, & besides is A Considerable Addition to their Fury,—The Duch &:C: have here built large Barns, wherein they put their Hay & Corn, & have their Stables & places for their Cows in them; the Beer here is very bad, & Muddy, which the Duch don't regard; the Malt is generally of Barly, & Some of wheat, The Indians, in Action, dress a Red Feather in their Heads & Make a Terrible Noise with their Shouting & Screaming. They are Excellent at curing Disorders by herbs gathered in the woods, they cure the french Disease[14] well, by herbs; they have got it, & other Disorders very much among them. When clearing Land, the Set fire to the Timber, & burn it to ashes, which they Scatter about on the ground; they make Charcoal of Wood; They never clear more Land than Serves for their Own Use

of the whole country, which was formerly theirs they have now but a small Share, they Sold their Land for Rum, & Trifles, like Sailors, who, when they have mony, are never Easy till they get rid of it. December the 27th. a party of them left Sir Williams House, with some mony he gave them, & went to a Tavern, (soe they call every litle house, which sells Rum) four Miles from Fort Johnson, where, a Bear & wild Turky was prepared for them; for which they at Once laid down ten Dollars, & paid for Rum besides, phaps twenty Dollars. Venison is not in season in Winter; the Hunters kill them for their Skins & Eat the Flesh.

There is an Act past, (& a Reward of half a Crown,) against killing Pheasant: Duck & other wild fowl. Fowl are in Season in May; & they say there are some Moor Fowl. Some Families have spruce Beer, which is very wholesome, & of which the french made great use; the Trees are not easily found, as they doe not grow in Many Places.

Sir William, has the Nameing of all officers, & has had the Albany Regim^{t}. of Militia since the year 1744 being then made privy Councellor; the Regim^{t}: consists of 5000 Men; 'tis a great Command, as they are subject to the military Laws, he marched with them Several Times this War.

An Indian Letter or Message is A String of Wampum. It freezes there soe hard in One Night as to shut up the Rivers, on which One may walk next morning. The Mohawk River is 300 yards broad, and is soe hard frozen in one Night, as people may walk over it; Decem^{r}. the 28th. it was soe cold as to freeze almost any thing even by the fire's side: The frost is soe intense, that if you walk in Leather Shoes & Gloves, you are frost bitten. Gent: drink Punch at Victuals at 12 o'clock in the Day even in Winter, & tho: always cold they would chuse in winter to have a hard frost & snow on the Ground, 'tis wholesomer; & they can the more Easily ride down their Corn on they Ice to Albany, and bring their Fireing home. The Cat-fish is very good there, & weigheth about 70 Lb, only in the River Mohanangaely,[15] near fort Pitt, which River runs to the Mohio [Ohio]. 'tis about 78 years Since Philadel^{a}. was built. The finest Land, & most Cleared in America is there abouts. Sir William had 70 men allowed him by the Governm^{t}: this War in his Fort.

if a married person here, be 3 years without hearing from his wife, or a woman from her husband, they are allowed by the Laws to marry again, the Person being supposed Dead. Indians chiefly live on boiled Indian Corn. One Gallon of Molosses., which is but 2^{s}. Ster., sufficient for a Barrell of Spruce Beer. The more to the North, the better the Furr; tis much better, & vastly plentier, in the Canada than in the Country of Albany.

January the 3^{d}. bad disagreable Cold Weather, Rain, then a very hard frost & great Snow.

A Duch Parlour has Always a bed in it. & the man & woman of the House Sleep in it. their Beds are good, for the Mind noe other Furniture. The Europeans, are hardier, & bear the Cold better than the Natives in America, Except the Indians.—the New England Men are lazy, & not Esteemed as good Soldiers, as the Men of the Other Provinces, nor soe good Farmers, & are as easily distinguishd. as the County Cavan Men in Ireland. Yorkers the best, being mostly Europeans. Officers wore noe Swords here during the whole War, in Action, but a kind of Bayonet, which was more handy in the Woods. Sir Willm. every winter has 4 Men, & 2 Horses employed for fireing. Viz^t. 2 men for cutting & 2 to bring home the Wood; the Wood is Lynder [basswood], or a kind of Sycamore, or Mulbery tree . . 3^d. of January. [*my Urine still foul*] The Duch boil their meat, & then roast it, & use grease for sawce. In order to clear Land, they cut the Trees at the height of three feet from the Ground, & then they perish in One year; the Sugar—Wood in two years.—

They put Horses in Stocks to Shoe them, which is very dangerous. Indians mourn more, by goeing Naked than by wearing black, they often doe the former. they catch Horses with salt tho: ever soe wild, or young; the Horses will follow one like Dogs, after tasting it Twice. Roots of all Sorts will keep all Winter without being frozen in A Cellar. Days in summer, in Ireland are about 2 hours longer than here, & in Winter Two hours Shorter, being here Nine hours long in Winter &c—

The light used in Mills & houses here generally is pich^d.-pine Nots; The Indians have it in their Canoes fishing, & by it in the Night doe see Salmon & spear them. The Indians have particular Hunting Ground for Each Tribe, & never intrude upon One another's Places. 6^s. English for knitting a pair of Cotton Stockings.

January the 8th: 1761 Receiv^d. the Acc^t. of the Kings Death,[16] which, was sudden; at Kensington.

The houses having noe window shuts above Stairs in the Country are much colder than in Europe it freezes so hard. January the 11th. 1761 That Strong Punch in 20 Minutes, is covered with a Scum of Ice, & Ink on a Table is frozen, before the fire, the wind being generally at N.West.—

There is about a foot of Snow, on the ground all the Winter, & back in the woods about four foot;—February generally is the Month of great Snow.

The Dutch not very polite, they Smoke in Ones Parlour, thoe not asked to sit down, & always seat themselves without bidding. Their Children at Seven year Old, Smoak, & their Parents think it a great Qualification. Sir William Actually had not above 1100 men Engaged at Lake George & them raw & undisciplined Soldiers, which obliged him to Expose himself greatly in Action, against 2200 French; he was soe hoarse in the Engagem^t. with calling to the Troops, & running along the Lines, as not to be able to speak, untill he got a Lemon, & sucked the Juice, & Notwithstanding his wound, which affects him still, did not keep in his Tent, but was very active. To know whether Ice be Strong Enough to bear you, let fall an ax, on it, And if it does not get to the Water, you may safely venture on it.

Monsr. Bernier (Aid-d-Camp, to Baron Deskeau at Lake George—Engagement) Commissary General in Canada, informed Sir Willm., & shewed him A Return, of the Regular Troops at Montreal, when taken; They had light Battallions, which consisted in all of 2150 Men. The take the shoes of their Horses in Spring, & let them goe without them, till Winter. New England Rum freezes, & Madeira, [unless] the Cellar be Warm & Closely Stopped. Wood Cocks goe from here in October, to Carolina, & towards the Missisippi. Sir William was very near being perished in a snow squall, coming from Schenectedy to his Own house; his Strength was soe Exhausted, as to be obliged to take hold of a big Dog (he had with him) by the Tail, which helped to an House, very near him; It was late in the Night, & the People could hardly hear him, it blew soe hard. The Panther is very Dangerous to be met with, it holloos like a human Creature. & is soe Nimble as to leap on One, at above 40 yards Distance, & immediately drives his Claws in you. Common Rum at Montreal in Novem^r. 1760 was 14^s. English per Gallon, & Shrub 20^s. The Most of the French there were ruined by having Paper mony, which now will not pass current, A vast Scarcity of Provisions all over Canada, this Winter. Our Troops get some meat for Salt from the Inhabitants, they not having any ab^t. Montreal. Indian Meal is very good to fatten Catle. Some People have an Indian's Skin for a Tobacco Pouch. America in General a very hilly Country, Virginia the flattest & very good Land.

January the 13th. 1761. The Weather soe Excessive Cold, That Maderia at 50£ English   Pipe botled in a Room, where a good fire is kept, is quite frozen; Lemon Juice in Large Botles, 3 parts Strong frozen, Jamaica Rum alsoe quite frozen in a Room with fire in it; & the Strongest Rum, left out over Night is quite frozen in the Morning. this is as Severe a Winter as hath been for some years, Bread soe frozen that there is noe Eating it. the best way to thaw frozen Meat is in cold Water.—

January the 14th. 1761, walked over the Mohawk River; I have seen One Indian, who would not drink Rum, & would drink Water Only; their Skin is thicker than any Christians; & when sickly they shut up their Houses, & goe into the Woods. they have Now, in January 1761 & had two years agoe, An Epidemical Distemper which comes with a pain in the head, & Back, & in four, or 5 Days Time, carries of Numbers of em it is attended with a fever, the Indians eat always leaning. Dutch, & Germans great One to the other, the Latter are vastly Superior. The Dutch hate both English & Irish, & Eat hogs Lard on their Bread, instead of Butter, with Tea; the Use the Grease of fryed Bacon with Sallets, in stead of Oil, & mix it up with their Hands for they never use forks; the Each Cucumbers sliced, in Buttermilk. A Constable's fees for bringing a Person before a Justice is—1^s.-6^d. Currency. A summons 1^s. A warrant 1^s., the first Mile 6^d., he furnishes a Slea, the Rest of the way.

Noe fresh Meat (except with Gent:men in Winter), nor Meat Markets even at Skenectady, or Albany, they keep the Rams, from the Ewes later than in Europe On Acct. of the Snow in Winter.

Sir William fasted five Days, & only Eat two grains of Indian Corn. A firelock at Ticonderoga went off by accident, & hit him with seven grains of Shot, but were almost Spent. The Indians are great Eaters, yet can fast, ten, or twelve Days on Water: They know in the Woods, whether People passed by, lately by the impression on the Leaves, & their Numbers, by the Paths they make.

They send their Squaws 30 Miles into the Woods for Venison, & know their way by broken Twigs which the Men break at every 3 or 4 Miles. Indians cross any River on floating Rafts. 50 Men with Snow Shoes, tho: the snow be six foot Deep, will make an excellent Road, A Person cannot goe into the Woods in Winter without Them. the flesh of a Woodcock is the best Bait for A Salmon.—

Brick burners have 5^s. English per Day, Battoemen 7^s. per Day. Indians indure great Pain: the frost gets down the Chimneys.

January the 18th. 1761: the Snow 28 Inches deep, it is generally dry; to be seen here a litle Bird like a Linnet, but crook-billed like a Hawk.—

A Saw Mill saws 500 Logs per Day Each worth 15^d. English. Indians had noe pay, but more Expensive. My Indian Name is Ariwanughne.

Indians know all Medicinal herbs; the Men of them goe mostly bare headed.

Merchants have 150£ per Cwt. for European Goods; they dont use Mares here in Draught.—

January the 23d. Extreme Cold, & a very hard frost. if one walks two Mile in European Shoes & gloves, he is frost bitten; Numbers of our Troops in marching last Winter suffered vastly soe, & were rendered incapable of Service, having lost Toes, & Fingers, & some feet Obliged to be cut of; above 100 suffered. When they Encamp in the Woods, have large Fires at their feet, & Sleep on the Branches of Trees, & Sometimes a shade of them round them.

January the 24th. 1761, [*My Urine Still Foul.*] The Weather soe cold that handling Brass, or Iron leaves a Blister on the Fingers: & in Bed People are cold even with ten Blankets on. They are remarkable at Philadelphia for making rifled Barrell Gunns, which throw a Ball above 300 yards, vastly well, & much better than any other Barrells. People here in general Shoot very well with Ball, but don't doe much with Shot. The Dutch all wear their hair (which buckles[17] like Candles) or Night Caps, they wont be at the Expence of Wiggs, The Men of them sleep in their Breeches, & Stockings, & the Women in their Pettycoats. A Slea carries five Barrells of wheat.

There is a sort of whiskey distilled from Peaches, & Rotten Apples, it is called Brandy: 'tis mostly made in the lower part of Philadelphia; Should a person be thirsty at Night, he stands a bad Chance, unless he drinks Rum, every Other Liquor being frozen.

January the 25th. 1761, Saw People with their Ears quite froze. Dutch Girls get Noe fortunes, when they marry, nor, untill their Fathers die, the Estate being Equally Divided between the Sons. Negroe Women Suckle white Children in the West Indies, & a great many here. There are many free Negroes here. who have good Estates; most Indians have their Ears cut, & Trinkets in them, & their Noses, which they Think a great Ornament: They very often have boiled bear & deer skins, on which they use to sleep, & Eat them for want of food: Sir William very often lay in the wods, in very wet & severe weather, without any Covering, & had his Sadle for a Pillow. The Dutch have Scarcely any Notion of Distinction of Persons or compassion, Sir Willm. has had many Escapes from them, being often waylayed by No.—being often way-layed by Numbers of them, & had at one Time, at Albany [20] 8 lusty Dogs of them upon him, of which he Got the Better by the assistance only of one Irish man, & almost destroyed them. & a Mob of them assembled the 18th. of January 1761, at Skenectady, at 11 o' th' Clock at Night, murdered two Irish Men: The Next Day all the Irish, in Town, got together & offered five pounds for the sight of a Dutchman, but None. dare appear; The Magistrates there (who are all Dutchmen) Summon'd The Rioters/their Country men, to appear before them, and Only fined them, to the Number of 14 men, 7£ 16^s. per man for the Murder. if the Irish had been the Guilty, they w^d. have them certainly hanged. However the friends of the deceased, & the gent:men of Ireland in these Parts, have appealed to the Courts at New york. 25th. of January 1761, great Snow, & next Day, very wet weather, & at Night a hard - - - frost, & a Storm at North west—

The Dutch are more afraid of Sir William than any man Living, he is the only person can keep them in order. There are noe highwaymen in America, but great Horse Stealers. Wooll grows in A Season or two on West India Sheep here, & hair on Woolly Sheep there. Wolves destroy many Horses & other Catle, & very dangerous (if provoked) for Christians to meet. The Duch in their Sleas run, as hard as they can, up the hills, & Easily down.

January the 28th. Rain, & always more moderate upon a thaw, Snow yet two foot deep; Beef killed the 1st. of Decem^r, is quite fresh, & very good Roasted in April, or as long as the frost continues; 'tis hung up in a Garret, & the Boiled kept close in Tubbs.

February the 6th. 1761, very cold with hard frost, & snow. The Duch take 10£ currency Bail for a Murderer—if the Murderer be a Duchman. Hickorry Wood per Chord 1£-11^s. English, ash 1£-6^s-0^d, the sap of sugar Wood makes very wholesome, & good Beer with Hops & Yeast.

4C of Hay in January 1761 Generally 16^s Eng^{sh}.—There is about 2 Guineas for clearing an Acre of Land. Rogers[18] & Butler[19] were backward with Sir Willm. at one Time, when he thought himself Surrounded by the french, & Indians, & only 4 men, & a Squaw Stayed with him. Canada lies N. N. East from albany towards the Missisippi.—

Indians this year, have given a Deer, or Bever Skin for a Spoonful of Rum. If a Drunken Indian comes among Sober Ones, they all fear him, & will not medle with him, but run away & hide themselves.—

Five french Caughnawags rowed Sir Will^{ms}. whale Boat, up to Montreal. There is noe Oath in the Indian Language. Noe Salt in North America; they had it here from the West Indians in January 1761 at 6^s. per Bushel.

February the 7th. Rain, & pretty warm Weather; they here get their fat Catle mostly from New England. they dont sow as much Corn there as in long Isle.—

February the 8th. Great Rain & foggy Weather.—This Day there was A Woman buried in Sir Will^{ms}. field close by his House. February the 15th. Fogg rain frost & snow. 16th. pretty warm, at Night cold with a fogg & some Rain. 17th. great cold & a frost. 18th. great Snow, & a thaw. 19th. really warm Weather, & thaws fast; 2 foot of snow yet on the Ground up the Country, but not soe much Downwards.

February the 17th. seen two white Lambs of Sir William's, 'twas very hard for them to Live, having noe Grass. At Montreal this Winter, Butter was Sold at 3^s. English per Lb. Bad Sugar the same per Lb, & a quarter of Mutton sold at a Pistole. Things were Dearer at Fort Detroit. The Reason is, because the french got noe Supplies from home these two years past. About Detroit the Country is good, clear, & fine; the french have great Setlem^{ts}. there, & a great furr-trade. It is thought, English Traders will make a vast Profit, both there & in Canada in Exchange for their Goods. At the Isle Aunois[20] there is a fine clear Country, it is a great Branch of the Missisippi. Chicksaws thereabouts, a very warlike Nation, but amount, not to above 300 fighting Men. The Chenessies [Genesee Senecas] near Oswegoe a fine, flat, open Country, and a great Nation of Indians there. At the Time Fort Edward was attacked, & taken by Mons[r]. Moncalme, Sir William wanted to goe to the Relief of it; but Gen[l]. Webb would not consent to it; 5000 Volunteer's offered to goe with him.

The french Indians are very honest, of which there were several Examples, at Montreal this Winter. The french Indians near Detroit offered Sir William a fine, Island Eight Miles long, & three broad. A Member of the Albany Assembly, (a Duchman, & indeed the most of his fraternity) will sell 1[d]. milk, 1[d] straw, &.c.

February the 18th. I heard an Indian playing many European Tunes, & pretty well on the Fidle. New Orleans, is the chief french Town on the Missisippi. About fort Mobile on the Gulf Florida, there is a great french Setlem[t]. not above 1800 french Regulars in Louisiana; the French have a Lieuten[t]. Governor, there Subject to the Orders of the Governor of Canada. Louisiana, a sickly barren Country, but about Isle Aunois a very fine One.

February the 19th. I went over the Mohawk River in a Slea, tho. a great thaw, & Rain for three or four Days before. Wolves & foxes came about 7 o'Clock this Night into Sir William's yard to a Dead Cow. 20th. Feb. a great thaw Rain & Cold.

Feb. 16th. There were New Members of Assembly Chosen at Schenectady, and the Week before at Albany: And at both Places, there was as Eager a Competition between Candidates, and as great a Corruption of Parties as in Europe.

February the 21st. very great Rain, & 18 Inches of Snow on the Ground; 22[d]. went over the Mohawk River, in a Slea, tho there was great Rain & a Constant thaw for 7 or 8 Days before, this Night a violent Storm: 23[d]. Snow, frost, & Extream Cold, & Ice as Strong as ever; I was at a great Schechems [sachem's] funeral at fort Hunter, he was interred in fine Indian Shoes, Stockings, &.C. the Indians behaved vastly decent, & shewed Sincere Grief. formerly they used to have their Guns, Axes, &.C. put in the Ground with them, immagining they were to hunt in the Other Country to the East (meaning the other World) & be merry. (it seems, that, by Instinct, they fell in, with the Notion of the Generality of the people in the Time of Paganism; as the Poets &.C. say.)—

America in general is vastly remarkable for fine Navigable Rivers & Creeks, in which are plenty of Fish. if one gets a Dutch Girl with Child, 'tis not minded.

February the 24th. I Eat Roast Beef killed in Novem[r].; Tripes &.C. are here kept up, & in Season untill april. I seen but 3 Dutchmen, who wore wigs, & them black, their Cloaths in Town are always of the Same Colour; They are at noe Expence by Mourning, which they don't take much to heart, but Sincere Enough for their nearest friends, And just soe are most Europeans in this Part of the World. Traders get great Profit. Generally there is very litle Wind in the Country; the woods, I fancy, break it off; if it blow here in Winter as in Europe there would be noe bearing with the Cold; &c—

February the 24th. frost & very cold Weather, but Clear. Noe medium in this Climate, the Summer always Excessive hot, and the winter as Cold; the Latter End of Septem^r. & the Month October is the most Agreable Time, being somewhat Temperate.

February the 25th. Great frost, & cold,. 45 out of 50 men of the province of New England, near Lake George in the year 1755 w^d. not march for their officers, & acknowledged themselves Cowards, & Signed their Names, to that Purpose. All Trees here almost Lean, to the S.East, Occasioned by the Wind being Generally from the North West. Great Quantity of wheat, Sent from this Country to the west Indies, & get Rum, Sugar &.C^a. in Exchange. Pine Buds in spring used by way of Tea, & Buds of Red Deal Excellent against the Gravel.

Feb. 26th. Great Snow, A Sergeant at one of the Indian Castles requested as a favour of the Indians not to make their Broth soe very rich having put vast quantities of Lice into it for that Purpose.

Indians pluck their Beard, & know how to trace their Game in Winter. 27th. Seen, an Indian dressed like a white Man, with a Wigg. &.C. the Indians have a Method of calling Deer to them, by immitating a Fawn. There is Plenty of Game at the Ohio, & Virginia, Indians, good Archers, can kill anything with Bows & Arrows. 27 & 28 February, constant Snow. A Buffelo larger than an Horse. Prodigious Horses not now very plenty. A Slea Load of Hay 20 C^{wt}. is 1£-17^s.-0 En. at Albany 1£-0^s.-0^d. En. only up this Country. A Skipple, wch. is the Measure used here for Grain, contains—3—Pecks.—

February the 28th. ther is Snow 4 foot deep; & March the 1st. I had this Day the honour, at Fort Johnson, to be made a chief Sachem, or Prince, in a grand Council of the Six Indian Nations, being the first white Man ever admitted to that Rank (my brother Excepted) amongst them.

Virginia horses are the best, & hardiest in America the have mostly Tobacco, & not much Corn in that Province. March the 4th. Stormy Weather, the 5th. Snow & frost. my Brother had four horses killed this Winter by Wolves.—

My Brother gets Lime Stones carried, ten Miles, upon Sleas, at Nine Shillings currency per Load. Shaving here in Winter is vastly disagreable & painful. March the 7th. very cold & hard frost. 12£-10^s currency Patent fees to the Governor here for every 1000 Acres of Land; Snakes Birds, Squirrells, &.C. are not Strong untill about the beginning of June. The Indians affirm, that if you tie an Eel skin round y^r. Leg, noe Snake will Ever come near you.—

Their heads boiled, & hogs Lard thrown into it, will poison Balls. 8th. of March Snow; 9th. Snow, & a thaw. the Pigeons in Winter goe to the Southward, & return the Latter End of March. 10th. some frost but moderate fine Weather. A grand Council of the heads of the Six Indian Nations, held at Fort Johnson, some of whom came 400 Miles to it. they complain greatly of our breach of Promise to them, having told them, before Canada was taken, That, if they w^d. Join us against it, we w^d. doe fine things, & find that we now want to shake them off: which is not good Policy by any Means, as it is in their Power almost to ruin us. An Indian will give you your Demand having No Notion of your imposeing upon him. the Mothers have the intire disposal of their Daughters. If an Indian takes you for a Mate, or friend, he will doe any thing for you, & Expects the same from you; but must have the greatest opinion of you before they commence Such a friendship. Indians Act quite Secure in Action, they think vastly of loseing any of their Men; They look upon me, as their great Mate, being Brother to Sir William, & having besides their own good Opinion of me.

10th. of March, a very cold frost, the 11th. a hard frost, & Excessive Cold; the 12th. great Rain, & at Night frost & Snow. 13th. cold windy Weather; the Morning of the 14th. very fine, & a hard frost with a great Storm in the afternoon. the 15th. Extream cold, & a very hard frost. the 16th. the weather as Cold, & the Ice as Strong almost as any Time this Winter with 3 foot of Snow on the Ground: but not near soe deep, towards Albany, or York; but towards Oswegoe more than here; They have not soe much Snow, in Winter, in Virginia, but are more Sickly than these Parts, Neither is the Winter soe Severe at Philadelphia, as here.

16th. of March my Urine quite foul, & I find my health, a good deal impaired, which I impute to the want of Exercize. The Province of New york, & some others gave 50£ Ster. by way of bounty Money, to Serve this last Campaign, & had their Pay besides. There is here 2s.-6d. currency Quit Rent, per 100 Acres.—

The Cherokees took a Disgust to us, for delaying Soe long the Attack of Fort d-Qesne,21 they had near 600 men of their Nation there, who Stayed with our Army under Genl. Forbes, untill the Midle of Septemr. & then declared they would goe home before the bad Season came on, having 700 Miles to Travel. upon which the Genl. stripd. them of their Cloaths, Arms &.C. given them by the Governr. on the Borders of Virginia:—

On their Return home, having noe Ammunition to kill Game, they killed Catle; we repulsed them. & soe the war bgan: They made Peace with us, at Fort, Johnson a year or two before, & it is thought by Some, that the five Nations could have made up this Breach. Oats sold the 16 March at 3s. currency, per Skipple, Pease at 5s., Wheat at 5s., & Barley about the same. before the war, Oats used to be but 1s.-3d.-Currency, wheat 3s., Pease 2s. March the 17th. cold frosty Weather, A great Meeting at my Brother's House to drink St. Patrick, & most got vastly drunk. The 18th. frost Hail & Rain. 19th. frost. 20th. a great Thaw. 21st. & 22d. a fog & heavy Rain. March the 21st. I got on Horse back for the first Time Since Novemr.; Snow still in the Woods 3 foot Deep: And People Extremely Sickly, having a Disorder, which comes with a Pain in their Side, attended with a fever of which they generally die in 4 Days. About 24£ currency Patent fees for 1000 Acres of Land to the Governor, officer, Surveyor Genl; &c: of which the Governor gets 12£-10s. The 23d. of March there was a Bullock killed at Skenectady, & sold at 5d. Ster per Lb. Sugar wood, Hickerry & Butter Nut, grow on the richest Soil. Oak on poor Land. the Sugar Wood, Butter Nut, & Hickery are the best fireing. Trees in general are very Straight, & there is a great Quantity of Pine.

March the 23d. A Thaw, about 9 'Clock this Morning, the Mowhawk River broke up at Fort Johnson, the Ice carried every thing before it, & really appeared dreadful. the 21st. March I saw the wild Pigeons in great flocks, at which the Duch are very much rejoiced, as they Chiefly live on them till Winter. they are alsoe a great Relief to Others, particularly the Negroes, who live on Salt provisions all Winter. People crossed the Mohawk River the 22^d. of March, in Sleas & on Horseback. At Fort Hendrick the Roads are very bad: the Snow is 3 foot deep in the Woods; And on the Clear about a foot deep; fine Sleighing in the Woods, but noe where Else.

March the 24th. Some frost, but the weather very fine, and quite pleasant, were it not, for the Snow on the Ground: Vast quantities of Ice, on the Land, along the River, driven there by the River's breaking up.

March the 25th. the Ice not broke at Several places up the River, nor at Albany, the Roads are Scarcely passable, there is Some frost, but the Weather like our April, those two, or three Days past.

26th. of March; Shoals of wild Pigeons fly very high, & some wild Duck: very litle Snow on the low, clear Lands, Some frost in the Morning, but fine weather, and a quite warm Sunshine.

27th. of March; Some Rain, & sultry weather. People ride over the Ice, about 4 Miles up the River, & at several other Places: Terrible Thunder, & lightening, with Wind, Rain & a fog: Noe passing the River over Ice, but towards Canada, where the Lakes are not broke up, but Still firm. It generally blows hard in a Thaw.

28th. March, frost, & pretty cold, 29th. the Weather very fine, and almost as warm as our Summer. 30th. the weather the same, & the River quite broke up in all Places.—

Wood-cocks came here, A week agoe, not much larger than our Snipe, & some Wild Geese; Now very little Snow, even in the Woods; 31st. the Weather much the same.

April the 1st. cold windy weather, 2^d. & 3^d. mild, 4th. very stormy with hail, rain Snow & frost, 5th. cold, 6th. very cold windy weather, with frost & Snow. 'tis dangerous being in the Woods, lest trees would fall on one.—

7th. of April, Punch frozen, & the Weather as cold as any Time in Winter, & at Night great Rain, 8th. wet weather, but much milder, 9th. cold & frosty, 10th. much the same, 11th. cold & hazy: the Lakes towards Canada not broke up, as yet, and Snow in some parts of the Woods; but None on Clear Ground. Castle cumber Land[22] & about. it is a very fine deep rich black soil, & they are now preparing to sow their Spring Grain: they have 2 Bullocks behind, & one Horse before in the Plow. they have Roots of all Sorts, and very large Successively from one Season to Another: there is noe Eating Butter or Milk, on Acc^t. of the Cows feeding mostly on Onions in the wood, which last but about a forthnight, & by that Time are too rank, for they grow only in rich Land. Indians formerly did not Sport or marry untill 30 years of Age, for they immagined it infeebled them; And when going to War, are not very fond of their Wives, on the same Acc^t.: The Duch were the first Traders, with them at Albany. there was an Advertisement, this Winter, published by the Select Men of Boston, to warn People, to hang, or Chain up their Dogs, for fear of an Infection of the Small Pox. A good Saw-Mill saws, in 24 hours, 16 Logs of 13 Boards Each, at 1^s. per Board.

Wood cocks breed here in Meadow Ground & River Banks, & have 7 at a Time: I shot One this 11th. of April full of Eggs. The spring, & Fall, are the best Times for Sporting. tho: the fowl is not in Season. but Poeple here dont mind that, as I fancy they doe not know it: The black duck take trees, the Wood cocks fly by flocks & pitch towards Night on a green Spot.

12 of April, the Weather very fine; Roads very bad,—Horses are very badly broke, over all America; Traders very busy going to Montreal &:C:

Major Rogers computes there are about 30, or 40,000 Indians at Detroit, and towards Missilamakinac [Michilimaackinac], & very warlike Nations. The Dutch salt Cabbage in the fall, on which they chiefly live with Bread. There are many Instances of both Men & women recovering after being Scalped they pull it off from the back of the Head.—

the 13th. fine Summer Weather: the 14th. cloudy fine weather, & some Rain towards Noon. Parsons keep publick Houses in this Country. When Deer, lick Trees in Night Time; if a lighted Candle be left in the Tree which It licks, that one may see him; & then stand at a litle Distance, one may Easily kill him. Pheasants here are not quite so large as our Grouse.

April the 15th. many Indians going out on their Spring Hunt, take Snow Shoes with them, as the Snow is Still 4 foot Deep in many places backwards in the Woods, the weather being very cold with Hail, Snow & Rain.—

16th. vast Rain, but very warm at Noon; & at Night cold with a Strong wind; 17th. very cold & a Mist, 18th. frost & pretty cold, 19th. frost in the morning, but fine weather; 20th. a fine morning, but a very wet afternoon, both which Days a Lutheran Church was kept in my Brothers Barn, which 250 People attended. There is 3^s. currency for Swearing an Oath over all America; the Doors are open in all Houses, the whole Nights: A Smith has 45£ Currency, per Annu^m, & meat & Drink: Any Tradesman 8^s. & a Lahourer 3^s., who are very Scarce:—

The Province of New Yorks Quota for the year 1761 are 1785 Men; & 15£ bounty: they have 1^s-3^d. per Day, & Cloaths: my Brother often soe much fatigued with Indians this War as to faint several Times. Barly sowed here in May, may be cut in six weeks; Peas, Oats, Summer wheat, Potatoes, Gardening the 1st. of May; Buckwheat in June: Indian Corn, the 1st. of May, 3 foot Distance, 4 or 5 Grains in a Drill; weed it well, when about 4 Inches high, & put a litle Dung or fresh Ground to it; & when about a foot high dung it round in litle hillocks. The Acre & Barrell not soe large here as in England, the Indian Corn ought to be planted in the best Ground. 21st. an heavy Mist but Mild Weather, 22^d. fine weather in the Morning, but great Rain towards Night. This morning I set out from Fort Johnson for Albany, & came in a Battoe to Schenectady—was 5 hours by the way in company with my Brother 23^d. great Rain, the Streets of Albany the Dirtiest I ever Saw, & worse than Edinburgh in Scotland for litle Houses; the lands about Albany are a bad poor Soil, produceing Nothing hardly but Pine Trees, &. 24th. warm weather: The reason the Duch doe not pave the Streets of Albany, is the Dread of the Stones wearing the Iron of their Cart wheels:. There are 1200 Regulars in Carolina: & Postage free for officers by Lord Loudon; The Bread at Albany is very Good & white: That Town, & up the Mowhawk River, is reckoned the Montpellier of America, & certainly 'tis the healthyest: 25th. vast Rain & Cold; 26th., fine weather; I set out this Morning from Albany for N:York on board one of their Sloops, about 150 Miles, on a very pleasant River, but a barren poor Soil, mostly all along, & vast high Mountains appearing very wild, tho: there are many Setlers; & a fine fish-pond, well stored with fish, on the Top of the highest Mountain, in the high lands; 50 Miles from New York I took up Coll. Eyers[23] & some other officers, whose Sloop, runn aground; 27th. & 28th. foggy wet weather, 29th. landed at N.York at 6 o'Clock in the Morning: The India^{ns}: Sometime use the Bark of Trees, for Tobacco; a Gent: at Albany drank 27 Bowls of Punch one Night.

Trees are in blossom, and Aspargus very plenty the 15th. of April Ins^{tt}.—

The 29th. I dined with Genl. Amherst, & the 30th. with the President:[24] And this Day 3 Men of war, & Transports with 3 Regim^{ts}. Embarked, 'tis thought for Gaudelope, but more probably, for Carolina. Officers, from the highest to the lowest, game here, to a very Surprizing Degree; (I was taken in for some Pieces) & they spend a vast Deal of Mony at Taverns; how they can doe soe, is what I can Scarcely Guess. the weather proved very fine the 29th. & 30th. of April Inst. &c.

May the 1st. Cloudy weather with Rain. The best Madeira in the year 1746 bought in the Islands of Madeira for 12£ Sterl. & 'tis Now 32£ Sterl.—2^d. & 3^d. of May moderate, fine warm Weather like our Summers; There is a fish here called Bass, plenty & Cheap, & another fine large flat Fish, & Now Pease, & Beans are about 3 Inches high, & Garden things in a Manner as forward as in Europe; there were Radishes 6 Days agoe: 4th. of May wet Foggy weather & a very great Storm, the Cellars almost all overflowed: 5th. clear in the morning with a brisk N.West wind & after-wards some Rain, the 5th. 6th. 7th. & 8th. fine weather at Noon, but Cold bleak winds tho. Southerly. the 9th. of May Sailed for Bristol, on board the Belle Sauvage Snow Captn. Lewis, & came to Sandy Hok 30 Miles from York, 10th. Wind bound, the wind blowing Easterly. Pease are blossomed since the 6th. of May. An Horse at a Livery Stable will cost 2^s-9^d. Cur^y. per Night here—I have been much afflicted these five or six Days past with the Rheumatism in my Right Hand & Arm. 13th. of May sailed from Sandy Hook: that Night & next Day very hard Gales of Wind & foggy; 15th.—16th, 17th, Cold, & quite thick & hazy weather with hard Squalls, & Calms: 18th. Hard Gales of wind. Our Course to England is East by South, for 100 Leagues, untill Nanticut Coasts are cleared, & then East & by North: Generally foggy thick weather on this Coast, during Summer & fall, & indeed the winter winds are mostly from the East, with a fog, but when westerly Clear. tis vastly disagreable on Board, having 10 Cabbin Passangers, 2 women, & two young Parsons, all bad Companions, a Shipboard. &C. People have been remarkably frost Bitten this Winter, pticularly in Canada. &c London is 11 Degrees more to the North than New York: London being in 51^{Do} . . . 35^M. & New York in 40 &c. Degrees North Latitude. 19th. very hard Gales of wind, 20th. much the same. run 200 & odd Miles in 24 hours, for 2 Days, the sea very high, & I am quite Sea Sick, 21st. & 22nd. the same weather; the Rheumatism still in my hand, and the Wind at

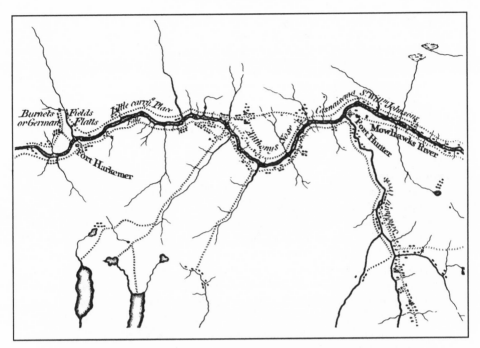

9. Detail from *Communication between Albany and Oswego* (Kitchen 1772). The map shows both Mohawk and Euro-American settlements in the Mohawk Valley, as well as principal trails in the years just before the outbreak of the Revolutionary War. The Lower Castle was located at Fort Hunter. The Upper Castle (Indian Castle site) is shown as six dots opposite the mouth of East Canada Creek just east of "Little carry^g Place."

South West. We goe a Degree & half to the South of Newfound Land Banks: I Scalded my right hand very much, the 22^d. Day with a ketle of boiling Water. the Cook's Cabhouse being on fire, upon which Occasion we made use of the water, & happily Extinguished it tho twice on fire. &.C.

24th. vastly Strong Squals of Wind, with heavy Rain. 25th. pretty fine Weather; 26th. 27th. fine Summer Weather. From the Twenty Ninth Day of May, to the 7th of June, A Constant hard Gale of Wind at N.East quite against us. 4th. June seen Curvo, one of the western Portugese Isles about 400 Leagues from the Lizard, & seen here Several Turtles, but the weather too bad to Send out a Boat. From the 7th. to the 10th. of June fresh North East Gales. 10th. Saw Tercera Island, & Angra the Town, One of the Western Isles—330 Leagues from the Lizard: There are Several Turtles about these Islands but not soe good as in the west Indias. the 11th. in the afternoon, a hard Gale of wind which carried off all our Top Masts, try sail, Mast, & Sprit Sail, 4 Men got on the Yards, but fortunately none carried over Board, nor much hurt. we certainly cut a very miserable Figure, & the wind at North west. I have a Constant Heart-burn & am Stomach Sick. 15th. the Wind Easterly & soe cold that a Person, at Noon, can with great Pleasure bear a Wide

Coat. the wind these three weeks is very Severe against us. 16 the Wind Still against us, at N.East. & very cold, tho in Latitude 44. 7 Degrees more to the South than London the Weather more moderate, tho. noe South Wind almost the 4 weeks. There was a Sailor flogged in Boston by order of the Select men, for kissing his wife in the Streets on Sunday tho. after three years absence: And a Stallion brought to a whipping Post, & lashed, by said Order, for covering a Mare on the Sabbath Day. these things are upon Record in Boston, as having happen'd not many years agoe, 17th. wind Still at North East—the 19th. the Weather moderate, & Light Air from the N west. 20th. June, Wind, S.West, & South East, & at Night very hard Squalls of wind & Rain, 21st. wind at N.west but Light Airs: We sounded at 12' O'Clock, & found Ground, & Judge ourselves 12 Leagues Eastward of Cape Clear, & 65 Leagues from Lundy

We saw a Vessel this Morning, which lost her Top mast, & Two More a Brigg, & a Snow, in sight—the Brigg chaced by the Snow, which was a french Privateer: 22^d. a light wind, & against us, we were Chaced by a Large Ship, which proved the Venus Frigate, & came up with us & took us for one of the Privateers, there being four privateers in sight almost between here & Bristol. 23^d. the Venus Chaced the Snow Privateer, & came up fast with her, but towards Night, a very thick Fogg & calm came on, & we lost both Ship & Privateer, the wind being quite against us: We saw Cape clear at about 8 League's Distance. 24th. a Fog Rain, & a Strong cold wind against us, & have been these four Days under great apprehensions of being taken, & still are being—80 Leagues from Lundy & we begin to be in want of most Things, & have noe Prospect of a Fair wind: The Winds (Except for few Days) have been from the East, these five Weeks past; hard Fortune! 25th. light airs at S: west, Just at Day break:

This Morning we seen a Vessel, but can't tell what she was, being foggy weather, & believe they, being to Winward, did not see us, we were a litle afraid, having but two old Guns; at Noon, we were Chaced by a large Ship, which proved the Venus; we had at Night a hard Gale of wind, at N:N:East: 26th. The wind Still blows very hard at N:N:East. We saw several Sail, & the Venus in Company, & seen the English Land, at half an hour after '12, near Biddiford, & 20 Miles N: of Lundy.—but the wind was Contrary to get up Bristol Channell. I am quite Sea sick. the Venus tells us of four french Privateers off Lundy, Viz^t. A Snow, a Brigg, Cutter, & Lugsail Boat, the Two last generally under Land; At Night it blew Excessive hard from the East: 27th. Landed at Apple Door in Devonshire near Biddiford 150 Miles from Bristol, & same Distance from Bath; There are here about 2000 french Prisonners; July the 3^d. I set out from Bath for London, & arrived there that Night. There are at Bristol about 1500 french Prisonners.

ENDNOTES

1. In New York State Library.
2. Richard Tyrrell, a cousin of Warren and Sir William.
3. Pad. An easy-paced horse.
4. Trenton, N.J.

5. I.e., for fermentation.
6. Indian dish of corn and beans.
7. Iroquois at La Gallette, near Oswegatchie on St. Lawrence River.
8. Pierre Francois Rigaud, Marquis de Vaudreuil.
9. Bottom lands.
10. Canajoharie.
11. Sir William's Indian name.
12. Allegheny.
13. Distant from.
14. Venereal disease.
15. Monongahela.
16. George II died Oct. 25, 1760.
17. A crisp curl. To put the hair in a buckle; i.e., to fasten it in shape like a candle.
18. Robert Rogers.
19. Col. John Butler.
20. Illinois.
21. Fort Duquesne.
22. Near present site of Johnstown.
23. William Eyre.
24. Cadwallader Colden, president of the council.

Journal of Joseph Bloomfield

1776

Joseph Bloomfield

Joseph Bloomfield was a soldier and fourth governor of New Jersey. He was born in 1755, and he was commissioned a captain in the 3rd New Jersey regiment in 1776. His regiment was ordered to Canada, but the American retreat from Quebec redirected him first to Fort Stanwix and later to Fort Ticonderoga. He kept a journal of his service in New York, which has been edited and published recently by Lender and Martin (Bloomfield 1982). The portion of the journal reproduced here covers the days May 15-27, July 23, July 24-31, 1776, when Bloomfield (1982:46-55, 81-93) spent time in the Mohawk Valley. The period from May 28 to July 21 has been omitted because it is not as pertinent to the purposes of this volume. The period is actually split between volumes 1 and 2 of Bloomfield's journal, for he began a new volume on July 24, 1776. Footnotes and the superscripted numbers leading to them, which were inserted by Lender and Martin, have been omitted as unnecessary here. In one case we have clarified the deletion with an additional bracketed insertion. All other bracketed insertions were provided by Lender and Martin.

Bloomfield had a long and productive career, serving as governor from 1801 to 1812. President Madison appointed him brigadier general at the outbreak of the War of 1812. Once again he was ordered to participate in an abortive invasion of Canada. He later returned to New Jersey, where he died in 1823.

D.R.S.

WEDNESDAY THE 15th. of May (vid. 31st. Inst.) Last Night Seeley Simkins, Benjn. Simkins, Ebenezer Woodruff, Lewis Thomson, Uriah Maul & James Logan Deserted from me after Stealing a Watch & sundry other Things from the Company. William Magra also a Soldier in my Company died last Night & this Eveng. was buried in form, the whole Regmt. with the Field-Officers & Chaplain attending, who Prayed with & Addressed the Soldiers. Afterwards five Men fired three rounds over his Grave & the Men were Dismissed greatly admiring the respect Shewn one of their Brother Soldiers. Engaged on a Court Martial. Tried John Brewer of Col. Dayton's Regmt., Capn. Sharp's Compy. for Desertion. Sentenced to receive 25 Lashes & return to his duty. Robert Barry for Drunkeness & Disobedience of Orders Sentd. to receive 25 Lashes. Michael Calen for Theft, Embezzlement & Selling the Publick Stores Sentenced to be carried to the Post with a Halter about his Neck & to receive 39 Lashes for Theft, also 39 Lashes for making way with the Congress Stores, be carried back with a Halter about his Neck to the Guardhouse & be confined 8 Days on Bread & Water & return to his duty. Spent the Eveng. & Supped with Mr. Caldwell our Chaplain at Mr. Henry's.

Thursday the 16th. May. Set all day upon the Genl. Court Martial. Tried Thoms. Price for Desertion & Embezzleing the Publick Stores sentenced to receive the same Punishment ordered yesterday for Callen. Sundry others were tried some discharged & some Sentenced to receive Punisht.

Friday the 17th. of May. By directions from Major Genl. Schuyler, Brigadr. Genl. Sullivan Ordered our Regmt. to Parade at 6 O'Clock this morng. compleat in Arms & 350 of our best Men were picked out & supplied with flints Powder & Ball & five days Provisions on a secret Expedition. At 4 P.M. our Detachmt. of 350 Men with Col. Dayton, Major Barber, Capts. Potter, Patterson, Ross, Sharp, & myself with subalterns accordingly, our Surgeon, & Worthy Chaplain sett out & Marched as far as Cripple Bush Eight miles from Albany where we halted & Pitched our Tents. Lay this Night being the first time I ever slept in a Tent. This day was observed throughout the Continent as a Day of Fasting & Prayer by Order of the Congress.

Albany Saturday the 18th. of May 1776. Struck our Tents by 4 this Morning & Marched through a Scotch mist of Rain to Schenectady 18 Ms. from Albany where the Committee Desired the Inhabitants to Billet our Troops which was done & our Officers & Men were treated with great kindness. Dined with Dr. Prickett in company with Dr. Dunham & Mr. Gaulidet, appointed my Ensign on the present Expedition. At 3 P.M. crossed the Mohawk River opposite Albany & Marched eight Miles then Pitched our Tents & Lodged.

Sunday the 19th. of May. Proceeded on our March early this Morning. At 8 [A.M.] passed by the elegant Buildings of Col. Guy Johnson & Col. Claus, Son in Laws of Sr. Wm. Johnson, & now in England doing America all the Mischief in their Power. At xi passed by the very Neat and Elegant Buildings that the late Sr. Wm. Johnson lived in, generally called Fort or Castle William on the Eastside of the Mohawk river and within four Miles of the lower Castle of the Mohawk Indians called Fort Hunter, which we passed by 12 O'Clock alarming the Indians along this delightfull Country not a little & who appeared at a distance to be collecting. Here our Regmt. Landed & our Col. ordered advanced Flank & Rear Guards to our Partisan. At 4 P.M. arrived at Johnstown, pitched our Tents at the upper End of the Town, our Troops being greatly fatigued with their march & heavy Burden of Provisions. Brought my Arms, Blanket, & Napsack with 6 days Provisions to Johnstown, being with Capts. Sharp, Ross, & Lieut. Mc.Mihell, the only officers who did not on the road put their Napsacks in the Carriage Waggons. My Ambition was too great to see the Men loaded and myself, with no burthen, Nay I prided myself in Marching at the head of the Regmt. with as heavy if not heavier load than the Soldiery though I must Acknowledge

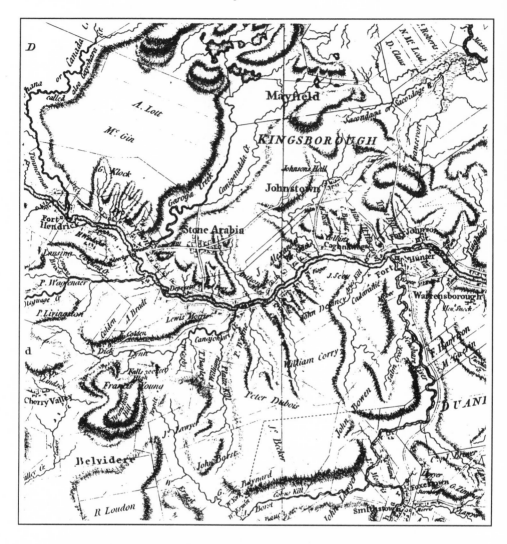

10. Detail from *A Chorographical Map of the Province of New York in North America* (Sauthier 1779). Fort Hendrick is shown near the eastern boundary of lands owned by the Upper Castle Mohawks at the beginning of the Revolutionary War. The Lower Castle was located at Fort Hunter. "Caghnawaga" refers to a Euro-American settlement on the present site of Fonda.

my inclination frequently almost induced me to through [throw] my Napsack & Blanket into the Waggon. We were here informed that Sr. John Johnson had left John's Town with most of the Male Inhabitants & all the Highlanders, Dutch & Irish about it with 50 Indians, that they were embodied Armed and intended to Attack us Very probably this Evening. Col. Dayton ordered me to Mount Guard with 68 Men, Lt. Mc.Mihell, Lt. Mc.Donald & Ensign Anderson Subalterns, for the security of the Camp. Mounted guard all Night, visiting the 22 Centories [sentries] out at a time round the Camp every hour. The Vigilance now required made me forget my fatigue entirely. The officers & Men lay in the Tents on their arms. The forepart of the Night we could frequently hear the Indian Warriors yell the War-hoop or Alarum in a most hideous manner and this added to the Darkness of the Night, being in a strange Country surrounded with woods added greatly to our apprehensions of being attacked which made our Centeries as Watchful as Night-Owls. Though the Officers and Soldiers were anxious to engage the Enemys of their Country, yet they wished for the Daylight for such bloody business. The latter part of the Night all quietness, no alarms or Accident happening in the Camp.

Monday. 20. [May, John's-Town]. This morning the Commissioners appointed by Genl. Schuyler to treat with the Indians arrived in Town & at twelve, Abraham, the Indian King accompanied by the Sachems & Indian Warriors painted & dressed in their Warlike Manner also arrived and the Treaty was opened by the Indians demanding in a haughty manner of our great Warrior (as they called Col. Dayton) what He meant by coming into their country with armed Troops & whether He was for Peace or War? To which Col. Dayton replied that He came not to molest our Brothers the Mohawks but to suppress the Highlanders & others who had taken up arms against the Congress & hoped our Brothers the Mohawks would not interfere in our Family Quarrel with great-Britain. They replied that we came to take Sr. John's Life, their good old Friend Sr. Wm. Johnson's Son, That they loved Sr. Wm. who was their Father, for his sake they would protect his son, that Sr. Williams blood ran in their Veins, was mixed with their Blood, and they would stand by him. After much more altercation the treaty was adjourned till tomorrow, the Indians first promising that their Warriors should be peaceable till the Treaty was over. It is worth remarking that the Interpreter after the Indians spoke delivered their Speech in Dutch to our superintendant & who delivered it to Colo. Dayton & the Commissioners in English. It is really surprizeing to see what an assuming behaviour those Savages put on whilst in Council. They sett in their Indian painted warlike dress with their Indian Tomahawks with Pipes (the handle of the Tomahawk being the Tube & the head of the Hatchet the Bole) and smoking with such a confident air of Dignity & Superiority as if they were above all other beings mad[e] and their Authority extended over the whole Earth. My curiosity induced me to pay a Visit alone this morning to Johnson-Hall, which is a Very beautiful large & elegant Build[ing] with two Forts built by Sr. Wm. in the time of the last War about half a Mile from Town on a small eminance with a fine Stream of Water which runs about 5 Rod off before the Hall. My excuse to see the Hall was to Wait on Miss Peggy Watts (a Sister of Lady John Johnson's & who I was formerly Acquainted with) & who I said I understood was at the Hall. Lady Johnson received and treated me with the greatest Politeness talked freely upon the present unhappy Times & seemed to have the greatest fortitude for a Woman considering the situation her Houshd. was in. She shewed me Sir Wm. Johnson's Picture, which was curiously surrounded with all kinds of Beads of Wamphum, Indian curiositys and Trappings of Indian Finery wh. He had received in his Treatys with different Indian Nations, Curiositys suficient to amuse the curious. She shewed me also the Johnson coat of arms, good old King Hendrick's Picture &c. &c. In short, I returned pleased with my feigned Visit, greatly pleased with Johnson-Hall and the worthy *Lady indeed* (though a Tory who is in Possession of it). Our Detachment parraded in the Evening and took Possesion of the Court-House, Goals, & Church for the security of the Troops in case Sr. John & his party should attack us & who we are informed are embodied to the number of 500 in the woods about five Ms. off & intend acting in a hostile manner, of repelling force by force. Pitched our Tents before the Court House & Church.

Tuesday. 21 [May]. This morning the Indian Treaty was again Opened. Our great Warrior (Col. Dayton) told the Mohawks by the Interpretor that if they offered to take up the Hatchet or oppose his Warriors in their present Expedition He would break the Covenant Chain, He would burn their upper & lower Castles on the Mohawk River, would burn all their houses, destroy their Towns & Cast the Mohawks with their Wifes & Children off of the face of the Earth; on the contrary if they would be still and let us alone in a Family Quarrel, his Young Men (meaning the Soldiery) Should not come near nor molest their Castles &c. At the same time our Detachment with the Drums & fifes were parrading & made a most martial appearance through the street. I believe this had a good effect, these savages cant bear to be supplicated, it makes them think they are of great consequence. The only way is to strike Terror into them. This is the way the brave & politic good old Sr. Wm. Johnson used to treat with them. Upon this the Indian Chiefs & Warriors withdrew for one hour, then returned appeared more mild, submissive & peaceable. Said they were determined not to meddle with our Family Quarrell; all they wanted was to be assured Sr. John should not be killed. We might do as we pleased with the Highlanders, upon which our Chief (Col. Dayton) told them not a hair of Sr. John's head should fall to the ground. We loved him also for his Father's sake, what we was a going to do would be for Sr. John's benefit. We should destroy [illegible] and those Indians who opposed us only, after which some friendly speeches past. The Covenant Chain was promised by both to be brightened and the Hatchet buried. Our Chief desired them not to let their Young Men imprudently come about our Camp, especially in the Night, for fear our Young Warriors & Young Men might be rash & take their Scalps. The Indian Chiefs promised that their Young men should stay at home & not hunt till we were gone out of the Country. Then this great & mighty Council broke up, after drinking plentifully of Toddy, which was the best drink the place good [could] afford. The Wine (if they ever had any) Rum & all the Provisions of the place were taken off by Sr. John & his Party, which makes every article of the Provision kind very Scarce & consequently extravagantly dear—Butter 3/6 per lb., Milk 1/6, Butter without Milk 1/4, Cyder /10 & small Beer /6 pr. Quart, Eggs 2/pr. Doz. and every thing else accordingly dear.

I will now give a description of John's-Town, with my sentiments of its importance.

John's-Town lies in Tryon-County New-York Government, forty five M. West-Nor:W. from Albany, four M. from the Mohawk-River between the upper (called Fort *Hendrick*) and lower (called fort *Hunter*) Mohawk Castles, Twelve Miles from Ionandago [Onondaga], from whence a Creek communicates with the North-River, and from whence there is a communication to Canada by land. The noted Tory rascals White & others went this way & were taken up by our Troops at lake Champlain.

By Examination of several Persons, Wigs & Tories it appears that Sr. John can raise of his own Tenants about 300, Scots and as many Dutch & Irish, that they have arms & ammunition. The warriors of the lower Castle are generally Tories & altho. they have professed themselves satisfyed yet they are not to be trusted, especially as they are much attached to Sr. John. The Missionary & school-Master in their Town: of this we had a most striking proof at the last treaty with Col. Dayton for notwithstanding their Warriors in their last speech gave the most solemn Assurances of their resolutions to abide by the Covenant made with the six Nations, their countenances expressed a Very different language, and evinced to every bystander that we are indebted to their Neutrality in arms to fear not to attachments.

The Town contains about 30 houses, mostly small half Stories. The Country round the Town is fertile & capable by cultivation to supply a great quantity of Provisions. It is well situated to connect the North & Mohawk Rivers to tamper with the Indians, to connect [the] Tories below with those above, And in case we should be unfortunate on either side to fall upon us—fall upon a Weaker party—cutt off a retreat and take the advantage of the fluctuating Passions of Mankind, that any circumstance might be improved against us. It [is] very evi-dent Sr. John's Tenants are against us from the very circumstances of their being Tenants & otherwise in debt to Sr. John & dependant upon him, till their cir-cumstances are altered they cannot nor will not be our Friends. There appears but two Methods of securing this Country in our Interest: The One, to keep a Garrison here to support the Wigs and over awe the Tories; The other, of plant-ing Wigs in the room of Tories. The situation of the Town for a Garretson: For the middle and highest Part are a large Court house of Brick with a good well contiguous to it, and Church of Stone on opposite sides of the street about twenty rod distant from each other, about 100 rod from these and about 40 Rod from the upper part of the Town Sou: East upon ground much higher than the Town and the highest of any near it is a large Goal strongly built with stone, with three feet Walls with a well of good Water close to it. A little labour would render these places Very strong and whoever possest them first would not be easily disposse-sed and from whence a Scouting Partie could be Sent through the Country to distress the Tories, To press Provisions if necessary &c.

A description of Johnson-Hall was given in Yesterday's Remarks &c.

A Proclamation was this day published & sent by Col. Dayton through the Country, warning the Scotch Highlanders & all others who had taken up arms against the Congress to come in with their Wifes Children & Affects and they should be well treated; and all those who failed of immediately coming in should be dealt with the Utmost severity & suffer accordingly.

Lieut. Col. White came to Johns-Town this Eveng. with the remainder of our Regt. & Proviss. for the whole. Lieut. Elmer of my Company being left in Albany with the care of the Baggage & Sick.

Wednesday. May 22. I was early this Morning directed by Col. Dayton to take a file of Men & go to Johnson Hall with my side arms only & wait on Lady Johnson with a Letter, The substance of which was to demand the key of the Hall & drawers in the Rooms with directions for her immediately to Pack up her own apparel only and go to Albany, that an Officer & a Guard should wait on her Ladyship to Albany if she choses. Accordingly I went to the Hall & after directing the Sarjant of My Guard to place Centuries round the Hall & Fort I asked for her Ladyship who was then a Bed and after waiting an hour she came into the Parlour. I gave her the Letter with assuring her Ladyship it gave me Pain that I was under the disagreable necessity of delivering her a letter that must give her Ladyship a great deal of uneasiness and which my duty obldiged me to do in obedience to the orders of my superier Officer. She hastily broke open the Letter & immediately burst into a flood of Tears, wh[ich] affected me, so that I thought proper to leave her alone. After some time she sent for me, composed herself, ordered the Keys of the Hall to be brought in & given to me & which I desired might lay on the Table till the Coll. came. After which I breakfasted with her Ladyship & Miss Jenny Chew whose Father is in England Acting the part of a Violent Tory. After Breakfast Col. Dayton & Major Barber came & we in the presence of her Ladyship or Miss Chew Examined every Room & Every Drawer In Johnson-Hall & Sr. John's office, but found no Letters of a publick Nature inimical to the cause worth mentioning.

This search gave me an opportunity of fully satisfying my curiosity in seeing everything in Johnson-Hall. To give a particular Acct. would exceed the bounds of my Journal, only I'll say that we saw all Sr. William's Papers of all the Treaties He made with the different Indian-Nations, with Medals of Various sorts sent him from Europe & samples of others which He had distributed at his Treaties to the Indians &c., with innumerable Testimonials &c., all which placed Sr. William Johnson's Character in a Very important station of life and greatly merited the warmest thanks of his Country. But when we reflected on Sr. John's (his Son's) Conduct, it afforded a contrast not to be equalled. Whilst we admired and commended the Wisdom, Prudence, Patriotic Spirit, Ardor & Bravery of the Father, we could but detest and discommend the foolish imprudent, treacherous & base Conduct of the son, who, instead of Walking in the Paths of his good old Father in supporting the Liberty of America & thereby Merit the applause of his Country, He has basely endeavored and still is endeavoring to destroy the Libertys & Propertys of his Native Country, and to cutt the Throats of Those, who feared, loved & fought under the command of his Valiant Father, and who now (with a degree of Tenderness & Respect) are obldiged to search the Hall built by the good industrious old Baronet (& in which He dyed) to discover and detect the Young Profligate Knights Treacherous Villany. Lady Johnson treated us all with the greatest complaisance & Politeness, and begged of the Coll. to let her stay in the Hall for the present, assureing him that it was not in her power to send Sr. John any supply of Provisions, that she heard from Sr. John a Monday last, when she sent him a large supply of Provisions & that Sr. John informed her by Letter, He should make the best of his way with his Party to Niagara, which the Coll. had reason to believe true as the Testimony of several on Oath both Wigs & Tories, confirmed the same & therefore He permitted Lady Johnson to stay in the Hall for the Present, Ordering Centuries to be kept around The house to prevent Provisions being sent from thence to Sr. John.

This afternoon the Coll. had his hands full with Examining Tories, Scotch-Men &c. &c. who came to deliver themselves up.

Thursday. 23. [May]. This day taken up in examining Scotch, Dutch & Irish Tories who came to deliver themselves to the Coll. It is not uncommon here to hear the different English Scotch, Dutch & Indian Languages talked at one time. P.M. Parties were sent out to secure some Tories & who were brought in Accordingly.

It is very surprizeing to see what a consternation & fright the Tories in this County are thrown into. Those miserable Wretches are afraid to be seen by any of the Soldiery, which is the Reasen we are so Scanty of fresh Provisions, Butter, Eggs &c. They behave with the greatest servility imaginable when brought to the Coll. & make all the Promises for their future good behaviour that can be desired, upon which they are usually dismissed

The Committee of this County sitt every day & afford the Coll. all the Assistance in their Power.

Friday. May 24. John's-Town. This day taken up as yesterday in Examing Tories. At 6 P.M. I was ordered to take a Party of Men with Lt. Gifford & go to the house of the Noted Tory Rascal Alexr. White, Esqr. High Sheriff of this county and Examine his Papers & if I thought Necessary to bring him with me, which was no sooner said (as the old saying is) than it was done. I arrived at White's house on the Mohawk River 5 Miles from this place in 70 Mins. Searched his house found neither Letters Arms or ammunition. White assured me upon his Honor that He had not acted directly or indirectly in the present cause since he gave his Obligation not to, & had his parole from New-York Goal. After this examined two more Tory houses-Col. Butler's for one, who is now in Niagara Superintendant of Indian Affairs, but without effect. Returned by xi with a good appetite for my supper. Capn. Sharp with 60 Men & two 2 subalterns were ordered on a Party to take Possession of a Mill about 20 Miles to the Northwd. to cutt off any Stores going from thence to Sr. John's Party &c.

Sunday. May 26. John's-Town. This Morning we were informed Independency is declared by the Congress which greatly pleased our Regmt.

By direction of the Coll. I waited on the Church Wardens of the Church in Town; got the Keys of the Church, in wh[ich] the Revrd. Mr. Caldwell preached to our Regmt. true Wiggism for the first time I dare-say & Prayed for the Congress, that ever it was done in this Church. Our officers took Possession of Sr. John's & the Governor's Pews which with the Pulpit &c. were hung in Black in mourning for good old Sr. William who built this elegant Church. It has a noble Steeple with a good Bell and an excellent sett of Organs which we also made use of, so that we had Presbeterism preached in an Episcopal Church in taste. O Tempora! O Mores! Qui Mutantur. Mounted Guard this night. Lt. Tuttle, Lt. Coxe [Cox] & Ensign Patterson subalterns. Wet & Rainy. Went over to Johnson-Hall & relieved the old-guard myself.

Monday. May 27. John's-Town. By order of the Coll. waited this morning on Lady Johnson with a Letter directing her to prepare to go to Albany tomorrow morning. Breakfasted with her Ladyship who said she would be ready in obedience to the orders. P.M. waited on her Ladyship again desireing her to name the officer (as the Colonel intended one should Wait on) she would choose to Accompany her to Albany, upon which she desired me to attend her, to inform the Colonel she was most acquainted with & therefore preferred me before any other officer. This day our Regt. was reviewed by Col. Dayton Judge Duer & the Committee of Tryon County who was greatly pleased with the Alertness of the Men & thought we were well disciplined Troops, when it well knew we are yet raw & unexperienced.

Tuesday. 23. [July]. Notwithstanding it is mentioned to have been wrote the 23d of July, I have sett the accts. down as my time & business wd. allow. The following is a brief description of the Indian-Nations attending the Treaty, by the various Accounts I have collected, vizt.

The five Nations consist of so many Tribes or Nations joined together by a league or confederacy like the united Provinces, and without any superiority. This union has been time immemorial. They are known & distinguished by the Mohawks, Oneydaes [Oneidas], Onondagas, Cayugas, & Seneka's. The Tuskaroras, after a War it is said they had with the People of Carolina, fled to the five Nations, and are incorporated with Them; so that now, indeed, they properly consist of six Nations. Each of them is again divided into three different Tribes, who distinguish themselves by three different arms, viz, the Bear, the Tortoise and the Wolf; The sachems put that belonging to their Tribe to every publick Paper.

They think themselves by Nature superior to the rest of Mankind, and assume the Name of Ongue-honwe, that is, Man surpassing all others. This Opinion gives them that carriage, which has been so terrible to all the Nations of North-America; and that Opinion they have taken such care to [impress?] on all their Neighbours, that on all Occasions they yield to them the most submissive Obedience. They have such absolute Notions of Liberty, that they allow of no kind of Superiority, and banish all servitude from their Territories.

An old Mohawk Sachem, in a poor Blanket & dirty shirt, Issues his orders, with as arbitrary an authority as a Roman dictator. The Authority of their Sachems who govern in publick affairs as well that of their Captains consists wholly, and is only obtained by the good Opinion the Nation have of the Wisdom & integrity of the former, and of the Courage & Conduct of the latter; and they loose it by a failure in those Virtues.

Their Instruments of War are Muskets Hatchets, and long sharp-pointed Knives; these they always carry about with them. The Hatchet in war-time, they stick in their girdle behind; and they have the art of directing & regulating its motion, so, that though it turns round as it flies, the edge always sticks in the tree, near the place they aim at. The use of bows & arrows is not entirely laid aside, except among the Boys, who use them with surprizeing dexterity. Their Castles or Towns are generally square surrounded with Pallisadoes, without any bastions or out Works. They express peace by the metaphor of a Tree & fire, and all Indians make use of a Hatchet or ax as an emblem of War.

Wampum is the current money among the Indians, it is of two sorts, white & purple; the white is worked out of the inside of the great Conques [conch], into the form of a Bead, & perforated, to string on Leather. As the Indians live far from the Sea, our people make & sell the Purple or exchange them for Beaver-skins &c. and many, at Albany particularly, make a handsome living by that Trade. The purple is worked out of the inside of the muscle [mussel] shell; they are wove as broad as one's hand, & about two feet long; these they call belts, & give and receive at their Treaties, as the seals of Friendship; for lesser matters, a single string is given. Every bead is of a known Value and a belt of a less Number is made to equal one of the greater, by so many as are Wanting, fastened to the belt by a string.

One hundred of those Beads are usually valued at 4*l*. per 200, 8*l*. & so on, & in this manner they trade & barter with each other & with all that deal with them.

I will now describe the Indian-Dance mentioned a Saturday Evening July 20. The Indians were painted after their usual manner, Red, Black, blue & every colour in their power. Those who dance are Naked, except their Breach-Clout & Ornaments. Those who dance are the Youngest Men. The Chiefs are Spectators & Conductors. The middle State conduct the music. One beats upon a Keg over the head of which is streached a skin. The others round him join their Voices, He who beats setting the tune. Their Notes are few, but soft, & all keep time & Tune with the greatest exactness. Every one who sings has two little sticks which He beats together in concert with the Drum. Round these the Dancers perform after their manner, which consist of Violent exertions & according to some rules. Once in the space of two Minutes, they step with a shout in which they exert their Voice to the Utmost. The Singers are grave & the Dancers full of pleasantry. After a little pause the Music begins & the dance goes on they stomp violently upon the ground & Exert themselves to great fatigue. This dance seems calculated to enure to harden & to render the Muscles Vigorous. In the midst of the dance one of chief Warriors who was a spectator steps forward & strikes with a stick, which produced a instant pause. In a short speech He related his warlike exploits, the Prisoners & Scalps taken from other Nations appealing to those who were Witness, and then finished with a present of a little paint wrapped up in paper which he had received from the Commissioners for that purpose. This was received by all with great marks of applause. Some time after, another Chief & then another did in like manner. This custom is intended in the time of their mirth to Inspire them with a thirst for War & an emulation to have the like Opportunity publickly to relate their gallant deeds. The Seneka's are taller & better proportioned than the other Indians present or the whites, And from their healthful fleshy appearance, are more temperate & better fed than the other Indians.

Every Indian-Nation has something peculiar in their own Customs & Manners different from each other.

The Indians in general are tall & straight in their limbs, beyond the proportion of the whites. Their bodies are strong; but of such a species of Vigour, as is rather adapted to endure much hardship, than to continue long at any servile works: it is the strength of a beast of prey, rather than a beast of burthen. Their Bodies & heads are flattish, the effects of Art fro[m] the Squaa's carefully brace their Children or papoosses's till they walk alone on a Broad board to which they lace the Infant with broad Cloths carrying them on their shoulders in all their Journies, for Most of them for the sake of the Presents given at the Indian Treaties, take their whole Familys with them, carrying & lugging such Papoosse's as are unable to walk in this slavish manner. The Cottages in the meantime, are shut up & there being no furniture to lose, a string or thong of leather serves for a lock. Their features are regular but their countenances fierce; their Hair (those that wear it) long in general Very black, lank & Very strong. They have no beards owing to custom of continually drawing it out by the roots with twisted wires. The colour of their skin a reddish brown, admired amongst them; and improved by the const. use of Bear's fat & paint. They in general go naked except a Clout which they wear to cover their Nakedness, Once in a While throwing a Blanket over their Shoulders. The Squaa's dress in the same manner, only they always wear a striped Blanket, striped with Red or Yellow ferryiting [ferreting] or Ribbons agreable to their quality in life & and those stripes are generally on the middle of the Blanket & covered with silver & brass Broaches of all sizes.

Their only Occupations are hunting & War; Vide Friday June 28th. remarks. Agriculture is left to the Women. Merchandize they contemn. When their Hunting Season is past, which they go through with much patience, & in which they exert Ingenuity, and their Provisions laid up, they pass the rest of their time in an entire indolence. They sleep half the day in their Tents, they loiter & jest among their Friends, and they observe no bounds or decency in their eating & drinking. They are excessive fond of spirituous Liquors, and the desire of acquiring these is a principal End they pursue in their Treaties with us: & from this they suffer inexpressible Calamities, for haveing once begun to drink they can preserve no measure, but continue a succession of drunkenness as long as their means of procuring liquor last. In this condition they lie exposed on the ground to all the Inclemency of the seasons, which wastes them by a train of the most fatal Disorders. They perish in rivers & marshes, they tumble into the fire, they quarrel & Very often murder each other. And in short excess of Drinking, with us highly Criminal, & which is not generally Very pernicious in its effects as among this uncivilized People, who have not art enough to guard against the consequences of their Vices, is a public calamity. The few among them who live free from this evil, enjoy the reward of their temperance in a robust & healthy old age. The Disorders which a Complicated Luxury has introduced & supported amongst us are strangers to the Savages.

The Education of the Indians from their Infancy is solely directed to fit their bodies for this mode of Life, & to form their Bodies & Minds to endure the affliction of the greatest evils.

As I said before, Almost the sole Occupation of the Indians is war, or such Exercises as qualify him for it. His whole Glory consists in this: and no man at all is considered till he has increased the strength of his Country with a Captive or adorned his Hut with the Scalp of one of its Enemies. And these Scalps are so many evidences of the Trophies of their Bravery.

The Character of the Indians is striking. They are grave even to sadness, upon any serious Occasion; observant of those in Company, respectful to the old, of a temper cool deliberate, by which they are never in haste to speak before they have thought well on the matter, & are sure the person who spoke before them has finished all he had to say; they have therefore the greatest contempt for the vivacity of our People who interrupt each other, & frequently speak altogether.

Nothing is more edifying than their behaviour in their public Councils & Assemblies; every man there is heard in his turn, According as his Years, Wisdom, or service to his Country, have ranked him. Not a Word, not a Wisper, not a murmur is heard from the rest, whilst He speaks; no indecent condemnation, no ill-timed applause. The younger sort attend for their Instruction. Here they learn the History of their Nation; here they are inflamed with the songs of those who celibrate the Warlike Actions of their Ancestors; and here they are taught what are the Interests of their country, & how to pursue them.

Their habitations are Very small, consisting only of a little cottage, in the middle of which is their fire-place: here both they and the Animals they breed, live promiscuosly. They have a particular fondness for Dogs, & never are without three or four little curs in their huts; a hog or two, and a little poultry, with some earthen ware, as pots and jugs, & the Cotton which their Wifes spin, constitute the whole Inventory of an Indian's effects. Their beds consist of two or three sheep-skins without Pillows or any thing else; and on these they sleep in their usual squatting posture; and as they never undress, appear always in the same garb.

The above Acct. of the Indians must serve for the present, as I shall be daily more & more acquainted with their manners. I will sett down hereafter promiscusly such observations as Occur & strike my fancy, considering at the same time, my *time* & business.

Awoke & arose to business agreable to Orders of Yesterday & with our Worthy active Parson, laid out the lines of the Fort & sett the fatigue-Party to work, & who by Night finished the lines being (2 feet wide & 4 feet deep) so as to be ready for the Pickquets, which began to be brought in this Evening being large heavy & 20 feet long. These Pickquets when put up will defend our Lines, and with the Natural situation of the Place & a deep Ditch in front of the stockade will make our fortification formidable to our Enemys; especially as on the different angles will be placed small Artillery to secure the Lines in case of a close

Attack. Within this stockade is included a convenient House suitable for the officers & a Very large Barn which will serve for Barracks for the Soldiery, also a
Very good Well. 500 Men can fight at once on the Lines & it is so constructed as
to be defended by half that Number of Men.

In the Evening went to the General's Bowry. Whilst there an Express came to
the General, from Genl. Washington informing him all was well at New-York.

Also the Rev'd Mr. Kirkland & some of the principal Chiefs from the Oneida-
Castle, particularly the Chiefs *White-Skin & Grasshopper,* who treated me with a
good deal of kindness when at the Oneida-Castle (see June 28 antea).

After the usual salutation of *Sago*-ongh Ottachagousola (How do you do
Brother, or Friend?) & shaking of hands they sat down beside the General &
Commisss. The Genl. ordered Liquor & Pipes immediately, Light his Pipe &
drank to them, by wishing them Welcome & signifying He was glad to see them
in health & peace, which was interpreted to them. They in their turn by their
Chief *Grasshopper* (which is his name in their languague being
Cheeastawaliosottee) said "They were glad to see the General & Commissioners
that God had permitted them to meet again in [Health?] to drink one another's
health & smoak a friendly Pipe together."

White-Skin drank their Health & the United States wishing them prosperity.
After smoaking a Pipe or two & hearing the News, they retired, it being first
Settled that the Treaty should open in two days hence, as all the Onendagoes &
Tuscaroras will then arrive.

Returned to camp with my fellow-Lodger who are at present—Col. Dayton
being down from fort-Stanwix otherwise called Fort Schuyler, Mr. Timothy Ed-
wards one of the Commissioners of Indian-Affairs, The General's aid-de-Camp
being Major Livingston from Elizth. Town, and the worthy Mr. Calldwell my
Assistant in fortyfying Fort [entry incomplete].

The following being the *Lord's-Prayer* in the Mohawk Tongue, may serve as a
specimen of the Indian-Language in general, there being but little Variation, except in the pronunciation. (vizt.)

The Lord's Prayer: Ra, odereanayent ne Royaner.
Songywanika ne Karongyage tighsideron, wasaghnadogeaghtine.
Sarayert sera iewa, tagserra Eighniawewan, siniyought Karongy-
agough, onioghwansiage. Niyadwighniseroge taggwanadara
nondaghsik nonwa: Neonitondag warighwiyoughston, siniyught oni
Jakwadadouighwiyoughstan i: Neonitoghsadaghgwasarineght, de-
waddatdennageraghtangge nesane sedjadagwaghs me Kondighse-
rokeanse, kea sayanertsera ne naagh, Neoni, ne kaeshatste, Neoni ne
Onweseachtakne siniyeheinwe Neoni siniyekeinwe.

AMEN.

The *Mohawk*-Nation pronunce their Words long soft, full, low & with
suprizeing sweetness. The *Oneydoes* [Oneidas] on the contrary pronunce their

words very short harsh & with a great deal of roughness. The Seneka & Cayugas Language differs considerably from both.

Wednesday. July the 24th. German-Flatts on the Mohawk-River. Arose Very early this Morning. Immediately attended & have been engaged all day in overseeing the fortification now erecting in this place, by direction of Major-Genl. Schuyler, as before mentioned July 22d. Col. Coxe's Militia drew Pickets all day. Dined with the General Commissioners & officers of the Army, who had a Visit paid them after Dinner by the Chiefs, Sachems & Warriors to the amount of near 100. of the Oneydoes, who arrived to day, & came to pay their Respects & Return the belts which summoned them down, to the General.

Genl. Schuyler made them a speech, which they readily answered, Complimenting one another Very highly, after which the Genl. ordered Pipes, Tobacco & Grogg (as is usual upon such Occasions) to Drink each other's Health, at the same time, thanking the supreme being that they were permitted to meet, & smoak a friendly Pipe together & prepare to kindle a Council-Fire. After much conversation in which they shewed a great deal of Wit & pleasantry, as it was interpreted to us. They parted in the Evening with the usual Greetings.

The following may serve for a description of this Country.

The German-Flatts lye on the Mohawk-River about 40 or 50 Miles above John'stown, is one or two miles wide & 5 or 6 long, exceeding rich & fertile. On either side are very high mountanous Hills, over these Mountains the Land is flat & rich. The Mohawk-River seems to run all the way from Schinactaday to Fort-Schuyler, which lies at the head of the River through a ridge of Hills & Mountains with a rich Valley between, which is very rich & fertile & where the Dutch the Inhabitants of this fertile Country raise Vast Quantitys of Peas which they carry down the Mohawk-River in Batteaus to Albany, & is what we call the *Albany Peas*. At the Head of these Flatts is my present Post, where on the Northside of the Flatts a Creek makes out called Lower-Canada Creek about one third as large the River. Upon both sides of this Creek & up & down the river lies the famous Tract of 120,000 Acres of the finest Land in America, belonging to Sr. William Johnson's Estate; whose Family by being Tories, have forfeited his & their other Estates to the Colonies.

This Country, particularly this Place is remarkable for Fogs. Almost every morning a Fog like a Cloud ariseth from the rivers or Mountains & falls like a fine Rain, or if it does not fall in this mist it generally falls in heavier Showers before Night.

Here I see that passage of the Psalmist (mentioned 104th. Psm: 8th. Verse) remarkably fulfilled: where speaking of the Waters, He saith, *"They go up by the Mountains, They go down by the Valleys, unto the place thou hast founded for them."*

Here we see the vapour rise, sometimes in smaller Columns and sometimes in larger; and presently form a Cloud, which breaks over the Mountains & pours down upon us. By this means the Country is watered.

These are some of the wonderfull Works of God, of whose Goodness the Universe is full.

Thursday. July 25. 1776. Engaged all day in overseeing the Picquets brought in as yesterday. Wrote home to my friends today, by an Express from Genl. Schuyler to Genl. Washington.

Invited Joseph an Indian Sachem & 2 others of the Onandagoes & Abraham, a Lieut. of the Stockbridge Indians, to drink tea with me, which they Accepted & behaved with a good deal of Modesty. This Joseph was in the American-Army at Boston last Summer & staid some time this spring with Genl. Washington in New-York where he was greatly caressed & Dined every day with his Excellency.

Friday. 26. [July]. Began this morning & Engaged all day in raising the Pickets & securing the stockade. I forgot to mention that last Evening I restored Jonathan Lummis & Thomas Parker mentioned before (July the 17th.) to their former station of Corporals. Spent the Evening at the Generals.

Saturday. 27. [July]. Necessity drove me to order a Court-Martial today wh. made the following report.

> At a Regimental Court-Martial held by order of Capt. Bloomfield at the German-Flatts July 27th. 1776. Capt. Garret Veadder President, Lieut. Wm. Gifford, Pendleton, Cannon & Elmer members.
>
> Michael Reynolds of Bloomfield's Coy. accused of Lodging out of Camp in disobedience of orders, Nonattendance at Roll-Call this morning & attempting to leave the Company without leave. (after mentioning the Evidence) The Court Martial considering the above crimes do sentence him, to be led to the post stripped & tyed thereto for the space of a quarter of an hour & afterwards dismissed to his duty with the stoppage of One Weeks pay from his wages.
>
> GERRIT S. VEEDER
> Presdt. & Capn.

Which was approved in the following manner. "I approve of the above Sentence & order it put immediately into Execution." JOS. BLOOMFIELD.

At the Roll-Call in the Evening the Companies were drawn round the Adjutant's Daughter (the Whipping-Post so called), The Prisoner tyed up & was exhorted by our Chaplain for his base Conduct & the Soldiery warned against bringing themselves to such a shamefull Punishment. I also spoke to my Company & the Prisoner, told them it gave me a great deal of Pain to see One of their Brother-Soldiers punished; but, at the same time, when I reflected He was not originally Inlisted with me but taken up as a Deserter from the 2[d.] Pennsilvania Battn., it was some alleviation of my Anxiety &c. &c. &c. After Prayers the Prisoner was released & Expressing himself in a haughty manner that He was punished, through spite, I ordered him immediately to be again Confined in the Guard-house. vid. July 31.

Sunday. July 28. Attended Meeting (with the Companies under my Command in form) & heard the Revd. Mr. Kirkland Indian Missionary from the Presbeterian Synod preach to the Indians in the Oneida-Language, the Oneidoe's being professors of the Christian-Religion & Presbeterians, attended in general. The Mohawk Nation, who are Episcopalians, also attended, & the Gentlemen of the Army, & some few Indians of the other Nations out of curiosity.

Mr. Kirkland first sang an Indian-Psalm, Prayed first in English, & then in Indian, Sang another Psalm in Indian & then Preached to them from [blank] (as he afterwards told us). After Sermon and Anthem well sung in the Oneida-Tongue & then the Congregation was dismissed after Prayers & the Blessing both in the English & Indian-Languages.

The great attention serious, solemn & devout Behaviour of those poor Savages, with the sweetest, best & most harmonious singing I ever heard, excited the steady attention & admiration of all present, & was an Example to the whites & at the same time a Reproof to the Christians, who haveing the Gospel allmost daily preached to them, pay no great attention (it being an old Story) & frequently behave with the greatest Rudeness during Divine service. The Oneydoes excel in singing. They carried all the parts of Music with the greatest Exactness & harmony.

Though I did not understand a word that was said, Yet I never paid greater attention or was more improved in attending divine Worship.

When I observed & Reflected with what reverence & solemnity the almost naked Savages, (the Men haveing a Clout only round them & the Women a skirt & Blanket wh. they covered themselves except their faces entirely) unless some few of the Heads & Chiefs & their squaas who were elegantly dressed with mockinsens Leggins &c. &c. after their Indian Fashion, I say, their devout Behaviour struck me with Astonishment & made me blush with shame for myself and my own People. In short we all came away after service greatly pleased with the Indians & Conscious of our own Inattention & want of Reverence during divine services in general. P.M. Attended Divine service with the Companies as in the Morning; when our Very Worthy & Patriotic Chaplain Preached (in the Presence of Genl. Schuyler & the officers of the Army & sundry Indians who returned our Complyment paid them in the Morning by their also attending Divine Worship deliverd in the English Language) from 2 Sam: X.12 "Be of good Courage, & let us play the Men for our People, & for the Cities of our God; & the Lord do that which seemeth him good." This Text being very suitable to the Occasion, was Delivered with a great deal of Judgement & applied particularly to those who bore the Military Character in such a Manner as to engage the attention of his Audience & Edify all present.

It is worth remarking that Very early in the Morning I heard the Dutch Domine preach in the High-German-Language, so that I heard Divine-Worship Delivered in three Tongues today. Besides I heard in the different Companies I was in, the following Languages spoke—1st. English, 2d. High-Dutch, 3d. Low-Dutch, 4th. French, 5th the Mohawk, 6th. Oneydoes, 7th. Senekas, 8th. Cayugas, 9th. Tuscaroras & 10th. the Onondagoe-Languages. The most of those Tongues I heard daily spoke and one Person in particular a frenchman can speak French, English Low-Dutch & the five Indian-Languages.

I must also observe, that whilst the Religious Oneydoes were at their worship in the Morning, the Atheistical Seneka's Onondagoes & Cauyugas who believe there is no God & make a jest of all Religion were beating their Tub singing, Dancing & Carrusing in the most profane Manner. The Tuscaroras are Papists by Profession but in fact have no Religion. In short, the various scenes of this day I shall never forget, & hope whenever I reflect on it will excite a grateful sense of thankfulness to the supreme being who has placed me in such a situation in Life as to enjoy so many advantages above those poor Savages.

Monday. July 29. 1776. Engaged all day in overseeing the Erecting Pickets at the Fortification &c. &c. Two Grand matches were made up between the Oneydas & Tuscaroras at Ball, or what the Scott's call Golf. Near 100 Dollars worth of their Ornaments were staked each time, which were gained by the Tuscaroras. The Oneydas had been used to beat them at all set matches for many years till this day. At these Matches the Ornaments staked are generally collected from the Women who generously give some of their wampum, silver, Bead Bracelets, others their Earrings, nose-Jewels & Pins. Others give Necklaces, belts &c. & all kinds of Indian-Ornaments. They are remarkably fair in their play. Nothing that has the appearance of Cheating nor any Wrangles are seen on these Occasions. When the boys play together, or shoot for Coppers, all is fair & honest, & Courteous. The Indians when sober are remarkably cautious. They will hardly ever say or do a Thing that will give offence. If one supposes he has ground of offence or has received an Injury he will not shew it unless Drunk & has an opportunity for Revenge. This caution undoubtedly arises from their form of Government or rather being without Government. We are not afraid of offending because secured by the force of Government from revenge. This security they have not, & most therefore screen themselves by caution.

The Genl.-Officers of the Army; & all the Indians, Men & Women, attended at the matches at Ball to day.

This day I also saw in the field an Indian Squaa with two Babes, born in her hutt about three days before, & soon after her arrival. She was now out with them more than half a mile from Camp. The Mother & Infants appeared Very well. They were both bound upon their Boards or Cradles according to Custom, & one of them was carried by the Mother & the other by a little sister. The same Woman a few Years ago was taken in Travail upon the Road to a Treaty. She only halted by the wayside a few Minutes with another female friend till they received the stranger, bound it up, & marched after in the rear of the Company. With many of them it is a Custom to send the Newly delivered Woman out to Chop a Load of Wood & Carry it home upon her Back. This they say brings all the Joints & Bones to their place again. And their Women have been seen to be taken in Labour while out cutting their Wood. They lay down their ax wrap the Papoosses in their Blankets & bring them home upon their loads of Wood. I shall be more particular in giving an Acct. of the Indians & a description of their Play, before mentioned when my time will permit. See hereafter August 29th.

Tuesday. 30. [July]. Engaged between the hours of 2 & 3 P.M. on a Genl. Court-Martial for the trial of Lieut. Wm. McDonald (vid. Aug. the 1st.) This

P.M. rode out in the Generals-Coach with Major Livingston, the Generals Aid-de-Camp, the Genl's Secretary Mr. Larson, Capt. McGee & other Gentmn. on Horseback. After riding over the German-Flatts we crossed the Mohawk-River 3 miles from this place. Drank Tea at Mr. Shoemakers & returned at 6, when the General & Gentm. of the army were much engaged in observing a total Eclipse of the Moon being most of the Time Visible.

Wednesday. July 31. 1776. Engaged on the Court-Martial as Yesterday. This day Tesconindoe [Skenandoa] the Head-Warrior of the Oneydoes Dined with me. He made me a present of a Red-Belt or sash worked with beads as a Testimony of his regard, ariseing I suppose from my Visiting him when at the Oneyda-Castle & treating him with familiarity since He has been here. I forgot to mention or rather had not time to enter the Proceedings of a Regimental-Court Martial on Monday last.

> At a Regimental Court-Martial held at the German-Flatts July 29th. 1776. by order of the Commanding Officer, whereof Capt. Vosburgh is President, Lt. Pendleton, Bates, Solsberry, & Ensign Thomas are members. (after mentioning the Evidence which is very lengthy.) The Court takeing into Consideration the Cases of the abovementioned Persons John Cook, Luke Jinnins, & James Newman do adjudge them guilty of Gameing & Cards to the Value of £7:00:0 & upwards & Order that they immediately make each other as good as they were before & pay four Shillings fine & be returned to their duty.

To which the following Assent was given:

> I have Considered of the Sentences of the Court against the respective Prisoners within mentioned & do approve of the same except the fines imposed on John Cook &c. which is hereby remitted except so much as will pay for every Pack of Cards at the rate of 1*l*. [shilling] per pack that is as will be hereafter publickly destroyed by order of the officers of the respective Companies in this place agreable to the orders of this day.
>
> JOS. BLOOMFIELD. 29th. July 76.

Michael Reynolds mentioned 27th. Inst. haveing shewed great contrition for his misbehaviour &c. &c., he meant the Soldiers & no officer; was discharged.

Visit to Schenectady

1780

François-Jean de Beauvoir, Marquis de Chastellux

Beauvoir was a professional soldier who wrote one of the more readable of many descriptions of the United States published after the American Revolution. He was born in 1734 and by the age of 21 was already a colonel. At about the same time, he volunteered to be the first Frenchman inoculated against smallpox, a risky experimental procedure at the time. He survived inoculation and 25 years later saw to it that French soldiers under his command in America were also inoculated.

Beauvoir was a major general with the French Expeditionary Forces, and his *Travels in North America* was originally intended only as a kind of round-robin letter for his friends back home. He was well published in several subjects, and it turned out not to be difficult to persuade him to publish his observations on America. He had already published literary works and philosophy, spending some time under the tutelage of Voltaire. He was a man of letters, whose personality and ability to speak English endeared him to leaders like Franklin, Jefferson, and Washington. He became Marquis de Chastellux in 1784 with the death of his older brother. He married late, in 1787, and died suddenly the next year at the age of 54. He never knew either his son, who would be born four months later, or the French Revolution that would soon follow.

The brief passage that follows is part of a two-volume translation of Beauvoir's *Travels in North America*, edited by Howard C. Rice, Jr. (Chastellux 1963:206-209). Rice's footnotes and the superscripted numbers leading to them have been deleted from this reprinting. Readers wishing to know more about Beauvoir and his works should refer to Rice's excellent introduction. The passage is as useful in conveying the prejudices and humor of Beauvoir as it is in describing the Mohawk Valley and its inhabitants.

D.R.S.

December 27, 1780: Albany—Visit to Schenectady

THE 27TH IN THE MORNING, learning that the rivers were not yet frozen over, but seeing that the weather was fairly good but very cold, I wished to take advantage of it to go to Schenectady. This is a town situated fourteen miles from Albany, on the Mohawk River. It excites some curiosity from being built in the very country of the Indians; from its being picketed, that is to say, surrounded with lofty palisades like their villages, and from their still retaining some habitations there, which form a sort of suburb, to the east of the town. It was rather late when I thought of this ride, and it was noon before I got a sleigh; but General Schuyler had assured me that I should be there in two hours, on the supposition, doubtless, that my sleigh would have better horses than it did. I found the roads very difficult, and the horses even more difficult than the roads; for they would not pull, and if M. de Montesquieu had not himself taken the reins, and pressed forward with more vivacity than their meek driver, I believe I should still be there in the snow, with which this country is covered six months in the year. The country which lies between Albany and Schenectady is nothing but an immense forest of spruce trees, untouched by the axe. They are lofty and robust, but well spaced; and as nothing grows under their shade, a line of cavalry might traverse this wood without breaking ranks or defiling. It was three o'clock, and I was half dead with cold when I reached Schenectady. This town stands at the foot of a small declivity, on your coming out of the woods; it is regularly built, and contains five hundred houses within the palisades, without counting some dwellings which form a suburb, and the Indian village adjoining this suburb. Two families, and eight inhabitants, are reckoned to a house. Beyond the town, to the westward, the country is more open and the land very fertile; it produces a great deal of grain with which they carry on a great trade. I alighted at Colonel [John] Glen's, the quartermaster general of this district, a lively, active man. He received me in the politest manner; an excellent fire and two or three glasses of toddy warmed me sufficiently so that I could ask him a few questions and set out again immediately, for night was coming on, and the Vicomte de Noailles expected me for dinner at five o'clock. Colonel Glen lent me horses to return to Albany, and was so good as to conduct me himself into the Indian village. As we were preparing to set out, one of these savages entered his house: he was a messenger dispatched by their hunters, and came to announce that a party of one hundred and fifty Senecas and several Tories had been seen a few miles from Saratoga, and that they had even carried off one of their young men. This messenger spoke very good French and very bad English; born of a Canadian, or perhaps European, father, he had mixed with the savages, amongst whom he had lived twenty years, from preference for this unrestricted life (*libertinage*) rather than from any other motive. The news he brought was not very encouraging for the journey I was planning for the morrow or the day following, but I gave little credit to it, and I was in the right.

The Indian village Mr. Glen conducted me to is nothing but an assemblage of miserable huts in the woods, along the road to Albany. He took me into the hut of a savage from the Sault Saint Louis, who had long lived at Montreal and spoke good French. These huts are like our barracks in time of war, or like those built in vineyards or orchards, when the fruit is ripe and has to be watched at night. The framework consists only of two uprights and one crosspole; this is covered with a matted roof, but is well lined within by a quantity of bark. The inner space is rather below the level of the ground, and the entrance by a little side-door; in the middle of the hut is the fireplace, from which the smoke ascends by an opening in the roof. On each side of the fire are raised two platforms, which run the length of the hut and serve as beds; these are covered with skins and bark. In addition to the savage who spoke French, there was in this hut a *squah* (the name given to the Indian women), who had taken him as her second, and was bringing up a child by her first husband; two old men composed the remainder of this family, which had a melancholy and poor appearance. The *squah* was hideous, as they all are, and her husband almost stupid, so that the charms of this society did not make me forget that the day was advancing and that it was time to set out. All that I could learn from the Colonel, or from the Indians, was that the state gives them rations of meat and sometimes of flour; that they also possess some lands, where they sow Indian corn, and go hunting for skins, which they exchange for rum. They are sometimes employed in war, and are commended for their bravery and fidelity. Though in subjection to the Americans, they have their chiefs, to whom application is made for justice, when an Indian has committed any crimes. Mr. Glen told me that they submitted to the punishments inflicted on them; but could not comprehend that it was right to punish them with death, even for homicide. Their number at present is 350, which is constantly diminishing, as is that of the tribes called the Five Nations. I do not believe that these five nations can produce four thousand men in arms. The savages of themselves therefore would not be too much dreaded, were they not supported by the English and the American Tories. As an advanced guard they are formidable, as an army they are nothing. But their cruelty seems to augment in proportion to their decrease in numbers; it is such as to render it impossible for the Americans to consent to have them longer for neighbors; and a necessary consequence of a peace, if favorable to Congress, will be their total destruction, or at least their exclusion from all the country this side of the lakes. Those who are attached to the Americans, and live in some manner under their laws, such as the Mohawks in the neighborhood of Schenectady and a part of the Oneidas, will ultimately become civilized, and be intermingled with them. This is what every feeling and reasonable man should wish, who, preferring the interests of humanity to those of his own fame, disdains the little artifice so often and so successfully employed, of extolling ignorance and poverty, in order to win acclaim in Palaces and Academies.

I had time to meditate on such matters as these, and on many others besides, as I journeyed by the sole light of the snow, through these majestic woods, where silence reigns by night and is seldom disturbed by day. I did not arrive at the lodgings of the Vicomte de Noailles until nearly eight o'clock; supper, tea, and conversation detained me there until midnight. Nothing, however, was decided respecting our journey, and the news we had received about the rivers was not yet satisfactory.

Diary of Peter Sailly on a Journey in America in the Year 1784

1784

Peter Sailly

Peter Sailly (1754-1826) emigrated to the United States from his native France in 1784. Soon afterward he settled near what is today Plattsburgh, New York, situated in the Lake Champlain region, and became engaged in the fur trade, the manufacture of potash, and the lumber business. He was an associate justice of the Court of Common Pleas (1788-1796), elected to the State Assembly in 1803, and served a single term in Congress (1805-1807). He returned to Plattsburgh in 1807, assuming the post of collector of customs, which he held until his death.

Sailly's short account is of a trip to the interior of New York following his arrival at Philadelphia. He sailed up the Hudson River to Albany and then traveled overland to Johnstown, the former home of Sir William Johnson. From here, he and a small party proceeded west through the Mohawk Valley to Fort Stanwix and a nearby Oneida Indian village. The next day they continued south to Schuyler Lake and the headwaters of the Susquehanna River, returning once again to the Mohawk, and then back to Albany. He passed through Saratoga on his way to Plattsburgh, where he would buy land.

Sailly's papers and a manuscript memorial were presented to the New York State Library. They were published as *Peter Sailly (1754-1826), A Pioneer of the Champlain Valley* by Bixby (1919). Bixby's footnotes have been eliminated here.

W.A.S.

1784, MAY 11.—I arrived at Philadelphia.

May 14.—Left Philadelphia to examine the iron works near Newark; accompanied by the proprietor.

May 17.—I left Newark to visit Mr Faesch, the proprietor of the iron works at his house. Left there on the 18th for New York, where I arrived the same day.

May 19.—I embarked on the Hudson river for Albany, by the way of Poughkeepsie, with the intention of exploring the interior of the country.

May 20.—We arrived within view of West Point; a large fort, where the Americans had their principal forces during the late war. The tide and the wind being adverse, we were obliged to anchor. I profited by the delay to examine this locality, celebrated both from its position, which renders it almost impregnable and from the treason of General Arnold. To reach the first fort on the south, I ascended, with great labor, a mountain and some very large rocks. I found the mountain covered with walnut trees, and fragrant with roses, aromatic herbs and wild vines in blossom. I had scarcely reached the summit, and was within fifty paces of the fort, when the captain made the signal to leave, which obliged me to descend the mountain in haste and not without danger. In ascending, as we passed around the forts and redoubts I counted ten *terre-pleins* upon the heights, where the sides are nearly impracticable. The Hudson river, a magnificent stream, runs through a deep channel between two chains of high mountains. The mountains are not cultivated and can not be.

May 20.—I landed at Poughkeepsie, where I expected to find Mr Dezong, a gentleman I had seen in New York, and who intended to be my traveling companion.

May 21.—This day at Poughkeepsie, a small and pleasant village, but the environs of which are not very pleasing, with the exception of the country seat of Mr Livingston, which is upon the borders of the river, in a most charming location. I forgot to notice, that I passed in sight of two villages between West Point and Poughkeepsie, called New Windsor and Newburgh; but they did not equal the smallest villages in France.

May 22.—I left Poughkeepsie for Albany in company with Mr Dezong on horseback. The country between these two places is fine and well cultivated. We passed three small villages. The roads were very good.

May 23.—Arrived at Albany which is 84 miles from Poughkeepsie and 168 miles, or 56 French leagues from New York. Here the valley enlarges and presents a charming appearance. Albany, situate upon the North or Hudson river, is a flourishing village, very advantageously located, particularly for the fur trade with the Indians.

May 24.—This day at Albany, where I had several letters of introduction to deliver.

May 25.—Left Albany for Schenectady, by the way of the falls of the Mohawk. These falls are sixty feet high, and present a most magnificent appearance. Schenectady is eighteen miles from Albany. It is a pleasant village with fine houses upon the banks of the Mohawk river. It numbers about 450 inhabitants. The country is beautiful along the Mohawk from a point six miles above the falls to Schenectady.

May 26.—Left Schenectady for Johnstown, about twenty-four miles distant, and five miles from the Mohawk river. The country between these two villages is indifferently good. The borders of the Mohawk are contracted by the surrounding hills. Johnstown contains sixteen dwellings, a church, court house and jail. The house of General Johnson is one-fourth of a mile from the village. All his property has been confiscated by the state; against which he took part in the late war. The commissioners were at Johnstown to take legal proceedings concerning his property, consisting in this section, of about fifty thousand acres of land and forests. The soil is good about this place. Johnstown is situated upon a small stream which turns several mills, and upon which forges could be built. There are but few fish in the river and game is not abundant.

May 27, Sunday.—We took a walk seven or eight miles in the woods, north of the village. We saw fine oaks and pines from three and one-half to four feet in diameter and sugar maples two and one-half feet.

May 28.—I went about twelve miles from Johnstown, to the house of Madam, the widow Paris, whose husband was killed by the English at the commencement of the late war. He was their terror. This brave man was Colonel of Militia, originally from l'Orient, France, I believe. He has a brother in Philadelphia with whom I am acquainted; and had also many friends in Nantes. His widow has a mill in good condition, but it lacks water. She manufactures potash. Near her residence we passed through a section of country called "Stone Arabia." It is one of the finest sections I have seen in America. The cultivated land is about eight miles in length by two miles in width and lies upon an elevated plain along the immense forests which border upon the Mohawk. The soil is fertile and the inhabitants will be prosperous if they do not again undergo the evils of war, from which they have suffered by the loss of their houses and cattle, stolen and burned by the Indians. They have since then built a small fort into which they can retreat in case of any new incursion, if peace does not render the tardy precaution unnecessary.

May 29.—Colonel Melcher, Captain Dezong and myself left Johnstown with the intention of visiting Fort Stanwix and the Indians of Lake Oneida. We purpose to sleep at German Flats, a section celebrated in North America for its beauty and the richness of its soil. The valley here expands and forms a beautiful plain, which the Mohawk river divides in the center. A fine stream called Canada creek, traverses a portion of the German Flats and joins its waters with the Mohawk. The inhabitants have suffered more from the late war than in other sections, as their neighbors, the Indians, have treated them with greater severity, having burned their houses, stolen their cattle and brought other misfortunes upon them. It would seem that Nature itself were in league with the enemy to desolate the country, for the land, naturally fertile, has been unproductive the present year. The most beautiful country in the world now presents only the poor cabins of an impoverished population who are nearly without food and upon the verge of starvation. The German Flats are about forty miles from Johnstown.

May 31.—We continued our route toward Fort Stanwix. Our progress being retarded by several events of little interest, we were obliged to sleep in a small Indian village, composed of four or five cabins, and containing between twenty-five and thirty inhabitants. These Indians dwell upon the borders of the Orisque [Oriskany], a branch of the Mohawk. We were received with a cordiality we have not found in any other part of America, and which is not always found in France. They gave us salmon, which they catch in Oneida lake, twenty-four miles higher up, where the main body of the tribe resides. This little tribe, which forms the main part of the Onontagues [Onondagas], one of the Six Nations of Iroquois, numbers about two hundred families. They were the friends of the

United States in the late war. The savages gave up to us their beds, which are made of a blanket spread upon a bedstead eighteen inches high. The couch is of the bark of trees. These Indians show nothing of the savage except in dress. Many of them conversed in English with my companions, with as much spirit and ease as we could ourselves assume. I found them much more polite than the peasants of France, who are the most civilized and polished of that class in Europe. We saw several fine and very tall men; one young man of twenty-two years, who was tall and well proportioned, with a most martial figure and address. Few men in Europe are by nature as noble in appearance (aussi distingués de la nature). The females are inferior; rendered so by labor, harsh treatment and their unbecoming dress.

Upon the borders of the Orisque General Herkimer gained a battle over the English and their Indian allies, commanded by M. de St Leger, a man of French parentage but born in Ireland. This engagement took place in the woods, while General Herkimer was on his way to relieve Fort Schuyler, then besieged by the English. About four miles before reaching the Indian village we saw Fort Schuyler, which is no more than a rampart of earth, now overgrown with thorns and bushes.

July 1.—Prepared to continue our journey, but the horse of Mr Dezong becoming lame we returned to sleep at German Flats. Col. Melcher continued on. The whole country on both sides of the Mohawk is very fine. The lands are excellent. About five miles above German Flats are immense forests of primitive growth. The ground is covered with old and decayed trees which render the roads difficult. The mosquitoes are extremely troublesome. This section must sometimes become the most beautiful and richest in America. It contains a fertile soil, rich meadows and a great number of lakes and rivers filled with fish.

July 3.—We started to visit Lake Schuyler and several other small lakes in its vicinity. We passed through a forest twenty-four miles in length from German Flats over a road blocked up, at every step, by fallen trees. At the lake we found the land to be of very inferior quality, if we except the bottom lands, but these latter are exposed to annual inundations during the rainy season. Lake Schuyler is six miles long, in some places two miles wide and in others less than one mile. We passed over it in a canoe, as far as its outlet, which forms part of the Susquehanna river, sixteen miles below. We caught many fine fish in the lake with lines, with which we were provided. On our arrival we let loose our horses on the banks of the lake, but the next day, Sunday, mine could not be found. I think it was stolen by some hunters who were near the lake. The lake is full of fish and two streams of considerable size enter into it, but the land is so level near the lake that it is not possible to construct mills. A small piece of elevated land which we saw at the head of the lake, where there is an old house inhabited and several acres fit for cultivation, presents a favorable place for building a mill. There is not much current, yet, by making a dam to retain the waters about two hundred and fifty paces higher up, a mill could be turned twelve hours during the twenty-four and the dam would cause no further expense.

This is the most favorable section in the world for fishing and the chase. We found in the lake large quantities of pike and perch, and at certain season salmon are caught. Deer, bears and beaver abound in the forest bordering on the lake, and in the surrounding country are to be found partridges, hares and pigeons in great numbers.

On Monday the fifth we started on our return to German Flats, without obtaining any information about my horse. We visited an ancient Indian village while descending the Mohawk. This is a fine section and the lands are of better quality. Mills and forges can be built upon a large stream which traverses the country and empties into the Mohawk. We continued our route for Johnstown, where were the commissioners of the State, who propose to make a road to an iron ore mine upon a mountain near the borders of the Mohawk. Certain points upon this river present advantageous sites for forges. There is but little commerce upon the Mohawk. The inhabitants are poor since the war. It is nevertheless a desirable location as this part of America will soon be thickly peopled. The rich lands will attract settlers. A merchant here can only sell in exchange for grain and peltries. With both of these he can do well in New York. Wheat can not be sold as it is received. It must be made into flour. New York then receives it for her own consumption and for shipment to the Islands [West Indies]. It is of great importance to a merchant on the Mohawk that he own a mill, some land, a house and a little stock. With these he can carry on a very good business.

July 7.—I returned to Fort Henry, twenty-four miles from Johnstown, upon the Mohawk, to purchase some excellent lands, but I could not agree with the proprietors as to the terms.

July 10.—Arrived at Albany.

July 11, Sunday.—I saw Mr Gilliland who owns lands upon Lake Champlain. As the price and terms of payment were satisfactory, and the lands were represented to be very good, I determined to look at them. Mr Gilliland could not leave until Thursday the 15th, and the same night we slept at Saratoga; a locality celebrated in America from the surrender of General Burgoyne with an army of seven thousand men to the American General Gates. We saw the encampments of the two generals and the ground where two battles were fought between them. Saratoga is twenty-four miles from Albany and comprises a great extent of territory, but little cultivated. General Schuyler has a large farm upon the borders of the North river. A small and rapid stream empties near his house upon which he has built several mills. There are a number of mills along the borders of the North river. The land in this section is of poor quality.

Journey to the Oneidas

1784

François Marbois

François Marbois (1745-1847), who later had the title of Marquis de Barbe-Marbois conferred upon him, was secretary of the French legation to the newly formed United States from 1779 until 1785. By this time Marbois was already an experienced diplomat, having served as a representative of his government to the Diet of the Empire at Ratisbon (Regensburg), Dresden, and at the Court of Bavaria. Marbois was also a prolific writer who produced, among other works, a book entitled *Historie de la Louisiane et de la cession de cette colonie* (1829), which stemmed from his appointment by Napoleon to act as negotiator for the cession of Louisiana to the United States. It was for Marbois that Thomas Jefferson wrote his *Notes on the State of Virginia*.

Marbois had traveled extensively in the United States and wished to see, at first hand, its native inhabitants. He chose to visit the Oneida. Arriving first at Albany, he met, by chance, an expedition about to make its way to Fort Stanwix (Schuyler) where the first treaty negotiations following the Revolutionary War were about to begin between the federal government and the six Iroquois tribes. Leading this party was the Marquis de LaFayette, James Madison, and Oliver Wolcott, one of three federal commissioners sent to treat with the Indians.

Before leaving for Indian country, Marbois and his companions visited the Shaker community at Niskayuna, which clearly fascinated the Frenchman. The party then continued west into the Mohawk Valley, badly ravaged in the recent war. Once at Fort Stanwix, where there was a great deal of activity as preparations were made for the treaty deliberations, Marbois traveled to an Oneida village, probably Oriske, where he encountered an old acquaintance, the sachem "Great Grasshopper." On October 2, Marbois returned to Fort Stanwix. By now, Indians from many different tribes had arrived for the soon-to-begin treaty conference. Following the signing of the treaty, Marbois left for Albany.

Marbois's record of his journey is in the form of a letter to Mlle d'Alleray. It was published in its entirety in *Our Revolutionary Forefathers: The Letters of François, Marquis de Barbe-Marbois* (1929). Endnotes and the superscripted numbers leading to them in the 1929 edition have been dropped here.

W.A.S.

SEPTEMBER 14, 1784. I am having my vacation, mademoiselle; we have neither Congress nor Committees, and I am taking advantage of the circumstance to see the country. Here I am at New Brunswick, in the Jerseys.

I was traveling with my wife, and the falls of the Passaic were the first object for which we stopped. We climbed the hill at once, for the falls are seen from above, at which you will be surprised, for usually waterfalls are seen from below. This one can be seen only from the top of the rock. The pool into which it drops cannot be seen without going right up to the edge, and it is necessary to lean over to see into the depths. My wife approached it while I was looking at some bushes, and when I turned around I saw her leaning over the precipice. I shuddered, I did not dare run up to her to bring her back; indeed, I was afraid of making her realize her danger. The noise of the fall prevented me from making her hear me, I stretched out my arms to her. She calmly went on looking, walked along the dangerous ledge, and finally came back to rescue me from my mortal terror.

I visited forts which the English occupied a year and a half ago, and which are given over to-day to a flock of sheep and a few cows. They browsed peacefully on the grass which grows on the slopes of the walls, they scaled the ramparts by breaches which they have made, and in a few years they will have ruined these works which the enemy erected at so much expense and with so little result.

I will not tell you anything about New York. We are on our way to go to the settlement of the savage Oneidas.

September 23. We embarked with our horses and our carriage in a sloop which took us up the Hudson, as far as Albany, in three days. The sea goes up one hundred and sixty-four miles above New York. Five years ago I saw these same banks covered with tents and soldiers; five years ago people did not venture on the Hudson without the precautions necessitated by the nearness of the enemy. To-day everything breathes liberty, everything enjoys abundance, and peace attracts to the banks of the river a prodigious number of immigrants from Europe and even from the neighboring states. It is in that way that the little village of Hudson has been established, which is peopled in large part with immigrants from Rhode Island and Massachusetts. We stopped and saw forty fine houses, all built in the course of the last year. Several days ago the residents met to deliberate concerning two objects greatly differing in importance; the question was whether to build a church or a dance hall. You will perhaps think that our Presbyterians did not waver, and that the church is already being finished; but the advocates of pleasure had the advantage. The dance hall is being finished; the building of the church is put off. It will be built in less hard times.

Our traveling on the water had no remarkable incidents, except perhaps the meeting with an old blind fisherman. Our pilot told us that for more than thirty years he has come every day in his boat to the same spot to throw in a line. He told us the news of his district, he asked us where we came from, and in the evening retired to his log cabin which you see from here. They tell the story of a newcomer who started one day to fish in the same spot. The old man objected, calling his attention to the fact that for a number of years he had fished there without catching anything, and that he had a right to the first fish. In disembarking I found the Marquis de Lafayette, the Chevalier de Caraman, and Mr. Madison, a delegate from the Congress, ready to start to go to see several savage tribes, and we soon joined parties to go together.

We had heard a great deal about the American "convulsioners." For three years this sect has made progress in America. We wanted to see their chief establishment, which was on our way, and to the ordinary motives of curiosity M. de Lafayette joined that of desiring to examine at close range phenomena which have a great similarity to those of "Mesmerism."

It was on Sunday that we left for Niskayuna, the principal place of their group; this village is difficult to reach, and we were obliged to go on foot to look for them. We heard, as we drew near, melancholy but fairly melodious music. We found the Shakers at their religious exercises. They were assembled to the number of about one hundred and forty or thereabouts, in a hall built of wood. A large fire warmed the hall. The women were on one side, and the men on the other, all standing. They made room for us. We heard three preachers in succession. They had no distinction of clothes or rank. In their sermons they attempted to give us an idea of their principles and beliefs, but I was persuaded that the characteristic doctrine of their belief is not yet well established. One of them, in speaking of marriage, called it contrary to the example of the Saviour who was never married,—to use his terms "never had any carnal connection with a woman." He praised Origen highly and in his discourse made use of figures which the least scrupulous orator would have avoided. Another inspired man cited the words of St. Paul, "If you marry, you do well; if you do not marry, you do better."

They cure wounds and claim to cure even fractures, by mere laying on of hands, accompanied by faith in Jesus Christ. They believe themselves inaccessible to sin. An old woman,—and it was their prophetess, the "elect lady,"—was, they believed, immortal. Her death, which happened about six weeks ago, embarrassed them a little. They explained it in so ridiculously mystical a way, that I spare you the details; it is enough to tell you that, a place having become vacant in heaven, through some promotion, it was necessary to fill it, and that the "elect lady" was preferred above all the rest of her flock. Before prophesying this woman used almost always to get drunk on spirits. The makers of poor jokes who saw her in that condition used to say that THE SPIRIT had taken possession of her. Her violent tremblings during her periods of being possessed, and her immoderate use of liquors, undoubtedly hastened her end. These enthusiasts were persuaded that this holy matron sat in the Council of the Almighty three times a week. She had worked several miracles. They told me that one day when a great crowd of people had gathered at Niskayuna to witness the resurrection of a dead man, she had said the customary prayers and was about to proceed to the miracle when an American officer stopped her and said that he, like her, had received the gift of raising the dead. She wished to oppose any attempt on his part, and to be the only one to exercise the gift of doing marvels; but the people were curious to see whether the officer was an impostor and insisted, and the holy matron went away threatening him with divine anger. At once he drew his sword, and running up to the dead man cried in a terrible voice: "Come to life, come to life, or I will kill you!" The dead man naturally came to life at once.

This trembling should not cause them to be confused with the old-fashioned Quakers; they have a horror of being compared with them. M. de Lafayette, who is skilled in magnetism, wished to experiment on one of them. While he hypnotized him with all his force, the poor man told us his history. "I fell one day from my carriage," he told us. "I wounded my leg. A charitable man came to help me while I was unconscious. When I came to myself, I was cured. I experienced a complete change in my feelings and inclinations; I renounced the world and its ways; I have followed the ways of these men who are so perfect; and from that moment I have been infinitely happy."

The Shakers are seized with their movements at any time, on any occasion, while they cultivate the earth, while they are cutting trees, while traveling on foot, or on horseback. We saw them in this condition during their rest, and during conversation. The convulsion does not interrupt anything; the most usual movement is to turn the head from left to right, with eyes closed or raised towards the sky, with an expression which proclaims ecstasy, anguish, and pain. We noticed that the women shed tears, were pale and downcast, and that their face reanimated itself only when the convulsion was at an end. The men raised their arms, trembling; their knees gave way and knocked together. Often while all their members shook, they would seem to have a seizure under which they would succumb, but it was the end of the ecstasy. The head turned less rapidly, and when the crisis was over, they sighed deeply, like people relieved at length of excessive anxiety, or coming out of a painful swoon.

They are all thin, and most lack color. Their convulsive dances do not bring their color back. They pirouette on a single leg, with a surprising rapidity, their head moves from right to left and often a dizziness seizes them in the middle of the dance. Those whom we heard preach had no convulsions while they spoke. All the people whom we saw had a serious, rational, and reflective expression. There were more old than young people. Some are good farmers, others artisans well thought of in their profession. They could only be considered useful citizens, if their discipline did not tend to shorten their lives, and if their rules about marriage did not lead to the extinction of the society. It is regenerated only by converts.

Those who are distant from the churches of their denomination have no hesitation in performing the duties of their religion in other churches. Furthermore, nothing is so common in this region as for all sorts of sects to borrow each others churches, and although the dissenters are divided into more than thirty sects of all denominations, they go to each other's churches without repugnance. They believe that their worship is just as acceptable to the deity in whatever place it is offered, and the experiment of the United States proves in the most complete manner that tolerance is absolutely without inconvenience there. At Annapolis the room where they play comedies six days in the week is used as a church on Sunday.

I remember that one day they were making, in the presence of Franklin, an enumeration of the different beliefs in the United States. Thirty or so were mentioned. "You forget the most numerous," he told us, "it is that of the 'tarry at homes.'"

We continued our journey across superb country, but where everything recalled the war to us. We had divided up the duties. M. de Lafayette was in charge of the cavalry, M. de Caraman was in charge of lodging, Mr. Madison directed the march, and I was cook for the troop. We had a bag of corn meal which was a great resource, tea, and chocolate. They furnished us with butter in abundance, and if we asked for milk, great wooden pails of it were immediately filled and brought. We used to make a soup which became famous throughout the region, and often our hosts, instead of feeding us were fed by us. Cloaks and rugs were one of our great resources. I except, to be sure, M. de Lafayette, who seemed to be immune to the extremes of the seasons. He had taken, to protect himself from the rain, a cloak of gummed taffeta, which had been sent him from France wrapped up in newspapers. The papers had stuck to the gum, and there had not been time to get them off, so that the curious could read, on his chest or his back, the *Journal de Paris,* the *Courier de l'Europe,* or news from other places.

In spite of the devastation to which the two banks of the Mohawk were a prey, the population there makes rapid growth. We found families of ten or twelve children, large and small, all in one bed. We were new sights for them, in a region where it is very rare to see strangers traveling for curiosity. Little Indians served us as domestic servants, and there was nothing which they refused to do. If we asked for a candlestick, an urchin four or five years old was placed near us with a candle in his hand. If we seemed discommoded by the heat, another took the place of screen for us. Often the honor of turning a wooden spit, which we had invented to cook our meat, troubled the peace of the family and made a division between brothers. One day we happened to tell a little savage to turn the spit, and we showed him how his hand should move from bottom to top. He followed the lesson, but after having resisted the hot fire for a long time, he was obliged to give up this confidential duty to another. The latter started to turn in the opposite direction, the first made fun of his clumsiness, and after several remarks, blows followed and hair was pulled out. We asked the cause of this fight. The interpreter told us that the boy who had been turning the spit first had hit his successor because the latter was turning it backwards, and would unroast the chickens.

We began to meet savages more frequently, and everything told us that we were about to leave the white man's settlements to enter the territory of the Indians. All the scattered houses were still surrounded by stockades, with which, during the late war, they had been protected against the barbarians, and which had not always been sufficient to stop their ravages.

We found the roads worse than we could have imagined. After having traveled miles in the carriage, we were forced to give it up, on account of the continual danger of upsetting and the extreme fatigue of the horses. I left my phaeton at the "German flats" and turned my two large carriage horses into riding horses. The coverings with which I had fortunately provided myself served me as saddle, and in that half-savage equipage we made the rest of the journey to Fort Schuyler. That is the place determined upon for negotiations between three commissioners sent by the Congress, and the chiefs and warriors of the six savage nations who live in the neighborhood of the Great Lakes which separate the United States from Canada. We found a great number of them assembled, but the commissioners had not yet arrived. The Indians had hurriedly built cabins in which they lodged with their families; some even, in spite of cold and frost, had merely shelters of branches of trees whose dried leaves protected them against neither wind nor rain. One of these cabins was filled with presents intended for the Indians. The other served as lodging for Mr. Kirkland, a missionary established amongst them for about twenty years. We shared his room, which was prepared for the commissioners from the Congress.

We wished to see the Indians in their villages, and to get acquainted with their customs as well as so short a residence would allow, so as to judge for ourselves the changes which had taken place among them since the last accounts of travelers who have visited them.

Indeed Europeans who are curious to know them must not lose time, for the advance of the European population is extremely rapid in this continent, and since these nations live largely by hunting and fishing, they cannot remain in the neighborhood of cultivated regions. They go farther away, and soon it will be necessary to look for them beyond the Mississippi or in the ice-covered regions around Hudson Bay. In a few centuries, even, when civilization will have extended its effects over all the world, people will be tempted to regard the reports of travelers as the ingenious dreams of a philosopher who is seeking the origin of society and is tracing the history of its advances from his imagination.

We had distributed our provisions amongst all the caravans, as if we had feared a famine or as if we had to travel in the desert. It was a mistake; we lacked nothing.

The tribe of the Oneidas is the second among the six who are confederated and to whom we give the collective name of the Iroquois. It possesses sixty square miles or twenty square leagues of a region of which the fertility surpasses anything that can be imagined. We were frequently stopped by torrents and brooks, which in digging out their beds have uncovered the earth twelve or fifteen feet deep, and we were surprised to see that the uncovered soil was just as rich as that on the surface, and resembled artificially made top-dressing. Moreover, in the parts of this region which are cultivated, they never have to let the land lie fallow. Wheat is grown without interruption, or if the crop is sometimes changed, it is at the end of seven or eight years. Then they sow some other kind of grain, and the next year begin to cultivate wheat again: one or two years of rest is enough.

It is not here, however, that the best cultivated farms are found. I have told you that we left them in entering the country of the Indians. Here everything is wild, and as soon as you go a little distance from the trodden paths, you think yourself separated from all human creatures by an immense distance. Several times I stopped a few minutes in one of these spots: there reigned a profound silence; one could give himself up to his reflections in peace. In a century, and perhaps sooner, agriculture and commerce will give life to this savage desert. This rock will furnish stones to the city which will be built on the banks of that stream. There will be a bridge here and a quay there. Instead of this marsh there will be a public fountain; elegantly dressed ladies will stroll in the very place where I walk carefully for fear of rattlesnakes: it will be a public park, adorned with statues and fountains. A few ancient trees will be exhibited as the precious remains of the forest which to-day covers the mountain. I see already the square where the college, the academy, the house for the legislature, and the other public buildings will be placed. Do not take this for a dream, for beginning with Philadelphia there are twenty cities on this continent which, a hundred years ago, had no more existence than this one which I have just built. All these details are not very closely related to our journey to the Oneidas. But I keep the promise I made you to write without order and without method; hosts of objects present themselves to me as I write, and I am much more embarrassed to keep them out of my journal than to find something to put into it.

What is really barbarous and wild are the roads which lead from Fort Schuyler to the Oneidas. One of our servants exhorted us in good faith to complain to the *intendant* of the province of the wretched state of the bridges and highways in his department.

We had to make a way for ourselves on horseback through the wood, following as well as we could a path worn by the Indians, who always go on foot. The brooks keep in existence a muddy marsh, into which we sank at each step. Trees of immense height and girth fall from age in all parts of the forest, and make the path difficult for men on horseback, although nothing prevents the native from climbing over them. We traveled in dark and rainy weather; we lost our way once, but our guides found it soon. The trees served them as compass; they recognized the north by the bark, which is brown and more covered with moss on that side than on the south. After having gone through this deep forest, sometimes on foot, sometimes on horseback, and after crossing the rivers by fording them, and sometimes by swimming our horses, we arrived, very wet and very tired, in the territory of the Oneidas.

We had no other encounters on the road, except one with an old man sleeping in a marsh and covered with half-frozen mud. Our guides woke him and learned that the day before he had been to the fort, where he pawned his gun for a little cask of brandy. His intention was to take it back to his village, but having given in to the temptation to taste it, he had emptied the cask and passed a very cold night in deep drunkenness.

We had five little casks of brandy, or to use the expression which those who are especially fond of it use, five "breasts of milk." Five Indians each carried one of them, but this burden did not slow down their march, and in spite of the difficulty of the road they followed us quickly, and sometimes even outdistanced us. One of them seemed to me tired, and I said to my driver,

"Frantz, try to make yourself understood by this man, and persuade him to give you his keg. Your horse will carry it easily."

The Indian had lead at his ears, bones hung at his nose, and his face was painted with bands of different colors. He had heard me, and turning towards me said in excellent French,

"I will give up the keg to your driver, but only to please you, for I do not feel the burden of it."

Surprised to hear the man speak thus, I said,

"Let us go along together, and tell me how you learned to speak our language so well."

"My name is Nicholas Jordan," he told me. "I was born at Longpré-les-Corps-Saints, a village on the Somme, between Amiens and Abbeville. I went to Canada, thirty years ago, as secretary to M. de Vilmon de Beaupré. Soon came the war between France and England. The savages took part. I fell into their hands, with some other Frenchmen. They were burned and eaten. Witness of their fate, I expected to share it. I was already half smeared over with the black color with which they paint those who are destined to die, and the stake to which I was to be attached was surrounded with fagots, when an interpreter came to tell me that the nation recognized me as one of its members, and that I should be free if I consented to marry the daughter of the king or sachem. She had lost her husband a little while previous. This princess had seen me unclothed, and in spite of my white color had had me asked if I would take her for my wife. I replied quickly that it would give me the greatest pleasure in the world. I abridge the story; I need only add that I was at once adopted by the whole family; the widow herself unbound my hands; and the marriage was concluded a few days later.

"My wife was a rich match," said Jordan to me. "Her dowry consisted of six hundred pins, one hundred needles, linen cloths, vermilion, a gun, powder and shot, a club, a knife, twenty bundles of furs, two pots, a house, a cow, and a garden crossed by a stream in which the fishing belongs to me. She had also a dozen scalps; to the Indians these are family jewels, and are kept as we keep the flags or cannon taken from the enemy. I had been treated with extreme severity during my brief captivity, but as soon as the savages had adopted me, I experienced great humanity from them. They taught me all that my new situation made necessary. I learned to hunt as they do, to strip a tree of its bark, to build a cabin, to guide a fishing boat. I learned soon how a man can live for a month on foodstuffs which are very small in volume.

"I remembered, however, my friends and my country. My wife was not as beautiful as a woman from Picardy, and she got drunk when she had liquor. I missed France. One day I deserted the village, and I admit that I carried off the pot and the gun, but I was recaptured by the savages of a neighboring tribe. They took me back to the Oneidas, who did not impose on me the harsh treatment that I feared. They gave me back to my wife. Since that time I have sometimes had the desire to see my country again, and I have written a great many letters to my family, but having received no reply I have insensibly got used to the way of living of these people. I have several children, I have brothers and other adopted relatives. I have seen the French again in a land from which I thought them excluded forever. Their victories and their successes have brought me greater consideration among the savages. I no longer think of leaving them; my age, my children, fix me here forever, and I shall regret my country less than in the past, since I can hope from time to time to see Frenchmen again."

As we traveled, we met several Indians traveling, the women, according to custom, carrying the heaviest burdens. Jordan told me that they were Stockbridge savages; a nation which remained in the state of Massachusetts, in the midst of a civilized people. The Oneidas offered them a piece of land six miles square, and the Stockbridges, to the number of about six hundred, are on their way to occupy it. The Oneidas have also invited the Narragansett Indians, a nation which inhabited a little district near Charlestown in the state of Rhode Island. It is reduced to about a hundred individuals who have accepted the offer. There are also, in Connecticut, a few remains of the Mohican nation and of the Niantics. They all seem disposed to join the Oneidas, since they cannot preserve their customs and usages amongst the civilized nations, and move away when they can.

The women carried almost all the baggage on their backs, in large baskets rather like those of our villages. The basket is supported by a band around their forehead. I am told that some of these squaws sometimes carry very heavy loads of wood from the forest to the village, which is a quarter of a mile away. The men do not show much pity when they see them bent over from their burdens.

A white flag raised on the principal cabin indicated to us the Council House, or as our people say, the Town Hall. We found the chiefs and warriors of the nation assembled there. They received us with the hospitality which they show towards all those who are not their enemies. I found an old acquaintance, a venerable chief whose name is the Great Grasshopper. I had seen him in Philadelphia in 1781. He received us clothed in a Bavarian court hunting costume which M. de la Luzerne had given him then, and which he wears on all important occasions. After the customary compliments, they brought us a large salmon which had just been caught. We had milk, butter, fruit, and honey in abundance. We prepared our supper ourselves, and a set of table utensils, which was in our baggage, was a great resource. We drank from goblets of wood, and M. de Lafayette, as a distinction, had one of glass mended with gum.

We expressed a desire to see their dances, and at once one of the principal men stepped out, and blowing on a horn called the young men of the village and told them to dress for the dance, and to go without delay to the Council House to amuse the strangers. This cabin was composed of a single room twenty-four feet by eighteen. On each side were the beds on which we were to spend the night. In the middle was a sort of alley, which was the dance room. Towards each end of the central passage, there was a fire of which the smoke went out the roof or through cracks left by the badly joined bark. This cabin had been got ready for our reception.

The dance began. The dancers were young men, some dressed as warriors, others in clothes which they had received from the English or in those which [word missing] had given them. It was a thoroughly ridiculous variety of colors.

The men's usual dress is the covering or cloth which sometimes is bound round their loins and sometimes covers their whole body; it replaces the skin robes with which they used to cover themselves before the arrival of the Europeans on this continent. All have shirts but they wear them seven or eight months without ever taking them off. We gave them several entire suits, without noticing that they did not ever use the third piece, so not knowing what to do with it, some of them cut it into two pieces and put half on their heads, the day of the masquerade.

A warrior wears a crest of braided feathers in his hair; his face is painted with horizontal bands about an inch wide. Each band is of a different color, white, red, black, blue, green, yellow, according to their fancy. They put long red or black feathers through holes which they make in their nostrils, a ring or pendants of lead or silver hang down before their mouths. They fasten bells to their arms or their feet; they wrap the body with a piece of red or black cloth; they carry a bow and arrow, and a club, and they have a gun when they are actually fighting or hunting. They have bare thighs, and legs covered with cloth gaiters or animal skins. The leather strip over their shoulders from which a tomahawk hangs, their belt which has a dagger in it, and their traveling pouches, are embroidered. The strange dress which their warriors wear does not improve their appearance, but its strangeness is not so disagreeable to an European as the sight of an Indian clothed in European fashion, in a coat and a braided waistcoat, having long dirty sleeves, wearing a hat with turned up edges, and almost naked from the belt to the legs. They have their hair painted red, and their ears pierced in a hideous fashion, falling almost to their shoulders—they hang leaden rings in them to stretch them more. Their skin is a yellowish brown. They grow old very young. Liquor, intemperance, hunger, exercise, forced marches, ruin their health before the age of 35 or 40 years, and in general these children of nature are not at all what the writers of Europe say, who have never seen them. It is necessary, of course, to make certain distinctions between those who come into a more frequent intercourse with us and those who are at some distance. The latter are less corrupted, and more robust, and their appearance, really barbarous, pleases me more than the mixture of barbarousness and civilization which one finds amongst the Oneidas.

The dancers were as impatient to show themselves as we to see them. The dance begins with a gentle movement. It consists in turning in succession one after the other around fires lighted in the cabin. They sing, themselves, the music to the noise of which they dance; it consists of only two notes, and the poem consists of this one word: "Joy." These monotonous articulations were interrupted at times by a general cry of the dancers; they stopped for an instant and began again, with a motion which grows quicker and finally becomes so rapid that the fatigue seems to us unsupportable. Their chiefs joined rarely in their dances; they considered these amusements beneath their serious position. Some women came and joined them, but they followed each other without mingling with the men.

The women are dressed with care and a sort of decency, and in spite of their frequent marches have little feet. They have modest countenances while dancing; the men leap from one foot to the other and strike the earth sharply; they dance without leaving the floor, sliding their feet. All keep time with perfect precision. When the dance had lasted two hours, we told the interpreters to ask the dancers to retire. It was not easy. The interpreters pretended that we gave them leave to go out of politeness and so as not to tire them; and the dancers, not to be outdone, suggested that they would keep on till daylight. Since drunkenness had been added, the two first arguments which were conducted with them had no effect. The chiefs did not want to send them away, and indeed did not have the power. Finally one of the dancers, who had formerly acted as a servant to M. de Lafayette, took pity on us and talked so eloquently that the maskers dispersed and we were free to go to bed.

I saw their war dance under other conditions. A little drum was the only military instrument which they used. They marched up to a line, came together, bent, advanced, and retired, in rhythm; they separated into two parties; their disagreeable death cries were heard. The fight began, they imitated all the actions which take place in their wars; they scalped, they took prisoners, they pretended to torture them, to burn them—in short we saw enough not ever to want to fall into their hands.

Jordan translated to us several of their songs; they contain no ideas and no imagination. Their simplicity is not accompanied by any feeling which could make it valuable. The music is limited to two notes, as in their dances, but the time is just as marked, and as far as I could observe, all the couplets have the same number of verses and all the verses have the same rhythm.

As for their eloquence, I have read a great many of their discourses, both those prepared and those delivered without preparation. There are several in which I noticed sound judgment, but none of those characteristics of vigor or imagination which it would seem should characterize eloquence amongst savages as well as in our communities. The eloquence of the savages is limited to a dozen strange and unnatural figures. When they go to war, they raise the hatchet against their enemies; when they make peace they bury the hatchet under a large tree; they cover it with earth and stones so that no one can find it. They bury the bones of their killed friends, so that they cannot rise to excite them to begin the war again. They rub the chains of an agreement of peace, so that it shall remain clear and bright. They accept presents because they contribute to the preservation of this chain from rust which might destroy it. Such are the metaphors constantly repeated in their solemn speeches. Nothing is rarer in their harangues than the method and order which even a country man possesses, if he is really eloquent, and they heap up all sorts of incoherent ideas and facts, without paying attention to their natural relationship.

They build a cabin of bark very quickly and skillfully. A savage surprised by night in a forest gets out of the difficulty more easily than a European. In an hour he will have built a shelter. He lights a fire, and waits for daylight comfortably enough. In such a case the European will sleep in the open air and cannot protect himself against rain.

If we take our information from the travelers who have visited the tribes which are most distant from European establishments, the Indians there are less wicked and less corrupt. Those whom I have seen do not appear admirable to me. It is possible that their intercourse with us, and the introduction of strong liquor have helped to deprave them; however it may be, they are really children who are managed by promises, threats, and presents; who are hurt easily, who can be quieted as easily; whose hate and friendship are rarely lasting, and who seemed to me to have no dominant passion except the love of strong drink.

In the midst of a serious discussion they will interrupt the speakers to tell the interpreter to call our attention to the fact that there is too much water in the "brandy wine" which we had given them, and that they would prefer to drink it pure. It is, however, very rare to see them drunk in a formal conference, and those at which we were present were solemn and decorous.

When we were ready to return to Fort Schuyler, they told me that my horses had been lost, and that they had been hunted for unsuccessfully since morning. They were neither surprised nor uneasy but merely gave several orders. I promised a reward, and at the end of a half-hour I saw stones rolling down from the mountains, and the horses came back to me themselves. You must know, to understand the story, that during all the time that we spent in the village, our horses were at liberty in the midst of pastures and immense forests, and that except for the incident I have just mentioned, they neither strayed nor were led away. Moreover, the Indians here seem less inclined to theft than those of the South Sea, and although our cabin and our tents were opened to everyone, and although they were not guarded, nothing was stolen from us.

The furnishings of an ordinary cabin consist of a black earthenware pot, a mortar, pestle, and two cooking pots. I had a red cloak which was widely and frequently admired; I could hardly get along without it, and I was very much afraid that some Indian would come to tell me that it was missing, and that I should have to get out of it by giving a rug or by making other presents.

We were on the point of departure, when two young men of twenty-eight and twenty-five years, one of whom appeared drunk, began to quarrel. The conversation became more and more animated. One of the two struck the other with his club violently, and the one who was hit started to cry and appeared to wish to return the blows which he had received, when an old man took him by the arm and held him down on the ground until some women had come; they led the other from the cabin. The old man was father of the two young men, and his son, although vigorous, made no effort to get out of his arms. The brothers even became reconciled. The offended one smoked half a pipe and presented it to the aggressor who finished it, and peace was made. One of the two brothers had followed the English army, and the other had joined the American.

I have reason to believe that some of our servants got married during their brief residence in the village, for at the moment of our departure we saw several squaws still adorned with wedding ribbons, and the separation was very touching. Since a missionary has come to live with the Oneidas, these marriages entered into for the sake of hospitality, are very rare amongst them, and if they proposed one to M. de Caraman, he would by no means allow himself to be seduced.

On returning to the fort, we were surprised to find again the Indian whom we had already met while going to the village. This wretched man, when he got home and came out of his drunkenness, had realized that he had to redeem his gun at any price. He had sold it for a little keg of brandy, he believed that another keg would buy it back. He obtained this liquor by pledging one of his cooking pots. He was carrying the brandy to the fort, when he succumbed a second time to an irresistible temptation. He opened the "breast of milk," and had fallen into the same state of drunkenness in which we had already found him several days before.

During our absence from the fort, Indians had arrived from several districts, and on our return we found some of them from eight different nations. There were Mohawks, Oneidas, Onondagas, Cayugas, Stockbridges, Senecas, and other nations from Canada amongst whom the men from Sault St. Louis were the most noteworthy, and almost all spoke French.

The power with whom they were treating had assumed the responsibility of feeding them during the conferences. We were present at several distributions of meat, flour, and rum. They were without order and without limit; the same Indian received allotments several times, though he had received all he needed, and the commissioner at the distribution dared refuse no-one for fear of giving offense. They love profusion, and waste more than they consume; they think it silly and even mean to weigh out what one needs to live; they prefer to receive less but to have it unmeasured than to receive it with scales in hand. They regard this wasting and spoiling of the means of subsistence as a mark of greatness.

To-day, October second, my thermometer was three degrees below zero. A wooden basin of water which was three feet away from a large fire which we had made, was frozen on top. The cold had driven me from my bed, I wrapped myself in coverings and put myself near the fire. I had been writing since six o'clock this morning, when I heard a child of seven or eight months old, with a very bad cold, crying as hard as its cough permitted. It was the child of a squaw who was undressing it to plunge it into the Mohawk River which flows twenty fathoms from our tent. I approached and saw the child come out from this bath and express well-being and happiness by its movements and its voice. The mother dried it with a coarse blanket, put it into its cradle, and carried it on her back. The good example made an impression on me, and I bathed in the same place as the little savage, with the same repugnance, the same pleasure, and the same success.

I again found the Indian with whom I had talked. I write you from his cabin, near his fire, with the ink which he made for me by pounding sassafras charcoal and moistening it with gum. A tortoise shell serves as writing desk and the paper is the thin bark of a maple tree.

It is through him that I am at this moment collecting five or six barrels of ginseng which I intend to send to France, for you may be sure I have not forgotten that it is from this place that that plant can be transplanted with the greatest probability that it will prosper. You know that the Chinese are passionately fond of it, and that Tartary did not furnish it abundantly enough, so that before the discovery of the plant in America they paid for it with its weight in gold.

Though many travelers say that the savages are naturally grave and melancholy, we have not had occasion to make this observation. On the contrary we have been perpetually disturbed by their dances and their singing, day as well as night. They dance around large fires and the one which burns near our tent often attracts them.

Furthermore, their gaiety ceases when they are busy with public affairs; they show themselves grave and serious, and give their most particular attention.

We were witnesses of the reconciliation of the Oneidas with their enemies. Although both dwelt, for several days, near the fort, and in spite of the cessation of hostilities, communication had not been reëstablished between them. The "Great Grasshopper," covered with the mantle which the Chevalier de la Luzerne had given him, and followed by five other savages dressed with the same care, went to the cabins of the Senecas. They walked stiffly, and stopped from time to time. The chief of the Senecas came out and went to receive them at some distance. They sat on the grass and compliments were exchanged by the two chiefs. They smoked the pipe of peace and separated. The next day the visit was returned by the Senecas to the Oneidas with the same sort of dress and the same formalities. Seeing this ceremonial, I thought myself at the Diet of Ratisbon.

They have vague ideas in regard to the immortality of the soul and a future life. When a savage dies, they bury his arms with him, they put food into the grave in which he is to be interred, and if he is a famous warrior, they paint his face with startling colors, so that when he arrives in the other country, its guardians will receive him without hesitation and assign him an honorable place. At the death of one of the chiefs, the funeral ceremonies are nothing extraordinary, but after they are over, mourning still continues. It consists of the Indians' not leaving their dwellings for several days, and not permitting any mark of happiness, not even a smile. The chief persons of nearby regions come to the number of fifty or sixty, and sometimes more, to suffer with their friends.

"Brothers," they say to them, "the sun which gave you light has set. It is night. You will walk in darkness and fear. Your fires are put out, your guide is no longer here. Your hair is disheveled, your eyes are fixed on the ground. Where is the prey destined for your hunters? Why do not fish come any longer to your nets? Your tribe suffers from famine. Your ears are closed. Tears cover your breasts."

Then they sit in a circle and chant a lugubrious hymn, keeping time by swaying from left to right. During the hymn they make plaintive noises which have no meaning. Suddenly one of the strangers gets up, and looks at the new chief and cries with joy.

"Brothers, your sun has returned, the light shines for you, your enemies tremble, your chief puts them to flight. Shake off the ashes which cover your hair, raise your eyes towards the forests where game is waiting for you. Your lines are weighted down with fish; your fields promise an abundant harvest. Brothers, we rejoice in your good fortune."

Just so at the funerals of our monarchs, a high official, breaking his wand of command, says three times, "The King is dead," and then suddenly, "Long live the King."

Nothing is more usual than to see them, in the midst of severely cold weather, when fever or some illness torments them, jump into half frozen water. This remedy kills or cures them. They cannot be persuaded that it is fatal in smallpox. They also use many superstitious practices against their diseases. The friends and relatives of the sick person assemble, and cook a pig or a stag. Each eats a piece while addressing several magic words to the dying person. They sing, they cry, and often he recovers.

I should have begun perhaps, by telling you of their marriages, except that they are made without any ceremony. It is usually the mothers who make the arrangements. They seldom choose the handsomest man or best warrior. It is the best hunter who is preferred. The future husband presents his fiancée with a stag's foot. She gives him an ear of Indian corn, and the emblems of their duties having been exchanged, the ceremony is over.

A girl and a young man may love each other for several years without saying a word. They show their feelings only by a few affectionate smiles which they make when they meet while going from one cabin to the other. To be sure, this reserve exists only among those who have been carefully brought up, and in the lower classes there are less reserved young ladies who go themselves to wake up their lovers with the sound of a flute. Boys from the age of five or six are put on guard against these inclinations, and the old men never cease repeating that it is unworthy of a warrior to fall in love with a woman before having distinguished himself in war or hunting.

Suicide is very rare among the savages. The "Swimming Salmon" told me that he had known only two in several years. Ambition was the cause of the first. A young warrior had for neighbor another young warrior already famous for his fine deeds, cherished by the old men of the tribe, and sure to gather round him a considerable number of other warriors as soon as they had to march on the enemy. His rival was constantly annoyed by his praises, and confided in his mother the pain which he felt. She told him not to lose courage, that in the next war he could distinguish himself also. The war came and the ambitious young man could not distinguish himself as he had hoped. On his return he said good-bye to his mother, saying, "Your promises are not fulfilled, but my neighbor will not rejoice in the scorn which people have for me." He went out of his cabin, leaned against a maple tree, and stuck a dagger into himself.

Another young man loved passionately a young girl of the tribe of the Bear, the noblest of the three tribes of the Oneidas. He could not obtain her, and his mother encouraged him to deserve her by killing more beavers than his rivals. Whether through bad luck or lack of skill he almost always came back with empty hands. He had reason to think himself loved, and the girl never passed near him without looking at him with a friendly smile. His mother, witness of his despair, resolved to ask her in marriage. Her parents replied that the young man was always one of the last in hunting and took nothing, and that he was not more skillful in fishing, and they refused their daughter. His mother brought back this reply. He said that there was no more happiness for him in this country, and that he was going to another. He went to the borders of Cayuga, gathered several poisonous plants, pressed out the juices into a shell, and died at the end of three hours.

When married people do not get on, they freely leave each other. The idea of an indissoluble contract which binds a man to a woman without the privilege of withdrawing, is as foreign to their spirit as is voluntary slavery.

Quarrels between individuals are settled by the parties themselves, either by the judgment of arbiters whom they choose, or by force. If it happens that an Indian kills his adversary by some treachery, the crime is not proceeded against, either by society or by any public magistrate. It is the relatives of the assassinated person who pursue the malefactor, and often he gets out of it by retiring to a neighboring tribe. Sometimes a relative of the dead man kills the murderer. He is killed in his turn, and the process lasts till the extinction of one of the two families. Sometimes, however, presents put an end to this butchery.

The Indians have kept a great respect for the King of France. They talk with veneration of the French nation, although their relations with it have been at an end for over twenty years. They love liquor passionately, but they say that the French were real fathers to them, because they refused them this poison, which the English furnished in abundance.

Several naturalists believe that the Indians have no beard, and have given very specious reasons for it. The truth is that they pull it out with care as soon as it begins to grow, and that they pull the hair out of their whole body in the same way. Some of them, however, do not take the trouble, and their beards descend to their breasts.

The women are more susceptible to jealousy than the men; one sees them often beating their rivals with their fists, pulling their hair, and skinning their faces, while the man, a tranquil spectator of the fight, awaits the result, and decides in favor of the bravest.

"Their superstition is extreme," said Mr. Kirkland to me, "and only to speak of those with whom I have lived most, I have almost been a victim of their doubts. I baptized one of their children, and I had neglected to take my stole. A strange Indian present at the ceremony, told them that I was an impostor and not really a priest. For the first time, I saw them forget the respect which they had always shown me. I excused myself as well as I could."

They seem to love glory, but like other people they have strange ideas of it. Sometimes men come to find the priest and say to him, "Father, our hands itch, our feet are beginning to grow into the ground; do you need our bows and our tomahawks?" If the chief does not judge it suitable to accept their offer, they go away, and at their own risk challenge and fight some members of a neighboring tribe.

To-day I met a rather fine looking squaw, whose color and bearing did not seem quite savage. I asked her in English who she was. She pretended at first not to understand. Pressed with my questions she told me that she had formerly served at the home of a planter in the State of New York, but that she had tired of the position of a servant and had fled, and that the Indians had welcomed her, and that she lived very happily among them. "The whites," she told me, "treated me harshly. I saw them take rest while they made me work without a break. I ran the risk of being beaten, or of dying of hunger, if through fatigue or laziness I refused to do what I was told. Here I have no master, I am the equal of all the women in the tribe, I do what I please without anyone's saying anything about it, I work only for myself,—I shall marry if I wish and be unmarried again when I wish. Is there a single woman as independent as I in your cities?"

An American officer in General Sullivan's expedition, in 1779, told me what follows. The Indians had committed frightful ravages on the frontier, and the Congress had resolved to punish them severely. It had ordered the general to destroy their settlements entirely. He planned his march so that he went towards the region where we now are. "The Indians," this officer told me, "fled from their settlements when we approached, and we found their cabins entirely deserted, but some soldiers who went into the forest to cut wood discovered an old Indian woman who had hidden under cut branches. She was brought back to be questioned, and did not doubt that we planned to kill her. Her fears had deprived her of speech; she raised and lowered her clasped hands as if to beg us to spare her life. The interpreter hastened to tell her that we did not wish to harm her, and that we should only ask her questions about the route of the Indians. She shed tears and with eyes fixed on heaven gave thanks to the Great Being. She told us all that she knew. The general had her given clothes and provisions.

"On our return, at the end of two months, we found her again, in the cabin where we had left her. She was squatted near a little fire, idle and without a living being who could give her any consolation in her abandonment. Infirm and incapable of getting her food, she ate each day a small portion of the provisions which we had left her. Her only care was to keep up her fire. Separated forever from her family, from her friends, from the society in which she had lived for almost a century, she passed long days in inactivity, having no other future than hunger, hearing round her neither the voices of men nor any noise which would give her pleasant ideas or revive her waning spirits. She did not seem less attached to life than a young woman of twenty in the midst of abundance and pleasure. We believed that she would be glad to go along with us, and we promised her all the attentions which humanity could bestow; but the love of freedom, the horror of any restraint, the attachment to the spot which had seen her birth, and where she had passed her whole life, made her reject our offers. We left her provisions for several months. This poor creature expressed her gratitude as well as she could, and when we left the place, she followed us a little distance and took leave of our general by clasping him to her bosom."

They have no acquaintance here with the cruel tests through which an Indian must pass among the nations of the South in order to become the chief of the tribe, for it is birth which gives the right to command. I did not expect to find a nobility established amongst savages. But there are amongst the Oneidas three families which from all antiquity have had a right to the chiefs of the nation. Sometimes, however, their choice falls upon a man of the common people, when he has merited this honor by several brilliant deeds, or by some important service rendered the nation. These chiefs have a great influence over the nation, but one cannot say that they command it. Although the wisest, they are not the most sober. They cannot resist a bottle of rum. Drunkenness is the more frightful amongst these people because it serves them as excuse for frightful crimes and because they are never punished when liquor is the cause. During general festivals two or three Indians are instructed to take care that no harm occurs. These guards hide their arms and observe the greatest sobriety while the others get drunk. If, contrary to ordinary custom, they happen to get drunk themselves, they are held responsible for what happens.

I saw, amongst the Oneidas, a tomb on which the earth and stones seemed new. They told me it was that of an Indian murdered a few days before. They showed me the murderer, who did not mingle with the most distinguished; but no one thought of punishing the crime. They suspected him of wishing to fly to the Onondagas, to shelter himself from pursuit by the relatives of the murdered man.

We were present at the opening of the peace conferences between the commissioners from the Congress and the savages. There were several speeches. The setting was in the open air, in spite of a penetrating cold. The savages were squatted in a circle, and several dry branches burned in the center. They never fail to light fires for very solemn occasions. They listened to the orators with a particular attention. Chiefs and women were present. The warriors, armed as if for battle, were presentable in appearance, but the others were clothed in the strangest and most ridiculous manner. One was dressed up with the skin of a bear, and looked like that animal. The possession of a wig had been the cause of a quarrel a few days before. These grotesque figures contrasted strangely with the gravity of the orators. The most noteworthy of the latter had a piece of cloth floating over his shoulders, he had his arms stretched out, a proud air, a loud voice, and we listened very attentively to the interpreter who was translating his discourse, but we found nothing in it equal to the expectations which his appearance had caused.

October 26, 1784. We had fulfilled the chief purpose of our journey, which was to see the savages. Nothing kept us any longer at the fort. We rented a small boat in which there was just room for eleven people, including five rowers, and we descended the Mohawk river very comfortably and in the finest weather in the world. We found our carriages again, and we are back at Albany.

Travels of a Gentleman from Milan

1790

Paolo Andreani
Translated by Elisabeth Ruthman

Count Paolo Andreani lived from 1763 to 1832. He traveled in the United States and Canada in 1790-1791, adding to journals that he began keeping as early as 1783. The American Philosophical Society holds microfilm copies of Andreani's manuscripts (Film 604). The originals remain in the possession of his descendants in Milan. The portions reproduced here have not been previously published or translated into English.

Andreani traveled to London early in 1790, where he obtained letters of introduction from General Frederick Haldimand. These included one to Joseph Brant, who was by now living at the Six Nations Reserve in Ontario. Andreani traveled to Albany and up the Mohawk River, reaching Oneida by late August. There he presented a letter of introduction from Philip Schuyler to Samuel Kirkland, missionary to the Oneidas (Kirkland 1980:202, 234). He questioned Kirkland about the Oneida and Seneca languages, noting that he had acquired standard word lists for over 200 languages in his travels.

By the time of Andreani's visit, most, if not all, Mohawks had left their valley. He consequently focused most of his attention on the Oneidas. Comments on the Tuscaroras and Onondagas are also offered. Andreani was also fascinated by the Shakers, who had recently established their principal community near Albany.

D.R.S.

About the Oneidas

THIS IS ONE of the six confederated nations, namely Tuscarora, Seneca, Mohawk, Oneida, Onondaga, and Delaware, covering a large area bordered by the state of New York, the state of Pennsylvania, and the Canadian lakes, and owned today under state deeds and sovereign guarantees. The borders of their territory are the eastern bank of the Susquehanna River on the south, the Ontario and Oneida lakes on the north, and small rivers on the east and the west forming the other two borders. Thus they represent about one degree in latitude and two in longitude. The land could easily provide subsistence to a population a hundred

318

thousand times larger than that presently inhabiting the nation, if only the inhabitants wanted to devote themselves to agriculture, and live from the products of the land; but since the savages do not adjust well to labor, and prefer a wandering life and the uncertain subsistence of the hunt, they complain about the limited territory they can scour, and quite often go hunting beyond the prescribed boundaries.

The land these Indians inhabit is one of the richest and most fertile on our globe. It is generally of open plains, cut from time to time only by small rivers and hills, and full of lakes abounding with fish and salubrious waters. But with the exception of small cultivated fields that are found close to their dwellings, all the rest is covered by the thickest forests, in which abound several species of quadrupeds and birds. The Oneida town covers an area of about five miles clear of trees, in which are found, scattered here and there, a few of the savages' houses. The whole population does not amount to five hundred inhabitants.

Except for the Mohawk, this nation is one of the oldest of the confederacy. Its language differs little from that of the Mohawk, and it has embraced Christianity since the beginning of this century, with the exception of about 1/9 of the population which continues to be pagan, and perhaps more precisely without religion of any sort. It is not easy to say if they have embraced Christianity because of the major interest they have always had with the European colonies or because of their amenability to persuasion. But we have attended a holy service celebrated by a Protestant missionary [Samuel Kirkland] who resides among them and we have been generally surprised by their dignity and the pleasing melody of their singing of the psalms translated into their language. Those who are Christian observe Sundays with scrupulous attention, even abstaining from playing games and hunting. The rest laugh at these religious practices, but it is impossible to say if they are worse than the others in their manners.

The physical constitution of these Indians is not apt to give one an impression of great robustness, unlike the Indians living on the banks of the Mississippi. Men are thin, and generally of medium stature; but the women are absolutely frail, small, and very thin. Since there are few families among the Oneida that have preserved their Indian blood without mixing with European blood, the complexion of some of them is not as yellow as found elsewhere, and a few have a little more hair on the chin and genitals, as it is not customary among them to shave. Their clothing consists of a shirt falling to the mid-thigh, which remains loose. In winter they cover themselves with a wool blanket, which has the double function of serving as bedding. The thighs are completely naked, except for a cloth which goes between them and covers the genitalia. Some of them wear a sort of woolen legging and leather moccasin, but this is usual only among the wealthiest, and especially in winter. On festive days they adorn themselves with silver ornaments, such as neckbands, bracelets, etc., and the women's only different clothing from the men is a skirt that circles the upper thighs. They like to adorn themselves with feathers, ribbons, and bizarre ornaments of all sorts, creating all together elegant clothing. Some of the men fashion for themselves a head crown with animal feathers or flowers, and others pile a prodigious quantity of fake hair on their heads, which falls in large curls, in all directions, and which completely disfigures them. In this nation nowadays those who are accustomed to paint themselves are few, and those few are found among the men. We have observed only two women who had painted a red line across their head, and some color on the cheeks. Among the men this painting requires a great deal of time since they execute it with care, representing at times stripes of different colors, and at times animal figures. This bizarre usage, common to all nations of savages, must have had its origin in the southern regions where the land, covered with an enormous quantity of mosquitoes of all kinds and shapes, has forced the inhabitants to find a means of protecting themselves from being stung by those annoying animals. Once the custom of painting oneself began, it must have very quickly become common also among the northern nations, where mosquitoes are fewer in number and less stinging. It came to be introduced as part of the warriors' adornment so as to inspire fear in the enemy with an incandescent face. We have done various studies of this custom in different circumstances and we have had the same answer, which matches that probability very well.

Another bizarre custom among Indians, the custom of cutting one's ears in different parts and adorning one's nostrils, lips, etc. with pieces of silver or with whatever decoration, is gradually being abandoned among the Oneidas. The cutting of the ears is particular only to the men, among them those who call themselves warriors. But since almost all the inhabitants are included in that category, one would erroneously think this usage was an intrinsic part of the savage man's ornamentation. The origin of the custom is said to have been to demonstrate that they do not quail at shedding their own blood, nor at suffering; and certainly this operation is very painful especially when executed as it is with the use of ordinary scissors. During our visit among this nation we have witnessed one of these operations, and the fifteen-year-old young man who was enduring it was screaming so loudly and piercingly that his shrieks could be heard for more than a mile. We have seen an Oneida whose ears' edges fell nine and seven-eighths inches, and the ornaments hanging on each side weighed seven ounces.

We have reported earlier that the physical constitution of the women in this nation is poor, and having endeavored to investigate the cause, we could assign no other reason than the custom of nursing the offspring for about two years or more, which must naturally contribute to weakening the mother and the child. The women's poor physical constitution may also be due to their hard labor since they cultivate the fields, cut firewood, build part of the housing, and carry their children and the household utensils on their shoulders during the winter travels. Such long nursing of the children must without doubt contribute to weakening them, and we have observed a son who was 27 months old and entirely fed from his mother's milk and who, under the appearances of sturdiness and good health, could absolutely not stand on his own feet. It is only at the age of three that they begin to walk on their own.

The most common diseases in this nation are the inflammatory fevers brought on by the immoderate use of hard liquor, and various kinds of venereal diseases. Infusions of different herbs help the first and the second of these disorders, and

infusions of medicinal plants are the remedy for all complicated and simple illnesses. We could not ascertain which herbs they would use in such various circumstances because the doctor had been absent from the village for several
months, and since this group keeps its trade secrets, the nature of the medicinal
plants is only explained to those who pay to be initiated. The difficulty is in
knowing how to divine the nature of the illness; and since the cleverest at this art
among us are often deceived, it should not be surprising if a few of the ignorant
savages also frequently did not succeed. The missionary who has resided in this
nation for more than twenty-five years has assured us that, in cases of serious
illness, few are cured. What has greatly surprised me has been to be assured that
the most complicated venereal disease could be cured in four or five days. An
old man of about sixty told us he was infected, and prior to our departure he was
perfectly cured, as far as the external sores were concerned. It would remain to
be determined if the cure was yet entirely complete. We will have the opportunity to observe this fact more thoroughly at first hand.

The frequent intercourse that this nation has had with European colonies, and
the religious principles with which they have become accustomed since they
have embraced Christianity, have had a great influence on their customs. We can
call the Oneidas semicivilized savages, and although a few of them do not profess any religion, nevertheless by living together, a similarity in principles results. Hospitality is common to all Indians, and the kindness which they offer to
a foreigner is really to be admired. On that occasion the whole family busies
itself to take care of him and the men go hunting to provide sufficient food
supplies. The various family members love each other greatly and their filial love
is no less than that which exists among us. There is no formality of any kind in
marriage. Whenever the parties are satisfied they unite without celebrating any
rite, as long as the missionary does not oblige them to renew their vows in
church—which often happens after the consummation. Those who are Christian
only separate from their wives in cases of proven adultery, which however happens less than one would think in a country where women have all possible freedom and are left alone for several months while the husbands are called on
distant travels. But it is not true that in all similar cases the marital separation is
generally observed. The husband is often satisfied with beating his wife. It is true
that such excesses occur on days of national celebration or dances—which usually fall on the occasion of some treaty or to entertain some foreigner, and even
other excesses of various finds are frequent, because the Indian who has no
means to procure for himself a daily ration of liquor, uses it with excess when it
becomes available. The women who also participate [in drinking] with pleasure
become more joyful and more libertine, while some men end up quarreling and
fighting among themselves. The closing of a dance always ends in blood and
scares whoever attends it for the first time.

The Oneidas are, like all Indians, prone to laziness and we believe that they
would not go hunting if they did not have to. They have developed a certain liking for gardening, and almost every family grows a field of green vegetables and
one of Indian corn; but the men are rarely involved in such labor. They stay

home lying about, smoking pipes and playing games while the wives ruin themselves at hard labor in the field. At night they retire early, sleeping on bare
benches, covered only with a blanket. They get up early in the morning. In winter, their first activity is to sit around a fire and smoke a pipe; in summer, to sit
around smoking embers and discussing public matters, in which they are forever
interested, as they do not have anything else to do. They are accustomed to
smoky fires inside their dwellings to protect themselves from insects. After a
while, they often go hunting with gun or bow. In the meantime the wife puts a
kettle of Indian corn on to boil with some vegetables, enough for family needs
for the whole day. If a hunter is lucky, he returns with his prey, or often leaves it
on the field where he killed it, sending his wife to carry it since it would be
shameful for him to carry such burden when he has someone to do it for him. In
such a situation a man carrying firewood would be mocked by all his neighbors.
After all this, he lies down on the bed and without asking, expects to be served a
meal when it is ready; and then the wife calls all the children to share what there
is and, preparing equal portions, lets each take his share to eat when he pleases.
In general mealtime is from around four to five P.M.

The Oneidas are only hunters, almost disinterested in fishing, although there is
a beautiful lake in their territory which bears their name, full of excellent fish,
and extending for twenty-five miles from east to west. The six winter months are
the best for hunting. Bear, deer, fallow deer, and martens are the only animals
they seek, since their skins sell well, and during the hunting season they feed
themselves for the most part with the meat from these animals. Some white men
who had spent time with Indian hunters said that when it is well boiled, bear
meat has an excellent taste (Note: On our trip along the Northwestern Canadian
Great Lakes we had to eat this food and found that it tasted foul and unwhole-
some. *Young bear* is a little more tolerable.) They use in turn the rifle or the
bow, and handle these two deadly instruments with remarkable dexterity. For the
most part they hunt with friends, and if one of them has no luck or no dexterity,
they quite willingly divide their prey with him, as long as he does not refuse to
help with the cleaning and initial preparation of the skins.

In the harvest months this nation does not leave the village—except in case of
some extraordinary requirement. And during this time the men play almost everyday a game which consists of making a ball fly. Each player is supplied with a
sort of racquet about four feet and six inches long, somewhat curved at the end,
and netted with a bowstring, which is used to throw the ball. The player who
succeeds in catching the ball with this instrument, juggling it while preventing
others from touching it, until he can perform a given number of turns in a large
field, is victorious. These turns require dexterity and agility in running; we have
attended one game which lasted two and a half hours, in which a large sum was
at stake on both sides. The other pastime consists of racing to a certain goal on
foot or on horseback. Whenever these games are played for money or for goods,
the women attend and they get to encourage their sides with their horrible
screams. The silliness of the Indians is such that we have seen one of them run
on horseback around a field for about seven hours, dressed so as to be hardly

recognizable to his friends, and looking like a buffoon to those who were watching him. We not observe other than that he was a warrior, and thus respected in the nation.

It would be difficult to talk clearly about this nation's government since those who have often visited it or have remained there for a long period have never taken the trouble to study its principles. During our brief visit we have had a great deal of difficulty acquiring any general idea. There are two kinds of offices, one hereditary among the families, the other conferred only on pure merit; and those who are invested enjoy a preeminent rank in the nation and at the councils. There are three chiefs in the first category, and the number of assistants is undetermined. The succession to these hereditary titles is only established among the sons of women to the exclusion of men, in such a way that the son of a sister is preferable to one's own son. This heir to the title of chief must be appointed by his predecessor while he is still alive; but when at times a chief dies without having appointed a successor, the council assembles and selects a chief among the closest relatives of the deceased, always observing the laws of female descent. The chiefs elected by merit are elected by the council and they must all agree. A good warrior, a good politician, or a good speaker, is elected chief warrior and sits at the council. At times a simple action, which anywhere else would be considered foolish, can among Oneida Indians qualify a man to be considered for chief; for example, a man who crosses an immense tract of land and reaches a faraway nation, carrying with him some sign of his origin, could become, and is indeed often considered as a chief. When one of the hereditary chiefs is still young, he must attend the council for five years without the liberty of speaking, and a tutor speaks and acts for him.

This nation has no written laws, either civil or criminal; nevertheless, there are frequent examples of thefts, offenses, and homicides, considering the small number of inhabitants who make up this nation. In the first case, the thief has nothing to suffer but public indignation, and when this becomes too great he is obliged to exile himself. In the case of a homicide, the murderer has nothing to fear from the government and must only protect himself from the scheming of the closest relative of the deceased, who is the only one expected to avenge the offense; and if he is a courageous man, he never misses seizing the offender in some narrow passage and murdering him. For every such case the council gathers and dispenses advice to prevent similar recurrences. With regard to the civil laws, they are not even written, but they are judiciously observed. In case one dies without descendants, the council gathers and divides the property of the deceased in equal parts among his friends; if he has direct descendants, then the estate is passed to the natural heirs.

In its construction, this nation has embraced in part the custom of the neighboring European colonies, and instead of building a longhouse with several berths all around as they used to do, now they build a room in which they put various beds. As far as we are concerned, we feel that their original way was better, with the exception of the hearth, which being placed in the middle of the room is more likely to smoke.

The Oneida population does not amount to more than seven hundred souls, among whom about a hundred and fifty are warriors. Most of them live in the town of the same name. A few years ago this nation was rapidly dwindling annually, but according to a census conducted by a missionary, it has increased for the last six years.

When I asked those living here what impression the sight of the first white man made on them, I was assured that the latter then came to be called *askéànt,* that is to say, men without blood. They called themselves however, *Ongwéhoenwe,* that is to say, real men.

Whenever some visitor of distinction comes to visit their region, the chiefs quickly assemble in council to decide if he must be greeted or not. [In our case] they gathered on Sunday, after the evening service, and after a while we were invited to proceed to their place of assembly. We entered a miserable hut where we found the chiefs, about twenty-five of them, assembled and seated according to their rank. Among the first ones, we noticed Skannondòo who had received us in his house with the greatest hospitality. He invited us to sit next to him, and had someone ask us if we had something to say to the nation. The interpreter translated the compliments we gave, after which the most important chief addressed us in these words: "Father (this is how they call foreigners) we, your sons are always happy and ready to receive with friendship those who come in the Great Canoe (this is how they call the ships, from beyond the Great-lake, the sea) to visit the Oneidas, and we compliment you that God preserved you from the many dangers which are found in such immense crossing, and that you have reached us safely. Keep, O Father, the love that your Brothers have always demonstrated, and we can always be in peace. The King, the Chiefs, and the War Chiefs thank you for your visit, and ask you to stay with them in the Great Island until the sun turns." At the end of this speech the chief who had pronounced it got up and came to shake my hand, which is what all the others did too, one by one. Since they had affairs to discuss, we took leave and left them assembled.

About the Tuscaroras

We shall only say a few words about this nation, because in reality it differs very little from the one we have just discussed, and also because of the brief visit we had among them. This nation is only composed of eighty families and their number dwindles every day. It has been incorporated in the six nations for some time, being originally from North Carolina and Virginia. Always persecuted by wars, they were obliged to leave, wandering for a long time until they were received and incorporated by the Oneidas under the supposition that they were a branch of the Oneidas because of some analogies in the language. Today they live at the northwest of the Oneidas, and follow almost the same customs.

About the Onondagas

The road which goes from the Oneidas to the capital town of this nation is about thirty miles long, across dark and dense forests, in which we constantly meet bears and rattlesnakes. A big dog attacked one of these animals and he got bitten. An Indian who was accompanying us followed the rattlesnake on horseback through the woods, caught up with it and killed it. It was of a monstrous shape, and had twenty-nine joints on its tail. The wounded leg of the poisoned dog started to swell, and then the swelling went to his head and he died, amidst spasms and acute suffering. He lived only forty-two minutes after being bitten. We can infer from this example how cautious the travelers must be, and the natives too, since even when the wound can be cured, if the medicine is not quickly administered it is of no use. The guides invited us to follow a bear track, and to witness their hunting ability. The bear was of a normal size, and although it was close to its cubs and wanted to defend them, when wounded (but not that much) by a first shot, instead of hurling itself against its assailant or trying to defend itself, it tried to run away. Since it was losing a lot of blood, it was easy to kill it.

The principal village of this nation, which bears its name, is neither as considerable nor as populated as the Oneidas'. The houses here are all built Indian style, a few of them are more than sixty feet long and have four hearths at different distances. They sleep at night in the lower berths and spend the day at the same place next to the fire. The upper sections are used to store domestic tools and food supplies.

Near the Onondaga lake, to the east, are several springs with very salty water, which seem to indicate some large build-up of fossilized salt in the bowels of the earth, since the water is too far away to assume a connection between the sea and the aforementioned springs. A white man was granted permission by the Indians to make salt at one of the springs, and he established forty-eight cauldrons there from which he was collecting two thousand pounds of salt a day. Since the only cost for the firewood necessary to the evaporation of the water is the trouble to carry it, the profits are great. A hundred pounds of water contain around 34-36 pounds of salt.

This nation cultivates even less than the Oneidas and they are also poorer, being forced to buy various articles for primary subsistence. For the rest it differs little in its customs from the latter, with the exception of the religion, since they have not embraced Christianity like the Oneidas. In the event of homicide or theft, they act in the same way as was described for the Oneidas, and also as far as the succession to office and heredity are concerned.

They have a notion of a supreme being, who must have created the world, and who punishes after death those who did not conduct themselves well. According to them, life in the future consists of a continuous wandering around the world, sometimes rejoicing, if deserving of reward, or suffering, if deserving of punishment. The religious ceremonies are reduced to a single day of the year, during the month of January, and consist of the sacrifice of three white dogs and one barrel of tobacco. The people, preceded by the chiefs, gather around a large fire and after having adorned the victims with flowers, throw them into the flames, the chief pronouncing the following words: "We hope that these animals we are sending you will please you, o Ayenniyo (God)." And then throwing a few small parcels of tobacco: "And that you use this tobacco to smoke." The ceremony ends with dancing around the sacred fire, singing some hymn at the same time, which for a lack of a good interpreter we were unable to translate.

There is no religious formality of any sort in marriage; so a few of them live with two wives and change them at will. It is rare that a man ends his life with his first wife. When a man separates from his wife, he only takes a single son with him, and very often he denies having any: they all remain on the shoulders of the wife. There is no great ceremony at funerals. Only the neighbors, and at times the whole village, gather in the deceased's house, bringing with them their own food supplies because they linger to feast. We were unable to discover the origin of this custom.

We will end our description of the Six Nations Indians, by relating here under a small vocabulary and some of their principal grammatical rules.

The Mohawk language, of which the Oneida is but a derivation, has general rules. Its inhabitants never close their lips when they speak, and as a result, they do not use labial letters.

They pronounce the *a*, the *e*, and the *i* like in Italian.

The Mohawks pronounce the letter *v* but never the letter *d*; and the Oneidas pronounce the *d* instead of the *v*. The Senecas use neither one, and substitute instead the letter *h*.

MOHAWK,   *Raniha* for father
ONEIDA,   *Laniha*
SENECA,   *Hanih*

A whole sentence is often expressed in one word. The few words listed in the following vocabulary are accented in order to facilitate their understanding and pronunciation. The grave (`) is placed on long syllables, and the (') accent on the short. There are a lot of guttural letters in this language, some pronounced louder, others more softly. In the first instance, they are expressed with *gh,* in the second with *hh.*

The two following examples relate to the use of *R, L,* and *H* in the three languages.

MOHAWK: *Rawegh*   They say   *Raosare,* his knife
ONEIDA: *Laweagh*   *Laosale*
SENECA: *Haweagh*   *Hoganysaith*

Personal pronouns:
Iih, I; *ise,* you; *laouhha,* him; *aouhha,* her; *ongyouhha,* we; *tiouhe,* you (plural); *Lonouhha,* they (masculine); *onouhha,* they (feminine).
Agwawea, my/mine; *sawea,* your/yours.

Active verb: I say

Wagilov	I say
Wahagilov	you say (singular)
Wahhelou	he says
Wagealou	she says
Waaggnilow	we say
Wisinilou	you say (plural)
Wahanilou	they say (masculine)
Waggnilou	they say (feminine)
Wagélone	I said
Engilou	I will say
Agilou	I can say
Aougweange	I could, I would have said
Aiseange	you could, you would have said
Ahaweange	they could, they would have said
Ayalou	they could say
Waailou	they say
Yondou	it is said

Laniha	Father
Lageniha	my father
Yaniha	your father
Saggneniha	our father (to the two of us)
I'waniha	our father
Swanika	your
Lodiniha	their father

A few words in the following languages:

ITALIAN	ONEIDA	SENECA
God	*Nych o Raweniyo*	*Haveniyo*
The earth	*Oghweatsya*	*Owéentja*
The sun	*Kalaghkwa*	*Kaahkwa*
The moon	*Eghuida*	*Owenida*
The star	*Ojestock*	*Ajestock*
The tree	*Kalonda*	*Kéonda*
The world	*Oghwhentoyagwekow*	does not exist
The father	*Laniha*	*Hanih*
Son	*Ondadyéa*	
Daughter	*Sagoyéa*	
Mother	*Agnolha*	*Noiyéah*
Man	*Ongwe*	*Ongwe*
Woman	*Onheghtyea*	*Agouheghteya*

Young woman	*Kayadase*
Boy	*Laxaa*
Wheat	*Onuste*
Girl	*Ixaa*
Gold	*Osinkwala* (meaning yellow)
Silver	*Oghwista*
Iron	*Kanhyouhughwe*
Water	*Oghnega*
Fire	*Oziste*
Rain	*Ogeanolaghsela*
Dry	*Yostatheagh*
Humid	*Yonanaweagh*
Winter	*Goghsetage*
Summer	*Agenhage*
Spring	*Toyogenhondi* or *Keangwedightsi* (anticipated Spring)
Fall	*Kannenage*
Church	*Onoghsadogeaghte*
Milk	*Ononda*
Fish	*Kensiyoh*
Bread	*Kanataloh*
Wine	*Onegweaghtala n Kagh* (This means a red-colored liquor, and is the usual expression. The following word is more expressive, elegant, and sacred. Properly pronounced it does not have the harshness that it seems to have at first glance.) *Oheahhaladasehhouhtselaggelé*
Cow	*Teyonhoghshiwalonde*
Horse	*Yagoghsatas* (it means a creature which carries something on its back)

This animal has received various names in the savages' different countries, according to the first impression it made on their mind when they first saw it. The Seneca call it *Kayendaneghkwe,* that is to say, animal carrying firewood. They call the wild beasts *Kalliyo.*

The following are some sentences in the Oneida language which a visitor would use the most:

How are you? *Esghananktisone*
Where do you come from? *Cazzanonquatinonta-se?*
Is this the way to Oneida? *Neca-neca-judati Kanonaloale*
Do me the favor *Aschitanlé*
I thank you for your thoughtfulness *Gniavan-ne Waschitanle*
This dish is very good *Cawalaeon-Cahia-na*
How many children do you have? *To ni savilaja?*

Are you married? *Saniaconcan?*
What is your name? *Ot je sajatz?*
Is this your house? *I-neca-sanonsoté?*
Do you want to feed me? *Atsqui-ne-aschequanonte?*
I love your daughter *Chenon wese ne sejana*
She is truly beautiful *Cajetas*
If I were an Indian I would marry her *Togat conqueonwe a canaghe tajon-chiatieche*
I wish to learn your language *Ikel-e ajavan acalonche-tsi suavannotan.*
Please do not trouble yourself *Tacan tan con niconlaalan*
I like this country very much *Vanconvesquanie ne canto.*

Small Vocabulary of the Onondaga Language

Onondaga	*Otiseanagada*
God	*Avennyo*
The earth	*Vovenga*
The sun	*Kalaqua*
The moon	same as the sun, with the epithet, *by night*
The stars	*Ozzistennoqua*
A tree	*Kalonta*
The world	*Ongwe*
Father	*Kenigho*
Son	*Ontatawa*
Daughter	*Hé-en*
Mother	*Aho-ho*
Man	*Longwe*
Woman	*Ae-én*
Boy	*Laksaa*
Girl	*Exaa*
Wheat	*Onéca*
Gold	*Oxinkwala*
Silver	same as in Oneida
Iron	*Odeganzla*
Cow	*Tionaqualunt*
Horse	*Cossatens*
Water	as in Oneida
Fire	*Ozista,* only differs from Oneida in the ending
Rain	*Ostaluntiun*
Dry	*O-en*
Humid	*Iuszatan*
Winter	as in Oneida
Summer	*Kagenhage*
Spring	*Kanguitetzi*
Fall	*Kannenage*

Church	as in Oneida
Milk	*Ononasa*
Poison	*Oziunda*
Bread	*Oaqua*

About the Shakers

Whoe'er travels from his country, sees
Things he thought were far away
And when he recounts them afterwards, he is
Not believed and is considered a liar.
                    Ariosto, ORLANDO FURIOSO

Among the most extravagant and absurd religious sects that men invented in a moment of delirium, we can without doubt include the one we are going to talk about. As far as we know, there is no other sect today to which this one compares. If the reports are correct, this sect originated in England, or more exactly, Ann Lee, considered to be its founder, was born in England. The sect does not appear to have been known anywhere in Europe or America before her time. It is impossible to assert what was the character of this woman. According to her followers, we should consider her as a chosen woman who is mentioned in the twelfth chapter of John's revelations; while her enemies, on the other hand, draw a frightening picture of her, probably exaggerated. Both groups seem far from the truth. She arrived in America from Europe in 1774 with three or four of her first followers. After wandering for a while in Pennsylvania and recruiting a few followers, they came to New York State where they bought a tract of land in a place called Nisqueunia [Niskayuna], about nine miles north of Albany. They remained there unnoticed, barely known by their neighbors. In this first establishment founders and converts continued their crafts, such as blacksmith, shoemaker, which still represent today their principal occupations.

They lived quietly in Niskayuna until around 1783. At that time, their number and wealth having considerably increased, some of them moved to the New Lebanon Valley where we visited them and where the main establishment is found today. They bought there twelve thousand acres of land and created a beautiful village in which most of their artisans reside. The others, who are farmers, live scattered in the surrounding countryside. The obnoxiousness of this sect has not failed to attract other followers, and there are four hundred of them just in this place, a considerable number if one takes into account the fact that they have only recruited in a sparsely populated country. Since they do not allow the propagation of the species among themselves, they must continuously enroll more converts in order to remain in existence. Among them everything is held in common and nothing in private. The leaders keep a common purse, where they put the individual daily earnings, providing each one with necessities. And since one of their religious principles is to work hard and to be industrious, it is easy to believe that they never lack money. These sectarians' eccentricities are not restricted to doctrinal matters, but are even extended to their way of praying. We will first talk about this.

They have two churches in this village, or more exactly there are two houses in which they gather on Sundays. The novices have free access to one of these churches, and all the persons curious to attend their assemblies are usually allowed to do so. But only the advanced can enter the other church and when in assembly, they do not admit anyone else. We can only say a few words about this second group because we would have to rely on someone else's testimony who maybe never have entered that church, and we would then be subject to error.

The shape of the church in which the novices gather is oblong, clean, but without any ornament or pictures, even though it would be the proper place to put the statue of madness. They started entering at eight in the morning, following the custom of admitting the men in one group to the west and the women in another group to the east. As they entered they took places in an orderly fashion, always standing up, since there are few benches, principally for visitors. They thus formed two triangular battalions, one of men, and the other of women. One of the leaders was at the center of those two divisions, and after a few convulsive contortions of the head and shoulders, and after spitting several times, he uttered with a clear voice certain words which had no connection. This is how he started: "Order Christ . . . our well-being . . . Your example . . . ah, seriousness . . . listen to the one who speaks . . . Will you believe him? . . ." and similar broken-up monosyllables. During this extravagant beginning they were all attentive and demonstrated from the outside a religious restraint. Then he added: "Prepare yourselves for the holy service." This preparation consisted in changing the triangular shapes of the two battalions in two quadrilaterals. Before forming the second figure and while still observing the greatest silence, the men took off their jerkins and tied their shirt sleeves with ribbons. Standing in place and looking in the face some of their leaders from both sexes who were lined up along the wall, they waited for one of them to intone a mystical song, or more precisely a song with made-up words, to the tune of which both squadrons started dancing, forming various prescribed figures while turning at the same time on both feet. In this dance, everyone dances on his own, without touching the partner or changing the configuration, staying at the same place, beating the feet in cadence, while a few of them accompany themselves by singing. The more the dance progresses, the more the imagination heats up, and then the contortions and convulsions are carried to excess. From time to time the leader stops his intonation and the dancing stops. They rest without changing the configuration, or leaving their respective places, except for removing their clothes. They remain dancing like this all day long, and we have seen them in continuous contortions and movement from eight in the morning to six in the evening.

As strange as their way of adoring God may seem, we must trust testimonies that appear to be devoid of partiality and assert that today this sect is not as ridiculous nor as scandalous as it once was. Ann Lee introduced many eccentricities and indecencies, which we mention with great disgust. At the time no order, dignity, or reserve were observed in the temple. All the sect members could do as they pleased, and while some preached, others lay down on the floor, faking convulsions, others smoked pipes, and others discussed extraneous things amongst themselves. During the dance, unbelievable things happened. Both sexes were naked, and they danced together without propriety nor circumspection. But such dishonorable behavior does not occur any longer, and everyday they have modified a little more their oddities.

At the same time that the novices are assembled in this church, the advanced are gathered in theirs. It is not easy to say what practices they observe in this church. The doors are shut, and no stranger is admitted, so that the voices of their neighbors', who imagine that scandals and foolishness were committed there, could well be nothing more than slanders.

We should report here what the religious maxims and the belief of this sect are, but we must confess that after having taken the trouble to read certain manuscripts and to converse with some of their leaders, we are far from seeing the truth, and we perhaps have reason to believe that they themselves ignore what they adore, and what they believe. One leader in the advanced group is the general director of the whole congregation, and what he orders is executed; what he says is believed. So he orders them to believe in the holy scripture, but at the same time, he interprets it as he wishes. They call themselves the followers of the second apparition of Christ As a result they consider all the other sects to be adorers of the antichrist. According to them, no man was saved after the apostles departed this world. But the point in which they differ the most from any other sect is their observance of the abstinence of union between the two sexes, not allowing marriage among them nor the propagation of the species. The rise, the propagation of the scripture must be understood only for the propagation and the increase of the true belief. It is good however that such observance be scrupulously observed and since they have to enroll new members in order to survive, this absurd and strange sect will fortunately not last long.

If one wanted to deduce from their present customs the virtue of their religion, the inquiry would be in their favor. But what does it prove besides the power of fanaticism? Their domestic life is excellent. They live frugally and are laborious and industrious. They work to cultivate the fields as they take care of their forges in their various manufactures, and their fields are better cultivated than those of their neighbors, and the products from their hands fetch a higher price at the markets because they are of superior quality. When making a contract, they are trustworthy, loyal, honest and straight, without losing their natural shrewdness and discernment. At home they are friendly with each other, and the pain of one is the pain of all. If one abused the order of absolute chastity, he would be expelled from the congregation; pregnant women would also be expelled. But we hear only of a few such cases, which is hard to believe, considering the intimate union in which both sexes live together, sharing the same quarters. How can you reconcile principles so different, customs so excellent, so strange, so ridiculous to such absurd principles?

The followers must first start to confess their past life and all their sins to one of the leaders. Some leaders want them to communicate all this to the whole congregation. After formally renouncing ownership and the use of sex, he is immediately accepted among them and enters the church. The power of God manifests itself through the convulsions and the gesticulations that they start performing, and the greater those signs, the more frequent they are, as signs of progress toward perfection, and the more the holy grace works in them. Such are their practices and sentiments. And thus an obscure and ignorant woman, out of insanity or vanity, has been able to increase the number of oddities in this world, and to adorn it with a new trophy, the image of madness.

Journal of Travels, Principally by Water, from Albany to the Seneca Lake

1791

Elkanah Watson

Elkanah Watson was born on January 22, 1758, and died on December 5, 1842, in Port Kent, New York. From the age of 19 to near the end of his life of nearly 85 years, Watson wrote extensive journals and correspondence. He revised and compiled much of this by 1820, at which time he published his *History of the Rise, Progress, and Existing Condition of the Western Canals in the State of New York*, from which much of the following narrative is taken. His son, Winslow Watson, completed the compiling and editing of these and other journals for publication in 1856, under the title *Men and Times of the Revolution; or Memoirs of Elkanah Watson*. He published an indexed and more easily used version a year later in 1857. Unfortunately, the younger Watson chose to rework the material and present some of it in the third person, a decision that robs the text of much of its vitality. Both editions also eliminated some material of interest contained in the portion on the Mohawk River published in 1820. Footnotes found in the originals have been omitted from this edition.

The first portion of the Watson journals reproduced here includes his narrative of the later part of his 1788 trip up the Mohawk, which is taken from the 1857 publication (pp. 310-318). It was on this trip that he began to perceive the potential of the valley as a canal route. The second portion covers his 1791 trip over much of the same ground and is taken from the 1820 publication (pp. 25-40). There is information here about the inhabitants, the boats already using the river, and Watson's speculations about future canal development. Italicized passages are as they appeared in the original publications. They probably represent passages underlined for emphasis in the original manuscript.

Watson was with Franklin and Adams in Europe during the Revolution, and he carried messages between Paris and London during preliminary peace negotiations. He settled in Albany in 1789 and helped push a canal law through the legislature by March 1792. The result was the set of canal locks and canals that served Durham boat traffic until the Erie Canal was completed in 1825. Watson served as a director of the Western Canal Company. Despite his various accomplishments as a journalist, diplomat, and politician, the epitaph over his grave credits him only as the founder and first president of the Berkshire Agricultural Society.

D.R.S.

1788

SEPTEMBER, *1788.*—From Colonel Sterling's, I began to traverse the wilderness bordering upon the Indian territory. The road is almost impassable; I was upwards of three hours in reaching the Mohawk, opposite old Fort Schuyler, a distance of only six miles. Here I reluctantly forded the river, being alone and without a guide, and both shores being alive with savages. Having fasted twenty-four hours, in consequence of a severe head-ache the day previous, I was by this time excessively hungry and fatigued. As there was no tavern, and there were only a few scattered houses, I proceeded to an old German log house, on the margin of the river, and implored for something to eat. At length, after much difficulty, I prevailed on an ill-natured German woman, to spare me two ears of green corn, and some salt.

The road from thence to Whitesborough continued as bad as possible, obstructed by broken bridges, logs, and stumps,—my horse, at every step, sinking knee-deep in the mud. I remained one day recruiting at the log house of Judge White, the founder of the settlement, and slept in his log barn, with horses and other animals. Whitesborough is a promising new settlement, situated on the south side of the Mohawk river, in the heart of a fine tract of land, and is just in its transition from a state of nature to civilization. The settlement commenced, only three years since. It is astonishing to see what efforts are making, to subdue the dense and murky forest. Log houses are already scattered, in the midst of stumps, half-burnt logs, and girdled trees. I observed, however, with pleasure, that their log barns are well filled. A few years ago, land might have been bought for a trifle; at present, the lots bordering upon the river, have advanced to three dollars per acre, and those lying a few miles back, to one dollar per acre. Settlers are continually pouring in from the Connecticut hive, which throws off its annual swarms of intelligent, industrious, and enterprising emigrants,—the best qualified, of all men in the world, to overcome and civilize the wilderness. They already estimate three hundred brother Yankees on their muster list; and, a few years hence, they will undoubtedly be able to raise a formidable barrier, to oppose the incursions of the savages, in the event of another war.

At Oriskany, I passed a small tribe of two hundred Indians, the remnant of that once powerful Mohawk nation, which was the former terror and dread of the New England frontier. On ascending a hill, I approached the place where the intrepid General Herkimer was drawn into a fatal ambush and miserably defeated, in 1777. Herkimer was a gallant, but inexperienced leader, and here perished, with nearly half his army, formed of the patriotic yeomanry of the Mohawk valley. Just before reaching this sanguinary battle-field, I met with two Germans, familiar with the incidents. They conducted me over the whole ground;

and, in corroboration of the fact, of which they assured me, that many of the slain who were scattered through the woods were never interred, I saw numerous human bones, strewn upon the service [surface] of the earth. This movement was intended to succor Fort Stanwix, then besieged by St. Leger.

I found myself, soon after leaving this consecrated spot, alone in the woods, in the midst of a band of Indians, "*as drunk as lords.*" They looked like so many evil spirits, broken loose from Pandemonium. Wild, frantic, almost naked, and frightfully painted, they whooped, yelled, and danced round me in such hideous attitudes, that I was seriously apprehensive, they would end the farce, by taking off my scalp, by way of a joke. I had luckily picked up the word *Sago,* the salute of friendship, of which I made frequent use, constantly extending my hand to the most active among them, by whom it was cordially accepted.

On my arrival at Fort Stanwix, I saw the whole plain round the fort covered with Indians, of various tribes, male and female. Many of the latter were fantastically dressed in their best attire,—in the richest silks, fine scarlet cloths, bordered with gold fringe, a profusion of brooches, rings in their noses, their ears slit, and their heads decorated with feathers. I noticed among them some very handsome countenances and fine figures.

I luckily procured a sleeping-place, in the garret of the house in which Governor Clinton and the eight other commissioners,—also John Taylor, Esq., of Albany, Indian Agent,—Egbert Benson, Esq., of New York, and a man with a large white wig, of the name of Dr. Taylor,—were quartered. The sight of this wig fixed the attention, and excited the mirth, of many of the Indians; one of whom I observed making strong efforts to smother a laugh in the Doctor's face, since nothing could appear more ludicrous and grotesque to an Indian, than a bushy white wig. The object of this great treaty, is to procure a cession, by the Indians, of territory lying west of Fort Stanwix, in this State, and extending to the great lakes. Fort Stanwix was built in 1758, by the British Government, at a cost of sixty thousand pounds sterling, and is situated on an artificial eminence, near the river; a large area round it is entirely cleared. Here Colonel Gansevoort, in 1777, sustained a terrible siege, until relieved by Arnold, when St. Leger made a precipitate retreat, abandoning most of his camp equipage and munitions. The French Ambassador, Count de Moustier, and the Marchioness de Biron, are now encamped within the Fort, under a marquee formerly used by Lord Cornwallis. This enterprising and courageous lady has exposed herself to the greatest fatigues and privations, to gratify her unbounded curiosity, by coming all the way from the city of New York, to witness this great and unusual assemblage of savage tribes.

On contemplating the position of Fort Stanwix, at the head of bateau navigation on the Mohawk river, within one mile of Wood Creek, which runs west toward Lake Ontario, I am led to think, that it will in time become the emporium of commerce between Albany and the vast western world. Wood Creek is indeed small, but it is the only water communication with the great Lakes; it empties into the Oneida Lake, the outlet of which unites with the Onondaga and Oswego, and discharges into Lake Ontario at Fort Oswego, where the British have a garrison. Should the Little Falls ever be locked, the obstructions in the Mohawk river be removed, and a canal between that river and Wood Creek at this place be formed, so as to unite the waters flowing east with those running west, and other canals be made, and obstructions be removed to Fort Oswego,—who can reasonably doubt, that, by such bold operations, the State of New York will have in her power, by a grand measure of policy, to divert the future trade of Lake Ontario, and the great lakes above, from Alexandria and Quebec to Albany and New York?

The object of the present treaty, is the purchase of an immense territory, estimated at eight millions of acres, and now owned, and chiefly inhabited, by the Six Nations of Indians. The sovereignty of this tract has been in dispute, between Massachusetts and New York. These States have at length made an amicable division, assigning four millions of acres to each. The former has since sold her right of domain to a company of adventurers, who have purchased prëemption from the Indians. New York has, by this treaty, accomplished the same result. This vast territory, therefore, is now opened, without any impediments, to the flood of emigration which will pour into it from the East. Many hardy pioneers have already planted themselves among the savages; and it is probable, that the enthusiasm for the occupation of new territory, which now prevails, will, in the period of the next twenty years, spread over this fertile region a prosperous and vigorous population.

I left Fort Stanwix, with the intention of passing down Wood Creek to Lake Ontario, indulging the idea of extending my tour to Detroit. Under the strong presentiment, *that a canal communication will be opened, sooner or later, between the great lakes and the Hudson,* I was anxious to explore its probable course. A hard rain commencing, and the obstacles I found to exist in the creek, induced me to abandon the arduous enterprize, and return to Fort Stanwix. The attempt afforded me the gratification of sailing west, for the first time, in the interior of America.

I continued several days at the Treaty, passing my time most agreeable, in associating with the Commissioners; and, I was much diverted with the novel and amusing scenes exhibited in the Indian camp. The plain in the vicinity of the fort, has already been laid out into a town-plot; a few houses have been erected, and also saw-mills, and other improvements, at the distance of a mile on Wood Creek.

A young Indian, named Peter Otsequett, a Chief of the Oneidas, was attending this Treaty. He had just returned from France, having been in that country for several years, under the patronage of the Marquis de La Fayette, by whom he was taken when a boy. He is probably the most polished and best educated Indian in North America. He speaks both French and English, correctly; is familiar with music and many branches of polite and elegant literature; and, in his manners, is a well-bred Frenchman. He is, however, a striking instance of the moral impracticability of civilizing an Indian. There appear to exist natural impediments to their amelioration. While visiting the Catawba Indians, a year since, I became acquainted with a young Indian, who had been educated at a prominent college; but had already fallen into the degradation of his native savage habits, and was to all intents an Indian. It is noticed that each year, in its progress, wears off the European polish of Otsequett, and brings him nearer to the savage. Ten days ago, I was introduced to him, a polite and well-informed gentleman; to-day, I beheld him splashing through the mud, in the rain, on horseback, with a young squaw behind him, both comfortably drunk.

My curiosity satisfied, I sent my horse toward Albany, and embarked on board of a returning bateau, and proceeded down the Mohawk to Little Falls, anxious to examine that place, with an eye to canals. We abandoned ourselves to the current of the river, which, with the aid of our oars, impelled us at a rapid rate. We met numerous bateaux coming up the river, freighted with whole families, emigrating to the 'land of promise.' I was surprised at the dexterity with which they manage their boats, and the progress they make in poling up the river, against a current of at least three miles an hour. The first night, we encamped at a log hut on the banks of the river; and, the next morning, I disembarked at German Flats.

The meanderings of the river, according to my estimate, about doubles the distance in a direct line. We passed a valuable tract of sixteen thousand acres of land, situated on the north side of the river, which has been granted by the State to Baron Steuben. From Schenectady, I pursued the road across a thickly settled country, embracing many fine farms, to Ashley's Ferry, six miles above Albany. On the east side of the river, at this point, a new town has been recently laid out, named Vanderheyden. This place is situated precisely at the head of navigation on the Hudson. Several bold and enterprising adventurers have already settled here; a number of capacious warehouses, and several dwellings, are already erected. It is favorably situated, in reference to the important and growing trade of Vermont and Massachusetts; and, I think, it not only bids fair to be a serious thorn in the side of New City, but in the issue a fatal rival.

I spent a day in examining this locality, and then walked on the banks of the Hudson, a distance of three miles, to New City, where I continued several days. This place is thronged with mercantile emigrants, principally from New England, who have enjoyed a very extensive and lucrative trade, supplying Vermont and the region on both banks of the Hudson, as far as Lake George, with merchandise; and receiving, in payment, wheat, pot and pearl ashes, and lumber. But, as I remarked, I think Vanderheyden must, from its more eligible position, attain the ultimate ascendency.

I crossed the river at Half-Moon, a small hamlet containing about twenty dwellings; and, about a mile from this place, I visited the Cohoes Falls, on the Mohawk River. Nothing so much charms and elevates my mind, as the contemplation of nature in her bold and majestic works. Fixing my position on the margin of the bank, which descends in an abrupt precipice of about seventy feet, I beheld the volume of the Mohawk, plunging over a fall of about the same height, and nearly perpendicular. The barrier of rocks,—the lofty banks,—the roaring and dashing of the waters,—and the cloud of mist, presented a spectacle of surprising sublimity. The river divides, immediately below the Falls, into three branches, and empties into the Hudson, nearly opposite New City. The bed of the stream is filled with rocks, among which it rushes and surges in terrific impetuosity.

As to ascending by locks from the Hudson to the Mohawk River, it appears to me, that the obstacles at this place will be much greater, than to cut a canal across the pine plains, into a grand basin, back of Albany. I took passage, in a bateau at New City, to Albany, for the purpose of sounding the river. The result of my examination satisfied me, that, in ordinary tides, five or six feet may be carried to within a mile of New City, and from thence to that town fifteen to eighteen inches. The tides sensibly rise and fall, as far up as Vanderheyden. Upon careful investigation and mature reflection, it appears to my mind, that Albany is one of the most favorable positions in America for the future enjoyment of a vast internal commerce. It is favorably situated, in reference to the trade of Vermont and the extensive eastern country. It may control the fur trade of the lakes; it must occupy the avenues which penetrate into the valley of the Mohawk; and it will be the depot of the produce from the luxuriant territory of the Genesee.

1791

Thursday, September 1, 1791.—I left Albany, with Jeremiah Van Rensselaer, Esq. on our way westward. Traversed a pine barren, sixteen miles, to Schenectady; a considerable town, on the south side of the Mohawk river. Considering Albany as the northern capital of this state, and Schenectady at least the fourth town in rank, as to age and size,—and that this road has been the only channel of communication between these two places, for about one hundred and seventy years, its present shameful state is a matter of regret and astonishment;—apparently following the direction of original Indian footpaths, whereas the nature of the ground will admit of a spacious turnpike road; which, I am confident, may be established at a moderate expense, compared with its great importance. I spent the day in preparing for our water expedition, and viewing this old town.

Schenectady is handsomely laid out, on the margin of the Mohawk, in a pleasant valley. It contains about three hundred houses, and sixteen hundred inhabitants, mostly of Dutch descent.

The fur trade has vanished, and with it their enterprize. Although they are situated in a country abounding in resources, yet they will not depart from their old track, and strike off into a new road, which would lead them to affluence.

September 2.—This morning we despatched two batteaux, with six men, and ample provisions and stores, for a six weeks' voyage, for thirteen persons, including Gen. Van Cortland, Stephen N. Bayard, Esq. and two servants. We proceeded on by land to meet our batteaux and fellow travellers, at Herkimer.

Between Schenectady and Johnstown, the country along the river, is thinly peopled, much woods, hilly, stony, and an infamous bad carriage road. The bridges are not only in a ruinous state, but absolutely dangerous; some impassable, and altogether too narrow for convenience and safety.

The present road system is disgraceful to this fine state, and calls loudly for a radical change. We were driven by a stupid fellow; sometimes rattling us over stones and rocks, as if the d—l was at our heels,—and then creeping along over a level road, as if going to a funeral. Such, O man, is the perverseness of thy nature! The town of Johnstown is pleasantly situated, four or five miles from the Mohawk river, and north-west of Albany. The philanthropic Sir William Johnson, was the founder and father of this village.

September 4.—We proceeded on our journey with a miserably covered waggon, and in a constant rain, till night; which brought us to Maj. Schuyler's mills, in Palatine, settled by the descendants of German emigrants, intermixing on all sides with the enterprising sons of the east, between whom mutual prejudices run high. These will gradually subside by intermarriages, and other modes of intercourse. Thus far the German, and Dutch farmers, have been, in a manner, totally remiss in cultivating the first rudiments of literature; whereas the descendants of the English, in New-England, have cherished it as a primary duty. Hence the characteristics of each people are distinctly variant. When literature shall begin to shed its benign rays over this benighted race,—should our wise law-makers open their arms to embrace, and cherish its general diffusion, as a leading object of legislation,—then, and not till then, the Germans, the Dutch, the Yankees, will soon dismiss all local, illiberal prejudices and distinctions; and in twenty or thirty years the shades of discordance will be hardly perceptible. The whole will amalgamate, and all will be dignified by the general name of *Americans;* speaking the same language, and possessing the same genius and education.

I have noticed with pleasure, that the German farmers begin to use oxen in agriculture, instead of horses. For this salutary commencement, they are indebted to New-Englandmen; on the other hand, I regret to add, that I have noticed that New-England farmers, settled in this country, have, in some instances, adopted the lazy, and unprofitable custom, of using horses instead of oxen.

I am induced to believe, should the WESTERN CANALS *be ever made, and the Mohawk river become, in one sense, a continuation of the Hudson river, by means of canals and locks, it will most clearly obviate the necessity of sending produce to market, in winter, by sleighs. On the contrary, it would be stored on the margin of the Mohawk, in winter, and be sent in the summer months, by batteaux, to be unloaded aboard of vessels in the Hudson. Whenever this glorious state of things shall exist, western farmers will find it infinitely to their interest to substitute oxen, even for the transportation of their produce, in place of horses.*

Five miles from Johnstown we descended into a flat country, the precise road I travelled in 1788, and crossed the same bridge where my horse decided my journey west. We pursued our course west, travelling on the north side of the river.

The bottoms, or low lands, are laid off in rich enclosures, highly cultivated,—principally by industrious Germans. Narrow roads, and contracted bridges, still continue.

It is also to be regretted, that individuals should be permitted to annoy travellers, by interrupting the free passage of a public highway, by numerous gates, erected for private convenience. They should all be prostrated as public nuisances.

On the south side of the river, the country is thicker settled, and many pleasant situations, old farms, and wealthy farmers;—but evidently far behind those of Germany or England, in the profitable science of agriculture. We crossed a new wooden bridge, near Schuyler's mills, seventy-five feet long, with a single arch, supported by framed work above. I was glad to notice this, as an entering wedge to more extended improvements.

September 7.—This morning we ascended Fall hill, over a craggy road of one mile. From its summit, we commanded an extensive and picturesque view of the surrounding country in the north,—partly settled, but generally in Nature's original brown livery, spotted here and there with an opening.

We left the Little Falls on our right, and descended into the rich settlements of the German-flats. At Aldridge's tavern, near Fort Herkimer, we overtook our batteaux, all well; and embarked the same evening, steming fourteen miles, against a strong current, with an awning spread over our heads. Each boat was manned with three men; two in the bow, and one in the stern to steer, and occasionally rowing in still water,—and setting, with short poles, at the rapids, with surprising dexterity. In this mode, their average progress is three miles an hour, equal to treckschute travelling in Holland; but it is extremely laborious, and fatiguing to the men.

At night we encamped in a log-hut, on the margin of the river, with tag-rag, &c. and were *literally flea'd alive.*

September 8.—A pleasant sail of ten miles, this fine morning, brought us to old Fort Schuyler. Here we were joined by Gen. Van Cortland, and Stephen N. Bayard, Esq. waiting for us, which completes our number to thirteen.

From the Little Falls, thus far, the *river is nearly competent to inland navigation, with the exception of a serious rapid, and a great bend at the Germanflats, called wolf-riff,—which must be subdued, either by a cut across the neck of land, upwards, one mile, or by removing the obstructions.*

An Indian road being opened from this place, [now Utica,] to the Genesee country; it is probable the position at Fort Stanwix, and this spot, will become rivals, as to the scite of a town, in connection with the interior, when it shall become a settled country.

If however the canals should be constructed, I think Fort Stanwix will take the lead at a future day. Such was my impression when there in 1788. Since which, only a few houses and stores have been erected here; also a tolerable tavern, to administer comfort to the weary traveller, which I experienced the want of three years past. In the afternoon we progressed thirteen miles, meeting many obstructions, in consequence of the cruel conduct of the new settlers, (who are wonderfully increased since I was here last,) filling the river with fallen trees, cut on its margin,—narrowing it in many places, producing shoals where the deepest waters had been accustomed to flow, and impeding the progress of our boats.

We pitched our camp on the right bank of the river, in the midst of woods. All hands fell to work, soldierlike: we soon had a roaring fire, and our tents pitched,—open on one side to the fire, and closed at each end with canvass. We found an excellent substitute for feathers, by laying our buffaloes on hemlock twigs; although the ground was extremely moist, yet we were effectually protected from any inconvenience. We enjoyed a pleasant night, with ten times more comfort, than we could in the miserable log huts along the margin of the river.

This is the first time in my life, with all my vicissitudes, (with the exception of one night, when I was lost in the wilderness in North-Carolina, in 1777,) that I ever slept in the open air. We breathed of course in a free atmosphere, and slept soundly.

September 9.—At noon we reached Fort Stanwix,—to which place, *with some aid of art, the river continues competent to inland navigation, for boats of five tons burthen.* Emigrants are swarming into these fertile regions in shoals, like the ancient Israelites seeking the land of promise.

We transported our boats, and baggage, across the carrying-place, a distance of two miles, over a dead flat,—and launched them into Wood creek, *running west,*—huzza! It is a mere brook at this place, which a man can easily jump across.

In contemplating this important creek, as the only water communication with the immense regions in the west, which are destined to bless millions of freemen in the approaching century; I am deeply impressed with a belief, considering the great resources of this state, that the improvement of our internal navigation cannot, much longer, escape the decided attention of our wise law makers; especially as it is obviously practicable,—and when effected, it will open an uninterrupted water communication from the immense fertile regions in the west, to the Atlantic ocean,—and vice versa. But more of this, as I advance in my travels. *My mind being constantly absorbed with the subject, I shall not fail to notice every obstacle, and to my best judgment, to form plans, and make estimates. The particular spot I have contemplated for a canal, to unite the Wood creek with the Mohawk, is about two miles, through a swamp, to Oneida brook,—which, I presume, may be effected for ten thousand dollars.*

The situation at Fort Stanwix appears destined to become a great city. It lies in an open plain,—healthy, and exactly between the eastern and western waters. There is a large clearing round the old fort, and two or three scattering houses. No progress has, however, been made since I attended the treaty here in 1788, although the plan of a city is now contemplated.

On the Mohawk river we observed several block-houses, to which the distracted inhabitants fled for shelter and protection;—and also noticed widespread desolation, occasioned by the cruel depredations of the Indians, aided by those infamous white savages, the tories, in the late war; who pursued their warfare on the Mohawk, with unrelenting fury. My heart has been often pierced in this jaunt, as well as in the year 1788, with the groans and cries of widows and orphans. It seems to me, their wrongs *will be avenged,* and that the eternal justice of Heaven *will not sleep.*

September 10.—This morning our batteaux began to descend Wood creek, with the aid of a mill-dam, which had been previously filled just above. Some of our party, at the same time, descended by land, on a tolerable waggon road, to Canada creek, six miles.

Although aided by the sluice, we progressed with infinite difficulty. In many places the windings are so sudden, and so short, that while the bow of the boat was ploughing in the bank on one side, her stern was rubbing hard against the opposite shore. In some places our men were obliged to drag the boats by main strength; and in others, the boughs and limbs were so closely interwoven, and so low, as to arch the creek completely over, and oblige all hands to lie flat. These obstacles, together with sunken logs and trees, rendered our progress extremely difficult,—often almost impracticable.

Such, alas! is the present deplorable state of a very important river, which Providence has evidently intended for the most valuable purposes, yet to be realized. One thousand, perhaps twelve hundred, pounds, judiciously applied, under the eye of an experienced engineer, would render this communication extremely easy, at the same time of the utmost importance to the Union,—to the State,—and to individuals.

From a superficial view of this important creek, it appears to me the great difficulties may be surmounted:—*First,* by cutting away all the bushes and trees on its banks. *Second,* by cutting across the necks, and removing all sunken logs and trees;—and lastly, by erecting substantial sluices, or inclined planes, at given distances, so as to continue a head of water from sluice to sluice. *This creek, in its present state, may be considered a natural canal, from ten to twenty feet wide. If sluices were erected only to the height of the banks, with small locks, on inclined planes, it is probable they would be sufficiently high, and they could be well done, I am persuaded, for fifty pounds each.*

Batteaux which ascend the creek, at this season, are dragged by horses, travelling in the water, and frequently the descending boats; which is a work of incredible fatigue and difficulty.

The accession of Canada creek, more than doubles the size of Wood creek.

September 11.—Last night, and this day we were inundated by heavy rains, which our tent was unable to repel; in consequence we were all setting in the most uncomfortable manner.

In the intervals of showers we amused ourselves by catching fish. Salmon, Oswego bass, catfish, chubs, trout, and pike, are the fish common in this river. Salmon are sometimes caught at the mill-dam, at Fort Stanwix.

September 12.—At 3 o'clock we reached the royal block-house, at the east end of the Oneida lake. The innumerable crooks and turns in Wood creek, carried us to every point of the compass. We counted one hundred and eighty-eight distinct points of land, from Canada creek, on both sides. At a place called the Neck, four miles from Oneida lake, we measured seven paces across, and our boat had to go a mile round to meet us on the opposite side. A ludicrous scene took place this morning, which had nearly proved fatal to one of our men, by the name of Capron, who steered Gen. Van Cortland's boat. This fellow is a confounded glutton;—he devoured at a meal more salt pork than two common men, and was of great bulk. In the act of doubling short round a point of land, propelled by a swift current, immediately after gorging himself with pork, &c. and half asleep, a sly limb, which hung over the point, struck him across the breast, and capsized him fairly backwards, with a perpendicular plunge, to the bottom of the creek. As we were directly in the rear of that boat, I distinctly saw this neat exploit. He rose along side of our boat, like a young whale, spouting water from his nostrils and mouth, and splashing the surface with both his hands. We reached him just in time to save him from sinking a second time. He fastened himself on the side of our boat, but as it was impossible to get him in, the other boat came to our aid,—and, between both, we towed him ashore, to the great diversion of our men, who gave him three cheers, as he touched bottom with his feet.

Should the western canals be ever attempted, I am persuaded this creek may be shortened at least one third[.] The lands, on each side of Wood creek, are low, and heavily timbered with beach, maple, oak, elm, lynden, and near the lake, some white pine.

Bears are plenty, and deer scarce. Within two miles of the lake, the river suddenly widened; we took to our oars. Within one mile of the lake, Fish creek falls into Wood creek from the north, about one hundred feet wide. Thence to the lake the creek is bold and spacious. We caught a catfish as large as a common sized cod, measuring five inches between the eyes.

September 13.—This morning we wrote home by a boat coming from the west, loaded with hemp, raised at the south end of the Cayuga lake. *What a glorious acquisition to agriculture and commerce, do these fertile and extensive regions in the west present in anticipation! And what a pity, since the partial hand of nature has nearly completed the water communication from our utmost borders to the Atlantic ocean, that art should not be made subservient, in co-operation with nature, to complete the great work!—which would eventually promote the happiness of millions, and directly, or indirectly, the interest of every man in the state.*

Immediately after breakfast we embarked,—doubled a point of land, and entered the Oneida lake, with our sails filled to a light easterly breeze. The lake opened to our view, like an ocean, spreading before us;—we glided smoothly over its surface, and were delighted with a charming day. On the south is the Oneida reservation, at present inhabited by the Oneida nation of Indians. The country lies flat for eight or ten miles, and then swells into waving hills:—On the north it is generally low, and heavy timbered. Although I have traversed a considerable portion of the United States, in various directions, and have travelled extensively in Europe, yet this is the largest lake I have ever seen.

It is thirty miles long, and, on an average, from five to eight broad. We are now sailing parallel with the *Ontario ocean,* which I hope to see;—and at least enjoy, in delightful anticipation, *the prospect of a free and open water communication from thence, to the Atlantic, via Albany and New-York.*

In giving a stretch to the mind, into the womb of futurity, I saw those fertile regions, bounded west by the Missisippi,—north by the great lakes,—east by the Allegany mountains,—and south by the placid Ohio,—overspread with millions of freemen. Blessed with various climates,—enjoying every variety of soil,—and commanding the boldest inland navigation on this globe; clouded with sails, directing their course towards canals, alive with boats, passing and repassing,—giving and receiving reciprocal benefits from this wonderful country, prolific in such great resources.—Or, perhaps, passage boats, bearing distant travellers on their surface, with horses trotting on their embankments.

In taking this bold flight in imagination, it was impossible to repress a settled conviction, that a grand effort will be made to realize all my dreams,—perhaps delusive.

Near the west end of the lake, are two small islands;—on one of which resides a respectable Frenchman, who came from France a few years since, and has voluntarily sequestered himself from the world, and taken up his solitary abode upon this island, with no other society but his dogs, guns, and library;—yet he appears happy and content.

This lake is extremely turbulent and dangerous,—a small breeze producing a short bobbing sea, in consequence of shoal water.

The batteaumen commonly hug the north shore, as safest, as well as more direct, from point to point; which, on that side, project less into the lake, than on the south side shore. The wind soon rose to a brisk side gale, which occasioned such a dangerous agitation, as obliged us to make a harbour at twelve mile point,—near which we noticed two large bears, walking leisurely along the shore in majestic confidence.

On one of these islands, Dr. Woodruff, of Gansevoort's regiment, has often told me, was a tree of incredible magnitude, now prostrate.

We trolled with our lines, and caught some bass,—and the day concluded with heavy rains, and violent squalls;—in spite of our tents, we were much wet, and half smoked to death.

September 14.—Early this morning, we embarked, and proceeded across the lake, rowing, with a light breeze in our favour. We passed the seven mile islands, (already mentioned,) after stopping to breakfast on the north shore; soon after which the shores suddenly narrowed, and we found ourselves opposite Fort Brewenton, at the entrance of the Onondaga river, which is very shallow.

We landed near the old fort, where we found two families, and a handsome improvement. After refreshing ourselves, under the first Christian roof which had sheltered us in five days, we commenced descending the Onondaga river, with an easy current. The river is generally about three hundred feet wide, nineteen and three quarters of a mile to three river point. In this distance there are three or four pretty long rapids; *these obstructions can easily be removed, and a boat channel formed.*

We observed in many places on this river, small hills of stones,—which, we are told, are thrown up by salmon, where they cast their spawn, to protect them from other fish. These waters abound in catfish, salmon, bass, eel, and corperals, all very fine, and fat. They are caught in eel weires, formed by Indians thus:—Two walls of loose stones are thrown up, obliquely descending across the river, to a point,—where they are taken, at a small opening, in baskets, or eel pots. Salmon are caught at the Oswego falls in the night, by spearing them as they vault up the falls, by the aid of torch light.

The shore along the town of Cicero, is generally low, heavy timbered, and some pine ridges. In the course of the day we were incommoded by rain;—in the evening we pitched our tent at Mr. Moses De Witt's camp, at the Three-River-Point; who is surveying the military lands, (destined as gratuities for the troops of the New-York line, in the late war,) with a company of surveyors.

Here the Onondaga river from the east, and the Seneca river from the west, form a junction in majestic silence, without ripling or confusion. Their waters mingle in a spacious confluence, descending cordially a NW. course, into Lake Ontario, at Fort Oswego, twenty-four miles distant.

Fort Oswego is, at present, garrisoned by a captain's company of British red coats, in violation of the treaty of 1783;—but according to my calculations, this violent, and truly British aggression, will be of short duration. A high spirited, independent nation, will not long brook the insult.

We were visited in our camp, this evening, by several troublesome Indians, of the Onondaga tribe, attended by some young squaws, by whose persuasions we were finally relieved from their pressing importunities for *rum, rum!*—a terrible scourge among this unfortunate race of mortals, who have been cut off in millions, by its excessive use, since America was first peopled by Europeans. There are two or three families settled here. The situation is high, and healthy, fronting the communication with Canada,—and a central point from east, west, and north.

In my view, a large city will arise at this spot, during the ensuing century. *A canal communication, from hence to Oswego harbour, is necessary,—(although the obstacles are great at this point)—to complete the great chain of water communication from Ontario to the Hudson,—admitting the other points I have contemplated, are effected. To effect this part of the navigation will be a work of infinite difficulty, and great expense, as there is about one hundred feet fall to the lake.*

Dr. Belknap's Tour to Oneida

1796

Jeremy Belknap

Jeremy Belknap (1744-1798) and Jedidiah Morse (1761-1826) were both Congregational clergymen and scholars. Belknap was also a productive writer who published a series of essays and stories, along with his book, *History of New-Hampshire*. He conceived of and founded the Massachusetts Historical Society and was a member of the American Philosophical Society and the American Academy of Arts and Sciences. Morse, who published several acclaimed and widely read works on geography, was greatly interested in Indian affairs, which resulted in an appointment by the secretary of war in 1820 to visit and report on the border tribes. From this he proposed, among other things, that a separate state be created for Indian people. Morse was the father of Samuel F. B. Morse, the inventor of the telegraph, and Sidney Edward Morse, a prominent journalist.

Belknap and Morse had been named by the board of commissioners of the Society in Scotland for Propagating Christian Knowledge to visit the Oneida and Stockbridge Indians at their missions in central New York. These were directed by the Reverends Samuel Kirkland and John Sergeant. From information collected during their two-month journey, they produced a report that is in the form of a series of queries regarding the state of the missions and the Indians they served.

The Belknap report was first published in the *Collections of the Massachusetts Historical Society* (1882). It was reprinted in 1955 by the Museum of the American Indian, Heye Foundation. The two portions reproduced here cover the periods June 14 to 20 and June 27 to July 1, 1796. We have omitted footnotes and the marks referring to them that were part of the 1882 edition.

W.A.S.

THIS DAY [June 14] arrived the first division of the Federal troops, consisting of one hundred from West Point, who are going to take possession of the British posts of Oswego and Niagara. They immediately encamped on Pinxter-Hill west of the city, with their artillery in front. They are under the command of Captain Bruff.

I shall omit a particular description of Albany till my return from the Indian country, but cannot help remarking one very shocking sight which fell under my observation this day. I had been on the turret of the prison, which stands in an elevated situation, to take a view of the city, the river, and the surrounding country, which indeed was a very fine prospect. On passing through the prison yard I saw several coffins with human bones, open, partly above ground, and some bones scattered about the yard. These are said to be the coffins and bones of soldiers who died here in the wars of 1756, when a fort stood on this spot, the remains of some part of which are still visible. I inquired why this shocking spectacle was allowed, and was told it was owing to the negligence of the sheriff, whose business it was to have them covered. The hill has been dug away to make a situation for the prison, by which means the coffins were exposed.

Old Fort Orange, built by the Dutch, was situate at the shore of the river near the ferry, on the spot where De Witt's house is built.

Wednesday, June 15. Rode in company with the Lieutenant-Governor and Dr. Morse to the great fall called Cohoes, in Mohawk River. Its appearance from the bridge, about a mile below, is majestic, but more so from an eminence near it on the south side. The extent of the fall is about one thousand feet, if measured by the breadth of the river; but there is a very large projecting rock between the centre and the north shore, which makes the real extent greater. The perpendicular height is said to be sixty feet, and I believe this is not far from the truth. The rock over which the water flows is of the same kind with that which lines each shore,—a black, shelly [shale] rock, soft, and easily broken with any kind of instrument; but where the water runs over it is polished very smooth. At the foot of the fall the water was shallow, and several persons were fishing. We bought of them several very fine pike, which we carried to Lansingburg, and they were boiled for our dinner. These are the first of the kind which I ever tasted, and were very delicate eating. We came down again and crossed the bridge, which is eleven hundred feet long, built on sixteen stone piers. The ascent on the north side from the bridge is very steep, cut through the rock. It was at first thought impracticable to make a road here; but by experiment and perseverance they found it practicable, and even *ploughed* through the rock.

Passed through Waterford, a village at one of the sprouts of the Mohawk, in the township of Halfmoon; then crossed the Hudson to Lansingburg, and there dined. P.M., rode to Troy on a level road, ascended the high land to obtain a good prospect of the river, but could not gain the spot where we were told was the best view; the land had been newly fenced and the roads altered. Came down again, crossed the Hudson at Troy, and returned to the Lieutenant-Governor's seat. By the way saw a seine drawn on the bank of the river, and a sturgeon caught of seven feet in length. They cut his tail, and he bled to death in a few minutes. Evening visited General Schuyler, who proposed to carry me to Skenectada [Schenectady] to-morrow. The country through which we passed this day is well cultivated, chiefly the intervale lands of the Hudson and Mohawk Rivers; large fields of wheat and rye.

High-water at Albany at the same time as at Sandy Hook. The flood is just one hour later at the end of every ten miles up the river. At the end of sixty miles it is high-water in the river at the same time that it is low-water at the city of New York.

The climate of Albany is between the influence of the easterly Atlantic winds and the vapors of the great lakes. The wind is for the most part either north or south, following the course of the river.

Thursday morning, June 16. Rode with General Schuyler in his own carriage to Schenectada,—a town on the banks of the Mohawk, sixteen miles from Albany. The road chiefly pitch-pine land and deep sand. Some farms on the summit land. Dr. Morse went in a private carriage with Mr. Watson to see the glass-works, and came to Schenectada four or five hours after me. I got there at twelve o'clock, and went to see General Schuyler's new boat, in which he invited us to go up the Mohawk with him. He is going to Fort Stanwix to oversee the cutting of a canal from thence to Wood Creek. The boat was then painting, and the weather damp and wet. Before dinner it began to rain, and continued to rain all the P.M. and half the night, which deprived me of the pleasure of seeing this place as much as I intended.

The inhabitants were originally Dutch, as were those of Albany. Their descendants retain their language and manners, especially their fondness for smoking tobacco. General Schuyler carries his pipe, and smokes in his carriage and about the street.

The streets are regular; I think three in number. There are three places of worship, and a college called Union College. Dr. John Smith, brother to Samuel Stanhope Smith, of New Jersey College, is the president. A fine body of meadow adjacent to the town.

In the late war the Oneidas retreated to this place and encamped on the high land above the town, where they remained till the war was over, and then returned to their own country.

In the evening we determined to go in the stage, hoping to come down the river with the general at his return.

Friday, June 17. At five o'clock crossed the Mohawk River at Schenectada in the stage. Foggy, damp, unpleasant weather; roads wet and miry. Sometimes the mist would thicken to a shower, and sometimes be seen hovering on the summits of the hills. Before noon the weather grew clear and hot.

This A.M. we passed by "Guy Park," the seat of Guy Johnson, who married a daughter of Sir William, and succeeded him in the office of superintendent of the Indians, before the late war. It is a tract of one mile square on the north side of the river,—a large, well-finished stone house, which was much damaged and abused during the war. The whole estate now belongs to a Mr. Miles from Connecticut, who keeps an inn. He bought it for £950 New York money,—a mere trifle.

Passed by the first seat of the late Sir William Johnson, consisting of one large stone house and two stone stores and a stone barn, a good garden and orchard. Here Sir William first kept a trading-house and got his estate. He afterward removed further up the river, and four miles from the river, where he built an elegant seat, and lived in the latter part of his life in a very genteel style, and very hospitably, keeping a number of young Indian women about him in quality of concubines, and offering them in that respect to gentlemen who happened to lodge at his house. Many of his children and their descendants are now mixed with the other Indians, and are proud of reckoning their descent from him. The story of Hendrick's dream and Sir William's counter dream is generally believed to be true.

This day we dined at a house (Putnam's) just opposite the mouth of Skoharie [Schoharie] Creek, and, walking into the field as far as the brow of the hill, had a very fine view of the river, the creek, the church on Skoharie, and the site of Fort Hunter, which was built not far from one of the old Mohawk castles. Here was an Episcopal mission established in the reign of Queen Ann, and kept up till the beginning of the late revolution; a set of books and service of plate in the church.

P.M. Rode through a tract of land called Cagnawagha [Caughnawaga], part of the way on the intervale; passed a Dutch church; stopped at Conolly's, on the intervale, under a very steep, rocky hill, which is said to be a nest for rattlesnakes and hawks, and the people on the opposite side call it "Conolly's Rookery." This man came from the county of Down, in Ireland, and this plantation was given him by his brother. He has lived here about ten years. Passed by a projection of the rocky mountain, which is called "Anthony's Nose." Here the road is very narrow between the rock and the river, and goes partly over a wharf built with timber. The water here is said to be very deep. The rock rises in an angle of forty-five degrees. In the side of this mountain is a cavern fourteen by twelve feet square. The stage stopped, and some of the company went up to it. It is said there is another deeper cavity, which they could not find. One of the finest springs runs out of this mountain, a little westward of the "Nose," affording plenty of water to the thirsty traveller. On the opposite side, the mountain approaches the river, and the road is equally narrow as on the north side.

The next tract is called Canajohara [Canajoharie], from a creek which comes in on the south side, above the "Nose," and extends several miles. About five o'clock we crossed the river to the south, and rode under the mountain through a miry road, then on the intervale, then on the upland again, till we came to Ruff's, a dirty, noisy Dutch tavern, where we were obliged to lodge.

The lands through which we passed this day are all highly cultivated, and loaded with a luxuriant growth of wheat, rye, oats, and peas. Hops grow wild along the margin of the river and run over the bushes. There is a fruit called mandrake, very plenty in all this tract and above. It grows on a stalk from twelve to fifteen inches high, under a canopy of leaves. It has a fine smell, and some people are fond of it. Gooseberries and black currants are also very numerous. Some of the gooseberries are half ripe and have prickles on the fruit.

We were eleven in number in the stage this day, and very closely stowed,—four segars [cigars] smoking great part of the time.

At Skenectada met with Hugh White, Esq., from whom Whitestown took its name, and had his company all this and the next day up to Whitestown. He removed from Middletown, in Connecticut, about ten or twelve years ago, bought a large tract of land, and is now a kind of patriarch, having seen the lands advance from a rude wilderness to a well-cultivated and productive country.

Vast quantities of limestone all along the Mohawk River. The stone lies in horizontal laminæ in the quarry, and is easily taken out in any shape or size. The churches and some of the houses are built with it.

Saturday, June 18. Set out early in a *lesser* carriage with the same number as yesterday, except one: very much crowded, but we accommodated each other as well as we could. Breakfasted at Hudson's, at the mouth of East Canada creek,—a good tavern, seated on the same ground where Hendrick lived, the Mohawk sachem who was killed in Johnson's battle, 1755, near Lake George.

It is a beautiful eminence, commanding a pleasant prospect, and here are many apple-trees of at least fifty years old, called Hendrick's orchard. We had some of the cider, and it was excellent. Here was a fort, built by British troops in 1756, called "Fort Hendrick," the rampart, ditch, and glacis of which are visible; and here was found, about four years ago, a golden medal, which it is supposed was the property of some Indian chief. It was worth about seven dollars; had an Indian on one side and emblematic figure on the other. It was sold at Albany to a Mr. Lansing. This place I take to have been the lower Mohawk castle, as marked on Holland's map of New York, though I believe that near Fort Hunter was called the lower castle seventy or eighty years ago.

Before noon we passed by a church and a village which I suppose to have been the upper Mohawk castle marked in said map. This was the residence of Joseph Brandt before the war. There are several graves round the church, enclosed with square cases of wood, like pig-styes. Abundance of apple-trees, and many of a large size. Passed over the Fall mountain, a very fine tract of upland. Dined at a good house, Aldridge's, near Fort Herkemer, on the edge of German Flats. Fort Herkemer was a stone house surrounded with ramparts of earth, which are still visible. General Herkemer was killed during the late war, going to the relief of Fort Stanwix when besieged, 1777.

German Flats have been settled by the high Dutch about seventy years. They have been three times broken up by war. The land is excellent, both on the meadows and hills; very extensive fields of wheat, rye, oats, flax, and peas, but all overrun with charlock, so that they look like fields of mustard, and, being now in bloom, are all yellow. The Germans are not so good husbandmen as the Yankees.

Soon after leaving German Flats the road leaves the river, which we crossed to the north on a bridge. Just on the upper part of the Flats is a church and court-house, in Herkemer County. The county through which we have hitherto passed is Montgomery; both named after general officers belonging to this State, who lost their lives in defence of their country. Passed through thick woods; bad road, but good land,—beech, maple, walnut, and oilnut growth. After sunset, crossed the river to the south on a bridge to old Fort Schuyler, in the lower part of Whites Town.

Here the public stage ends. The house being full of people, and very noisy (there having been a muster of light horse this P.M.), we hired a wagon and proceeded four miles by moonlight to Colonel White's tavern at Whites-borough, where we arrived at half-past ten, much fatigued.

Lord's Day, June 19. Attended public worship, and heard Mr. Dodd preach all day. I had a letter to Mr. Jonas Plat, who kindly invited me to put up at his house, where I now am.

Monday, June 20. Preparing to go on horseback to the Indian settlements. This morning Captain Thomas, of Plymouth, came to see me, on his way to the military lands, and informed me of the death of Mr. Gorham, of Charlestown, two days after we left Boston. In this place is a post-office and printing-office, several very good houses, a wide and level road; and, though it has been inhabited but about ten years, Whitestown contains six parishes, three regiments of militia, and one troop of light horse. The road runs northwest and southeast. This place is situated southeast from Lake Ontario. A northwest wind brings the vapors from that and Lake Erie, and is generally a sign of foul weather. The climate is milder here, both in winter and summer, than in the same parallel to the eastward, and vegetation is more forward in the spring. The great lakes never freeze, and the country about them is warmed by the vapor of them in the winter; so far from the truth is the notion that the great lakes are the cause of our intensely cold northwest winds.

I am now in a region greatly elevated above the level of the ocean. Within twelve miles south of this place is a ridge of hills, not very high, from the south side of which the streams run into the Susquehanna, and twelve miles northwest from hence the streams run into Lake Ontario. The waters here discharge into the Mohawk, which is one mile distant to the north. This region enjoys settled weather more than Albany,—evenings and mornings cool, though the middle of the day be hot.

Distances:

—from Boston to Albany	180	miles.
to Skenectada	16	"
to Canajohara	40	"
to old Fort Schuyler	42	"
to Whitesboroough	4	"
	282	miles.
to Paris (Clinton settle[t])	7	"
to Mr. Kirkland's	1	"
to New Stockbridge	12	"
to Oneida village	6	"
The extent of our journey	308	miles.
Rode in the stage, going and returning	564	"
Rode on horseback, going and returning	52	"
	616	miles.

[June 21-June 26 omitted]

Monday, June 27. We had some expectation of going to Fort Stanwix, twelve miles distant to the northwest, and thence going down the Mohawk with General Schuyler, in his covered boat, to Schenectada. We this day received a letter from the General, informing us that his boat was gone down to fetch the engineer and his family, that he should be glad to see us at Fort Stanwix and bring us down by water to old Fort Schuyler, where he should stay four or five days, and that he would send us down by the first boat that he could detain. Considering that we should be delayed perhaps a whole week here, and considering also that this is a fever-and-ague country, that the disorder has begun rather earlier than usual, that Mr. Plat's wife (where I lodge) has it, and that General Schuyler himself is not free from it,—as we heard by Mr. Fish, of New Jersey, who saw him this morning,—we concluded it was best for us to go down by the stage, as we came up. After dining with Mr. Breeze, and waiting for the stage till six o'clock, we set off and came down this P.M. to old Fort Schuyler, and lodged at Mr. House's inn.

Tuesday, June 28. Rose at four. Waited till a quarter past five for the stage and company, then set off toward home. Three miles from old Fort Schuyler we met the first detachment of the troops destined for Oswego. They appeared to be about sixty or seventy in number, in a uniform of blue and red. A wagon followed containing their tents and baggage. After riding a few miles we met a boy on horseback, who inquired of us where we met the troops. We answered him, but knew not the reason of his asking till we got to Aldridge's. The driver knew him to be Aldridge's boy. This morning cloudy and rainy. In a shower we met two Dutch girls walking barefoot, and carrying their shoes in their hands,—an eminent instance of Dutch economy.

After fasting six hours and riding seventeen miles through very bad road, at ten A.M. we got some very welcome breakfast at Aldridge's (German Flats). Here we found the boats containing the baggage, ammunition, and stores of the troops, with the commanding officer, Captain Bruff, and the agent or purveyor, Judge Glen. The preceding afternoon they had had a quarrel with the Dutch boatmen who navigated the batteaux in which were the stores. They would have their own way to go or stop when and where they pleased, and it is as hard to turn a Dutchman as a mule out of his way. The captain could not speak their language; but he wanted the boats to be paraded *en militaire,* and guarded by night. (N.B. They had been six days on the water from Schenectada.) This bred a quarrel. The Captain fired his piece at them, and they came at him with the poles with which they set the boats against the stream. A conflict might have ensued had not the Captain's wife and daughter by their cries and entreaties prevailed. The arrival of the purveyor, soon after,—who, being a Dutchman, could speak to them in their own tongue,—helped to pacify the boatmen. But, to be sure of a superiority, the Captain had despatched Aldridge's boy (whom we met) to call back part of the troops, who had at least seventeen miles to travel in a retrograde progression to

come to the assistance of their commander. Both he and the Judge appeared to
be in great agitation, full of words, and not destitute of profaneness.

Dined this day at Indian Castle, and got some more of Hendrick's cider, which
is excellent. Lodged at Dwight's, a mile below the house where the stage puts up.
N.B. Dwight told me that the root called wake-robin is an effectual cure for the
poison of bushes and plants which usually affect the skin. It is bruised with milk,
and applied externally. In the night a heavy thunder-shower. The meadow was
full of fire-flies, and, the extent being great and the house high above it, I had a
singular amusement the preceding evening in viewing the incessant glimmering
of ten thousand of these insects, with now and then a flash of lightning to assist
the illumination.

Wednesday, June 29. Dr. Morse not well. Rode six miles to Conolly's, and
there breakfasted; but he ate nothing. Rode eleven miles more, and he was so ill
that we stopped at Putnam's,—a clean Dutch house opposite Schoharie Creek
and Fort Hunter,—and let the stage go on, the driver promising to return to-
morrow on purpose to fetch us, if he should be able to proceed. Employed a Dr.
Sanford as physician to Dr. Morse, and the good man and woman of the house
nursed him as tenderly as if he had been their own child. His disorder was chol-
era morbus. He was very ill all day and evening. At night got some rest by the
help of anodyne, and in the morning was better.

All the P.M. and A.M. of next day, Thursday, June 30, employed myself in
reading Wheelock's narratives, which I carried in my trunk; and observing the
warm, enthusiastic manner in which the business of converting Indians has been
conducted, and the changes which appeared in the conduct of the persons concerned when the ardor abated. *Tempora mutantur, &c.* About twelve o'clock the
extra stage came; and, Dr. M. being somewhat recovered, we set out for
Schenectada, twenty-one miles.

Stopped by the way at Miles's (formerly Guy Johnson's house); there met a Dr.
Sweet, who fell into conversation, and offered to conduct us to the *painted rock,*
which he said was about two miles down the river. Took him up in the carriage
and rode with him two miles. Then he and I left the carriage to search for the
rock. This ramble took up forty minutes, and I walked about two miles, partly
through woods and partly through fields. The rock is on the north bank of the
Mohawk, fifteen miles above Skenectada. It is a perpendicular ledge of limestone, with a pretty smooth surface and about twenty feet high. On the upper
part—which is easily accessible, the laminæ projecting in various
places—appear the remains of some red paint, which has been in the same situation for eighteen or twenty years. Imagination may conceive the paint to resemble almost any thing; but judgment cannot decide without the help of testimony.
The tradition is that it was painted by the Indians in memory of some canoes of
Indians who went thence to war, and never returned; that the painting represented canoes and men in them; and that this painting is frequently *renewed* to
preserve the memory of the event. Some add that the renewal is performed in the
night, or by some *invisible* hand. The fact is that there is a rock with some appearance of red paint, that the paint has been in some measure defended from the

weather by a projection of the rock *over* it, and that the place is easily accessible by similar projections *under* it. This is all that can be said with any certainty. As to the frequent renewal of the paint, &c., I was assured by Dr. Sweet that he had known it to be in the same condition as we saw it for eighteen years past; and a man whom we took as a pilot, who appeared to be about twenty-five years old, said it always looked just so since his remembrance.

We had a pleasant ride to Schenectada, and got there just at sun-set. This village is not a very *sightly* place either from a distance or when you are in it. The principal business is boat-building, for which there is a great call by reason of the continual increase of transportation on the Mohawk River for one hundred miles. Evening visited Mr. Duane. Lodged at Plat's.

Friday, July 1. Breakfasted with Rev. Dr. John Smith, president of the college here. It has a fund of fourteen thousand pounds, York currency; contains forty students. Part of the fund is to be applied toward the erection of a public building for college exercises, library, apparatus, &c.; but the scholars are not to live in barracks nor eat in commons. The classes are distinguished by different-colored ribbons worn over their shoulders in the form of sashes. The name of the institution is Union College. It began last fall. By the report of the regents, March, 1797, the property of this college is stated to be $42,422.60, and 1,604 acres of land. After breakfast rode sixteen miles to Albany, the wind driving the dust before us, so that we were fairly involved in a cloud the whole way. Stopped at McKean's, five miles from Albany, where we saw the spring-head of the projected aqueduct for the city. The water is very pure and cool, and there seems to be a good supply.

By reason of our detention at Johnstown, my stay in Albany will be so short that I shall not have time to visit every part. The old Dutch church is an object of curiosity without. Its appearance is more like a powder magazine than a place of worship. It is of stone, with a monstrous, high, pitched roof, in a pyramidal form, with a little cupola and bell. It is eighty years old, and was built over an older church in which divine service was performed all the time that the present one was building, so that they omitted but one Sunday. This is the tradition, and I was assured of the truth of it by Lietuenant-Governor Rensselaer, with whom I dined this day. There is nothing elegant in any of the public buildings of this city. The jail is, I think, the most sightly of them and the newest. Some of the streets are very narrow; but the new ones, particularly Watervliet, is wide and well paved. State Street is also wide; the old Dutch church is at the lower end, and the English church at the upper end. There is also a Presbyterian meeting-house; but the clergyman, McDonald, is silenced, . . . and has set up a bookstore. This man had a great share of influence whilst his wickedness was unknown; but he is now treated with as much disrespect as he deserves. It was he who wrote the letters to Scotland which were the occasion of our mission into these parts. There is also a Methodist church, a German Calvinist, and a German Lutheran,—six in all.

The old fur-traders in this city look very pleasant this day, on the occasion of the arrival of about twenty wagons loaded with furs from the northward. A renewal of this gainful business is anticipated; and this is one effect of peace and friendship with Great Britain, notwithstanding all the clamor that has been raised about the treaty.

The mayor of this city, Abraham Yates, died yesterday, and is to be buried tomorrow, but I cannot stay to see the funeral. It is said the whole city is invited to attend, and here none go to a funeral but those who are invited. The bell rings as ours do for fire. To a wedding everybody goes without invitation, and the married couple keep open doors for two or three days. The boys assemble round the door and expect cookies, *i. e.*, cakes, to be thrown out to them.

At Albany I parted with my companion, Dr. Morse, he intending to go down the river to New York next week. Lodged this night at Mr. Elkanah Watson's. Was much amused with the sound of cow-bells; all the cows of the city passing by his house on their return from pasture. At Skenectada the cows parade in the streets by night, and make dirty work before the doors. The whole town is a perfect cow-yard.

Visit to the Falls of Niagara
1800
John Maude

This brief narrative is part of a larger traveler's journal written by John Maude in 1800. Maude, an Englishman, traveled extensively in America from 1793 to 1803. Unlike many aristocratic English travelers, Maude was not inclined to ridicule what he saw. What comes through are the experiences of a curious and pleasant man, who was clearly enjoying himself.

Maude's journal was first published in London in 1826. An anonymous editor supplied footnotes containing largely superfluous information taken from another book cited as "Morse, 2ⁿᵈ edition, 1797." The footnotes have been eliminated here. In a few places new clarifications have been inserted in brackets.

The Hudson Valley portion of Maude's journal has been reproduced by van Zandt (1971), and the whole journal was reprinted by Lost Cause Press of Louisville in 1980. The portion reproduced here covers only Maude's travel from Albany up the Mohawk to Oneida Castle. Take note of Maude's references to canals along the Mohawk Valley. He passed through long before construction of the Erie Canal. However, several small canals had been built around major obstructions in the river by 1800, and there was brisk traffic in Durham boats carrying goods up and down this rare natural avenue for east-west travel in the new United States.

D.R.S.

Wednesday, July 2d.

4½ A.M. Started in the Stage for Utica; passed Miss Jay, the Governor's daughter, in the public stage waggon; passed General Oothout driving his own waggon.

7½ A.M. Schenectady, (Indian Name, signifying End-of-the-Woods) sixteen miles; Brownall's and Beal's Inn; breakfast—loin of veal, ham, strawberries, cheese, coffee, tea, tarts, preserved apples, &c. &c. Drove some miles through rich and fertile Flats on the banks of the Mohawk, worth one hundred and twenty-five dollars and upwards per acre; nineteen miles. Boats poling up the

Rapids, some difficulty in getting over them; water low; [Durham] boats draw about two feet.

Noon. Dine at Warren-Bush, or Tripe-Hill, thirty-three miles.

5 P.M. Canajoharee [Canajoharie], (Indian Name, signifying the Boiling Pot,) fifty-five miles. Mr. Elias Kane, fellow passenger, introduced me here to his brother Archibald, who has a well furnished Store, and carries on a very extensive business. Archibald has been nearly five years in partnership with his brother James, settled in Albany, who have in that time made a clear profit of fifty thousand dollars each; two other brothers are settled in New York, and one at Fort Anne, near Lake George.

A. and J. Kane took, in the course of last Fall and Winter, thirty-four thousand bushels of Wheat, which were bought on an average at one dollar and fifty cents per bushel, fifty-one thousand dollars, and sold at New York for one dollar and ninety-three and three quarters cents, sixty-five thousand eight hundred and seventy-five dollars. They took, also, in Potash two thousand five hundred barrels, worth on an average, twenty-five dollars per barrel, sixty-two thousand five hundred dollars. So that in these two ready money articles alone, they turned over upwards of one hundred and twenty thousand dollars.

A large family is no burthen in America; the prosperity of the K----'s is owing, in a great measure, to their number; it affords them an opportunity of playing into each others hands.

Mr. Archibald Kane kindly insisted on my passing the evening and taking a bed at his house, to which invitation I readily yielded. While we were engaged with a bottle of Claret, my servant was jockeying for a horse; the bargain was soon made, and I paid down the money first demanded, sixty-two dollars and fifty cents.

Scrub Pine and Oak barrens from Albany to Schenectady; then rich Flats on the Mohawk; Red and Ground Squirrels; Yellow and Black Birds, Robins, Crows, a Sea-Gull and Wild Ducks. Very cold Morning; pleasant day. Walked a few miles, by getting start whilst the horses were changing.

Thursday, July 3d.

Mr. A. Kane had breakfast for us at 5½ A.M.

6½ A.M. Started, Mr. K. and self, on horseback. I had brought saddles and bridles with me from New York, and had taken my place in the Stage no further than Canajoharee, having some expectation that I should buy a Horse there; my servant went on in the stage. Road along the banks of the Mohawk. Morning very foggy; passed Stage whilst breakfasting at Hudson's Indian Castle, sixty-seven miles. Fall-Hill, seventy-three miles, very steep; this declivity in the ground makes the Little-Falls of the Mohawk, which interruption in the Navigation is obviated by a [1795] Canal.

Noon. German-Flats, Aldridge's Tavern, eighty miles; here found the Stage again which had repassed us. Dined with the passengers. No better Land than these Flats; worth sixty dollars per acre; produce Wheat thirty bushels: and Maize seventy-five bushels per acre.

5 P.M. Proceeded; new Road very bad; the Stage wisely took the North side of the River.

8 P.M. Utica. (Fort Schuyler) ninety-six miles. Schwartz's Hotel, excellent house, miserably kept. Built by Boon and Lincklaen, (agents for the Holland Company,) the proprietors of a considerable number of the adjoining building lots; those East of these are the property of the Bleeker Family, on which the principal part of the present town is built—built too on short leases of fourteen years, after which the houses become the property of the owners of the soil, to the certain loss and probable ruin of the present Residents.

Utica is in the Township of Whitestown, and contains about sixty houses. No *genteel* family save Colonel Walker's, and he resides at a small distance east of the Town.

The great Genesee Road turns off at this place. An Act has lately passed for making it a Turnpike Road to Geneva and Canadarqua [Canandaigua], a distance of one hundred miles and upwards. The expense is estimated at one thousand dollars per mile; the road to be four rods in width. The Inhabitants of Utica subscribed to finish the first mile; they formed twenty Shares of fifty dollars each; these Shares they afterwards sold to Colonel Walker and Mr. Post, for forty-four cents the dollar, who have finished the first mile: thirty miles is expected to be finished before the Winter sets in.

Bridge here over the Mohawk, the River narrow, clear, and shallow; no fish; seven boats at the Wharf; heard a bullfrog; groves of sugar maple, a tree very common here.

Paid thirty dollars for a horse, which Lewis had bought before my arrival. Warm day.

Friday, July 4th

Noon; mounted our horses; passed Inman's.

1 P.M. Arrived at Whitestown; one hundred miles; White's Tavern; bad house; introduced to Mr. Fitzpatrick. About forty houses; genteel neighbourhood; excellent land; has produced, per acre, ninety bushels of marketable shelled Corn, (maize) exclusive of inferior of Hog-Corn, and of Wheat, about thirty-five bushels: three acres in the town sold, in one lot, four years ago, for three hundred and thirty-two dollars and fifty cents.

Observed some handsome Sugar Orchards; introduced by Kane to Mr. and Mrs. Platt, with whom took tea; Mr. P. a pleasant sensible young man, a correspondent of my friend Harper, member of Congress for South Carolina. Mrs. P. was a Miss Livingston, from Poughkeepsie. Saw a dwarf of eighteen years of age, not three feet in height. Very warm day, especially from 5 to 7 P.M. Some musquitoes.

Saturday, July 5th.

Started 5½ A.M. Woods; few Settlements.

8 A.M. Rome; (Fort Stanwix) White's Tavern, one hundred and twelve miles. Settled within six years; forty houses; situated midway between the heads of navigation of the Mohawk and Wood-Creek, on the Canal uniting those waters. Canal nearly two miles in length; two locks, one at each end; cost seventy-five thousand dollars; lock dues from two to four dollars agreeable to the load; much less expense and trouble than attended the portage, yet boatmen much dissatisfied. August 1st, Capt. Williamson informed me, that these lock dues were far from being so moderate as here mentioned;—that every bushel of wheat paid ten cents; of salt, twelve and a half cents; and a barrel of flour, fifty cents.

Visited the Canal in its whole length; water very low in the Mohawk and Wood-Creek; has sensibly decreased since the first settlement of the Country, which causes this navigation to become more and more tedious and laborious, insomuch that it is expected to be neglected as soon as the Turnpike Road is finished from Utica to Geneva and Canadarqua. Paid also a visit to Fort Stanwix and Blockhouse. The Mohawk is not here above ten or fifteen yards across, and two or three feet deep. Wood-Creek is not above six, seven, or eight feet in width at the head of navigation, and from twelve to eighteen inches in depth. As the boats draw two feet of water, they, during the present scarcity require every now and then a lock-full from the Canal, to assist in ascending and descending Wood-Creek. There is another route by which the Wood-Creek, the Canal, and the Mohawk, as far as Utica, may be avoided; it is from the Oneida Lake, to ascend Oneida Creek about three miles, from whence a road will require making to Oneida Castle, a distance of about three miles more, when you fall in with the Turnpike-Road within twenty miles of Utica. The advantage of this Route is that you substitute a good land for a bad water carriage, and save two thirds of the distance. You save also much time, and probably will not find it more expensive. Had salmon for dinner, caught in Wood-Creek.

4½ P.M. Proceeded.

7 P.M. One hundred and twenty miles; Baited at Langon's; small log hut; one hundred and twenty-six miles; Oneida mills;—good mills, built for the Oneida Indians.

9 P.M. One hundred and twenty-seven miles. Passed through Oneida Castle; six hundred Oneida Indians; a reservation of twelve miles square; cannot dispose of it. No bargain with those Indians, by individuals, good in law. Kane held a conversation with a young Squaw, and afterwards with an Indian youth, in their own tongue. The latter lived in a boarded house, the only one I saw in the Castle. At this Castle we fell in with the main Genesee Road.

10 P.M. Wemps's Tavern, one hundred and thirty one miles; good, civil, clean. Met here a Mr. Stewart. Road tolerable for two or three miles; then execrable to Oneida Mills; thence, very good to Wemps's. Struck into the Oneida Woods on leaving the Canal; new road; bogs every other step; little cleared land the whole route, (owing to its belonging principally to the Indians) land, however, excel-

lent. The Timber principally Beech and Sugar Maple. Birds the Whip-Poor-Will and the Hoot-Owl. Very warm day; full moon at 8 P.M. or could not have proceeded.

On a Mission Through the Mohawk and Black River Country, in the Year 1802

1802

John Taylor

Taylor was a missionary who was engaged by the Missionary Society of Hamp-shire County, Massachusetts, to assess the need for missionaries in northeastern New York. Hampshire County at that time comprised a much larger fraction of western Massachusetts than it does currently. The society was apparently not formally incorporated until February 1804 (Lockwood et al. 1926:1:372). There is no mention of Taylor on the list of officers.

This narrative comes from his journal of 1802 (Taylor 1849-1851:684-690). Taylor began his journey from his home in Deerfield on July 20, 1802. He reached the Mohawk Valley in only three days. He subsequently went all the way to Lake Ontario by way of Oneida Lake and the Black River before returning by a shorter route around the southern flank of the Adirondacks. He reached his home on October 12, 1802.

We have changed Taylor's abbreviations to complete English words where doing so makes his meanings clearer. Some abbreviations that are still common have been left as he wrote them.

D.R.S.

General Remarks

JULY 21*st* 1802.—I this day passed thro' the affecting scene of parting with my family, for the term of three months, to journey into the Northern counties of New-York, and to perform the duties of a missionary. May I and my family en-joy divine protection; and may the pleasure of meeting my family and people again, be greater than the sorrow of parting with them.

I expected to have obtained some information respecting the northern country from the Revd Mr Field of Cherlamont, but was disappointed, as he was not at home. Proceeded from Cherlamont, on the turnpike, over Housic mountain. The land on the mountain appeared to be good. I am not a little surprised that it has not been settled. When I came to the west side of the mountain, I found before I began to descend the most sublime prospect I had ever seen. The high moun-

362

tains, which present on all sides, apparently locking in with each other,—the scattered fields upon those mountains—the blooming appearance of vegetation—and the valleys below filled with houses—appearing to be sunk so low, as to be almost lost, was a prospect that led me into a train of agreeable and elevated reflections. Having passed down the mountain I came into the town of Adams, which is remarkable for limestone. 5 miles from Adams is Williamstown—The College consists of about 90 scholars—a president and 4 tutors. There are 2 eligant buildings—standing on elevated ground about 40 rods from each other. I put up with Dr Fitch—a valuable man—and has an agreeable family.

22^d—Left Williamstown about 8 o'clock—took the road to Albany across the mountains, on the ground of the proposed turnpike. After passing a high mountain, came into a valley, and into the town of Petersburgh, in the state of N. York. This town contains about 2900 inhabitants. There are 2 chhs. of Pedobaptists, and one of Saturday baptists. After passing in this valley about 3 miles, I rose another mountain, and for 10 miles found a most intolerable road. Passing off this stony and hard ground, I came down into Greenbush, a level country—for about 4 miles from the mountains the soil appears to be good—from thence to the river it is too sandy.

ALBANY, *July* 23, *at Trobridge's.*—At 11 o'clock left Albany. From Albany to Schenectada is a barren sandy plain—the road very bad in consequence of sand—but 3 or 4 houses in the whole 17 miles. Schenectada makes a singular appearance, being built in the old Dutch form—houses in general but one story, or a story and half, and standing endwise to the street. Its local situation is excellent, standing upon the south bank of the Mohawk—and there appears in every [thing] a simplicity, and neatness that is very pleasing.

Passed the Mohawk at Schenectada—found an excellent turnpike for about ten miles. Some very good meadow on the left. The country in general level. Soil, except in the meadows, a hard gravel, not very productive. Fields of grain, however, appear good. People in the midst of harvest. After about 10 miles from Schenectada, the country becomes more hilly. As we pass up the river into Montgomery county, we find for several miles but little intervale; what there is, appears to be good. On Tripe's, or Tribe's hill, about 20 miles above Schenectady, we have the prospect of a few hundred acres of excellent meadow, which was formerly the seat of the famous Hendrick, the sachem of the Mohawks. The ancient and elegant seat of Sir William Johnson I passed about 4 miles back. This is commonly called the *Old fort.* On Tribe's hill, I had great satisfaction and pleasure of meeting a Mr Plum, an old acquaintance from Westfield, and was treated with great kindness in his family—tarried with him until Monday the 25th; received correct and considerable intelligence from him respecting the country—especially in Montgomery county.

There is an apple tree on this hill, which I am credibly informed produces apples without a core or seeds. There is also in this town, what is called by the people the Jerusalem thorn. There is also a singular production called mandrakes—of which I have taken a rough drawing.

This place appears to be a perfect Babel, as to language: But very few of the people, I believe, would be able to pronounce Shibboleth. The articulation even of New-England people, is injured by their being intermingled with the Dutch, Irish, and Scotch. The character of the Dutch people, even on first acquaintance, appears to be that of kindness and justice. As to religion, they know but little about it—and are extremely superstitious. They are influenced very much by dreams, and apparitions. The most intelligent of them seem to be under the influence of fear from that cause. The High Dutch have some singular customs with regard to their dead. When a person dies, nothing will influence the connections, nor any other person, unless essentially necessary, to touch the body. When the funeral is appointed, none attend but such as are invited. When the corpse is placed in the street, a tune is sung by a choir of singers appointed for the purpose—and continue singing until they arrive at the grave; and after the body is deposited, they have some remarks made—return to the house, and in general get drunk. 12 men are bearers—or carriers—and they have no relief. No will is opened, nor debt paid, under 6 weeks from the time of death.

July 26th.—Left the river about noon, and turned to the North. Preached the afternoon to a body of people in the north-west part of the town of Amsterdam—people kind and friendly; soil good—very productive in wheat;—a silicious earth.

27th.—Left Amsterdam, and travelled 5 miles to Johnstown, a very pleasant village—containing one Dutch presbyterian chh. and an Episcopalian. The village is tolerably well built. It is a county town—lies about 4 miles from the River, and contains about 600 inhabitants. In this town there is a jail, court-house and an academy. About 3/4^{ths} of a mile from the centre of the town, we find the buildings erected by Sir William Johnson. After leaving this town, I passed about 10 miles in a heavy timbered country, with but few inhabitants. The soil, however, appears to be in general excellent—the country is a little more uneven than it is back in Amsterdam. After travelling about 10 miles in a tolerable road, I came to Stonearabe [Stone Arabia] (or Robby as the Dutch pronounce it.) This is a parish of Palatine, and is composed principally of High Dutch, or Germans. Passing on 4 miles, came upon the river in another parish of Palatine—a snug little village, with a handsome stone chh. Having travelled a number of miles back of the river, I find that there is a great similarity in the soil, but some difference in the timber. From Johnstown to Stonearabia, the timber is beech and maple, with some hemlock. In Stonearabia the timber is walnut, and butternut. The fields of wheat are numerous, and the crop in general is excellent. In every thing but wheat, the husbandry appears to be bad. The land for Indian corn, it is evident from appearance, is not properly plowed—they plow very shallow. Neither is the corn tended—it is in general full of weeds and grass, and looks miserably. Rie is large. Flax does not appear to be good—whether this is owing to the season or the soil, I know not. Pease appear to flourish—so do oats; but the soil, I believe, is too hard, and clayey for Potatoes—they look very sickly.

I perceive, as yet, but one great defect in the morals of the people—they are too much addicted to drink.

The back part of the County of Montgomery consists of some pine plains; but in general the lumber is beach and maple. A good grass and wheat country. Sacondaga creek heads in Mayfield—runs N. E. and empties into a branch of North river, about 20 or 30 miles above Halfmoon.

Manheim, 8 miles from the Stone chh. in Palatine. This town is about 7 miles square. One Dutch Reformed chh. Vacant. Mr Dysling supplies about half the time in this town and half in Palatine: a Swiss, and a good character, and a man of learning. Passing on from Manheim, we find the mountains drawing to a point, upon the 2 sides of the river. When we come to the river, there is only a narrow pass for about 3/4^{ths} of a mile between the river and the foot of the rocks. When we come to the Falls the scene which presents is sublime. We now enter Herkimer county—and a small village of the town of Herkimer, called Little Falls, by which the canals pass, which were constructed in '95. The length of the canal is 3/4^{ths} of a mile. There are 6 locks. The appearance of the falls is sublime. The village is built upon a ledge of rock. It promises fair to be a place of business as to trade, as all produce of the Royal grants will naturally be brought here to be shipped. They have a new and beautiful meeting-house, standing about 40 rods back on the hill, built in the form of an octagon. I am now, July 27th, about 30 rods from fall mountain on the south. Between this and the mountain is the Mohawk, and a bridge over it, in length about 16 rods. Between this and the bridge is the canal. On the right, about 40 rods are the falls, or one bar of the falls in full view. The falls extend about 3/4^{ths} of a mile. Upon the whole, this place is the most romantic of any I ever saw; and the objects are such as to excite sublime ideas in a reflecting mind. From the appearance of the rocks, and fragments of rocks where the town is built, it is, I think, demonstrably evident, that the waters of the Mohawk, in passing over that fall, were 80 or 90 feet higher in some early period than they are now. The Rocks even an hundred feet perpendicular above the present high water mark, are worn in the same manner as those over which the river passes. The rocks are not only worn by the descent of the water, but in the flat rocks are many round holes worn by the whirling of stones—some even 5 feet deep and 20 inches over. If these effects were produced by the water, as I have no doubt they were, then it follows as a necessary consequence, that the flats above, and all the low lands for considerable extent of country, were covered with water, and that here was a lake—but the water having lowered its bed, laid the lands above dry.

28th—About the middle of the afternoon I left the Little Falls, and turned 8 miles North in the town of Fairfield. Fairfield is, in general, on high land; a little part of it, thro' which I passed is broken ground. It is, however, taken together, an excellent township. It is worthy of remark, that these highlands, in this part of the world, which at a distance appear to be mountains, when you approach them, dwindle into mere gradual and gentle ascents; and there is but a mere trifle of unprofitable land to be found in the country. There is a great similarity in the nature of the soil—it is a loam with a little sand—mingled with a considerable quantity of white clay. In passing to the North from Fairfield to Norway—6 miles—I find that the hills increase in magnitude, but none so steep but that they may be tilled. Norway is an excellent township. But of this town and the town in this vicinity, I shall give a further description when I return to them.

July 29*th*—Left Norway for Utica, about 22 miles to the south-west. In passing out of this town, I saw a daughter of M*r* Joshua Sweet—appears to be comfortably situated. About 3 miles from the center of Norway, we go down from the uplands, and come upon White Creek, a very useful stream. Here the hills are rugged. We rise from the creek again into uplands—pass on a few miles, and go down upon Canada creek. This is a river a little larger than that of Deerfield. After crossing the river. We begin to rise a mountain which is patent land. We go on 10 miles thro' this mountain, which is the highest in those parts—but all good passable land. At the foot of this mountain, we enter into a corner of the town of Skyler. From thence we go about 6 miles to the river road—pass a few miles in Deerfield, and pass the Mohawk in Utica. This is a very pleasant and beautiful vilage; but it is filled with a great quantity of people of all nations and religions. I put up at M*r* Baggs'—saw the lady of the Hon. C. Phelps Esq*r* on her way from Canadaigua to Suffield, in a common Dutch waggon, covered with tow cloth. My health is good—something wearied with travelling. Determined to visit Norway, on my return home.

30*th*—From Utica to Whitesborough, is 4 miles—pleasant riding. Whitesborough is not so large and flourishing a place as I expected to find. It is, however, a pleasant village. Dined at D*r* Mosley's. In the afternoon rode out 9 miles to Clinton. This is a flourishing place. The land is the best I have seen since I left home, and is the best tilled. The people are principally from Connecticut. On my way to this town, saw Capt. Mitchel, and his daughter who married a Rice. Meeting with Mitchel and his family was a pleasing scene. In all this part of the country there is no waste land; and indeed the original Whitestown—appears to be the garden of the world. Was treated with the greatest kindness and attention in Capt. Mitchel's family—which, as far as I am able to judge, is in a good situation. His farm is now in the bloom, and its appearance is pleasing.

31*st*—Parted with my good friend Mitchel and his family—returned back to Whitesborough—spent the afternoon very agreeably and profitably with M*r* Dodd, the minister. The situation and buildings of Whitesborough may be seen in my rough draught.

August 1*st*, *Sunday.*—Preached for M*r* Dodd, in a schoolhouse. Audience devout, and attentive—a great mixture of people, as respects nations, and religions.

Afternoon at Utica—put up with Lawyer Clark from Lebanon. There is but a handful of people in this [place] who have much regard for preaching, or for any thing but the world. 8 years last spring there were but 2 houses in the present town plot. There is now above 90—Lodge at Baggs'.

August 2*d*.—Started for Floid—rode 11 miles to a Capt. Rice's. Preached in the evening. I know not what remarks to make upon the inhabitants of this town—a half a dozen excepted, they seem to be the fag-end of man in disorder, and confusion of all kinds. The baptists have some regularity; but the methodists are producing the scenes which are transpiring in Kentucky. Women here methodists, pray in their families instead of the men—and with such strength of lungs as to be distinctly heard by their neighbors. I had almost as many nations, sects, and religions present to hear me preach, as Peter had on the day of Pentacost. In this town there is an excellent character, Esqr Dier—he tells me that Clinton has given commissions to 5 men for Justices, in this place—one of whom is a renegade Irishman, without character and without prayer; and the other has no bible in his house. In fact, this is a most miserable place,—as to inhabitants. The land is good—too good for such inhabitants.

3^d and 4th.—At Trenton. This town is a part of the Holland Patent. Boon's settlement is within the circle of this town. The land is tolerable—some of it very good—well watered—about 130 voters.

—Found on some of as high land as any in the town, rocks and stones containing sea shells petrified into stone, and forming parts of stones. This is another evidence that the Mohawk at the Little Falls was once obstructed by the rocks—and yet the lands in this town were a part of a large lake. Timer—beech, maple, ash, birch, and bass.

5th, 6th, 7th, 8th, 9th, & 10th—STEUBEN. This patent is on the height of land between the Mohawk and the Black river—some of the headwaters of both are in this town. Standing on a hill, near the centre of the town, we have an extensive prospect on 3 sides;—to the N. W., about 35 miles, we see the Oneida Lake—south we see the settlements of New Hartford and Clinton—Clinton Academy is in full view. We can here see the tops of the Catskill mountains—S. E. & S. W. the tops. It is said that upon the tops of the trees Ontario is in sight. Upon this height of land, I found in a number of places sea shells which form constituent parts of rocks and stones. This land is so high that this singular fact cannot be accounted for by supposing that the rocks at the Little Falls, were once united; for this land is evidently much higher than the mountain at that place. The face of the country is here rough and uncouth; something stony—yet no hills so steep as to render any land useless. Between this and Clinton is about 4 miles of low flat land—very rich, and heavy timbered. Unsettled; and, indeed, but a very little part of this county is settled. A considerable part of the lands which are settled, are to hire on lease—the inhabitants have not the right of soil. 10$ is the common price for 100 acres annual rent; but most of these leases are for perpetuity. About 1-3^d of the people in Steuben are Welsh—who are industrious and prudent beyond all example. I am now at the house of the first settler who came into the town, Esqr Siser's.

Here I find the grave of the once active and enterprising STEUBEN. He lies in a swamp, under a Hemlock, with a bier standing over the grave, and a few rough boards nailed to some trees to keep the cattle off. Alas! what is man! that the great STEUBEN should be suffered to lie in such a place—and without a decent monument.

A few rods from this swamp, we find the place of his former residence—of which I have taken a rough drawing. This is a very healthful situation. The house faces the south—and there is a gradual descent for about 80 rods, and an opening about 50 rods wide. The seat of this great man was not indeed a palace, nor what we should suppose would afford contentment to the mind of an enterprising nobleman: It consists of 2 log houses—one at the end of the other—containing in the whole 3 rooms—unsealed. It is, however, a decent loghouse. The Baron died in a fit of numb palsy.

Crops in this town much injured by rust. Winter wheat is open to winter kill—the lands, though high, are very wet. There is, however, some low, rich land, of the nature of marsh. The prospect on the height of land in this town is extensive.

WESTERN, *Wednesday,* 11*th.*—In passing from Steuben west, we descend for about 2 miles—and come to a branch of the Mohawk—and pass a tract of excellent land—heavy timbered, and well watered. In about 2 miles from this Eastern settlement in this town, we come to another settlement, in which we find Gen. Floyd, one of the signers of Independence, and one of the members of Congress during the whole of the American war with great britain. He is about 70 years of age—retains in full his powers of mind. He spends the summers in this place, and the winters on his seat on Long Island. He is a gentleman of immense property: and is now building an elegant seat upon the banks of the Mohawk.

It is incredible how thick this part of the world is settled—and what progress is making in opening the wilderness and turning it into a fruitful plain. The land in this town is most excellent—crops are rich. The same evil operates here, however, as in many parts of this country—the lands are most of them leased. This must necessarily operate to debase the minds and destroy the enterprise of the settlers—altho' the rent is small—only /9 an acre; yet if men do not possess the right of soil, they never will nor can feel independent. And what is as great an evil, they will always be under the influence of their landlords. Lodged at Gen. Floyd's—on the night of the 12th—Thursday.

Friday, 13*th.*—Passed on 4 miles to the west to a settlement on the bend of the Mohawk—a flat and rich country—land here a black loam;—it is a meadow, and much of it is made ground. Crossed the Mohawk, and put up with Esqr Wicks—treated with the greatest respect. A woman by the name of Anderson called to see me—she was a bush of Enfield—a Mr Wills, originally from Shelburn, called on me. In this part of the county may be found all the shades of character, from the most ignorant and abandoned, to the most virtuous and excellent. Society is in a miserable state—it is, however, progressing on towards order. There is a mixture of all sects, which will undoubtedly for a long time retard religious order. In consequence of the imprudence of the methodists, and their erroneous sentiments, party spirit in matters of religion, it is to be feared, will soon arise. In this town there is one congregational chh.—small.

Saturday, 14th.—Rode 3 miles to the west. The face of the country level, and excellent—heavy timbered. Inhabitants very thick—log-houses may be found in every direction. The people appear to be cheerful, and are all under the influence of a hope of better times—the happiest situation, I believe that men can be in. Over all the face of this country, may be found in great plenty the petrified sea shells—some in rocks, and some in stones. Timber—is beech and maple, generally; some ash, and a little bass.

Monday, 16^(th).—At Mr Lord's—who has 2 sisters with him—all of whom are children of Benjamin Lord of Norwich—and are my cousins. They are comfortably situated—have a good farm, and a good framed house. The west part of Western is in a fine tract of land, and many of the inhabitants are good characters, and persons of some property.

Tuesday, 17^(th).—At Eli Bush's—in the Northwest corner of the town. All his children but one are with him; and he is in a flourishing situation, and appears to enjoy himself well. A mile and a half west is Fish creek, which supplies all this part of the world with the best of salmon. The people are not allowed to take them with seins, but stabs. This river is peculiar. The banks, for miles, are almost perpendicular—and are from 50 to 150 feet above the water. It is very rapid, and rocky. It arises from a pond in which the salmon spawn. This part of the town is on high lands; yet the ascent is so gradual as hardly to be perceivable. We are now in sight of the Oneida lake.

The sea shells, petrified into stones, are very thick on this land. Face of the country very pleasant. Crops of corn, oats, and grass, equal if not superior to any I have seen. Water pure. It is, in fact, a noble country, and needs nothing but clearing to make it a fruitful garden. However strange it may appear, yet it is a fact, goods of all kinds are cheaper here than in the county of Hampshire. Salt is 7/6—or by the barrel 6/.

ROME, Wednesday, 18^(th), at Esqr Hathaway's. This is a pleasant village, upon the banks of the Mohawk. The old Fort Stanwix stands about 30 rods from the river. It is regularly built: the intrenchment is very deep. In the centre of the fort stands the old block house. This can better be described by my drawing.

It is a very great singularity, that the waters of the Mohawk and those of Wood Creek, which run in opposite directions, should here come within a mile of each other—and should admit of a communication by water through canals. This communication is of incalculable benefit to this part of the world. Produce may be sent both ways. Sunday, after meeting, took tea at Pease's.—He appears to be a man of business, and is gaining property. He has a family, and a sister with him, who appears to be a very likely person.

Journal of a Trip from New Jersey to Oneida Lake

1802

Friedrich Rohde

Translated by Charles T. Gehring

The most that is known about the author and the circumstances of this description of the Mohawk Valley appear on the title page to the journal from which the following extract was taken: *Observations about various unique mineralogical formations on a journey from New Barbadoes Neck* [near Hackensack, New Jersey] *to Oneida Lake. For his friend and former colleague the inspector of mines in Nassau Siegen, Mr. Engels. Collected and written down by Friedrich Rohde. New Barbadoes Neck in the State of New Jersey, 1802.* It is possible that Rohde, "a geologist from Siegen, a center for iron ore mining near Cologne, Germany," had emigrated to the United States and settled in New Jersey. A trip three years earlier in the Hudson Valley may have prompted him to return on a more extensive scientific expedition to the western regions of New York. With a companion, whom he only describes as a "friend," Rohde carefully collected specimens of mineralogical deposits, which he intended to send back to his friend and former colleague in Westphalia for analysis.

The trip north begins in Bergen County, New Jersey, near present-day Hackensack, on the first of August 1802. Traveling by stagecoach Rohde proceeds along the west side of the Hudson River until Albany. Along the way he is fascinated by the production techniques in a nail factory, local customs, and, of course, geological formations. By August 6 he has reached the Coxsackie area just south of Albany. The following extract begins at this point. Of particular interest are Rohde's observations on the Palatine Germans who had settled in the Mohawk Valley several decades before the American Revolution. Rohde also exhibits a keen eye for commercial improvements, such as his remarks on a proposed canal to connect the Mohawk and Hudson rivers, and his forecast for the growth and development of the western regions of the state. He also is struck by the apparent disregard Americans have for damage to the environment. The following extract ends on August 19. Rohde was forced to cut short his trip and retrace his steps because of the illness of his companion. On September 9 he returned to his residence in New Jersey.

The original manuscript of Rohde's journal is held by the Westfälisches Wirtschaftsarchiv [Westphalian Economic Archives] in Dortmund, Germany. This is the first time that Rohde's journal has been published in either German or in English translation. The translation was made from a photocopy of the original by Charles T. Gehring. Place names and personal names appear exactly as they do in the manuscript. The endnotes are also Rohde's. Identification of names and comments on the contents appear within brackets.

C.T.G.

August 6

THE ROAD from the last-mentioned owl field or Oxsakie [Coxsackie: on the previous day Rohde was informed that the name derived from the local Indian *moagh sachy* or 'place of the owl'], one of the most level and beautiful wheat fields and pastures, where there was a church and other attractive buildings, led us along outcroppings of most likely limestone ridges for 7 miles. They bordered us like walls, sometimes hanging over because of chunks breaking loose and tumbling down. About 16 miles west of Oxsackie there is supposed to be an iron works. The place is called Newderham [New Durham]. Along several hills and kills, of which the first one is called Hahne Crey Kill (Cock's crow stream), we saw slate again. In Coeymans, a small place with a church, we had breakfast. A cliff, perhaps 1 mile away to the west, seemed to me to have suffered a recent rupture, and with this perspective I believed to have discovered sandstone in it on account of the yellowish color. However, to be sure, I hurried over to it and found what I had thought before; namely, that it was limestone, the block that had tumbled down and was lying below was larger than a common log house. This confirmed that this rock cliff was nothing more than a continuation of the previous mountains and ridges we had been traveling near, and that all of them, especially at their peaks, are covered with limestone. The yellow color found in the recent rupture was calcareous earth [calcium oxide] that had liquified long ago and was now hardened. Upon my return I inquired about the rupture and collapse of this cliff and was told that it happened 14 years ago on a Sunday and made a terrible noise; however, otherwise did not cause the least damage. Continuing our journey, we passed the Coemans [Coeymans] Kill, which has such a fall near the North River that 4 mills are driven by it within a half mile, and each one has a distinct head of water. The slate crops out here in banks; almost forming natural dikes. A little ways up stream there was a brick yard, where mostly bricks were made. From here to Albany the slate always predominated, and is especially visible in and along Loorman's [i.e., Noorman's] Creek in banks and ridges. In Albany we put up at the Tontine Coffee House and stayed overnight there. This place has grown quite extraordinarily in the last few years. The ship traffic on the North River and the warehousing of commercial products from the western part of the State of New York, and its associated business, make this place very lively. They are brought (primarily wheat) partly by water on the Mohawk River to Schenectady and from there by hand to Albany, or directly to this place in sleighs, especially in the winter when there is usually a good snow cover. I was assured that often 1,000 to 1,500 sleighs, some traveling 150 to 200 miles, come into this city in one day, for the most part loaded with wheat but also with oats, peas, and rye. Here they either warehouse their products, taking goods or money on account, or they sell or trade their produce at once.

August 7

It is 16 miles from Albany to Schenectady, over sandy flats and a knoll covered with inferior wooded growth, where there is not the slightest indication of stone or rock. Here and there you see a tavern with little cultivated land. Schenectady is a considerably larger place but by its appearance not quite as prosperous. There is even an academy in this place, which was formerly funded by the state. There must be, however, very few students, or they must be kept in their cells, for I did not see a single one. The Mohawk River flows closely past the city; however, from there to the North River there is a 72 foot fall, for which reason all goods coming down the Mohawk are unloaded here and transported to Albany in wagons, and so vice versa whenever goods are sent from there to the western parts of the country. There have already been long deliberations about connecting the Mohawk with the North River by means of canals and locks, and thus achieve shipping through it. However, it seems that it has been not as much impeded up to now by its impossibility as the cost of its construction. Nevertheless, there is talk about it again, and there is no doubt that the adventurous American will clear all obstacles from his path, and also accomplish this useful work for the benefit of a large part of this country. Shipping had almost made me forget my chief objective, if some stone buildings and the hearthstones of beautiful blue slate in the tavern had not reminded me of it. Upon my inquiry about it, I was told that they are quarried about 2 miles to the east below the aforementioned knoll, over which we had passed. Therefore it seems that slate also serves as a substratum for those sand dunes. From where and how the sand came to settle on it or how it was produced, I am unable to explain. If the esteemed mining board member Voigt himself cannot determine this (see his splendid book *The Practical Orology*, p. 148), why would anyone hold it against me, a forlorn miner?

August 8

Today on this dear Sunday we continued on. First we crossed the Mohawk with the ferry and then traveled along the same at varying distances from it so swiftly on a new turnpike that we covered 16 miles in 2½ hours. Whether and how mineralogical observations can be made in this way, is easy to judge. Meanwhile, I give it as good as I could get it [*gebe ich's so gut als ich's kriegen konnte*]. That smacks of the English, I give it as good as I could get it. Well then! This is the way it is. There was washed up and rounded off gravel along the road, and about another 6 miles there was slate in a small creek, and after a few miles secondary limestone. McKorks Tavern, where we ate breakfast, was built of secondary limestone, and it was a large, solid structure. Four miles from Schenectady, and about 10 miles farther is the district called Amsterdam. A recently constructed trip hammer, with which scythes and shovels were manufactured, was situated along the road; also an oil mill. I was told that bloomery iron is also made there, and that the iron ore was quarried a short ways from Schenectady. Beautiful, steep and flat hills accompanied the Mohawk from here on in varying distances on both sides, and the plains lying in between them and river consist of the most bountiful fields and meadows. Some clumps of granite lying along the road most likely was floated here from afar. Two miles farther at Cuylers Mill, a short stop provided me with enough time to be able to sample the species of stone lying under the mill, but deposited here from afar, and take along the pieces entered under No. 5. I leave it you to append the proper and fitting names to them. In Brides Tavern, in the district called Caghnawahga [Caughnawaga], we took our midday meal. Behind it was a hill rising to the north, consisting of slate and wacke, which also was found in and near the road from there on, mixed, however, with pieces of limestone. Thereafter the road led us through cultivated fields until Conolli's Tavern, a short distance from Antonius Nose in the so-called Mohawk highlands. Behind this house about 3 to 400 yards distance, the hills stretching along the river are rather high and bare. Presumably it is a sort of wacke or more likely trap. Our host called it rotten stone that flies into small cubical pieces when struck.[1] The eastern hill on the opposite side is not as precipitous, with cultivated fields and houses visible here and there. The Indians, who are known by the name, Mohawks, formerly had their chief settlement here, of which our obliging host showed us the ruins, especially those where the chief or king had his storage cellar, which, however, appeared to be no more than old sink holes, separated from one another by about 10, 15 to 20 paces. This tribe took the English side in the last war under the leadership of a certain Johnston. However, they sought refuge in Canada when events turned against them.

August 9

Night quarters already bad in several respects but made considerably worse by the heat, was cause enough to rush on all the earlier. The base of the so-called Antonius Nose[2] consisted of granite and related species of stone, some samples of which are entered under No. 6. I had no time to examine the species of rock in this outcropping; however, I surmise that there is slate and wacke, and that there is limestone at the peak. The height of this nose was considerable, and I am not exaggerating when I estimate it to be 60 German fathoms [*Lachter*]. The hills connected with it nearby are steep and bare both in front and back. A few miles farther there were several slides down which timber is rolled. This leads you to believe that there are wooded flats or hills to be found on the heights, just as the rock covered with calcium oxide in several defiles at the base of this mountain is a sign that its surface and peak consist of limestone, and so farther on for another 4 to 5 miles, where the rock gradually flattens out and crops up in layers, and continues almost to the Lower Canada Creek. No. 7 is a gradation of milk-colored silica or quartz, which I broke off from a rounded chunk lying along the turnpike road. These can be found frequently here and there. I also took it along to add to the collection. A German church, the Palatine Church, is built of these limestone slabs, together with many other buildings. This is also the original name of the district here, because it was first settled by Palatine Germans, who also did this construction work. The first colonists settled down right among the Indians. However, they multiplied so rapidly and vigorously that the Indians grew mistrustful and finally fell into open warfare in order to drive them out. Now and then you can still see the ruins of forts and old blockhouses that served these Mohawk Germans as refuges in emergencies. The outcome was that the Indians moved on, the Germans kept their property, and to this day maintain it as conquered land and their possession. These former compatriots of ours do not have the best reputation and are accused of great immorality. However, what can you otherwise expect from people who grew up among and with the Indians and afterwards even went to war against them and emerged victorious? Your intelligence would be insulted if you were told that it was wicked, but this can be asserted justly by the schools. Besides this, the too widely practiced freedom and the democratic fraud, in this otherwise magnificent land, have no less an inappropriate influence on humanity than on these so-called Mohawkers. But enough of this! I still want to report without fail on the end of this day that our journey today took us through the most beautiful meadows and an exquisite cultivated region; along the previously mentioned creek, which we had to cross by means of a dilapidated bridge, beautiful outcroppings of slate layers jutted out.

August 10

The place of our last overnight quarters, which consisted of a few recently built houses, in addition to saw and gristmills, was called Manheim from here on for a good ways, and was inhabited mostly by Germans. From here to the little falls of the Mohawk (Little Falls) slate probably makes up the foundation rock, which, however, is usually covered with layers of limestone on the attending heights. There is a specimen of it under No. 8. Although there were some beautiful farms along this road, you generally see either poor ones or completely uncultivated stretches, which annoyed me all the more as I had sided with the Germans up till now, and had thought that their industry and economy compensated for the other accusations directed at them. Yet, should a dispute that exists between the inhabitants and the arrogant proprietors of this district command the greatest interest? Next to Little Falls the Mohawk has certainly created a passage with the greatest force and thereby laid bare on both sides such rock walls that it produces a frightful and yet pleasant sight. In the greatest haste I was only able to break off a few pieces from it, and they can be found under No. 9. The falls themselves amount to a perpendicular elevation of 42 feet. About 5 to 6 years ago, a mile long canal with 6 different locks was built there to facilitate navigation. If you look at the many drill marks along the canal, which mostly were made though a solid, thick wacke rock, it is easy to conclude that this enterprise prompted a considerable capital investment. In the river itself, right next to the canal, the violence of the water can be observed most clearly. You can see down there extraordinary pot-shaped excavations, which are none other than the work of Neptune. If Noah had not found solid ground again on Mount Ararat and landed there, you would think that he had unloaded the ballast from his ark at this falls. An area of 3 to 4 *morgen* [6 to 8 acres] is covered with enormous blocks that were probably torn from the higher cliffs and mountains and split open on the ground. It affords the eye with an unpleasant sight; however, you are compensated for it by the magnificent fields and meadows on the approaches to German Flats. Shortly before Herkemer, which place and county were named in honor of a general who was supposed to have performed much good service, there was visible at a crumbling elevation, where the new turnpike cut through, 3 to 4 exposed layers of gravel sand; but no solid rock. At the foot of which we crossed on a scandalous bridge the Upper Canada Creek, which flows into the Mohawk a short distance from here, and in which I likewise could not discover any solid rock. Meanwhile, the extruded stones in the stream lead you to no other conclusion than that they consisted of slate. A sample that I found on a pile being collected for the walling up of a cellar, is recorded under No. 10. However, there must be limestone nearby, and presumably up on the heights. We ate breakfast in Herkemer, not at all a bad place, where there is a courthouse, a jail, and a wretched church, and a German one to boot. On account of the heat, which in the forenoon had already climbed to 84 and in the afternoon even to 87 degrees, we also took our midday meal there. The greatest part of the inhabitants are Germans; and as the saying goes, from a somewhat better shot and corn than those Mohawkers. The mountain range, which approaches here on the opposite and approximately southwesterly side of the Mohawk, is, as already mentioned above, softly rolling, and you cannot help but believe that Master Kobale [*Kobold*: in German superstition a house spirit and a gnome who works in the mines and forests] must make his residence in there. According to Morse's Gazetteer there is supposed to be a lead works in this county; however, I was unable to gather any further information about it, which surely would have happened if the works had been in operation. However, lead works will hardly come into fashion in this country soon, because this metal can be imported from England cheaper than it can be produced here on account of the high wages. In the afternoon we traveled through a landscape that for the most part has been recently cultivated until Utica. Formerly Fort Schuyler, a small city, where there were scarcely 3 houses 8 years ago, and now 150 can be seen; some rather stately. Indeed, a rather attractive building, a hotel, has been constructed of brick by some Hollanders on speculation, which, however, has not yet corresponded to its expectations, but, on the contrary, stands there under lock and key.

August 11

From Utica to Whitestown; only 4 miles. This place, also a beautiful small rural city, has to inspire the travelers' admiration for the rapid growth and the settlement of uncultivated regions. In 1785 the Indians still had possession of this tract of land, but were bought out in connection with the rapid increase of their so-called Christian expellers, for the most part Yanky's,[3] and presumably withdrew farther to Oneida Lake. If you dare believe the accounts of the inhabitants and Morse's *Gazetteer*, then the region here is one of the most productive in all America, because one acre produces 36 to 40 bushels of wheat, where otherwise a harvest of 25 bushels is regarded as considerable. The mineralogist, however, will find even a greater sterility here, and scarcely any deposited stones anywhere. They were just ready here to lay the foundation of a new church, and had to gather the stones for it from the heights 2 miles away. The largest share was gray wacke, and a few pieces of fine-grained granite. Upon our return trip I had the time to take a short walk on the road to Paris, also a new town, where good educational institutions are supposedly being erected. You will find some samples of the various sorts of stone lying along the road, which however are not indigenous, under No. 10½. I found slate in a small ravine. About 7 miles from just before Paris, there is supposed to be an ironworks and some forges. I was unable to learn any details about it, and time and rainy weather would not permit me to go there myself.

August 12

Today it was just a short trip from Whitestown to Rome, formerly Fort Stanwix. The entire region is even more recently developed than the one mentioned yesterday. Only at Oriscany Creek was there an attractive and stately house and garden, as well as a grist and saw mill, which belonged to the owner of this district. Otherwise you see almost exclusively log houses until near Rome, where it also looked somewhat better as in the previously mentioned place. The millions of stumps, dried or half-burned trees, 120 to 130 feet long, lying by the thousands crisscrossed over one another alongside the road, does not afford the most pleasant sight. Many German foresters would cry, perhaps even shutter, if he saw this spectacle, and at the same time thought of the future. Along the entire way there were no stones to be found, except for a few deposited chunks; some rather large. Near Rome is, without a doubt, the highest point of our entire journey so far. This is demonstrated by the two rivers that have their source close by. The Mohawk and Wood Creek take different courses, the first to the east and the latter to the west. For facilitation of navigation the two have been connected by a 3 mile long canal, and both sides provided with locks, through which the ships easily pass and continue their course. I will not attempt to ascertain the rise above sea level from New York to Rome; nevertheless, I believe that it could be easily 450 to 500 feet. However, there is no solid primary stone; on the contrary, there is nothing but deposited gravel, clay, loam, sand, and mold. The extensive and good quality clay provides the opportunity for a brick yard, which is set up in completely open piles with some openings among them. The wood is shoved in the latter, set afire, and maintained until the bricks are done, which very seldom takes place on their exteriors and tops. Nevertheless these are also used for chimneys. They know as little about pan tiles here as they do in the entire country. Only in the cities are they used on account of the danger of fire; and they are mostly especially glazed imported ones. Roofing slate is also used. I have to note in parenthesis that even these are to be produced shortly in this country not far from the North River, as a certain company in Albany has decided to look for coal, and probably even transport it, if they find it, which is most probable, judging by the quantity of slate.

August 13

Today we made a trip to the new settlement in Scriba's Patent, as far as the road allowed, which was only carved out 3 years ago; it is about 15 miles wide and reaches to Esquire Bloomfield, who is an agent for it, and who has established a saw mill. In Fish Creek, which we crossed over on a recently constructed bridge, there appeared once more banks of a hard, blue slate; also, fragments of it lay along the road and the aforesaid creek. Every type of wood, beech, sugar maple, fir, and hemlock, a variety of the same, are extraordinarily strong and long. The aforesaid Esquire Bloomfield assured us that he often finds firs of 160 feet long and 3 feet in diameter, and can use them entirely as sawing logs. Fish Creek is extraordinarily rich in fish and especially salmon that come out of Oneida Lake in the spring and fall into the small waterways, this one in particular, presumably on account of its fresh water, and climb its pure and stony bottom in order to spawn. For this reason the Indians stipulated upon selling this district that the woods for ½ mile wide on either side should not be cut down, because they believe that by denuding the creek of woods would harm the fishing. The 14th was a rest day and on the 15th we went back to Rome on the same road. For this reason I have nothing further to relate.

August 17

The highway from Rome to Rotterdam on Oneida Lake is new and of such a quality that it can only be passed over with great difficulty. For this reason we decided to go by water on Wood Creek, and then cross over the lake. On account of a light rain this morning, it was almost 10 o'clock when we boarded, or more accurately, got into a small open vessel. It was about 60 [4] feet long, 7 to 8 feet wide in the middle and quite pointed fore and aft. It is provided with a flat bottom and is called a bateau or flat bottom. The method for setting these bateaux in motion is threefold: with a favorable wind on open and deep water it is done with a sail; also with oars; however, in narrow winding rivers clogged with wood it is done with setting poles that are metal tipped below and crooked above. At the beginning of our trip through the above-mentioned canal as well as through the greatest part of Wood Creek until some miles from the lake, where a rather large river is formed by the entry of Fish Creek, the latter demanded such difficult methods and disagreeable labor, and especially made more difficult first by the shallow water and then by the countless trees, bushes and even planks and bark that come down from Gilbert's saw mill nearby, impeding navigation, so that the boatmen from time to time had to cut through a tree recently fallen in or across the river, and create an opening, or even climb out to lighten up the boat, lifting it up and away over logs lying on the bottom. In addition, this river runs through an extraordinary amount of bends, even though 12 canals or cuts have already been dug in order to facilitate as well as shorten navigation, that the boatmen, of whom two stand forward and one behind, must have much skill in order to keep it from smashing into the bank or heaps of wood. Under these conditions we traveled mostly very slow until Gilbert's Tavern, which is 6 miles by water and 5 by land from Rome. Between this place and the lake there is no house, where an honest man could spend the night. For this reason, at the urging of our boatmen, who explained that it would be too late to enter the lake, we decided to stay here.

They are in the process of constructing several canals, dams or dikes, and locks here for the facilitation of navigation in the oft-mentioned Wood Creek, and had up to 80 at work for this purpose, over whom a certain Mr. Huntington was employed as superintendent. One of these works was complete, the second almost finished, and the third not yet begun, but with the hope to complete it still before winter. I took the opportunity to converse with the aforesaid superintendent about the strata of the soil through which the aforementioned locks were dug. I received the following report from him: "The first stratum was a sandy loam, the 2d bluish clay, the 3d gravel, the 4th again clay, and the 5th again gravel, in which a still rather healthy oak tree was found, as well as a walnut with its outer green bark. Here at the required depth no stone stratum was found; only scattered loose stones." Carelessly I neglected to ask about the thickness of the aforesaid strata. However, as the total depth amounts to 12, at most 14 feet, then it is easy to judge that none of them is considerable. How deep such primal rock is to be found under here is a question that must remain unanswered for the present. The entire neighboring region from Rome up to and below the lake, and for several miles farther on both sides, is mostly level with few elevations. Even the Conassoraga Mountains are low hills, and as it seems from a distance suitable for cultivation, because here and there cultivated land is already evident.

August 18

We started off early, and after many difficulties already mentioned yesterday, we arrived safely at Lake Oneida toward 3 o'clock in the afternoon. However, it was so rough and turbulent on account of a strong west wind that our boatman would not dare a crossing at this time; but he did believe that the wind would die down by sunset, and would then row across all the easier. So we put up with it. The boatmen made a fire and cooked their dinner (midday meal) of pork and potatoes, which they enjoyed just as much with a glass of Madeira wine and brandy grog, as we did our cold ham. I used this time to make some observations about the types of earth along Wood Creek. I intentionally say types of earth, because you do not get to see stones, except for some small piles of gravel worked together by the salmon near the confluence of Fish Creek in which they conceal their eggs, and now half jut up out of the water. The upper layer of earth consists of the so-called sandy loam (lime mixed with sand). Below this lies a very sticky clay of a pale yellow or grayish color in layers up to two inches thick, which, of course, only crops out here and there, but quite often covered with deposited sand. It would be too much to say, if you wanted to assert that the earth strata from Rome to the lake maintained itself in the same way, but in general I think it is the case; not doubting that deviations exist in various respects. The above-mentioned layered and horizontally-oriented clay strata are not affected in the least by the current, which often is supposed to be quite torrential, especially as a result of snow and heavy rain. At least the boatmen assured me of this, and the oldest of them even said, that he has been traveling up and down here for 30 years, and has never noticed any change in these banks. The land on both sides of the river, through which it works its serpentine way in the above-mentioned bends, is level and still completely covered with every species of wood. It is supposed to flood over now and then with the melting snow, which often reaches a considerable depth. The herbs, hops, grape vines, oats, rye, and the like that grow along the banks indicate, nevertheless, that the soil would have to be very fertile. Viewed as totally wild, perhaps they would become domesticated if they had more air and sun. Here and there a flower rose up among them, whose redness matched the most beautiful crimson. What they are called, however, I do not know. An experienced botanist could without fail make hundreds, even thousands of discoveries and collections here, if the mineralogist grows drowsy from boredom. The sun gradually set, the wind abated, and the sea grew calm enough so that we were able to strike out on our course toward 7 o'clock. The wind had turned more toward the north, preventing us from making sail. For this reason the entire lake had to be rowed across. This progressed all the slower because of the contrary wind; nevertheless, we reached Rotterdam, our destination, safely but somewhat frozen after midnight, going for 1 o'clock.

August 19

Rotterdam is a newly undertaken settlement similar to Scriba itself, where a store, saw and grist mill, brandy distillery, pottery works, and the like have been established. In time it will be an attractive place because it is conveniently located for the ship traffic on account of the creek that flows through it, which they can enter when the wind comes up; also, as a landing for goods required in the interior of the country, for whose transport the necessary arrangements are already being made. The location of the place is pleasant, and has a splendid view of the sea and the mountains on the other side. There is no primal rock to be seen at all near this place, and to go into the interior of this still wood-covered land, would be dangerous without a guide, and extremely difficult with one, especially since while we have been here, heat, thunderstorms, and rain alternate almost constantly with one another. A light sandy and viscous ground makes up the cultivating soil, in which all sorts of produce, garden vegetables as well as fruit thrive wonderfully. Under this comes clay of various types and colors, from which bricks as well as pottery are already made, and it has been found good for both purposes. The layers of earth below this still lie undiscovered, and the few springs present there are hardly 6 feet deep, telling us little in the matter. At the lake there are various sorts of displaced types of stone; some samples of which can be found under No. 11. Where they come from is anybody's guess. Without a doubt I could have more of the same, however, I was already embarrassed to pack up so many. There are fish of all sorts in the lake as well as in the rivers and streams, and indeed of the best type, such as salmon, trout, pickerel, but somewhat different from ours in Germany, eels and many others of the same in great abundance; also, in the forests there is game, stags and does that closely resemble our German game in shape as well as size right down to the horns. One of which is included here as a sample. There are also still some bears, wolves, and panthers; however, disproportionately more of the latter than of the former. An inhabitant of Rotterdam single-handedly killed 24 of the former last fall, as well as a female wolf with 5 of her young last spring; and 2 years ago a panther was killed in the neighborhood. Near the water here you frequently see wild ducks of many varieties, and forest fowls; also, predators such as foxes, wild cats, martens, otters, and the like. Beavers are already rare. In the lake itself there are small islands where thousands of sea gulls lay their eggs, and are gathered and used in quantity by the whites and Indians living in the area. It is said that they are similar to chicken eggs. Another water fowl, the loon, as big as a small goose and a stinking fish eater, also lays both of its eggs along the banks of these small islands, of which one is white and the other grayish-black, and is supposed to be as thick as a goose egg. These are also used. Cattle breeding is no less good, and the best pastures can be established along the lake as well as the creeks. However, as the world for the time being still lies open here in every way, the inhabitants take no trouble to come to the assistance of nature, but rather expect, as do most Americans, everything from its bounty. On the south side of the lake the Indians, as they are commonly called, or rather the natives of America still possess a considerable stretch of land on Oneida Creek, which forms their border to the east. The place where they reside is called Oneida Castle. Although they live right in the middle of civilized people, come in contact and do business with them almost daily, they nevertheless still remain true to their old dress, lifestyle, and customs. Their dress consists of a linen smock [*Frock*] or *Beiderwand*, which is very similar to a German coachman's smock; around the loins they wear a flap of blue woolen cloth 15 to 18 inches wide, and that is their summer wear. They cover their hair, which hangs down straight in their faces, with neither hats nor caps; however, I did see some few of their women (squaws) wearing round felt hats, and draped with *Blanquets* (woolen blankets). Their king (chief), I was told, was bred by a white, a German to boot, and a Negro in Canada; and is consequently a mulatto. However, he conducted himself so well in the war that the Indians elected him to this important position. His name is Lewis or Louis. He and his co-regent Conkebud are members of the New York Free Masons society, and have in appreciation of this honor bequeathed 200 acres to the society. The total number of Indians living in Oneida Castle is given at 600 souls, among whom there are about 80 warriors. A description of this people does not exactly suit my purpose, and several writings note that my observations perhaps should be regarded as useless. But *nulla regula sine exceptione* [no rules without exceptions]. A rather long stay, brought about by the indisposition of my friend, gave me much time and therefore the opportunity for it, and in consideration that I am writing for a friend and countryman, I gathered up everything I thought proper and carelessly threw it in.

According to our travel plans we intended to continue on by water on the Onondago, and then farther until Fort Oswego; from there on Lake Ontario until Mexico, another Scriba-like settlement, and then return from there by land. However, for the above stated reason this was postponed to another time. We decided to return from here, and began after a 10 day stay. Thus I was robbed of not only seeing a large tract of the country, some navigable rivers and the rather large Lake Ontario, but also some possibly useful observations on one or another subject.

ENDNOTES

1. Mr. Ferber in his *Oryctography of Derbyshire*, p. 24 refers to a species of stone called rotten stone, which, however, has completely different constituents than this Mohawk rotten stone, because this one does not effervesce in any way with nitric acid.
2. Along the North River, not far from Pigskill [Peekskill], there is also a similar high angular elevation called Antonius Nose [Big Nose, west of Fonda]. Its base is also granite, as I had the opportunity to notice 3 years ago.
3. Yanky's is a derisive name for all inhabitants from the states located east of New York; it comes from the name of an Indian tribe that once lived there. The English derisively call all Americans Yanky's.
4. This is without a doubt a error in calculation. On the Mohawk, which is larger than Wood Creek, I did not see a single one of this length; the largest are between 30 to 40 feet.

De Witt Clinton's Private Canal Journal

1810

De Witt Clinton

De Witt Clinton was born in 1769 in Orange County, New York, the son of James Clinton, an American general in the Revolution, and Mary De Witt, a descendant of Dutch settlers. Trained in the legal profession, Clinton was introduced to the world of politics by his uncle George Clinton, governor of New York. In 1797 he was elected to the New York Assembly as a Republican; a year later he became a state senator. In 1803 he resigned his position in state government to become mayor of New York City. Clinton held this office for all but two annual terms until 1815.

During one hiatus from the mayoralty (1810) he was appointed to a legislative commission charged with exploring a route for a canal from the Hudson River to Lake Erie. Clinton led the canal movement, which resulted in the enactment of laws in 1816 and 1817 authorizing the construction of the Erie Canal. His identification with this major public work led to his election as governor in 1817.

The Erie Canal was built between 1817 and 1825. It was an incredible feat of engineering that stimulated the construction of canals throughout the country. More important, it proved to be an enterprising act of government initiative for promoting economic development. The dramatic decline of shipping rates, from $100 a ton before the canal to $5 after, opened up the Genesee country in western New York, making it cost effective to ship eastward bulk cargoes such as lumber, potash, and wheat, in return for manufactured goods. The original construction debt of $7 million was soon paid off. The surplus revenue, which rapidly accumulated from the canal's instant popularity, was deposited in banks to be loaned out for further economic development. "Clinton's Ditch," as it was derisively called by opponents during its construction, had become a major factor in promoting economic growth in the Northeast by connecting the Hudson River with the Great Lakes. The 363-mile-long canal also contributed greatly to the populating of the Midwest by immigrants pouring into New York City. New York's achievement set off a "canal fever," which led to the rapid development of a nationwide transportation network.

The personal journal kept by Clinton while serving as canal commissioner in 1810 was first published in a volume edited by William W. Campbell (1849).

The following account of the Mohawk Valley comes from pages 29 to 63 of this work.

C.T.G.

ON THE 30TH of June, 1810, I left New York for Albany in the steamboat, in company with Mr. Eddy, his son, and Mr. Osgood's son and nephew. A servant by the name of Thomas Smyth, whom I had engaged to attend me, and to whom I paid a month's wages in advance, disappointed me, and in waiting for him I had nearly lost my passage. The weather was warm, and the boat crowded. We arrived at Albany before daylight on Monday morning, and put up at Gregory's tavern.

A meeting of the Commissioners was held according to appointment, at the Surveyor-General's office, and all were present except Col. Porter, who did not arrive until evening. It appeared that Mr. De Witt had engaged Mr. Geddes to attend us as surveyor from Utica. Morris and Van Rensselaer agreed to make the jaunt by land; the other Commissioners determined to proceed by water. Mr. Morris was to be accompanied by his wife, and Mr. Sharpless, a painter; and Mr. Van Rensselaer by his brother-in-law, Mr. Patterson. General North was to take boat with us at Utica.

We employed ourselves in laying up the necessary stores for our voyage, having previously drawn from the Treasury $1500, in favor of Mr. Eddy. A mattrass, blanket, and pillow, were purchased for each Commissioner; but we unfortunately neglected to provide ourselves with marquees and camp-stools, the want of which we sensibly experienced.

On the 3d July, we set out in carriages for Schenectady, and put up at Powell's Hotel. We found that Mr. Eddy had neglected to give directions about providing boats, and that Mr. Walton, the undertaker, who is extensively engaged in transporting commodities and merchandize up and down the river, had notice of our wishes only yesterday. He was very busy in making the requisite preparations. He had purchased a batteaux, and had hired another for our baggage. It being necessary to caulk and new paint the boats—to erect an awning for our protection against the rain and sun, and to prepare a new set of sails, we had no very sanguine hope of gratifying our earnest desire to depart in the morning, although we exerted every nerve to effect it.

July 4th. On consulting with Mr. Walton about our departure, he informed us that this being a day of great festivity, it would be almost impracticable to drag the men away. We saw some of them, and found them willing to embark as soon as the boats were ready, and we therefore pressed the workmen with great assiduity.

The true reason for this anxiety, was the dullness of the place. Imagine yourself in a large country village, without any particular acquaintance, and destitute of books, and you will appreciate our situation. Schenectady, although dignified with the name of a city, is a place of little business. It has a Bank, a College, and Court-house, and a considerable deal of trade is carried on through the Mohawk;

and all the roads which pass to the westward on the banks of that river necessarily go through this place. A great portion of the crowd that visit the Mineral Springs at Ballston and Saratoga also visit Schenectady. With all these advantages it does not appear pleasing, and we endeavored to fill up the gloomy interval between this time and our departure, by viewing the pageantry which generally attends this day.

There were two celebrations, and two sets of orators—one by the city and one by the College. The feuds between the burghers of Oxford and Cambridge, and the students of those Universities, appear to be acted over here. In the procession of the students, we saw a *Washington Benevolent Society,* remarkable neither for numbers nor respectability. The President was a Scotchman, of the name of Murdoch, and certainly not a warm Whig during the war.

This place is known in history as the scene of a terrible massacre. On the 9th of February, 1690, it was destroyed by a party of French and Indians from Canada, and its inhabitants murdered. It then contained a church and forty-three houses. Those that escaped would have perished in a violent snow-storm, had they not providentially met sleighs from Albany, which of course returned immediately with them. This account has reached us by tradition, and was given to us by Henry Glen, Esq., and old inhabitant.

On receiving information that our batteaux were ready, we embarked at 4 o'clock in the afternoon. Our boat was covered with a handsome awning and curtains, and well provided with seats. The Commissioners who embarked in it, were De Witt, Eddy, Porter, and myself; and the three young gentlemen beforementioned also accompanied us. The Captain's name was Thomas B. Clench, and we were provided with three men, Freeman, Van Ingen, and Van Slyck. In our consort, were the Captain, named Clark, three hands, three servants, and about a ton and a-half of baggage and provisions. We called, ludicrously at first, our vessel the *Eddy,* and the baggage-boat the *Morris.* What was jest became serious and when our batteaux were painted at Utica, these names were doubly inscribed on the sterns in legible characters.

A crowd of people attended us at our embarkation, who gave us three parting cheers. The wind was fair, and with our handsome awning, flag flying, and large sail, followed by another boat, we made no disreputable appearance. We discovered that our mast was too high, and our boat being without much ballast, we were not well calculated to encounter heavy and sudden gusts. These boats are not sufficiently safe for lake navigation, although they frequently venture. A boat went from this place to the Missouri in six weeks. The river was uncommonly low. Goods to the value of $50,000 were detained in Walton's warehouses, on account of the difficulty of transportation. After sailing a couple of miles, a bend of the river brought the wind in our faces. Our men took to their poles, and pushed us up against a rapid current with great dexterity, and great muscular exertion. The approach of evening, and the necessity of sending back to Schenectady for some things that were left, induced us to come to, for the night, at Willard's tavern, on the south bank of the river, and three miles from the place of departure.

This tavern is in the 3d ward of the city of Schenectady. In the election of 1809, the first after the establishment of the county, a great disproportion was discovered between the Senatorial and Assembly votes, which could not be accounted for on fair principles. A greater number of persons testified that they had voted for the Republican candidates, than there were ballots in the box; and there could not be the least doubt, but that Republican tickets had been taken from the box, and Federal ones substituted. This tavern was located as the scene of the fraud. The boxes were kept here one night, and, it is said, locked up in a bureau, left there for the express purpose, as it is supposed. The tavern-keeper and some other accomplices, perpetrated the atrocious deed. The present incumbent looks as if he were capable of any iniquity of the kind.

The south road leads in front of the house. While here, we had an opportunity of seeing the pernicious effects of these festivals, in the crowds of drunken, quarrelsome people, who passed by. Among other disgusting scenes, we saw several young men riding Jehu-like to the tavern, in a high state of intoxication, and their leader swinging his hat, and shouting, "Success to Federalism." A simple fellow handed me a handbill containing the arrangements for the procession, and was progressing in his familiarities with the rest of the company, when he was called off by the landlord, who, in a stern voice, said "Come away, Dickup;" and poor Dickup, alias *thick-head,* immediately obeyed.

July 5th. We rose with the sun, expecting to start at that time, but we were detained by our Captain, who had gone to Schenectady, until nine o'clock. The high wind then subsided, and it had rained considerably in the night. In the rear of the house, we ascended a high and perpendicular hill, from whence we had a delightful view of Schenectady, and the flat lands forming the valley of the Mohawk.

The advertisements in the tavern indicated attention to manufactures. Two machines, for preparing and carding wool and cotton, were announced as ready for operation.

In the course of the day we passed three boats and a raft. The general run in going to Utica, and returning to Schenectady, is nine days. One of the boats was from Utica, and could carry ten tons.

We had with us Wright's Map of the Mohawk, made from an actual survey at the expense of the Canal Company. This map exhibited the distances, the names of places, the rapids, rifts, and currents, with great accuracy, and was singularly useful.

Between fifteen and sixteen miles from Schenectady, we passed the first settlement made by Sir William Johnson, in this country. It is handsomely situated on the right bank of the river, and must have been selected by him on account of its vicinity to the Mohawk Castle. There is here, a handsome two-story brick house, which was recently owned by one Stanton. He had but two daughters, who were courted by a carpenter and mason. He withheld his consent until they had erected this house. Like Jacob, they undertook the service; and the death of the old man has placed them in the building made by their hands.

In dried mullen [mullein] stalks we discovered young bees in a chrysalis state, deposited there by the old ones, and used as a nest. We also saw, on the banks of the river, the shell of the common fresh water muscle.

About sixteen miles from Schenectady, we saw, on the left bank of the river, a curious specimen of Indian painting. On an elevated rock was painted a canoe, with seven warriors in it, to signify that they were proceeding on a war expedition. This was executed with red ochre, and has been there for upwards of half a century.

We dined on board the boat, and, after a hard day's work, arrived at Cook's tavern, on the north side of the river, about 8 o'clock, P.M. The wind was violently adverse, the rapids frequent and impetuous. The Morris staid about a mile behind, which was no favorable indication.

Sir William Johnson had a son and two daughters by a German woman, with whom he cohabited. The son, Sir John, succeeded him in his title, and now resides in Canada. One of his daughters married Guy Johnson, the other Col. Claus, whose estates were confiscated. Sir William gave each of his sons-in-law a mile square on the river, and built for them spacious and, in that time, magnificent stone houses, with suitable out-buildings. Cook's tavern was called Guy Park, and belonged to Guy Johnson. The place was sold by the Commissioners of Forfeitures, and is now owned by John V. Henry, Esq., of Albany, who rents it for $500 a-year. The house is well kept.

July 6th. Started at 5 o'clock. About nineteen miles from Schenectady, passed the former seat of Sir William Johnson, on the north bank of the river. It is now used as a tavern. After he erected Johnson Hall, at Johnstown, and resided there, this house was occupied by his son. It is a large, double, two-story stone building, with two stone offices, and other elegant appurtenances. In those days it must have been considered a superb edifice.

After breakfasting at a log house, occupied by Mrs. Loucks, we proceeded on our voyage, and passed the mouth of Scoharie [Schoharie] creek, which discharges itself on the left bank, about twenty-two and a half miles from Schenectady. A fort was erected here by Gov. Hunter, the friend and correspondent of Swift, and called Fort Hunter, after him. On the west side of the creek, there is a beautiful flat country, on which was situated the castle, or chief village, of the once powerful tribe of the Mohawks. There is a convenient bridge over the creek at this place.

We landed here at a fine spring, for a few moments; and in imagination I was carried back to the time, when this country was occupied by roving barbarians and savage beasts, when every trace of civilization and refinement was excluded. The chief employment and supreme delight of the savage was to slake his thirst at the spring, to gorge himself with flesh, and to plant the arrow in the bosom of his enemy. In course of time, he felt the power of the man of Europe. He struggled against his arts and his arms, and after the lapse of two centuries, he is banished from the country which contains the bones of his forefathers; and the powerful nation of the Mohawks, which formerly struck terror as far as the Mississippi, is now dwindled down into absolute insignificance.

On our way up we passed Caughnawaga Village, which is about twenty-nine miles from Schenectady, and contains a church. It is pleasantly situated on the north side of the river. On the south side, opposite to one Dockstedder's, a wooden pitchfork was thrown at our batteaux, from an elevated bank. It just passed over the boat, and if it had struck it, might have killed a man. As it passed close to one of the hands, they felt a proper indignation, and immediately stopped the batteaux. The ruffians, who were making hay on the lowlands, scampered off, and left their rakes and forks to the mercy of the enraged boatmen, who took their revenge in breaking them.

We lodged this night at Dewandalaer's tavern, thirty-four miles from Schenectady, in Palatine, on the north side of the river. This is a good although a small log house. We had four beds in one room, and although the cotton sheets, which are generally used in the country, were not so agreeable as linen, yet we passed a comfortable night. The landlord owns a farm of 600 acres, 180 of which are on the Mohawk flats. About twenty years ago it cost him $7.50 an acre. He had but twenty sheep. We saw peas, hemp, and flax, growing in one field on the lowlands. The flats must produce excellent hemp, but this profitable commodity is almost entirely neglected. The hard winter has proved nearly fatal to the wheat crop. Land on the bottoms can rarely be purchased; it is worth $100 per acre. This place formerly belonged to Major Fonda. His house was burnt by a party Indians and Tories, during the last war, who came from Canada, and swept the country as low down as Tripe's Hill. Near this place they were defeated by the militia. A short distance below De Wandalaer's, you pass a remarkable rock called the Nose. The mountains here are high, and are like the Highlands of the Hudson on a small scale. The river must have burst a passage for itself. The opening of the mountains exhibits sublime scenery.

I saw at this house a pamphlet written by Cheetham, entitled, "The New Crisis, by an old Whig." This family are, it seems, connected with the Van Vechtens, of Albany, and the pamphlet was probably transmitted to be used as a powerful political engine.

7th July. We commenced our journey at 5 o'clock; and in order to facilitate the passage of our batteaux over Kater's Rapid, which extends a mile from this place, and which is among the worst in the river, we walked to the head of it. And here Mr. Eddy, who was complimented with the title of Commodore and the conduct of expedition, disburthened his pocket of a towel, which he had negligently put into it at the tavern where we slept, with particular injunctions to deliver it safely. This trifling incident excited some merriment; and we were happy to catch even at trifling incidents in order to beguile the time, which the slowness of our progress, the sameness of the scenery, and the warmth of the weather, began to make tedious.

In order to furnish as much amusement as possible, we put our books into a common stock, or rather into a trunk, and appointed one of the young gentlemen keeper of the library. The books, which were most extraordinary, were a treatise on Magic, by Quitman (this I purchased at Albany), and a pamphlet on Religion, by Mr. D. L. Dodge, a respectable merchant in New York, with an answer by a

Clergyman, (these were furnished by Mr. Eddy). Quitman's Treatise is a labored
argument against Magicians, and to disprove their existence. Dodge's work is
principally levelled against war, breathes a fanatical spirit, and is completely
refuted by the adversary's pamphlet. As a specimen of his reasoning, take the
following:—

"If a good man does not resist an assailant and submits to be killed, he will go
to heaven. On the contrary, if he kills the assailant, he may probably send a soul
to hell, which if spared, may be converted and saved to life everlasting."

Dodge's pamphlet, weak as it is, has given him a great name among the Quakers; and, through their recommendation, he is now a trustee of the New York
Free School.

We were not, however, without other amusements. A one-horse wagon, driven
tandem, came up to Shephard's tavern in great style, and formed an admirable
burlesque of the fops of our cities who sport in that style.

Shephard's house is thirty-nine miles from Schenectady, on the north side of
the river, and close to Canajoharie bridge, which passes over the Mohawk. It is a
large handsome house, dirty and unaccommodating, although much frequented.
Here is a small village of two or three stores, two taverns, asheries for making
pot and pearl ashes, and about eight houses. We relished our breakfast but very
indifferently. The swarms of flies which assailed the food, were very disgusting;
and custards which were brought on the table, *mal apropos* exhibited the marks
of that insect as a substitute for the grating of nutmeg.

At the distance of forty-two and a-half miles from Schenectady, passed Fort
Plain on the south side and in Minden. It derives its name from a block-house
which was formerly erected here. There is a church near it, and it is marked erroneously in Wright's map, Canajoharie. An occurrence took place, near here,
during the war, which excited much sensation among the superstitious. A Tory,
from Canada, was apprehended and executed as a spy, in the army commanded
by Gen. James Clinton. His friends were gratified with his body for interment;
and when the company were assembling in a cellar-kitchen, a large black snake
darted through the window, and ran under the coffin, and could not be found.
This affair made a great noise, and the superstitious Germans interpreted it as an
omen favorable to the Whig cause, considering the black snake as a devil, anxious to receive his victim, and anticipating a delightful sacrifice. A mile above
Fort Plain, we passed under the third bridge, the Schenectady one included, and
a mile above this bridge we passed the Lower Palatine church, on the north side
of the river. The Higher Palatine church is a few miles higher up.

At half after one, and forty-five miles from Schenectady, we passed a boat
which left Utica yesterday, at 12 o'clock; and five miles further, we overtook and
passed a Durham boat, with a load of eight or ten tons, which left Schenectady
on Tuesday for Utica. The *Eddy* can carry but three tons. We purchased a basket
of eggs, at one shilling per dozen, and some fine butter, at fifteen cents per
pound, also nine fishes taken by a spear, weighing from one pound to one and a-
half each, and eighteen inches long, for four shillings altogether. We shot a fine
bittern, and one of our men speared a large snapping-turtle. The wind became

fair for a while; the air was cool, the country pleasant, and our epicures were anticipating a fine dinner on shore, when, to evince the fallacy of human wishes, lo! a black vapor, not larger than a man's hand, appeared in the West, and in a short time magnified itself into a dark, portentous cloud, surcharged with electrical matter, and covering the western horizon. We were compelled to encounter the rain-storm by coming to, under the bank, with our curtains down, and in this situation we took our cold dinner and sipped our hot wine. After the rain, which continued until three o'clock, the thermometer stood at 81°. The thighs and fleshy parts of the turtle we caught, were filled with leeches. We pursued our voyage through a damp, disagreeable afternoon, and about evening arrived at Pardee's Tavern in Manheim, on the west side of East Canada Creek. The town on the south side of the river is called Oppenheim. Pardee's is fifty-one miles from Schenectady. He keeps a store and excellent tavern, also the Post-office. There is a bridge over the Canada Creek near his house, and the Mohawk and Schenectady turnpike run close by it. Here we met Jaspar Hopper and his family going to the Ballston Springs. The house was crowded in the evening, by militia on their way from a regimental inspection. They conducted themselves with great decorum. Mr. Pardee says that the expense of land and water transportation is about equal, but the former is to be preferred on account of its superior safety and convenience.

July 8th, Tuesday. We continued our voyage at six o'clock, and arrived at the Little Falls at ten. It had rained the whole night, and the morning was introduced by the vocal music of the woods. Thousands of birds of different kinds had assembled in a grove near to Pardee's, which they made to ring with their songs. The blackbird and the robin appeared to be the principal performers in this great concert of nature.

On our way, we were spoken to by James Cochran and brother in a phæton, and Francis A. Bloodgood and family in a coach, who informed us, that our colleagues were waiting for us at Utica. We passed a loaded Durham boat in its descent from Utica, and fifty-six miles from Schenectady we passed the house of the gallant General Herkimer, who was mortally wounded at the battle of Oriskany, and who died here. His house is on the south side, and was protected by pickets during the war. This brave man is honored in the memory and affections of his country. A county, a town, and a village, are called after him. He was of German descent, and the ground where he received the fatal wound, was covered with the dead and dying of his gallant countrymen. From his house to the Little Falls, the water is deep and still.

Little Falls

This village is built upon rocks of granite—contains about thirty or forty houses and stores, and a church, together with mills.

As you approach the falls, the river becomes narrow and deep, and you pass through immense rocks, principally of granite, interspersed with limestone. In various places you observe profound excavations in the rocks, worn by the agitation of pebbles in the fissures, and in some places, the river is not more than twenty yards wide. As you approach the western extremity of the hills, you will find them about half-a-mile from top to top, and at least, three hundred feet high. The rocks are composed of solid granite, and many of them are thirty or forty feet thick, and the whole mountain extends, at least, half-a-mile from east to west. You see them piled on each other, like Ossa on Pelion; and in other places, huge fragments scattered about in different directions, indicating evidently a violent rupture of the waters through this place, as if they had been formerly dammed up, and had forced a passage through all intervening obstacles. In all directions you behold great rocks exhibiting rotundities, points, and cavities, as if worn by the violence of the waves or pushed from their former positions.

The general appearance of the Little Falls indicates the existence of a great lake above, connected with the Oneida Lake, and as the waters burst a passage here and receded, the flats above formed and composed several thousand acres of the richest lands. Rome being the highest point on the Lake, the passage of the waters on the east side left it bare, and the Oneida Lake gradually receded on the west side, and formed the great marsh or swamp now composing the head waters of Wood Creek. The whole appearance of the country, from the commencement of Wood Creek to its termination in the Oneida Lake, demonstrates the truth of this hypothesis. The westerly and northwesterly winds drive the sand towards Wood Creek, and you can distinctly perceive the continual alluvions increasing eastward by the accumulation of sand, and the formation of new ground. Near the Lake you observe sand without trees—then, to the east, a few scattering trees, and as you progress in that direction, the woods thicken. In digging the canals in Wood Creek, pine-trees have been found twelve feet deep. The whole country, from the commencement to the termination of Wood Creek, bears the indications of made ground. An old boatman, several years ago, told Mr. De Witt, that he had been fifty years in that employ, and that the Oneida Lake had receded half-a-mile within his recollection. William Culbraith, one of the first settlers at Rome, was arrested, in digging a well, by a large tree which he found at the depth of twelve feet. This great Lake—breaking down in the first place to the east, the place where its waters pressed the most, and then to the west, where its recession was gradual—forms an object worthy of more inquiry than I had time or talent to afford. The Little Falls are the Highlands in miniature; and the Mohawk here, ought to be considered as the Hudson, forcing its way through the mightiest obstacles of nature. It being rainy the whole day and night, after breakfasting, we continued here until the next morning at four o'clock, when we continued our voyage.

The Mohawk and Schenectady turnpike passes through this place. It is in the town of Herkimer, and at the commencement of the locks, a line of division between the counties of Montgomery and Herkimer runs. The town of German Flatts is on the opposite side of the river, which is connected with this place by an excellent bridge.

The proprietors of this place were originally Fin and Ellis, Englishmen, who made their fortunes in this State and returned to their native country. The land now belongs to their heirs. They sent a clerk named John Porteus, a Scotchmen, who resided here and took care of their concerns. He kept a store and mills. He had a daughter who is married to Wm. Alexander, the principal trader of this village. The lots are leased for ever at three dollars per annum, and are 60 by 120 feet. Alexander being the agent of the canal company, we had frequent interviews with him, and were not a little entertained with the bathos he attempted in his conversation.

The tavern here is kept by one Carr, and is a good one. We saw here the *New York Spectator,* and a federal paper called the *American,* printed in the village of Herkimer, by J. and H. Prentiss. I had the pleasure of seeing my friend J. C. Ludlow, Esq., on a tour to Quebec, accompanied by Joshua Pell and Augustus Sacket. They left New York on Tuesday last in the steamboat, and came from Albany in the mail stage. The Inland Lock Navigation Company was incorporated in 1792, and has a capital of $450,000, of which the State owns $92,000. They have five locks at the Little Falls, two at the German Flatts, and two at Rome, besides their works in Wood Creek.

All their improvements might now be done at less than half the original expense. General Schuyler, the original superintendent, was inexperienced. The locks at the Little Falls were originally built of wood, which rotting, stone was substituted; and those at Rome were made of brick, which not standing the frost, were replaced also by stone. There is a fine stone quarry a mile and a half from the Little Falls, of which the locks were made; and they were first built of wood from ignorance that the country contained the stone. This quarry is no less curious than valuable. The stones divide naturally as if done by tools. The wooden locks here put the Company to an unnecessary expense of 50,000 dollars—10,000 dollars a lock. An old church at the German Flatts was built of stone taken from that quarry, and yet this escaped the notice of the Company. The artificial bank of the canal was supported in the inside by a dry wall which cost 15,000 dollars. This is found worse than useless. It served as a sieve to carry off the water and to injure the banks, and it has become necessary to remove it. The bridges of the canal are so low that we were obliged to take down our awning.

In one year the income of the company was 16,000 dollars. This, after all expenses, would have afforded a dividend of 5 per cent. There never has been but one dividend of 3 1/2 per cent. Alexander supposes that a million dollars worth of produce may pass down the canal annually, and as much up in goods. The toll is received at the Little Falls by Wm. Alexander, and at Rome by George Huntington.

The following amount of tolls received at the Little Falls was furnished us by Mr. Alexander:—

1803,	.	.	.	.	.	10,916 59
1804,	.	.	.	.	.	9,749.36
1805,	.	.	.	.	.	10,178.05
1806,	.	.	.	.	.	7,235.30
1807,	.	.	.	.	.	10,972.61

1808,	.	.	.	.	4,700.08
1809,	.	.	.	.	4,723.41
1810, as yet,	.	.	.		4,313.83

The rates of toll have been reduced since 1808, in order to meet the charges for transportation by land.

In April and May ast here passed the falls,	151 boats.
In June, ...	91 "
	242

Two boats passed through the locks in our presence—one a Durham boat from Ithaca with potash, part of which came from Owego. This boat draws when full loaded, 28 inches of water, and can carry 100 barrels of potash, or 240 of flour. It paid in lockage at Rome $16 50.

Miscellaneous

The mountain which forms the south-western extremity of the Falls is very elevated and called Fall Hill. A turnpike runs at its foot adjacent to the river. This mountain is the barometer of the Little Falls; if covered with fog in the morning, it invariably denotes a rainy day.

In entering from the east into the narrow part of the river at the Little Falls, we saw on the north side large holes dug, which we were told were made by money-seekers from Stone Arabia.

We saw excellent window-glass made in a factory in Oneida, and japanned and plain tin-ware is made for wholesale and retail in this place. The rainy weather induced me to procure thicker stockings; for a pair of coarse worsted I paid 11s., and for two pair of cotton half stockings, 6s. 6d. each.

9th July.—As before-mentioned we departed from the Little Falls at four o'clock, with an intention of reaching Utica, in which we succeeded, after a laborious day's work, at ten o'clock at night.

We met two empty boats going down to Schenectady, which had been to Utica with goods; as the wind was favorable, they probably reached their place of destination this day. We breakfasted at the toll-keeper's at the German Flatts, 64 miles from Schenectady.

The canal here is through the Flatts, a delightful body of low lands, which look like the flats of Esopus, and were first settled by the Palatines. The canal is 1 1/4 mile long, 24 feet wide, and 4 feet deep. The land through which it is cut cost the company 120 dollars an acre. It is furnished with a guard lock to prevent too great a flux of water. The embankments afford a delightful walk and the expense of cutting the canal could not exceed that of a good turnpike. A lock here cannot, with economy, be more than 6,000 dollars. The lock was filled in five minutes for our boat to pass. The canal here ought to have been extended further to the east, in order to have avoided another difficult rapid, and this could have been done at a trifling expense.

The village of German Flatts is a small place on the south side of the river and near the toll-house. The first Indian treaty, after the peace, was made at it. It contains a stone house which was picketted during the war and was called Fort Herkimer. The stone church was also used as a fort during that period, and the loop-holes for seeing through are still visible.

A bridge crosses the river 65 miles from Schenectady, and leads to the village of Herkimer, a flourishing place. The river is narrow at this place, and the West Canada Creek from the north falls into it, on the east side of the bridge.

We dined on the south side of the river about 71 1/2 miles from Schenectady; in the open air, at a saw and carding mill owned by a Mr. Meyer; 74 miles from Schenectady we passed under a new bridge, and a mile further we saw the commencement of Cosby's manor. This may be considered the commencement of a new country; the hills retreat from the river, the land grows better, the river narrows, and beach and sugar maple supply the place of willow bushes which cover the banks below. About 79 miles on the south side, there was a tree 60 feet high with an umbrella top, and two-thirds of the elevation without branches. It is said to be an *unique* in this country, and to be visited by strangers who do not know what it is. Mr. De Witt and Col. Porter went out of the boat to examine it; the distance of its branches prevented them from determining its kind, but they supposed it to be the Cucumber-tree, which is rarely seen on the east side of the Genesee river.

Wild or Indian Hemp was in great plenty on the branches of the river, also a beautiful wild flower, whose botanical name is *Oscis,* and of which there are six different kinds in the western country.

There is also abundance of Mandrake or Wild-lemon, a delicious fruit as large as a Love-apple. Its leaves are large, and it is about a foot or eighteen inches high. It is a plant, not a shrub.

Morris and Van Rensselaer having pre-occupied Baggs' tavern, where we intended to quarter, we put up at Billinger's tavern in Utica.

Utica

July 10th.—The Board met, all present, and adjourned to meet at Rome on the 12th instant.

Utica is a flourishing village on the south side of the Mohawk; it arrogates to itself being the capital of the Western District. Twenty-two years ago there was but one house; there are now three hundred, a Presbyterian Church, an Episcopal, a Welch Presbyterian, and a Welch Baptist; a Bank, being a branch of the Manhattan Company, a Post Office, the office of the Clerk of the County, and the Clerk of the Supreme Court. By the census now taking, it contains 1,650 inhabitants. Two newspapers are printed here.

The situation of the place is on low ground, a great part of which is natural meadow. It derives its importance from its situation on the Mohawk, the Seneca turnpike which communicates with the heart of the Western country, and the

Mohawk and Schenectady turnpike, which leads to Schenectady on the north side of the Mohawk, independently of a good free road on the south side.

Produce is carried by land from Utica to Albany for 8s. per 100 lbs.; by water to Schenectady, for 6s. When the Canal Company reduced the toll, the wagoners reduced their price, in order to support the competition. Country people owe merchants, and pay their debts by conveyances of this kind, and in times when their teams are not much wanted for other purposes.

Utica bears every external indication of prosperity. Some of the houses are uncommonly elegant; the stores are numerous and well replenished with merchandize. The price of building lots is extravagantly high. Lots, correspondent to double lots in New York, sell here from four to eight hundred dollars. The Bleecker family own 1200 acres in the village and its vicinity, and by at first refusing to sell, and by leasing out at extravagant rates, they greatly injured the growth of the place. They seem now to have embraced a more liberal policy. They have made a turnpike of two miles, and a bridge over the Mohawk, to carry the traveling through their estate; and they have opened streets for sale. They recently sold 2 1/2 acres at auction, for $9,000. The land was divided into 25 lots, fifty by one hundred feet. Judge Cooper of this place bought, about ten years ago, 15 acres for $1,500, which would now sell for $20,000.

The capital of the Manhattan Bank is $100,000. The building is improperly situated close by stables, and is much exposed to fire. In consequence of the trade with Canada, specie is continually accumulating here. It affords a great facility for the transmission of money to and from New York. A small Bank in Connecticut, named the Bridgeport Bank, of which Doctor Bronson is President, discounts notes here through a private agent. Having made an arrangement with the Merchants' Bank of New York, to take its notes, they became in good credit, and had an extensive circulation. As the Branch did not receive their notes in payment, they were constantly accumulating a balance against the institution. With a view to meet this evil, and to turn the tables on the adversary institution, the Branch now take the Bridgeport notes. I found that it is projected by the Directors to increase the stock of the Bank to $500,000; to distribute it in the village, and to maintain its dependence upon, and connection with, the Manhattan Company, in order to prevent it from becoming a federal institution.

The town of Whitestown contains, besides Utica, two considerable villages, West Hartford and Whitesborough. This district of country has twenty-two lawyers.

I met here Bishop Moore, on a diocesan visitation to confirm the members of his Church. Also, Col. Curtenius. Dined at Mr. Kip's, who lives in handsome style, and who received us with great hospitality.

July 11th. Morris and Van Rensselaer were to travel by land as before; here we met Gen. North and the Surveyor. We proceeded by land to Whitesborough, four miles from Utica, and there we divided, some of the company continuing to go by land and others taking to the boats.

Two miles from Utica we visited a famous cheesemaker, named Abraham Bradbury, an English Quaker. He has rented a farm of 163 acres, for $500 per annum. He keeps thirty-six cows, and makes upwards of 400 cheeses a-year. Besides the cheese, the milk will support a great number of hogs. He is assisted by his wife and two sisters. His cheese is equal to the best English cheese that is imported, and he vends it for 1s. 3d. per pound. Notwithstanding his high rent, he clears upwards of $1000 a-year by his establishment.

On Sauquoit Creek, a mile from Whitesborough, there is a large manufacturing establishment for spinning cotton. The works go by water. It is owned by a Company, and is denominated the Oneida Manufacturing Society. The stock is said to be profitable, and to be forty per cent above par. It employs forty hands, chiefly young girls, who have an unhealthy appearance. It is on Arkwright's plan, and contains 384 spindles on six frames.

Whitesborough contains the Court-House, and is a handsome village. Several lawyers reside here on account of the Court-House. The federal candidate for Governor has a handsome house. Eight miles from Utica we passed Oriskany, where Herkimer's battle was fought.

We arrived at Rome for dinner, and put up at Isaac Lee's house, which is a large double three-story frame building, called the Hotel. He rents it and ten acres of land from Dominick Lynch, for $250 a-year.

Rome is on the highest land between Lake Ontario and the Hudson, at Troy. It is 390 feet above the latter; sixteen miles by land and twenty-one by water from Utica, and 106 miles by water from Schenectady. It is situated at the head of the Mohawk River and Wood Creek, that river running east and the Wood Creek west. You see no hills or mountains in its vicinity; a plain extends from it on all sides. It has a Court-House, a State Arsenal, a Presbyterian Church, and about seventy houses. Its excellent position on the Canal, which unites the Eastern and Western waters, and its natural communication with the rich counties on Black River, would render it a place of great importance, superior to Utica, if fair play had been given to its advantages. But its rising prosperity has been checked by the policy of its principal proprietor. When he first began to dispose of his lots, he asked what he called a fine of £ 30, and an annual rent of £ 7 10s., for each lot for ever. His subsequent conduct has been correspondent with this unfavorable indication, and has given Utica a start which Rome can never retrieve.

Two lots, sixty-six by 200 feet, sell from $200 to $250. Wild land in the vicinity sells from $10 to $12 50 per acre, and improved land for $25. A Company was incorporated the last session of the Legislature, for manufacturing iron and glass, and half the stock is already filled up. The place has a Post Office and four lawyers. Rome being on a perfect level, we naturally ask from what has it derived its name? Where are its seven hills? Has it been named out of compliment to Lynch, who is a Roman Catholic?

Rome was laid out into a town, after the Canal was made or contemplated. It derives its principal advantages from this communication. Independent of the general rise it has given to Lynch's property, it has drained a large swamp for him near the village, which would otherwise have been useless; and yet he demanded from the Company, at first, $7,000, and at last, $5,000 for his land, through which the Canal was to pass. The appraisers gave him but nominal damages—one dollar.

The Canal at Rome is 1 3/4 miles long; 32 feet wide at top, and from 2 1/2 to 3 feet deep. The locks are 73 feet long and 12 wide; 10 feet lift on the Mohawk, and 8 feet on Wood Creek.

July 12th. The Commissioners had a meeting here; all present. Adjourned to meet in Geneva. At this meeting the Senior Commissioner was for breaking down the mound of Lake Erie, and letting out the waters to follow the level of the country, so as to form a sloop navigation with the Hudson, and without any aid from any other water.

The site of Fort Stanwix or Fort Schuyler is in this village. It contains about two acres, and is a regular fortification, with four bastions and a deep ditch. The position is important in protecting the passage between the lakes and the Mohawk river. It is now in ruins, and partly demolished by Lynch, its proprietor. Since the Revolutionary War a block-house was erected here by the State, and is now demolished. About half a mile below the Fort, on the meadows, are the remains of an old fort, called Fort William; and about a mile west of Rome, near where Wood Creek enters the Canal, there was a regular fort, called Fort Newport. Wood Creek is here so narrow that you can step over it.

Fort Stanwix is celebrated in the history of the Revolutionary War, for a regular siege which it stood. And as this and the battle of Oriskany are talked of all over the country, and are not embodied at large in history, I shall give an account of them, before they are lost in the memory of tradition.

After having dined on a salmon caught at Fish Creek, about eight miles from Rome, we departed in our boats on the descending waters of Wood Creek. And as we have now got rid of the Eastern waters, it may be proper to make some remarks on the Mohawk River.

This river is about 120 miles in length, from Rome to the Hudson. Its course is from west to east. The commencement of its navigation is at Schenectady. It is in all places sufficiently wide for sloop navigation; but the various shoals, currents, rifts, and rapids with which it abounds, and which are very perspicuously laid down on Wright's map, render the navigation difficult even for batteaux. The Canal Company have endeavored, by dams and other expedients, to deepen the river and improve the navigation, but they have only encountered unnecessary expense; the next freshet or rise of the river has either swept away their erections or changed the current. Mr. Weston, the engineer, from a view of the multifarious difficulties attendant on such operations, proposed to make a canal from Schoharie Creek to Schenectady, on the south side of the river; he only erred in not embracing the whole route of the Mohawk. The valley formed by that river is admirably calculated for a canal. The expense of digging it will not exceed that of a good turnpike. The river is good only as a feeder.

The young willows which line the banks of the river, and which are the first trees that spring up on alluviums, show the continual change of ground. No land can be more fertile than the flats of this extensive valley. The settlements here were originally made by migrations from Holland and Germany. The grants under the Dutch Governor were from given points on the Mohawk, embracing all the land south or north, meaning thereby to include only the interval land, and deeming the upland as nothing. Chief-Justice Yates said, that he recollected a witness to state in Court that he had travelled from Kinderhook to Albany and found no land.

The Mohawk is barren of fish. It formerly contained great plenty of trout—it now has none. The largest fish is the pike, which have been caught weighing fourteen pounds. Since the canal at Rome, chubb, a species of dace, have come into the Mohawk through Wood Creek, and are said to be plenty. A salmon and black bass have also been speared in this river, which came into it through the canal. It would not be a little singular if the Hudson should be supplied with salmon through that channel. The falls of the Cohoes oppose a great impediment to the passage of fish; but the Hudson is like the Mohawk, a very sterile river in that respect.

We saw great numbers of bitterns, blackbirds, robins, and bank swallows, which perforate the banks of the river. Also, some wood-ducks, gulls, sheldrakes, bob-linklins, king-birds, crows, kildares, small snipe, woodpeckers, woodcock, wrens, yellow birds, phebes, blue jays, high-holes, pigeons, thrushes, and larks. We also saw several king-fishers, which denote the presence of fish. We shot several bitterns, the same as found on the salt marsh. The only shell fish were the snapping turtle and muscle.

We left Rome after dinner—five Commissioners, the surveyor, and a young gentleman. Morris and Van Rensselaer were to go by land and meet us at Geneva.

We went this day as far as Gilbert's Tavern on the north side of the creek, six and a-half miles by water, and four and a-half miles by land, from Rome.

We saw a bright red-bird about the size of a blue-bird. Its wings were tipped with black, and the bird uncommonly beautiful. It appeared to have no song, and no one present seemed to know its name. I saw but three besides in the whole course of my tour, one on the Ridge Road west of the Genesee River. It is, therefore, a *rara avis*.

On the banks of the creek were plenty of boneset, the Canada shrub, said to be useful in medicine, and a great variety of beautiful flowering plants. Wild gooseberry bushes, wild currants, and wild hops were also to be seen. The gooseberries were not good; the hops are said to be as good as the domestic ones. In the long weeds and thick underwood we were at first apprehensive of rattlesnakes, of which we were told there are three kinds—the large and the small, and the dark rattlesnake. But neither here nor in any part of our tour did we see this venomous reptile. The only animals we saw on this stream were the black squirrel and the hare, as it is called in Albany, a creature white in winter, of the rabbit kind, although much larger.

About a mile from the head of the creek we passed a small stream, from the south, called Black or Mud Creek. Above Gilbert's the Company have erected four wooden locks, which are absolutely necessary, at a small expense, when compared with their stone locks at the Little Falls, which cost $500. The Company have also shortened the distance on the whole route of the creek about four miles, the whole distance being about 28 miles, by cutting canals to meet the serpentine bend of the stream. It is susceptible of being shortened, so as to make only sixteen miles. The State reserved a thousand acres on the south side, from Gilbert's down to the Oneida Lake, to be applied to the improvement of the navigation. This land is overrun by squatters. From some causes which cannot be satisfactorily explained, unless connected with our mission, the stock of this Company can now be bought for $200 a share—the nominal value is $250.

We passed, on the north side of the creek, the appearance of an old fortification, called Fort Bull. The remains of an old dam, to impede the passage of a hostile fleet, and to assist the operations of the fort, were also to be seen. Although there is now a road on that side of the creek, yet in those days there could have been no marching by land with an army. The transportation of provisions must have been impracticable by land; and, indeed, the general appearance of the country exhibits a sunken morass or swamp, overgrown with timber and formed from the retreat of the lake.

Gilbert's house is a decent comfortable house, considering the little resort of travelers. The grounds around it are overflown by the creek, and the situation unhealthy. He had procured fresh salmon from Fish creek for us, at 6d. a lb. We found it excellent. In the neighborhood of Gilbert's there is said to be good bog ore; we saw specimens furnished by a man who had come to explore the country for that purpose.

We rose early in the morning, and breakfasted at the Oak-Orchard, six miles from Gilbert's on the south side of the river. The ground was miry, and in stepping into the boat, my foot slipped, and I was partly immersed in the creek. The captain assisted me in getting out. The dampness of the weather, and the sun being hardly risen, induced me, for greater precaution, to change my clothes. This trifling incident was afterwards magnified by the papers into a serious affair.

Near Gilbert's, the Canada Creek comes in from the north side, a mile west the Rocky or Black Creek, from the south. At Oak-Orchard the first rapid commences; as the creek was extremely low, we requested the locks to be left open above, two or three hours before we started. This furnished us with a flood of water, and accelerated our descent. We found, however, that we went faster than the water, and had frequently to wait. The creek was almost the whole distance choked with logs, and crooked beyond belief; in some places after bending in the most serpentine direction for a mile, it would return just below the point of departure. From Wright's survey, the distance—

	Miles.	Chains.
From Gilbert's to the mouth of the creek, by the old route—is	21	24
By the present route, as improved by the Canal Company,	17	61
On a straight line, which is practicable for a Canal,	9	44

We stopped at Smith's, a German, who lives on the south side of the creek, and about eight miles from the Oneida Lake. The creek is sandy, and very winding from this place,—the sand, accumulated at such a distance from the lake, demonstrates the truth of my theory respecting the formation of the ground from Rome to the lake. Smith is not forty years of age, and has been settled here fifteen years. He has six daughters, five of whom are married; two sons, twenty-five grand-children, and one great-grand-child, who almost all reside in his vicinity. The female part of his descendants were assembled to rake his hay; their children were brought with them, and the whole exhibited a picture of rural manners and rude industry, not unpleasing.

About six miles from the lake we saw the remains of a batteaux, sunk by the British on their retreat from the siege of Fort Stanwix.

Four miles from the lake we dined at one Babbits', on the north side of the creek. We found, on such occasions, our own provisions and liquors, and were only provided with house-room and fire for cooking. The family were obliging and simple. They had been forewarned of our approach, and their attention was turned towards the contemplated canal. As they are the proprietors of the soil, which was purchased from General Hamilton, they were apprehensive that the canal would be diverted from them, and pass through Camden, and the old lady said she would charge us nothing, if we straitened the creek and lowered the lake. The only potable water here is from the creek, which is very bad, and no other can be procured, as the creek is on a level with the surrounding country. The family furnished us with tolerable vinegar, made of maple juice. The old lady, on being interrogated as to the religion she professed, said that she belonged to the church, but what church she could not tell. The oracle of the family was a deformed, hump-backed young man, called John. On all occasions his opinions were as decisive as the responses of the sybil; and he reminded us of the Arabian Night's Entertainment, which represents persons hump-backed as possessed of great shrewdness. John told us a story of Irish Peggy, a girl whom he described as going down in a batteaux, so handsome and well-dressed that she attracted him and all the young men in the neighborhood, who visited the charming creature; that on her return some weeks afterwards, she looked as ugly as she had been before beautiful, and was addicted to swearing and drunkenness; that she had been indirectly the cause of the death of three men; that one of them, a negro, was drowned in a lock, who had gone to sleep on the deck of the boat, in order to accommodate her and her paramour; that another fell overboard, when she had retired with her gallant, and prevented by it assistance that might have saved him; and that the third one experienced a similar fate. The commodore did not fail to extract a moral from John's story, favorable to the cause of good morals; and admonished him to beware of the lewd woman, "whose house is the way to hell, going down to the chambers of death."

A boat passed us at this house, which speared a salmon with a boat-hook in passing under a bridge. The frequent passage of boats, and the shallowness of the waters, terrify the salmon from ascending in great numbers beyond this place.

We passed James Dean's old house on the right, about two miles from the lake. He first went among the Oneidas as a silversmith, vending trinkets. He afterwards acted as an interpreter, and coaxed them out of large tracts of land. He is now rich, a Judge of Oneida county, has been a member of Assembly, and is a prominent Federalist.

Fish Creek enters Wood Creek, a mile from the lake, on the north side. It is much larger and deeper, and derives its name from the excellent fish with which it abounds, up to the Falls, which are ten miles from its mouth. It is frequented by great numbers of salmon; and we saw Indians with their spears at work after that fish, and met two canoes going on the same business, with their pine knots and apparatus ready for the attack. The Indians have reserved the land on each side of this creek, in order to secure themselves the benefit of fishing.

The confluence of these streams makes a considerable river from this place to the Oneida Lake, deep, wide, and gloomy, and resembling the fabled Avernus. You can see the track of its black and muddy waters a considerable distance in the great basin into which it discharges.

We arrived at Mrs. Jackson's tavern, at seven o'clock, near the mouth of Wood Creek, which enters Oneida Lake from the north-east. To the west, the eye was lost in the expanse of waters, there being no limits to the horizon. A western wind gently agitated the surface of the waters. A number of canoes darting through the lake after fish in a dark night, with lighted flambeaux of pine knots fixed on elevated iron frames, made a very picturesque and pleasing exhibition. We walked on the beach, composed of the finest sand, like the shores of the ocean, and covered with a few straggling trees. Here we met with an Indian canoe, filled with eels, salmon, and monstrous cat-fish. In another place we saw the native of the woods cooking his fish and eating his meal on the beach. We could not resist the temptation of the cold bath. On returning to the house, we found an excellent supper prepared; the principal dish was salmon, dressed in various ways.

The salmon come into this lake in May, and continue till winter. They are said to eat nothing. This is the season of their excellence. They formerly sold for one shilling a-piece; now the current price is sixpence a pound. The salmon are annoyed by an insect called a tick, and run up into the cold spring brooks for relief.

Near this tavern there are to be seen the marks of an old fortification, covering about one-eighth of an acre, and called the Royal Block-House. In this place, Col. Porter and the young gentlemen made a tent of the sails and setting poles, and, with the aid of a fire and our mattrasses, had a good night's lodging. The other Commissioners slept in the house; the window panes were out and the doors open. The resort of Indians and the sandy ground had drawn together a crowd of fleas, which, with the musquitoes, annoyed us beyond sufferance the whole night. Some of the family sat up late; the creakings of a crazy old building and the noise of voices, added to our other annoyances, completely deprived us of rest. The house was in other respects a comfortable one. The ice, which we used to correct the badness of the creek water, had a pleasant effect.

We found here a new species of mullen [mullein], with a white bushy top of flowers. Sometimes the top was yellow. The common mullen was also plenty.

References Cited

Bayard, Nicholas
    1692   *A Narrative of an Attempt Made by the French of Canada Upon the Mohaques Country.* Transcription in the Montgomery county Department of History and Archives, Fonda, New York.

Belknap, Jeremy
    1882   Dr. Belknap's Tour to Oneida, 1796. *Collections of the Massachusetts Historical Society.* Boston.

    1955   *Dr. Belknap's Tour to Oneida, 1796.* Museum of the American Indian, Heye Foundation. New York.

    1792   *History of New-Hampshire.* 3 vols. Published privately, Boston. Reprinted by Arno Press, New York, 1972.

Bixby, George S.
    1919   *Peter Sailly (1754-1826), A Pioneer of the Champlain Valley, with Extracts from his Diary and Letters.* New York State Library History Bulletin 12. The University of the State of New York, Albany.

Blaeu, Willem Janszoon
    1635   *Nova Belgica et Anglia Nova.* Amsterdam.

Block, Adriaen
    1614   *First Figurative Map.* Copy in New York Public Library, Stokes Collection. Facsimile produced by Holland Village, Inc., 1986.

Bloomfield, Joseph
    1982   *Citizen Soldier, The Revolutionary War Journal of Joseph Bloomfield.* Edited by Mark E. Lender and James Kirby Martin. New Jersey Historical Society, Newark.

Bogaert, Harmen Meyndertsz van den
    1988   *A Journey into Mohawk and Oneida Country, 1634-1635.* Translated and edited by Charles T. Gehring and William A. Starna. Syracuse University Press, Syracuse.

Campbell, William W.
    1849   *The Life and Writings of De Witt Clinton.* Baker and Scribner, New York.

Chastellux, François Jean
    1963   *Travels in North America in the Years 1780, 1781 and 1782.* 2 vols. Translated and edited by Howard C. Rice, Jr. University of North Carolina Press, Chapel Hill.

Danckaerts, Jasper
    1867   *Journal of a Voyage to New York and a Tour in Several of the American Colonies in 1679-80, by Jaspar Dankers and Peter Sluyter of Wiewerd in Friesland.* Translated and edited by H.C. Murphy. Long Island Historical Society, Brooklyn.

1913   *The Journal of Jasper Danckaerts*. Scribner's Sons, New York. Edited by Bartlett B. James and J. Franklin Jameson. Reprinted 1941 and 1969 by Barnes and Noble.

DHSNY = O'Callaghan, E.B. (editor)

1849-51   *Documentary History of the State of New York*. 3 vols. Weed, Parsons, and Company, Albany.

Donck, Adriaen van der

1655   *Beschryvinge van Nieuvv-Nederlant*. Evert Nieuwenhof, Amsterdam.

1656   *Beschryvinge van Nieuvv-Nederlant*. Evert Nieuwenhof, Amsterdam.

1841   Description of the New Netherlands... Together with Remarks on the Character and Peculiar Customs of the Savages or Natives of the Land. Translated by Jeremiah Johnson. *Collections of the New York Historical Society*, Second Series, 1:125-242.

1968   *Description of the New Netherlands*. Edited by Thomas F. O'Donnell. Syracuse University Press, Syracuse. Reprint of the 1841 edition.

Eccles, W.J.

1969   Bochart de Champigny, Jean. *Dictionary of Canadian Biography* 2:71-80.

Franquelin, B.L.

1684   *Carte de la Louisiane*. Copy in the Library of Congress, Washington, D.C.

1688   *North America*. Copy in the Library of Congress, Washington, D.C.

Gehring, C.T., and R.S. Grumet

1987   Observations of the Indians from Jasper Danckaerts's Journal, 1679-1680. *William and Mary Quarterly* 44:104-120.

Grassmann, Thomas

1969   *The Mohawks and Their Valley, Being a Chronological Documentary Record to the End of 1693*. J.S. Lischynsky, Schenectady.

Greenhalgh, Wentworth

1677   Observations of Wentworth Greenhalgh in a Journey from Albany to ye Indyans Westward; Begun May ye 28th 1677 and Ended July ye 14th Following. State Paper Department of Her Majesty's Public record Office, London.

1849-51   Observations of Wentworth Greenhalgh in a Journey from Albany to the Indians Westward Begun 28th May and Ended 14th July 1677. Documentary History of the State of New York (DHSNY), edited by E.B. O'Callaghan, vol. 1, pp. 11-12. Weed, Parsons and Company, Albany.

1853-83   Observations of Wentworth Greenhalgh in a Journey from Albany to the Indians Westward Begun 28th May and Ended 14th July 1677. Documents Relative to the Colonial History of New York (NYCD), edited by E.B. O'Callaghan, vol.3, pp. 250-252. Weed, Parsons and Company, Albany.

1860-63   Observations of Wentworth Greenhalgh in a Journey from Albany to the Indians Westward Begun 28th May and Ended 14th July 1677. Calendar of State Papers—Colonial Series, America and West Indies, 1677-80:95-97, 217. State Paper Department of Her Majesty's Public Record Office, London.

Herrick, James W.
    1995   *Iroquois Medical Botany*. Edited by Dean R. Snow. Syracuse University Press, Syracuse.

Jameson, J.F. (editor)
    1909   *Narratives of New Netherland, 1609-1664*. Barnes and Noble, New York.

Johnson, Warren
    1962   Journal of Warren Johnson. In *Sir William Johnson Papers*, edited by M.W. Hamilton, vol. 13, pp. 180-214. The University of the State of New York, Albany.

Johnson, William
    1921-65 *Papers of Sir William Johnson*. 14 vols. Edited by J. Sullivan, A.C. Flick, A.W. Lauber, M.W. Hamilton. The University of the State of New York, Albany.

JR=Thwaites, R.G. (editor)
    1959   *The Jesuit Relations and Allied Documents 1610-1791*. 73 vols. Pageant, New York.

Kirkland, Samuel
    1980   *Journals of Samuel Kirkland: 18th-Century Missionary to the Iroquois, Government Agent, Father of Hamilton College*. Edited by Walter Pilkington. Hamilton College, Clinton, New York.

Kitchen, T.
    1772   Communication between Albany and Oswego. In *Islands of the West-Indies* by Thomas Mante, facing page 61. Strahan and Cadell, London.

Lockwood, J.H., E.N. Bagg, W.S. Carson, H.E. Riley, E. Boltwood, and W.L. Clark (editors)
    1926   *Western Massachusetts, A History, 1636-1925*. 4 vols. Lewis Historical Publishing Company, New York.

Marbois, François
    1829   *Historie de la Louisiane et de la Cession de cette Colonie*. Firmin Didot, Paris.
    1929   *Our Revolutionary Forefathers: The Letters of François, Marquis de Barbe-Marbois*. Translated and edited by Eugene Parker Chase. Duffield and Company, New York.

Maude, John
    1826   *The History of the Late War in North-America, and the Islands of the West Indies, Including the Campaigns of MDCCLXII and MDCCLXIV against his Majesty's Indian Enemies*. Strahan and Cadell, London. Reprinted by Lost Cause Press, 1980.

Megapolensis, Johannes, Jr.
    1909   A Short Account of the Mohawk Indians, by Reverend Johannes Megapolensis, Jr., 1644. In *Narratives of New Netherland, 1609-1664*, edited by J.F. Jameson, pp. 163-180. Barnes and Noble, New York.

NYCD = O'Callaghan, E.B. (editor)
    1853-87 *Documents Relative to the Colonial History of the State of New-York.* 15 vols. Weed, Parsons and Company, Albany.

Radisson, Peter Esprit
    1885   *Voyages of Peter Esprit Radisson, Being and Account of his Travels and Experiences Among the North American Indians, from 1652 to 1684.* Publications of the Prince Society, Vol. 16. Boston.
    1967   *Voyages of Peter Esprit Radisson, Being and Account of his Travels and Experiences Among the North American Indians, from 1652 to 1684.* Reprint of the 1885 edition. Burt Franklin, New York. Sauthier, Claude Joseph

Rumrill, Donald A.
    1985   An Interpretation and Analysis of the Seventeenth Century Mohawk Nation: Its Chronology and Movements. *The Bulletin and Journal of Archaeology for New York State* 90:1-39.

Sauthier, Claude Joseph
    1779   *A Chorographical Map of the Province of New York in North America.* William Faden, Charing Cross, London. Copy in New York State Archives (747), Albany.

Schuyler, Peter
    1854   Major Peter Schuyler's Report to Governor Fletcher. In Documents *Relative to the Colonial History of the State of New-York* (NYCD), edited by E.B. O'Callaghan, vol. 4, pp. 16-19. Weed, Parsons and Company, Albany.

Snow, Dean R.
    1995a   Microchronology and Demographic Evidence Relating to the Size of Pre-Columbian North American Indian Populations. *Science* 268:1601-1604
    1995b   Migration in Prehistory: The Northern Iroquoian Case. *American Antiquity* 60:59-79.
    1995c   Mohawk Valley Archaeology: The Collections. *Matson Museum of Anthropology Occasional Papers 22.* The Pennsylvania State University, University Park.
    1995d   Mohawk Valley Archaeology: The Sites. *Matson Museum of Anthropology Occasional Papers 23.* The Pennsylvania State University, University Park.

Snow, Dean R., and William A. Starna
    1989   Sixteenth Century Depopulation: A View from the Mohawk Valley. *American Anthropologist* 91:142-149.

Starna, William A.
    1980   Mohawk Iroquois Populations: A Revision. *Ethnohistory* 27:371-382.

Taylor, John
    1849-51 Journal of the Rev. John Taylor, on a Mission Through the Mohawk and Black River Country, in the Year 1802. *In Documentary History of the State of New York* (DHSNY), edited by E.B. O'Callaghan, vol. 3, pp. 673-696. Weed, Parsons and Company, Albany.

Trigger, Bruce G. (editor)
    1978   *Northeast.* Handbook of North American Indians, vol. 15, W.C. Sturtevant, general editor. Smithsonian Institution, Washington, D.C.

Van Zandt, Roland
    1971   *Chronicles of the Hudson; Three Centuries of Travelers' Accounts.* Rutgers University Press, New Brunswick, New Jersey.

Visscher, Nikolaus
    1685   *Novi Belgii*. Copy filed as *New England, New York, Pennsylvania, and New Jersey in 1685*, Library of Congress, Washington, D.C.
Watson, Elkanah
    1820   *History of the Rise, Progress, and existing Condition of the Western Canals in the State of New York*. D. Steele, Albany.
Watson, Winslow C. (editor)
    1856   *Men and Times of The Revolution; or Memoirs of Elkanah Watson*. 1st ed. Dana and Company, New York.
    1857   *Men and Times of The Revolution; or Memoirs of Elkanah Watson*. 2nd ed. Dana and Company, New York.
Wilson, James G.
    1895   Corlear and His Journal of 1634. *The Independent* (October 3, 1895) 47:1-4.
    1896   Arent Van Curler and His Journal of 1634-35. *In American Historical Association Annual Report for 1895*, pp. 81-101.

THE Iroquois AND THEIR NEIGHBORS

Laurence M. Hauptman, *Series Editor*

Other titles in the series include: